THEORIES IN CONTEMPORARY
PSYCHOLOGY

Theories in Contemporary Psychology

SECOND EDITION

EDITED BY

Melvin H. Marx
University of Missouri–Columbia

AND

Felix E. Goodson
DePauw University

Macmillan Publishing Co., Inc.
New York

Collier Macmillan Publishers
London

Macmillan Publishing Co., Inc.
866 Third Avenue, New York, New York 10022

Collier Macmillan Canada, Ltd.

Library of Congress Cataloging in Publication Data

Marx, Melvin Herman, ed.
    Theories in contemporary psychology.

    First published in 1951 under title: Psychological theory.
    Includes bibliographies and index.
    1. Psychology—Methodology—Addresses, essays, lectures.   I. Goodson, Felix E., (date)   joint ed. II. Title. [DNLM: 1. Psychology.   BF38 T394]
BF38.5.M35   1976   150'.19   75-14310
ISBN 0-02-376880-0

Printing: 1 2 3 4 5 6 7 8   Year: 6 7 8 9 0 1 2

PREFACE

IT IS *tempting to construe the remarkable changes that have been occurring in our discipline during the past decade as a major revolution. Certainly we have moved into a period of questioning and doubt: about our facts, our research techniques, our theories, even the definition of our subject matter. The mirror within which we saw ourselves in 1963, when the second edition of this book was published, now provides a vague series of overlapping, sometimes conflicting images. Our faith in the old scientific verities that sustained and inspired us then has been shaken, and like the adolescent child searching for his lost saints, we are floundering about. We believe that psychology is experiencing not revolution, but the inevitable pendulum swings that must be expected in any viable discipline. We are in a period of ferment and consolidation, which is healthy.*

In the dozen years since the appearance of the 1963 edition of this book a large number of important changes have occurred or are in process: (1) a resurgence of interest in mind as central to the subject matter of psychology; (2) a correspondingly reduced faith in the tenets and applications of strictly objective behaviorism; (3) a renewed interest in philosophical issues and perspectives; (4) some clear indications of increasing interest in broad, integrative theories, as complements to the more typical narrow type of theory; (5) appreciable reduction in certain formerly pronounced interests, such as comparative psychology, and trends, such as mathematical models.

We have attempted to select material reflecting all major contemporary trends in psychological theory. To this end an active search for appropriate material has been made. Over 400 recent articles were examined with an eye toward finding not only those that established or represented major trends but those that provided balanced representation of the shifting positions and emphases in our field. Many excellent articles are not included, some because of space and balancing requirements, others no doubt because of unconscious selection biases. We do admit, but do not apologize for, one perspective that seems to run counter to the prevailing trend: a commitment to precision and orderly procedures in both experimentation and theory development, as will be noted in some of the early selections in the book.

The organization of the present volume differs markedly from that of the two previous editions, which appeared in 1951 and 1963. The first part consists of a variety of papers reflecting the theoretical climate of contemporary psychology. These issues are considered particularly important as background materials without which the more strictly "psychological" issues cannot be fully appreciated. The second part is concerned with methodological problems in theory construction, with special reference to psychology. The more clearly substantive issues are covered in the third and final part of the book. These issues are organized around the concept of three levels of data and analysis—experiential, physiological, and behavioral—with synthesizing and integrating trends covered in the final section.

The degree of change in theoretical psychology since the first edition of this book in 1951 is reflected in the fact that only two of the original selections are still included (selections 1 and 2), primarily to provide some historical flavor of the orthodox views of the earlier era. Nevertheless, the primary objective of the book remains as stated in the preface to the first edition: "to encourage a more critical understanding and a sounder utilization of the principles of theory construction." We retain the strong conviction that, with the marked changes in viewpoints toward theory occurring since the previous editions, it is now even more important that all well-trained graduate students in the various branches of psychology be familiarized with the major problems and techniques of theory construction. Sophistication in theory evaluation and criticism is desirable even for those students trained in a more positivistic manner. The empirical components of research are most often emphasized in scientific courses, even more so perhaps in the apprenticeship system now characteristic of the more effective graduate training programs. But training students in experimentation needs to be supplemented by training in interpretation, and the present work is predicated on the premise that sloppy interpretations can best be counteracted by familiarizing students with some of the problems that beset the theorist.

We wish to acknowledge the kindness of the authors, editors, and publishers who have granted permission to reproduce papers. We also most gratefully acknowledge the assistance of many of our students during years of teaching these materials, and of several colleagues who kindly gave advice on special points, notably W. A. Hillix, John Mueller, and George Morgan.

Kathleen Marx and Cheryl Goodson did the typing, manuscript preparation, permission requests, and other necessary technical and clerical tasks. We wish to express here our sincere gratitude for their assistance.

M. H. M.
F. E. G.

CONTENTS

Part I
THEORETICAL CLIMATE

Part II
THEORY CONSTRUCTION

Part III
LEVELS OF ANALYSIS

Part I
THEORETICAL CLIMATE

IN THIS first division of the book the reader is introduced to the transition that has taken hold and has been gathering momentum since the publication of the last edition of this volume more than a decade ago. Then there was a much greater demand for precision and orderly procedures in theory development. Although a dramatic shift toward informality and relaxation of rules has occurred, scientific rigor is as important as it was a decade ago, perhaps even more so because of this shift.

The first section in this part, "Classical Positions," provides some of the flavor of the traditional methodology and standards concerning theory in psychology. Although these have been radically questioned by many, they nevertheless constitute an important part of the contemporary "climate" for theory in psychology.

The second section, "Historical Perspectives," contains a variety of points of view, each of which brings to the reader some interpretation of past events on contemporary problems.

The following section, "Shifting Paradigms," documents the transition that has occurred within psychology over the past decade. The two focal points of this transition are, methodologically, a radical relaxation of the old rules and standards for psychological research and theory building and, substantively, a return to an active concern with problems of the mind.

The final section of this part is "Philosophical Perspectives." In addition to the long-argued "mind–body problem," some of the more recent developments in the philosophy of science are sampled.

CLASSICAL POSITIONS

THE *papers by Stevens and MacCorquodale and Meehl defend the importance of clarity and precision in the analysis and definition of constructs. Stevens's paper is a review of what may now be regarded as a kind of "golden era" in psychological theory and has been extremely influential over the nearly four decades since it first appeared. The paper by MacCorquodale and Meehl stimulated a great deal of interest in the problem of theoretical representation of assumed internal functions and signaled the start of a preoccupation with that problem that has now largely subsided. This is not to say, by any means, that the importance of the basic problem is any less than it ever was; rather, in the light of its neglect as theoretical fashions have shifted, the need to look carefully and critically into how such representations are made may be even greater at the present time.*

1

OPERATIONISM AND LOGICAL POSITIVISM

S. S. STEVENS

THE scientist has always been proud of his hard head and his tough mind. When William James (1914) sat in judgment and divided the universe of temperaments into the tough- and tender-minded, the scientist knew where he belonged. He was happy to run with the goats, for he was an empiricist and he loved facts in all their crude variety. He was skeptical and cautious of word, and to "isms" of all kinds he was peculiarly unresponsive. The tender-minded were the rationalists. They had faith in intuition and were awed by the power of the mind. It was their opinion that by taking thought they could discover absolute principles of truth answering to the criteria of coherence and consistency and that, armed with these principles, they could legislate the bounds of science. They were

FROM S. S. Stevens, Psychology and the science of science, *Psychological Bulletin,* 1939, 36, 221–263. Reprinted by permission of the author, the *Psychological Bulletin,* and the American Psychological Association.

the sheep whose wool shone white under the light of reason. They were most numerous in departments of philosophy.

Undoubtedly these two types are still with us, but it is the purpose of this review neither to shear the sheep nor tame the goats. Instead, its purpose is simply to invite attention to some recent developments in what we might call the Philosophy of Science.

The tough-minded scientist has always known that he could screen his integrity against the seductive pipings of the rationalist by ignoring philosophy. The tender-minded philosopher, gifted with his superior dialectic, has usually despaired at the stubborn naïveté of the scientist and has determined to leave the unrefined fellow to grovel alone, while he, the philosopher, calmly demonstrated the impossibility of proving anything by induction. Suddenly, however, we find, on the one hand, a coterie of philosophers plying us with what, if it is not science, is certainly not the brand of stuff we have ordinarily pigeonholed as philosophy; and, on the other hand, we are beset by a host of scientists of all disciplines campaigning for what, if it is not philosophy, is surely not the science we are used to.

The philosopher, Benjamin (1937a), says of these scientists:

They begin with science, they talk about science, and they end with science, yet they do not conform at all to the tradition of scientific writing. . . . Their repeated reference to philosophical issues tempts one to classify them with this group, yet the writings approach these problems in a new spirit and with a new method, which seem quite foreign to traditional philosophy.

And concerning the widespread groups of philosophers participating in this movement, Reichenbach (1938) observes:

Though there is no philosophic system which unites these groups, there is a common property of ideas, principles, criticisms, and working methods. . . . It is the intention of uniting both the empiricist conception of modern science and the formalistic conception of logic . . . which marks the working program of this philosophic movement.

So numerous and insistent are the words of those who have been seized by the spirit of this movement that they swell the pages of several new journals—journals whose subject matter defies simple classification.[1] There are articles by philosophers, mathematicians, and scientists. But it is more than a mere scrambling of the sheep and the goats. A common spirit animates most of these writings. The common theme, despite its fundamental simplicity, despite differences of interpretation by newborn

[1] Some representative journals are: *Erkenntnis*, begun in 1930; *Philosophy of Science*, begun in 1934; and *International Encyclopedia of Unified Science*, begun in 1938. The advisory boards of these last two publications read like a who's who in science and philosophy. It would be a passionate optimist, however, who would expect such a band of hardy individualists to be entirely of one mind. Many of them have not yet spoken.

enthusiasts, and despite the disparagement of misunderstanding, is probably to be esteemed as a truly great advance in the Philosophy of Science, or the Science of Philosophy.

Numerous phrasings of this central theme have been cast by authors interested in various aspects of it, but they all assert essentially that *science seeks to generate confirmable propositions by fitting a formal system of symbols (language, mathematics, logic) to empirical observations, and that the propositions of science have empirical significance only when their truth can be demonstrated by a set of concrete operations*. There are thus two separate realms of discourse: the *formal* (or rational) and the *empirical*. It is the business of the philosopher to labor with the formal and discover and perfect the rules of the scientific language, and it is the business of the scientist to apply the formal symbolic model to the observable world in such a way that the concepts he generates will satisfy the rules of operational criticism.

Elementary as these notions may appear, the development of their implications has commanded the interest of both tough- and tender-minded. The movement has proved disastrous for metaphysics, challenging for logic, and salutary for science. Philosophers and scientists in essential agreement are astonishing enough, but here we have them pleading for a common method. In this strange harmony we are witnessing the birth of a new discipline: the Science of Science. It is a triumph for self-consciousness. The science-makers are asking themselves how they make science and are turning on that problem the powerful empirical weapons of science itself; while at the same time a tough-minded outcropping among the philosophers is carefully combining the metaphysics out of logic in order to investigate more easily the common linguistic structure of science. In this quest the philosophers, like the scientists, resort to empirical methods. Witness the spirit of philosophy as exemplified by Nagel (1938):

It is difficult for me to take seriously the various attempts made historically by philosophers to legislate to the sciences just what they can and cannot investigate . . . on the basis of a deductive theory of mind and nature. . . . Furthermore, it seems to me an integral character of skilled workmanship to insist upon the fact that no statement or proposal has any meaning apart from the methods which are or may be employed to establish or execute them.

In succeeding pages we shall see how operationism, beginning at one end in the laboratories of scientists, evolved an enterprise co-ordinate with that of Logical Positivism, Physicalism, and Scientific Empiricism which, beginning at the other end of the armchairs of philosophers, settled on the problem of the proper scientific use of logic. And we shall see how the natural issue of this mating came to make up the unifying principles of the Science of Science. We shall see how this movement concords with "behavioristics," which is a behavioristic psychology tuned up to keep pace with a fast-moving logical criticism. And finally, we shall see what the impact of this movement means for some specific problems in psychology, and what is indicated as the future rôle of psychology in this scheme.

Operationism

Ten years ago Professor Bridgman, the expert on high-pressure phenomena, wrote a book[2] called *The Logic of Modern Physics* (1928). It has been judged an excellent book, animated by the single idea that "in general, we mean by any concept nothing more than a set of operations; *the concept is synonymous with the corresponding set of operations.*" This dictum stands forth in what many have found to be objectionable nakedness, but, throughout more than 200 well-stocked pages, Bridgman demonstrates what he means by analyzing the operational meaning of the basic concepts of physics. There is nothing rationally a priori in his method (at least he honestly *tries* to exclude metaphysics). His introductory confession is: "The material of this essay is largely obtained by observation of the actual currents of opinion in physics." In this empirical spirit he observes the behavior of his colleagues and finds that what is considered an *explanation* "consists in reducing a situation to elements with which we are so familiar that we accept them as a matter of course, so that our curiosity rests." The reduction of the "situation" is made in terms of operations, but do we thereby arrive at exact and certain knowledge? No. "We never have perfectly clean-cut knowledge of anything, but all our experience is surrounded by a twilight zone, a penumbra of uncertainty, into which we have not yet penetrated," and consequently "no empirical science can ever make exact statements." The degree to which any of the laws of science wear the penumbrous halo can be told only by inspecting the operations which the laws are intended to generalize.

Bridgman's book is rich in example but poor in precept. That its author has occasionally been misunderstood has perhaps been due largely to this fact. The book gives numerous examples of operational method without prescribing explicitly what operational method is; it talks of "operations" without giving an explicit definition of the term; and it discourses on natural laws without pointing out how we get from particular operations to generalizations. In short, it is a thoroughly inductive enterprise, and the reader is often allowed to make the induction by himself. Nevertheless, the spirit of the book is unmistakable and its message is simple and powerful.

Philosophers rose to protest, or sometimes to defend, the notion of "operational meaning" because it assures the automatic elimination of even the choicest propositions of metaphysics: "If a specific question has

[2] For additional comments on some of the books and papers cited in this review, see the "Bibliography." [In the original publication.—Ed.]

meaning," says Bridgman, "it must be possible to find operations by which an answer may be given to it." No operations, no meaning! And so, as we have said, philosophers, and others, rose to protest. Finally, the pressure pushed Bridgman temporarily from his Harvard laboratory and on to the lecture platform at Princeton where he spoke what became another book: *The Nature of Physical Theory* (1936).

To say that this second book pleased all who were disciples of the first book is perhaps not quite true. The author had been able to say in his first book that fortunately he would "be able to get along with a more or less naïve attitude toward" psychology and epistemology, but in his second work he boldly lays hold on thought, language, and experience. Bridgman's discussion of these concepts was what the world had been waiting for, but once out of the well-charted sea of physics and adrift in epistemology, the author's bark, if we are to believe the critics, appears to have lost its rudder. One cannot avoid the impression that criticism of this second book has been of unmerited severity, but perhaps severe criticism is what must be expected by a man who challenges us with issues as vital as those proposed by Professor Bridgman. Objection has been made to such statements as: "In the last analysis science is only my private science." "What," asks editor Malisoff (1936), "can an operationist mean by a 'last analysis'?" Bridgman says his purpose in sailing the epistemological waters is "to map out the possibilities and limitations of the human mind in dealing with the problems presented to it." "Our complaint," criticizes A. F. Bentley (1938), "is not that he makes this inquiry, but that in it he employs all the bad devices he had ejected from physics." Some of his devices are assertions crutched on such terms as "essentially," "absolutely," and "intuitively." Nevertheless, Bridgman's critics agree that his discernment in physics remains as fine as ever—he is still simple and hardheaded. In physics he is an operationist, and it is in physics that we should judge him, if we are to presume to do so.

Just as Bridgman had set out to apply and make explicit the principles by which Einstein shattered the physicist's notion of the absolute, so did others seize upon the opportunity to try out these principles in other fields. Psychologists, long self-conscious of their own self-consciousness, were particularly alert to this budding self-inspection on the part of the modern masters of physics. If the physicists could examine the methods of their science-making and evolve helpful principles, perhaps psychologists could do likewise. Such, at least, was the attitude of those who were happy to confess blindness to any fundamental dichotomy between the methods of psychology and physics.

Operationism in Psychology

But psychology is more difficult than physics—at least psychologists often find it easier to get themselves into a mess in their field than physicists do in theirs. Of course, when the physicist strays into psychology, the result is apt to restore the psychologist's ego-level, but if the physicist fumbles it only serves to show that when doing open-field running among psychological concepts the critic must hold the ball more tightly. In view of the difficulty of keeping a grip on the operational principle, it is not surprising to find evidence of dissension among the psychological apologists [Professor Bills (1938) calls them "apostles"]. In spite of much scattered writing, the case for operationism in psychology has perhaps never been adequately briefed, but a few of its consequences have been made explicit, and some interesting applications have appeared.

We all remember Tolman's *Purposive Behavior in Animals and Men* (1932). Whatever dismay we may have felt at the superabundance of his glossary, the fact remains that in coining the words of his new language he appealed most directly and explicitly to experimental operations. The book is a monument in the methodology of definition. In much the same spirit, Professor Tolman has more recently prepared for us "an operational analysis of 'demands'" (1936a). In his own field of expertness we find McGeoch making a critical inquiry into the possibility of "learning as an operationally defined concept" (1935). Boring treats of "temporal perception and operationism" (1936) in a short, poignant demonstration of how a classical problem turns out to be specious when its defining operations are made explicit. Seashore and Katz propose to bring order to the chaotic discipline of abnormal psychology by "an operational definition and classification of mental mechanisms" (1937). Lundberg, the sociologist, would do the same for the social sciences by replacing spineless intuitionism by "quantitative methods in social psychology" (1936), the foundation for which would be concepts operationally defined. And finally, Kantor examines "the operational principle in the physical and psychological sciences" (1938) and concludes that the principle, properly enlarged, can be employed to the psychologists' advantage. Now, these are not all of those who have taken notice of Bridgman's proposals. Nor do all these commentators see eye to eye with Bridgman or with each other regarding certain fundamentals. Futhermore, it is becoming alarmingly obvious that the phrases "operationally defined" and "operationally sound" are acquiring the sort of positive valence which leads to their being bandied about in indiscriminate fashion by writers who suppose that they can meet the operational test by announcing good intentions. Operationism is being threatened by its friends—largely, perhaps, because of the inherent difficulty of making a rigorous formulation of it.

What, then, are we to understand by operationism? All that any one man can do is to present his own version, and this I did in a series of articles in 1935 and 1936 (1935a, 1935b, 1936). There are some points there which invite revision, but, in general, the sins appear to be those of omission. The statement there needs expansion, but obviously this review is not the place for it. A résumé is more in order.

First, however, it must be emphasized again that the development of operational principles is properly an empirical undertaking. What do the science-makers do? What methodology has the maximum survival value? When do propositions have empirical validity? In short, operational principles are induced generalizations rather than a priori fiats. They are therefore subject to the usual hazards and uncertainty of inductive propositions. This empirical aspect of operational criticism has never been sufficiently stressed, and it is not surprising that operationists have sometimes been regarded as self-appointed legislators who try to prescribe rather than discover.

These, then, are some of the generalizations which I propose as verifiable:

1. Science, as we find it, is a set of empirical propositions agreed upon by members of society. This agreement may be always in a state of flux, but persistent disagreement leads eventually to rejection. Bridgman does not agree to this social criterion of knowledge and it was against this notion that he aimed a part of his Princeton lectures (1936). We must ask him, however, to produce the negative case. A physical law to which only Bridgman agreed would not be a part of physics—not, at least, until he won converts, and then there would be agreement.

2. Only those propositions based upon operations which are public and repeatable are admitted to the body of science. Not even psychology knows anything about private experience, because an operation for penetrating privacy is self-contradictory.

3. What becomes acceptable psychology accrues only when all observations, including those which a psychologist makes upon himself, are treated as though made upon "the other one." Thus, we make explicit the distinction between the experimenter and the thing observed. This distinction is obvious in physics; in psychology it is equally valid.

4. Although a particular experimenter may himself become the object of study by another experimenter, and he in turn by still another, at some stage of such a regress an independent experimenter *must be* (i.e., is always) assumed. The recognition of this "experimenter-regress" unravels many knots in psychology.

5. A term denotes something only when there are concrete criteria for its applicability; and a proposition has empirical meaning only when the criteria of its truth or falsity consists of concrete operations which can be performed upon demand.

6. When we attempt to reduce complex operations to simpler and simpler ones, we find in the end that discrimination, or differential response, is the fundamental operation. Discrimination is prerequisite even to the operation of denoting or "pointing to," because whenever two people reduce their complex operations for the purpose of reaching agreement or understanding, they find that unless they can each discriminate the same

simple objects or read the same scales they still will not agree. Agreement is usually reached in practice before these most elementary operations are appealed to.

7. There are two types of propositions: *formal* and *empirical*. The formal propositions are arrays of symbols without empirical reference. They are language, mathematics, and logic *as such*. Empirical propositions are those in which these arrays of symbols have been identified with observable events. Sometimes the two types of propositions intermingle and trouble results. For avoiding the obscurity of pseudo problems this distinction between the formal, syntactical model (symbols) and the operations for which it is made to stand is of prime importance. Hypotheses, for example, can be only formal statements—operationally empty—until they are demonstrated (see Appendix II*). Within the formal realm we speak sometimes of mathematical operations, but here we mean the manipulation of symbols carried out according to certain conventional rules. These are not the operations of operationism.

Although we shall have more to say later about the contrast between the formal and the empirical, at this point we might do well to see how history occasionally sets them off from one another and thereby emphasizes their distinctive natures. Historically, the algebra of complex numbers (numbers of the form $x + iy$, where x and y are real numbers and i is the square root of -1) was developed from the purest of purely mathematical motives. The rules for the manipulation of these numbers (their addition, multiplication, division, etc.) were worked out in conformity with the conventional laws of ordinary algebra and interesting relations were discovered. Gauss, for example, set a landmark in algebra by proving that every algebraic equation in one unknown has a root and that all roots of such equations are complex numbers (see Bell, 1937, p. 232). In Gauss's time these numbers were simply abstract symbols which could be combined according to the rules of the game we call algebra. They proved nothing about the empirical world or about science: they constituted, as they still do, a purely *formal* system. Then, with the advent of alternating electric currents, came also the need for a simple, effective "model" to represent electric circuits; and the electrical engineers discovered that if they let x stand for resistance, iy for inductive reactance, and $-iy$ for capacitative reactance, they could manipulate these symbols according to the rules of complex algebra and obtain new combinations of the symbols which they could then identify with some measurable aspect of an electric circuit. In other words, this formal system was found useful as a model, and out of its utility has grown the modern intricate theory of alternating currents. Therefore, when we can identify these complex numbers with various aspects of a circuit, we can say that the

* In the original publication.—Ed.

propositions containing these symbols are *empirical* propositions, testable by concrete operations.

These seven bald assertions about operationism are perhaps too brief to be convincing, but they may recommend the fuller development in the three papers already referred to. In the meantime we might profit by considering what operationism is not—still, of course, in only one man's opinion. Misunderstandings have been numerous and many of them could have been headed off had someone signaled what is non-operational. Let us, then, look at a few of operationism's contrasts.

What Operationism Is Not

1. It is obviously not a new school of psychology. Rosenzweig (1937) presented an admirable argument to show that the schools of psychology are really more complementary than antagonistic, but he was worried about operationism. He should stop worrying.

2. It is not a set of rules telling how to be a bright and original scientist. It does not even tell how experiments should be carried out. It has no precepts. At the risk of breeding disappointment we must say of operationism, as James (1914) said of pragmatism, that, "at the outset, at least, it stands for no particular results. It has no dogmas, and no doctrines save its method." Furthermore, its method is one which is applied *after* the scientific proposition has been made: it provides criteria for determining whether what *has been* said is empirically meaningful. In short, it tests inventions, but does not tell how to invent.

3. It is not opposed to hypotheses, theories, or speculation. It seeks merely to discover criteria by which these things may be detected and labeled. It is not opposed to poetry, art, or religion. It wants only to know the difference between these things and science. It wants to know under what conditions the consorting of science with metaphysics breeds pseudo problems. Scientists as people may be opposed to pseudo problems, but operationism's business, as a principle of criticism, is to discover them.

4. It is not a guarantee of agreement as to tastes or theories, but it points out how agreement as to facts is achieved by men capable of making the same fundamental discriminations. Operationism wants, most of all, to discover the bases of such agreement. What are the procedures which compel agreement among those engaged in open-minded pursuit of science? As to compelling agreement on tastes—that is probably a job in applied eugenics.

5. It is not positivism. The blemish on positivism was that in its reaction against rational metaphysics it pretended to base *everything* in science on experience. Operationism, however, acknowledges the rôle of the rational methods of mathematics and logic—formal disciplines which do not appeal to experience for verification, but only to conventions. Science

uses these formal systems as models for representing its data. To deny them is to cure the disease by burying the patient.

When it is a matter of the significance of *empirical* rather than of *formal* propositions, needless to say, operationism adopts an uncompromising positivistic attitude.

6. It is not behaviorism. Like positivism, behaviorism erred in denying too much. Operationism does not deny images, for example, but asks: What is the operational definition of the term "image"? Of course there are different behaviorisms, and some of the renovated brands are truly operational. Tolman (1936b) has a variety which he dubs explicitly "operational behaviorism"—and perhaps it is. It is certain that the behavioristic emphasis has served capably in blasting a path through subjectivity, and without this path an objective Science of Science could not march.

7. It is not monism. It asks only whether any operational meaning can be given the proposition that there is but one irreducible substance or attribute. Can the truth or falsity of this proposition be put to experimental test? If not, we face a pseudo problem.

8. It is not dualism. Here again the problems raised are pseudo problems, because the propositions are not testable. As Bills (1938) so aptly says, "Parallelism would automatically reduce to a double-aspect formula, because where two sets of defining operations coincide perfectly they become identical operationally." Of course there can be no quarrel, except on the grounds of utility, with any arbitrary dividing or classifying of facts, but pseudo problems can be avoided only provided we remember that these classes are arbitrary.

The division of concepts into the categories of subjective and objective is justifiable—if at all—only on pragmatic grounds, and only *provided* both types of concept answer the operational test. Bills believes that "mentalistic" concepts like percept, image, and idea can be operationally defined. So do I. Kantor, however, is disturbed. He detects dualism. But Bills "cannot agree with Kantor that there is any necessary dualism implied in Stevens' position." Neither can Stevens. If we admit to our store of empirical science only those concepts which are operationally founded, can we not classify them according to our purposes?

Kantor (1938) would appear to supplant dualism with a kind of realism. Now, realism is a metaphysical doctrine, and perhaps Kantor did not intend a realism. Nevertheless, he appears to defend the proposition: Nature is not the same as our knowledge of nature. Operationism must here again pose its perhaps tiresome, but necessary, question: Can any operations be formulated which will either prove or disprove this proposition? If not, it is operationally meaningless, however much "emotional meaning" it may pack.

9. Finally, operationism is not pluralism. It should be apparent by now that operationism is not consonant with any "ism" which asserts something about the ultimate nature of reality.

The Problem of Generality

There is one more criticism we must take seriously before we continue. It has been urged that operationism reduces to a vicious particularism; that there is no provision for generalization, that instead of unification in science a strict servility to the operational principle nourishes an ever-expanding multiplicity of concepts. Here is what the critics say:

Margenau, in "Causality in Modern Physics" (1931), which he addressed to the philosophers, states that operationism "cannot be tolerated as a general directive. For, in the first place, it would, if carried to its consequences, dissolve the world into an unmanageable variety of discrete concepts without logical coherence."

Lindsay, in "A Critique of Operationalism in Physics" (1937), says: ". . . logically the operational method . . . implies that each concept is tied to a definite operation."

Lindsay and Margenau together, in their book *Foundations of Physics* (1936)—a book which has brought them merited high praise—state: "On the basis of purely operational definitions, all concepts are strictly empirical and isolated" (p. 412).

Bills, in his excellent address on "Changing Views of Psychology as Science" (1938), says: "One of the ideals of scientific concept-makers is to reduce all concepts to a few fundamental ones. . . . Yet this is not, by any means, the likely outcome of operationally defined concepts. . . . For there is no universal set of operations."

Waters and Pennington, in their careful criticism of "Operationism in Psychology (1938), assert: "The fact that the concept, for Bridgman, is *synonymous* with a corresponding set of operations cannot be over-emphasized. The slightest change in any aspect of a set of operations would mean, therefore, a new concept and would demand, likewise, a new symbol for its designation. A multiplicity of concepts could scarcely be avoided."

Since Bentley (the critic, not the psychologist), in his flashy tirade on "Physicists and Fairies" (1938), has a point to make here, we will let him speak first. He refers to Lindsay and Margenau when he says: "By distorting Bridgman grossly enough, either man can, of course, readily destroy what he has distorted. Both men distort alike; first by insisting 'operations' must be all hands and no mind; second by alleging that no operation in this world can have anything to do with any other operation, not even with its own repetitions of itself."

Whether there is distortion or not, the fact that so many have pounced on this supposed snare in operationism means that the rules and procedure for generalizing from operations must sometime be made explicit. These rules obviously can be stated, because science does generalize, and operationism seeks only to discover how scientists do what they do.

The process of generalization proceeds on the basis of the notion of classes. All objects or events satisfying certain criteria we call members of a class and to that class we assign a name or symbol. Common nouns originate in precisely this fashion, and it is apparent at once that no empirical proposition is ever without some element of generality. Classification can proceed only when we have criteria defining the conditions for class-inclusion, and these criteria are essentially operational tests. Thus the statement, "Dobbin is a horse," asserts that Dobbin is a member of a class. This proposition is empirically meaningful only provided its truth or falsity can be demonstrated by concrete procedures. Does Dobbin satisfy the criteria of the class, *horse?* If he is a certain size and shape, is covered with hair, feeds on oats and hay, etc., we are happy to acknowledge him as a full-fledged horse. But how do we know he meets our tests? Here we resort to that fundamental operation we have already called discrimination. If we can discriminate crucial differences between Dobbin and other animals we have named horses, we reject Dobbin as something not horse. In other words, we "correlate" our discriminations—those made on Dobbin with those made on other objects—and the "goodness" of the correlation determines where we shall classify the beast.

It may be objected that we can always tell Dobbin from other horses, i.e., discriminate differences, but we still would resent the suggestion that he is not a horse. The answer is that a certain latitude is always allowed —we seldom resort to j.n.d.'s in a case like this—and the amount of the latitude determines the precision of the concept. As Bridgman has insisted, no concept is without its halo of uncertainty, its penumbra. No empirical class is ever watertight; we can always plague the taxonomist with the borderline case.

On the basis of elementary discriminations, then, we make our first rudimentary classes and in doing so we have made the first step toward generalization. From there we advance to form classes of classes[3] and to discover the relations between classes—always, at the empirical level, in keeping with operational criteria. Occasionally we find that from a certain point of view two classes satisfy the same criteria, or are related by a simple law, so that we are enabled to combine them into a more inclusive class under a more generic tag. Nevertheless, in all of these classifications and combinations the same simple rule is followed: We combine operations when they satisfy the criteria of a class; and the concept of that class is defined by the operations which determine inclusion within the class.

The matter can be illustrated by referring again to that example which appears to have been the jumping-off place for the critics: the concept of

---

[3] This *empirical process* of forming classes of classes should not be confused with the *logic* of classes, in which the provision for an infinite hierarchy of classes led to the antinomies discovered by Russell. The empirical process has no *necessary* relation to a formal system of logic.

length. Bridgman's argument is that we measure the length of the table and the distance to a star by two different sets of operations and we have, therefore, two different concepts of length. True enough. And Bridgman proceeds thence to show that when dealing with very large distances or very minute ones, or with distances where velocities are involved, we do well to keep in mind the differences in our defining operations. However, in his concern for the perils of promiscuous class-matings he forgot to tell us when combining is legitimate. Length measured with a rod is different from length measured with a transit, but under certain statable conditions we can muster operations to determine the relation of these two sets of measurements, and, if they meet the proper criteria, we combine them to form a larger class defining length. Of course, if we had no operations for comparing the two lengths, we should have to veto their combination. In short, then, we can and do generalize the concept length, but we do it with operational sanction.

The Philosophical Movement

Just ten years ago, the year Bridgman published his *Logic of Modern Physics*, there appeared in Vienna a company of scholars bound together by mutual admiration and a common *Weltauffassung*—a scientific philosophy. Their discussions under the leadership of Professor Schlick accomplished a unitary enthusiasm which came to concrete form in the organization of *Der Wiener Kreis*.[4] The avowed intention of this "Circle"

4 Some of the members of the Vienna Circle follow:
Moritz Schlick (1882–1936) fathered the group. Under his professional paternalism the Circle met, discussed, and found its unity. (Schlick's unfortunate death, at the hand of a crazed student, occurred as he was climbing the steps of the lecture hall.)
Otto Neurath (b. 1882) contributed his own brand of enthusiastic originality. His spirited support of radical new theses provided important inspiration. Neurath coined the designations "Physicalism" and "Unity of Science."
Rudolph Carnap (b. 1891) labored with the problem of syntax—the logical rules of language. His energetic attack on the problem of the actual construction of a fundamental syntax for the "physical" language has created a whole new field of inquiry.
Philipp Frank (b. 1884), a theoretical physicist, applied the new theory of knowledge to the problems of physics.
Hans Hahn (1879–1934), a mathematician, investigated the foundations of mathematics and exact science in the light of the scientific *Weltauffassung* of the Circle.
Friedrich Waismann distinguished himself with an investigation of the logical foundations of mathematical thinking.
In addition to these members of the Vienna Circle there were other groups whose scientific philosophy was so similar as to be scarcely distinguishable. In fact, one of the impressive aspects of this recent philosophical movement is the manner in which a common *Weltauffassung* appeared almost simultaneously among widely scattered groups of scientists, mathematicians, and philosophers. There was the Warsaw Circle, which boasted such able logicians as Tarski (b. 1901) and Lukasiewicz (b. 1878). At Berlin, prior to the recent cultural eclipse, there was another Circle whose out-

was to replace philosophy by the systematic investigation of the logic of science which, for Carnap, is "nothing other than the logical syntax of the language of science." There are but two kinds of acceptable propositions: *formal* and *empirical*. Formal propositions concern syntax. They state the rules and procedures for combining words or symbols and have no empirical reference. Empirical propositions are assertions about the observable world and their truth or falsity can be tested by means of observational procedures. Since metaphysics consists of statements not susceptible to empirical test, it is either an array of syntactical (formal) sentences or else it is technical nonsense. Mostly it is nonsense. Philosophy must be purged of it; and, once purged, it becomes the business of philosophy, says the Circle, to investigate the rules of the language we use in formulating our scientific propositions. The goal of such philosophical research is to provide a secure foundation for the sciences.

This movement was not, of course, without its antecedents. Its most immediate point of departure was the famous *Tractatus Logico-philosophicus* (1922) by Russell's pupil, Ludwig Wittgenstein. The "Tractus" exhibited the close connection between philosophy and syntax; it made clear the *formal* nature of logic and showed that the rules and proofs of syntax should have no reference to the meaning (empirical designation) of symbols; and it showed that the sentences of metaphysics are pseudo propositions. But the roots of these notions can be traced even back beyond Wittgenstein. All who, like the positivists, struck out at metaphysics; all who, like Kant, sought to conciliate analytic (formal) methods with the synthetic (empirical); and all who, like the British empiricists, assaulted philosophy with logical weapons have something in common with the Vienna Circle. Hume, in particular, except when he was assuming the existence of a transempirical world, caught the spirit. He winds up his "Enquiries Concerning Human Understanding" (1902) with this counsel:

If we take in our hand any volume; of divinity or school metaphysics, for instance; let us ask, *Does it contain any abstract reasoning concerning quantity or number* [formal questions]? No. *Does it contain any experimental reasoning concerning matter of fact and existence* [empirical questions]? No. Commit it then to the flames: for it can contain nothing but sophistry and illusion.

A philosophy as distinctive as that of the Vienna Circle must inevitably become an "ism," and its disciples, Blumberg and Feigl (1931), lost no time in introducing the Circle's program to American scholars under the title of "Logical Positivism." A. F. Bentley (1936) promptly raised the question as to whether Logical Positivism is either logical or positive, but in spite of some obvious disadvantages, the name is not entirely unreason-

standing advocate was Reichenbach (b. 1891). Logicians Russell (b. 1872) and Frege (1848–1925) fall into the same tradition, and in America C. W. Morris (b. 1901) is perhaps the best-known expositor of the common program. For a more complete listing of names, see Neurath's "Historische Anmerkungen" (1930).

able. Bentley, as his readers know, loves a *bon mot* and has a low threshold for alarm—he is aroused to criticism easily but not unpleasantly. The name Logical Positivism quite properly suggests the union of the formal and the empirical—a union which, in a well-ordered scientific household, is possible and legitimate.

Logical Positivism proposes to tell us how such a household should be run. A certain division of labor is required. The scientist, in his special field, continues to investigate the empirical relations among the variables he has at hand and these relations he represents by some form of symbolic language. The philosopher complements the scientist by probing the nature and the rules of this symbolic language. Statements about the empirical domain are called object-sentences; statements about language-forms are syntactical sentences. In any special science, such as psychology, both types of sentences frequently occur, because the psychologist must tell us not only about his facts, but also how he intends to use his words and symbols—he must provide his own definitions (see Appendix I*). The philosopher, on the other hand, can point out the logical implications of the psychologist's language and help him guard against the vicious combinations of the two types of sentences which lead to pseudo propositions.

Under this program it is not, however, the task of the philosopher to legislate for science. Science can use any logic it finds useful. Carnap (1937b), at this point, proposes a Principle of Tolerance to allay our fears: "It is not our business," he says, "to set up prohibitions, but to arrive at conventions." "*In logic,*" he continues, "*there are no morals.* Everyone is at liberty to build up his own logic, i.e., his own form of language, as he wishes. All that is required of him is that, if he wishes to discuss it, he must state his methods clearly, and give syntactical rules instead of philosophical arguments." Consequently, he who sets out to scrutinize the logic of science must renounce the proud claim that his philosophy sits enthroned above the special sciences. He works in the same field as the specialist, only with a different emphasis. He ponders the logical, formal, syntactical connections. He studies rules which are basically nothing other than conventions and matters of free choice. Hence the labors of the philosopher in that which is his only legitimate domain, the logic of science, are bound to be barren unless they are pursued in close coöperation with the special sciences.

Logical Positivism, then, seeks (1) to clarify the language of science, and (2) to investigate the conditions under which empirical propositions are meaningful. The language of science (including syntax, logic, and mathematics) consists of arrays of words or symbols which we assemble according to certain rules. The analytic propositions of syntax and mathematics are absolutely necessary and certain, once the rules of the game

---

* In the original publication.—Ed.

have been laid down. These propositions neither tell us anything about the empirical world, nor can they be confuted by experience. They can no more be proved "true" than can the conventional rules of the game of chess (see below). They simply record our determination to use words and symbols in a certain fashion.

Mathematics, under this view, is a completely rational and deductive system and nothing is contained in one formula which is not implicit in all formulas. This, to many, is a fearful thought. Poincaré (1913) voiced his apprehension by asking: "If all the propositions it enunciates can be deduced one from the other by the rules of formal logic, why is not mathematics reduced to an immense tautology? . . . Shall we admit that the theorems which fill so many volumes are nothing but devious ways of saying that A is A?" The answer appears to be that regardless of how inventive mathematical discoveries may appear to be, they contain nothing not already implicit in the fundamental postulates of the system. The outcome of our symbol-juggling surprises and delights us and fills us with the illusion of discovery, simply because of the limitations of our minds. A man of sufficient intellect would disdain the use of logic and mathematics, for he would see at a glance all that his postulates and definitions implied. He would be aware of all possible discoveries under the rules. The rest of us, however, must continue to do our mathematics stepwise, proceeding from one tautological transformation to the next, and being surprised at the result.

The second aim of Logical Positivism—to discover the conditions of empirical meaning—leads to the notion that an object-sentence is one which is verifiable by means of some concrete procedure. At this point operationism and Logical Positivism are essentially indistinguishable and we shall say no more about them, except to note an error.

This is an error which the Logical Positivists themselves have acknowledged and corrected (cf. Carnap, 1937a, p. 11), but since the slip was made in what is commonly regarded as psychological territory, we had best have a look at it. The Vienna Circle committed the all too common fallacy: It claimed to find a difference between *knowledge* and *immediate experience* (see Blumberg and Feigl, 1931). Knowledge is communicable, but the immediately given is private and noncommunicable. This from the mouth of a Logical Positivist! Indeed, by all the rules they have proposed, this sentence is not a testable proposition, for how shall we demonstrate the existence of the noncommunicable? But, as already indicated, the Logical Positivists have not been stubborn about insisting that it makes sense to talk of the private content of immediate experience as being different from the discriminable and reportable relations between experiences. Their past lapse in this regard is interesting only because it shows how easy it is for even the well-intentioned to talk nonsense when they invade this field of psychology. In "The Operational Definition of Psychological Concepts" (1935b) I have tried to demonstrate that an empirical (operational) definition of immediate experience is possible provided we note precisely what its advocates do when we ask them to indicate an example of it. Almost invariably they point to a situation involving an elementary discrimination such as: "I see red." Elementary discriminations, then, are what is meant by the immediately given, and discriminatory reactions, of course, are public and communicable.

Physicalism

As thoroughgoing empiricists the Logical Positivists hold that all meaningful scientific propositions are derived from experience. More precisely, all such propositions are reducible to *protocol-sentences*—sentences relating to the simplest elements of experience. This notion, I take it, is equivalent to the operationist's view that complex propositions are shown to be meaningful when they can be reduced to simpler propositions for which there are operational tests. The simplest propositions of all would be those relating to elementary discriminations. Now, if all scientific propositions are reducible in this fashion, including propositions expressed in what is called *physical language*, it must follow that *all* propositions are translatable into the physical language—a language similar to that of contemporary physics. This is the thesis of Physicalism.[5]

Physicalism was christened by Neurath (cf. 1931). Contrary to what the name suggests, it is not a metaphysical doctrine asserting that everything is physical, for such a proposition can have no testable meaning. It is, on the other hand, a thesis relating to language: The physical language is a universal language of science and the individual languages used in any subdomain of science can be equipollently translated into the physical language. Innocent as this assertion about language may appear, it is charged with far-reaching implications for psychology. In fact, the examples used to illustrate Physicalism make it appear that the doctrine was aimed directly against psychology—at least against the kind peddled by philosophers.

Physicalism makes it clear that the traditional but somewhat antiquated

---

5 This is a somewhat oversimplified statement of Physicalism. Furthermore, Carnap (1937a) has recently introduced extensive qualifications and changes into the original views of the Vienna Circle regarding the relation of the various "languages" of science. His reasons for preferring the physical to the psychological language (pp. 9 ff.) do not appear to me to be binding, especially if the psychological language is made operational. If that is done, the choice becomes one based on convention or convenience. We could express all physics in psychological language, but that would be more traumatic to tradition than if we were to express all psychology in the physical language. The name Physicalism justifiably appeals to many as an unhappy designation, because it arouses prejudices by suggesting the primacy of a materialistic physics.

problem of psychophysical dualism is exclusively a problem of syntax. Using the common "material mode" of speech we might say: To every psychical state there is a corresponding physical state of the body and the two are lawfully connected. Couched in this form, such a sentence is a veritable gold mine for pseudo problems. Physicalism would throttle these problems by saying: All sentences purporting to deal with psychical states are translatable into sentences in the physical language. Two distinctly separate languages to describe physics and psychology are therefore not necessary. And in this assertion we have Physicalism's denial of metaphysical dualism. It is the Logical Positivist's way of saying that psychology must be operational and behavioristic.

The philosopher, Hempel (1935), calls this kind of psychology *logical behaviorism*. It differs from the primitive American stamp in that it does not prescribe that research shall be limited to stimulus-response connections. It is not, properly speaking, a theory *about psychology* at all, but only a logical theory about psychological sentences. The psychologist may study anything he pleases, but any verifiable psychological proposition he may utter is equivalent to some proposition in the physical language. An operationist would certainly agree to this notion. In fact, an operationist would point out that this view is correlative with his own dictum that any meaningful psychological proposition, even though it pertains to a toothache, is reducible to public, concrete operations.

The Unity of Science

How we get from Physicalism to the thesis of the *unity of science* is obvious indeed. If every sentence can be translated into the physical language, then this language is an all-inclusive language—a universal language of science. And if the esoteric jargons of all the separate sciences can, upon demand, be reduced to a single coherent language, then all science possesses a fundamental logical unity.

This idea of a unified basis for science, introduced into the Vienna Circle by the imaginative originality of Neurath, has launched a whole new movement in scientific philosophy. The newly begun *International Encyclopedia of Unified Science* is tangible testimony to the vigor and seriousness of the enterprise.[6] Annual congresses provide a forum where

6 Neurath (1937) describes *unified science* as *encyclopedic integration*. The new "Encyclopedia" is to be constructed like an onion. The heart of the onion will be two introductory volumes consisting of twenty pamphlets, and in these volumes will be laid the foundations for a logical unity which will make possible future integration of scientific disciplines. The first layer of the onion enclosing the heart will be a series of volumes to deal with problems of systematization in special sciences, including logic, mathematics, the theory of signs, history of science, classification of the sciences, and the educational implications of the scientific attitude. Still outer layers will concern even more specialized problems. The encyclopedia will not

the thesis is developed (Fifth Annual Congress . . . held at Harvard University, September 5–10, 1939); and out of this intellectual format there is emerging a substantial basis for an empirical and universal Science of Science. But before we inspect this newest of sciences—one which is obviously still warm in the womb of its philosophy-mother—let us look backward a few centuries.

How many men, since ancient Thales proposed that all is water, have dreamed the dream of a universal science is beyond a guess. The dream has taken many forms—mostly impracticable—for the history of science is a story of diversification and specialization proceeding almost geometrically with time. If there is unity in so much arborescence, where are we to find it? Certainly not in subject matter where differentiation is the rule. Perhaps, then, in method and logic.

In 1666 the twenty-year-old Leibnitz (Bell, 1937) dreamed his own dream about the unity of science and recorded it in *De Arte Combinatoria*. He himself called it a schoolboy's essay, but in it he proposed to create *"a general method in which all truths of reason would be reduced to a kind of calculation. At the same time this would be a sort of universal language or script, but infinitely different from those projected hitherto; for the symbols and even the words in it would direct the reason; and errors, except those of fact, would be mere mistakes in calculation."* How long would it take to create this logistic? Leibnitz thought a few chosen men could turn the trick within five years. But chosen men were not at hand and two centuries passed before the creation of a universal symbolic logic was even begun. Almost another century of labor has been needed to lay a foundation in logic and syntax so tangible that many men together could vision the unity of science.

Leibnitz, though, if any single man, was father to the idea. He hoped for a universal logicalization of human thinking by means of a general calculus and a general terminology. He conceived a formal discipline to include a theory and art of forming signs to represent ideas and a general calculus giving a universal formal method of drawing consequences from the signs. Then, if two men were to find themselves in disagreement as to anything except matters of observation, they would settle their argument by calculating the right answer. Leibnitz' inspiration is perhaps not with-

---

be an alphabetical dictionary and its creators hope, quite piously, that it will not become a mausoleum but remain a living intellectual force.

At the present writing only three numbers (1, 2, and 5) of the "Encyclopedia" have appeared, but it is already clear that, although there is great community among the contributors, detailed unanimity is absent. As to the problem of unity in science, for example, Carnap finds as yet *no unity of laws* in science, but only *unity of language;* Lenzen finds a basis for unity in the fact that all science starts from experience; Neurath would get his unity by means of *encyclopedic integration;* Russell says the unity is essentially one of method; and Dewey hopes for unity by promulgating what he calls the scientific attitude.

out its utopian aspect, but it cannot be denied that the modern logic of science has made progress towards Leibnitz' goal.

Perhaps our progress has not always been of the sort that would have delighted the boy of twenty, for metaphysics was no triviality in 1666. Today, however, it is clear that the unhappy symphonies of pseudo propositions that are metaphysics have all too frequently thwarted our efforts at clarification. Logical analysis has unmasked metaphysics; at least that is one of the boasted achievements of the recent philosophical movement. Opinion will probably never be unanimous on this issue, but disclosure of the empirically meaningless aspects of metaphysics is intimately bound to the other advances claimed by the Logical Positivists. By way of review at this point, these are some of the achievements of the modern movement:

1. It has been demonstrated that a unified language of science is possible. The syntax of this language is to be discovered by careful analysis of linguistic usage in science. And what unity there is in science is to be found in the unity of its logic and syntax.

2. Linguistic analysis has revealed the all-important distinction between the *formal* and the *empirical* aspects of science. Formal science consists of the analytic statements established by logic and mathematics; empirical science consists of the synthetic statements established in the different fields of factual knowledge.

3. The statements of logic and mathematics derive their validity from conventions, and, from the point of view of empiricism, they are materially empty and constitute a closed system of tautologies. Logic deals with language only—not with the objects of language. Likewise, mathematics deals with symbols—not with the objects which the symbols represent.

4. Empirical propositions have meaning when there exists a concrete procedure (a set of operations) for determining their truth or falsity. Empirical significance attaches only to testable or confirmable sentences.

5. What we have called the "truth" of an empirical proposition is something which can never be absolute. Repeated tests of an object-sentence can add to its probability but never clinch its certainty. Induction, as Hume pointed out, is not a watertight method of proving anything empirical.

6. The notion that all scientific sentences are translatable into a common form—the physical language—requires of psychology a behavioristic approach. Psychology so conceived is called *behavioristics*.

These alleged achievements of the philosophers have been attained in the same spirit professed by the operationists: an empirical study of the actual doings of science-makers. Little wonder, then, that the two groups, although differing in emphasis, have arrived at substantially the same generalizations. Furthermore, these studies investigating the science-makers are the beginnings of a Science of Science. Like all other sciences, this one began before it was founded. Its founding and christening are of very recent date. They coincide with the harvesting of its first fruits.

The Science of Science

These first fruits of the Science of Science, it would appear, are the positive advances of operationism, of Logical Positivism, and of all who have looked seriously into the rules under which science is created. Except for these fruits, of which many are still green and some may even turn out to be wormy, the Science of Science comprises little more than an optimistic program. The fullest account of this program is supplied by C. W. Morris in his excellent essay on the "Foundations of the theory of signs" (1938b).

Morris is a philosopher at Chicago, and many will want to ask: What good is a science in the hands of philosophers? The obvious retort is that all our major sciences passed their childhood in the mansion of philosophy and only after they had grown tough and empirical were they bold enough to desert the tender-minded parent. It may be that once again a band of curious men have turned up in some unsuspected corner a new science with which they will charm away a few hardy scholars and leave the parental mansion tenanted by the tender-minded.

Let us turn now to an outline of the scientific study of science. Morris calls it "Metascience" or "Scientific Empiricism." Morris is enthusiastically full of new terms; in fact, a difficulty with his account is that he is overly generous in his willingness to enrich our vocabulary. Much of his coinage, however, is choice and merits more extensive circulation. Morris defends the thesis that *it is possible to include without remainder the study of science under the study of the language of science, because the study of that language involves not merely the study of its formal structure but its relation to the objects it designates and to the persons who use it.* Language is a system of signs or symbols and the general science of signs is to be called *Semiotic*. Semiotic has a double relation to the other sciences: It is both a science among the sciences and an instrument of the sciences. It is not a "superscience" but rather a common science among the others. Every scientist at some stage of his work must embody his results in linguistic signs, and consequently he must be as careful with his linguistic tools as he is in designing his apparatus or in making his observations. In his enterprise, the scientist unites empiricism with methodological rationalism, and Semiotic studies how this marriage is consecrated.

The study divides itself into three dimensions or levels, which we shall discuss in turn:

1. Syntactics is the study of the relation of signs to signs.
2. Semantics is the study of the relation of signs to objects.

3. Pragmatics is the study of the relation of signs to scientists.

Syntactics refers to the formal disciplines commonly called logic, mathematics, and syntax, where the relation of signs to one another is *abstracted* from their relation to objects and to users or interpreters. At present this is the best developed branch of Semiotic, but in the field of the logical syntax of language there is still greater labor to be done. The investigation of language from the syntactical point of view is at once both complex and fruitful. It has been possible accurately to characterize primitive, analytic, contradictory, and synthetic sentences, and to show that many sentences which are apparently object-sentences (and so concern things which are not signs) turn out under analysis to be pseudo object-sentences which must be interpreted as syntactical statements about language. An astonishing number of the scientist's sentences are syntactical in this sense (see Appendix I*). They are propositions without material content.

Ayer (1936, p. 63) gives us a "striking instance" of the way in which propositions which are really linguistic are often expressed in such a way that they appear to be factual. At first glance, the proposition, "A material thing cannot be in two places at once," looks quite empirical, but critical inspection shows that "it simply records the fact that, as a result of certain verbal conventions, the proposition that two sense-contents occur in the same visual or tactual sense-field is incompatible with the proposition that they belong to the same material thing." The proposition, then, is a definition—it records our decision as to how we shall use the term "material thing." As this example suggests, the scientist frequently couches in the material idiom the propositions which he really intends as definitions, and thereby he tends unwittingly to generate pseudo problems out of his use—or misuse—of signs.

Of course, science is not the only activity in which we use signs. The artist, the musician, and the traffic cop are notable sign-users. What their various signs express or designate concerns semantics; what the effect of these signs is on society and the individual concerns pragmatics; but we can also inquire under what rules the signs are made, combined, and transformed, and that is syntactics.

Semantics refers to the rules determining under what condition a sign is applicable to an object or situation. Thus, the operational rule[7] laid down

---

* In the original publication.—Ed.

[7] In discussing operationism I have used the words *term* and *proposition*, *applicability* and *truth* (Stevens, 1935b, 1936). In keeping with the spirit of Semiotic I ought perhaps to say that *terms* have *applicability* under semantical rules when the criteria governing their use are operational criteria. Then, sentences formed by combining these *semantically* significant terms into propositions are *empirically* significant (have truth-value) when their assertions are confirmable by means of operations. In other words, there is a justifiable distinction between the operational meaning of words and symbols (semantical significance) and the operational meaning of empirical

by Bridgman for determining the meaning of a term is, I take it, essentially a *semantical rule*. And the so-called "applicational definitions" used by the Logical Positivists to state when a term shall apply to an object come under this heading (cf. Blumberg and Feigl, 1931). Within the study of these rules belong all the problems relating to the correlation between the signs which comprise a scientific treatise and the discriminable aspects of the physical world to which the signs are meant to apply. The simplest semantical rule is that governing an *indexical* sign. Such a sign designates what is pointed at at any instant. The denotation of the sign is based upon the operation of pointing, which in turn, of course, involves an act of discrimination. We have already noted that discrimination is the simplest and most basic operation performable.

Many of the problems of semantics belong to psychology. Morris sees in the experimental approach made possible by behavioristics great promise for determining the actual conditions under which certain signs are employed. Unfortunately, rules for the use of sign-vehicles are not ordinarily formulated by the users of a language; they exist, rather, as habits of behavior, and semantics wants to know what these habits are and how they come to be established. Many pertinent experimental studies have already been made by psychologists seeking the conditions of concept formation and judgments of similarity, but more are in order. Tolman's discovery of sign-gestalts functioning in the life of the rat discloses semantics among the rodents, and Lashley's effort to discover what range of patterns are considered equivalent by the rat when he uses them as signs for food directs attention to the problem of functional substitutivity (to use Professor Boring's term) among symbolic forms.

The game of chess is frequently suggested (cf. Carnap, 1934, and Reichenbach, 1938) as an example of a system of conventional formal rules applicable to concrete objects and situations. Perhaps at this point we can better illuminate Semiotic by examining this ancient pastime. First let us consider a set of signs. We shall use three groups of symbols: (1) the letters *a, b, c, d, e, f, g,* and *h;* (2) the numbers 1, 2, 3, 4, 5, 6, 7, and 8; and (3) certain other signs such as Kt, B, Q, K, etc. Next we shall set up conventional rules for manipulating these symbols by allowing only combinations in which 1 sign from each of the three groups appears, such as, for example, Kt *c* 4. This combination shall be transformable into other combinations, depending upon the first symbol, Kt. Thus:

$$\text{Kt } c\, 4 \longrightarrow \text{Kt } e\, 5$$

But we shall not be allowed to write:

$$\text{Kt } c\, 4 \longrightarrow \text{Kt } d\, 5$$

---

propositions. I am not certain, however, that Morris would distinguish between empirical and semantical propositions in the same way.

Now, when we have stated all the rules governing these signs, what do we have? Quite plainly, what we have is a formal system—a set of signs governed by syntactical rules. We are engaged in the pursuit of syntactics.

Anyone who is a chess player will have guessed by now that these syntactical rules were *abstracted* from the game of chess. The point is that we can abstract them in this way and study them with no reference to anything beyond themselves. On the other hand, we can use them as a "model" to describe chess. In order to use them in this way we proceed to set up *semantical rules*. We say: Let the letters stand for the rows and the numbers for the columns of a chess board; let Kt stand for a particular small object (called a knight) which sits on a square of the board; then define Kt c 4 as equivalent to the statement that there is a knight on the square of co-ordinates c and 4; and define Kt c 4 $\longrightarrow$ Kt e 5 as equivalent to the statement that the knight is moved from c 4 to e 5. These semantical rules are statements about the use of language—they merely record our decisions as to how we shall use certain signs—and as semantical rules they are not empirical propositions. (This distinction between semantical and empirical statements was not made sufficiently explicit in operationism, but it needs to be stressed.)

We create an empirical statement as soon as we say that Kt c 4 is true, i.e., that there is, in fact, a knight on c 4, because this statement can be operationally verified. We can look to see whether our knight is there on c 4, or elsewhere. If the knight is on c 4 the statement is confirmed as true and if the knight is not on c 4 the statement is unconfirmed and is false. On the other hand, the statement "Kt c a" can never be considered an empirical proposition, because this combination of signs violates the rules of syntax and is meaningless—it cannot be tested operationally.[8]

From our game of chess we can abstract still another dimension or aspect. We can ask: What is the relation of these rules to chess players? Is the game hard or easy? What is its place in society, etc.? Here we are broaching pragmatical questions.

Pragmatics, as a part of Semiotic, studies the relation of signs to scientists. Here belong the problems as to how the scientist, as a behaving organism, reacts to signs; how science, as a social institution, interacts with other social institutions; and how scientific activity relates to other activities. This, indeed, is the aspect of Semiotic most challenging to the psychologist. It is the problem of the interpretation of signs. What is their effect on the man who sees or hears them? How do they determine behavior? How are they used and abused in shaping human destiny? A nebulous problem, one might complain, and overwhelmingly complex. "Yes, but none the less real and pressing," must be the answer.

[8] Note the similarity between the statement "Kt c a" and Ayer's example discussed above. To say that a knight cannot be on c and a at the same time is very like saying that an object cannot be in two places at once. Both statements follow directly from the rules of our syntax and are therefore nonempirical sentences.

The term "pragmatics" obviously suggests the philosophy known as pragmatism. The word was deliberately chosen to be thus suggestive. (In Semiotic we should say that the *pragmatical* aspect of the word is one of suggestiveness.) Pragmatism, more effectively than ever before, directed attention to the relation of signs to their users and assessed this relation as an aid in understanding intellectual activities. Pragmatics, as part of Semiotic, pays tribute to the achievements of Peirce, James, Dewey, and Mead, but it must not be thought identical with pragmatism as a philosophy.

Both pragmatism and pragmatics agree that the interpreter of a sign-vehicle is an organism whose "taking-account" of the sign consists in a *habit to respond* to the vehicle as it would to the thing designated by the sign. We thus find the problem of pragmatics cast in such a form that it can be handled by behavioristics—we deliberately avoid talking about the subjective effects of signs unless these effects are disclosed by public operations. Not only do we react to the signs appearing in sober scientific propositions, but our habits of response carry over to situations where signs obey neither semantical nor syntactical rules. We are often delighted by senseless jingles and moved to strong emotions by what analysis shows to be gibberish. In propaganda, where syntax is usually not violated, but where semantical relations are sometimes distorted, the pragmatical effects (the induction of some form of behavior) may be profoundly disturbing. Clearly, psychology has a stake in the solution of all these problems arising in pragmatics.

One more facet of this many-sided problem deserves our interest. What Morris calls *descriptive pragmatics* occurs when a sign used by a person is employed as a means of gaining information about the person. The psychoanalyst studies dreams for the light they throw upon the dreamer, not to discover whether there are actually any situations which the dreams denote. Likewise, we may study the statements of newspapers and politicians, not as empirical propositions, but for their ability to disclose the faction whose interest is being served by this form of propaganda. And in much the same spirit, the psychiatrist inspects the signs used by his patient in order to diagnose an abnormality. The pragmatical aberrations found among the psychoses are extremely illuminating, for occasionally a patient lets his system of signs displace completely the objects they once stood for; the troublesome world of reality is pushed aside and the frustrated fellow gets his satisfaction in the domain of signs, oblivious to the restrictions of syntactical and semantical rules. The field of psychopathology thus holds great promise as a place to apply Semiotic and discover some of its laws.[9]

9 Count Alfred Korzybski has written a bulky work called *Science and Sanity* (Lancaster: Science Press, 1933), in which he contends that in the miseducation of our youth we teach them semantical rules based upon static Aristotelian classifications which they must then use in dealing with a fluid dynamic universe. Such

There can be no doubt that in the realm of human behavior the concept of sign holds a key place. And if, as the pragmatists contend, mental phenomena are to be equated to sign-responses, psychology bears an intimate relation to the science of signs. The theory of signs—being the co-ordinated disciplines of syntactics, semantics, and pragmatics—is the core of a unified science. "Indeed," exclaims Morris (1938b), "it does not seem fantastic to believe that the concept of sign may prove as fundamental to the sciences of man as the concept of atom has been for the physical sciences or the concept of cell for the biological sciences."

Epilogue

That then, in all too brief review, is the manner in which the Science of Science has been staked out. Whoever would probe the making of science can learn all the answers by inspecting thoroughly the language of science. The investigator must remember, however, that *this language is an intersubjective (public) set of sign-vehicles whose usage is determined by syntactical, semantical, and pragmatical rules.* By making the Science of Science coextensive with the study of the language of science we have set spacious bounds to this field of inquiry—there is ample room for a variety of talents, and to bring all the diverse areas under cultivation will require co-operation among the specialties.

Three features of this lusty embryonic science stand out with particular prominence.

First, the rational and the empirical elements in science are disentangled and then reassembled according to a straightforward, workable plan. The formal, rational, analytic, a priori, deductive side of creative thinking, which has always been so dear in the hearts of James's "tender-minded," neither rules nor is ruled by the empirical synthetic, a posteriori, inductive wing. Neither side can be called a usurper when both are understood, for they are not even in competition. Their union is achieved, not after the manner of Kant, who held out for a bastard hybrid which he called the "a priori synthetic judgment," but in conformity with the relation of sign to object.

Secondly, it is proposed that in our study of the science-maker we begin with the *products* of his activity—his finished propositions—rather than with his "experiences" or any other phase of his earlier behavior. This is a sensible place to begin. If we were to study the manufacture of any product, such as automobiles, we should probably find it useful first to ascertain what an automobile is and then to discover the conditions under

---

semantical habits are enough out of tune with reality to drive many people crazy. Korzyski would cure the resulting insanity by renovating the patient's semantics. Whatever our opinion about this etiology and cure, it is plain that much of Korzybski's concern is with what Morris would call pragmatics—the effect of signs upon the users of signs.

which it comes into being. Science manufactures sentences, and we, as curious mortals, ask: What is a sentence and how is it made? The *complete* answer to this question is the Science of Science.

Thirdly, does it not appear that the Science of Science must go directly to psychology for an answer to many of its problems? Is it not also plain that a behavioristic psychology is the only one that can be of much help in this enterprise? A sign has semantical significance when an organism will react to it as it would to the object which the sign supplants. The psychologist works out the laws under which different stimuli evoke equivalent reactions. Signs, as stimuli, can be combined and utilized extensively in the control and direction of behavior, both individual and social. The entire activity of the scientist as a sign-using organism, constitutes, therefore, a type of behavior for which behavioristics seeks the laws. If there is a sense in which psychology is the propaedeutic science (cf. Stevens, 1936), it is undoubtedly in its ability to study the behavior, *qua* behavior, of the science-makers.

Perhaps we are too close to this young Science of Science either to judge its value or see clearly how it came to be. We shall forego the value-judgment, since it would merely disclose the author's particular prejudice (already clear, no doubt), but an observation about the movement's immediate ancestry is not entirely out of order. It now appears, in retrospect, that the Science of Science emerged as the reasonable outcome of revolutions in the three major fields: physics, psychology, and philosophy. These revolutions occurred almost independently, but a general community of spirit among them led directly to extensive cross-fertilization. Operationism as a revolution against absolute and undefinable concepts in physics, behaviorism as a revolution against dualistic mentalism in psychology, and Logical Positivism as a revolution against rational metaphysics in philosophy were the three forces whose convergence into a common effort is effected by the Science of Science.

Finally, the purpose of this review has been to call the attention of those of us who are psychologists to the critical principles involved in scientific method as evolved in recent scientific and philosophic movements. We have had little to say concretely about psychology or its facts, and undoubtedly many will be impatient with so much non-experimental discourse. "Who cares about philosophy?" they will say. "What matters is the product of the laboratory." While such robust empiricism is admirable, we must ask the indulgence of these tough minds. We must ask them to bear with us while we inspect our logical tools as carefully as we do our other apparatus. And we must ask them to weigh the implications for psychology of this statement by Quine, the logician (1936):

The less a science has advanced the more its terminology tends to rest upon an uncritical assumption of mutual understanding. With increase of rigor this basis is replaced piecemeal by the introduction of definitions. The interrelationships recruited for these definitions gains the status of analytic principles; what was once regarded as a theory about the world becomes reconstrued as a convention of language. Thus it is that some flow from the theoretical to the conventional is an adjunct of progress in the logical foundations of any science.

REFERENCES

AYER, A. J. *Language, truth and logic*. London: Gollancz, 1936.

BELL, E. T. *Men of mathematics*. New York: Simon and Schuster, 1937.

BENJAMIN, A. C. *An introduction to the philosophy of science*. New York: Macmillan, 1937 (a).

———. The operational theory of meaning. *Phil. Rev.*, N.Y., 1937, **46**, 644–649 (b).

BENTLEY, A. F. The positive and the logical. *Phil. Sci.*, 1936, **3**, 472–485.

———. Physicists and fairies. *Phil. Sci.*, 1938, **5**, 132–165.

BILLS, A. G. Changing views of psychology as science. *Psychol. Rev.*, 1938, **45**, 377–394.

BLUMBERG, A. E., and FEIGL, H. Logical positivism. *J. Phil.*, 1931, **28**, 281–296.

BOAS, G., and BLUMBERG, A. E. Some remarks in defense of the operational theory of meaning. *J. Phil.*, 1931, **28**, 544–550.

BORING, E. G. Temporal perception and operationism. *Amer. J. Psychol.*, 1936, **48**, 519–522.

BRIDGMAN, P. W. *The logic of modern physics*. New York: Macmillan, 1928.

———. A physicist's second reaction to Mengenlehre. *Scripta math.*, 1934, **2**, 3–29.

———. *The nature of physical theory*. Princeton, N.J.: Princeton Univ. Press, 1936.

———. Operational analysis. *Phil. Sci.*, 1938, **5**, 114–131.

BRUNSWICK, E. Psychology as a science of objective relations. *Phil. Sci.*, 1937, **4**, 227–260.

BURES, C. E. The concept of probability. *Phil. Sci.*, 1938, **5**, 1–20.

CAMPBELL, N. R. *Physics: the elements*. Cambridge: Univ. Press, 1920.

CARNAP, R. On the character of philosophic problems. *Phil. Sci.*, 1934, **1**, 5–19.

———. *Philosophy and logical syntax*. London: Kegan Paul, 1935 (a).

———. Les concepts psychologiques et les concepts physiques sont-ils foncièrement différents? *Rev. Synthèse*, 1935, **10**, 43–53 (b).

———. Testability and meaning. *Phil. Sci.*, 1936, **3**, 419–471; 1937, **4**, 1–40 (a).

———. *Logical syntax of language*. London: Kegan Paul, 1937 (b).

DINGLE, H. *Through science to philosophy*. Oxford: Clarendon Press, 1937.

EINSTEIN, A. On the method of theoretical physics. *Phil. Sci.*, 1934, **1**, 163–169.

FEIGL, H. The logical character of the principle of induction. *Phil. Sci.*, 1934, **1**, 20–29 (a).

———. Logical analysis of the psycho-physical problem. *Phil. Sci.*, 1934, **1**, 420–445 (b).

HEMPEL, C. G. Analyse logique de la psychologie. *Rev. Synthèse*, 1935, **10**, 27–42.

HUME, D. *Enquiries concerning the human understanding and concerning the principles of morals* (2nd ed.). Oxford: Clarendon Press, 1902.

JAMES, W. *Pragmatism.* New York: Longmans, Green, 1914.

KANTOR, J. R. The operational principle in the physical and psychological sciences. *Psychol. Rec.,* 1938, **2**, 3–32.

LEWIN, K. The conceptual representation and the measurement of psychological forces. *Contr. Psychol. Theor.,* 1938, **1**, No. 4, 1–247.

LINDSAY, R. B. A critique of operationalism in physics. *Phil. Sci.,* 1937, **4**, 456–470.

LINDSAY, R. B., and MARGENAU, H. *Foundations of physics.* New York: Wiley, 1936.

LUNDBERG, G. A. Quantitative methods in social psychology. *Amer. Sociol. Rev.,* 1936, **1**, 38–54.

MALISOFF, W. M. The universe of operations (a review). *Phil. Sci.,* 1936, **3**, 360–364.

MARGENAU, H. Causality in modern physics. *Monist,* 1931, **41**, 1–36.

———. Methodology of modern physics. *Phil. Sci.,* 1935, **2**, 48–72, 164–187.

McGEOCH, J. A. Learning as an operationally defined concept. *Psychol. Bull.,* 1935, **32**, 688 (abstr.).

———. A critique of operational definition. *Psychol. Bull.,* 1937, **34**, 703–704 (abstr.).

McGREGOR, D. Scientific measurement and psychology. *Psychol. Rev.,* 1935, **42**, 246–266.

MENGER, K. The new logic. *Phil. Sci.,* 1937, **4**, 299–336.

MORRIS, C. W. Scientific empiricism. *Int. Encycl. Unif. Sci.,* 1938, No. 1, 63–75 (a).

———. Foundations of the theory of signs. *Int. Encycl. Unif. Sci.,* 1938, No. 2, 1–59 (b).

NAGEL, E. Some theses in the philosophy of logic. *Phil. Sci.,* 1938, **5**, 46–51.

NEURATH, O. Historische Anmerkungen. *Erkenntnis,* 1930, **1**, 311–314.

———. Physicalism: the philosophy of the Viennese Circle. *Monist,* 1931, **41**, 618–623.

———. Unified science and its encyclopedia. *Phil. Sci.,* 1937, **4**, 265–277.

POINCARÉ, H. *The foundations of science.* New York: Science Press, 1913.

QUINE, W. Truth by convention. In *Philosophical essays for Alfred North Whitehead.* New York: Longmans, Green, 1936, p. 90.

RASHEVSKY, N. Foundations of mathematical biophysics. *Phil. Sci.,* 1934, **1**, 176–196.

———. Physico-mathematical methods in biological and social sciences. *Erkenntnis,* 1936, **6**, 357–365.

REICHENBACH, H. *Experience and prediction.* Chicago: Univ. of Chicago Press, 1938.

ROSENZWEIG, S. Schools of psychology: a complementary pattern. *Phil. Sci.,* 1937, **4**, 96–106.

SCHLICK, M. De la relation entre les notions psychologiques et les notions physiques. *Rev. Synthèse,* 1935, **10**, 5–26.

SEASHORE, R. H., and KATZ, B. An operational definition and classification of mental mechanisms. *Psychol. Rec.*, 1937, 1, 3–24.

SOMERVILLE, J. Logical empiricism and the problem of causality in social sciences. *Erkenntnis*, 1936, 6, 405–411.

STEVENS, S. S. The operational basis of psychology. *Amer. J. Psychol.*, 1935, 47, 323–330 (a).

———. The operational definition of psychological concepts. *Psychol. Rev.*, 1935, 42, 517–527 (b).

———. Psychology: the propaedeutic science. *Phil. Sci.*, 1936, 3, 90–103.

STRUIK, D. J. On the foundations of the theory of probabilities. *Phil. Sci.*, 1934, 1, 50–70.

TOLMAN, E. C. *Purposive behavior in animals and men.* New York: Appleton-Century, 1932.

———. An operational analysis of 'demands.' *Erkenntnis*, 1936, 6, 383–390 (a).

———. Operational behaviorism and current trends in psychology. *Proc. 25th Anniv. Celebr. Inaug. Grad. Stud.* Los Angeles: Univ. of S. Calif. Press, 1936, 89–103 (b).

WATERS, R. H., and PENNINGTON, L. A. Operationism in psychology. *Psychol. Rev.*, 1938, 45, 414–423.

WEINBERG, J. R. *An examination of logical positivism.* London: Kegan Paul, Trench, Trubner, 1936.

WITTGENSTEIN, L. *Tractatus logico-philosophicus.* New York: Harcourt, Brace, 1922.

WOODGER, J. H. *The axiomatic method in biology.* Cambridge: Cambridge Univ. Press, 1937.

2

THE INTERVENING VARIABLE

KENNETH MacCORQUODALE and PAUL E. MEEHL

As THE thinking of behavior theorists has become more sophisticated and self-conscious, there has been considerable discussion of the value and logical status of so-called "intervening variables." Hull speaks of "symbolic constructs, intervening variables, or hypothetical entities" (3, p. 22) and deals with them in his theoretical discussion as being roughly equivalent notions. At least, his exposition does not distinguish among them

FROM K. MacCorquodale and P. E. Meehl, On a distinction between hypothetical constructs and intervening variables, *Psychological Review*, 1948, 55, 95–107. Pp. 95–96 and 103–107 reprinted by permission of the authors, the *Psychological Review*, and the American Psychological Association.

explicitly. In his presidential address on behavior at a choice point, Tolman inserts one of Hull's serial conditioning diagrams (8, p. 13) between the independent variables (maintenance schedule, goal object, etc.) and the dependent variable ("behavior ratio") to illustrate his concept of the intervening variable. This would seem to imply that Tolman views his "intervening variables" as the same character as Hull's. In view of this, it is somewhat surprising to discover that Skinner apparently feels that his formulations have a close affinity to those of Tolman, but are basically dissimilar to those of Hull (7, pp. 436, 437). In advocating a theoretical structure which is "descriptive" and "positivistic," he suggests that the model chosen by Hull (Newtonian mechanics) is not the most suitable model for purposes of behavior theory; and in general is critical of the whole postulate-deductive approach.

Simultaneously with these trends one can still observe among "tough-minded" psychologists the use of words such as "unobservable" and "hypothetical" in an essentially derogatory manner, and an almost compulsive fear of passing beyond the direct colligation of observable data. "Fictions" and "hypothetical entities" are sometimes introduced into a discussion of theory with a degree of trepidation and apology quite unlike the freedom with which physicists talk about atoms, mesons, fields, and the like. There also seems to be a tendency to treat all hypothetical constructs as on the same footing merely because they are hypothetical; so that we find people arguing that if neutrons are admissible in physics, it must be admissible for us to talk about, e.g., the damming up of libido and its reversion to earlier channels.

The view which theoretical psychologists take toward intervening variables and hypothetical constructs will of course profoundly influence the direction of theoretical thought. Furthermore, what *kinds* of hypothetical constructs we become accustomed to thinking about will have a considerable impact upon theory creation. The present paper aims to present what seems to us a major problem in the conceptualization of intervening variables, without claiming to offer a wholly satisfactory solution. Chiefly, it is our aim here to make a distinction between two subclasses of intervening variables, or, we prefer to say, between "intervening variables" and "hypothetical constructs," which we feel is fundamental but is currently being neglected.

We shall begin with a common-sense distinction, and proceed later to formulations of this distinction which we hope will be more rigorous. Naively, it would seem that there is a difference in logical status between constructs which involve the hypothesization of an *entity, process,* or *event* which is not itself observed, and constructs which do not involve such hypothesization. For example, Skinner's "reflex reserve" is definable in terms of the total available responses without further conditioning, whereas Hull's "afferent neural interaction" involves the notion of processes within the nervous system which presumably occur within the objective physical system and which, under suitable conditions, we might observe directly. To take examples from another science in which we psychologists may have less stake in the distinction, one might contrast the notion of "resistance" in electricity to the notion of "electron." The resistance of a piece of wire is what Carnap has called a *dispositional concept,* and is defined by a special type of implication relation. When we say that the resistance of a wire is such-and-such, we mean that "so-and-so volts will give a current of so-and-so amperes." (For a more precise formulation of this see Carnap, 1, p. 440.) Resistance, in other words, is "operational" in a very direct and primitive sense. The electron, on the other hand, is supposedly an *entity* of some sort. Statements about the electron are, to be sure, supported by means of observational sentences. Nevertheless, it is no longer maintained even by positivists that this set of supporting sentences exhaust the entire *meaning* of the sentences about the electron. Reichenbach, for example, distinguishes *abstracta* from *illata* (from Lat. *infero*). The latter are "inferred things," such as molecules, other people's minds, and so on. They are believed in on the basis of our impressions, but the sentences involving them, even those asserting their existence, are not reducible to sentences about impressions. This is the epistemological form, at rock bottom level, of the distinction we wish to make here. . . .

On the basis of these considerations, we are inclined to propose a linguistic convention for psychological theorists which we feel will help to clarify discussion of these matters. We suggest that the phrase "intervening variable" be restricted to the original use implied by Tolman's definition. Such a variable will then be simply a quantity obtained by a specified manipulation of the values of empirical variables; it will involve no hypothesis as to the existence of nonobserved entities or the occurrence of unobserved processes; it will contain, in its complete statement for all purposes of theory and prediction, no words which are not definable either explicitly or by reduction sentences in terms of the empirical variables; and the validity of empirical laws involving only observables will constitute both the necessary and sufficient conditions for the validity of the laws involving these intervening variables. Legitimate instances of such "pure" intervening variables are Skinner's *reserve,* Tolman's *demand,* Hull's *habit strength,* and Lewin's *valence.* These constructs are the behavioral analogue of Carnap's "dispositional concepts" such as solubility, resistance, inflammability, etc. It must be emphasized that the setting up of a definition or reduction for an intervening variable is not a wholly arbitrary and conventional matter. As Carnap has pointed out, it often happens that we give alternative sets of reduction sentences for the same dispositional concept; in these cases there is empirical content in our statement even though it has a form that suggests arbitrariness. The reason for this is that these separate reductions for a given dispositional concept imply that the empirical events are themselves related in a certain way. The notion of amount of electric current can be introduced by several different observations, such as deposition of silver, deflection of a needle, hydrogen separated out of water, and so on. Such a set of reductions has empirical content because the empirical statements together with the reductions must not lead to contradictions. It is a contingent fact, not derivable from definitions alone, that the deposition of silver will give the same answer for "amount of current" as will the deflection of a needle. A similar problem exists in Hull, when he sets up "momentary effective reaction potential" as the last intervening variable in his chain. In the case of striated muscle reactions, it is stated that latency, resistance to extinction, and probability of occurrence of a response are all functions of reaction potential. Neglecting behavior oscillation, which does not occur in the formulation for the second two because they involve many repetitions of the situation, this means that the empirical variables must be perfectly correlated (non-linearly, of course). The only possible source of variation which could attenuate a perfect correlation between probability of occurrence and resistance to extinction would be actual errors of experimental measurement, since there are no sources of uncontrolled variation left within the organism. If we consider average latency instead of momentary latency (which is a function of *momentary* effective reaction potential and hence varies with behavioral oscillation), latency and resistance to extinction should also be perfectly correlated. It remains to be seen whether the facts will support Hull in giving simultaneously several reductions for the notion of reaction potential.

As a second linguistic convention, we propose that the term "hypothetical construct" be used to designate theoretical concepts which do *not* meet the requirements for intervening variables in the strict sense. That is to say, these constructs involve terms which are not wholly reducible to empirical terms; they refer to processes or entities that are not directly observed (although they need not be in principle unobservable); the mathematical expression of them cannot be formed simply by a suitable grouping of terms in a direct empirical equation; and the truth of the empirical laws involved is a necessary but not a sufficient condition for the truth of these conceptions. Examples of such constructs are Guthrie's M.P.S.'s, Hull's r_g's, S_d's, and *afferent neural interaction*, Allport's *biophysical traits*, Murray's *regnancies*, the notion of "anxiety" as used by Mowrer, Miller, and Dollard and others of the Yale-derived group, and most theoretical constructs in psychoanalytic theory. Skinner and Tolman seem to be almost wholly free of hypothetical constructs, although when Skinner invokes such notions as the "strain on the reverse" (7, p. 289) it is difficult to be sure.

We do not wish to seem to legislate usage, so that if the broader use of "intervening variable" has become stuck in psychological discourse, we would propose alternatively a distinction between intervening variables of the "abstractive" and of the "hypothetical" kind. Since our personal preference is for restricting the phrase *intervening variables* to the pure type described by Tolman, we shall follow this convention in the remainder of the present paper.

The validity of intervening variables as we define them cannot be called into question except by an actual denial of the empirical facts. If, for example, Hull's proposed "grand investigation" of the Perin-Williams type should be carried out and the complex hyperspatial surface fitted adequately over a wide range of values (3, p. 181), it would be meaningless to reject the concept of "habit strength" and still admit the empirical findings. For this reason, the only consideration which can be raised with respect to a given proposed intervening variable, when an initial defining or reduction equation is being written for it, is the question of convenience.

In the case of hypothetical constructs, this is not so clear. Science is pursued for many reasons, not the least of which is *n Cognizance*. Since hypothetical constructs assert the existence of entities and the occurrence of events not reducible to the observable, it would seem to some of us that it is the business of a hypothetical construct to be "true." It is possible to advance scientific knowledge by taking a completely "as if" attitude toward such matters, but there are always those whose theoretical-cognitive need dictates that existential propositions should correspond to what is in fact the case. Contemporary philosophy of science, even as represented by those who have traditionally been most cautious about discussing "truth" and most highly motivated to reduce it to the experiential, gives psychologists no right to be dogmatic about the "as if" interpretation of theoretical knowledge (cf. especially Carnap, 2, p. 598, Kaufmann, 4, p. 35, Russell, 6, Introduction and Chapter XXI, and Reichenbach, 5, *passim*). We would find it rather difficult to defend the ingenious conditioning hypotheses developed in Hull's series of brilliant papers (1929–) in the *Psychological Review* on the ground that they merely provide a "convenient shorthand summarization of the facts" or are of value in the "practical manipulation" of the rat's behavior. We suspect that Professor Hull himself was motivated to write these articles because he considered that the hypothetical events represented in his diagrams may have actually *occurred* and that the occurrence of these events represents the underlying truth about the learning phenomena he dealt with. In terms of practical application, much (if not most) of theoretical psychology is of little value. If we exclude the interesting anecdotes of Guthrie, contemporary learning theory is not of much use to school teachers. As a *theoretical* enterprise, it may fairly be demanded of a theory of learning that those elements which are "hypothetical" in the present sense have some probability of being in correspondence with the actual events underlying the behavior phenomena, i.e., that the assertions about hypothetical constructs be true.[1]

Another consideration may be introduced here from the standpoint of future developments in scientific integration. Even those of us who advocate the pursuit of behavioral knowledge on its own level and for its own sake must recognize that some day the "pyramid of the sciences" will presumably catch up with us. For Skinner, this is of no consequence, since his consistent use of intervening variables in the strict sense genuinely frees him from neurophysiology and in fact makes it possible for him to impose certain conditions upon neurophysiological explanations (7, pp. 429–431). Since he hypothesizes nothing about the character of the inner events, no finding about the inner events could prove disturbing to him. At most, he would be able to say that a given discovery of internal processes must not be complete because it cannot come to terms with his (empirical) laws. But for those theorists who do not confine themselves to intervening variables in the strict sense, neurology will some day become relevant. For this reason it is perhaps legitimate, even now, to require of a hypothetical construct that it should not be manifestly unreal in the sense that it assumes inner events that cannot conceivably occur. The "as if" kinds of argument sometimes heard from more sophisticated exponents of psychoanalytic views often seem to ignore this consideration. A concept like *libido* or *censor* or *super-ego* may be introduced initially as though it is to be an intervening variable; or even less, it is treated as a merely conventional designation for a class of observable properties or occurrences. But somewhere in the course of theoretical discussion, we did find that these words are being used as hypothetical constructs instead. We find that the libido has acquired certain hydraulic properties, or, as in Freud's former view, that the "energy" of libido has been converted into "anxiety." What began as a name for an intervening variable is finally a name for a "something" which has a host of causal properties. These properties are not made explicit initially, but it is clear that the concept is to be used in an explanatory way which requires that the properties exist. Thus, libido

1 It is perhaps unnecessary to add that in adopting this position we do not mean to defend any form of metaphysical realist thesis. The ultimate "reality" of the world in general is not the issue here; the point is merely that the reality of hypothetical constructs like the atom, from the standpoint of their logical relation to grounds, is not essentially different from that attributed to stones, chairs, other people, and the like. When we say that hypothetical constructs involve the notion of "objective existence" of actual processes and entities within the organism, we mean the same sort of objective existence, defined by the same ordinary criteria, that is meant when we talk about the objective existence of Singapore. The present discussion operates within the common framework of empirical science and common sense and is intended to be metaphysically neutral.

may be introduced by an innocuous definition in terms of the "set of sexual needs" or a "general term for basic strivings." But subsequently we find that certain puzzling phenomena are *deduced* ("explained") by means of the various properties of libido, e.g., that it flows, is dammed up, is converted into something else, tends to regress to earlier channels, adheres to things, makes its "energy" available to the ego, and so on. It is naive to object to such formulations simply on the ground that they refer to unobservables, or are "hypothetical," or are not "statistical." None of these objections is a crucial one for any scientific construct, and if such criteria were applied a large and useful amount of modern science would have to be abandoned. The fundamental difficulty with such theories is twofold. First, as has been implied by our remarks, there is the failure explicitly to announce the postulates concerning existential properties, so that these are introduced more or less surreptitiously and *ad hoc* as occasion demands. Secondly, by this device there is subtly achieved a transition from admissible intervening variables to inadmissible hypothetical constructs. These hypothetical constructs, unlike intervening variables, are inadmissible because they require the existence of entities and the occurrence of processes which cannot be seriously believed because of other knowledge.

In the case of libido, for instance, we may use such a term legitimately as a generic name for a class of empirical events or properties, or as an intervening variable. But the allied sciences of anatomy and physiology impose restrictions upon our use of it as a hypothetical construct. Even admitting the immature state of neurophysiology in terms of its relation to complex behavior, it must be clear that the central nervous-system does not in fact contain pipes or tubes with fluid in them, and there are no known properties of nervous tissue to which the hydraulic properties of libido could correspond. Hence, this part of a theory about "inner events" is likely to remain metaphorical. For a genuine intervening variable, there is no metaphor because all is merely short-hand summarization. For hypothetical constructs, there is a surplus meaning that is existential. We would argue that dynamic explanations utilizing hypothetical constructs ought not to be of such a character that they *have* to remain only metaphors.

Of course, this judgment in itself involves a "best guess" about the future. A hypothetical construct which seems inherently metaphorical may involve a set of properties to which hitherto undiscovered characteristics of the nervous system correspond. So long as the propositions about the construct are not stated in the *terms* of the next lower discipline, it is always a possibility that the purely formal or relational content of the construct will find an isomorphism in such characteristics. For scientific theories this is enough, since here, as in physics, the associated mechanical imagery of the theorist is irrelevant. The tentative rejection of libido would then be based upon the belief that no neural process is likely to have the *combination* of formal properties required. Strictly speaking, this is always problematic when the basic science is incomplete.[2]

Summary

1. At present the phrases "intervening variable" and "hypothetical construct" are often used interchangeably, and theoretical discourse often fails to distinguish what we believe are two rather different notions. We suggest that a failure to separate these leads to fundamental confusions. The distinction is between constructs which merely abstract the empirical relationships (Tolman's original intervening variables) and those constructs which are "hypothetical" (i.e., involve the supposition of entities or processes not among the observed).

2. Concepts of the first sort seem to be identifiable by three characteristics. First, the statement of such a concept does not contain any words which are not reducible to the empirical laws. Second, the validity of the empirical laws is both necessary and sufficient for the "correctness" of the statements about the concept. Third, the quantitative expression of the concept can be obtained without mediate inference by suitable groupings of terms in the quantitative empirical laws.

3. Concepts of the second sort do not fulfill any of these three conditions. Their formulation involves words not wholly reducible to the words in the empirical laws; the validity of the empirical laws is not a sufficient condition for the truth of the concept, inasmuch as it contains surplus meaning; and the quantitative form of the concept is not obtainable simply by grouping empirical terms and functions.

4. We propose a linguistic convention in the interest of clarity: that the phrase *intervening variable* be restricted to concepts of the first kind, in harmony with Tolman's original definition; and that the phrase *hypothetical construct* be used for those of the second kind.

5. It is suggested that the only rule for proper intervening variables is that of convenience, since they have no factual content surplus to the empirical functions they serve to summarize.

6. In the case of hypothetical constructs, they have a cognitive, factual reference in addition to the empirical data which constitute their support. Hence, they ought to be held to a more stringent requirement in so far as our interests are theoretical. Their actual existence should be compatible with general knowledge and particularly with whatever relevant knowledge exists at the next lower level in the explanatory hierarchy.

2 We are indebted to Dr. Herbert Feigl for a clarification of this point.

REFERENCES

1. CARNAP, R. Testability and meaning, Part IV. *Phil. Sci.*, 1937, **4**, 1–40.
2. ———. Remarks on induction and truth. *Phil. & phenomenol. res.*, 1946, **6**, 590–602.
3. HULL, C. L. *Principles of behavior.* New York: Appleton-Century, 1943.
4. KAUFMANN, F. *Methodology in the social sciences.* London: Oxford Univ. Press, 1944.
5. REICHENBACH, H. *Experience and prediction.* Chicago: Univ. of Chicago Press, 1938.
6. RUSSELL, B. *Inquiry into meaning and truth.* New York: Norton, 1940.
7. SKINNER, B. F. *Behavior of organisms.* New York: Appleton-Century, 1938.
8. TOLMAN, E. C. The determiners of behavior at a choice point. *Psychol. Rev.*, 1938, **45**, 1–41.

HISTORICAL PERSPECTIVES

NO CONCEPT in the field of the philosophy and history of science has been more influential over the past decade than that of the scientific paradigm as conceptualized by Kuhn. The paper here reprinted reports his basic early position. The following selection, by Shapere, is a contemporary critique of the Kuhnian notions, in the form of a wide-ranging book review; it suggests the degree of ferment that has been produced by the paradigm concept.

The excerpt from Veatch is an interesting comparison of humanistic and scientific productivity. Veatch examines what he sees as the significantly more enduring character of literary and artistic productions as compared with scientific ones; he concludes that the relatively ephemeral nature of most scientific work is a necessary function of the way in which scientific progress operates.

The next two selections are fascinating historical analyses of scientific issues. Brush's paper is a comprehensive review of the recurrent changes in the treatment of the history of science, focusing on the need to introduce a greater degree of realism into historical perspectives. Frankel then provides an insightful historical treatment of the major threats to "reason"; such a treatment is especially timely during the present period in which there are so many challenges to the "establishment" on intellectual as well as political and social grounds; the historical precedents outlined by Frankel should help in evaluating many such contemporary challenges to intellectual processes.

In the final selection in this section we turn somewhat more directly to psychology. Jaynes presents a wide-ranging historical inspection of the variegated character of science. In so doing he provides an introduction for the next section, in which some of the recent convulsive changes in psychology are examined.

3

TRADITION VS. INNOVATION

Thomas S. Kuhn

I am grateful for the invitation to participate in this important conference, and I interpret it as evidence that students of creativity themselves
possess the sensitivity to divergent approaches that they seek to identify
in others. But I am not altogether sanguine about the outcome of your
experiment with me. As most of you already know, I am no psychologist,
but rather an ex-physicist now working in the history of science. Probably my concern is no less with creativity than your own, but my goals,
my techniques and my sources of evidence are so very different from
yours that I am far from sure how much we do, or even *should*, have
to say to each other. These reservations imply no apology: rather they
hint at my central thesis. In the sciences, as I shall suggest below, it is
often better to do one's best with the tools at hand than to pause for contemplation of divergent approaches.

If a person of my background and interests has anything relevant to
suggest to this conference, it will not be about your central concerns, the
creative personality and its early identification. But implicit in the numerous working papers distributed to participants in this conference is an
image of the scientific process and of the scientist; that image almost
certainly conditions many of the experiments you try as well as the conclusions you draw; and about it the physicist-historian may well have
something to say. I shall restrict my attention to one aspect of this image
—an aspect summarized in one of the working papers by the sentence,
'[The basic scientist] must lack prejudice to a degree where he can look
at the most "self-evident" facts or concepts without necessarily accepting
them, and, conversely, allow his imagination to play with the most
unlikely possibilities' (Selye, 1959). In the more technical language supplied by other working papers (Getzels and Jackson, 1963), this aspect
of the image recurs as an emphasis upon 'divergent thinking . . . the freedom to go off in different directions . . . rejecting the old solution and
striking out in some new direction.'

I do not at all doubt that this description of 'divergent thinking' and
the concomitant search for those able to do it are entirely proper. Some

FROM Thomas S. Kuhn, The essential tension: tradition and innovation in scientific
research, in C. W. Taylor and F. Barron (Eds.), *Scientific creativity: Its recognition
and development*, Wiley, 1963, pp. 341–54. Copyright © 1963 by John Wiley & Sons,
Inc. Reprinted by permission of John Wiley & Sons, Inc.

divergence characterizes all scientific work, and gigantic divergences lie at the core of the most significant episodes in scientific development. But both my own experience in scientific research and my reading of the history of sciences lead me to wonder whether flexibility and open-mindedness have not been too exclusively emphasized as the characteristics requisite for basic research. I shall therefore suggest below that something like 'convergent thinking' is just as essential to scientific advance as is divergent. Since these two modes of thought are inevitably in conflict, it will follow that the ability to support a tension that can occasionally become almost unbearable is one of the prime requisites for the very best sort of scientific research.

I am elsewhere studying these points more historically, with emphasis on the importance to scientific development of 'revolutions' (Kuhn, 1962). These are episodes—exemplified in their most extreme and readily recognized form by the advent of Copernicanism, Darwinism or Einsteinianism—in which a scientific community abandons one time-honored way of regarding the world and of pursuing science in favor of some other, usually incompatible, approach to its discipline. I have argued in the draft that the historian constantly encounters many far smaller but structurally similar revolutionary episodes and that they are central to scientific advance. Contrary to a prevalent impression, most new discoveries and theories in the sciences are not merely additions to the existing stockpile of scientific knowledge. To assimilate them the scientist must usually rearrange the intellectual and manipulative equipment he has previously relied upon, discarding some elements of his prior belief and practice while finding new significances in and new relationships between many others. Because the old must be revalued and re-ordered when assimilating the new, discovery and invention in the sciences are usually intrinsically revolutionary. Therefore, they do demand just that flexibility and open-mindedness that characterize, or indeed define, the divergent thinker. Let us henceforth take for granted the need for these characteristics. Unless many scientists possessed them to a marked degree, there would be no scientific revolutions and very little scientific advance.

Yet flexibility is not enough, and what remains is not obviously compatible with it. Drawing from various fragments of a project still in progress, I must now emphasize that revolutions are but one of two complementary aspects of scientific advance. Almost none of the research undertaken by even the greatest scientists is designed to be revolutionary, and very little of it has any such effect. On the contrary, normal research, even the best of it, is a highly convergent activity based firmly upon a settled consensus acquired from scientific education and reinforced by subsequent life in the profession. Typically, to be sure, this convergent or consensus-bound research ultimately results in revolution. Then, traditional techniques and beliefs are abandoned and replaced by new ones. But revolutionary shifts of a scientific tradition are relatively rare, and extended periods of convergent research are the necessary preliminary to them. As I shall indicate below, only investigations firmly rooted in the contemporary scientific tradition are likely to break that tradition and give rise to a new one. That is why I speak of an 'essential tension' implicit in scientific research. To do his job the scientist must undertake a complex set of intellectual and manipulative commitments. Yet his claim to fame, if he has the talent and good luck to gain one, may finally rest upon his ability to abandon this net of commitments in favor of another of his own invention. Very often the successful scientist must simultaneously display the characteristics of the traditionalist and of the iconoclast.[1]

The multiple historical examples upon which any full documentation of these points must depend are prohibited by the time limitations of the conference. But another approach will introduce you to at least part of what I have in mind—an examination of the nature of education in the natural sciences. One of the working papers for this conference (Getzels and Jackson, 1963) quotes Guilford's very apt description of scientific education as follows:

[It] has emphasized abilities in the areas of convergent thinking and evaluation, often at the expense of development in the area of divergent thinking. We have attempted to teach students how to arrive at 'correct' answers that our civilization has taught us are correct. . . . Outside the arts [and I should include most of the social sciences] we have generally discouraged the development of divergent-thinking abilities, unintentionally.

That characterization seems to me eminently just, but I wonder whether it is equally just to deplore the product that results. Without defending plain bad teaching, and granting that in this country the trend to convergent thinking in all education may have proceeded entirely too far, we may nevertheless recognize that a rigorous training in convergent thought has been intrinsic to the sciences almost from their origin. I suggest that they could not have achieved their present state or status without it.

Let me try briefly to epitomize the nature of education in the natural sciences, ignoring the many significant yet minor differences between

[1] Strictly speaking, it is the professional group rather than the individual scientist that must display both these characteristics simultaneously. In a fuller account of the ground covered in this paper that distinction between individual and group characteristics would be basic. Here I can only note that, though recognition of the distinction weakens the conflict or tension referred to above, it does not eliminate it. Within the group some individuals may be more traditionalistic, others more iconoclastic, and their contributions may differ accordingly. Yet education, institutional norms, and the nature of the job to be done will inevitably combine to insure that all group members will, to a greater or lesser extent, be pulled in both directions.

the various sciences and between the approaches of different educational institutions. The single most striking feature of this education is that, to an extent totally unknown in other creative fields, it is conducted entirely through textbooks. Typically, the undergraduate *and* graduate student of chemistry, physics, astronomy, geology or biology acquires the substance of his field from books written especially for students. Until he is ready, or very nearly ready, to commence work on his own dissertation, he is neither asked to attempt trial research projects nor exposed to the immediate products of research done by others, that is, to the professional communications that scientists write for each other. There are no collections of 'Readings' in the natural sciences. Nor is the science student encouraged to read the historical classics of his field—works in which he might discover other ways of regarding the problems discussed in his textbook, but in which he would also meet problems, concepts and standards of solution that his future profession has long since discarded and replaced.

In contrast, the various textbooks that the student does encounter display different subject-matters, rather than, as in many of the social sciences, exemplifying different approaches to a single problem field. Even books that compete for adoption in a single course differ mainly in level and in pedagogic detail, not in substance or conceptual structure. Last, but most important of all, is the characteristic technique of textbook presentation. Except in their occasional introductions, science textbooks do not describe the sorts of problems that the professional may be asked to solve and the variety of techniques available for their solution. Rather, these books exhibit concrete problem solutions that the profession has come to accept as paradigms, and they then ask the student, either with a pencil and paper or in the laboratory, to solve for himself problems very closely related in both method and substance to those through which the textbook or the accompanying lecture has led him. Nothing could be better calculated to produce 'mental sets' or *Einstellungen*. Only in their most elementary courses do other academic fields offer as much as a partial parallel.

Even the most faintly liberal educational theory must view this pedagogic technique as anathema. Students, we would all agree, must begin by learning a good deal of what is already known, but we also insist that education give them vastly more. They must, we say, learn to recognize and evaluate problems to which no unequivocal solution has yet been given; they must be supplied with an arsenal of techniques for approaching these future problems; and they must learn to judge the relevance of these techniques and to evaluate the possibly partial solutions which they can provide. In many respects these attitudes toward education seem to me entirely right, and yet we must recognize two things about them. First, education in the natural sciences seems to have been totally unaffected by their existence. It remains a dogmatic initiation in a pre-established tradition that the student is not equipped to evaluate. Second, at least in the period when it was followed by a term in an apprenticeship relation, this technique of exclusive exposure to a rigid tradition has been immensely productive of the most consequential sorts of innovations.

I shall shortly inquire about the pattern of scientific practice that grows out of this educational initiation and will then attempt to say why that pattern proves quite so successful. But first, an historical excursion will reinforce what has just been said and prepare the way for what is to follow. I should like to suggest that the various fields of natural science have not always been characterized by rigid education in exclusive paradigms, but that each of them acquired something like that technique at precisely the point when the field began to make rapid and systematic progress. If one asks about the origin of our contemporary knowledge of chemical composition, of earthquakes, of biological reproduction, of motion through space, or of any other subject matter known to the natural sciences, one immediately encounters a characteristic pattern that I shall here exemplify with a single example.

Today, physics textbooks tell us that light exhibits some properties of a wave and some of a particle: both textbook problems and research problems are designed accordingly. But both this view and these textbooks are products of an early twentieth-century revolution. (One characteristic of scientific revolutions is that they call for the re-writing of science textbooks.) For more than half a century before 1900, the books employed in scientific education had been equally unequivocal in stating that light was wave motion. Under those circumstances scientists worked on somewhat different problems and often embraced rather different sorts of solutions to them. The nineteenth-century textbook tradition does not, however, mark the beginning of our subject-matter. Throughout the eighteenth century and into the early nineteenth, Newton's *Opticks* and the other books from which men learned science taught almost all students that light was particles, and research guided by this tradition was again different from that which succeeded it. Ignoring a variety of subsidiary changes within these three successive traditions, we may therefore say that our views derive historically from Newton's views by way of two revolutions in optical thought, each of which replaced one tradition of convergent research with another. If we make appropriate allowances for changes in the locus and materials of scientific education, we may say that each of these three traditions was embodied in the sort of education by exposure to unequivocal paradigms that I briefly epitomized above. Since Newton, education and research in physical optics have normally been highly convergent.

The history of theories of light does not, however, begin with Newton.

If we ask about knowledge in the field before his time, we encounter a significantly different pattern—a pattern still familiar in the arts and in some social sciences, but one which has largely disappeared in the natural sciences. From remote antiquity until the end of the seventeenth century there was no single set of paradigms for the study of physical optics. Instead, many men advanced a large number of different views about the nature of light. Some of these views found few adherents, but a number of them gave rise to continuing schools of optical thought. Although the historian can note the emergence of new points of view as well as changes in the relative popularity of older ones, there was never anything resembling consensus. As a result, a new man entering the field was inevitably exposed to a variety of conflicting viewpoints; he was forced to examine the evidence for each, and there always was good evidence. The fact that he made a choice and conducted himself accordingly could not entirely prevent his awareness of other possibilities. This earlier mode of education was obviously more suited to produce a scientist without prejudice, alert to novel phenomena, and flexible in his approach to his field. On the other hand one can scarcely escape the impression that, during the period characterized by this more liberal educational practice, physical optics made very little progress.[2]

The preconsensus (we might here call it the divergent) phase in the development of physical optics is, I believe, duplicated in the history of all other scientific specialities, excepting only those that were born by the subdivision and recombination of pre-existing disciplines. In some fields, like mathematics and astronomy, the first firm consensus is prehistoric. In others, like dynamics, geometric optics and parts of physiology, the paradigms that produced a first consensus date from classical antiquity. Most other natural sciences, though their problems were often discussed in antiquity, did not achieve a first consensus until after the Renaissance. In physical optics, as we have seen, the first firm consensus dates only from the end of the seventeenth century; in electricity, chemistry and the study of heat it dates from the eighteenth; while in geology and the non-taxonomic parts of biology no very real consensus developed until after the first third of the nineteenth century. This century appears to be characterized by the emergence of a first consensus in parts of a few of the social sciences.

In all the fields named above, important work was done before the

2 The history of physical optics before Newton has recently been well described by Ronchi (1956). His account does justice to the element I elaborate too little above. Many fundamental contributions to physical optics were made in the two millennia before Newton's work. Consensus is not pre-requisite to a sort of progress in the natural sciences, any more than it is to progress in the social sciences or the arts. It is, however, pre-requisite to the sort of progress that we now generally refer to when distinguishing the natural sciences from the arts and from most social sciences.

achievement of the maturity produced by consensus. Neither the nature nor the timing of the first consensus in these fields can be understood without a careful examination of both the intellectual and the manipulative techniques developed before the existence of unique paradigms. But the transition to maturity is not less significant because individuals practised science before it occurred. On the contrary, history strongly suggests that, though one can practise science—as one does philosophy or art or political science—without a firm consensus, this more flexible practice will not produce the rapid pattern of consequential scientific advance to which recent centuries have accustomed us. In that pattern, development occurs from one consensus to another, and alternate approaches are not ordinarily in competition. Except under quite special conditions, the practitioner of a mature science does not pause to examine divergent modes of explanation or experimentation.

I shall shortly ask how this can be so—how a firm orientation toward an apparently unique tradition can be compatible with the practice of the disciplines most noted for the persistent production of novel ideas and techniques. But it will help first to ask what the education that so successfully transmits such a tradition leaves to be done. What can a scientist working within a deeply rooted tradition and little trained in the perception of significant alternatives hope to do during his professional career? Once again limits of time force me to drastic simplification, but the following remarks will at least suggest a position that I am sure can be documented in detail.

In pure or basic science—that somewhat ephemeral category of research undertaken by men whose most immediate goal is to increase understanding rather than control of nature—the characteristic problems are almost always repetitions, with minor modifications, of problems that have been undertaken and partially resolved before. For example, much of the research undertaken within a scientific tradition is an attempt to adjust existing theory or existing observation in order to bring the two into closer and closer agreement. The constant examination of atomic and molecular spectra during the years since the birth of wave mechanics, together with the design of theoretical approximations for the prediction of complex spectra, provides one important instance of this typical sort of work. Another was provided by the remarks about the eighteenth-century development of Newtonian dynamics in the paper on measurement supplied to you in advance of the conference. The attempt to make existing theory and observation conform more closely is not, of course, the only standard sort of research problem in the basic sciences. The development of chemical thermodynamics or the continuing attempts to unravel organic structure illustrate another type—the extension of existing theory to areas that it is expected to cover but in which it has never before been tried. In addition, to mention a third common sort of research problem, many scientists constantly collect the concrete data (e.g., atomic weights, nuclear moments) required for the application and extension of existing theory.

These are normal research projects in the basic sciences, and they illustrate the sorts of work on which all scientists, even the greatest, spend most of their professional lives and on which many spend all. Clearly their pursuit is neither intended nor likely to produce fundamental discoveries or revolutionary changes in scientific theory. Only if the validity of the contemporary scientific tradition is assumed do these problems make much theoretical or any practical sense. The man who suspected the existence of a totally new type of phenomenon or who had basic doubts about the validity of existing theory would not think problems so closely modeled on textbook paradigms worth undertaking. It follows that the man who does undertake a problem of this sort—and that means all scientists at most times—aims to elucidate the scientific tradition in which he was raised rather than to change it. Furthermore, the fascination of his work lies in the difficulties of elucidation rather than in any surprises that the work is likely to produce. Under normal conditions the research scientist is not an innovator but a solver of puzzles, and the puzzles upon which he concentrates are just those which he believes can be both stated and solved within the existing scientific tradition.

Yet—and this is the point—the ultimate effect of this tradition-bound work has invariably been to change the tradition. Again and again the continuing attempt to elucidate a currently received tradition has at last produced one of those shifts in fundamental theory, in problem field and in scientific standards to which I previously referred as scientific revolutions. At least for the scientific community as a whole, work within a well-defined and deeply ingrained tradition seems more productive of tradition-shattering novelties than work in which no similarly convergent standards are involved. How can this be so? I think it is because no other sort of work is nearly so well suited to isolate for continuing and concentrated attention those loci of trouble or causes of crisis upon whose recognition the most fundamental advances in basic science depend.

As I have indicated in the first of my working papers, new theories and, to an increasing extent, novel discoveries in the mature sciences are not born *de novo*. On the contrary, they emerge from old theories and within a matrix of old beliefs about the phenomena that the world does *and does not* contain. Ordinarily such novelties are far too esoteric and recondite to be noted by the man without a great deal of scientific training. And even the man with considerable training can seldom afford simply to go out and look for them, let us say by exploring those areas in which existing data and theory have failed to produce understanding. Even in a mature science there are always far too many such areas, areas in which no existing paradigms seem obviously to apply and for whose exploration few tools and standards are available. More likely than not the scientist who ventured into them, relying merely upon his receptivity to new phenomena and his flexibility to new patterns of organization, would get nowhere at all. He would rather return his science to its pre-consensus or natural history phase.

Instead, the practitioner of a mature science, from the beginning of his doctoral research, continues to work in the regions for which the paradigms derived from his education and from the research of his contemporaries seem adequate. He tries, that is, to elucidate topographical detail on a map whose main outlines are available in advance, and he hopes—if he is wise enough to recognize the nature of his field—that he will some day undertake a problem in which the anticipated does *not* occur, a problem that goes wrong in ways suggestive of a fundamental weakness in the paradigm itself. In the mature sciences the prelude to much discovery and to all novel theory is not ignorance, but the recognition that something has gone wrong with existing knowledge and beliefs.

What I have said so far may indicate that it is sufficient for the productive scientist to adopt existing theory as a lightly held tentative hypothesis, employ it *faute de mieux* in order to get a start in his research and then abandon it as soon as it leads him to a trouble spot, a point at which something has gone wrong. But though the ability to recognize trouble when confronted by it is surely a requisite for scientific advance, trouble must not be too easily recognized. The scientist requires a thorough-going commitment to the tradition with which, if he is fully successful, he will break. In part this commitment is demanded by the nature of the problems the scientist normally undertakes. These, as we have seen, are usually esoteric puzzles whose challenge lies less in the information disclosed by their solutions (all but its details are often known in advance) than in the difficulties of technique to be surmounted in providing any solution at all. Problems of this sort are undertaken only by men assured that there is a solution which ingenuity can disclose, and only current theory could possibly provide assurance of that sort. That theory alone gives meaning to most of the problems of normal research. To doubt it is often to doubt that the complex technical puzzles which constitute normal research have any solutions at all. Who, for example, would have developed the elaborate mathematical techniques required for the study of the effects of interplanetary attractions upon basic Keplerian orbits if he had not assumed that Newtonian dynamics, applied to the planets then known, would explain the last details of astronomical observation? But without that assurance, how would Neptune have been discovered and the list of planets changed?

In addition, there are pressing practical reasons for commitment. Every research problem confronts the scientist with anomalies whose sources he cannot quite identify. His theories and observations never quite agree; successive observations never yield quite the same results; his experiments have both theoretical and phenomenological by-products which it would take another research project to unravel. Each of these anomalies or incompletely understood phenomena could conceivably be the clue to a fundamental innovation in scientific theory or technique, but the man who pauses to examine them one by one never completes his first project. Reports of effective research repeatedly imply that all but the most striking and central discrepancies could be taken care of by current theory if only there were time to take them on. The men who make these reports find most discrepancies trivial or uninteresting, an evaluation that they can ordinarily base only upon their faith in current theory. Without that faith their work would be wasteful of time and talent.

Besides, lack of commitment too often results in the scientist's undertaking problems that he has little chance of solving. Pursuit of an anomaly is fruitful only if the anomaly is more than non-trivial. Having discovered it, the scientist's first efforts and those of his profession are to do what nuclear physicists are now doing. They strive to generalize the anomaly, to discover other and more revealing manifestations of the same effect, to give it structure by examining its complex interrelationships with phenomena they still feel they understand. Very few anomalies are susceptible to this sort of treatment. To be so they must be in explicit and unequivocal conflict with some structurally central tenet of current scientific belief. Therefore, their recognition and evaluation once again depend upon a firm commitment to the contemporary scientific tradition.

This central role of an elaborate and often esoteric tradition is what I have principally had in mind when speaking of the essential tension in scientific research. I do not doubt that the scientist must be, at least potentially, an innovator, that he must possess mental flexibility, and that he must be prepared to recognize troubles where they exist. That much of the popular stereotype is surely correct, and it is important accordingly to search for indices of the corresponding personality characteristics. But what is no part of our stereotype and what appears to need careful integration with it is the other face of this same coin. We are, I think, more likely fully to exploit our potential scientific talent if we recognize the extent to which the basic scientist must also be a firm traditionalist, or, if I am using your vocabulary at all correctly, a convergent thinker. Most important of all, we must seek to understand how these two superficially discordant modes of problem solving can be reconciled both within the individual and within the group.

Everything said above needs both elaboration and documentation.

Very likely some of it will change in the process. This paper is a report on work in progress. But, though I insist that much of it is tentative and all of it incomplete, I still hope that the paper has indicated why an educational system best described as an initiation into an unequivocal tradition should be thoroughly compatible with successful scientific work. And I hope, in addition, to have made plausible the historical thesis that no part of science has progressed very far or very rapidly before this convergent education and correspondingly convergent normal practice became possible. Finally, though it is beyond my competence to derive personality correlates from this view of scientific development, I hope to have made meaningful the view that the productive scientist must be a traditionalist who enjoys playing intricate games by pre-established rules in order to be a successful innovator who discovers new rules and new pieces with which to play them.

As first planned, my paper was to have ended at this point. But work on it, against the background supplied by the working papers distributed to conference participants, has suggested the need for a postscript. Let me therefore briefly try to eliminate a likely ground of misunderstanding and simultaneously suggest a problem that urgently needs a great deal of investigation.

Everything said above was intended to apply strictly only to basic science, an enterprise whose practitioners have ordinarily been relatively free to choose their own problems. Characteristically, as I have indicated, these problems have been selected in areas where paradigms were clearly applicable but where exciting puzzles remained about how to apply them and how to make nature conform to the results of the application. Clearly the inventor and applied scientist are not generally free to choose puzzles of this sort. The problems among which they may choose are likely to be largely determined by social, economic or military circumstances external to the sciences. Often the decision to seek a cure for a virulent disease, a new source of household illumination or an alloy able to withstand the intense heat of rocket engines must be made with little reference to the state of the relevant science. It is, I think, by no means clear that the personality characteristics requisite for pre-eminence in this more immediately practical sort of work are altogether the same as those required for a great achievement in basic science. History indicates that only a few individuals, most of whom worked in readily demarcated areas, have achieved eminence in both.

I am by no means clear where this suggestion leads us. The troublesome distinctions between basic research, applied research, and invention need far more investigation. Nevertheless it seems likely, for example, that the applied scientist, to whose problems no scientific paradigm need be fully relevant, may profit by a far broader and less rigid education than that to which the pure scientist has characteristically been exposed. Certainly there are many episodes in the history of technology in which lack of more than the most rudimentary scientific education has proved to be an immense help. This group scarcely needs to be reminded that Edison's electric light was produced in the face of unanimous scientific opinion that the arc light could not be 'subdivided,' and there are many other episodes of this sort.

This must not suggest, however, that mere differences in education will transform the applied scientist into a basic scientist or vice versa. One could at least argue that Edison's personality, ideal for the inventor and perhaps also for the 'odd-ball' in applied science, barred him from fundamental achievements in the basic sciences. He himself expressed great scorn for scientists and thought of them as woolly-headed people to be hired when needed. But this did not prevent his occasionally arriving at the most sweeping and irresponsible scientific theories of his own. (The pattern recurs in the early history of electrical technology: both Tesla and Gramme advanced absurd cosmic schemes that they thought deserved to replace the current scientific knowledge of their day.) Episodes like this reinforce an impression that the personality requisites of the pure scientist and of the inventor may be quite different, perhaps with those of the applied scientist lying somewhere between.[3]

Is there a further conclusion to be drawn from all this? One speculative thought forces itself upon me. If I read the working papers correctly, they suggest that most of you are really in search of the *inventive* personality, a sort of person who does emphasize divergent thinking but whom the United States has already produced in abundance. In the process you may be ignoring certain of the essential requisites of the basic scientist, a rather different sort of person, to whose ranks America's contributions have as yet been notoriously sparse. Since most of you are, in fact, Americans, this correlation may not be entirely coincidental.

REFERENCES

GETZELS, J. W., and JACKSON, P. W. (1963), 'The highly intelligent and highly creative adolescent,' in C. W. Taylor and F. Barron, (eds.), *Scientific Creativity: Its Recognition and Development*, Wiley, pp. 161–72.

JONES, F. A. (1908), *Thomas Alva Edison*, New York, pp. 99–100.

KUHN, T. S. (1962), *The Structure of Scientific Revolutions*, University of Chicago Press.

PASSER, H. C. (1953), *The Electrical Manufacturers, 1875–1900*, Cambridge, Mass.

3 For the attitude of scientists toward the technical possibility of the incandescent light see Jones (1908), and Passer (1953, pp. 82–83). For Edison's attitude toward scientists see Passer (1953, pp. 180–81). For a sample of Edison's theorizing in realms otherwise subject to scientific treatments see Runes (1948).

RONCHI, V. (1956), *Histoire de la Lumière*, trans. J. Taton, Paris.

RUNES, D. D. (ed.) (1948), *The Diary and Sundry Observations of Thomas Alva Edison*, New York, pp. 205–44 *passim*.

SELYE, H. (1959), 'What makes basic research basic?' *Saturday Evening Post*, vol. 231, p. 30.

4

CRITIQUE OF THE PARADIGM CONCEPT*

DUDLEY SHAPERE

SINCE its publication in 1962, Thomas Kuhn's *The Structure of Scientific Revolutions* has become one of the most popular attempts of all time to interpret the nature of science. It has proved an important step in a movement away from the positivistic empiricism that has held sway, among both philosophers and working scientists, for well over two generations. Writers in many disciplines have adopted the book's fundamental notion of "paradigm" in analyses of their subject matter and controversies. The book has had an impact also on a wide body of laymen, even, on occasion, being cited as authority by spokesmen of the New Left.

The thesis of the original edition was that "particular coherent traditions of scientific research" (p. 10), which Kuhn called "normal science," are unified by and emerge from "paradigms." Paradigms are "universally recognizable scientific achievements that for a time provide model problems and solutions to a community of practitioners" (p. x). Kuhn conceived of a paradigm as not identifiable with any body of theory, being more "global" (p. 43) and generally incapable of complete formulation. He held it to include "law, theory, application, and instrumentation together" (p. 10), consisting of a "strong network of commitments, conceptual, theoretical, instrumental, and methodological" (p. 42), and even "quasi-metaphysical" (p. 41); it is, he claimed, "the source of the meth-

* This is a review of T. Kuhn, *The Structure of Scientific Revolutions* (2nd ed.), 1970; and I. Lakatos and A. Musgrave (Eds.), *Criticism and the Growth of Knowledge*, Vol. 4, 1970.—Ed.

FROM D. Shapere, The paradigm concept, *Science*, 1971, *172*, 706–709. Copyright 1971 by the American Association for the Advancement of Science.

ods, problem-field, and standards of solution accepted by any mature scientific community at any given time" (p. 102), permitting "selection, evaluation, and criticism" (p. 17). "Normal science" consists of working within and in the light of the paradigm, making it more and more explicit and precise, actualizing its initial promise "by extending the knowledge of those facts that the paradigm displays as particularly revealing, by increasing the extent of the match between those facts and the paradigm's predictions, and by further articulation of the paradigm itself" (p. 24). In the course of such articulation, however, "anomalies" arise which, after repeated efforts to resolve them have failed, give birth to the kind of situation in which a scientific revolution can take place:

Confronted with anomaly or with crisis, scientists take a different attitude toward existing paradigms, and the nature of their research changes accordingly. The proliferation of competing articulations, the willingness to try anything, the expression of explicit discontent, the recourse to philosophy and to debate over fundamentals, all these are symptoms of a transition from normal to extraordinary research. . . . Scientific revolutions are inaugurated by a growing sense . . . that an existing paradigm has ceased to function adequately in the exploration of an aspect of nature to which that paradigm itself had previously led the way [pp. 90–91].

New candidates for fundamental paradigm are introduced; ultimately one may become accepted, often necessitating "a redefinition of the corresponding science" (p. 102). Kuhn emphasized that scientific revolutions are "non-cumulative developmental episodes in which an older paradigm is replaced in whole or in part by an incompatible new one" (p. 91).

Kuhn's views diverge radically from those dominant since Mach and Ostwald, developed in the outlook of the Vienna Circle and its intellectual associates, and paralleled in the views of Bridgman and Frank and a host of more recent thinkers. Whereas those views tended, at least in their heydays, to separate sharply "fact" (or "observation" or "operation") from "interpretation"—thus claiming to preserve the "objectivity" of science—Kuhn emphasizes the dependence of what counts as a "fact," a "problem," and a "solution of a problem" on presuppositions, theoretical or otherwise, explicit or implicit. Likewise, he attacks traditional "development-by-accumulation" views of science—views according to which science progresses linearly by accumulation of theory-independent facts, older theories giving way successively to wider, more inclusive ones. In these respects, Kuhn's book has had an undeniably healthy influence on discussions of the nature of science, bringing them to a closer inspection of science and more in line with what recent scholarship has revealed about its history.

Despite these beneficial effects, however, Kuhn's views as expressed in the first edition have faced severe criticism. Two main types of objections have been raised. Those of the first type revolve around ambiguities in the notion of "paradigm." For that term, although at the outset it is applied to "a set of recurrent and quasi-standard illustrations of various theories," which are "revealed in . . . textbooks, lectures, and laboratory exercises" (p. 43), ultimately appears, as the reader may have gathered from the passages quoted above, to cover anything and everything that allows the scientist to do anything. The assertion that a scientific tradition is paradigm-governed then appears to become a tautology, and all the wealth of Kuhn's historical analysis becomes irrelevant. On the other hand, the term is so vague that, in particular cases, it is difficult to identify what is supposed to be the paradigm. (This problem is, of course, compounded by Kuhn's insistence that the paradigm is not, and in general cannot be, completely expressed.) Furthermore, the vagueness of the term makes the distinction between "normal" and "revolutionary" science seem a matter more of degree than of kind, as Kuhn claims: expression of explicit discontent, proliferation of competing articulations, debate over fundamentals are all more or less present throughout the development of science. And similarly for the distinction, drawn with uncompromising sharpness by Kuhn, between different "traditions" in science: far from there being such sharp discontinuities, there are always guiding factors which are more or less common, even among what are somewhat artificially classified as different "traditions." Finally, "commitment" to such guiding factors does not in general seem to be as rigid as Kuhn suggests.

The second major type of objection against Kuhn's first-edition view has to do with the relativism in which it apparently eventuates. In emphasizing the determinative role of background paradigms, and attacking the notion of theory- (or paradigm-) independent "facts" (or any such independent factors or standards whatever), Kuhn appears to have denied the possibility of reasonable judgment, on objective grounds, in paradigm choice; there can be no good reason for accepting a new paradigm, for the very notion of a "good reason" has been made paradigm-dependent. And certainly, though in some passages Kuhn denied this implication of his view, in most he gloried in it: "the competition between paradigms is not the sort of battle that can be resolved by proofs" (p. 147), but is more like a "conversion experience" (p. 150); "What occurred [in a paradigm change] was neither a decline nor a raising of standards, but simply a change demanded by the adoption of a new paradigm" (p. 107); "In these matters neither proof nor error is at issue" (p. 150); "We may . . . have to relinquish the notion, explicit or implicit, that changes of paradigm carry scientists and those who learn from them closer and closer to the truth" (p. 169). Objectivity and progress, the pride of traditional interpretations of science, have both been abandoned. Indeed, Kuhn's relativism did not stop here: for not only is there no means of rationally assessing two competing paradigms; there is no way of comparing them at all, so different is the world as seen through them (or—in an alternative formulation that is in many ways more consonant with Kuhn's general thesis—so different are the worlds they define). "The normal-scientific tradition that emerges from a scientific revolution is not only incompatible but often actually incommensurable with that which has gone before" (p. 102). Kuhn carried this view to the point of holding that if the same terms continue to be used after a scientific revolution (like "mass" after the replacement of the Newtonian by the Einsteinian "paradigm") those terms have different meanings.

In this new edition, Kuhn has altered little of the original text; however, he has added a 36-page "Postscript" (p. 174 ff.) reviewing and attempting to meet criticisms that were made of the first edition. This discussion is supplemented by opening and closing essays by Kuhn in *Criticism and the Growth of Knowledge*, a collection of papers—the others are by Paul Feyerabend, Imre Lakatos, Margaret Masterman, Karl Popper, Stephen Toulmin, John Watkins, and L. P. Williams—discussing Kuhn's ideas in relation to those of Popper. (There is good reason to compare the two; for despite the differences that emerge from the discussions in that book, Popper's contention that there is no rationale in the introduction of new "conjectures" in science, but only in the exposure of such conjectures to tests potentially falsifying them, and Kuhn's insistence, at least in the first edition, and despite a number of contradictory statements, that there is no rationale in the introduction of a new paradigm, but only in the attempt to "articulate" the paradigm and make it deal successfully with "anomalies," are basically similar. There is room here to discuss only Kuhn's contributions to this volume; the paper by Lakatos, however, may be recommended as being particularly important and provocative.)

It is important to recognize the extent—and the significance—of Kuhn's withdrawal from his original position. With regard to the concept of paradigm, Kuhn now wishes to distinguish two different senses of the term.

On the one hand, it stands for the entire constellation of beliefs, values, techniques, and so on shared by the members of a given community. On the other, it denotes one sort of element in that constellation, the concrete puzzle-solutions which, employed as models or examples, can replace explicit rules as a basis for the solution of the remaining puzzles of normal science [p. 173].

For the former, broader sense Kuhn suggests the name "disciplinary matrix," distinguishing four components of such matrices (pp. 182–86): "symbolic generalizations," "metaphysical paradigms," "values," and "exemplars," the "concrete puzzle-solutions" referred to above. All these elements were lumped together in the first edition; "they are, however, no longer to be discussed as though they were all of a piece" (p. 182). This distinction, however, is of little help to those who found the earlier concept of "paradigm" obscure. Contrary to Kuhn's complaint, few critics failed to see that the *primary* sense of "paradigm" had to do with the "concrete puzzle-solution." The difficulty was, rather, that Kuhn never adequately clarified how the remaining factors covered by that term were related to (embodied in) the concrete examples in such a way that the whole outlook ("paradigm" in the broader sense) of the tradition would be conveyed to students through such examples. Nor did he clarify the ways in which, through the concrete examples, this general paradigm determined the course of scientific research and judgment. Yet it was precisely the unity, and the controlling status, of paradigms that constituted the appeal and the challenge of Kuhn's original view: the contention that there was a coherent, unified viewpoint, a single overarching *Weltanschauung*, a disciplinary *Zeitgeist*, that determined the way scientists of a given tradition viewed and dealt with the world, that determined what they would consider to be a legitimate problem, a piece of evidence, a good reason, an acceptable solution, and so on. (The affinities of Kuhn's view with 19th-century Idealism run deep.) Does he now hold that this "constellation" that makes up the disciplinary matrix is just a loosely associated assemblage, each of whose components has its own separate and separable function? (And Kuhn offers precious little discussion of those functions.) Certainly Kuhn's emphasis here is on the distinction between the components rather than on any unity underlying them; but if this is his new view, then—especially when it is coupled with his apparent abandonment (to be discussed below) of the controlling status of the paradigm—Kuhn will have abandoned what was, however obscure, one of the most provocative and influential aspects of his earlier view. Perhaps this would be—if the remaining elements of his new position prove consistent with this view—for the best. For it could then be argued that he has moved in the direction of a salutary concern with the details of scientific reasoning—for example, with specific ways in which specific background presuppositions may influence scientific judgment and activity—rather than with sweeping but vague generalities that are ultimately tautological. But in any case it would not be the old Kuhn. (It should be remarked that Kuhn still, in spite of his critics' attacks, maintains the sharp distinction between "revolutionary" and "normal" science; indeed, the latter and its characteristic activity of "puzzle-solving"—a notion which Kuhn uses far too lightly—acquire in his essays in *Criticism and the Growth of Knowledge* an even more central role.)

But it is in his attempt to meet the charge of relativism that Kuhn's most striking retreats from his original extreme position occur. Now, what counts as a scientific problem is not determined, at least completely, by the paradigm: "Most of the puzzles of normal science are directly presented by nature, and all involve nature indirectly" (*Criticism*, p. 263); there is, apparently, a paradigm-independent objective world (nature) which presents problems that a paradigm must solve. Further, paradigms no longer, apparently, determine, at least completely, what counts as a good reason:

> It should be easy to design a list of criteria that would enable an uncommitted observer to distinguish the earlier from the most recent theory time after time. Among the most useful would be: accuracy of prediction, particularly of quantitative prediction; the balance between esoteric and everyday matter; and the number of different problems solved. . . . Those lists are not yet the ones required, but I have no doubt that they can be completed. If they can, then scientific development is, like biological, a unidirectional and irreversible process. Later scientific theories are better than earlier ones for solving puzzles in the often quite different environments to which they are applied. That is not a relativist's position, and it displays the sense in which I am a convinced believer in scientific progress [pp. 205–206].

No, that is not a relativist's position; but it is a far cry from Kuhn's first-edition attack on the view of scientific change as a linear process of ever-increasing knowledge (to say nothing of its view that there is no such thing as an "uncommitted observer"), and its defense of the view that what happens in a scientific revolution is "neither a decline nor a raising of standards, but simply a change demanded by the adoption of a new paradigm." It is, in fact, for better or for worse, a long step toward a more conventional position in the philosophy of science—one that makes a distinction between the "given" and the "interpretation" (or "theory") and holds that the latter are adequate to the extent that they account for the former.

It appears, then, that Kuhn now believes that the conceptual guiding factors in science research are more diverse and complicated in their functioning, and that there are objective factors that are independent of and exercise some constraint on them ("nature cannot be forced into an arbitrary set of conceptual boxes"—*Criticism*, p. 263). Such sober retrenchment is not, however, consistent with Kuhn's simultaneous adherence to many of his old views. Despite his claim that his view does not imply "either that there are no good reasons for being persuaded [in favor of a new paradigm] or that those reasons are not ultimately decisive for the group" (p. 179), he still tells us,

> What it should suggest, however, is that such reasons function as values and that they can thus be differently applied, individually and collectively, by men who concur in honoring them. If two men disagree, for example, about the relative fruitfulness of their theories, or if they agree about that but disagree about the relative importance of fruitfulness and, say, scope in reaching a choice, neither can be convicted of a mistake. Nor is either being unscientific [pp. 199–200].

But if there are, as Kuhn suggests here and elsewhere, no constraints on what one can assert in the name of "values," it seems gratuitous to speak of *reasons* in such contexts. And yet this seems to be the sort of thing Kuhn intends when he speaks of "good reasons" for adopting a new paradigm (for example, after telling us that his view does not imply "that the reasons for choice are different from those usually listed by philosophers of science: accuracy, simplicity, fruitfulness, and the like" [p. 199], he declares that "such reasons function as values" in the sense just discussed). It is a viewpoint as relativistic, as antirationalistic, as ever.

Particularly unhelpful is Kuhn's reply to the charge that his view of paradigm "incommensurability" implies that competition of communication between different paradigms is impossible. This is partly due to his residual ambiguity regarding the extent to which paradigms determine meanings and views of "nature": for in the absence of a clear idea of the extent of that determination, it is impossible to be clear about the extent to which meanings determined by one paradigm can be expressed in the language of another. This ambiguity in turn destroys the effectiveness of his suggestion that Quine's views on translation can help alleviate the difficulty: for Quine's views (briefly, that "radical" translation is indeterminate in that it depends on some "analytic hypothesis" which is highly arbitrary, though subject to some constraints) are not obviously consistent with Kuhn's first-edition view of paradigm determination of meanings, hypotheses, and standards. Finally, Kuhn's strange view of neural stimuli and processes and their relation to meanings and knowledge muddies the situation still further: on the one hand, we read that "people do not see stimuli; our knowledge of them is highly theoretical and abstract" (p. 192); but on the other hand—when he is trying to face the problem of incommensurability—he says that "the stimuli that impinge on [the adherents of two different paradigms] are the same" (p. 201). It is thus unclear whether what we consider to be stimuli is paradigm-independent or is relative to our paradigm (for Kuhn does call our knowledge of them "theoretical"). Beyond these contributions to confusion, Kuhn's discussion (pp. 202–204; *Criticism*, p. 266 ff.) fails utterly to come to grips with the issue. He now admits (in denial of complete paradigm-determination of meanings) to a great deal of overlap of meanings, and this, he claims, helps to circumscribe the areas of communication breakdown between adherents of different paradigms. But how are mutual understanding and comparison of adequacy to be achieved with regard to *those* areas, once located? His answer is simply that competing scientists proceed to observe one another and "may in time become very good predictors of each other's behavior. Each will have learned to translate the other's theory and its consequences into his own language and simultaneously to describe in his language the world to which that theory applies" (p. 202). But this begs the question, amounting merely to an assertion that such translation is possible. Kuhn has not succeeded in showing how he can retain paradigm incommensurability in the sense of the first edition while allowing cross-paradigm communication and comparison.

In summary, then, Kuhn appears to have retreated from his earlier position in just those respects in which it was most suggestive, important, and influential, and to have retained aspects which many have felt were the most objectionable features of his earlier view. Finally, the consistency of what he has retained with his apparent departures from his former view is certainly open to question. And it is far from being unambiguously clear what his current view really is. He seems to want to say that there are paradigm-independent considerations which constitute rational bases for introducing and accepting new paradigms; but his use of the term "reasons" is vitiated by his considering them to be "values," so that he seems not to have gotten beyond his former view after all. He seems to want to say that there is progress in science; but all grounds of assessment again apparently turn out to be "values," and we are left with the same old relativism. And he seems unwilling to abandon "incommensurability," while trying, unsuccessfully, to assert that communication and comparison are possible.

These issues come to a head in Kuhn's proposals as to what must be done if a complete understanding of science is to be obtained, and what the character of that understanding will be once obtained. For the fundamental question is, Do scientists (at least sometimes, even in "revolutionary" episodes) proceed as they do because there are objective reasons for doing so, or do we call those procedures "reasonable" merely because a certain group sanctions them? Despite the ambiguities and inconsistencies of many of his remarks, Kuhn's tendency is clearly toward the latter alternative. Though occasionally tentative ("Some of the principles deployed in my explanation of science are irreducibly sociological, at least at this time"—*Criticism*, p. 237), in most passages he asserts his view categorically: "The explanation [of scientific progress] must, in the final analysis, be psychological or sociological. . . . I doubt that there is another sort of answer to be found" (*Criticism*, p. 21). "Whatever scientific progress may be, we must account for it by examining the nature of the scientific group, discovering what it values, what it tolerates, and what it disdains. That position is intrinsically sociological" (*Criticism*, p. 238). We must study scientific communities not as one of several steps in clarifying the nature of science (in attempting, say, to separate the irrational from the rational components as a prelude to analyzing the latter); it is the *only* step. What the community says is rational, scientific, is so; beyond this, there is no answer to be found. An alternative to this view is to think of sociology as able to bring to our attention the kinds of biases which scientists should learn to avoid, as interferences, hindrances to good scientific judgment. For Kuhn, however, such biases are an integral, and indeed the central, aspect of science. The point I have tried to make is not merely that Kuhn's is a view which denies the objectivity and rationality of the scientific enterprise; I have tried to show that the arguments by which Kuhn arrives at his conclusion are unclear and unsatisfactory.

5

SCIENCE AND HUMANISM

HENRY B. VEATCH

MOST people accept as true the sentence with which Aristotle begins his Metaphysics: "All men by nature desire to know." What is not so readily accepted is the fact that "knowledge" is not a univocal concept and that our human ways of knowing, as well as the kinds of knowledge that result from them, may be deceptively multiple and various. . . .

It will be illuminating to contrast humanistic and scientific knowledge in action, so to speak, with reference to a test case which may check this inveterate and uncritical tendency of ours to write off humanistic knowledge altogether, as if it were not properly knowledge at all when compared with what one finds in the sciences. The test case that I would propose has to do with the common employment in the humanities of so-called philosophical or literary classics. It will hardly be disputed that the traditional and even continuing way of studying either literature or philosophy is in terms of what people have generally called classics, even though these are no longer the classics of Greece and Rome. It is hard to imagine even the most up-to-the-minute contemporary phi-losopher who does not spend a great portion of his time and effort over the texts of Wittgenstein, Heidegger, Merleau-Ponty, or Bergmann. And why? Because the philosopher in question is convinced that the text he is studying is in some sense or other a truly classic one—that is, one that stands out from others just in virtue of the decisive excellence that it is presumed to have.

Or again, suppose that in a course in contemporary literature the in-structor assigns something of Alan Ginsberg, or Susan Sonntag, or Eldridge Cleaver. The instructor's choice of authors is guided by con-

FROM H. B. Veatch, The what and the why of the humanities, The *Key Reporter,* 1972, 37 (4). Pages 2–4 and part of page 8 reprinted by permission of the author, *The Key Reporter,* and Phi Beta Kappa.

siderations of the superior excellence of the writers selected—perhaps not excellence absolutely, but excellence of a certain kind and in a certain genre. It is evident that the authors selected, by the very fact that they have been chosen, are being treated as classics, whether the actual term be used or no.

Contrast, though, the sciences. Would it be wrong to say that in the sciences there just aren't any classics at all—or at least not any that we might call operative classics? To be sure, it is easy to point to any number of great works in science that have been literally epoch-making in the history of science—Newton's *Principia*, Darwin's *Origin of Species*, Einstein's special and general theory of relativity. Even though such works have been incomparably decisive in the development of science, can it really be said that they have ever been used and studied by scientists in the manner of classics? How many contemporary physicists, for example, have read and proceeded to reread and even to return time and again to the texts of Einstein's papers on relativity in the way in which, say, almost every young philosopher in the present-day analytic tradition finds himself going back again and again to Wittgenstein's *Tractatus* or to his *Investigations*?

Now this is not to deny that it has become increasingly fashionable in recent years to take the history of science more seriously. Many scientists of the highest reputations have done a great deal toward making not only scientists themselves, but even the general public, much more conscious of the history of science, and of the startling revolutionary achievements of the great men of science.

All the same, has this new-found interest in the history of science had any marked effect upon the actual discipline and practice of science? Does the ordinary chemist or biologist or geologist or physicist feel that a first-hand acquaintance with the work of Avogadro, or of Mendel, or of Lyell, or of Galileo is absolutely essential to his proficiency and the fruitfulness of his work is his particular scientific discipline? In other words, an interest in scientific classics and in the history of science generally is not an interest that is proper and pertinent to science as such, but rather, like any other interest in history, is a humanistic interest; it bears fruit in a deepened and broader understanding of man and of man's characteristic human achievements; but it contributes nothing, at least not directly, to the advancement of science itself.

Why, though—and here our main question returns to plague us— why is there this difference between the sciences and the humanities, in that the pursuit of the one would appear almost invariably to involve a study of classics, whereas to the other, classics are a matter of comparative, if not of complete, indifference? In answer to this question, we shall hazard an explanation in terms of a contrast between humanistic knowledge and scientific knowledge which, I am afraid, is far from being the currently fashionable one, or even one that many have heard of, and which yet may prove ultimately to be the only sound and defensible one.

First, then, as to humanistic knowledge, we assume in literary no less than in philosophical works, the concern of the author is to "tell it like it is." That is to say, a poet such as Alan Ginsberg, no less than a Dante or Sophocles, is a man with something to say, and what he has to say has to do with the truth about ourselves as human beings and our human predicament. Not only that, but the poet, and to a lesser degree perhaps the philosopher too, does not merely wish to tell it as it is, but also to move us to respond to that truth appropriately.

As students of the humanities, we acknowledge ourselves to be but men who want to know and understand what the score is, and what we can expect in the way of a life on earth, as well as how we can make some sense of our lives and avoid making utter fools or knaves of ourselves. We turn then for instruction to just those works that we have been calling classics—that is to say to those men who as writers have "told it like it is" and whose words have the ring of truth.

It is painfully obvious that no set of classics, however chosen, ever speaks with but a single voice or purveys a single truth. Thus if Blake no less than Donne, or George Herbert no less than Aristotle, are all equally classics, how can one possibly say that through classics, and only through classics, do we come to know the truth? Is it not the case instead that many truths, rather than the truth, and many truths diametrically opposed and even contradictory to one another—in other words, downright errors no less than truths—these are what are mediated by any study of classics, whatever such classics may be and however chosen?

Humanistic knowledge cannot be attained merely by swallowing key truths in formulas and capsules. There is no way of either coming to know or continuing to know what the truth is about reality and about ourselves, without at the same time becoming ever more sensitive to and understanding of the ways of errors as well.

Why would there seem to be nothing quite comparable to this in science? Why is it that scientific knowledge is apparently indifferent to such things as might be called classics, whereas humanistic knowledge finds its only proper nourishment and sustenance directly in the classics? We shall no longer accept as a truism that the reason science has no truck with classics is because science is concerned only with objective facts, whereas the humanities are concerned rather with our subjective human responses to the facts and with the literary and artistic embellishments that these entail. Our thesis is, if anything, just the opposite; it is precisely because science is not really concerned with knowing the nature of things, or the way things are, that it finds itself indifferent to anything on the order of classics, whose sole justification for being classics is just that they do open our eyes to the truth and to what is our true human predicament, set down as we are in the midst of things and encompassed by a reality that is not of our own making.

If such a thesis sounds utterly paradoxical, even fantastic, let us qualify it a bit by conceding that, no doubt historically, science has not been so indifferent to achieving knowledge of the real, as it would now appear to have become. Not only that, but we concede that many practising scientists are not aware of the radically non-realistic orientation that their discipline has come to have, and hence may think of themselves in their role as scientists as being concerned simply with trying to observe and to describe the facts as they are. Yet when one considers the distinctive character of the modern scientific enterprise, as this has been brought into focus by recent philosophers of science, then one begins to see that the real thrust of the scientific enterprise is not aimed at anything like a knowledge of reality or the nature of things at all. Oversimplifying somewhat, one might say that there are at least two dominant features or factors that have been operative in the methodology of science that have made this result inevitable—one is what might be called the nature of scientific data; and the other, the nature of scientific hypotheses, theories and explanation generally.

First, as to the data. Surely all of us, nonscientists no less than scientists, know that although the entire fabric of science is erected on the data of observation and experiment, such data as they function in science are hardly the data of our ordinary experience. Rather they are those bare, but presumably public and reproducible data such as pointer-readings, impressions on a photographic plate, etc. In this sense what may be considered to be given to the scientists as data are not at all the things of our everyday experience—tables and chairs, men and mice, night and day, winter and summer, sunlight and clouds; rather the only properly acceptable data of the scientist are more like those bare sense data which the philosophers of 25 years or so ago were wont to make so much of—momentary patches of color, of sounds, of odors, of tastes, etc.

What's more, these properly scientific data prove to be singularly uninformative, particularly when it comes to anything suggestive of ordered patterns or causal laws in terms of which the things and events in nature could possibly be made intelligible. Ever since Hume it has become something of a truism that no causal connection can ever be observed to hold between the data of sense; and as for inductive inferences from such data, these just don't seem to have any properly logical warrant of any kind.

What, then, has been the result of this seeming frustration in any and all efforts to find meaning or intelligibility in the data of experience, or at least in such data of experience as the scientist may properly accept? The answer is to be found in that second factor of the modern scientific situation which we mentioned above, the factor of scientific hypotheses and theories. For in effect what the scientists have tended to do is that, not being able to find meaning or intelligibility in the actual facts and data of science, they have, as it were, fabricated and imposed a kind of intelligibility upon the data from the outside in the form of scientific theories and hypotheses. Thus Sir Karl Popper, the distinguished contemporary philosopher and logician of science, quotes with favor and even with some furbishing of the text on his own part, a well-known passage from the 'Preface to the second edition of Kant's *Critique of Pure Reason:*

When Galileo let his balls run down an inclined plane with a gravity which he had chosen himself; when Torricelli caused the air to sustain a weight which he had calculated beforehand to be equal to that of a column of water of known height; . . . . then a light dawned upon all natural philosophers. They learnt that our reason can understand only *what it creates according to its own design: that we must compel Nature to answer our questions,* rather than cling to Nature's apron string and allow her to guide us. *For purely accidental observations, made without any plan having been thought out in advance, cannot be connected by a . . . law*—which is what reason is searching for.

Moreover, the very logic of this conception of the nature of scientific theories and hypotheses, and of the objectives they serve tends to have consequences that far outrun anything that either Kant or Popper would seem to have realized. For if a scientific hypothesis be not in any way derived from the facts or data of observation, then even supposing such a hypothesis to have been pretty well corroborated and borne out by empirical test and experiment, it can scarcely be concluded from this that the hypothesis is to be regarded as properly an account or description or reflection of the facts or of the way in which things are. It simply provides a convenient and useful ordering device with respect to the manifold sensory data—an ordering device, be it logical or linguistic or mathematical, which the human mind or the mind of the scientist devises for the purpose of helping him get about, as it were, among the data, associating them one with another, making predictions from certain ones to others, and thus putting them to various calculable uses. As C. I. Lewis, a perceptive philosopher of a generation ago, very tellingly put it, a scientific hypothesis is really but an intellectual or "conceptual go-cart" that enables the scientists to "get over the intervals" between the sensory data.

If scientific theories are no longer to be regarded as sources and means through which we as men can come to a better understanding of the nature of things, if as theories they are not even supposed to disclose the truth about things, but only what might be called the truth of our human predictions, manipulations, and devices for the control of nature, then it is little wonder that scientific treatises in which theories of this sort are presented and expounded can hardly function in the manner of classics. For the excellence of theories so conceived is not to be gauged by their approximation to the truth, or by the insights which they offer into the nature of reality, but only by what we might call in the crude sense their pragmatic consequences. Consequently, once a theory comes along that works better than its predecessor, then that predecessor, so far from being able to attain the status of a classic, can hope for no better fate than death and discard. Indeed, if theories or explanations in science are to be respected, not for their being testimonies to human understanding and insight into the nature of the real, but simply for their being testimonies to human inventiveness and ingenuity, then it stands to reason that it will be only the latest and the most ingenious invention that will count, all others being but so many outmoded devices that no longer work. As such, they may be either simply consigned to the dust heap, or else treated as mere museum pieces in the history of science, but of no further use whatever in science itself.

6

FACT AND FANTASY
IN THE HISTORY OF SCIENCE

Stephen G. Brush

An editorial in the Washington *Post,* bemoaning double-talk from both sides during the last presidential election campaign, suggested that public reporting of the campaign, being harmful to the ideals of young readers, might be a proper target for censorship (1):

It is time to consider whether this campaign ought not to be rated X for children, on the grounds that young and inexperienced minds might form the impression that our national politics is mainly composed of hypocrisy and cynicism. Adults know that to be wrong, of course, but there is not much in the current campaign by which to prove it.

Such proposals are equally appropriate to a variety of subjects similarly remote from the realm of sex, which the term "X-rated" connotes (2). My concern in this article is with the possible dangers of using the history of science in science education. I will examine arguments that

from S. G. Brush, Should the history of science be rated X? *Science,* 1974, 183, 1164–1172. Copyright 1974 by the American Association for the Advancement of Science.

young and impressionable students at the start of a scientific career should be shielded from the writings of contemporary science historians for reasons similar to the one mentioned above—namely, that these writings do violence to the professional ideal and public image of scientists as rational, open-minded investigators, proceeding methodically, grounded incontrovertibly in the outcome of controlled experiments, and seeking objectively for the truth, let the chips fall where they may (3).

As is customary, "science" will be identified primarily with physics and early astronomy; these subjects usually furnish the successful examples of the scientific approach to be emulated in other fields.

The Conventional Description of Scientific Behavior

The introduction of historical materials into science courses is often motivated by the desire to give the future scientist not only facts and technical skills, but also the correct attitude or general methodology. His teachers want him to respect the standards of impartiality, logical rigor, and experimental verification of hypotheses and to refrain from excessive theorizing about new or unexplained phenomena on the basis of metaphysical, mystical, or theological preconceptions. As the philosophers of science put it, he should be able to distinguish between the "context of discovery" and the "context of justification"—scientific hypotheses may come in an undisciplined way from the creative mind, but they must ultimately face the test of comparison with experiment and observation (4).

Science textbooks generally place a strong emphasis on the experimental character of science. As Charles Kittel and his colleagues say in *The Berkeley Physics Course* (5, p. 4):

Through experimental science we have been able to learn all these facts about the natural world, triumphing over darkness and ignorance to classify the stars and to estimate their masses, composition, distances, and velocities; to classify living species and to unravel their genetic relations. . . . These great accomplishments of experimental science were achieved by men of many types. . . . Most of these men had in common only a few things: they were honest and actually made the observations they recorded, and they published the results of their work in a form permitting others to duplicate the experiment or observation.

Obviously any historical materials that might raise doubts in the students' minds as to whether their heroes—men like Galileo Galilei, John Dalton, or Gregor Mendel—really did follow these precepts would undermine the purpose of the course and would therefore not be appropriate.

Another virtue often mentioned in textbooks is skepticism about established dogma. The scientist must be brave enough to question and criticize anything his teachers or his society may tell him, at the risk of ostracism, denial of financial support, or worse. Only in this way can a scientist hope to make a positive contribution to his subject. Obviously, if an historian of science were to suggest that most scientists, most of the time, are simply working out routine problems according to agreed procedures, his help would not be welcome in teaching science. There is only one established dogma in science—that scientists do not blindly accept established dogma (6).

Nevertheless the emphasis on teaching "scientific method" is not very noticeable nowadays in courses for the science major, especially in physics courses. Statements by such physicists as P. W. Bridgman, that there is no such thing as scientific method (7), have apparently had some impact, and the usual approach is to assume that the student will absorb the correct attitude as he learns the subject matter and works in the laboratory. But in courses for the nonscience major, in which there is not much subject matter and perhaps no laboratory work at all, the discussion of methodology is much more explicit (8). Indeed, many educators feel that the only justification for requiring all students to take a science course is to show them how legitimate (that is, physical and biological) scientists work, in order that they may learn a method they can apply in their own disciplines in the social sciences and humanities. Thus Daniel Bell writes that "as part of a general education all students should be aware of the nature of . . . hypothetical-deductive thought" as it has been developed in science (9, p. 248). Bell, a sociologist, quotes biophysicist John Platt's statement that some fields in science move more rapidly than others, in part because "a particular method of doing scientific research is systematically used and taught" (10, p. 347). This method relies on "devising alternative hypotheses for any problem, devising crucial experiments, each of which would, as nearly as possible, exclude one or more hypotheses" (9, p. 251). The procedure is said to have been particularly effective in the Watson-Crick determination of the structure of DNA and in more recent research in molecular biology, as well as in physics.

History in Science Teaching

The history of science has always exerted a strong attraction on some scientists, and they have often advocated the historical approach in teaching science. For some, this means no more than an extension of the usual technique of "searching the literature" pertaining to a research topic. In extreme cases, this can lead to the publication of series of annotated sources or of gigantic bibliographies (11). Such projects, initiated by scientists who maintain that they have primarily in mind the needs of other scientists and students, often turn out to be of considerable value to historians of science, in spite of occasional snide remarks that the publications are "not really history."

One occasionally encounters claims that new discoveries have been inspired by reading about much earlier work that was not successful at the time and hence did not make its way into the textbooks (12). Ernst Mach, a physicist who devoted considerable time to historical studies, wrote (13):

They that know the entire course of the development of science, will, as a matter of course, judge more freely and more correctly of the significance of any present scientific movement than they, who, limited in their views to the age in which their own lives have been spent, contemplate merely the momentary trend that the course of intellectual events takes at the present moment.

In spite of such statements, most science teachers have not been willing to make more than a superficial use of history in training scientists. (Perhaps they realize that Mach's own faulty judgment of physical theories in the early decades of the 20th century is an eloquent refutation of his statement.) They apparently agree with J. B. Conant's argument that, while knowledge of the history of science may help a scientist to function better outside the laboratory, it has nothing to teach him about the methods of research he will need in order to make new discoveries (14). F. S. Allen, an historian who has surveyed the changing opinions of scientists on this subject, concludes that "since the 1950's, most scientists have not viewed a history of science course as a legitimate subject in the curriculum" (15, p. 270).

It has even been argued that historical readings would actually be harmful to a science student. As Thomas S. Kuhn has pointed out, in the great classics of science the student "might discover other ways of regarding the problems discussed in his textbook, but . . . he would also meet problems, concepts, and standards of solution that his future profession has long since discarded and replaced" (16, p. 344). Thus he might be led to waste his time doing work that would not be acceptable for publication in science journals. (This seems to be the fate of many bright people who try to break into a scientific discipline from the "outside," without having gone through the orthodox training process.)

Conant and other influential science educators have nevertheless strongly urged the use of history in science courses designed for non-science majors, and many such courses and textbooks have met with some success (17). Moreover, in recent years the publication of some exceptionally penetrating articles and books on 20th-century physics has caused many teachers to conclude that such historical studies might indeed challenge their brightest students. The debates of Albert Einstein, Niels Bohr, Erwin Schrödinger, Werner Heisenberg, Paul Ehrenfest, and others on the fundamental problems of relativity and quantum mechanics have attracted renewed attention, especially now that these theories are no longer regarded as beyond criticism.

One symptom of the revival of interest in this subject is the International Working Seminar on the Role of the History of Physics Education, organized by Allen King and held at the Massachusetts Institute of Technology in July 1970, under the sponsorship of the Commission on Physics Education of the International Union of Pure and Applied Physics (18). Supposedly, the participants were all agreed that history of science is useful in teaching, and the purpose of the seminar was to organize concrete steps toward collecting and preparing materials, guidelines, and so forth for teachers who might like to use history but know very little about it. The participants made considerable progress along these lines, and the proceedings of the seminar have now been published. The proceedings include discussion and recommendations: listings of books, films, translations of classic papers, and so forth (19). But some doubts were raised at this meeting about whether history and science teaching really go together as well as many participants assumed. Martin Klein played the devil's advocate by pointing out that history and science are inherently different kinds of disciplines; bringing them together is likely to do violence to one or the other. The scientist wants to get at the essence of a phenomenon, and to do so he must strip away all complicating features or contingencies peculiar to time, place, and the personality of the observer. Yet for the historian those are the essence of history; if the detail of past events were to be eliminated, nothing significant would be left. Again, when the science teacher introduces historical materials, he must do so in a very selective way, since his real purpose should be to teach modern theories and techniques more effectively; he can only take from the past that which seems to have significance in the present. The result may be a series of fascinating (and often mythical) anecdotes, but it is surely not history as the historian understands it.

Subversive Aspects of the History of Science

It can be argued that the historical approach, while it may distract students by loading a course with superfluous information, does give the instructor an opportunity to discuss conceptual problems that are often overlooked in conventional teaching (20). Yet the science teacher may be justified in following his instincts to ignore history, especially if his purpose is to train scientists who will follow the currently approved research methods.

By "history" I mean simply the most accurate or authoritative account that an historian of science can give of the way a discovery was made, a theory was developed and accepted or rejected by scientists, and the mutual influences of research in different areas of science or of science and other kinds of human activity. History is not merely an unchanging record of facts, but also the interpretations proposed by each new generation of historians.

Many people still believe [with George Sarton, who called Auguste Comte the founder of history of science (21)] that the purpose of the historian is to record the process of cumulation of positive knowledge, not forgetting that there have been errors and confusion along the way, but also not forgetting to identify them clearly as such. (Sarton also specifically stated that what may appear as error to one generation of historians might be seen as neglected truth by the next.) A modern historian of science, Charles C. Gillispie, has eloquently argued the thesis that science progresses by using "objectivity" to separate truth from error (22). Sarton and Gillispie may be taken as representatives of the traditional view, which is probably still held by a majority of scientists.

In recent years, some historians of science have been moving toward another conception of their role, based on the notion that scientists often operate in a subjective way and that experimental verification is of secondary importance compared to philosophical arguments, at least in some of the major conceptual changes that have occurred in science. If this notion is correct, then the historian must do more than document the application of objectivity to scientific problems. He must be prepared to analyze the philosophical, psychological, and sociological aspects of scientific work, to explain how certain problems came to be considered "scientific" and how particular standards happened to be accepted for evaluating solutions to those problems. He may also have to account for scientific change in terms other than those of linear progress from error toward truth.

This reorientation of the historical interpretation of science is usually considered to have begun with the publication of Alexandre Koyré's Galilean studies in the 1930's (23). Here one finds Galileo described not as the first modern experimental physicist, but as a Platonist who helped to replace the Aristotelian world view by a mechanistic one, employing the tools of logical arguments, rhetorical persuasion, and mathematical deduction. From the narrowly empirical viewpoint, Galileo could hardly be said to have made any positive contributions to knowledge (apart from his telescopic observations)—his theories did not even explain everyday experience as well as those of the Aristotelians. But Koyré argues that (24):

. . . [W]hat the founders of modern science, among them Galileo, had to do, was not to criticize and combat certain faulty theories, [but] to correct or to replace them by better ones. They had to do something quite different. They had to destroy one world and to replace it by another. They had to reshape the framework of our intellect itself, to restate and reform its concepts, to evolve a new approach to Being, a new concept of knowledge, a new concept of science—and even to replace a pretty natural approach, that of common sense, by another which is not natural at all.

This picture of Galileo was already beginning to infiltrate textbooks two decades ago, for I have taken this quotation from the first edition of

Gerald Holton's *Introduction to Concepts and Theories in Physical Science,* published in 1952. In this book, Holton also pointed out that the supposedly objective "facts" with which the scientist deals are useless without some interpretation, and the latter is inevitably linked to theory and to metaphysical preconceptions. These sentiments were not new, but they had rarely been expressed so forcefully in a science textbook.

Koyré's interpretation of Galileo was not universally accepted, but it did acquire considerable support among other historians of science. For example, A. Rupert Hall wrote in 1964 of the battle between the geocentrists and heliocentrists in the 17th century (25, p. 71):

There was no proof for either side: there was only the choice between *this* way of regarding things which belonged to antiquity, and *that* which belonged to Galileo and modern science . . . the number of instances of his offering a precise piece of experiment in support of his notions is small indeed. Even the positive assertions of experimental verification made by Galileo have been doubted. . . . Sufficient-reason considerations and mathematical arguments were of greater effect in winning support for the law of falling bodies than any experiments. . . . Galileo is above all aware that the senses must be educated and assisted to perceive realities. Thus one could *know* the true nature of the moon without the telescope: that instrument simply makes reality easier to discover. . . . A Platonist, a Copernican, a mechanical philosopher could not possibly be a naive empiricist; and it was hardly more possible for him to be, systematically, a follower of the hypothetico-deductive logic.

By 1970, such views had become so widespread that philosopher of science Paul Feyerabend could make the following statement with scarcely any documentation (26, pp. 64–65):

The reader will realize that a more detailed study of historical phenomena like these may create considerable difficulties for the view that the transition from the pre-Copernican cosmology to Galileo consisted in the replacement of a refuted theory by a more general conjecture which explains the refuting instances, makes new predictions, and is corroborated by the observations carried out to test these new predictions. And he will perhaps see the merits of a different view which asserts that while the pre-Copernican astronomy was in trouble (was confronted by a series of refuting instances), the Copernican theory was in even greater trouble (was confronted by even more drastic refuting instances); but that being in harmony with still further inadequate theories it gained strength, and was retained, the refutations being made ineffective by *ad hoc* hypotheses and clever techniques of persuasion.

Other examples of historians' debunking of the discoveries of Nicolaus Copernicus, Galileo, Antoine Laurent Lavoisier, Dalton, Mendel, and Robert A. Millikan might be cited, but Richard Westfall's article on Isaac Newton (27) should suffice: "If the *Principia* established the quantitative pattern of modern science, it equally suggested a less sublime truth—that no one can manipulate the fudge factor quite so effectively as the master mathematician himself" (27, p. 752). Westfall, being quite familiar with Newton's work, had no difficulty in shooting down the suggestion that Newton's ploys could be considered acceptable scientific procedure (28).

Meanwhile, the suggestion that scientific change may result primarily from theoretical arguments or subjective factors was being generalized into a new description of scientific revolutions by Kuhn (29). Kuhn's scheme undermines conventional ideas of scientific behavior in two ways. First, he argues that the (proper) function of scientific education is *not* to produce skeptics who will continually challenge existing dogma, but rather to train highly competent "puzzle-solvers" who will be content to work within the agreed framework of rules and theories—the current "paradigm" governing "normal science" (30, p. 341). Second, he describes revolutions as changes from one paradigm to another by a process that is more like a "conversion experience" than a reasoned debate based on objective evidence (29, p. 151). Since the paradigm includes not only a theory, but also a set of criteria for determining what problems are worth solving and how one recognizes a solution when he has it, there may not be any mutually agreed basis for determining whether the new paradigm is better than the old. Thus, successive paradigms tend to be "incommensurable," and doubt is cast on the cherished idea that science makes cumulative progress. Moreover, according to Kuhn, scientists do not test theories by a hypothetico-deductive process at all: "Once it has achieved the status of a paradigm, a scientific theory is declared invalid only if an alternative candidate is available to take its place" (29, p. 77), and then the choice is made on at least partially subjective grounds. Although the revolution may be initiated by the failure of the old paradigm to account for some crucial piece of experimental data or observation, its outcome may be a new paradigm that fails to account for other data or observations that were explained quite well by the old paradigm. (For example, the failure to observe stellar parallax in the 17th century was a strong argument against the heliocentric theory and a confirmation of the geocentric theory.)

There is no need to review here the controversy generated by Kuhn's thesis (31); I will mention only one publication to illustrate the considerable discomfort it has caused those concerned with science education and their failure (in my opinion) to come to grips with the basic problems it raises. Israel Scheffler, professor of education and philosophy at Harvard University, views with alarm the tendency I have just been describing (32):

That the ideal of objectivity has been fundamental to science is beyond question. The philosophical task is to assess and interpret this ideal: to ask how, if at all, objectivity is possible. This task is especially urgent now, when received opinions as to the sources of objectivity in science are increasingly under attack. The notion of a fixed observational given, of a constant descriptive language, of a shared methodology of investigation, of a rational community advancing its knowledge of the real world—all have been subjected to severe and mounting criticism from a variety of directions.

The overall tendency of such criticism has been to call into question the very conception of scientific thought as a responsible enterprise of reasonable men. The extreme alternative that threatens is the view that theory is not controlled by data, but that data are manufactured by theory; that rival hypotheses cannot be rationally evaluated, there being no neutral court of observational appeal nor any shared stock of meanings; that scientific change is a product not of evidential appraisal and logical judgment, but of intuition, persuasion, and conversion; that reality does not constrain the thought of the scientist but is rather itself a projection of that thought. Unless the concept of responsible scientific endeavour is to be given up as a huge illusion, the challenge of this alternative must, clearly, be met. . . .

What Scheffler characterized as the "extreme alternative" is really not an unfair description of the conclusions that have emerged from some recent historical studies. In addition to the reinterpretation of Galileo's work mentioned above, it has been alleged that Dalton and Mendel "cooked" the supposedly experimental data they presented in support of their theories of chemical atomism and heredity, respectively (33). Einstein refused to let experimental "facts" shake his belief in the validity of relativity theory, and in this he was supported by H. A. Lorentz (34). Paul Dirac stated that a theorist should prefer beautiful equations to uglier ones that yield closer agreement with experimental data (35), and Max Planck stated that new theories rarely get accepted by rational persuasion of the opponents—one simply has to wait until the opponents die out (36).

Einstein identified the fallacy in assuming that scientific theories are tested by observations when, in 1926, he replied to Heisenberg's statement that only observable magnitudes must go into a theory. After all, asked Heisenberg, didn't you stress this requirement in formulating the theory of relativity? Einstein replied, according to Heisenberg (37, p. 63):

Possibly I did use this kind of reasoning, but it is nonsense all the same. Perhaps I could put it more diplomatically by saying that it may be heuristically useful to keep in mind what one has observed. But on principle, it is quite wrong to try founding a theory on observable magnitudes alone. In reality the very opposite happens. It is the theory which decides what we can observe.

A year later, when he formulated his indeterminacy principle, Heisenberg recalled Einstein's assertion that "It is the theory which decides what we can observe" and realized that, once that principle had been deduced from quantum mechanics, it was no longer vulnerable to experimental disproof. The processes involved in an experiment or observation must themselves satisfy the laws of quantum mechanics, hence "experiments are unlikely to produce situations that do not accord with quantum mechanics" (37, p. 78).

Scheffler argues that scientists simply should not behave this way, and he proposes an alternative philosophy of objectivity. But when the scientists who have laid the foundations of modern physics confess that their theory is not controlled by data, the prospects for enforcing objectivity on the scientific community are substantially diminished (38).

Theory and Experiment: Additional Historical Examples

I now turn to three examples of scientific behavior which I have uncovered in my own research in the history of science. In the first case, an apparently well-established theory of the nature of heat was rejected, not because of any new experimental evidence or theoretical calculations pertaining directly to heat, but because of new experimental and theoretical work in optics. In the second case, a theory of the nature of gases was clearly refuted by experimental tests (according to at least one proponent of the theory) but was accepted anyway. In the third case, a particular interatomic force law, derived by fitting experimental data, was abandoned in favor of another force law, which was in worse agreement with the data, primarily because of theoretical calculations. While these decisions were made in the first instance by individual scientists, their colleagues did not protest the irrationality of the decisions but simply followed the leader; hence these cases provide legitimate evidence for the behavior of the scientific community. Moreover, they do not involve major conceptual revolutions such as those mentioned earlier; they pertain, rather, to the less spectacular kind of theory change that is more typical of ordinary scientific activity.

The Wave Theory of Heat (39, 40). Any physics textbook will report that the equivalence of heat and mechanical energy was established by the experiments of James Prescott Joule in the middle of the 19th century. Some will also state that Joule thereby overthrew an earlier theory, the "caloric theory," which identified heat as a substance rather than a form of energy. Here, it might seem, is a classic historical illustration of the essential role of quantitative experimentation in exposing fallacious theories, an example eminently suitable for pedagogical purposes.

Unfortunately for the physics teacher, this traditional account of the origin of thermodynamics leaves out one very important fact. At the time Joule did his work, in the 1840's, the caloric theory had already been abandoned by most physicists. The reason was not the earlier experiments of Count Rumford and Humphry Davy (circa 1800), showing that heat can be generated by friction; those experiments were indeed well known, but they failed to shake the faith of early 19th-century scientists in the materiality of heat. Instead, the crucial experiments were those on radiant heat and light. The investigations of William Herschel,

Macedonio Melloni, and others showed that radiant heat has all the qualitative properties of light: it can be reflected, refracted, even polarized. Thus, by the 1820's, it was generally accepted that whatever theory might be adopted to explain the physical nature of light, a similar theory must be adopted for heat. I say "heat," not just "*radiant* heat," for at that time the modern distinction between radiant and other kinds of heat was not recognized. In fact, many theorists believed that all heat is essentially radiant.

Before 1820, the conviction that heat and light are essentially the same kind of phenomenon was favorable to the caloric theory of heat, since light was assumed to be composed of material particles rather than of the motions of particles. But when Augustin Fresnel succeeded in establishing the wave theory of light, by a combination of brilliant theoretical and experimental arguments, physicists were quick to draw the obvious conclusion that heat must also have a wave nature—that is, it must consist of vibrations of the same ethereal medium that was then considered responsible for the propagation of light.

The transition from the caloric to the wave theory of heat took place gradually, but inevitably, in the 1830's. Most of the phenomena that had been explained in terms of caloric could be explained in terms of *vibrations* of caloric, or ether, as it had come to be called. The theory was enunciated in its most explicit form by André-Marie Ampère. He did not try to show that the new conception of heat had any marked advantages over the old one in explaining thermal phenomena. The change was motivated solely by the desire for a unified theory of both heat and light. It is easy to demonstrate the widespread acceptance of the wave theory of heat by examining almost any physics textbook or encyclopedia article on heat published between 1830 and 1845 (41).

Supporters of the wave theory of heat insisted at first that their hypothesis was distinct from the older ideas of heat as atomic motion, since the "waves" involved only the vibrations of the ether. But once the association of heat with motion had been revived and made respectable, it was not long before the further assumption emerged that ether vibrations could induce or interact with atomic vibrations. There is some evidence that it was just this line of reasoning that led Sadi Carnot, C. F. Mohr, W. R. Grove, Hermann von Helmholtz, W. J. M. Rankine, and J. J. Waterston to conclude that heat can be described as a form of mechanical energy.

The Kinetic Theory of Gases (42). By the middle of the 1850's, the adoption of the principles of energy conservation and thermodynamics had created a strong presumption in favor of the ancient idea that heat is simply the energy of motion of atoms in a vacuum. This motion would be especially simple in a gas, if one could assume that the atoms (or molecules) moved in straight lines at a constant speed until they encountered other atoms or the sides of a container. Of course this assumption required that the wave theory of heat be consigned to oblivion, or at least limited to radiant heat phenomena, so as not to complicate the description of atomic motion with ether-drag corrections. Yet it was not at all obvious that the ether could be legitimately ignored, so the early kinetic theorists—Waterston, Rudolf Clausius, and James Clerk Maxwell—hedged their bets by treating the kinetic theory as a hypothesis that might be refuted.

It was in this cautious spirit that Maxwell wrote his first paper on the kinetic theory of gases (43). His caution was justified, for he discovered that two deductions from the theory were in conflict with known experimental facts about gases. First, there was the remarkable theoretical prediction that the viscosity of a gas of elastic spheres is independent of density and increases with temperature. Maxwell wrote to G. G. Stokes, who had done considerable work in hydrodynamics, to ask about experimental evidence on this point and learned that the only data known at the time (an observation Edward Sabine made in 1829) suggested that the viscosity of air does vary with density. This nonconfirming instance was duly noted by Maxwell in his paper.

The second difficulty of the kinetic theory was the disagreement of theoretical and experimental values of the ratio of specific heats. In this case, there was no doubt that the kinetic theory was refuted; as Maxwell told the British Association for the Advancement of Science in 1860, "This result of the dynamical theory, being at variance with experiment, overturns the whole hypothesis, however satisfactory the other results may be" (44, p. 15).

Fortunately for the progress of physics, Maxwell did not take seriously such a naive version of the hypothetico-deductive method. Instead, he continued to develop the kinetic theory and inspired others to follow him. He also conducted a series of experiments on gas viscosity himself and found that viscosity does not change appreciably over quite a large range of densities. This result was confirmed by several other experimenters and became one of the strongest arguments in favor of the validity of the kinetic theory. Stokes later admitted that the analysis of the Sabine experiment had implicitly involved the assumption that the viscosity of air vanishes at low densities; this assumption is so natural that it might have survived indefinitely had it not been for Maxwell's theory. In this case the theory refuted the experiment.

The other discrepancy was not so easily eliminated, and Maxwell refused to accept the artificial models of diatomic molecules proposed by Ludwig Boltzmann and others to explain the experimental specific heat ratios. Yet he would not abandon an otherwise plausible and successful theory simply because it failed to account for *all* the experimental facts. Those scientists who did suggest that the theory be abandoned, later in the 19th century, did so not because of this difficulty, but because of more deep-seated philosophical objections. For those who believed in a positivist methodology, *any* theory based on invisible and undetectable atoms was unacceptable, regardless of how well its predictions had been confirmed by experiments (45).

Interatomic Forces (46). The specific heats discrepancy and much else was cleared up by the development of quantum mechanics in the first part of the 20th century. During the same period, elaborate techniques for solving the Maxwell-Boltzmann equations of kinetic theory were worked out by David Enskog and Sydney Chapman (47). These techniques made it possible to compute the gas transport coefficients (viscosity, heat conduction, and diffusion) for any of a large class of hypothetical interparticle force laws. It was thus natural to suppose that by detailed comparison of experimental and theoretical coefficients one could determine the true law of force, at least for the simplest case of spherically symmetric rare gas atoms. A comprehensive program along these lines was undertaken by J. E. Lennard-Jones, beginning in 1924.

Lennard-Jones proposed to represent the interatomic force law by a function of the general form

$$F(r) = -ar^{-n} + br^{-m}$$

where negative values of F correspond to attractive forces and positive values to repulsive forces. It was expected that the exponent m would be greater than n, corresponding to a combination of a short-range repulsive and a long-range attractive force. By combining data on gas viscosity and virial coefficients with some information on the crystalline lattice spacing for the solid state, Lennard-Jones was able to show that n should be about 5 for helium, argon, and neon. Values of the index m varied from 9 to 21 for these gases, depending on the relative weights given to gas and crystal data.

The conclusion that long-range attractive forces between neutral rare-gas atoms vary inversely as the fifth power of the distance was no sooner established by experiment than it was overturned by theory. Quantum-mechanical calculations by S. C. Wang, J. C. Slater, R. Eisenschitz, and F. London led to the conclusion that this force should vary inversely as the seventh power of the distance. Accordingly, Lennard-Jones proposed in 1931 that his indices should be assigned the values $n = 7$ and $m = 13$. The latter value was not based on quantum mechanics at all, but simply on the fact that it is easier to do certain theoretical calculations in gas theory if m^{-1} is just twice n^{-1}. (Specialists will know that n^{-1} and m^{-1} are the exponents of $1/r$ in the corresponding potential energy function; this is the origin of the "6, 12" potential.) In fact, quantum mechanics leads to a different functional form, e^{-kr}, for the repulsive component of the force law.

Another surprising aspect of this story is that the Lennard-Jones force law (with $n = 7$ and $m = 13$) continued to be described and used as the "most realistic" function in many works on statistical mechanics for the next 30 years, despite the absence of any experimental basis for this claim. Within the last decade, it has finally been realized that neither this nor any other simple function can give an accurate representative of the interatomic force law in a manner satisfactory to both theorists and experimentalists.

The conclusion I would draw from these examples is not that experiments are unimportant in the choice of theories, but that direct experimental tests of hypotheses are often given less weight than the conformity of the hypothesis with a general theoretical superstructure or with more prestigious theories in related branches of science. One might still argue that the superstructures and prestigious theories are themselves established by objective experimental tests—but that is precisely what many historians of science now deny.

The Science Teacher as Whig Historian

The problem of objectivity is closely associated with another issue now being debated by historians of science—the so-called Whig interpretation of history. This phrase was introduced about 40 years ago by historian Herbert Butterfield to characterize the habit of some English constitutional historians to see their subject as a progressive broadening of human rights, in which good "forward-looking" liberals were continually struggling with bad, "backward-looking" conservatives (48). In the last few years, historians of science have applied the term to the accounts of scientific progress that tended to judge every scientist by the extent of his contribution toward the establishment of modern theories. Such an interpretation looks at the past in terms of present ideas and values, rather than trying to understand the complete context of problems and preconceptions with which the earlier scientist himself had to work (49).

My favorite enunciation of the Whig attitude in the history of science is the one found in the Marquis de Laplace's *Mécanique Celeste:* "When we have at length ascertained the true cause of any phenomenon, it is an object of curiosity to look back, and see how near the hypotheses that have been framed to explain it approach towards the truth" (50).

One might say that Whig history is precisely what the science teacher wants—he is interested only in those earlier developments that led up to today's established theories and laws. And, just as the Whig historian assumes that anyone who opposed a liberal reform must have been motivated by selfish interests rather than concern for human rights, so the science teacher assumes that anyone who fails to move toward modern (that is, correct) ideas when the path has been pointed out to him must be acting non-objectively—he has not accepted the true scientific method.

The rejection of Whig history is made quite explicit in writings such as H. F. Kearney's recent book on the scientific revolution of the 16th and 17th centuries (51). Kearney describes, not a progressive change from primitive to modern theories, a replacement of error and confusion by truth and clarity, but a complex interaction between three traditions, or paradigms: the "organic," the "magical," and the "mechanical." [These correspond to what are sometimes called Aristotelian, Hermetic, and Newtonian viewpoints, except that Newton himself may have been influenced by the magical tradition, as were Copernicus, Johannes Kepler, Giordano Bruno, and William Gilbert, according to some historians (52).] In their enthusiasm for relating scientific theories to the philosophical and cultural movements of earlier centuries, historians of science have begun to de-emphasize the technical content of those theories that makes them significant in modern science. The result is a widening gap between the goals of the historian and of the science teacher.

Spare the Objectivity and Spoil the Student?

I do not want to give the impression that subjectivism has been generally accepted by historians of science (there are too many outstanding counter-examples) or that future historians can never return to the old notion that scientists are governed by objective standards. My point is that, if science teachers want to use the history of science, and if they want to obtain their information and interpretations from contemporary writings by historians of science rather than from the myths and anecdotes handed down from one generation of textbook writers to the next, they cannot avoid being influenced by the kind of skepticism about objectivity which is now so widespread. They will find it hard to resist the arguments of the historians, especially if they bother to check their original sources. [Once it has been pointed out that in Galileo's statement, "I have discovered by experiment some properties of [motion]," the words "by experiment" were added in an English translation and do not appear in the original Italian version, it is hard to maintain the traditional faith in Galileo's empiricism (53). Of course, this kind of historical debunking can go too far; Koyré's suggestion that many of Galileo's experiments were imaginary, because he could not possibly have obtained the results he reported, has been refuted in several cases by Thomas Settle, Stillman Drake, and James MacLachlen (54).]

I do not know how science teachers are going to respond to the new historical interpretations. So far, most teachers seem to have ignored them. One way of dealing with unorthodox but occasionally successful behavior is to argue that it is permissible only for those scientists whose intuition is good enough to lead them to the right answer, regardless of the experimental evidence. Thus, the authors of *The Berkeley Physics Course* quote Dirac's statement (35, p. 47):

It seems that if one is working from the point of view of getting beauty in one's equations, and if one has a really sound insight, one is on a sure line of progress. If there is not complete agreement between the results of one's work and experiment, one should not allow oneself to be too discouraged, because the discrepancy may well be due to minor features that are not properly taken into account and that will get cleared up with further developments of the theory.

Galileo would have applauded such a statement, but the authors of the textbook add a caution to the physics student: ". . . most physicists feel the real world is too subtle for such bold attacks except by the greatest minds of the time, such as Einstein or Dirac or a dozen others. In the hands of a thousand others this approach has been limited by the inadequate distribution among men of 'a sound insight'" (5, p. 6). Thus the student is urged to assume realistically that he is not going to be an Einstein or Dirac, but merely another soldier in the ranks, who must learn the established rules for puzzle-solving within the framework of the current paradigm. His systematic labors will lead to the cumulative growth of normal science and may even, if he is lucky, uncover an anomaly that could be seized on by a rare genius to initiate a scientific revolution. But the good soldier should go no further since he will not know how to find or establish a new paradigm.

By adopting this approach, one implies that there are two kinds of scientists: the average scientist, who must obey the rules, and the genius, who will know when to break them. This may indeed be a realistic description of the scientific community, but I wonder what would happen to the morale of this community if such a description were taught to students. Is the occasional Galileo or Einstein to be considered an expectant father who will not get a ticket if he races the stork to the hospital at 100 miles per hour? Or a millionaire who escapes paying income taxes? And one must not forget that experimental results have also been twisted to support false doctrines, such as the caloric theory of heat, by first-rate scientists who apparently thought they had a license to give priority to their own insights rather than to the data (55, p. 140).

On the basis of the examples I have studied, I suspect that improper behavior is not peculiar to a handful of great scientists but is characteristic of a much larger group. Indeed, the burden of proof would seem to be on anyone who claims that a majority of scientists habitually use the hypothetico-deductive method in the strict sense (that is, rejecting a theory if it fails to agree with all experimental facts).

If my interpretation of current historical thinking is correct, the science teacher who wants to use historical materials to illustrate how scientists work is indeed in an awkward position. Perhaps one must finally ask: Are the standards of objective scientific method worth preserving, even as ideals that are rarely attained in practice? Or do we distort our understanding of the nature of science by paying lip service to such standards?

Conclusions

I suggest that the teacher who wants to indoctrinate his students in the traditional role of the scientist as a neutral fact finder should not use historical materials of the kind now being prepared by historians of science: they will not serve his purposes. He may wish to follow the advice of philosopher J. C. C. Smart, who recently suggested that it is legitimate to use *fictionalized* history of science to illustrate one's pronouncements on scientific method (56). On the other hand, these teachers who want to counteract the dogmatism of the textbooks and convey some understanding of science as an activity that cannot be divorced from metaphysical or esthetic considerations may find some stimulation in the new history of science. As historian D. S. L. Cardwell has argued (57, p. 120):

. . . [I]f the history of science is to be used as an educational discipline, to inculcate an enlightened and critical mind, then the Whig view . . . cannot do this. For it must emphasize the continuities, the smooth and successive developments from one great achievement to the next and so on; and in doing so it must automatically endow the present state of science with all the immense authority of history.

He suggests that the critical mind might be inhibited by seeing the present as the inevitable, triumphant product of the past. The history of science *could* aid the teaching of science by showing that "such puzzling concepts as force, energy, etc., are man-made and were evolved in an understandable sequence in response to acutely felt and very real problems. They were not handed down by some celestial textbook writer to whom they were immediately self-evident" (57, p. 120).

The past may give some hints on how to survive the most recent recurrence of public hostility to science. Rather than blaming historians such as Kuhn for encouraging antiscientific attitudes, as one physicist did in a public address in 1972 (58), one might consider this criticism of the older style of science history, published in 1940 by W. James Lyons (59, p. 381):

The historians of science are responsible, it would appear, for the unpopularity of science among those most acutely affected by the depression. In their clamor to enhance the scientific tradition, and hoard for science all credit for the remarkable and unprecedented material advances which studded the century and a quarter preceding 1930, these historians have been more enthusiastic than accurate . . . science emerged [in the popular mind] as the most prominent force responsible for making this modern world so startlingly different from all preceding ages. Thus when, for many people, the modern world, in spite of all its resources, began to slip from its role of "best of all imaginable worlds," science came in for a proportionate share of blame. Had a more accurate picture of the part science has played been presented, science would not now be the object of so much suspicion and resentment.

In more recent times, hostility to science has been intensified by the image of the "objective," robot-like scientist lacking emotions and moral values. If the new approach to the history of science really does give a more realistic picture of the behavior of scientists, perhaps it has a "redeeming social significance." Then, rather than limiting the conception of science to the strict pattern allowed by traditional local standards, one might try to change those standards in such a way as to reflect the freedom that the boldest natural philosophers have always exercised.

REFERENCES AND NOTES

1. See the Washington *Post* (24 September 1972), p. B-6.
2. I know of only one case in which a statement about the sexual behavior of a scientist was expunged from a book intended to be read by students. When the Physical Science Study Committee reprinted a part of Arthur Koestler's *The Sleepwalkers* as a volume in the "Science Study Series" one sentence was eliminated from Kepler's recollections of his adolescent experiences. See *The Watershed* (Doubleday, Garden City, N.Y., 1964), p. 25.
3. At the end of an enthusiastic review of Giorgio de Santillana's *Reflections on Men and Ideas* [*Isis* 62, 105 (1971)], A. Rupert Hall warned his colleagues in the history of science: "Do not buy this book for second-year physics majors" (p. 106). I don't know if his reasons were the same as the ones presented in this article.
4. H. Reichenbach, *Experience and Prediction* (Univ. of Chicago Press, Chicago, 1938), pp. 6–7 and 382–384.
5. C. Kittel, W. D. Knight, M. A. Ruderman, *The Berkeley Physics Course*, vol. 1, *Mechanics* (McGraw-Hill, New York, 1962).
6. It might be suggested that there is another established dogma: Scientists are not supposed to be concerned about personal priority rights in a discovery. I omit this topic since it has been thoroughly treated by Robert Merton [*Am. Sci.* 57, 1 (1969)].
7. P. W. Bridgman, *Reflections of a Physicist* (Philosophical Library, New York, 1955); the statement is frequently quoted—for example, in *The Project Physics Course, Reader I* (Holt, Rinehart & Winston, New York, 1970), pp. 18–19.
8. O. P. Puri, G. H. Walker, E. Burt, C. S. Kiang, J. D. Wise, W. P. Thompson, H. Rogers, *Concepts in Physical Science* (Addison-Wesley, Reading, Mass., 1970), pp. 9–10; J. G. Reilly and A. W. Vander Pyl, *Physical Science: An Interrelated Course* (Addison-Wesley, Reading, Mass., 1970), pp. 2–8; J. A. Ripley, Jr., and R. C. Whitten, *The Elements and Structure of the Physical Sciences* (Wiley, New York, ed. 2, 1969), pp. 5–10. Discussions of scientific method tend to be more elaborate in biology texts. See, for example, P. B. Weisz, *Elements of Biology* (McGraw-Hill, New York, ed. 3, 1969), pp. 3–12.
9. D. Bell, *The Reforming of General Education* (Anchor, New York, 1968).
10. J. R. Platt, *Science* 146, 347 (1964).
11. W. Ostwald, *Klassiker der exakten Wissenschaften* (Englemann, Leipzig, 1889–); J. R. Partington, *A History of Chemistry* (Macmillan, London, 1961–1971); D.

ter Haar, *Selected Readings in Physics* (Pergamon, Oxford, 1965–). See the comments on "what happens when a scientist turns to history" by L. P. Williams [*Victorian Stud.*, 9, 197 (1966)].

12. G. P. Thomson, J. J. *Thomson and the Cavendish Laboratory in His Day* (Nelson, London, 1964), p. 54 (on the discovery of the Zeeman effect); C. Truesdell, *Essays in the History of Mechanics* (Springer-Verlag, New York, 1968), pp. 305–333; G. Sarton, *The Life of Science* (Schuman, New York, 1948), pp. 43–44; R. B. Lindsay, *The Role of Science in Civilization* (Harper & Row, New York, 1963), pp. 120–122.

13. E. Mach, *The Science of Mechanics,* trans. by T. J. McCormack (Open Court, La Salle, Ill., ed. 6, 1960), pp. 8–9.

14. J. B. Conant, *Am. Sci.* 48, 528 (1960). For some reasons that "history of science bores most scientists stiff," see P. B. Medwar, *The Hope of Progress* (Doubleday Anchor, Garden City, N.Y., 1973), p. 101.

15. F. S. Allen, *Educ. Rec.* 48, 268 (1967).

16. T. S. Kuhn, in *Scientific Creativity, Its Recognition and Development,* C. W. Taylor and F. Barron, Eds. (Wiley, New York, 1963), pp. 341–354. Similar fears are suggested by the title (although not the text) of the article by J. L. Synge, "Is the study of its history a brake on the progress of science?" [*Hermathena* 91, 20 (1958)]. (I am indebted to F. Tipler for this reference.)

17. In his autobiography, Conant describes the original of the Harvard committee on general education, which produced a report advocating the use of history in teaching science. Since Conant thought that the professors who were not involved in war work might feel left out of things, he decided to give them the job of drawing up plans for education in the postwar world [J. B. Conant, *My Several Lives* (Harper & Row, New York, 1970), p. 364].

18. For a report on the recommendations of the seminar and further details, see S. G. Brush, *Phys. Teach.* 8, 508 (1970).

19. S. G. Brush and A. L. King, Eds., *History in the Teaching of Physics* (University Press of New England, Hanover, N.H., 1972); S. G. Brush, Ed., *Resources for the History of Physics* (University Press of New England, Hanover, N.H., 1972); H. Kangro, Ed., *Classic Papers in Physics* (Taylor & Francis, London, 1972–).

20. S. G. Brush, *Phys. Teach.* 7, 271 (1969).

21. G. Sarton, *The Life of Science* (Schuman, New York, 1948), p. 30.

22. C. C. Gillispie, *The Edge of Objectivity* (Princeton Univ. Press, Princeton, N.J., 1960); see the extract from Maxwell's 1871 inaugural lecture at Cambridge University, which Gillispie uses as the foreword to his book.

23. A. Koyré, *Études Galiléennes* (Hermann, Paris, 1966), reprint of three articles published separately, 1935–1939.

24. Quoted in G. Holton, *Introduction to Concepts and Theories in Physical Science* (Addison-Wesley, Reading, Mass., 1952), pp. 21–22, from A. Koyré, *J. Hist. Ideas* 4, 400 (1943), p. 405.

25. A. R. Hall, in *Galileo: Man of Science,* E. McMullin, Ed. (Basic Books, New York, 1967), pp. 67–81. A good critical analysis of the historical problem of proving that the earth moves was published about this time [R. Palter, *Monist* 48, 143 (1964)].

26. P. Feyerabend, *Stud. Hist. Philos. Sci.* 1, 59 (1970). For a persuasive argument that the example of the geocentric-heliocentric transition can be used to present science as a "reasonable activity" to students, see A. Romer, *Am. J. Phys.* 41, 947 (1973).

27. R. S. Westfall, *Science* 179, 751 (1973).

28. G. McHugh, *ibid.* 180, 1118 (1973); R. S. Westfall, *ibid.,* p. 1121.

29. T. S. Kuhn, *The Structure of Scientific Revolutions* (Univ. of Chicago Press, Chicago, ed. 2, 1970).

30. ———, in *Scientific Creativity*, C. W. Taylor and F. Barron, Eds. (Wiley, New York, 1963), pp. 341–354.

31. For a concentrated dose of this controversy, see I. Lakatos and A. Musgrave, Eds., *Criticism and the Growth of Knowledge* (Cambridge Univ. Press, London, 1970). Comments by scientists are discussed, for example, in W. J. Fraser, *Science* **173**, 868 (1971).

32. I. Scheffler, *Science and Subjectivity* (Bobbs-Merrill, Indianapolis, Ind., 1967), pp. v–vi.

33. L. K. Nash, *Isis* **47**, 101 (1956); J. R. Partington, *Ann. Sci.* **4**, 245 (1939); G. de Beer, *Notes Rec. R. Soc. Lond.* **19**, 192 (1964); L. C. Dunn, *Proc. Am. Philos. Soc.* **109**, 189 (1965); B. L. van der Waerden, *Centaurus* **12**, 275 (1968).

34. On Einstein's attitude, see G. Holton, in *Science and Synthesis* (Springer-Verlag, New York, 1971), pp. 45–70. See also the letter from Einstein to Max Born, 12 May 1952, in *The Born-Einstein Letters* (Walker, New York, 1971), p. 192. H. A. Lorentz, in an address at Leiden in 1926, mentioned the results of D. C. Miller, which some people thought would refute the theory of relativity, but which Lorentz maintained would, even if verified, only "indicate the existence of some unknown cause"; "relativity will be quite safe" [*Collected Papers* (Nijhoff, The Hague, 1935), vol. 8, p. 415].

35. P. A. M. Dirac, *Sci. Am.* **208**, 45 (May 1963). See also the statement, "It is also a good rule not to put overmuch confidence in the observational results that are put forward until they have been confirmed by theory," attributed to Eddington by G. S. Stent [*The Coming of the Golden Age* (Natural History Press, New York, 1969), p. 31]. Stent says this is "a realistic description of the psychological dynamics that obtain at the frontier of scientific advance."

36. M. Planck, *Philosophy of Physics* (Norton, New York, 1936), p. 97; *A Scientific Autobiography and Other Papers* (Williams & Norgate, London, 1950), pp. 33–34.

37. W. Heisenberg, *Physics and Beyond* (Harper & Row, New York, 1971).

38. In a private communication, I. Scheffler has pointed out that he locates objectivity not in the individual behavior of scientists, but in the "institutionalized controls by which science itself evaluates theoretical novelty" [see also (*32*, p. 72)]. I suppose one must then ask whether, in the historical cases cited in this article, other scientists followed the leader and thus collectively failed to exert these institutional controls. My opinion is that this is indeed what happened, but there is not enough space to debate the point here. Scheffler has published a further criticism of Kuhn's theory in *Philos. Sci.* **39**, 366 (1972).

39. S. G. Brush, *Br. J. Hist. Sci.* **5**, 145 (1970).

40. R. J. Morris, *Proc. Okla. Acad. Sci.* **42**, 195 (1962).

41. A. M. Ampère, *Bibl. Univers,* **49**, 225 (1832); *Ann. Chim. Phys.* **58**, 432 (1835); *Philos. Mag.,* ser., 3, **7**, 342 (1835); T. S. T[raill], in *Encyclopaedia Britannica* (Edinburgh, ed. 7, 1842), vol. 11, p. 180; M. Somerville, *On the Connection of the Physical Sciences* (Key & Biddle, Philadelphia, 1834), p. 195; W. Whewell, *History of the Inductive Sciences* (Parker, London, 1837), vol. 2, pp. 180–184. [Other references are given in another article (*39*).]

42. S. G. Brush, *Am. J. Phys.* **39**, 631 (1971).

43. See his letter of 1860 to Stokes and statements quoted in S. G. Brush (Pergamon, Oxford, 1965), vol. 1, pp. 27, 150, and 171.

44. J. C. Maxwell, *Rep. 30th Meet. Br. Assoc. Adv. Sci.* (1860), p. 15. This short but important summary of Maxwell's conclusions was not included in his *Sci-*

entific Papers, published by Cambridge University Press in 1890 and reprinted by Dover in 1952 and 1965.

45. S. G. Brush, *Synthese* **18**, 192 (1968); J. T. Blackmore, *Ernst Mach* (Univ. of California Press, Berkeley, 1972).

46. ———, *Arch. Ration. Mech. Anal.* **39**, 1 (1970).

47. See S. G. Brush, *Kinetic Theory* (Pergamon, Oxford, 1972), vol. 3, which includes an English translation of Enskog's monograph, and reprints of Chapman's shorter papers.

48. H. Butterfield, *The Whig Interpretation of History* (Bell, London, 1931), pp. 1–13.

49. See J. Hexter, *Reappraisals in History* (Northwestern Univ. Press, Evanston, Ill., 1961).

50. P. S. de Laplace, *Celestial Mechanics*, trans. by N. Bowditch (Chelsea, New York, 1966), vol. 4, p. 1015.

51. H. F. Kearney, *Science and Change 1500–1700* (McGraw-Hill, New York, 1971).

52. The suggestion that Copernicus was an adherent of Hermetism, deriving from the writings of Frances Yates on Bruno, has been denounced by Copernican scholar Edward Rosen. Rosen asserts that "out of Renaissance magic and astrology came, not modern science, but modern magic and astrology." See his article in *Historical and Philosophical Perspectives of Science*, R. H. Stuewer, Ed. (Univ. of Minnesota Press, Minneapolis, 1970), pp. 163–171; see also M. Hesse, *ibid.*, pp. 134–162. The importance of the role of mysticism and pseudoscience in the origin of modern science in Western Europe, as well as in ancient Chinese science, has been stressed by other historians of science: see, for example, O. Neugebauer, *Isis* **42**, 111 (1951); J. Needham, *The Grand Titration, Science and Society in East and West* (Univ. of Toronto Press, Toronto, 1969), p. 162. See also J. E. McGuire and P. M. Rattansi, *Notes Rec. R. Soc. Lond*, **21**, 108 (1966).

53. A. Koyré, *Isis* **34**, 209 (1943); but see also P. P. Wiener, *ibid.*, p. 301.

54. T. Settle, *Science* **133**, 19 (1961); S. Drake, *Isis* **64**, 291 (1973); J. MacLachlan, *ibid.*, p. 374.

55. T. S. Kuhn, *Isis* **49**, 132 (1958).

56. J. C. C. Smart, *Br. J. Philos. Sci.* **23**, 266 (1972). Herbert Feigl has admitted that "A few of us [philosophers of science] . . . for some time rather unashamedly 'made up' some phases of the history of science" [*Historical and Philosophical Perspectives of Science*, R. H. Stuewer, Ed. (Univ. of Minnesota Press, Minneapolis, 1970), p. 3].

57. D. S. L. Cardwell, *Mem. Proc. Manchester Lit. Philos. Soc.* **106**, 108 (1963–64).

58. L. Eisenbud, "Science for antiscientists," speech given at the American Physical Society meeting, Washington, D.C., 26 April 1972. Kuhn has protested "the description of my views as a defense of irrationality in science," but to no avail; see his article in *Boston Studies in Philosophy of Science*, R. C. Buck and R. S. Cohen, Eds. (Reidel, Dordrecht, 1971), vol. 8, pp. 137–146, and (29), p. 186.

59. W. J. Lyons, in *Science in America*, J. Burnham, Ed. (Holt, Rinehart & Winston, New York, 1971), pp. 377–384.

60. This article is based in part on research supported by the National Science Foundation. The author thanks Peter Bowman for his helpful suggestions.

7

THE HISTORY OF IRRATIONALISM

CHARLES FRANKEL

ALTHOUGH the 20th century has been marked by an almost unbroken series of challenges to the authority of rational methods of thought, the current clamor against these methods probably has certain unique features. On the whole, established churches and governments have not encouraged it. It is not associated with any widespread popular movement of moral or religious revivalism, nor is it, in the minds of most of those identified with it, a conservative movement whose purpose is to restore authority and recover old values. On the contrary, they think of it as, among other things, an effort to relieve oppression and injustice and to break through to new heights of vision radically liberative for the human spirit. Indeed, this movement is mainly a creature of what is called, or miscalled, the "liberal Establishment." Both in the United States and abroad, its most sympathetic audience comes primarily from the more comfortable and better educated classes, and its central inspiration and emotional thrust have been sustained by people belonging to universities and other institutions whose traditional commitment, officially, has been to the practice and propagation of rational inquiry.

Nevertheless, despite the setting and auspices of the present revolt against reason, it is essentially not new in its content. I speak, of course, not of irrationalism in behavior or in the organization of society; in both of these, unhappily, a certain spirit of creative innovation still manifests itself. I speak of irrationalism as a studied and articulated attitude, proudly affirmed and elaborately defended, which pronounces science—and not only science, but, more broadly, logical analysis, controlled observation, the norms and civilities of disciplined argument, and the ideal of objectivity—to be systematically misleading as to the nature of the universe and the conditions necessary for human fulfillment. Despite the new language, half jargon and half slang, in which this irrationalism is expressed, the actual assertions on which it rests can be found in classic treatises on mysticism and in the utterances of many traditional philosophers and poets. The breathtaking departures from the thoughtways of industrial civilization, or of Western civilization, that are announced each month or each week are simply updated and, usually, bowdlerized versions of views that go back to the Greek mystery cults and the pre-Socratic philosophers Heraclitus and Parmenides.

FROM C. Frankel, The nature and sources of irrationalism, *Science*, 1973, **180**, 927–931. Copyright 1973 by the American Association for the Advancement of Science.

What validity is there in the claims that this irrationalism puts forward to be accepted and believed?

Although current irrationalists speak out of very different kinds of experience (1), the degree to which they rest their case on the same set of fundamental propositions is striking. These can be reduced, I believe, to five.

1. The universe man inhabits is divided into two realms—one of appearance, the other of reality. The former is marked by accident, doubt, uncertainty, coldness, alienation. In the second, doubt is dispelled, time and death have no sting, one is embraced by a world congruent with one's deepest desires, and discord and trouble are dissolved in an encompassing sense of harmony and coherence.

2. The reason that people mistake appearance for reality is that their definitions of reality rest on biased presuppositions which their culture, class, and practical concerns impose upon them. "There is no such 'condition' as 'schizophrenia,' but the label is a social fact and the social fact a *political event*," says R. D. Laing (2, p. 100). In the same vein, Theodore Roszak writes, "*Reality* marks out the boundaries of what might be called the collective mindscape, the limits of sane experience" (3, p. xxiv). Irrationalists differ as to the best way to break loose from this enslavement to collective prejudice, but they agree that truth and reality are achieved only when experience is approached in nakedness of mind. Thus, criticizing Freud, Roszak writes: "What Freud never wished to face squarely was the fact that the line we draw between the world Out There and the world In Here must be predicated on metaphysical assumptions that cannot themselves be subjected to scientific proof" (3, pp. 74–75).

3. Human nature exhibits this ontological dualism between appearance and reality. A war goes on inside each person between the "cerebral" and the "emotional," the "conscious" and the "intuitive," the "empirical" and the "rhapsodic." And when the rational department attempts to extend its domain beyond its own rightful borders, it dehumanizes man and devalues nature. To quote Roszak again (3, p. 96):

Our proud, presumptuous head speaks one language; our body another—a silent, arcane language. Our head experiences in the mode of number, logic, mechanical connection; our body in the mode of fluid process, intuitive adaptation; it sways to an inner purposive rhythm. . . . It may seem that to speak this way is to deal in a crude dichotomy of human nature. It is. The dichotomy that tears at our personality *is* crude; but I did not invent it. I have only inherited it, like you, from the antiorganic fanaticism of Western culture.

4. The unmistakable sign that we have gone astray is when we arrive at states of consciousness in which subject and object are distinguishable. Thus, science is to be distrusted on principle, for it rests on the distinction between the subjective and the objective. Describing the diverse

influences playing on the "sensitivity training" movement, Kurt Back writes (4, pp. 207–208):

Perhaps the common thread . . . is the rejection of the intellectual aspect of life or, in somatic language, the influence of the cortex. . . . It is a concerted effort to turn away from the emphasis on intellect, on tool-making abilities of the human animal, on classification, in short, on mediation of any experience through reflection, and to push the participants toward a direct experience that is not thought about and not analyzed.

Similarly, we know we have gone wrong morally and emotionally, according to irrationalism, when we feel separate from other human beings, or alienated from nature, or divided within ourselves. The possibility that, in the irreducible nature of things, there can be discordances between the human creature and its environment—that nature can be less than a perfect fit for man—is not contemplated. If there is discordance, human beings are responsible: we are doing or thinking something wrong. Specifically, when we are dissatisfied with our place in the scheme of things, it is because we have allowed the so-called "rational" mode of comprehension to dominate the others. Roszak writes, "The greatest truth mankind learned from its ancient intimacy with nature [is] the reality of spiritual being." And he argues that, if we forget this, we "will lack psychological completeness" (3, p. 8). Evidently, what does not make us psychologically complete cannot be true.

5. Accordingly, all human problems, cognitive, emotional, and social, are reducible to a loss of harmony—harmony between man and his environment, his head and his heart, his ideas and his instincts. Thus, beyond its assertions about the nature of man and the universe, irrationalism offers an image of the good life. It is a life free from unrest and unease—a life released, through passionate ecstasy or rapt contemplation, from the regretfulness of time, the vexations of decisions, and the risks of fallibility. Whether or not one agrees with irrationalism, it is easy to understand why it has been perennially attractive. It offers the vision of a kind of peace and unequivocal acceptance and commitment from which the normal perils, pains, and worries of human existence have been removed.

But what of the soundness of these five propositions?

First Proposition Examined

Irrationalism is not alone in distinguishing between "appearance" and "reality." The scientific process regularly does the same thing, in two ways. First, it resists or reinterprets the gross evidence of our senses (consider Copernicus and Galileo, for example) in response to the demands of over-arching laws and theories. Second, it pierces the curtain of established belief, replacing ideas supported by conventional opinion or official authority with other ideas, for which independent and impersonal evidence exists.

Indeed, it is passing difficult to understand why the myth persists among many educated people that rational inquiry thins out the world or deprives human experience of its extra dimensions of meaning. Thanks to science, the present world makes available to those who will do their homework subatomic particles, DNA, marginal utilities, relative deprivations, the Minoan culture, the story of evolution. This adds immeasurably to the import to be found in daily existence, to the connections to be drawn, to the implications to be read, to the "unseen things" to be adduced.

What science and rational methods *have* done to "denude" nature is, first, to have introduced ideas for dealing with it that require specialized study and that are not easily available to the man on the run, and, second, to have deprived nature of her anthropomorphic and animistic qualities. This latter, above all, is responsible for most of the assaults upon science. It presents a nonhuman environment no longer perceived as subject to moral law or shaped to the size of human emotions. That this is the character of the natural universe is, admittedly, a harsh lesson to learn. For the sake of argument, agree that it may even be a false lesson. Still, it draws a sharper distinction between "appearance" and "reality" than does anything in the scheme of philosophical irrationalism.

It is against this background that Roszak's preference for the deliverances of "the dark mind" are, I think, best understood. Why, he asks, should we prefer the deliverances of our minds when awake to the deliverances of our minds when they dream (3, pp. 84 and 87)?

We in the contemporary West may wake each morning to cast out our sleep and dream experience like so much rubbish. But that is an almost freakish act of alienation. . . . It is the physicist's time we march to, time as time would be if there were no living thing to transform existence into experience; time such as machines can measure out in the lockstep of equal and abstract measures. The most threatening heresy of the dark mind lies precisely in this: it brings us to the still center of time's axis, where the turning wheel no longer turns. . . . It is just this lawless defiance of literalness and necessity that the intolerant waking mind rejects. . . .

But the "intolerant" waking mind, if one looks closely at the matter, merely rejects the idea that our dreams, shot through with moral and emotional import and constructed to the shape and dynamic of our fears and wishes, are as solid a basis for a veridical account of nature as the experiences of our more consciously critical and disciplined waking lives. Of course, logicians and scientists often forget or ignore their dreams and push them below the threshold of consciousness. But this implies no philosophical or intellectual commitment special to them. Mystics and rhapsodists do the same thing. I know of no scientifically informed individual, or partisan of reason in philosophy, who, as a matter of principle, dismisses dream experiences as "so much rubbish." Dreams are often a springboard to remarkable inspiration, in science as well as in poetry; and, at the very least, dreams tell a good deal, if analyzed, about the nature of the human self and human experience. But that necessary analysis is not performed while one is dreaming.

In fact, it is a caricature to suggest that we in the contemporary world ignore "the dark mind." Our interest in dreams is not less than that of our ancestors; like them, we try to tell our fortunes from our dreams. It is only in our method of inquiry into dreams, and in our theories about their causes, that we differ from them.

In sum, when one looks at the issues with some concern for facts and intellectual precision, irrationalism's distinctiveness lies, it seems to me, not in the fact that it asserts a difference between "appearance" and "reality," but in the fact that it applies a priori standards in determining what "reality" must be. It knows in advance that this "reality" must meet the human heart's desires, even the wildest desires welling up in our nighttime visions. In contrast, when scientific investigation distinguishes between what is "real" and what is only "apparent," the distinction is always specific, made in a particular context and as a consequence of a particular inquiry.

Is "Rational Inquiry" a Deception?

The irrationalist asserts that the methods of so-called "rational inquiry" are also compromised: they rest on presuppositions and therefore tailor the conception of reality to antecedent standards. Is this charge a just one? I think not. It involves a triple fallacy.

First, no inquiry of any kind is possible, nor is any commerce of the human creature with its environment, without assumptions of, at least, specialized and selective thrustings and responses of the organism. The irrationalist regularly suggests that he conducts his own explorations of reality without falling prey to this necessity of human existence: he floats on the Sea of Experience, absorbing all, imposing nothing. But such a mental performance would teach nothing, yield nothing; it would be an encounter with the unidentified, the indefinable, the unpicturable, the unrememberable. Moreover, from a psychological point of view, such a performance is impossible. Even in dreams, when something outside the dreamer's control seems most powerfully to take charge of him, his wishes, fears, and inveterate assumptions are patently present. That the irrationalist makes his own assumptions is illustrated by Laing's stunning statement that there is no such thing as schizophrenia and that the label "schizophrenic" is "a social fact and the social fact a political event." But what is a "social fact," and what is a "political event"? Do not these phrases also carry a load of assumptions with them?

The second fallacy is the notion that all presuppositions, merely because they are presuppositions, are equally impositions on the nature of things. But the fact that a process of thought called "scientific" rests on presuppositions does not put it on the same level with every other process of thought. Everything depends on the specific content and character of the presuppositions in question and on the controls that exist for checking, correcting, or rejecting them. Thus, we may agree or not with the soundness, say, of Freud's basic ideas, but, Roszak to the contrary notwithstanding, drawing a line at a certain point between "the world Out There" and "the world In Here" does not involve an unargued metaphysical assumption that is ever after free from correction. The line as we draw it is an invitation to conduct investigations in certain ways. If the investigations come up with nothing, or with monstrous findings incompatible with the stock of our well-tested beliefs, we have reason to draw the line differently.

Rational methods, whether in the law, physics, child-rearing, or personal hygiene, begin with presuppositions that are supported by successful experience in the past. They are sustained only as long as they meet successive challenges and serve as elements in explanatory frameworks that guide inquiry to reliable new results more effectively than do alternative frameworks. Such presuppositions, meeting, as they do, carefully elaborated standards of intersubjectivity, reflect the coordinated, but uncommanded, assent of a community of disciplined observers. "Reason" is often described in ethereal language. From a sociological point of view, however, it is simply the name for forms of behavior by which individual beliefs are concerted without recourse to force or authority. It codifies the elementary principles of courtesy without which the maintenance of a liberal civilization is impossible.

Nor does this mean that the scientific community is like a closed club that maintains its insular view of the world by establishing special conventions which prevent any alien point of view from breaking through. The intellectual history of science is a series of revolutions. In contrast, irrationalist thought turns and returns upon itself.

The third error in the irrationalist position derives from its own controlling preconception. The irrationalist holds that any presupposition is necessarily misguided because it is inevitably partial and selective and therefore distorts reality. This is the Wholistic Assumption—the view that all things are internally related in such a way that they are parts of one single organic entity, so constituted that if it changes in any one respect it must change in every other respect. The assumption persists from Parmenides to F. H. Bradley; it is recurrent among mystics. Jonathan Edwards stated it simply and lucidly when, as a very young man, he resolved to conduct his scientific studies so as to show "how the Motion, Rest, and Direction of the *Least Atom* has an influence on the motion, rest and direction of every body in the Universe; and to show how, by that means, every thing which happens, with respect to mote, or straws and such little things, may be for some great uses in the whole course of things, throughout Eternity . . ." (5)

But this assumption, although it expresses a hope that many men of great poetic and religious feeling have fervently entertained, is not one on the basis of which anybody can consistently think or act. It would involve his wrenching into unrecognizable shape common notions on which he inevitably relies.

For example, in everyday life, as well as in science, the law, and other specialized activities, we often speak of the "nature" of a thing or a person, or the "character" of an event. When we do so, we do not mean to include all of that thing's or event's relations and traits, possible as well as actual, accidental as well as essential. This is because intelligible discourse requires us to define and limit the subject matter of the discourse and to indicate those features of it from which, in terms of some explanatory framework, others of its salient features can be deduced and explained. The "nature" of a thing, in short, is only a selected subset of interrelated properties of that thing. To discard this notion is to say that there is never anything such as accident or irrelevance; it is to say, indeed, that there is no distinction to be drawn between a consecutive argument and a nonconsecutive one.

It is this Wholistic Assumption that lies behind the statements of writers like Laing that the distinction between sanity and insanity is a purely conventional or political one. But do such propositions as that fire burns and knives pierce rest for their confirmation entirely on conventions and political fiat? And must an individual be at one with all Reality in order to escape the charge, when he asserts such propositions, that he is a victim of sectarian prejudices?

Dualistic Psychology of Irrationalism

The irrationalist's theory of human nature is steeped in the tradition of the dualistic psychology it condemns. It talks about "reason" as though it were a department of human nature in conflict with "emotion." But "reason," considered as a psychological process, is not a special faculty, and it is not separate from the emotions; it is simply the process of reorganizing the emotions, of setting up a plan for satisfying them, a scheme of relative priorities constructed in relation to the resources and constraints of surrounding circumstance. As Hume said, reason is, and of necessity must be, the slave of the passions.

To be sure, reasoning is a process with a certain emotional tone and conative thrust of its own: it involves the feeling of controlling one's feelings, of delaying final judgment, of actively entertaining alternative ideas, and of judging all ideas, one's own as well as other people's, by the same tests. The strength of the rational emotion, accordingly, is not usually equal to that of our first-order emotions. It is only under comparatively rare circumstances, and normally under fairly artificial conditions, that the second-order emotion, which is the emotion of reason, can become intense and self-sustaining, and can yield an excitement equivalent to that caused by emotions such as love, hate, and awe. This is why the mores and institutions of the scientific community and the civilities of liberal society are so important. They nourish and reward rational emotion and provide social procedures that make up, in part, for the weakness of reason as an aboriginal component of human psychology.

As a pragmatic matter, what irrationalism asks is that society invest less—or nothing at all—in maintaining the institutions, and the codes of ethics and etiquette, which have proved necessary to support the emotion of reason. Only an extraordinarily sanguine attitude about the inherent reasonableness of man's instinctual life, only a confident faith, belied by all experience, in the unforced, providential symmetry between the needs of human nature and the structure of the universe, can explain the willingness to take such a one-sided chance on human impulse and spontaneity. Far from introducing a note of disharmony, reason is a harmonizer; for it is our first-order emotions, our spontaneous impulses, which are disharmonious one with another.

The Irrationalist and Original Sin

The belief in the universe's total and perfect integration with human needs also underlies the irrationalist notion that, when reality is genuinely understood, all forms of separateness and division—within the self, between individuals, between the "subjective" and the "objective"—will disappear. The assumption is that problems of choice between competing desires will not arise; that no activities such as planning or the conservation of scarce resources will be needed; that no conflicts will arise over the distribution of these resources. (Or is it the assumption that these difficulties, which characterize the world of appearance, will be left to a class of Helots, practicing the arts of reason, to solve, while the emancipated enjoy Reality in its higher kindness?)

In brief, for the irrationalist, the universe is good; it is man, rational man, who has willfully made it evil, all by himself. Irrationalism, behind its long arguments and often impenetrable rhetoric, is an attempt to solve the ancient problem of Evil and to restate the ancient myth of the Fall.

Prometheus and the Lotos-Eater

It is in this context that the irrationalist's notion of the good life may be evaluated. Although the spokesmen of irrationalism make much of words like "ecstasy" and "rhapsody," the vision they offer of how men should live is essentially passive and wistful. It is not the image of Prometheus or Odysseus that they offer, it is that of the Lotos-Eater. The dream is of a scheme of things in which human beings face no difficult dilemmas and all good things are equally possible. What, after all, is the imperative for rationality in action? It is simply that, in human life, appearances are deceptive, impulses and desires at cross-purposes, and time, energy, and resources limited. Irrationalism asks us to believe that these constraints do not exist in the world, not when it is rightly understood; irrationalism asks us further to believe that rational methods, which emerge to mitigate these constraints, are their cause.

Why Irrationalism?

The above consideration of the assertions on which contemporary irrationalist doctrine rests also tells us something, I believe, about its sources.

Undoubtedly, there are special features of the current scene that help to explain the particular audiences, the popularity, and the language and style of this irrationalism. Among these features are the marketing needs and habits of a competitive economy, the peculiarities of the position of youth, the drug culture, and the anti-intellectual implications of much that passes these days for "advanced" educational, psychological, and philosophical theory. The eagerness of liberal clergymen to be identified with what is, or seems, new must also be taken into account.

There are other factors. One is the damage done by uncontrolled technological change; another is the discredit done to scientists' reputation for common sense and common humanity by individuals—some of them scientists, some of them charlatans—who present, in relation to complex and grievous human problems, simplistic notions that parody scientific method. Considerable damage has also been done by scientists, among whom social scientists are perhaps the most notable, who exaggerate the amount of sound and applicable knowledge they have and who offer confident solutions to social problems—solutions that, when tried, turn out to be only a mixture of pious hope and insular moral judgments.

But when the nature and the antiquity of the arguments for irrationalism are considered, we become aware, I think, that the quarrel between supporters and opponents of rational methods represents an ancient division in the Western soul. In the disagreements between the Sophists and the Pythagoreans, Aristotelian and Augustinian Christians, Dominicans and Franciscans, Coleridge and the Utilitarians, Henri Bergson and

Bertrand Russell, we have successive reprises of this drama. It rises to fever pitch when scientific discovery accelerates and when the discoveries that science makes seem more and more subversive of inherited beliefs, social creeds, habits of action, laws, or the soundness of old and cherished hopes and hates. Under these circumstances, irrationalism offers a promise of relief and immunity. There can be no doubt that, although it points only clumsily at an evil, that evil is there. The careful rational methods by which knowledge and technique have been advanced have only rarely been used to examine the purposes to which this knowledge and intelligence are harnessed. It is natural that science, in such a setting, should seem to be a Frankenstein to those who are threatened by it.

Nevertheless, to use words George Santayana wrote 70 years ago in a letter to William James, it is "intolerable that we should still be condemned to give the parsons and the 'idealists' a monopoly of indignation . . ." (6). Those who look beyond reason have no monopoly, either in fact or in logic, on recognizing the frivolity, inanity, ugliness, and cruelty that are abroad in the world. Without reason, furthermore, indignation can be undiscriminating; and appeals to "conscience" and "morality" become only the demand that others acclaim one's prejudices.

I would add one final point. It often seems to me that disagreements over "rationalism" and "irrationalism," at least in their milder phases, stem from a misunderstanding. A matter of taste and style is mistaken for a matter of ultimate moral and cognitive significance, leading to the kind of sweeping assertions that I have considered. But once the issues I have discussed are set aside, there still remains, of course, a difference. It is the difference between Haydn and Wagner or between Voltaire and Rousseau.

Thus Roszak, describing what he calls "the hard-edged cerebral elegance of the Enlightenment," says that "it wanted no more and would tolerate no more of life than sound logic, good prose, and exact numbers might accommodate" (3, p. 280). But the music of Mozart, a major product of the Enlightenment, can hardly be described simply as "cerebral." Don Giovanni offers a view of life in which values other than sound logic, good prose, and exact numbers are given, as I recall, serious attention. It is possible to enjoy both the poetry of Pope and that of Blake; it certainly ought to be possible, if one can't abide one or the other, to follow a policy of live and let live. Must we really demand the resolution of radical metaphysical disagreements or suggest that we occupy different levels in the hierarchy of salvation because our preferences differ in such matters?

The policy of mutual toleration was also a product of the Enlightenment, and it expressed that age's conception of rational dealings between human beings. I presume that when irrationalists attack the ideal of rationality, few of them mean to attack this practical proposal for coexistence. To that extent, they, too, make obeisance to reason.

REFERENCES

1. A sample of recent books speaking for irrationalism in the sense here described includes: R. D. Laing, *The Politics of Experience* (2); G. Leonard, *The Transformation* (Delacorte, New York, 1972); T. Roszak, *Where the Wasteland Ends* (3). Lionel Trilling has described Roszak's earlier *The Making of a Counter-Culture* (Doubleday, New York, 1969) as "perhaps the best-known and also the best-tempered defense of the ideologized antagonism to mind" [*Times Literary Supplement* (17 November 1972), p. 1384]. Other irrationalist writers who have obtained a considerable following include Norman O. Brown and Carlos Castañeda. Tom Wolfe [*The Electric Kool-Aid Acid Test* (Farrar, Straus & Giroux, New York, 1968)] presents an account, in the mode of the new journalism, of irrationalism in the context of the drug culture. Kurt W. Back (4) offers an outsider's analysis and evaluation of the nature, setting, social origins, and incidence of "sensitivity training" and "the encounter movement."
2. R. D. LAING, *The Politics of Experience* (Penguin, Baltimore, 1967).
3. T. ROSZAK, *Where the Wasteland Ends* (Doubleday, New York, 1972).
4. K. BACK, *Beyond Words* (Russell Sage, New York, 1972).
5. J. EDWARDS, "Things to be considered, or written fully about," in *Benjamin Franklin and Jonathan Edwards: Selections,* C. Van Doren, Ed. (American Books, New York, 1920), p. xv.
6. *The Letters of George Santayana,* D. Cory, Ed. (Scribner, New York, 1955), p. 81.

8

THE ROUTES OF SCIENCE

JULIAN JAYNES

I WRITE this in a scorn of the unity of science. My impulse is a disturbed feeling that, as science folds back on itself and comes to be scientifically studied, it is being caricatured into a conformity which is nonsense, into a neglect of its variety which is psychotic, into a nagging and insistent

FROM J. Jaynes, The routes of science, *American Scientist*, 1966, **54** (1). Pages 94–98 reprinted with permission of the author, *American Scientist*, and the Society of Sigma Xi.

attention to its cross-discipline similarities which are of a trivial importance. And having just returned from a fortnight walking tour of a variety of countryside, reading at evening some volumes in the history of science, I want to venture an extravagant metaphor which brings out the differences as I see them between the two extremes of the scientific continuum.

Physics is like climbing a mountain: roped together by a common asceticism of mathematical method, the upward direction, through blizzard, mist, or searing sun, is always certain, though the paths are not. The problem of each new generation is easy: rope on, test the pitons, follow the leader, look out for better lay-backs and footholds to the heights. A source book in its history is a simple and inspiring matter; it is ledge to ledge upward. This clear? Well, no, even though physics text books try to structure our perception so. But the disorder is on the ledges, never in the direction.

Psychology is so different! Instead of the difficult simplicity of physics, psychology is full of an easy complexity. While physics gains in truth when most quantitative, psychology when most quantitative is of least scope, though the sweetness of elegance lingers over. And with its infinity of problems throughout the evolutionary scale, its Baroque experimental paradigms with which it attempts them, with its own criteria of excellence that change from one area to another, from one point of view to another, with its laws that are laws of themselves, and its embarrassed shiftiness from objective to subjective languages and back to describe its purposes and observations, it is less a mountain than a huge entangled forest in full shining summer, so easy to walk through on certain levels, that anyone can and everyone does. The student's problem is a frantic one: he must shift for himself. It is directions he is looking for, not height. And the direction out of the forest is unknown, perhaps nonexistent, nor is it even certain that that is what he is meant to do. Multitudes cross each other's paths in opposite directions with generous confidence and happy chaos. The bright past and the dark present ring with diverging cries and discrepant echos of "here is the way!" from one vale to another. Ear-plugs and blinders curiously replace bootcleats and pitons. If less invigorating than mountain climbing, it is, or should be, more fun for adventurists. And being closer to an altitude where most people live, psychology is ununited and unisolated with the necessity of difficult techniques in common, and so shows a remarkable variety of behavior corresponding to the variety of the terrain. In this forest, its history shouting with opinions clashing in the darkness of evidence, its tangled variety of paths, some overgrown with disuse, some broadened with fashion, and others weaving somewhere under the strange shrieks of religious and political vested interests hidden high in the foliage, in all this challenge of complexity and divergence, is it possible that psychology could or should pattern itself on physics? That a forest is like a mountain? Can all complexity be reduced to simplicity as in physics if we work hard enough?

What rubbish that it was once thought so! The time was not so distant when, following Mach's attempt to unify all science about "sensations," and the physicalism of the Vienna Circle, Carnap could say "every sentence of psychology may be formulated in physical language," not evidently realizing that that itself is a sentence of psychology and so on in infinite regress, which, since physical language cannot be infinite, negates Carnap's position, at least to me. How much truer, for example, to say that every statement of physics must reduce to a statement in psychology since it is the behavior of an organism! But such illogicality (to which Whitehead and Russell's Theory of Types does not apply) was never apparent then, back in the days when something called *The Encyclopedia for the Unity of Science* was first appearing, bluebook by bluebook from Chicago. Science then was thought of as a thing, unconscious of the metaphor of thingness. It was thought meaningful to speak of one science as being where another science was at a particular time, as if all were travelling the same road, or of the normal development of a science, as if the various "sciences" were so many tadpoles waiting on Froghood, and something more than mere academic conveniences. And even today, there are still individual scientists so timorous of their status as to think of it as a cult, a cult united by a mystique called "the scientific method," a cult that has nothing in common with ordinary rational activities, a kind of pure virginal objectivity that has to guard its beauty against the wrinkled advances of religion, art, or ethics like a Susanna among her peeping Elders. How long gone such notions!

And where was psychology in all this? Anxiously toadeating with the positivists. Weaned too quickly from philosophy, psychology mewled around for other dependencies. Accused of being not really a science, it nervously sprang to conform. It purified its journals into an objective aridity. It sophisticated itself above all other sciences in statistical and design techniques. It wrapped itself in cunning lingos that hid its softer parts from critical view. It followed Bridgman into operationism. It wandered the Gothic wonders of Hull's crumbling theorems or reduced into Skinnery descriptivism. I doubt if all that valiant nonsense could have taken place had it not been that the aggressive anti-intellectualism of naive behaviorism was frightening psychologists away from the marshes and bogs of the forest where perhaps its greatest adventures lie, and onto its drier, more barren knolls where the mountain of physics is most easily seen.

But that is history now, though I hope I've stepped on a few viable toes in the last paragraphs; I was stamping in the hope that I was. Rarely since World War II have there been similar attempts to confine the activities of psychologists into any particular laws or paradigms or methods. Although not always within academic departments of psychology, there has been a tremendous rise in various types of observation of both men and animals, in controlled and uncontrolled environments, with hosts of new variables both in and outside the organism, and observations where the very idea of a variable is eschewed, descriptive theories that do not pretend, though they may say something real of what lies behind the phenomena they are summarizing. While physics lends itself to the metaphorical verb "breakthrough," perhaps psychology's correlative verb is "breakout," as a previous attempt to throw an envelope around some aspect of research is suddenly seen to be a subjective barrier that is part of the psychodynamics of the scientist himself, and with the succession of generations gives way to the larger visions. Certainly, there is a sense now of an explosive expansion of vision in all fields of psychology, with more and more of the forest visible at each glance, vistas that would be strange and frightening to the battle-scarred veterans of a previous era, the Hunters and the Lashleys hunting and lashing (why not?) their half-imaginary opponents over the wastelands of behaviorism. Be it immediately said here that it is not behaviorism I object to, but behaviorism alone. Or anything that waves off whole areas as unimportant because they conflict with theory, and refusal to welcome wholeheartedly the multi-pathed nature of the endeavor. My point is that the history, philosophy, and sociology of one science should not be modeled on that of another, that there is no such thing as normal scientific progress, no one pattern of scientific activity, no one criterion of excellence though there may be of aesthetic satisfaction, that there is no one "scientific" method, and no one way of scientific history.

I erect this discussion of the unique divergent complexity of psychology as a background against which to consider some problems in the history of science and to praise a cluster of excellent new books in the history of psychology which represent these problems. As I have written elsewhere, there are three possible modes or cause-sets of intellectual history: *ethnographic*, or science as generated by culture and epoch; *biographic*, or science as generated by the lives and aspirations of scientists; and *doxographic*, or science as generated by previous science. Ideal scientific histories are mixtures of all three in which it is part of the historian's integrity to estimate in each new step which of the three cause-sets were most important. In any of the three there are two methods of composition or types, *representative* history, or writing history as it really was, making one's work representative of the time one is talking about, and *parapposite* history, which I have coined from *para* = near + *apposite* to mean history conceived as a dialogue of the present with the past. We do not attempt in parapposite history ever to resurrect archaic problems or the blind alleys of science, only to record its successes as they throw light on the problems of current interest.

Here again, we find a difference between sciences as to the applicability of this distinction. Representativeness and parappositeness coalesce in the history of physics. Physics is too theoretically simple to have many great errors and too technically difficult to invite them. Such errors as it does have are not blind alleys as they tend to be in psychology, but ledges on the upward climb. The Rutherford atom is not so much an error as a first approximation to Bohr, and so on. It is ledge to ledge, as in the succession (what a noble one) of Newton, Euler, Lagrange, Hamilton, etc. And that part of the thought of a particular age which is relevant to physics is also representative of its time. But in psychology, where every man, woman, and child is his own busy laboratory—theories of other people and animals being a necessity to ordinary life—representativeness is a much more difficult affair. Much of what a previous epoch was thinking in psychology may be quite irrelevant to current problems. These considerations suggest a law that might be stated: The narrower the topic, the more nearly parappositeness equals representativeness. In the rest of this essay, I am using these distinctions to ask questions of recent books in the history of psychology whose answers demonstrate a unique complexity unlike any other science.

The first point about all of the current work in the history of psychology is that none of it is or tries to be either representative or parapposite history of psychology as a whole. It is not even representative of the major ideas through time. If the material of these and most other books in the field is plotted against the age from which it comes, the most apparent characteristic of the resulting graph is the inevitable J-shaped dip through the long Medieval period. While the Greek heritage is usually given some representation, the huge Christian confusion of psychology and ethics, so important in cultural history, is carefully avoided. Nor should the dip in the Middle Ages be as deep as it is if a work is to be representative of history. It is, of course, quite true that, after the Roman defilement of its Greek sources and the huge oppressiveness thrown over science by the victory of Augustine's ideas after the fall of Rome in 410, there is nothing of intellectual originality in science written until 9th century Basra. But some thought was going on which a representative history would have to represent. And the Renaissance, particularly in psychology, occurred long before any of these books give an indication. I am referring particularly to that resplendent meeting of Arabic, Greek, Christian, and Hebrew ideas that coalesced so brightly in Islamic Spain just after 1000 A.D. The 16th century, that thrilling crescendo of adventure and exploration, the century that practically invented the idea of nature and so began modern biology, the century that had so much to show and so little to say, is never mentioned. And through later periods, books differ widely, some being more representative of some things than others, but none representative of the history of psychology as a whole.

Nor could any of the recent work be considered parapposite to modern psychology as a whole. Older histories, particularly when psychology was cramped up into psychophysics, could attempt parapposite history. But so broad is the spectrum of interest and endeavor, so free its viewpoint and methodology, that a parapposite history of modern psychology as a whole is unfeasible. How crisscrossing the paths are! How lesser trails are grown over with disuse! How some can never now be traced, while others may be reblazed and made clear by some new discoverer who makes it all parapposite to some new relevance! How many new ones are starting now that will go we know not where! If the history of a divergent and less sequentially dependent science like psychology is to be coherent, it must abandon all wish that it feel or look like the mountain climbing of physics. Its task must be the disentangling of confused paths. The more these paths are restricted to single topics, the more representative and parapposite history can coalesce into something sound and with meaning.

SHIFTING PARADIGMS

IN THE *first selection Joynson places a critical lens over our entire discipline, questioning not only its significance but the limitations of its methods and the appropriateness of its subject matter. From a British vantage point, this paper documents in particular some of the major facets of the recent movement away from the experimental and behavioral emphases that have tended to dominate modern psychology since the behaviorist revolution early in the century.*

The paper by Segal and Lachman gives historical perspective to the pendulum swings in psychology and suggests that a new movement may be in process. From an American vantage point, these authors apply a Kuhnian analysis, identifying 1960 as the turning point. Both forces external to psychology (e.g., computer technology, linguistics) and internal factors (e.g., the intransigence of certain problems long investigated by behaviorally oriented psychologists) are recognized as significant.

Next, Kagan defends the current trend toward relaxation and permissiveness, suggesting that ambiguity may be implicit not only in our subject matter but in the capacity of our techniques to cope with it. He stresses the shift from absolutistic to relativistic definitions of concepts, illustrating these changes by a wealth of observations from developmental psychology.

Kagan's position is reinforced by Deese, who notes that the formal experimental mode inherited from the physical sciences seems to be losing its priority in the study of psychological problems. The emphasis on internal (cognitive) rather than merely behavioral factors is continued in this selection.

9

BREAKDOWN OF
MODERN PSYCHOLOGY

R. B. Joynson

Nearly 80 years ago, in a paper entitled ' "Modern" Psychology: a Reflexion,' James Ward (1893) expressed his misgivings about the attempts, then just beginning, to treat psychology on a par with natural science. If we accept the judgement of some leading British psychologists, his fears may now be safely forgotten. In his *Introduction to Modern Psychology*, Zangwill (1950, preface) writes: 'It is my belief that the foundations of an empirical psychology have been securely laid during the past sixty years . . . a central biological science of psychology is in process of formation.' Again, Broadbent (1961, p. 11) writes: 'The advance of this branch of science threatens to make an impact upon our philosophies which will be at least as great as the impact of Darwinism.' But not everyone shares this assurance. James Gibson (1967, p. 142) remarks that psychologists 'seem to feel, many of them, that all we need to do is consolidate our scientific gains. Their self-confidence astonishes me. For these gains seem to me puny, and scientific psychology seems to me ill-founded. At any time the whole psychological applecart might be upset. Let them beware!' This paper asks how far Gibson's warning is justified.

In the numerous proposals which have been put forward for a scientific psychology, two ideas recur so frequently that they may fairly be regarded as representative. The first idea is that psychology is the study of behaviour rather than mind; of objects rather than subjects. This reflects the desire that the subject matter of psychology should be fundamentally akin to that of the natural sciences. The second idea is that the conditions which determine behaviour may be elucidated by experiment. This expresses the determination that the methods of psychology also should conform to the scientific ideal. Broadbent (1961, p. 35) combines these two features when he claims that 'the emphasis on objective methods of experiment . . . is now a generally accepted doctrine.'

This 'generally accepted doctrine' has often been criticized from a philosophical standpoint. But a more pragmatic approach will be adopted here. The reader is asked to consider what is supposed to be involved in the practical application of the doctrine, according to the

from R. B. Joynson, The breakdown of modern psychology, *Bulletin of the British Psychological Society*, 1970, **23**, 261–269. Reprinted by permission of the author and the British Psychological Society.

recommendations of its supporters. The outcome seems to justify Gibson's caution.

The use of the experimental method in psychology has too often been expounded with uncritical enthusiasm. Zangwill (1950, p. 5) describes its introduction as 'an intellectual advance of the first magnitude.' The only attempt which he then makes to explore any difficulties which there might be in applying it, comes in the phrase (with reference to studies of learning) that "it is obviously not possible to control every variable' (p. 49). But nothing is said of what these variables might be, of why it is difficult to control them, or of whether this materially limits the value of the work. Rather, the implication is that it does not. Consider also the manner in which Humphrey (1963) proceeds. The reader is given to understand that if there are 'many people in responsible positions who still feel misgivings about the psychological laboratory' (preface), this is because of 'the misunderstandings found among many humanists of what psychologists do in the laboratory and why they do it' (p. 1). The objections which Humphrey then lists have all been made to him by non-experimentalists, for example, the subjectivity of mind and the problem of measurement. No attempt is made to specify difficulties which the experimentalist might himself have discovered in his work. Again, when experimental psychology is presented to the medical profession (Summerfield, 1964), the impression is given—by the absence of any disclaimer or even cautionary note—that experiment in psychology may be taken to be as reliable as experiment in the biological sciences in general.

The need for a more careful examination of the method is in fact later suggested by Zangwill (1964, pp. 134–5) himself, when he writes that 'experimental psychology has not wholly justified the earlier confidence placed in it as a department of science. It soon becomes apparent that human reactions are influenced by internal no less than by external circumstances, and that experimental control of the former is difficult, if not impossible, to achieve. . . . The whole conception of experiment in psychology awaits clarification.' So long as it 'awaits clarification,' it would be advisable to refrain from describing it as 'an intellectual advance of the first magnitude.'

The Problem of Experimental Conditions

How far can the conditions which determine behaviour be identified and controlled? A standard exposition of experiment in psychology is given by Woodworth & Schlosberg (1954, p. 3):

Let us ask what kinds of conditions E (the experimenter) is able to vary and make his experimental variables. Since O (the subject or organism) certainly responds differently to different stimuli, there must be stimulus variables, S-factors, affecting the response. Just as certainly, the subject responds differently to the same identical stimulus according to his own state and intentions at the moment. There are O-variables . . . affecting the response. . . . The response depends on the stimuli acting at that moment and on factors present in the organism at that moment. This general statement can be put into the form of an equation, $R = f(S,O)$, which reads that the response is a function of S-factors and O-factors. . . . As to the control of these variables, we readily admit that stimuli can be controlled so far as they come from the environment, for E can manage the immediate environment consisting of the experimental room and the apparatus. But how can he control the O-variables? At first thought it seems impossible.

It will be seen that Woodworth & Schlosberg, like Zangwill, suggest that there may be difficulty in controlling O-variables, or internal circumstances. We shall return to this question. Here it may be noted that, if it is true that S-factors (external conditions) are relatively easy to control, and O-factors (internal conditions) relatively difficult, there might be a tendency for the experimentalist to exaggerate the significance of S-factors in the determination of response, and to minimize the significance of O-factors—for in this way he might persuade himself that his ideal was more nearly attained. This tendency is in fact often found. Many experimenters proceed, openly or tacitly, as if response may be treated as a function of external conditions alone. Their equation is $R = f(S)$. After a brief review of some notable instances of this over-simplification, we shall return to consider the problem of controlling internal conditions.

Standing in Awe of the Stimulus

Among the oldest examples of excessive reliance on the control of external conditions is that tradition of experiment on memory which originated with Ebbinghaus. Hunter (in Humphrey, 1963, p. 141) describes this as 'a body of knowledge unsurpassed in contemporary psychology for its precision and lawfulness.' The judgement is highly misleading. Irion (1959, pp. 546–559) states that 'the variability of technique among experimenters is enormous . . . gratuitous variation of practically every circumstance under which learning occurs, and this without plan or design, has made it impossible to compare results that should be, at least roughly, comparable.' He adds the cold comfort that 'this situation exists in most other areas of psychology, of course . . .' and concludes by referring to 'the present state of relative chaos.'

Much might be done, as Irion points out, to secure greater uniformity. But even more fundamental criticisms were made by Bartlett (1932, pp. 2–10), which have never been adequately answered. Bartlett noted that the pioneers of experimental psychology were trained either in physics or physiology, and argued that this biased them towards the attempt to 'control variations of response and experience by known varia-

tions of stimuli, and to explain the former in terms of the latter. . . .'
But this raised 'profound psychological difficulties. . . . The psychologist,
of all people, must not stand in awe of the stimulus. . . . To make the
explanation depend mainly upon variations of stimuli . . . is to ignore
dangerously those equally important conditions of response which belong to the subjective attitude and to predetermined reaction tendencies.'
Nor did Bartlett restrict his criticisms to studies of memory. For him,
the methods of the physical and physiological pioneers

have overspread the whole of psychological science. Yet all the while new problems, most of them concerned with conditions of response which have to be
considered as resident within the organism—or the subject—itself have been
forcing themselves to the front. . . . The external environment may remain
constant, and yet the internal conditions of the reacting agent—the attitudes,
moods, all that mass of determining factors which go under the names of temperament and character—may vary significantly. These, however, are precisely
the kind of determinants which are pre-eminently important for the psychologist.

They remain precisely the kind of determinants which are pre-eminently unimportant for many experimentalists. Yet Bartlett himself could
hardly protest. His own 'experiments' gave great scope for the expression
of internal conditions, but they did little to show how these conditions
could be brought under experimental control. Bartlett pointed cogently
to a major problem of experimental psychology. He was unable to offer
a solution.

The most famous version of the stimulus-determination position is,
of course, Watson's S-R formula. Originally propounded with revolutionary fervour, it has been slowly and painfully abandoned by most of
his followers. Eysenck (1965, p. 14) tells the story with agreeable
brevity:

Early in the history of psychology attempts were made to omit the organism
from the account, and to describe behaviour entirely in terms of stimulus-
response connections. This became known as S-R psychology, but it soon became obvious that the same set of stimuli might produce an entirely different
set of responses in different organisms, or even in the same organism at different times. This indeed is so obvious that it hardly needs saying, but obvious
things are sometimes neglected, and the reinstatement of the organism has
been a relatively recent occurrence.

Eysenck need not apologize for mentioning this obvious point once
more, for its neglect is endemic among experimentalists. Broadbent
(1961, p. 41) states that the modern behaviourist conceives psychology
as 'a science which relates events at the bodily senses ("stimuli") to
events at those parts of the body which act on the outer world ("responses").' His aim, apparently, is to compile 'a set of laws, each of
which said that when certain things are seen or heard by a man he will

perform certain actions' (p. 38). But this formulation does not seem to differ in any important way from the original S-R formula; and its weakness, in overlooking internal factors, does indeed seem obvious. If one attempts to devise a law stating what actions a man will perform when he sees or hears any common object, it rapidly becomes plain that the formulation places a grotesque weight on the external object as a determinant of response. But the organism is eventually reinstated. Broadbent later refers to Skinner's view that 'we ought simply to say what we do to the animal, what the animal does in return, and to find out regularities in the relation between these two kinds of observation' (p. 126)— the view, it seems, which Broadbent himself originally recommended. But this view is now to be rejected: 'Unfortunately, behaviour does not altogether lend itself to rules of that sort. On a simple observational level, an animal placed in the same situation does not always do the same thing . . . a rat, who normally responds to the sight of a runway by running eagerly along it, will not do so if he has been shocked in the food-box at the far end. B does not follow A if some other event has intervened' (p. 132). And later he writes: 'one cannot confine oneself in this way forever' (p. 182). . . . 'Perhaps the worst weakness of behaviour theory is its method of dealing with events inside the brain. One by one the simple theories, which treated only observed responses, have been eliminated. It is almost universally admitted now that even the behaviour of rats requires us to think of mechanisms operating purely inside their brains' (p. 188). . . . 'the next step in the analysis of behaviour is the construction of theories about the events within the skull' (p. 200). The *next* step! It is good to see the modern behaviourist struggling to free himself from Watson's primitive simplicities; but when he announces this 'next step,' as if it were the continuation of some triumphal march, he seems to forget that the aberrations of behaviourism have never been universally adopted, and that many before him have long since attempted this step: Hebb, Lashley and Kohler; James, Jackson and Flourens; Hartley, Cabanis and Descartes.

The experiments of Michotte (1963) provide a third example of over-reliance on the control of external stimulation. These have been warmly praised: 'a series of experiments perhaps unmatched in the history of psychology for their simple forcefulness and sustained collected march' (Oldfield, in Michotte, 1963, p. vii); 'one of the most important and valuable contributions to psychology in the last twenty years' (Vernon, 1964, p. 74) 'one of the great milestones in twentieth-century psychology' (Pickford, 1963, p. 369); 'one of the very few psychological classics of our time' (Zangwill, 1963, p. 224).

Michotte's work displays interesting ideas and marked ingenuity in the design of apparatus, but a more discriminating appraisal is required. Michotte's basic contention is that the perception of causality is an immediate response to definable configurations of stimuli, and that the type of causal impression received can be determined by appropriate manipulation of these stimuli. To establish this example of the formula $R = f(S)$, the following conditions, at least, must be met. First, the number of subjects must be large enough to demonstrate that individual differences are minimal, for individual differences imply varying internal conditions requiring identification and control. Second, subjects must have no prior knowledge of the experimenter's hypotheses, or commitment to them. Third, the experiments must be conducted under conditions where the subject is not exposed to the influence of others, and where his reports may be accurately recorded.

Michotte reports a main series of 72 experiments on mechanical causality, and a further 30 subsidiary experiments. With respect to the whole sequence, Beasley (1968, p. 405) comments that Michotte 'is most unspecific in reporting the numbers of subjects on which he carried out his experiments. . . . The amazing fact is that no details whatsoever are given about the subjects used in over 50 per cent of his experiments. . . .' With respect to the main series, the present writer's calculations show that there are only 10 experiments in which the number of subjects is recorded as greater than three; that in 11 experiments the number is recorded as three or less; and that in the remaining 51 experiments there is no record of the number at all. The first requirement is not met.

Who were the subjects? Michotte (1963, p. 40) states that 'the permanent staff of the laboratory, consisting of Professors Montpellier, Nuttin, and Michotte, as well as the assistants, took part in all of them.' (This is of course inconsistent with the fact that in 11 experiments three or less subjects are reported as used.) There is evidence that Michotte eventually realized the weakness of this procedure, but it is strange that Vernon (1964, p. 75) should write that 'Michotte cannot be faulted by the criticism . . . that the subjects knew beforehand what they were expected to see.' The second requirement is not met.

Michotte (1963, p. 40) also writes that 'some experiments, which required a large number of subjects, were also tried out on students. Others again, and these were of course the most important ones, have been repeated with very many observers (several hundreds) either during lectures . . . or in practical demonstration classes.' Perhaps it is not surprising that no further details are given of these crowded scenes, which violate the third requirement, and seem to form an educational rather than scientific exercise.

Other investigators, observing the above requirements, have found much evidence of the importance of internal factors—as revealed in individual differences, in effects of previous experience and variations of attitude, and in reports of constructive judgemental activities (Olum, 1956; Gruber et al., 1957; Gemelli & Capellini, 1958; Powesland, 1959; Beasley, 1968). Thus the case of Michotte, like that of Watson and Ebbinghaus before him, illustrates the uncritical eagerness with which the experimentalist tends to accept an application of the formula $R = f(S)$; only to discover, sooner or later, how inadequate it is. There are perhaps instances where the formula has greater plausibility, as with the sign stimulus which regularly evokes a particular pattern of response. But this seems to be a simple limiting case from which more complex behaviour may be expected to depart. In any case, the ethologists themselves stress that internal factors are important too (Tinbergen, 1951, p. 15). We next turn, therefore, to the problem of how these internal factors may be identified and controlled.

The Indirect Study of Internal Conditions

Woodworth & Schlosberg, it will be recalled, asserted that internal factors must certainly be taken into account; and they indicate two main ways of attempting 'to discover what goes on in the organism between the stimulus and the motor response' (1954, p. 2). (a) The first involves direct observation of such events, either physiological or introspective: 'Physiological recording instruments often reveal something of what goes on in the organism during emotion, and introspection can show something of the process of problem solution' (p. 3). (b) 'In another class of experiments . . . E does not attempt to find out directly what goes on in O, but hopes to find out indirectly by varying the conditions and noting the resulting variation in response' (p. 3). The class of indirect methods will be considered first.

The indirect method recommended by Woodworth is that of controlling O-variables through antecedent or A-variables. Hunger, an O-variable, can be controlled through time since last feeding, an A-variable; and the experimenter 'may find it more helpful and "operational" to speak of A- rather than O-variables, and to give our equation this modified form: $R = f(S,A,)$' (p. 3). As an example of this method, they write that 'a valuable analysis of what we are calling O-factors was offered by Clark Hull. . . . His ambitious project called for the identification of all these factors, the quantification of each factor with an appropriate A-factor, and the discovery of how the several factors combine into the momentary readiness for a particular response' (p. 4). But why should they call this project 'ambitious'—a word which suggests that success is hardly to be expected? Hull, after all, was only attempting to carry out, with respect to a restricted range of behaviour, the procedure which they are themselves recommending for experimental psychology as a whole; indeed, they are using his work to illustrate and defend that procedure. Is it perhaps a hint that it should not be taken too seriously? Such a hint is certainly needed, for the 'intervening variable' method has proved highly controversial.

Koch (1959, p. 735) writes that 'the overall tendency of the study is to call the intervening variable paradigm and much of the associated doctrine sharply into question, and to do this in almost every sense in which questioning is possible.' He summarizes the doubts in three main queries. First, it seems extremely unlikely that it will ever be possible to establish straightforward connections between antecedent variables and the supposed intervening variables which would be capable of being generalised over a wide range of situations. This is because to each intervening variable there will correspond a number of indicators, and interactions among these in new situations pose great problems of prediction. Second, there is an unknown relation between the specific variable whose function is examined in a single experiment and the class of variables to which this is supposed to belong. If, for example, a specific variable is said to indicate the influence of 'past training,' this is a loose formulation which asserts the function for a huge and indefinite class of empirical variables which remain unexamined. Third, it is doubtful whether it is really possible to find 'unambiguous linkage' to observable variables for many of the concepts which are of most significance for psychology, especially those concepts which refer to the meaning which a situation has for the organism. It would seem, then, that this method has not gained general support, and the onus of proof lies with those who wish to claim that it can achieve any wide validity.

Other methods, also indirect, have been proposed. Eysenck's criticism of the stimulus determination position, for its neglect of individual differences, has already been noted. 'I would like to suggest,' he again writes (1966, p. 2), 'that the root of many of the difficulties and disappointments found in psychological research, as well as the cause of the well-known difficulties in duplicating results . . . lies in this neglect of individual differences.' Most striking perhaps is the suggestion that differences in strain of rats was a major factor in the great Hull-Tolman debate: 'Hundreds of extremely able psychologists spent time, energy and a considerable amount of money . . . apparently quite pointlessly; must this sort of thing be repeated endlessly before we learn the lesson that individual differences . . . may not be pushed aside and forgotten when experiments are designed which purport to reveal universal truths?' (p. 26). Eysenck also provides much evidence that variance in experiments may be reduced by taking account of differences in major personality dimensions.

This is a cogent variation on Bartlett's theme. Is it also a satisfactory solution to the problem? Eysenck stresses that there are great practical difficulties. If one takes into account only three dimensions—introversion, neuroticism, intelligence—and selects subjects varying in each in only three degrees—high, medium, low—there will be 27 cells to fill, 'and the labour involved in filling all of them with equal numbers of subjects might be prohibitive.' But he continues (pp. 25–6),

However this might be, before deciding what is feasible it is often useful to know what is desirable; eventually psychology will have to face up to the problem that if investigators wish their results to be replicable, they must reduce the error variance drastically, and the only practical way of doing this is by some such device as I have here suggested. . . . No doubt designs will be much more complex and difficult, experiments will be more time-consuming and expensive, and background knowledge will have to be more extensive and less idiosyncratic; but all this is inevitable if we are serious in our scientific quest.

Unfortunately, the difficulties are not only practical. The identification of the major dimensions of personality remains debateable; but if this problem is waived, there is the more fundamental question of the nature of these O-variables and how they may be investigated. The observational basis of psychometrics lies in describing responses to mental tests; it claims to classify and measure this behaviour. It is then inferred that differences in some underlying O-factor must account for these differences in behaviour. But the O-factor is not directly observed. If it is shown that differences in the test situation correlate with differences in an experimental situation, it is reasonable to suppose that the same O-factor is at work. But its nature has still not been directly investigated; what has been demonstrated is that the system of classification applicable to test responses is also applicable to experimental responses. If this is to go beyond a descriptive psychology, the nature of the presumed O-factor must be elucidated. In this respect, psychometrics is in exactly the same position as experimental psychology; and Eysenck postulates physiological bases for his main dimensions in the same way that many experimentalists invent neural models. No doubt the classification of individual differences in behaviour, if reliably achieved, would provide powerful evidence about the O-variables involved; but the evidence remains indirect, and needs to be supplemented by other methods.

Among the most fashionable indirect methods, is the application of principles derived from cybernetics and information theory. It has been argued, notably by Gregory (1961), that the conventional direct physiological methods of ablation and stimulation suffer severe limits in the absence of knowledge of the overall design of the nervous system. Cybernetics, however, studies the general properties of control systems, in relative independence of their particular physical embodiment; and the psychologist, it is said, may use such principles as a guide to the groundplan, or 'block design,' of the control system of behaviour. In the case of inanimate mechanisms, the groundplan is formulated by the designer; but with animate organisms, this must be discovered. So the psychologist conducts 'input-output' experiments to determine the special form which cybernetic principles take in the field of behaviour. These principles may then help the physiologist to know what mechanisms to look for, when he attempts to establish the neural embodiment of the system.

Though the approach has undoubtedly suggested new ways of looking at certain features of behaviour, its novelty is easily exaggerated. Thus to the early behaviourist, 'purpose' was disreputable. The concept of feedback, with its promise of a physical mechanism, has encouraged the reintroduction of the term, often with the implication that this reflects scientific progress in psychology. In fact, what is psychologically valuable in the concept was plainly stated in the 're-entrant series' of Stout (1896, pp. 143–168). How far cybernetic principles have really advanced understanding of human purpose is an open question; while particular applications of the machine analogy remain precarious (Gauld, 1966). In the present context, however, the main limitation of the method is that it still does not enable the experimenter to achieve direct identification and control of internal factors. He can only make more or less plausible inferences about the properties of the system, in the light of external manipulation and general cybernetic theory; and familiarity with the limitations of the stimulus-determination position should prevent an over-sanguine estimate of the outcome. It might also be suggested that the physiologist would be capable of designing his own 'input-output' experiments if and when they were needed, and that if he required assistance he might seek it from the mathematicians and engineers who have developed this branch of knowledge. It remains to be demonstrated that the role of the psychologist could be more than peripheral and temporary. It is not, then, surprising if the speculative abstractions of the cybernetically minded psychologist have little attraction for those who recall that the interval between the stimulus and the response is occupied by the nervous system. 'If one is interested in the brain, rather than a hypothetical model,' writes Weiskrantz (in Summerfield, 1964, p. 49), 'this approach may be illusorily simple. The history of the "conceptual" nervous system, from Erasistratus, through Galen, Descartes and the stimulus-response psychology, is a very lengthy one, ante-dating even the history of its principal laboratory tool, the armchair. . . .'

The three indirect methods reviewed, recognise the importance of internal conditions. But they are in fact restricted to the control of external circumstances: this indeed is what makes them indirect. They are really variations on the formula $R = f(S)$, and like that formula they have not proved unambiguously successful. It would be excessive to assert that the methods so far considered can give no information of value; but it seems likely that, by themselves, they must remain partial and uncertain. We are forced to the conclusion that effective, agreed, advance can come only from the direct study of internal conditions.

The Direct Study of Internal Conditions

As means of direct study, Woodworth & Schlosberg recommended the methods of introspection and of physiology. Introspection may be set aside. Since Watson's day, it has been widely regarded as inappropriate in an objective science; and the would-be scientific psychologist usually ignores or disparages it, despite the protests of Burt (1962). There remains the physiological method, which is advocated by Zangwill (1950, p. 20) himself: 'it is urged that the elucidation of central nervous mechanisms in relation to behaviour is a central problem in modern psychological research.'

In so far as the experimentalist reaches this conclusion, he recognizes that the methods so far examined are of limited value, and the argument is thereby confirmed. At the same time, it would be generally agreed that the physiological approach faces great difficulties, in the limitations of contemporary knowledge and techniques; indeed, this is one reason why many prefer to continue with the methods already considered. Time, however, may diminish these difficulties. We should therefore attend to another perplexity, which the scientific psychologist himself raises: namely how, on this view, psychology is to be distinguished from physiology.

'Indeed you may wonder, as we proceed,' wrote Watson (1924, p. 11), 'whether behaviorism can be differentiated from that science.' Watson answered the question by saying that physiology 'is particularly interested in the functioning of the parts of the animal . . . behaviorism . . . is intrinsically interested in what the whole animal will do. . . .' This distinction is still the stock one. Humphrey (1963, p. 15) states that psychology studies 'the total functioning of the whole organism, as contrasted with the science of physiology, which tends to interest itself in part-functions.' Zangwill (1967, p. 294) states that physiology 'studies the activities of the organism one by one with special reference to the particular organs upon which they depend. Psychology, on the other hand, is concerned with the integrated activity of the organism as a whole.' Now it is not necessary, of course, that the distinction between psychology and physiology should be sharp and complete, for the frontiers of the various sciences are loose and permeable. But it is necessary that there should be a sufficient contrast of interest and aim to justify the retention of the two labels; and this is what these writers are trying to achieve.

But the conventional mode of distinguishing seems thoroughly inadequate, whether it is approached from the side of physiology or of psychology. In some respects, it is obviously true that the physiologist is primarily interested in the functioning of parts taken separately, as with the secretion of urine by the kidneys. But he is often also interested in what might be called the molar rather than molecular aspects of such functions as respiration and digestion; and the neurophysiologist in particular is interested precisely in the co-ordination of part-functions by the nervous system. Sherrington (1947, p. 2) gave the classic expression of this interest: after indicating that the physiologist is interested in the nutritive and conductive properties of nerves, he continues: '. . . a third aspect which nervous reactions offer the physiologist is the *integrative*. In the multicellular animal, especially for those higher reactions which constitute its behaviour as a social unit in the natural economy, it is nervous reaction which *par excellence* integrates it, welds it together from its components, and constitutes it from a mere collection of organs an animal individual.' Plainly then the main interest of the physiologist is not always in part-functions. Indeed, it is precisely because the nervous system has this integrative function that the biological psychologist regards its elucidation as so important in the explanation of behaviour. But what now is the difference between the psychologist and the neurophysiologist in their respective studies of the nervous system?—for clearly it is a difference between psychology and neurophysiology, rather than physiology in general, which the biological psychologist must establish. Sherrington supposed it was the business of the psychologist to study the psyche, for Sherrington was a dualist. But the biological psychologist shrinks before so unscientific a notion of his task. For Zangwill (1967, p. 294), 'the ultimate aim of psychology is to establish a system of general laws covering the whole field of higher nervous activity.' What then is the aim of neurophysiology?

Nor does the distinction seem satisfactory when approached from psychology. Watson, wanting to make psychology a natural science, faced a dilemma. He must avoid the Scylla of 'mentalism'—introspection is not a scientific method; but he must also avoid the Charybdis of physiology —psychology must not be defined in terms which make it indistinguishable from another science. Watson thought that the conception of a science of behaviour—establishing the laws connecting stimulus and response—provided an escape. As Farrell (1955, p. 176) writes of this tradition: 'Much of it has assumed that experimental psychology is strong enough to arrive at Laws of Behaviour—laws which will sit on a base of, at present, unknown neurological generalizations, but which will be synthesized with the latter in due course as these become known.' But this assumption has broken down. The stimulus-determination position has failed, and the modern behaviourist himself now asserts that the next step is the construction of theories about the events within the skull. It is necessary to regard these 'unknown neurological generalizations' as forming an essential part of the study of the conditions of behaviour, and not as a luxury which may be added later. How, then, is it possible to distinguish psychology from neurophysiology?

It would hardly be surprising if the attempt to maintain a distinction was abandoned. This is so. Zangwill (in Summerfield, 1964, p. 47) expresses the hope that 'a coalescence of neurology and psychology may ultimately be achieved.' If they cannot be distinguished, this is predictable. But what is the psychologist to contribute to this coalescence? The contribution of the neurologist is presumably a knowledge of neurology, perhaps 'a system of general laws covering the whole field of higher nervous activity.' Is the psychologist to offer the same thing? If he does, it is to be hoped that his laws will prove to be the same as those of the neurologist. But perhaps the psychologist has some distinctive principles of his own to contribute? At present, it seems that little is to be expected, for Zangwill (1964, p. 138) writes that 'Experimental psychology has produced many facts, a few generalizations, and even an occasional "law." But it has so far failed to produce anything resembling a coherent and generally accepted body of scientific theory.' In view of the difficulty which experimental psychology has experienced in identifying and controlling the large and important class of internal conditions, this is entirely understandable. Perhaps, however, the psychologist will have some basic principles to contribute in the future—for psychology, as we are perennially told, is a young science? But this, significantly enough, does not seem to be envisaged, for Zangwill (1964, p. 130) writes that 'It is indeed not too much to suggest that the neurology of today may well provide the psychology of tomorrow with its basic principles.'

But this is a great deal too much to suggest. For this is the outcome of that allegedly scientific psychology, which assured us that its foundations were securely laid, and foretold Darwinian triumphs. We now discover that, on its own admission, it has no coherent principles to offer, and expects neurology to provide them.

Conclusion

Our examination of the 'generally accepted doctrine' of objective experiment can only be regarded as thoroughly substantiating Gibson's contention that scientific psychology is 'ill-founded,' its gains 'puny.' Attempts to restrict inquiry to the study of external stimulation alone have repeatedly failed, as have attempts to include internal conditions by indirect methods. The conclusion which many psychologists then reach, that internal nervous mechanisms must be investigated, confirms Gibson's remarks. For no one would deny that contemporary knowledge of physiological mechanisms, in relation to those forms of behaviour in which psychology is primarily interested, is in its infancy. Indeed, for those who accept the conclusion, Gibson's comments can come as no surprise. What calls for surprise, from this standpoint, is for anyone to claim a knowledge of the scientific foundations of behaviour; for such a claim implies a level of neurological understanding not yet attained.

But further, it would not help psychology if this neurological understanding were forthcoming. The belief that the future of psychology lies in neurophysiology is futile, for as Scriven (1964, p. 168) writes, it is 'a future which lies after the grave, since that stage is no longer psychology.' Or as Stout (1896, p. 4) expressed it: 'it is incorrect to say that on this assumption his science becomes absorbed in physiology. It does not become absorbed; it simply ceases to exist in any form whatever.'

The history of modern psychology is a record, not of scientific advance, but of intellectual retreat. 'Ever since its stipulation into existence as an independent science,' writes Koch (1961, p. 629), 'psychology has been far more concerned with being a science than with courageous and self-determining confrontation with its historically constituted subject matter. Its history has been largely a matter of emulating the methods, forms, symbols of the established sciences, especially physics. In so doing, there has been an inevitable tendency to retreat from broad and intensely significant ranges of its subject matter, and to form rationales for so doing which could only invite further retreat.' The conception of objective experiment lies at the heart of this attempt to emulate the natural sciences; but it does not meet the case. Psychology has much to learn from the natural sciences, but it is stultifying to insist that its concepts and methods must conform to those of other sciences, or be rejected. This is the narrow rigidity of Watson (1924, p. 5) who 'decided either to give up psychology or else to make it a natural science.' It is only too plain that it is the former aim which the behaviourist has achieved. Perhaps, however, the time is coming when broader and more appropriate ideals will prevail, for we cannot continue to live on borrowed principles and abortive prophecies.

REFERENCES

BARTLETT, F. C. (1932), *Remembering*. Cambridge University Press.

BEASLEY, N. A. (1968). The extent of individual differences in the perception of causality. *Can. J. Psychol.* 22, 399–407.

BROADENT, D. E. (1961). *Behaviour*. London: Eyre & Spottiswoode.

BURT, C. (1962). The concept of consciousness. *Br. J. Psychol.* 53, 229–242.

EYSENCK, H. J. (1965). *Fact and Fiction in Psychology*. London: Penguin Books.

—— (1966). Personality and experimental psychology. *Bull. Br. psychol. Soc.* 19, no. 62, 1–28.

FARRELL, B. A. (1955). On the limits of experimental psychology. *Br. J. Psychol.* 46, 165–177.

GAULD, A. (1966). Could a machine perceive? *Br. J. Phil. Sci.* 17, 44–58.

GEMELLI, A. & CAPPELLINI, A. (1958). The influence of the subject's attitude in perception. *Acta psychol.* 14, 12–23.

GIBSON, J. J. (1967). In E. G. Boring & G. Lindzey (eds.), *A History of Psychology in Autobiography*, vol. 5. New York: Appleton-Century-Crofts.

GREGORY, R. L. (1961). The brain as an 'engineering' problem. In W. H. Thorpe & O. L. Zangwill (eds.), *Current Problems in Animal Behaviour*. Cambridge Univ. Press.

GRUBER, H. E., FINK, C. D., & DAMM, V. (1957). Effects of experience on perception of causality. *J. exp. Psychol.* 53, 89–93.

HUMPHREY, G. (ed.) (1963). *Psychology Through Experiment*. London: Methuen.

IRION, A. L. (1959). Rote learning. In S. Koch (ed.), *Psychology: A Study of a Science*, vol. 2. New York: McGraw-Hill.

KOCH, S. (ed.) (1959). *Psychology: A Study of a Science*, vol. 3. New York: McGraw-Hill.

―――― (1961). Psychological science versus the science-humanism antinomy: intimations of a significant science of man. *Am. Psychol.* 16, 629–639.

MICHOTTE, A. (1963). *The Perception of Causality*. London: Methuen.

OLUM, V. (1956). Developmental differences in the perception of causality. *Am. J. Psychol.* 69, 417–425.

PICKFORD, R. W. (1963). Review of Michotte (1963). *Br. J. Psychol.* 54, 369.

POWESLAND, P. F. (1959). The effect of practice upon the perception of causality. *Can. J. Psychol.* 13, 155–168.

SCRIVEN, M. (1964). Views of human nature. In T. W. Wann (ed.), *Behaviorism and Phenomenology*. Univ. of Chicago Press.

SHERRINGTON, C. (1947). *The Integrative Action of the Nervous System*. Cambridge University Press.

STOUT, G. F. (1896). *Analytic Psychology*, vol. 1. London: Sonnenschein.

SUMMERFIELD, A. (ed.) (1964). Experimental psychology. *Br. med. Bull.* 30, no. 1.

TINBERGEN, N. (1951). *The Study of Instinct*. Oxford Univ. Press.

VERNON, M. D. (1964). Review of Michotte (1963). *Br. J. soc. clin. Psychol.* 3, 74–75.

WARD, J. (1893). 'Modern' psychology: a reflexion. Mind 2 (n.s.), 54.

WATSON, J. B. (1924). *Behaviorism*. Univ. of Chicago Press.

WOODWORTH, R. S., & SCHLOSBERG, H. (1954). *Experimental Psychology*. New York: Holt.

ZANGWILL, O. L. (1950). *An Introduction to Modern Psychology*. London: Methuen.

―――― (1963). Review of Michotte (1963). *Q. J. exp. Psychol.* 15, 224.

―――― (1964). Physiological and experimental psychology. In J. Cohen (ed.), *Readings in Psychology*. London: Allen & Unwin.

―――― (1967). Psychology. In *Chambers Encyclopedia*, rev. ed. London: Pergamon Press.

10

HIGHER MENTAL PROCESSES[1]

Erwin M. Segal *and* Roy Lachman[2]

Anyone who has associated with research in learning and performance during the last decade knows that there have been significant changes in the research area. The changes do not necessarily hold for any individual, but the pattern of research and theory is very different from that in 1960. Rather than just sense the changes that have occurred, we analyzed this research domain to see if we could identify the major dynamics and forces of change.

We believe that there was an identifiable paradigm in psychology between 1930 and 1960 known variously as behavior theory, learning theory, neobehaviorism, or S-R psychology. We do not presume to say that all psychologists operated within this paradigm, as they did not, but a large percentage of American research psychologists agreed with each other on enough criteria for a paradigm to be established. Thus, the changes in this area of psychology are changes in an established science rather than preparadigmatic variation (cf. Kuhn, 1962). How are we to characterize these changes? Are the changes that have occurred in scientific psychology since 1960 merely due to conceptual refinement or are they due to a general change in the psychological Weltanschauung?

This article is divided into five sections. In the first two sections we discuss science in general during its stable and changing times. In the next two sections we apply the view of science we developed to experimental psychology during its recent stable and changing times. We end with a brief discussion of current cognitive psychology and a brief overview of the article.

Scientific Paradigms During Periods of Relative Stability

It is now generally agreed that any scientist's research flows from his particular point of view. His view partially originates in and develops from the characterization of the science by his predecessors. In order to

[1] A form of this article was presented at The Conference on Language and Higher Mental Processes, March 20 and 21, 1970, in Binghamton, New York. Work on this paper was partly supported by National Science Foundation Grant GB6530.

[2] Order of authorship is fortuitous; both authors contributed equally. The authors would like to thank Janet L. Mistler and Gail A. Bruder for their critical comments.

characterize its changes, we must discuss the science. We have been advised by a leading intellect of the twentieth century to look not at what the scientist says but at what he does (Einstein, 1933). One obvious place to look for what is actually done is graduate research training. Here, the operating characteristics of a paradigm in normal science are laid bare because graduate research training gives a considerable element of indoctrination in the prevailing paradigm.

An important facet of this indoctrination is the data base at a given point in time, that is, the first level of generalization, which includes the empirically discovered functional relations between operationally defined variables as well as empirical instances of results. Thus, both empirical laws and data are included (cf. Carnap, 1966). More correctly, the indoctrination concerns the dominant conception of the data base. Since the *unselected* data base of any science will encompass a collection that is enormous in size, the facets to which the student is exposed in the course of graduate training represent a process of considerable selectivity and omission. Facts that do not fit the prevailing paradigm are more susceptible to forgetting, not to say conscious omission, and appear with considerably lower probabilities in graduate lectures and publications than whose which support it. Selective forgetting, of course, is not the sole exit route for facts that do not fit the prevailing conceptualizations. It is not uncommon for such facts to be attributed to the work of incompetents, to be dismissed as uninteresting and unimportant, or even to be hidden in the files of the researcher who discovered them. Thus, a selective data base is transmitted from one generation of researchers to the next.

The data base, the student is advised, is a reflection of the fundamental concepts of the science. As the data and laws are mastered, the basic structure of the domain becomes apparent to the student. Learning this structure is like acquiring a set of "lenses" consisting of the accepted concepts and methods of a paradigm through which to view the basic regularities of the science. The student is not taught the details of the lenses through which he has to look to become a practicing scientist. He has to infer them from the elementary phenomena he is taught. If a description is attempted, the limited viewpoint of a scientist tends simply to be identified by a list of either pejorative or complimentary adjectives, depending upon whether the reviewer is friend or foe (e.g., Meehl, 1954). There seems to be no explanatory shortcut to understanding a system; it cannot be separated from the data it explains (Feyerabend, 1962). Thus, only a student of a science can fully understand it.

Every paradigm includes a variety of methodological commitments: the designs, procedures, and tools of inquiry. The student is enticed to learn both the procedures and the commitments. While any division of science, by subject matter or otherwise, will uncover obvious and necessary differences in methodology, such differences are frequently accidental consequences of subject-matter divisions (e.g., the archaeologist's pick and shovel and the astronomer's telescope). The relevant concern is that distinctive methodology may be regarded as uniquely suitable for an entire science, while, in fact, it is really appropriate to a paradigm within a science, a paradigm which entails a selective data base and coherent conceptual orientation. The research methodology of Skinner (1959), for example, includes the necessary apparatus to show the control of behavior by stimulus' and reinforcement conditions. His data are collected by a methodology that directly reflects his operating concepts and the facts he conceives to be relevant. The modified natural observation methods employed by ethologists such as Lorenz (1952) purport to deal with the same subject matter, that is, the behavior of organisms, but they reflect an entirely different set of concepts and relevant facts.

Scientists operating within the same paradigm can also employ methodologies as widely different as those of Skinner (1959) and Lorenz (1952). Insofar as a variety of empirical problems are acknowledged within a given paradigm, a variety of different methods can be developed to resolve these problems. In quantum mechanics, for example, naturally occurring cosmic radiation is studied in cloud chambers while man-made counterparts are studied in high-energy accelerators. Thus, although the paradigm defines the methods, it does not do so uniquely, and one cannot use similarity of methods as the basic criterion for identifying a single paradigm.

The essence of a paradigm rests with scientific concepts on the nature of things. Some of these concepts concern the relationships among other concepts. Such concepts reflect the scientist's grasp of entities and ideas which make up a vision of reality of the subject-matter domain. Such a vision of reality underlying a *limited* domain of science should not be mistaken for a comprehensive world view, which is typically formulated after some striking success in a scientific subject-matter area. Even Newton could not relate his gravitational theory to a systematic world view (Andrade, 1946). All-encompassing world views are frequently formulated by scholars in other disciplines, rather than by scientists. This does not stem from provincialism on the part of the scientific community. Giving a precise account of a subset of reality is a task which leaves little time for formulating comprehensive world views, although quite often the scientist does not have the temperament, inclination, or philosophical sophistication to attempt a world view.

Scientific Revolutions

At times during their history, several domains of knowledge have had changes in direction or orientation so major that they have been called revolutions. The most outstanding of these include the Copernican, the Newtonian, the Einsteinian, the Freudian, and the behaviorist revolutions.[3] In order to decide whether a revolution occurred recently, or is occurring in psychology today, we should have some guidelines on what it takes to have a scientific revolution.

We would like to propose the thesis that a scientific revolution is identified like a political revolution, on the basis of sociological criteria. One can conclude on the basis of political, theological, and social events that a scientific revolution has occurred, but one cannot identify a revolution on cognitive criteria alone. The conceptual changes in science that have most often been identified as revolutionary have had a cosmic effect on subsequent science and society. The primary criterion for an idea to have such an effect is the topic area in which it occurs. A topic has to be cosmic in scope to have revolutionary consequences. The most often cited scientific revolution is the Copernican, which had as its topic area the cosmos itself. It had, in addition, direct repercussions in such diverse areas as terrestrial physics and theology. A theoretical position with direct implications for the concept of the universe and the place of man in it cannot but be noticed by the educated laity. Other revolutions in science, such as the Newtonian and Einsteinian revolutions, were also directed at the cosmos and the basic concepts of physics. If they are defined by their social consequences, we cannot tell whether the Freudian and behaviorist revolutions are different ones, but we do know that both are directed at the concept of man. They changed the prevailing view that man is a rational being to a view in which man is affected by the accidental character of his physiology and environment.

Thus, the major revolutions in science over the last 500 years are those that caused a large number of the intellectual elite to change their conception of the nature of man or of the universe in which he lives. The *ideas* expressed by the leaders of these revolutions, however, are not in and of themselves the basis for claiming a revolution since most, if not all, of their central ideas had been expressed previously. What made them revolutions was their wide acceptance! Widespread acceptance, of course, can only be identified after it has occurred.

When a change in paradigm is identified retrospectively as revolutionary, two classes of individuals have accepted the change: the scientific community and the educated elite. New scientific conceptions with sociopolitical consequences are not judged by the layman on scientific grounds but solely on the basis of implications for proper human conduct broadly conceived. The scientist himself is not immune to such implications of his concepts and may make scientific judgments about these concepts using nonscientific grounds. Many deep conceptual changes in science, however, do not touch on issues of proper conduct, politics, or

3 Different readers have suggested the Darwinian, quantum mechanics, or Marxian revolution. Even scientists cannot agree as to what the most outstanding revolutions were.

common sense and, therefore, go largely unnoticed by the educated elite. In these cases, the issue is resolved entirely within the scientific community according to scientific criteria, and the change is not considered revolutionary. Consider, for example, the fixed stars. Classical cosmology, in addition to its conception of a geocentric universe, postulated an outer boundary identified as the sphere of the stars. The epicenter of the Copernican revolution was the conception of heliocentricity, but by the nineteenth century the universe was conceived as an infinite expanse populated throughout by solid bodies similar to our sun. Surely the shift from a finite to an infinite universe represented a conceptual change at least as great as that of Copernicus, but by then nobody cared. The implications beyond astronomy, implicit in the Copernican revolution, were no longer at issue.

Psychology of Complex Behavior 1930–1960: Period of Relative Stability

At no time in the history of psychology has there been general agreement on the detailed character of the science. From 1930 until at least 1960, however, a host of American psychologists articulated different positions which had at their core a similar set of methods and concepts. The most prominent of these, here identified as neobehaviorists, were Guthrie (1952), Hull (1943), Skinner (1938), Spence (1957), and Tolman (1932). The following is a brief discussion of several dimensions of their science in an attempt to capture the mood of that period.

The first of these dimensions is the data base. Although any claim of scientific fact can be accepted, ignored, or challenged, there was one set of facts that the neobehaviorists could accept to a remarkable degree; these were the data of animal learning. Included was the enormous aggregation of facts collected in classical, instrumental, and discrimination learning experiments. One of the primary reasons the neobehaviorists dominated scientific psychology during this period is that they could generally agree on what were the facts and which facts mattered. From the beginning of this period, however, a few of the facts were questioned and became the basis for extensive research efforts. These efforts reflected the optimistic consensus among all parties that challenges to the data base would be resolved empirically.

A second dimension relates to the neobehavioristic metatheoretical explanatory systems, which, unlike the data base, were several and varied. The many explanatory systems did not immediately become a source of controversy but, rather, provided a variety of theoretical options to members of the scientific community. Scientists with different notions of how psychological phenomena were best explained could easily find a suitable reference group. Hull's (1943) explanatory system, which was based on the hypothetico-deductive postulate structure of Newton's *Principia,* captured the imagination of many young psychologists. Here was "superscience"—psychologists were building a system to rival that of the most prestigious of all sciences. Few questioned whether Hull's conception was in fact being actualized or whether such a system was appropriate at that point in the history of psychology.

The raison d'etre for a science of psychology, for Skinner (1938), was specification of orderly change in behavior with manipulation of the conditions of stimulation. His explanatory system was radical empiricism: there was no a priori reason why a complete account of behavior would not be rendered by discovery and presentation of the functional relationships between relevant empirical variables (Skinner, 1950, p. 215). The major appeal of the Skinnerian explanatory system was diametrically opposite to that of Hull. One did not have to worry about mastering the details of a complex and abstract system; he could get right to work manipulating variables and, in so doing, establish the explanation for the behaviors observed.

The preferred explanatory system of Tolman (1938) was his own creation; there are no obvious antecedents to his particular formulation. In his explanatory system, every theoretical term was an intervening variable, ultimately defined in terms of at least two empirical variables. All theoretical concepts were established by antecedent conditions of stimulation and constitution and consequent measurements of behavior. From the very beginning, Tolman's metatheory offered an alternative to the other explanatory system, an alternative which gained importance when serious doubt developed concerning Hull's metatheory. The extent of his influence can best be seen in the work of Spence (1957), whose explanatory system is a direct outgrowth of Tolman's, although his theoretical concepts and formulations of law followed the lead of Hull.

A large cluster of research methods were available to and developed by the neobehaviorists. Skinner developed a research technology for carefully controlling the conditions of stimulation and exactly recording selected behavior. The others incorporated many of Skinner's techniques into their research methodology and added the statistical design procedures of Fisher (1935) and his students. With the addition of operationism, which was universally accepted by the neobehaviorists, the methodology was thought adequate to solve any of the deep problems of psychology. Indeed some psychologists still believe this to be the case. The neobehaviorists in concert had a vision of the ultimate character of psychological processes. All were influenced by the theory of evolution; they sincerely believed that the complex psychological processes of man could be reduced to subcomponents present in essentially the same form in the lower mammals. In particular, they were convinced that processes of learning—the change of behavior due to environmental conditions—

were the same whenever learning occurred. At that time this position appeared to be reasonable and received direct support in other sciences such as comparative anatomy. Additional justification came from the reductionist positions of physiology and organic chemistry.

The history of psychology has been plagued with problems that were not empirically resolvable, such as the mind–body problem, the fundamental elements of consciousness, and the nature of imageless thought. The neobehaviorists accepted positivism partially because it appeared to give a prescription for generating confirmable propositions. Also, the emphasis of the positivists on the intersubjective or public nature of valid scientific knowledge fit well with, and gave philosophical support to, the antimentalism and other behaviorist proscriptions already accepted.

Each leading neobehaviorist subscribed to a unique configuration of beliefs concerning the fundamental nature of behavior. All believed that the study of learning was at the core of scientific psychology and that advances in this field were an absolute precondition for developing coherent explanations in other fields of psychology, including higher mental processes. The historical formulation of associationism was a pivot concept, although the exact manner of its use was far from uniform. The establishing of connections, whether between S and R, or S and S, was considered a reasonable way to conceptualize all manner of behavior change including those involving complex behaviors. The neobehaviorists usually held two tenets which were related to their concept of association. First, these psychologists (with the exception of Tolman) believed that the associative connections could, in principle, be measured by instruments which either recorded overt behavior or were hooked up to the muscles or glands. Second, the neobehaviorists were convinced that the laws of conditioning (or learning) could be used to describe all the complex processes of behavior. Thus, the neobehaviorists had a vision of a reality which could be understood by the tools they already had.

All told, it is not difficult to understand the optimism of the period and the reasons why intellects of the highest order were seduced by S-R behaviorism. Indeed, some of the best of them attempted to apply the neobehavioristic prescriptions to the study of complex behaviors such as attitudes, verbal behavior, concept formation, language, and thinking (e.g., Gibson, 1940; Hovland, Janis, & Kelley, 1953; Miller & Dollard, 1941; Osgood, 1953; Skinner, 1957).

Cognitive Psychology Circa 1960: Period of Change

INFLUENCES FOR CHANGE EXTERNAL TO PSYCHOLOGY

Although a paradigm has a great deal of circularity built into its formulation, with the concepts determining the appropriate data and vice versa, it is not isolated from the world. The observed data, internal analyses of the paradigm, developments in other fields, and changing interests of scientists each furthered the decline of neobehaviorism.

Following World War II, striking advances occurred in several loosely related scientific fields including finite mathematics and probability theory, information theory, linguistic theory, and computer science. These fields all dealt with formal operations on symbolic entities. Since the neobehaviorist concepts had been generalized to verbal learning and concept formation, the scope of these achievements quite naturally attracted the attention of the psychological community. These various developments outside of psychology all had an important characteristic: their scientific credentials were impeccable. Many of the alternatives to S-R behaviorism within psychology had been vilified for their unscientific and metaphysical predilections, often justifiably. Charges of "unscientific" against these external influences would have seemed ludicrous; now a considerable selection of genuine scientific alternatives to neobehaviorism was available.

Starting with the publication of a text by Feller (1950) on probability, followed by an elementary elucidation of concepts in a book by Kemeny, Snell, and Thompson (1957) on finite mathematics, a large group of psychologists and their students were introduced to the power and simplicity of set theory and finite mathematics. These books and the many others on the same topic did not directly provide any substantive theories, but they did provide a way of formally characterizing many different kinds of hypotheses dealing with qualitative and discrete differences. Before the advent of new formalisms, a primary advantage of the behaviorist positions was that these were the only positions which had even the semblance of formal support. It is not clear whether other theoretical positions could have been formalized before the advent of finite mathematics, but in any case they were not. Now, however, for the first time one could discuss such concepts as attention, selection, cognitive states, or stimulus features with much rigor (e.g., Atkinson & Estes, 1963; Restle, 1961).

One of the most potent of the extrapsychological alternatives was information theory. Information theoretical concepts were applied to psychology almost immediately upon the publication of "A Mathematical Theory of Communication" by Shannon in 1948. Interestingly, the main thrust of information theory into psychology came not from its mathematical formalisms, the theorems, but rather from its conceptual characteristics. Information theory provided a rich source of hypotheses about psychological processes, mostly dealing with complex human behavior, and psychologists were quick to develop them. The result was the accumulation of a considerable literature of high quality. Information theoretic concepts such as uncertainty and structure provided viable alternatives to the concept of association and to the conditioning model (cf.

Garner, 1962); such alternative concepts were perhaps information theory's most serious blow to neobehaviorism.

Computer science had a manifold influence on psychology. Automata theory, programming technology, and computer principles provided a rich source of concepts, a methodology, and an explanatory formalism. These, singly and in concert, have been incorporated into a variety of approaches to psychological theory and research, which as a group is called the information-processing approach. General methodological and design characteristics of the approach have been described by Haber (1969) with special emphasis on perception and thinking. A new formalism for theory construction, computer simulation, is, of course, applicable independent of information-processing concepts and methodology, but the formalism and the concepts generally have been applied together, especially in the study of cognitive processes (cf. Reitman, 1965). The major concepts of the information-processing approach such as the flow charting of information, transformations of information, and stages in perception and thought offered a view of reality that contrasted sharply with the concepts of neobehaviorism.

Psychologists using this approach, rooted as it was in computer theory, could use a variety of mental concepts to describe mindless automata; the old behaviorist charge of mentalism was thus rendered irrelevant. It is interesting to note that Hull (1943) himself argued that the analogy with a "self maintaining robot" was an effective "prophylaxis against anthropomorphic subjectivism [p. 27]." Computer simulation was thus recommended in the abstract by a leader of the neobehavioristic movement. The appeal of this approach, along with some concurrent internal difficulties in S-R behaviorism, may account for the many defections from neobehaviorism (e.g., Bower, 1967; Mandler, 1967).

The most recent and most intensive undermining of neobehavioristic cohesion came from developments in linguistic theory. More than any other external influence, linguistics had an impact that cannot readily be separated from internal undermining. An excellent illustration is Skinner's application of his neobehaviorist methods and concepts to verbal behavior and Chomsky's analysis of that position. Chomsky (1959) reviewed Skinner's *Verbal Behavior* (1957), and neobehaviorism has not yet recovered. Although some disagree, we think that Chomsky clearly showed that Skinner's program could not be used to operationalize linguistic concepts and that it was neither a description nor a theory of language. Chomsky (1957, 1965) not only criticized the neobehavioristic position but offered positive alternatives. He demonstrated that language behavior could not be described meaningfully in terms defined solely by empirically delimited variables and also suggested that a formalism which generated sentences of natural language could be devised, provided that it contained certain abstract features. Miller (1962) called the attention of psychologists to Chomsky's theoretical formulations and demonstrated how they might be used as the basis of empirical research. This theoretical approach won many converts, talent that otherwise would have done research in the neobehaviorist tradition started intensive work within this new conceptual system. Evidence for this latter statement is the continuous dialogue between neobehaviorists and transformationalists and losses from the ranks of S-R behaviorism.

Our catalog of the external undermining of the S-R, neobehaviorist paradigm would be incomplete without some brief mention of developments in the philosophy of science. While neobehaviorists were accepting the tenets of logical positivism, this philosophy was coming under continuous and sometimes devastating attacks by other analytic philosophers. Psychologists generally were unaware of these attacks and of new approaches until quite recently. Among more recent work in the philosophy of science, the influential positions enunciated by Kuhn (1962) and Polanyi (1958) convinced many research psychologists that the conceptual frameworks within which science is conducted contain many arbitrary features. Such awareness could not but make research psychologists question their assumptions.

INFLUENCES FOR CHANGES INTERNAL TO PSYCHOLOGY

In 1954, the euphoria of many neobehaviorists was shaken by the publication of a conference report, *Modern Learning Theory* (Estes, Koch, MacCorquodale, Meehl, Mueller, Schoenfeld, & Verplanck, 1954). Although by then the four major neobehavioristic positions were considered to be theories of learning, the conclusions of the conference were that none were, in fact, coherent theories. In particular, none of the theories were formally adequate. They were not shown to be wrong, but more seriously, they *could not* be shown to be wrong because either they had essentially no formalism or they permitted contradictory deductions. Neobehaviorism has yet to recover.

The neobehaviorists started with essential agreement on the data base and the conviction that challenges to the data base would be resolved empirically. Little did they know what despair some of them would feel when the results of arduous experimentation yielded only one more tally in a box score, as occurred, for example, in the place versus response learning controversy. The basic issue was a seemingly simple empirical problem: Did organisms learn what response to make or where to go? Many studies were done, but the results were contradictory and neither position was established. Kendler and Gasser (1948) attempted to solve the problem by arguing that one of the "responses" a subject can learn is "approach," so place learning was identified as a subset of response learning. The discussion ended with Restle (1957) who claimed to resolve the issue by declaring it a pseudo-problem. What was called place or response learning depended on the locus of cues: if there were internal cues, it was response learning; if the cues were external, it was place learning. The original issue of what was associated to the cues was ignored. Thus, an issue that was to be resolved empirically floated away in a cloud of obscurity. Many other problems were "solved" in similar fashion such as latent learning, one-trial learning, and stimulus selectivity, among others.

As we have mentioned, most neobehaviorists believed that complex behaviors are mediated by essentially isomorphic mechanisms through much of the phylogenetic scale. This belief received shattering rebuffs during the last decade. Among the first to be disappointed were those neobehaviorists who did not wait until the empirical issues were resolved on animal subjects to apply the concepts and variants of the methodology to human complex behaviors. The empirical problems in the human domain were, if possible, more intractable than in the animal domain. Serial and paired-associate learning, two tried-and-true methods for investigating learning in humans, both presented problems unresolvable in terms of associations between elements. The stimulus in serial learning became an event that had no direct empirical correlate (cf. Young, 1968). The functional stimulus in paired-associate learning depended upon what was meaningful to the subject (Underwood, 1963). Subjects could use or not use associative connections as they chose (Jenkins, 1963; Postman & Stark, 1969). These and similar results supported the growing conviction that the data base gathered from animal studies was in no simple way capable of encompassing complex human behavior. Now, some even believe that there is a discontinuity between animal learning and human mental processes.

The neobehaviorists continue to hold antimentalistic convictions. Cautions against the value and reliability of human communication in the form of a verbal report continue to be offered. The Skinnerian wing of neobehaviorism believes to this day that verbal behavior is subject to the same laws and controlled by the same variable as the pecking response of pigeons. Their position represents one side of a controversy on the operant conditioning of verbal behavior (Holtz & Azrin, 1966). The other side of the controversy holds that verbal behavior is "conditioned" only when the human subject is aware that something is expected of him and is willing to do it. Whatever the resolution of the controversy, psychology changes. One of the central figures in this controversy has recently concluded:

Paradoxically, perhaps the most significant contribution of verbal conditioning research has been the stimulation of interest in verbal report procedures and in concepts such as "awareness" among psychologists who are inclined to insist that thoughts and ideas are beyond the limits of scientific inquiry [Spielberger & DeNike, 1966, p. 324].

Some psychologists became interested in complex symbolic processes themselves. This shift in interest oriented them to a new data base. This data base held obvious limitations for any system that depends upon learning defined as changes in the probability of responses. Miller (1965) pointed out that English-speaking adults can easily understand more than 10^{20} sentences. These obviously could not have been learned on an individual basis. If explanatory systems depending upon the changing probability of responses are not to become meaningless, one has to specify in a nontrivial fashion how to integrate response units into higher-order units. Claims that sentences are constructed by "autoclitic" responses to other responses (Skinner, 1957) do not meet this criterion. Also, understanding sentences is not clarified by discussing a systematic set of language habits such that, for example, "a," "the," and "this" are associated with one another by contiguous implicit responses, and "the" and "car" are associated explicitly such that all occurrences of the responses "the" would tend to elicit the response "car" (Staats & Staats, 1963). In addition to problems involving grammatical constructions, the need for conceptions other than the accumulation of S-R units is immediately apparent when one considers such behaviors as paraphrasing and understanding prose (Lachman & Dooling, 1968).

Psychology Circa 1970

The neobehaviorist position has been somewhat shaken since its heyday, but it still has adherents, although some individuals such as Bever, Fodor, and Garrett (1968) claim that an associationistic position, *in principle*, cannot account for certain higher mental processes. Others, such as Crothers and Suppes (1967), make the claim that associationism, *in principle*, can handle *any* complex mental phenomena. As things currently stand, Crothers and Suppes are right. Let us look at current neobehaviorism. Witness this statement by a leading S-R neobehaviorist: "an objective, functionalist, or even S-R viewpoint carries no necessary theoretical comments and no necessary aversion to postulating intervening processes [Cofer, 1968, p. 526]." A second distinguished S-R theorist states, "The least controversial, and perhaps most useful, interpretation of S-R associationism is to view it as a technical language system analogous to notations used to represent moves in a chess game [Kendler, 1968, p. 388]."

According to these spokesmen, by 1968 there were no precepts or limitations with which one could identify the neobehaviorist position. This situation was reached because the S-R psychologists as individuals successively modified their positions to account for the new conceptualizations, new formalisms, new methods, and new additions to the data base. They also became cognizant of problems in their explanatory systems. As far as we can tell, with the exception of the radical behaviorists who reject everything but their own research and rhetoric, the structure which was S-R behaviorism has no properties left. It, in short, has vanished. These psychologists, however, did not give up their conceptual lenses with which to view the world, but gained individualized new lenses to replace the old. It is just that for many psychologists their metatheoretical vocabulary lags behind their vision.

With the demise of S-R behaviorism, research in the higher mental processes has flourished (cf. Neisser, 1967). We cannot at this time specify what the future of psychology will be; however, we see the near future containing many and varied approaches. As to our original problem, are we in the midst of a scientific revolution? If the controversies in psychology lead to continuing debate by the nonscientific educated elite and the concept of man is at stake, as we think it is, then in several years we will be able to say that a revolution took place. We can say with assurance that deep conceptual changes in psychology have already occurred.

Summary

The basic naure of scientific paradigms during periods of stability and change was analyzed, and the results of this analysis were applied to scientific psychology. No particular aspect of a scientific viewpoint in isolation determines a paradigm and, surprisingly, a change in all may not signify a revolution. Revolutions are identified as such retrospectively, frequently by nonscientific criteria. Scientific psychology was in a stable period and was dominated by neobehaviorism for most of the middle third of the twentieth century. We present evidence that this domination was justified by both analytic and empirical considerations. After World War II, the bases for this domination began to dissipate. Major formal and theoretical advances outside psychology in finite mathematics, linguistics, computer technology, information theory, and philosophy of science are described. These gave rise to procedures and ideas applicable to formulations in competition with the behavioristic approaches. Problems within S-R behaviorism which were generally conceived to be empirically resolvable proved to be intractable. The strong neobehavioristic positions have weakened so considerably in the face of this competition that neobehaviorism can hardly be identified. Thus, the justification for the domination of psychology by neobehaviorism has eroded, as has the domination itself.

REFERENCES

ANDRADE, E. N. DA C. Isaac Newton. In Royal Society of London (Ed.), *Newton tercentenary celebrations, 15–19 July, 1946.* Cambridge, England: Cambridge University Press, 1947. (Reprinted in J. R. Newman [Ed.], *The world of mathematics.* Vol. 1. New York: Simon & Schuster, 1956.)

ATKINSON, R. C., & ESTES, W. K. Stimulus sampling theory. In R. D. Luce,

R. R. Bush, & E. Galanter (Eds.), *Handbook of mathematical psychology.* Vol. 2. New York: Wiley, 1963.

BEVER, T. G., FODOR, J. A., & GARRETT, M. A formal limitation of associationism. In T. R. Dixon & D. L. Horton (Eds.), *Verbal behavior and general behavior theory.* Englewood Cliffs, N.J.: Prentice-Hall, 1968.

BOWER, G. H. A multicomponent theory of the memory trace. In K. W. Spence & J. T. Spence (Eds.), *The psychology of learning and motivation: Advances in research and theory.* Vol. 1. New York: Academic Press, 1967.

CARNAP, R. *Philosophical foundations of physics.* New York: Basic Books, 1966.

CHOMSKY, N. *Syntactic structures.* The Hague: Mouton & Co., 1957.

————. Review of verbal behavior. *Language,* 1959, **35**, 26–58.

————. *Aspects of the theory of syntax.* Cambridge: M.I.T. Press, 1965.

COFER, C. N. Problems, issues, and implications. In T. R. Dixon & D. L. Horton (Eds.), *Verbal behavior and general behavior theory.* Englewood Cliffs, N.J.: Prentice-Hall, 1968.

CROTHERS, E., & SUPPES, P. *Experiments in second language learning.* New York: Academic Press, 1967.

EINSTEIN, A. On the method of theoretical physics. New York: Oxford University Press, 1933. (Reprinted in A. Einstein, *Ideas and opinions.* New York: Crown, 1954.)

ESTES, W. K., KOCH, S., MacCORQUODALE, K., MEEHL, P. E., MUELLER, C. G., SCHOENFELD, W. N., & VERPLANCK, W. S. *Modern learning theory.* New York: Appleton-Century-Crofts, 1954.

FELLER, W. *An introduction to probability theory and its applications.* New York: Wiley, 1950.

FEYERABEND, P. K. Explanation, reduction, and empiricism. In H. Feigl & G. Maxwell (Eds.), *Minnesota studies in the philosophy of science.* Vol. 3. *Scientific explanation, space and time.* Minneapolis: University of Minnesota Press, 1962.

FISHER, R. A. *The design of experiments.* London: Oliver and Boyd, 1935.

GARNER, W. R. *Uncertainty and structure as psychological concepts.* New York: Wiley, 1962.

GIBSON, E. J. A systematic application of the concepts of generalization and differentiation to verbal learning. *Psychological Review,* 1940, **47**, 196–229.

GUTHRIE, E. R. *The psychology of learning.* New York: Harper, 1952.

HABER, R. N. Perceptual processes and general cognitive activity. In J. F. Voss (Ed.), *Approaches to thought.* Columbus: Merrill, 1969.

HOLZ, W. C., & AZRIN, N. H. Conditioning human verbal behavior. In W. K. Honig (Ed.), *Operant behavior.* New York: Appleton-Century-Crofts, 1966.

HOVLAND, C. I., JANIS, I. L., & KELLEY, H. H. *Communication and persuasion.* New Haven: Yale University Press, 1953.

HULL, C. L. *Principles of behavior.* New York: Appleton-Century-Crofts, 1943.

JENKINS, J. J. Mediated associations: Paradigms and situations. In C. N. Cofer & B. S. Musgrave (Eds.), *Verbal behavior and learning.* New York: McGraw-Hill, 1963.

KEMENY, J. G., SNELL, J. L., & THOMPSON, G. L. *Introduction to finite mathematics*. New York: Prentice-Hall, 1957.

KENDLER, H. H. Some specific reactions to general S-R theory. In T. R. Dixon & D. L. Horton (Eds.), *Verbal behavior and general behavior theory*. Englewood Cliffs, N.J.: Prentice-Hall, 1968.

————, & GASSER, W. P. Variables in spatial learning. I. Number of reinforcements during training. *Journal of Comparative and Physiological Psychology*, 1948, 41, 178–187.

KUHN, T. S. *The structure of scientific revolutions*. Chicago: University of Chicago Press, 1962.

LACHMAN, R., & DOOLING, D. J. Connected discourse and random strings: Effects of number of inputs on recognition and recall. *Journal of Experimental Psychology*, 1968, 77, 517–522.

LORENZ, K. Z. *King Solomon's ring*. New York: Thomas Y. Crowell, 1952.

MANDLER, G. Verbal learning. In, *New directions in psychology*. Vol. 3. New York: Holt, 1967.

MEEHL, P. E. *Clinical versus statistical prediction*. Minneapolis: University of Minnesota Press, 1954.

MILLER G. A. Some psychological studies of grammar. *American Psychologist*, 1962, 17, 748–762.

————. Some preliminaries to psycholinguistics. *American Psychologist*, 1965, 20, 15–20.

MILLER, N. E., & DOLLARD, J. *Social learning and imitation*. New Haven: Yale University Press, 1941.

NEISSER, U. *Cognitive psychology*. New York: Appleton-Century-Crofts, 1967.

OSGOOD, C. E. *Method and theory in experimental psychology*. New York: Oxford University Press, 1953.

POLANYI, M. *Personal knowledge*. New York: Harper & Row, 1958.

POSTMAN, L., & STARK, K. The role of associative mediation in retroactive inhibition and facilitation. *Journal of Verbal Learnng and Verbal Behavior*, 1969, 8, 790–798.

REITMAN, W. R. *Cognition and thought*. New York: Wiley, 1965.

RESTLE, F. Discrimination of cues in mazes: A resolution of the "place-vs.-response" question. *Psychological Review*, 1957, 64, 217–228.

————. *Psychology of judgment and choice*. New York: Wiley, 1961.

SHANNON, C. E. A mathematical theory of communication. *Bell System Technical Journal*, 1948, 27, 379–423, 623–656.

SKINNER, B. F. *The behavior of organisms*. New York: Appleton-Century-Crofts, 1938.

————. Are theories of learning necessary? *Psychological Review*, 1950, 57, 193–216.

————. *Verbal behavior*. New York: Appleton-Century-Crofts, 1957.

————. A case history in scientific method. In S. Koch (Ed.), *Psychology: A study of a science*. Vol. 2. New York: McGraw-Hill, 1959.

SPENCE, K. W. The empirical basis and theoretical structure of psychology. *Philosophy of Science*, 1957, 24, 97–108.

SPIELBERGER, C. D., & DeNIKE, L. D. Descriptive behaviorism versus cognitive theory in verbal operant conditioning. *Psychological Review*, 1966, 73, 306–326.

STAATS, A. W., & STAATS, C. K. *Complex human behavior.* New York: Holt, Rinehart & Winston, 1963.

TOLMAN, E. C. *Purposive behavior in animals and men.* New York: Appleton-Century-Crofts, 1932.

————. The determiners of behavior at a choice point. *Psychological Review*, 1938, **45**, 1–41.

UNDERWOOD, B. J. Stimulus selection in verbal learning. In C. N. Cofer & B. S. Musgrave (Eds.), *Verbal behavior and learning.* New York: McGraw-Hill, 1963.

YOUNG, R. K. Serial learning. In T. R. Dixon & D. L. Horton (Eds.), *Verbal behavior and general behavior theory.* Englewood Cliffs, N.J.: Prentice-Hall, 1968.

11

THE NEED FOR RELATIVISM[1]

JEROME KAGAN

THE psychology of the first half of this century was absolutistic, outer directed, and intolerant of ambiguity. When a college student carries this unholy trio of traits he is called authoritarian, and such has been the temperament of the behavioral sciences. But the era of authoritarian psychology may be nearing its dotage, and the decades ahead may nurture a discipline that is relativistic, oriented to internal processes, and accepting of the idea that behavior is necessarily ambiguous.

Like her elder sisters, psychology began her dialogue with nature using a vocabulary of absolutes. Stimulus, response, rejection, affection, emotion, reward, and punishment were labels for classes of phenomena that were believed to have a fixed reality. We believed we could write a definition of these constructs that would fix them permanently and allow us to know them unequivocally at any time in any place.

1 Preparation of this paper was supported in part by research Grant MH-8792 from the National Institute of Mental Health, United States Public Health Service. This paper is an abridged version of a lecture presented at the Educational Testing Service, Princeton, New Jersey, January 1966.

Less than 75 years ago biology began to drift from the constraints of an absolute view of events and processes when she acknowledged that the fate of a small slice of ectodermal tissue depended on whether it was placed near the area of the eye or the toe. Acceptance of the simple notion that whether an object moves or not depends on where you are standing is a little over a half century old in a science that has 5 centuries of formalization. With physics as the referent in time, one might expect a relativistic attitude to influence psychology by the latter part of the twenty-third century. But philosophical upheavals in one science catalyze change in other disciplines and one can see signs of budding relativism in the intellectual foundations of the social sciences.

The basic theme of this paper turns on the need for more relativistic definitions of selected theoretical constructs. "Relativistic" refers to a definition in which context and the state of the individual are part of the defining statement. Relativism does not preclude the development of operational definitions, but makes that task more difficult. Nineteenth-century physics viewed mass as an absolute value; twentieth-century physics made the definition of mass relative to the speed of light. Similarly, some of psychology's popular constructs have to be defined in relation to the state and belief structure of the organism, rather than in terms of an invariant set of external events. Closely related to this need is the suggestion that some of the energy devoted to a search for absolute, stimulus characteristics of reinforcement be redirected to a search for the determinants of attention in the individual.

It is neither possible nor wise to assign responsibility to one person or event for major changes in conceptual posture, but Helson's recent book on adaptation-level theory (Helson, 1964), Schachter's (Schachter & Singer, 1962) hypothesis concerning the cognitive basis of affects, and Hernández-Peón's demonstration of the neurophysiological bases of selective attention (Hernández-Peón, Scherrer, & Jouvet, 1956) are contemporary stimulants for a relativistic view of psychological phenomena.

Three messages are implicit in the work of these men.

1. If a stimulus is to be regarded as an event to which a subject responds or is likely to respond then it is impossible to describe a stimulus without describing simultaneously the expectancy, and preparation of the organism for that stimulus. Effective stimuli must be distinct from the person's original adaptation level. Contrast and distinctiveness, which are relative, are part and parcel of the definition of a stimulus.

2. The failure of one individual to respond to an event that is an effective stimulus for a second individual is not always the result of central selection after all the information is in, but can be due to various forms of peripheral inhibition. Some stimuli within inches of the face do not ever reach the interpretive cortex and, therefore, do not exist psychologically.

3. Man reacts less to the objective quality of external stimuli than he does to categorizations of those stimuli.

These new generalizations strip the phrase "physical stimulus" of much of its power and certainty, and transfer the scepter of control—in man, at least—to cognitive interpretations. *Contrast, cognitively interpreted, becomes an important key to understanding the incentives for human behavior.* Since contrast depends so intimately on context and expectancy, it must be defined relativistically.

The issue of relativism can be discussed in many contexts. Many existing constructs are already defined in terms of contextual relations. The concept of authority only has meaning if there are fiefs to rule. The role of father has no meaning without a child. The concept of noun, verb, or adjective is defined by context—by the relation of the word to other constituents. We shall consider in some detail the ways in which a relativistic orientation touches two other issues in psychology: the learning of self-descriptive statements (the hoary idea of the self-concept), and even more fundamentally, some of the mechanisms that define the learning process.

The Concept of the Self

The development and establishment of a self-concept is often framed in absolute terms. The classic form of the statement assumes that direct social reinforcements and identification models have fixed, invariant effects on the child. Praise and love from valued caretakers are assumed to lead the child to develop positive self-evaluations; whereas, criticism and rejection presumably cause self-derogatory beliefs. The presumed cause-effect sequences imply that there is a something—a definable set of behaviors—that can be labeled social rejection, and that the essence of these rejecting acts leads to invariant changes in the self-concept of the child. Let us examine the concept of rejection under higher magnification.

The concept of rejection—peer or parental—has been biased toward an absolute definition. Witness the enormous degree of commonality in conceptualization of this concept by investigators who have studied a mother's behavior with her child (Baldwin, Kalhorn, & Breese, 1945; Becker, 1964; Kagan & Moss, 1962; Schaefer, 1959; Shaefer & Bayley, 1963; Sears, Maccoby, & Levin, 1957). These investigators typically decide that harsh physical punishment and absence of social contact or physical affection are the essential indexes of an attitude called maternal rejection. It would be close to impossible for an American rater to categorize a mother as high on both harsh beating of her child and on a loving attitude. A conventionally trained psychologist observing a mother who did not talk to her child for 5 hours would probably view the mother as rejecting. This may be a high form of provincialism. Alfred Baldwin[2] reports that in the rural areas of northern Norway, where homes are 5 to 10 miles apart, and the population constant for generations, one often sees maternal behaviors which an American observer would regard as pathognomonically rejecting in an American mother. The Norwegian mother sees her 4-year-old sitting in the doorway blocking the passage to the next room. She does not ask him to move, but bends down, silently picks him up and moves him away before she passes into the next room. Our middle-class observer would be tempted to view this indifference as a sign of dislike. However, most mothers in this Arctic outpost behave this way and the children do not behave the way rejected children should by our current theoretical propositions.

An uneducated Negro mother from North Carolina typically slaps her 4-year-old across the face when he does not come to the table on time. The intensity of the mother's act tempts our observer to conclude that the mother hates, or at best, does not like her child. However, during a half-hour conversation the mother says she loves her child and wants to guarantee that he does not grow up to be a bad boy or a delinquent. And she believes firmly that physical punishment is the most effective way to socialize him. Now her behavior seems to be issued in the service of affection rather than hate. Determination of whether a parent is rejecting or not cannot be answered by focusing primarily on the behaviors of the parents. Rejection is not a fixed, invariant quality of behavior qua behavior. Like pleasure, pain, or beauty, rejection is in the mind of the rejectee. It is a belief held by the child; not an action by a parent.

We must acknowledge, first, a discontinuity in the meaning of an acceptance-rejection dimension before drawing further implications. We must distinguish between the child prior to 30 or 36 months of age, before he symbolically evaluates the actions of others, and the child thereafter.

We require, first, a concept to deal with the child's belief of his value in the eyes of others. The child of 4 or 5 years is conceptually mature enough to have recognized that certain resources parents possess are difficult for the child to obtain. He views these resources as sacrifices and interprets their receipt as signs that the parents value him. The child constructs a tote board of the differential value of parental gifts— be they psychological or material. The value of the gift depends on its scarcity. A $10.00 toy from a busy executive father is not a valued resource; the same toy from a father out of work is much valued. The value depends on the child's personal weightings. This position would lead to solopsism were it not for the fact that most parents are essentially narcissistic and do not readily give the child long periods of uninter-

2 Personal communication.

rupted companionship. Thus, most children place high premium on this act. Similarly, parents are generally reluctant to proffer unusually expensive gifts to children, and this act acquires value for most youngsters. Finally, the child learns from the public media that physical affection means positive evaluation and he is persuaded to assign premium worth to this set of acts. There is, therefore, some uniformity across children in a culture in the evaluation of parental acts. But the anchor point lies within the child, not with the particular parental behaviors.

This definition of acceptance or rejection is not appropriate during the opening years. The 1-year-old does not place differential symbolic worth on varied parental acts, and their psychological significance derives from the overt responses they elicit and strengthen. A heavy dose of vocalization and smiling to an infant is traditionally regarded as indicative of maternal affection and acceptance. This bias exists because we have accepted the myth that "affection" is the essential nutrient that produces socially adjusted children, adolescents, and adults. The bias maintains itself because we observe a positive association between degree of parental smiling and laughing to the infant and prosocial behavior in the child during the early years. The responses of smiling, laughing, and approaching people are learned in the opening months of life on the basis of standard conditioning principles. This conclusion is supported by the work of Rheingold and Gewirtz (1959) and Brackbill (1958). However, phenotypically similar behaviors in a 10- or 20-year-old may have a different set of antecedents. The argument that different definitions of rejection-acceptance must be written for the pre- and post-symbolic child gains persuasive power from the fact that there are no data indicating that degree of prosocial behavior in the child is stable from 6 months to 16 years. Indeed, the longitudinal material from the Fels Research Institute study of behavior stability (Kagan & Moss, 1962) showed no evidence of any relation between joy or anxiety in the presence of adults during the first 2–3 years of life and phenotypically similar behaviors at 6, 12, or 24 years of age. The child behaviors that are presumed, by theory, to be the consequences of low or high parental rejection do not show stability from infancy through adolescence. This may be because the childhood responses, though phenotypically similar to the adult acts, may be acquired and maintained through different experiences at different periods.

It seems reasonable to suggest, therefore, that different theoretical words are necessary for the following three classes of phenomena: (a) an attitude on the part of the parent, (b) the quality and frequency of acts of parental care and social stimulation directed toward the infant, and (c) a child's assessment of his value in the eyes of another. All three classes are currently viewed as of the same cloth. The latter meaning of "rejection" (i.e., a belief held by a child) is obviously relativistic for it grows out of different experiences in different children.

Self-descriptive Labels

Let us probe further into the ideas surrounding the learning of self-evaluation statements, beyond the belief, "I am not valued." The notion of a self-concept has a long and spotted history and although it has masqueraded by many names in different theoretical costumes, its intrinsic meaning has changed only a little. A child presumably learns self-descriptive statements whose contents touch the salient attributes of the culture. The mechanisms classically invoked to explain how these attributes are learned have stressed the invariant effects of direct social reinforcement and identification. The girl who is told she is attractive, annoying, or inventive, comes to believe these appellations and to apply these qualifiers to herself. We have assumed that the laws governing the learning of self-descriptive labels resemble the learning of other verbal habits with frequency and contiguity of events being the shapers of the habit. Identification as a source of self-labels involves a different mechanism, but retains an absolutistic frame of reference. The child assumes that he shares attributes with particular models. If the model is viewed as subject to violent rages, the child concludes that he, too, shares this tendency.

Theory and data persuade us to retain some faith in these propositions. But relativistic factors also seem to sculpt the acquisition of self-descriptive labels, for the child evaluates himself on many psychological dimensions by inferring his rank order from a delineated reference group. The 10-year-old does not have absolute measuring rods to help him decide how bright, handsome, or likeable he is. He naturally and spontaneously uses his immediate peer group as the reference for these evaluations. An immediate corollary of this statement is that the child's evaluation is dependent upon the size and psychological quality of the reference group, and cannot be defined absolutely. Specifically, the larger the peer group, the less likely a child will conclude he is high in the rank order, the less likely he will decide he is unusually smart, handsome, or capable of leadership. Consider two boys with IQs of 130 and similar intellectual profiles. One lives in a small town, the other in a large city. It is likely that the former child will be the most competent in his peer group while the latter is likely to regard himself as fifth or sixth best. This difference in perceived rank order has obvious action consequences since we acknowledge that expectancies govern behavior. In sum, aspects of the self-descriptive process appear to develop in relativistic soil.

Learning and Attention

A second issue that touches relativistic definitions deals with a shift from external definitions of reinforcement—that is, reward or pleasure—

to definitions that are based more directly on internal processes involving the concept of attention. Failure to understand the nature of learning is one of the major intellectual frustrations for many psychologists. The query, "What is learning?" has the same profound ring as the question, "What is a gene?" had a decade ago. Our biological colleagues have recently had a major insight while psychology is still searching. The murky question, "What is learning?" usually reduces to an attempt to discover the laws relating stimuli, pain, and pleasure, on the one hand, with habit acquisition and performance, on the other. Pain, pleasure, and reinforcement, are usually defined in terms of events that are external to the organism and have an invariant flavor. Miller (1951) suggested that reinforcement was isomorphic with stimulus reduction; Leuba (1955) argued for an optimal level of stimulation, but both implied that there was a level that could be specified and measured. We should like to argue first that sources of pleasure and, therefore of reinforcement, are often relative, and second, that the essence of learning is more dependent on attentional involvement by the learner than on specific qualities of particular external events.

The joint ideas that man is a pleasure seeker and that one can designate specific forms of stimulation as sources of pleasure are central postulates in every man's theory of behavior. Yet we find confusion when we seek a definition of pleasure. The fact that man begins life with a small core set of capacities for experience that he wishes to repeat cannot be disputed. This is a pragmatic view of pleasure and we can add a dash of phenomenology to bolster the intuitive validity of this point of view. A sweet taste and a light touch in selected places are usually pleasant. Recently, we have added an important new source of pleasure. It is better to say we have rediscovered a source of pleasure, for Herbert Spencer was a nineteenth-century progenitor of the idea that *change in stimulation* is a source of pleasure for rats, cats, monkeys, or men. But, change is short-lived, quickly digested, and transformed to monotony. Popping up in front of an infant and saying peek-a-boo is pleasant for a 3-month-old infant for about 15 minutes, for a 10-month-old infant for 3 minutes and for a 30-month-old child, a few seconds. This pleasant experience, like most events that elicit their repetition a few times before dying, is usually conceptualized as a change in stimulation. The source of the pleasure is sought in the environment. Why should change in external stimulation be pleasant? The understanding of pleasure and reinforcement in man is difficult enough without having to worry about infrahuman considerations. Let us restrict the argument to the human. The human is a cognitive creature who is attempting to put structure or create schema for incoming stimulation. A schema is a representation of an external pattern; much as an artist's illustration is a representation of an event. A schema for a visual pattern is a partial and somewhat dis-

torted version of what the photograph would be. Consider the usefulness of the following hypothesis:

The creation of a schema for an event is one major source of pleasure.
When one can predict an event perfectly, the schema is formed. As long
as prediction is not perfect the schema is not yet formed. The peek-a-boo
game works for 15 minutes with a 12-week-old for it takes him that long
to be able to predict the event—the "peek-a-boo." Charlesworth (1965)
has demonstrated the reinforcing value of "uncertainty" in an experiment
in which the peek-a-boo face appeared either in the same locus every
trial, alternated between two loci, or appeared randomly in one of two
loci. The children persisted in searching for the face for a much longer
time under the random condition than under the other two conditions.
The random presentation was reinforcing for a longer period of time,
not because it possessed a more optimum level of external stimulation
than the other reinforcement schedules, but because it took longer for
the child to create a schema for the random presentation and the process
of creating a schema is a source of pleasure.

Consider another sign of pleasure besides persistence in issuing a particular response. Display of a smile or laugh is a good index of pleasure.
Indeed, Tomkins' (1962) scheme for affect demands that pleasure be
experienced if these responses appear. Consider two studies that bear on
the relation between pleasure and the creation of schema. In our laboratory during the last 2 years, we have seen the same infants at 4, 8, and 13
months of age and have shown them a variety of visual patterns representative of human faces and human forms. In one episode, the 4-month-
old infants are shown achromatic slides of a photograph of a regular
male face, a schematic outline of a male face, and two disarranged, disordered faces. The frequency of occurrence of smiling to the photograph
of the regular face is over *twice* the frequency observed to the regular
schematic face—although looking time is identical—and over *four times*
the frequency shown to the disordered faces. In another, more realistic
episode, the 4-month-old infants see a regular, flesh-colored sculptured
face in three dimensions and a distorted version of that face in which
the eyes, nose, and mouth are rearranged. At 4 months of age the occurrence of smiling to the regular face is over three times the frequency
displayed to the distorted version, but looking time is identical. There
are two interpretations of this difference (Kagan, Henker, Hen-Tov,
Levine, & Lewis, 1966). One explanation argues that the mother's face
has become a secondary reward; the regular face stands for pleasure
because it has been associated with care and affection from the mother.
As a result, it elicits more smiles. An alternative interpretation is that
the smile response has become conditioned to the human face via reciprocal contact between mother and infant. A third interpretation, not
necessarily exclusive of these, is that the smile can be elicited when the

infant matches stimulus to schema—when he has an "aha" reaction; when he makes a cognitive discovery. The 4-month-old infant is cognitively close to establishing a relatively firm schema of a human face. When a regular representation of a face is presented to him there is a short period during which the stimulus is assimilated to the schema and then after several seconds, a smile may occur. The smile is released following the perceptual recognition of the face, and reflects the assimilation of the stimulus to the infant's schema—a small, but significant act of creation. This hypothesis is supported by the fact that the typical latency between the onset of looking at the regular face (in the 4-month-old) and the onset of smiling is about 3 to 5 seconds. The smile usually does not occur immediately but only after the infant has studied the stimulus. If one sees this phenomenon live, it is difficult to avoid the conclusion that the smile is released following an act of perceptual recognition.

Additional data on these and other children at 8 months of age support this idea. At 8 months, frequency of smiling to both the regular and distorted faces is *reduced dramatically*, indicating that smiling does not covary with the reward value of the face. The face presumably has acquired more reward value by 8 months than it had at 4 months. However, the face is now a much firmer schema and recognition of it is immediate. There is no effortful act of recognition necessary for most infants. As a result, smiling is less likely to occur. Although smiling is much less frequent at 8 than 4 months to all faces, the frequency of smiling to the distorted face now *equals* the frequency displayed to the regular face. We interpret this to mean that the distorted face is sufficiently similar to the child's schema of a regular face that it can be recognized as such.

The pattern of occurrence of cardiac deceleration to the regular and distorted three-dimensional faces furnishes the strongest support for this argument. A cardiac deceleration of about 8 to 10 beats often accompanies attention to selected incoming visual stimuli in adults, school-age children, and infants. Moreover, the deceleration tends to be maximal when the stimuli are not overly familiar or completely novel, but are of intermediate familiarity. One hypothesis maintains that a large deceleration is most likely to occur when an act of perceptual recognition occurs, when the organism has a cognitive surprise. Let us assume that there is one trial for which this type of reaction occurs with maximal magnitude. If one examines the one stimulus presentation (out of a total of 16 trials) that produces the largest cardiac deceleration, a lawful change occurs between 4 and 8 months of age. At 4 months of age more of the infants showed their largest deceleration to the regular face (45% of the group: $n = 52$) than to the scrambled (34%), no eyes (11%), or blank faces (10%). At 8 months, the majority of the infants ($n = 52$) showed their largest deceleration to the scrambled face (50% to scrambled versus

21% to regular face). This difference is interpreted to mean that the scrambled face now assumes a similar position on the assimilation continuum that the regular face did 16 weeks earlier.

At 13 months of age these infants are shown six three-dimensional representations of a male human form and a free form matched for area, coloration, and texture with the human form. The stimuli include a faithful representation of a regular man, that same man with his head placed between his legs, the same man with all limbs and head collaged in an unusual and scrambled pattern, the man's body with a mule's head, and the mule's head on the man's body, the man's body with three identical heads, and a free form. The distribution of smiles to these stimuli is leptokurtic, with over 70% of all the smiles occurring to the animal head on the human body and the three-headed man, forms that were moderate transformations of the regular man, and stimuli that required active assimilation. The free form and the scrambled man rarely elicited smiles from these infants. These stimuli are too difficult to assimilate to the schema of a human form possessed by a 13-month-old infant. It is interesting to note that the regular human form sometimes elicited the verbal response "daddy" or a hand waving from the child. These instrumental social reactions typically did not occur to the transformations. The occurrence of cardiac deceleration to these patterns agrees with this hypothesis. At 13 months of age, the man with his head between his legs, the man with the animal head, or the three-headed man, each elicited the largest cardiac decelerations more frequently than the regular man, the scrambled man, or the free form ($p < .05$ for each comparison). Thus, large cardiac decelerations and smiles were most likely to occur to stimuli that seemed to require tiny, quiet cognitive discoveries—miniaturized versions of Archimedes' "Eureka."

It appears that the act of matching stimulus to schema when the match is close but not yet perfect is a dynamic event. Stimuli that deviate a critical amount from the child's schema for a pattern are capable of eliciting an active process of recognition, and this process behaves as if it were a source of pleasure. Stimuli that are easily assimilable or too difficult to assimilate do not elicit these reactions.

A recent study by Edward Zigler[3] adds important support to the notion that the smile indicates the pleasure of an assimilation. Children in Grades 2, 3, 4, and 5 looked at cartoons that required little or no reading. The children were asked to explain the cartoon while an observer coded the spontaneous occurrence of laughing and smiling while the children were studying the cartoons. It should come as no surprise that verbal comprehension of the cartoons increased in a linear fashion with age. But laughing and smiling increased through Grade 4 and then declined markedly among the fifth-grade children. The fifth graders understood the cartoons too well. There was no gap between stimulus and schema

3 Unpublished paper; personal communication.

and no smiling. Sixteen-week-old infants and 8-year-old children smile spontaneously at events that seem to have one thing in common—the event is a partial match to an existing schema and an active process of recognitory assimilation must occur.

The fact that a moderate amount of mismatch between event and schema is one source of pleasure demands the conclusion that it is not always possible to say that a specific event will always be a source of pleasure. The organism's state and structure must be in the equation. This conclusion parallels the current interest in complexity and information uncertainty. The psychologist with an information-theory prejudice classifies a stimulus as uncertain and often assumes that he does not have to be too concerned with the attributes of the viewer. This error of the absolute resembles the nineteenth-century error in physics and biology. This is not a titillating or pedantic, philosophical issue. Psychology rests on a motive-reinforcement foundation which regards pleasure and pain as pivotal ideas in the grand theory. These constructs have tended to generate absolute definitions. We have been obsessed with finding a fixed and invariant characterization of pleasure, pain, and reinforcement. Melzack & Wall (1965) point out that although the empirical data do not support the notion of a fixed place in the brain that mediates pain, many scientists resist shedding this comfortable idea. Olds' (1958, 1962) discovery of brain reinforcing areas has generated excitement because many of us want to believe that pleasure has a fixed and absolute locus. The suspicious element in this discovery of pleasure spots is that there is no habituation of responses maintained by electrical stimulation to hypothalamic or septal nuclei, and minimal resistance to extinction of habits acquired via this event. Yet, every source of pleasure known to phenomenal man does satiate—for awhile or forever—and habits that lead to pleasant events do persist for a while after the pleasure is gone. These observations are troubling and additional inquiry is necessary if we are to decide whether these cells are indeed the bed where pleasure lies.

We are convinced that contiguity alone does not always lead to learning. Something must ordinarily be added to contiguity in order to produce a new bond. Psychology has chosen to call this extra added mysterious something reinforcement, much like eighteenth-century chemists chose to label their unknown substance phlogiston. If one examines the variety of external events that go by the name of reinforcement it soon becomes clear that this word is infamously inexact. A shock to an animal's paw is a reinforcement, a verbal chastisement is a reinforcement, an examiner's smile is a reinforcement, a pellet of food is a reinforcement, and a sigh indicating tension reduction after watching a killer caught in a Hitchcock movie is a reinforcement. These events have little, if any, phenotypic similarity. What, then, do they have in common? For if they have nothing in common it is misleading to call them by the same name.

Learning theorists have acknowledged their failure to supply an independent a priori definition of reinforcement and the definition they use is purely pragmatic. A reinforcement is anything that helps learning. And so, we ask: What has to be added to contiguity in order to obtain learning? A good candidate for the missing ingredient is the phrase "attentional involvement." Let us consider again the events called reinforcements: a shock, food, a smile, each of these acts to attract the attention of the organism to some agent or object. They capture the organism's attention and maybe that is why they facilitate learning. Consider the idea that what makes an event reinforcing is the fact that it (a) elicits the organism's attention to the feedback from the response he has just made and to the mosaic of stimuli in the learning situation and (b) acts as an incentive for a subsequent response. The latter quality is what ties the word "reinforcement" to the concepts of motivation and need, but much learning occurs without the obvious presence of motives or needs. Ask any satiated adult to attend carefully and remember the bond syzygy-aardvark. It is likely that learning will occur in one trial. It is not unreasonable to argue that a critical component of events that have historically been called reinforcement is their ability to attract the organism's attention. They have been distinctive cues in a context; they have been events discrepant from the individual's adaptation level. If attention is acknowledged as critical in new mental acquisitions it is appropriate to ask if attention is also bedded in relativistic soil. The answer appears to be "Yes." The dramatic experiments of Hernández-Peón and his colleagues (1956) are persuasive in indicating that attention investment may not be distributed to many channels at once. One has to know the state of the organism. Knowledge of the organism's distribution of attention in a learning situation may clarify many controversial theoretical polemics that range from imprinting in chickens to emotion in college undergraduates. For example, comparative psychologists quarrel about which set of external conditions allows imprinting to occur with maximal effect. Some say the decoy should move; others argue that the young chick should move; still others urge that the decoy be brightly colored (e.g., Bateson, 1964a, 1964b; Hess, 1959; Klopfer, 1965; Thompson & Dubanoski, 1964). The quarrel centers around the use of phenotypically different observable conditions. Perhaps all these suggestions are valid. Moving the decoy, or active following by the infant chick, or a distinctively colored decoy all maximize the organism's level of attention to the decoy. The genotypic event may remain the same across all of these manipulations.

A similar interpretation can be imposed on Held's (1965) recent hypothesis concerning the development of space and pattern perception. Held controlled the visual experience of pairs of kittens. The only exposure to light was limited to a few hours a day when one kitten was placed in a gondola and moved around by an active, free kitten in an arena whose walls were painted in vertical stripes. After 30 hours of such experience each kitten was tested. The free kitten showed appropriate visual reactions. It blinked when an object approached; it put up its paws to avoid collision when carried near to a surface; it avoided the deep side of a visual cliff. The passive passenger kitten did not show these normal reactions. Why? Held, focusing on the obvious external variable of activity versus no activity, concludes that the sensory feedback accompanying movement is necessary to develop visual-motor control. This conclusion rests on the assumption that the passive kitten sitting in the gondola was attending to the stripes on the wall as intently as the free walking kitten. This assumption may be gratuitous. If the passive kitten were staring blankly—as many human infants do—then one would not expect these animals to develop normal perceptual structures. This interpretation may not be better, but it has a different flavor than the one suggested by Held.

A final example of the central role of attention is seen in Aronfreed's (1964, 1965) recent work on the learning of self-critical comments. Aronfreed states that the learning of a self-critical comment proceeds best if the child is first punished and then hears a social agent speak the self-critical statement. He interprets this result in drive reduction language. However, suppose one asks which sequence is most likely to maximize a child's attention to the adult's comment—Punish first and then speak to the child? Or speak first and then punish? The former sequence should be more effective. The punishment is a violation of what the child expects from a strange adult and recruits the child's attention to the adult. The child is primed to listen to the self-critical commendation and thus more likely to learn it.

DISTINCTIVENESS OF CUES

The above examples suggest that the organism's distribution of attention is a critical process that should guide our search for the bases of many diverse phenomena. One of the critical bases for recruitment of attention pivots on the idea of distinctiveness of the signal. Jakobson and Halle (1956) argue that the chronology of acquisition of phonemes proceeds according to a principle of distinctive elements. Distinctive elements capture the child's attention and give direction to the order of learning.

The importance of *relative distinctiveness of cues* finds an interesting illustration in the concept of affect. The concept of emotion has lived through three distinct eras in modern times. The pre-Jamesian assumed the sequence was: stimulus event—cognition—visceral response. James interchanged events two and three and said that the visceral afferent feedback occurred before the cognition. But Cannon quieted Jamesian ideas until Schachter's ingenious studies and catching explanations suggested that the individual experiences a puzzling set of visceral afferent sensations and integrates them cognitively. The language integration of visceral feelings, cognition, and context is an affect. This imaginative suggestion may be maximally valid for Western adults but perhaps minimally appropriate for children because of a developmental change in the relative distinctiveness of visceral cues.

Let us share a small set of assumptions before we proceed with the argument. Aside from pain and its surrogates, the major psychological elicitors of unpleasant visceral afferent sensations are violations of expectancies (uncertainty); anticipation of receiving or losing a desired goal; anticipation of seeing or losing a nurturant person; blocking of goal attainment; and anticipation of harm to the integrity of the body. Each of these event situations becomes conditioned to visceral afferent feedback early in life. These events—or conditioned stimuli—are salient and maximally distinctive for children and affect words are attached to the events, not primarily to the visceral afferent sensations. Thus, the 6-year-old says he is mad because mother did not let him watch television; he says he is sad because the cat died; he says he is happy because he just received a prized toy. Affect words are labels for a set of external events. With development, individuals—with the help of social institutions—learn to protect themselves against most of the unpleasant sources of visceral afferent feedback—against the apocalyptic horsemen of uncertainty, loss of nurturance, goal blocking, and bodily harm. Moreover, they erect defenses against recognizing these events. They defend against recognition that they are confused, rejected, unable to attain a goal, or afraid. Thus, when events occur that are, in fact, representations of these situations, the events are not salient or distinctive and are not labeled. However, the conditioned visceral afferent sensations do occur, as they always have in the past. In the adult, the visceral afferent sensations become more distinctive or salient; whereas, for the child, the external events were salient and distinctive. The adult provides us with the situation Schachter and his colleagues have described. The adult often has visceral afferent sensations but cannot decide why he has them or what they mean. So he scans and searches the immediate past and context and decides that he is happy, sad, alienated, uncommitted, or in love. The essence of this argument is that for the child the external event is more distinctive than the visceral afferent sensations and the affect word is applied to external events. In the adult, the visceral afferent sensations are relatively more distinctive and the affect words are more often applied to them.

The personality differences ascribed to children in different ordinal positions are the result, in part, of differences in relative distinctiveness of social agents. For the firstborn, the adult is the distinctive stimulus to whom to attend; for the second born the older sibling has distinctive value and competes for the attention of the younger child. Only children lie alone for long periods of uninterrupted play. A parent who enters the room and speaks to the infant is necessarily a distinctive stimulus. For a fifth born whose four older siblings continually poke, fuss, and vocalize into the crib, the caretaking adult is, of necessity, less distinctive and, as a result, less attention will be paid to the adult. The importance of distinctiveness with respect to adaptation level engages the heated controversy surrounding the role of stimulus enrichment with infants and young children from deprived milieux. The pouring on of visual, auditory, and tactile stimulation willy-nilly should be less effective than a single distinctive stimulus presented in a context of quiet so it will be discrepant from the infant's adaptation level. If one takes this hypothesis seriously, a palpable change in enrichment strategies is implied. The theme of this change involves a shifting from a concern with increasing absolute level of stimulation to focusing on distinctiveness of stimulation. Culturally disadvantaged children are not deprived of stimulation; they are deprived of distinctive stimulation.

The early learning of sex role standards and the dramatic concern of school children with sex differences and their own sex role identity becomes reasonable when one considers that the differences between the sexes are highly distinctive. Voice, size, posture, dress, and usual locus of behavior are distinctive attributes that focus the child's attention on them.

One of the reasons why the relation between tutor and learner is important is that some tutors elicit greater attention than others. They are more distinctive. Those of us who contend that learning will be facilitated if the child is identified with or wants to identify with a tutor believe that one of the bases for the facilitation is the greater attention that is directed at a model with whom the child wishes to identify. A recent experiment touches on this issue.

The hypothesis can be simply stated. An individual will attend more closely to an initial stranger with whom he feels he shares attributes than to a stranger with whom he feels he does not share attributes, other things equal. The former model is more distinctive, for a typical adult ordinarily feels he does not share basic personality traits with most of the strangers that he meets. The subjects in this study were 56 Radcliffe freshmen and sophomores preselected for the following pair of traits. One group, the academics, were rated by four judges—all roommates—as being intensely involved in studies much more than they were in dating, clubs, or social activities. The second group, the social types, were rated as being much more involved in dating and social activities than they were in courses or grades. No subject was admitted into the study unless all four judges agreed that she fit one of these groups.

Each subject was seen individually by a Radcliffe senior, and told that each was participating in a study of creativity. The subject was told that Radcliffe seniors had written poems and that two of the poets were selected by the Harvard faculty as being the best candidates. The faculty could not decide which girl was the more creative and the student was going to be asked to judge the creativity of each of two poems that the girls had written. The subjects were told that creativity is independent of IQ for bright people and they were told that since the faculty knew the personality traits of the girls, the student would be given that information also. The experimenter then described one of the poets as an academic grind and the other as a social activist. Each subject listened to two different girls recite two different poems on a tape. Order of presentation and voice of the reader were counterbalanced in an appropriate design. After the two poems were read the subject was asked for a verbatim recall of each poem, asked to judge its creativity, and finally, asked which girl she felt most similar to. Incidentally, over 95% of the subjects said they felt more similar to the model that they indeed matched in reality. Results supported the original hypothesis. Recall was best when a girl listened to a communicator with whom she shared personality traits. The academic subjects recalled more of the poem when it was read by the academic model than by the social model; whereas, the social subjects recalled more of the poem when it was read by the social model than the academic model. This study indicates that an individual will pay more attention to a model who possesses similar personality attributes, than to one who is not similar to the subject. Distinctiveness of tutor is enhanced by a perceived relation between learner and tutor.

Myths and superstitions are established around the kinds of experimental manipulations teachers or psychologists should perform in order to maximize the probability that learning will occur. When one focuses on the kind of manipulation—providing a model, giving a reinforcement, labeling the situation, punishing without delay—there is a strong push to establish superstitions about how behavioral change is produced. Recipes are written and adopted. If one believes, on the other hand, that a critical level of attention to incoming information is the essential variable, then one is free to mix up manipulations, to keep the recipe open, as long as one centers the subject's attention on the new material.

The most speculative prediction from this general argument is that behavioral therapy techniques will work for some symptoms—for about 20 years. A violation of an expectancy is a distinctive stimulus that attracts attention. The use of operant shaping techniques to alleviate phobias is a dramatic violation of an expectancy for both child and adult, and attention is magnetized and focussed on the therapeutic agent and his paraphernalia. As a result, learning is facilitated. But each day's use of this strategy may bring its demise closer. In time, a large segment of the populace will have adapted to this event; it will be a surprise no more and its attention getting and therapeutic value will be attenuated. Much of the power of psychoanalytic techniques began to wane when the therapist's secrets became public knowledge. If therapy is accomplished by teaching new responses, and if the learning of new responses is most likely to occur when attention to the teacher is maximal, it is safe to expect that we may need a new strategy of teaching patients new tricks by about 1984.

Let us weave the threads closer in an attempt at final closure. The psychology of the first half of this century was the product of a defensively sudden rupture from philosophy to natural science. The young discipline needed roots, and like a child, attached itself to an absolute description of nature, much as a 5-year-old clings to an absolute conception of morality. We now approach the latency years and can afford to relax and learn something from developments in our sister sciences. The message implicit in the recent work in psychology, biology, and physics contains a directive to abandon absolutism in selected theoretical areas. Conceptual ideas for mental processes must be invented, and this task demands a relativistic orientation. Learning is one of the central problems in psychology and understanding of the mechanisms of learning requires elucidation and measurement of the concept of attention. Existing data indicate that attention is under the control of distinctive stimuli and distinctiveness depends intimately on adaptation level of subject and context, and cannot be designated in absolute terms.

These comments are not to be regarded as a plea to return to undisciplined philosophical introspection. Psychology does possess some beginning clues as to how it might begin to measure elusive, relative concepts like "attention." Autonomic variables such as cardiac and respiratory rate appear to be useful indexes, and careful studies of subtle motor discharge patterns may provide initial operational bases for this construct.

Neurophysiologists have been conceptualizing their data in terms of attention distribution for several years, and they are uncovering some unusually provocative phenomena. For example, amplitude of evoked potentials from the association areas of the cortex are beginning to be regarded as a partial index of attention. Thompson and Shaw (1965) recorded evoked potentials from the association area of the cat's cortex—the middle suprasylvian gyrus—to a click, a light, or a shock to the forepaw. After they established base level response to each of these "standard" stimuli, the investigators presented these standard stimuli when the cat was active or when novel stimuli were introduced. The novel events were a rat in a bell jar, an air jet, or a growling sound. The results were unequivocal. Any one of these novel stimuli or activity by the cat produced reduced cortical evoked responses to the click, light, or shock. The authors suggest that the "amplitude of the evoked responses are inversely proportional to attention to a particular event [p. 338]." Psychology is beginning to develop promising strategies of measurement for the murky concept of attention and should begin to focus its theorizing and burgeoning measurement technology on variables having to do with the state of the organism, not just the quality of the external stimulus. The latter events can be currently objectified with greater elegance, but the former events seem to be of more significance. Mannheim once chastised the social sciences for seeming to be obsessed with studying what they could measure without error, rather than measuring what they thought to be important with the highest precision possible. It is threatening to abandon the security of the doctrine of absolutism of the stimulus event. Such a reorientation demands new measurement procedures, novel strategies of inquiry, and a greater tolerance for ambiguity. But let us direct our inquiry to where the pot of gold seems to shimmer and not fear to venture out from cozy laboratories where well-practiced habits have persuaded us to rationalize a faith in absolute monarchy.

REFERENCES

ARONFREED, J. The origin of self criticism. *Psychological Review*, 1964, **71**, 193–218.

———. Internalized behavioral suppression and the timing of social punishment. *Journal of Personality and Social Psychology*, 1965, **1**, 3–16.

BALDWIN, A. L., KALHORN, J., & BREESE, F. H. Patterns of parent behavior. *Psychological Monographs*, 1945, **58**(3, Whole No. 268).

BATESON, P. P. G. Changes in chicks' responses to novel moving objects over the sensitive period for imprinting. *Animal Behavior*, 1964, **12**, 479–489. (a)

———. Relation between conspicuousness of stimuli and their effectiveness in the imprinting situation. *Journal of Comparative and Physiological Psychology*, 1964, **58**, 407–411. (b)

BECKER, W. C. Consequences of different kinds of parental discipline. In M. L. Hoffman & L. W. Hoffman (Eds.), *Review of child development research*. Vol. 1. New York: Russell Sage Foundation, 1964. Pp. 169–208.

BRACKBILL, Y. Extinction of the smiling response in infants as a function of reinforcement schedule. *Child Development*, 1958, **29**, 115–124.

CHARLESWORTH, W. R. Persistence of orienting and attending behavior in young infants as a function of stimulus uncertainty. Paper read at Society for Research in Child Development, Minneapolis, March 1965.

HELD, R. Plasticity in sensory motor systems. *Scientific American*, 1965, **213**(5), 84–94.

HELSON, H. *Adaptation level theory: An experimental and systematic approach to behavior*. New York: Harper & Row, 1964.

HERNÁNDEZ-PEÓN, R., SCHERRER, H., & JOUVET, M. Modification of electrical activity in cochlear nucleus during attention in unanesthetized cats. *Science*, 1956, **123**, 331–332.

HESS, E. H. Two conditions limiting critical age for imprinting. *Journal of Comparative and Physiological Psychology*, 1959, **52**, 515–518.

JAKOBSON, R., & HALLE, M. *Fundamentals of language*. The Hague: Mouton, 1956.

KAGAN, J., HENKER, B. A., HEN-TOV, A., LEVINE, J., & LEWIS, M. Infants' differential reactions to familiar and distorted faces. *Child Development*, 1966, **37**, 519–532.

KAGAN, J., & MOSS, H. A. *Birth to maturity.* New York: Wiley, 1962.

KLOPFER, P. H. Imprinting: A reassessment. *Science,* 1965, 417, 302–303.

LEUBA, C. Toward some integration of learning theories: The concept of optimal stimulation. *Psychological Reports,* 1955, 1, 27–33.

MELZACK, R., & WALL, P. D. Pain mechanisms: A new theory. *Science,* 1965, 150, 971–979.

MILLER, N. E. Learnable drives and rewards. In S. S. Stevens (Ed.), *Handbook of experimental psychology.* New York: Wiley, 1951, 435–472.

OLDS, J. Self stimulation of the brain. *Science,* 1958, 127, 315–324.

————. Hypothalamic substrates of reward. *Physiological Review,* 1962, 42, 554–604.

RHEINGOLD, H., GEWIRTZ, J. L., & ROSS, H. Social conditioning of vocalizations in the infant. *Journal of Comparative and Physiological Psychology,* 1959, 52, 68–73.

SCHACHTER, S., & SINGER, J. E. Cognitive, social and physiological determinants of emotional states. *Psychological Review,* 1962, 69, 379–399.

SCHAEFER, E. S. A circumplex model for maternal behavior. *Journal of Abnormal and Social Psychology,* 1959, 59, 226–235.

SCHAEFER, E. S., & BAYLEY, N. Maternal behavior, child behavior and their intercorrelations from infancy through adolescence. *Monographs of the Society for Research in Child Development,* 1963, 28, No. 87.

SEARS, R. R., MACCOBY, E. E., & LEVIN, H. *Patterns of child rearing.* Row Peterson, 1957.

THOMPSON, R. F., & SHAW, J. A. Behavioral correlates of evoked activity recorded from association areas of the cerebral cortex. *Journal of Comparative and Physiological Psychology,* 1965, 60, 329–339.

THOMPSON, W. R., & DUBANOSKI, R. A. Imprinting and the law of effort. *Animal Behavior,* 1964, 12, 213–218.

TOMKINS, S. S. *Affect imagery consciousness.* Vol. 1. *The positive affects.* New York: Springer, 1962.

12

BEHAVIOR AND FACT

JAMES DEESE

MY purpose in presenting this paper is two-fold: First, I want to unburden myself of something of a crisis in my thinking about the uses of experimental psychology in the study of cognition, and, second, I want to

FROM J. Deese, Behavior and fact, *American Psychologist,* 1969, 24 (5), 515–522. Copyright 1969 by the American Psychological Association. Reprinted by permission.

talk about my current interests in research. Because I am assailed by severe doubts concerning the purposes and methods of experimental psychology, and because I am an experimental psychologist, such doubts reach crisis proportions.

The crisis and my current interests can be described together, for they are related. It was in pursuit of an answer to a particular question that I first became concerned about the purposes and functions of experimentation in psychological research. The question is: What happens when we understand something? How is a failure to understand different from understanding? This problem occurred to me in a particular context, but I soon became convinced that the concept of understanding is central to the analysis of memory, of meaning, and of a whole collection of other problems in cognitive psychology.

I shall begin by describing the nature of understanding as I view it. In order to do so, I shall use the term *fact* in the sense in which it is used in the title of this article. A fact is not necessarily some end product of formal psychological study. Rather, it is the result of any observation available to ordinary experience, and especially of those observations so universally and readily available that the special tools of formal scientific inquiry are not required for their discovery. Such a broad use of the term *fact* sometimes dismays experimental and other empirically minded psychologists, some of whom regard no fact as beyond the need for scientific investigation. Most of those psychologists have a firm faith in the philosophy of science developed in the early years of this century, a faith still represented in the official catechism of experimental psychology. My use is not intended to alarm those psychologists, but simply to dispense with the bone-wearying trivialities that encumber so much psychological research.

In this more general sense, the facts with which I am concerned focus on the nature of understanding and on the question of how we understand segments of the language. I do not mean to imply that there is some special capacity for understanding limited to language. In fact, I am prepared to defend the proposition that the metaphorical use of understanding in the phrases "understanding music" and "understanding art" is appropriate. However, most of my illustrations are drawn from language since my original concern with the matter developed from the study of semantics.

Certain linguistic segments—sentences, for example—can be interpreted by the use of other linguistic segments—other sentences. The term paraphrase is usually employed to describe such interpretation. Paraphrase, however, is only a particular result—one among many—of interpretation. The basic fact of paraphrase is that one individual can take a segment of language uttered by another individual and restate it in such a way that the hearer is pleased to accept the restatement as equivalent to the original. The familiarity of this fact should not blind us to its fundamental importance in linguistic studies. Of course, criticism, denial, questioning, and other reactions also depend upon interpretation. Paraphrase, however, occupies a particularly important role in linguistic theory. In the most general sense, linguistic interpretation depends upon the possibilities of equivalences between segments of the language, though its roots go deeper, as I hope to show.

Interpretation arises when there is understanding. Hence my interest in understanding and my view that it deserves status as a formal psychological concept. It need not be invented for the special case of interpretation, however. Understanding is a psychological rather than a linguistic concept, and it receives its main force from an introspectively discovered inward sense. There are two basic facts with which to begin: one is exemplified in the interpretation of linguistic segments, and the other is the existence of a state of understanding which reveals itself as an introspectively available process. To clarify that last point, then, understanding depends upon the availability of introspection. Each human being is capable of recognizing a state of understanding.

Thus, we say that we understand only when we mean to characterize a sense of how we feel about something. Since we are subject to external social controls, we generally assert the existence of understanding only when we are prepared to withstand at least some test of interpretation. Even so, sometimes we assert understanding only when we mean to be polite. Americans who have some commerce with Japan find very trying that nation's almost universal willingness to assert understanding in the interests of politeness. It is trying because understanding has a function, which is to signal the potential for interpretation. There is every reason to suppose that something like the deep structures and transformational operations of modern linguistic theory provide at least part of the ability responsible for interpretation. Thus, among other things, understanding reveals their availability in the service of a linguistic result of interpretation. There are nonlinguistic aspects to interpretation, such as imagery. However, the state of understanding itself does not imply that we operate upon each segment of a linguistic sequence so as to produce a series of ideas and images each of which, in some way, corresponds to a portion of that sequence. Clearly, many of the early commentators upon human thought took this point of view, and it has proven to be a sterile and inappropriate notion, whether embodied in a mentalistic or behavioristic theory. Understanding only signals the potential for appropriate imagery, linguistic operations, and other cognitive activity. The operations may not occur unless there is some challenge, either self-induced or external, to prompt them. In short, we may listen or read with no interpretation, but we rely on the vigil of understanding to signal the potential available in the tools of interpretation.

Understanding is a psychological concept that neither requires special psychological investigation to establish it nor generates any hypotheses for experimental test. The concept is required by certain evidence, but the evidence is of such a nature that psychological investigation of the matter would amount to the kind of gratuitous busy work that so often invokes scorn upon social scientists. Understanding is the inward sign of the potential for reacting appropriately to what we see or hear. The state of understanding is simply to be contrasted with similar situations when, in reaction to linguistic segments, it does not occur. Contrast the feeling of bafflement when we listen to someone whose English we cannot comprehend, or when we read something, the words of which we know but the totality of which we cannot grasp. In the latter case, we may attend to the words (and understand them as such) or we may allow our minds to wander. In either event, we are incapable of providing a reasonable interpretation of the sequence of sentences we hear or read.

The criteria for understanding are in the potential for an indefinite number of appropriate reactions, some linguistic and some not. Understanding does not imply universal agreement. The appropriate reaction may not be socially appropriate, or, from the point of view of society, we may think we understand when we do not. In such a case, I think it is reasonable to say that we actually do understand, but our understanding is not socially acceptable or consistent with external events. Sometimes there is no social agreement, and different interpretations may differ so widely as to be contradictory. Such is the case with nonreferential events, such as those in music and art. The important point, however, is that understanding *leads to no particular behavior*. Even when there is semantic agreement, the specific forms in which it occurs differ, and these may be of trivial importance. Thus, there is no way to link either understanding or interpretation with particular behavior. There is no way, then, to tie these concepts, in the traditional sense, to dependent variables or to particular measures of behavior. Even to tie the concept to something specific that still cannot be represented behaviorally—such as paraphrase—requires the introduction of an elaborate and sophisticated linguistic theory. Yet, I submit that the concept is central to the theory of human thought, and any attempt to eliminate or ignore it, in the interest of making psychology conform to the reputed canons of experimental inference, is worse than misguided. Such attempts are responsible for the sterility of much experimental study of cognition and for the fact that linguistic theorists surprised us when they produced a cognitive theory richer than most then available.

Psychology is the science of behavior only in a trivial sense. To say otherwise is like asserting that physics is the science of meter reading or that chemistry is a kind of elaborate cookery. And yet any concept without direct "behavioral implications" seems to have dubious status in the current market for psychological theory. Somehow the study of behavior at various levels and of various sorts has been confused with the whole of psychology. When we limit ourselves to the study of behavior, we make it difficult or even impossible for psychological theory. Our textbooks are filled with such barbarisms as "recognition behavior" or "thinking behavior." I used to say that we know so much more about human psychology than animal psychology because we can study ourselves directly and animals only indirectly. However, I have been corrected so often by didactic colleagues—who point out that we study animal behavior because it is simpler than human behavior—that I have stopped trying to make my point. But let me try once more. We have so much direct evidence as to the nature of our minds that we start with immeasurably more than does our colleague who genuinely and seriously tries to understand the mind of the dog or of the chimpanzee. That greater richness of information about human psychology requires us to use concepts which—without prejudice one way or the other—are not very useful to animal psychologists.

Even a more serious problem is that status of the independent variable and the experimental method generally in the study of thought. The heart of the experimental method lies in the ability to control some condition (the independent variable) upon which some other condition (the dependent variable) is said to be contingent. If the method is to be useful, the link of control over the independent variable must be simple and fairly direct. There should be no reasonable doubt that if the proper device is activated, the independent variable changes in a particular way —for example, when we move the optic wedge, the luminosity of the stimulus changes. It is equally important that the link between the independent and dependent variable be simple and direct. This aspect of experimentation is often forgotten, not only by psychologists, but by agricultural scientists and others who study problems in which there is no well-developed theoretical network for specifying the subtle and intricate links between independent and dependent variables. An indirect relation between independent and dependent variables must be supported by well-established and tested sets of intervening links, or the whole process of testing a theory becomes an exercise in futility. The traditional physical sciences, chemistry and physics, are preeminent in experimentation because of well-developed theory, not the other way around. No new series of experiments should be given the task of testing a very large and poorly specified series of intervening links, as were the learning-behavior theories of the 1940s and 1950s. The final absurdity of the postulate-test scorekeeping, exemplified in Hull's *A Behavior System* (1951) and elsewhere, has made most of us aware of this particular pitfall. However, we still find experimental psychologists performing experiments to test theories of this sort as a kind of magical rite. The tedium of these exercises is only relieved by the surprise value. Observations so seldom seem to be repeatable.

There are very few psychological variables that are linked together by a well-articulated theory, formal or informal, and most of them were discovered by the early experimentalists in the investigation of perception and the senses. In the study of the higher mental processes, despite nearly a century of investigation, the results have been little more than a long history of doubt, frustration, and trivial generalities. Despite the existence of an embarrassingly large number of experiments in which rote learning of some materials has been controlled and varied in time of exposure or trials, we still do not know whether there is some link between number of exposures and how well people learn (a condition we cannot even characterize adequately in behavioral terms, so we resort to the quagmire of concepts centering around response strength and associative strength). That the experimental psychology of rote learning has been unable to solve so simple and elementary a problem should lead us to question whether or not we are going about things in the right way. Certainly, almost anyone but an experimental psychologist would long ago have begun to entertain doubts.

This insistence upon doing experiments—the primary aim of which is not purely practical—in the absence of a well-developed network of links between independent and dependent variables has even infected the work derived from the fresh and important views supplied by generative theory in linguistics. To give people scrambled sentences and then find out how long it takes to disentangle them as a function of the structure of the sentences is to repeat all of the classical mistakes of the experimental psychology of the higher mental processes. First of all, it follows a familiar but dubious line of reasoning from structural complexity (measured, say, by sentence depth) through to solution time, reaction time, or some similar measure. The inductive leap assumes seldom-articulated principles of sequential rather than parallel processing of information and so many other things that they almost defy enumeration. Note that the dependent variable is not itself something of linguistic or direct cognitive significance, or even, in the usual case, some behavioral act. Rather it is simply how long it takes to do something (Miller & McKean, 1964—"average transformation time") or something as derived and unsupported by explicit reasoning as trials to learning (Miller & Isard, 1964). One gets the impression that these particular measures are chosen because we never really have thought of any good experimental methods for studying what is really interesting—the fact that people can do fantastically complicated operations upon sentences. We end up with the old tried and true measures that make nice graphs and upon which we can perform various model analyses of variances.

In short, we have been badly oversold on the classical experimental model as the means of studying such central aspects of human psychology as cognition. Too much evidence—obvious and available evidence—is ignored because it fails to conform to our prejudices about how empirical information arises. We have insisted upon the measurement of behavior to the extent that most of the things we observe in experiments have no relevance for the process of thinking, other than the empty observation that thinking, like most processes, takes a measurable period of time.

The problem is, I suspect, that the origins of a significant portion of cognitive events are simply unavailable for experimentation in the classical sense. It can be argued that the basic conditions of thinking are, at this stage, as remote for experimental study as interstellar space. That does not mean that we cannot apply the tools of science, only that we should consider whether the particular tools being used serve any genuinely useful purpose. Thinking does not occur as a reaction to a stimulus but as the result of activity, within an almost totally unmapped system, obeying instructions from within the system itself. The causes of ideas are beyond stimulus control in a direct and immediate way. They lie in a system, the complexity and richness of which we are only beginning to appreciate in a technical way (chiefly through the accomplishments of modern linguistic theory and the theory of automata).

The aspect of thinking with which I am concerned is the theory of meaning, specifically as it occurs in semantic studies. The psychological problem in semantic studies is to determine what happens when information, specifically information in the form of language, is interpreted. In the remainder of this paper I shall sketch some notions I have developed about the nature of interpretation, together with some of the implications that I think these notions have. I have presented the long, discursive foreword to these ideas because I want to explain the context in which these notions are presented. They are developed to describe and generate data not in the traditional sense but in the sense of giving prominence to the obvious observations of ordinary experience. I do not mean that one should abandon everything but the study of ordinary experience, but I do wish to give that which is so commonplace as almost to escape observation the importance it deserves by being common. Furthermore, I suggest that there is a significant role to be played by sophisticated and developed psychological techniques—such as those in multidimensional psychological scaling—for the amplification of ordinary experience, in solving certain puzzling problems that cannot be surmounted except by special methods.

Understanding signals to the individual that he is likely to be in a state in which, perhaps with a little effort, he can successfully interpret some information. So much I shall accept as fact. The function of understanding requires some more fanciful ideas, however. In fact, I am proposing a theory of the function of understanding. Understanding occurs when it is possible for an individual to conform some content (external information, semantic, or perceptual) to a conceptual category. Understanding, then, communicates that such a match is possible. The conceptual category provides the abstract structure of an interpretation. The interpretation itself consists of the content and the structure, although if it is to be put into some linguistic form (a paraphrase, etc.), it must engage the linguistic system (syntax). I am assuming that the linguistic system is independent and, in some well-specified sense, parallel to the device that produces the interpretation.

The fundamental character of interpretation, then, lies in the nature of the categories. I have named them categories after the model supplied by Kant in the *Critique of Pure Reason*. There is a parallel to the views of Kant on the nature of understanding. Understanding occurs when content is assimilated to categories. The categories are the possible or permissible modes of human thought, the forms into which we may cast our ideas. They can be defined either as structures or as relationships within the structures. I shall describe them as structures primarily, for these have more psychological reality. The relationships are often merely abstract ways of putting what is in the structure, and while these relationships may often be embedded in the linguistic forms that express the structure, they do so only in a kind of derived way. The primordial thought that gives rise to a linguistic interpretation is not itself linguistic; however, because language is our principal means of communication, it is almost impossible to express the nature of the structures without language. Almost but not quite impossible, for diagrams and other devices of deep, but generally neglected, cognitive significance are fundamentally nonlinguistic.

The fundamental categories of human thought are sought by beginning with a basic fact. Some cognitive operations are easier than others. That fact is so obvious as not to require special empirical demonstration, though the psychology of individual differences makes a contribution by describing, in reasonably exact if not always relevant ways, the precise order of difficulty. This contribution produces a host of subsidiary facts of considerable importance when examined in detail. Let me mention a few of these in this brief discussion.

It is generally more difficult for untutored people of moderate intelligence to solve logical problems when these are presented in abstract form rather than as concrete proposals about things and events. The tutored can solve problems by the application of some mechanical algorithm or computational device (as in doing exercises upon truth tables). The actual facts are complicated—for example, it is easier to mislead people when the problems are stated in concrete form. The errors of reasoning when faced with abstract problems, however, show that people of ordinary intelligence (college students of another and perhaps more selected generation) sometimes cannot comprehend problems when they are abstractly stated, although these same people can understand the same problems in a concrete form. We are familiar with Venn diagrams as aids to solution of problems in syllogistic reasoning. Resort to Venn diagrams, while providing an equivalence of sorts to the abstract problems, reveals a fundamentally different process at work, one that is much more general psychologically. There is a parallel between the more general psychological process and the logical one, but inevitably, because the two systems are in no sense equivalent, the psychological process must lead to error in solution, though the error is more likely to be systematic than random. In short, the human mind is a poor logical computer, perhaps as poor a logical computer as it is an arithmetic one. Of course, the human mind, coupled with external devices, such as pencil and paper, can perform remarkable logical operations.

What then are the categorical structures? I shall list some—but not all—examples. It would be very difficult to present a neat and tidy list, because the psychological evidence is not sufficiently precise. I should like to believe that the more important, in the functional sense, of these categories are close to and derived from underlying perceptual relations. And I do not mean simply that they are elements, among other things, that can appear in imagery; I mean that the relationships in thought are fundamentally perceptual in derivation. Thus it is possible that the relationship A implies B is not a fundamental operation, though the relationship A is inside of B, or B includes A is. Where the structures depart very far from the basic relations of sense perception, they often contain elements derived from more or less universal human relations— those of dominance, affection, etc. The characterization of the categories, which follows, may be regarded as tentative and exemplary.

Perhaps the most fundamental and general structure is that of grouping. Grouping occurs whenever objects, events, and ideas are perceived as containing something in common. The word something is used deliberately here to point to the fact that as often as not the ability to perceive grouping does not lead to the correct identification of the underlying features which account for or justify the grouping. The ability to identify attributes is, of course, evidence of another fundamental operation in interpretation, that is, the operation of contrast or antinomy. I have commented on this operation at length elsewhere; it will not be described here. Attribution and groupings are linked logically and less obviously psychologically. I say less obviously for, in the operation of the human mind, there is not always the kind of relation between these operations that there should be. There is, in fact, some slippage. The literature on concept formation as well as some recent experiments on changes in meaning (Deese, 1967) provide examples of the lack of correspondence between these operations. People try to justify various operations of grouping by inventing attributes that logically cannot do the job.

Grouping itself is revealed by a number of specific operations, perhaps the most important of which center around various judgments of similarity. Similarity, like attribution, is endlessly productive. Given some appropriate task or contest, anything may be said to be similar to anything else. The judgment, of course, can be justified by the invention of attributes, since attributes are, as well, endlessly invented. The productive nature of grouping and attribution is another fundamental fact about human thinking that is insufficiently explored by psychologists. In a recent dissertation, Johnson (1968) has begun the study of the way in which people solve analogies (similar to the Miller analogies) when the concepts entering into the analogies have been chosen at random. Johnson's random analogies are always solvable and justifiable by the invention of attributes, though there are large individual differences in the ability of people to perform the task with skill and imagination.

Another fundamental structure is that of classification. Classificatory structures are exemplified in Roget's semantic system used in the *Thesaurus* and in the Linnean system of biological classification. Abstractly, classificatory structures can be represented by branching trees in which each node represents some attribute that characterizes all concepts entered in the tree below that node. In English, the names attached to the nodes in such trees (and not all nodes will be in the lexicon, of course) indicate attributes and not the states of attributes. Thus, different aspects of attribution seem to be linked to grouping and classification. This, of course, reflects the different functions that grouping and classification have. The same content will be treated now by grouping and then by classification. If you ask students for definitions of ordinary words, the most characteristic reply mixes classification (by naming the superordinate) and grouping (by naming the state of an attribute). Thus, an orange is an edible fruit. However, for various purposes, now one and then another structure may be called upon.

The operation of classification is subordination and superordination. There is reason to believe that unaided human cognition deals only with the operation itself. That is to say, unaided human thought limits itself to considering a single node at a time. Ordinary folk think neither of the words employed by Roget to mark his concept trees as being in a classificatory structure, nor do they think of animals as being arranged in a Linnean structure except in local instances. The Linnean system, in order to be used by a human being, must be committed to memory by rote; even then only constant use will keep it viable. As a schema in thought, the picture of an abstract branching tree is generally a two-dimensional map, and that derives from another category.

Animals as well as plants are considered mostly as being in group structures. Motivated by the anthropological work on folk taxonomies, Henley (1968) has applied the methods of multidimensional scaling to animal names in English. Her results show that the most potent attributes for grouping are size and ferocity. Thus, big animals such as the elephant, horse, and camel are contrasted with small animals like the mouse, rat, and chipmunk. Fierce animals like the lion and the tiger (also large) are contrasted with tame animals like the (small) rabbit and the (big) cow. It is not that animals cannot be thought of in other ways, it is that judgments of similarity characteristically lead to this structure (more or less independently of the methods used to determine the structure). Furthermore, there is reason to believe that this general structure may have some cross-cultural validity (animal totems aside).

Any content, with some obvious exceptions, may be adjusted to any category. There is a kind of preference, based, I suppose, on the general shape of the content, for a given category paired with a given content. The preference for grouping animals becomes obvious after you free yourself from the learned Linnean system. Think of, in addition to size and ferocity, friendly animals versus unfriendly animals, your tribe's totem versus the neighboring tribe's totem. All of these are cross-classificatory and cannot be fitted onto a simple branching tree. The two-dimensional map for the grouping structure is not the tree but the feature table.

Groupings and classification have been mentioned first (with the resulting attribute structure) because they come closer than any other operations to being fundamentally intellectual rather than experiential. Those structures that most obviously rely on perception are various spatial structures. Spatial structures can be in one, two, or three dimensions. One-dimensional spatial representations are, of course, identical to scales and orders. There is some question as to whether one should regard one-dimensional scales as spatial. Introspection seems to deny a universal spatial representation to scales, but the work of my colleague DeSoto (1961) seems to point, in so many ways, to a spatial model in scaling that I shall subsume scaling under space. Given the spatiality, perhaps we should not use the term scale, for the scales of human thought seem to have a directional property (albeit one that is not directly a reflection of content). We order things low to high, left to right, and outward from the body. Perhaps this primitive spatiality, evident in our thinking about scales and orders, is as good a reason as any for subsuming scaling under spatial models.

Maps and graphs are familiar two-dimensional representations of real two-dimensional or, with projection or some arbitrary coding, three-dimensional experience. Ordinary maps are more abstract than reputed. Surprisingly, they are readily interpreted even by the untutored. Furthermore, maps of a high degree of abstraction are a cultural universal. Some primitive maps were so abstract, they were not recognized by Europeans for what they were. The Marshall Islanders, for example, possessed a complicated lattice system for portraying the location of islands in the sea together with the prevailing direction of wind and waves. Furthermore, things not inherently spatial (such as the Linnean classification) can be represented as a map or graph. Textbooks in physics and engineering uniformly use graphical representation for relations more efficiently presented as equations. The graph is possible to interpret intellectually, the equation can only be interpreted indirectly. Models or two-dimensional projections of models are universally used to represent abstract physical concepts to beginning students and nonphysicists.

I shall not sketch any additional candidates for fundamental cognitive structures. I think there are some. I have not settled in my own mind the cognitive status of a large number of possible operations. Certain operations, such as that of implication or equality (in the mathematical sense), may have no single cognitive operation associated with them. They require no interpretation other than the system of which they are a part and which, in contrast to the structures described, must be learned laboriously. I think they do not represent fundamental human intellectual categories, but I am not sure. We need to explore some of the basic facts about how these operations are used by people.

Certain other operations seem to be extensions of social relations. For example, the concept of ownership permeates language and thought. Such a device as the genitive of Indo-European languages seems to be a result of a cognitive structure, one based upon human social structure, fossilized in the grammar of language. Such a relation as ownership seems to have no physical and thus no spatial representation. Other relations, fossilized in the grammars of languages, do have possible spatial representations (most prepositions do, for example), and to the extent that they require any interpretation (meaning in the ordinary sense) other than those given by their strictly grammatical relations, they can be interpreted spatially. There is a device, called Language Lotto, designed to teach children grammatical concepts by pictures. The pictorial devices for prepositions are quite easy and obvious, but those for conjunctions, etc., are not. Perhaps these have no simple interpretation, other than their grammatical ones, in contrast to the prepositions.

Finally, other languages may reveal other structures. The list presented here is not very different from that derived by Casagrande and Hale (1967) from a semantic study of Papago—an American Indian language —but it does differ in detail. My real point, however, is that there are fundamental psychological issues at stake, issues that are suggested by readily available facts, facts that have scarcely entered into ordinary cognitive psychology, but that are far more important and fundamental than those derived from most experimentation. In fact, experimenting with thought, in the technical sense, must remain a relatively minor contribution to psychology. Experimenting, in the simple sense of making observations, is the source of much richer information. Determining how people define words, solve puzzles, and image is more closer to traditional psychometric observation than to the formal experiment.

Behavior as the goal in the study of thought is wrong, and the characteristic emphasis of the psychological laboratory on the measurable response and the controlling independent variable is responsible for the sterility of the study of thought. The really useful devices in the study of thought are often things that have evolved outside of traditional experimental psychology, in, for example, psychometrics and multidimensional scaling. The poverty of theory that has developed from experimenting is revealed, I think, by the inability of a generation of psychological thought about thought to stand up to the trenchant criticisms of the linguists. The model of experimenting taken from the physical sciences is useful as an aid in psychological research, but I have reached the conclusion that it no longer belongs in the center of psychology.

REFERENCES

CASAGRANDE, J. B., & HALE, K. L. Semantic relationships in Papago folk-definitions. In D. H. Hymes & W. E. Bittle (Eds.), *Studies in southwestern ethnolinguistics*. The Hague: Mouton and Co., 1967.

DEESE, J. Meaning and change of meaning. *American Psychologist*, 1967, **22**, 641–651.

DeSOTO, C. B. The predilection for single orderings. *Journal of Abnormal and Social Psychology*, 1961, **62**, 16–23.

HENLEY, N. E. A psychological study of the semantics of animal terms. Unpublished doctoral dissertation, The Johns Hopkins University, 1968. (*Journal of Verbal Learning and Verbal Behavior*, in press.)

HULL, C. L. *A behavior system*. New Haven: Yale University Press, 1951.

JOHNSON, M. G. The distributional aspects of meaning interaction in a grammatical context. Unpublished doctoral dissertation, The Johns Hopkins University, 1968.

MILLER, G. A., & ISARD, S. Free recall of self-embedded English sentences. *Information and Control*, 1964, **7**, 292–303.

MILLER, G. A., & McKEAN, K. A chronometric study of some relations between sentences. *Quarterly Journal of Experimental Psychology*, 1964, **7**, 297–308.

PHILOSOPHICAL PERSPECTIVES

THIS section is opened by Feigl, who presents both a defense of the orthodox or classical view of theories and some indications of the kinds of criticism that this view has been receiving.

In the next selection Feyerabend proposes the relaxation, if not the relinquishment, of certain generally accepted specifications concerning theory. He argues for as much freedom—"anarchy"—as possible in the development of scientific theories.

Wagoner and Goodson then introduce the ancient but still alive and kicking "mind–body problem." Their short conversation reflects some of the more common pro and con arguments on this problem.

A more extended examination of mind–body issues is presented in the form of a debate between philosopher Brand Blanshard and behaviorist B. F. Skinner. This debate is reminiscent of the much earlier debate on behaviorism by William McDougall and John B. Watson.

In the final selection of the section Horgan presents a thoughtful philosophical analysis of the mind–body problem as it relates to empirical evidence and so-called bridge laws. He suggests how philosophical factors can make a contribution when empirical differentiations are not feasible.

13

DEFENSE OF ORTHODOXY

HERBERT FEIGL

THE purpose of the following remarks is to present in outline some of the more important features of scientific theories. I shall discuss the "standard" or "orthodox" view, mainly in order to set up a target for criticisms, some of which I shall briefly sketch by way of anticipation. The standard account of the structure of scientific theories was given quite explicitly by Norman R. Campbell (7), as well as independently in a little-known article by R. Carnap (12). A large part of the volumi-

FROM H. Feigl, The "orthodox" view of theories: Remarks in defense as well as critique, in M. Radner and S. Winokur (Eds.), *Minnesota Studies in the Philosophy of Science*, Vol. 4 (Minneapolis: University of Minnesota Press, 1970). Pages 3–16. Reprinted by permission of the author and the University of Minnesota Press.

nous literature in the philosophy of science of the logical empiricists and related thinkers contains, though with a great many variations, developments, modifications, and terminological diversities, essentially similar analyses of the logical structure and the empirical foundations of the theories of physics, biology, psychology, and some of the social sciences. Anticipating to some extent Campbell and Carnap, Moritz Schlick, in his epoch-making *Allgemeine Erkenntnislehre* (38), championed the doctrine of "implicit definition." In this he was influenced by David Hilbert's axiomatization of geometry, as well as by Henri Poincaré's and Albert Einstein's conceptions of theoretical physics and the role of geometry in physics. These matters were then developed more fully and precisely in the work of H. Reichenbach, R. Carnap, C. G. Hempel, R. B. Braithwaite, E. Nagel, and many other logicians and methodologists of science.

In order to understand the aim of this important approach in the philosophy of science it is essential to distinguish it from historical, sociological, or psychological studies of scientific theories. Since a good deal of regrettable misunderstanding has occurred about this, I shall try to defend the legitimacy and the fruitfulness of the distinction before I discuss what, even in my opinion, are the more problematic points in the "orthodox" logico-analytic account.

It was Hans Reichenbach (36) who coined the labels for the important distinction between "analyses in the context of discovery" and "analyses in the context of justification." Even if this widely used terminology is perhaps not the most felicitous, its intent is quite clear: It is one thing to retrace the historical origins, the psychological genesis and development, the social-political-economic conditions for the acceptance or rejection of scientific theories; and it is quite another thing to provide a logical reconstruction of the conceptual structures and of the testing of scientific theories.

I confess I am dismayed by the amount of—it seems almost deliberate —misunderstanding and opposition to which this distinction has been subjected in recent years. The distinction and, along with it, the related idea of a rational reconstruction are quite simple, and are as old as Aristotle and Euclid. In Aristotle's account of deductive logic, mainly in his syllogistics, we have an early attempt to make explicit the rules of validity of necessary inference. For this purpose it was indispensable for Aristotle to disregard psychological factors such as plausibility and to formulate explicitly some of the forms of the propositions involved in deductive reasoning. This also required transforming the locutions of ordinary language into standard formal expressions. For an extremely simple example, remember that "Only adults are admitted" has to be rendered as "All those admitted are adults." Only after the standard forms have replaced the expressions of common discourse can the validity of deductive inferences be checked "automatically," e.g., nowadays by electronic computers.

Furthermore, Euclid already had a fairly clear notion of the difference between purely logical or "formal" truths and extralogical truths. This is explicit in his distinction between the axioms and the postulates of geometry. From our modern point of view it is still imperative to distinguish between the correctness (validity) of a derivation, be it in the proof of a theorem in pure mathematics or a corresponding proof in applied mathematics (such as in theoretical physics), and the empirical adequacy (confirmation or corroboration) of a scientific theory. In fairly close accordance with the paradigm of Euclid's geometry, theories in the factual sciences have for a long time been viewed as hypothetico-deductive systems. That is to say that theories are sets of assumptions, containing "primitive," i.e., undefined terms. The most important of these assumptions are lawlike, i.e., universal, propositions in their logical form. And, just as in geometry, definitions are needed in order to derive theorems of a more specific character. These definitions may be of a variety of kinds: explicit, contextual, coordinative, etc. They are indispensable for the derivation of empirical laws from the more general and usually more abstract assumptions (postulates). The "primitive" concepts serve as the definientia of the "derived" ones. The primitives themselves remain undefined (by explicit definition). They may be regarded as only "implicitly" defined by the total set of axioms (postulates). But it is important to realize that implicit definition thus understood is of a purely syntactical character. Concepts thus defined are devoid of empirical content. One may well hesitate to speak of "concepts" here, since strictly speaking even "logical" meaning as understood by Frege and Russell is absent. Any postulate system if taken as (erstwhile) *empirically uninterpreted* merely establishes a network of symbols. The symbols are to be manipulated according to preassigned formation and transformation rules and their "meanings" are, if one can speak of meanings here at all, purely formal. From the point of view of classical logic implicit definitions are circular. But as C. I. Lewis once so nicely put it, a circle is the less vicious the larger it is. I take this to mean that a "fruitful" or "fertile" postulate set is one from which a great (possibly unlimited) number of theorems can be (nontrivially) derived, and this desirable feature is clearly due to the manner in which the primitive terms are connected with one another in the network formed by the postulates, and also by aptness of the definitions of the derived (defined) terms.

In the picturesque but illuminating elucidations used, e.g., by Schlick, Carnap, Hempel, and Margenau, the "pure calculus," i.e., the uninterpreted postulate system, "floats" or "hovers" freely above the plane of empirical facts. It is only through the "connecting links," i.e., the "coordinative definitions" (Reichenbach's terms, roughly synonymous with the "correspondence rules" of Margenau and Carnap, or the "epistemic correlations" of Northrop, and only related to but not strictly identical with Bridgman's "operational definitions"), that the postulate system acquires empirical meaning. A simple diagram (actually greatly oversimplified!) will illustrate the logical situation. As the diagram indicates, the basic theoretical concepts (primitives) are implicitly defined by the postulates in which they occur. These primitives ($\bigcirc$), or more usually derived concepts ($\triangle$) explicitly defined in terms of them, are then

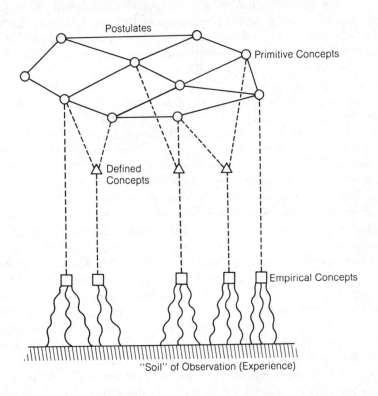

linked ("coordinated") by correspondence rules to concepts ($\square$) referring to items of observation, e.g., in the physical sciences usually fairly directly measurable quantities like mass, temperature, and light intensity. These empirical concepts are in turn "operationally defined," i.e., by a specification of the rules of observation, measurement, experimentation, or statistical design which determine and delimit their applicability and application.

Bridgman distinguished between "physical" and "mental" operations. What he had in mind is perhaps more clearly but also more cumbersomely expressed by distinguishing observational (cum mensurational-experimental) from logico-mathematical, e.g., computational, procedures.

Conceived broadly enough, these two types of "operations" cover the entire variety of specifications of meaning of any sort of scientific concept. But Bridgman's examples indicate that he focused his attention primarily upon concepts that are fairly close to the "plane of observation." One very elementary case is the concept of (average) velocity of a moving body for a given distance in space, and a corresponding interval of time: Determine, with yardstick or tape measure, etc., the distance, and with the help of a stopwatch or other chronometric devices the duration in question; these are examples of Bridgman's "physical" operations. Then divide the numerical result of the first by the numerical result of the second ("mental" operation of arithmetic division), and you have arrived at your result: the (average) velocity.

Clearly, highly theoretical concepts such as, for example, that of the "spin" in quantum mechanics, involve much more complex operations— of *both* types. Hence, I think it is advisable to speak of operational definitions only for "empirical" concepts. The meaning of theoretical concepts can be specified only by their place in the entire theoretical system involving the postulates, definitions, correspondence rules, and finally the operational definitions. These last are indicated by the "rootlets" that "anchor" the empirical concepts in the "soil" of experience, i.e., mensurational-experimental observations.

In view of the "orthodox" logical analysis of scientific theories it is generally held that the concepts ("primitives") in the postulates, as well as the postulates themselves, can be given no more than a partial interpretation. This presupposes a sharp distinction between the language of observation (observational language; O.L.) and the language of theories (theoretical language; T.L.). It is asserted that the O.L. is fully understood. Indeed, in the view of Carnap, for example, the O.L. is not in any way theory-laden or "contaminated" with the theoretical assumptions or presuppositions. In an earlier phase of positivism, for example in Carnap's (8), something like a language of sense data (actually a language of momentary total immediate experience) was proposed as the testing ground of all interpretive, inferential, or theoretical propositions. This was clearly the Humean doctrine of "impressions" brought up to date with the help of modern logic. Carnap, very likely influenced by Otto Neurath's and Karl R. Popper's criticisms, later proposed an intersubjective "physicalistic" O.L. as preferable to an essentially subjectivistic ("methodologically solipsistic") O.L. Hence, pointer readings and other similar objective or intersubjectively concordant "data" would serve as an observation basis. Sharply in contrast to terms thus referring to intersubjectively observable qualities and relations are the theoretical concepts. Terms like "electromagnetic field," "neutron," neutrino," and "spin" are understood only partially, i.e., with the help of postulates, explicit definitions, correspondence rules, and operational definitions. In the picturesque description of our diagram, it was said that there is an "upward seepage" of meaning from the observational terms to the theoretical concepts.

This, in brief outline, is the "orthodox" account of theories in the factual sciences. It has provided the guidelines for numerous axiomatizations of empirical theories. Various branches of theoretical physics (35), biology (40), especially genetics, psychology, especially learning theory (23), and the more recent voluminous output of P. Suppes and his collaborators at Stanford University in a wide range of subjects—all furnish examples of the many ways in which such reconstructions can be pursued. It is a matter of controversy just how fruitful or helpful strict axiomatizations are for the ongoing creative work of the theoretical scientists. If we disregard such relatively informal and "halfway" axiomatizations as can be found in the work of the great scientific innovators, such as Newton, Maxwell, and Einstein, it may well be said that the logicians of science work primarily by way of hindsight. That is, they *analyze* a given theory in regard to its logical structure and its empirical basis, but do not in any way add to the content of the theory in question. It seems to me that even this relatively modest endeavor can be useful in the following ways: (1) It enables us to understand a given theory more clearly; this is important at least in the teaching and learning procedures. (2) It provides a more precise tool for assessing the correctness of the logico-mathematical derivations on the one hand and the degree of evidential support (or else of disconfirmation) on the other. (3) Since no genuinely fruitful and important theory is "monolithic," but rather consists of a number of logically independent postulates, an exact reconstruction may well show which postulates rest on what empirical evidence.

It must be said immediately that all three of these contentions are being disputed nowadays. Regarding point (1), some criticisms concern the "partial interpretation" view. It is maintained, first of all, that the difference between observational and theoretical concepts is not all that sharp or fundamental; secondly, in this connection, it is urged that there are no observation statements that are free of theoretical presuppositions. Feyerabend even goes farther: He thinks that no neutral observation base exists and that none is needed for the testing of theories. He maintains that theories are tested against each other. If this were so, which I do not concede, then even the most liberal empiricism would have to be abandoned in favor of a, to me, highly questionable form of rationalism. But Feyerabend's construal of the history of scientific theories seems to me rather extravagant!

Furthermore, it is contended that we can understand scientific theories quite fully and that therefore the doctrine of "upward seepage" is all wrong. One reason why this criticism may seem justified is that the understanding of theoretical concepts and postulates rests on the use of analogies or analogical models. I would immediately admit the enormous importance of analogical conception and inference in heuristic and didactic matters. But it is a moot question whether analogical conception is part of the actual cognitive content of theories.

In regard to point (2), i.e., the separation of the assessment of the validity of derivations from the appraisal of the empirical adequacy of theories, I can hardly see any good grounds for criticism. To be sure, it is conceivable that the use of alternative, e.g., many-valued, logics might raise some questions here. But ever since the analyses of scientific explanation given on the basis of *statistical* postulates, especially by C. G. Hempel (20, 21), we have known how to explicate nondeductive derivations, which are actually the *rule* rather than the exception in recent science. Much more weighty are the questions regarding the precise analysis of the notion of evidential support or the "substantiation" of theories by observations (implemented whenever feasible by measurement, experimentation, or statistical design). I shall only mention here the radically different points of view of Carnap and Popper. Carnap has proposed a "logical" concept of probability, or of degree of confirmation of a hypothesis on the basis of a given body of evidence. Popper believes that the growth of scientific knowledge occurs through the severe testing of proposed hypotheses and that those hypotheses which survive such tests are "corroborated." Popper's "degree of corroboration," unlike Carnap's "degree of confirmation," is not a probability; it does not conform to the principles of the calculus of probabilities. The dispute between these two schools of thought still continues, but it is fairly clear that they are really reconstructing different concepts, each holding some promise of genuine illumination. There are also basic disagreements among the various schools of thought in statistical method. The controversies between the "Bayesians" or "subjectivists" and the "objectivists," e.g., those taking the Neyman-Pearson approach, might be mentioned here. It would lead us too far afield even to sketch in outline the various important points at issue.

Finally, in regard to point (3) we face the issues raised originally by Pierre Duhem, and more recently by W. V. O. Quine. Their contention is that theories can be tested only globally, in that it is (usually) the conjunction of all the postulates of a theory from which a conclusion is derived which is then either verified or refuted by observation. This contention is not to be confused with the (rather incredible) sort of assertion made on occasion by Sigmund Freud or his disciples that, as far as they are concerned, psychoanalytic theory is "monolithic," i.e., to be accepted or else rejected in its entirety. Duhem and Quine do not deny that the theories in the empirical sciences consist of *logically independent* postulates, or that they can at least be so reconstructed. What they deny is that the postulates can be independently *tested*. Prima facie this seems plausible, for in testing one postulate others are presupposed. The very use of instruments of observation and experimentation involves assumption about the functioning of those instruments. In the formal reconstruction of theory testing there are then always assumptions, or auxiliary hypotheses, or parts of general background knowledge that are, in the given context, taken for granted. A closer look at the actual history and procedures of scientific research, however, indicates that the auxiliary hypotheses, etc., have usually been "secured" by previous confirmation (or corroboration). And while, of course, even the best established hypotheses are in principle kept open for revision, it would be foolish to call them into doubt when some other more "risky" hypotheses are under critical scrutiny. Thus, for example, the astronomer relies on the optics of his telescopes, spectroscopes, cameras, and so on in testing a given ("far-out") astrophysical hypothesis. Similarly, the functioning of the instruments of experimental atomic and subatomic physics (cloud or bubble chambers, Geiger counters, accelerators, etc.) is taken for granted in the scrutiny of a given hypothesis in quantum mechanics or nuclear theory. All this is simply the practical wisdom that enjoins us not to doubt everything equally strongly at the same time. Even more to the point: It seems that the "pinpointing of the culprit," i.e., the spotting of the false assumptions, is one of the primary aims as well as virtues of the experimental or statistical techniques. Thus the hypothesis of the stationary ether was refuted by the Michelson-Morley and analogous experiments. It was definitely refuted provided the theoretical physicists did not resort to special ad hoc hypotheses. Ritz's "ballistic" hypothesis regarding the propagation of light, and electromagnetic radiation generally, was refuted by the observations of de Sitter on double stars. *Both* of these pieces of evidence are needed for a justification of Einstein's postulates in the special theory of relativity. Einstein's genius characteristically manifested itself when he guessed correctly in 1905 what de Sitter demonstrated only six years later. And there is some reason to believe that he did not explicitly utilize even the outcome of the Michelson-Morley experiment. Nevertheless, an objective confirmation of Einstein's theory does depend on these types of evidence.

Along with the "orthodox" view of the structure of scientific theories there goes an account of the levels of scientific explanation which, though often implicit, I formulated explicitly in one of my early articles (14). This account has been, perhaps somewhat sarcastically, referred to by Feyerabend as the "layer-cake" view of theories. I still think that this account is illuminating even though it needs some emendations. As a first crude approximation the account in question maintains that the ground level consists of descriptions; whether they are based on observation or inference does not matter in this context. On the first level we place the explanandum, i.e., the individual fact or event to be explained, or rather its linguistic or mathematical formulation. Logically speaking only singular sentences or conjunctions thereof should appear on this level. Immediately above this level are the empirical laws (deterministic or statistical, as the case may be). We can utilize these empirical (or experimental) laws in the explanation of the facts or events described on the ground level. These explanations usually strike us as rather trivial because they amount to simply subsuming the individual fact or event under a class specified in the empirical law. For example, the fact that a lens functions as a magnifying glass can be explained by Snell's laws of the refraction of light rays. Snell's law specifies the relation of the angle of incidence to the angle of refraction in terms of a simple mathematical function. Snell's law in turn can be derived from the wave theory of light. This theory already enables us to derive not only the laws of refraction but also those of propagation, reflection, diffraction, interference, and polarization. A still higher level of explanation is attained in Maxwell's principles of electrodynamics (electromagnetics). Here the phenomena of light are explained as a small subclass of electromagnetic waves, along with radio waves, infrared, ultraviolet, X rays, gamma radiations, etc. But in order to understand such optical phenomena as reflection and refraction, a theory of the interaction of the electromagnetic waves with various types of material substances is called for. In order to achieve that, the atomic and electron theories were introduced toward the end of the last century. But for a fuller and more precise explanation we can ascend to the next, and thus far "highest," level, viz. the theories of quantum physics.

This level-structure analysis makes clear, I think, the progress from empirical laws to theories of greater and greater explanatory power. To speak very informally, it is the fact-postulate ratio that represents the explanatory power of theories. The aim of scientific explanation throughout the ages has been *unification*, i.e., the comprehending of a maximum of facts and regularities in terms of a minimum of theoretical concepts and assumptions. The remarkable success achieved, especially in the theories of physics, chemistry, and to some extent recent biology, has encouraged pursuit of a unitary system of explanatory premises. Whether this aim is attainable depends, of course, both on the nature of the world and on the ingenuity of the scientists. I think this is what Einstein had in mind in his famous sayings: "God is subtle but He is not malicious"; "The only thing that is incomprehensible, is that the world is comprehensible." (There is serious doubt about the contention of a third well-known bon mot of Einstein's, "God does not play with dice.") Einstein's deep conviction of the basic determinism—at "rock bottom"—of nature is shared by very few theoretical physicists today. There may be no rock bottom; moreover there is no criterion that would tell us that we have reached rock bottom (if indeed we had!).

The plausibility of the level-structure model has been, however, drastically affected by Feyerabend's criticisms. He pointed out quite some years ago that there is hardly an example which illustrates strict deducibility of the lower from the higher levels, even in theories with 100 percent deterministic lawlike postulates. The simple reason is that in straightforward deductive inference there can be no concepts in the conclusion that are not present in the premises and definitions. Most of us thought that definitions, or else bridge laws, would accomplish the job. In fact, however, the lower levels which (historically) usually precede, in their formulation, the construction of the higher levels are, as a rule, incisively revised in the light of the higher level theory. This certainly was the case in the relations of Newtonian to Einsteinian physics, of Maxwellian to quantum electrodynamics, etc. When presenting the level scheme in my philosophy of science courses I have, for more than thirty years, spoken of "corrections from above" accruing to the lower level lawlike assertions. It is also to be admitted that while some of those corrections, within a certain range of the relevant variables, are so minute as to be practically negligible, they become quite significant and even indefinitely large outside that range. Moreover, and this is important, the conceptual frameworks of the theories of different levels are so radically different as to exclude any deductive relationships. Only if bridge laws help in defining the lower level concepts can the derivations be rendered deductive.

In disagreement with Feyerabend, I remain convinced that in the testing of a new theory, the relevant observation language must not be contaminated by that theory; nor need there be a competing alternative theory. If he contends that in most concerns of empirical testing there are presuppositions of a pervasive theoretical character, I would argue that those pervasive presuppositions, for example, regarding the relative permanence of the laboratory instruments, of the experimental records, are "theoretical" only from a deep epistemological point of view and are not called into question when, for example, we try to decide experimentally between rival theories in the physical, biological, or social sciences.

In conclusion I wish to say that the "orthodox" view of scientific theories can help in clarifying their logico-mathematical structure, as well as their empirical confirmation (or disconfirmation). It should be stressed, and not merely bashfully admitted, that the rational reconstruction of theories is a highly artificial hindsight operation which has little to do with the work of the creative scientist. No philosopher of science in his right mind considers this sort of analysis as a recipe for the construction of theories. Yet even the creative scientist employs, at least informally and implicitly, some of the criteria of logico-empirical analysis and appraisal which the logician of science endeavors to make fully explicit. Perhaps there is here an analogy with the difference between a creative composer of music and a specialist in musical theory (counterpoint, harmony, etc.). *Psychologically* the creation of a work of art and the creation of a scientific theory may have much in common. But logically, the standards and criteria of appraisal are radically different, if for no other reason than that the *aims* of art and science are so different.

According to the standard view correspondence rules are semantic designation rules. They merely provide an empirical interpretation of an erstwhile completely uninterpreted postulate system (pure calculus). Let me emphasize once more that this manner of regarding theories is a matter of highly artificial reconstruction. It does not in the least reflect the way in which theories originate. Correspondence rules thus understood differ from bridge laws in that the latter make empirical assertions. For example, if a bridge law states the relation between the mean kinetic energy of gas molecules and the thermometrically determined gas temperature, then this is, logically speaking, a matter of contingent empirical regularity. Nevertheless, in a complete theory of heat, i.e., statistical and quantum mechanical, the behavior of thermometric substances, e.g., alcohol, mercury, and gases, should in principle be derivable. Hence the bridge laws are to be regarded as *theorems* of the respective theories. This can also be formulated by saying that a logically contingent identification of empirical with theoretical concepts is thus achieved. This is surely part of what occurs in the *reduction* of empirical laws to theories, or of theories of lower level to a theory of higher level. Thus the theory of light rays (optics) is reduced to the theory of electromagnetic waves. Or light rays are identified with electromagnetic waves of certain wavelengths and frequencies. Similarly, ordinary (crystalline) table salt is identified with a three-dimensional lattice of sodium and chlorine atoms, etc., etc. The reduction of (parts of) psychology to neurophysiology is still scientifically and philosophically problematic and controversial, but if it were to succeed, it would involve the identification of the qualities of immediate experience with certain patterns of neural processes. In a unitary theory of perception the data of observation could then be characterizable as the direct-acquaintance aspect of brain states.

REFERENCES

1. ACHINSTEIN, PETER. *Concepts of Science.* Baltimore: Johns Hopkins Press, 1968.

2. ACHINSTEIN, PETER, and STEPHEN F. BARKER, eds. *The Legacy of Logical Positivism.* Baltimore: Johns Hopkins Press, 1969.

3. BRAITHWAITE, R. B. *Scientific Explanation.* Cambridge: Cambridge University Press, 1968.

4. BRIDGMAN, P. W. *The Logic of Modern Physics.* New York: Macmillan, 1927.

5. ———. *The Nature of Physical Theory*. Princeton, N.J.: Princeton University Press, 1936.
6. BUNGE, MARIO. *The Foundations of Physics*. Berlin, Heidelberg, and New York: Springer, 1967.
7. CAMPBELL, NORMAN ROBERT. *Physics: The Elements*. Cambridge: Cambridge University Press, 1920.
8. CARNAP, RUDOLF. *Der Logische Aufbau der Welt*. Berlin-Schlachtensee: Weltkreis-Verlag, 1928.
9. ———. *Foundations of Logic and Mathematics*, vol. I, no. 3 of the *International Encyclopedia of Unified Science*. Chicago: University of Chicago Press, 1939.
10. ———. "The Methodological Character of Theoretical Concepts," in H. Feigl and M. Scriven, eds., *Minnesota Studies in the Philosophy of Science*, vol. I. Minneapolis: University of Minnesota Press, 1956.
11. ———. *Philosophical Foundations of Physics*. New York: Basic Books, 1966.
12. ———. "Ueber die Aufgabe der Physik und die Anwendung des Grundsatzes der Einfachstheit," *Kant-Studien*, 28 (1923), 90–107.
13. COLODNY, ROBERT G., ed. *Beyond the Edge of Certainty*. Englewood Cliffs, N.J.: Prentice-Hall, 1965.
14. FEIGL, HERBERT. "Some Remarks on the Meaning of Scientific Explanation," in H. Feigl and W. Sellars, eds., *Readings in Philosophical Analysis*. New York: Appleton-Century-Crofts, 1949.
15. ———. "Confirmability and Confirmation," in P. P. Wiener, ed., *Readings in Philosophy of Science*. New York: Scribner's, 1953.
16. ———. *The "Mental" and the "Physical": The Essay and a Postscript*. Minneapolis: University of Minnesota Press, 1967.
17. FEYERABEND, PAUL K. "Problems of Empiricism," in R. G. Colodny, ed., *Beyond the Edge of Certainty*. Englewood Cliffs, N.J.: Prentice-Hall, 1965.
18. ———. "How to Be a Good Empiricist—A Plea for Tolerance in Matters Epistemological," in B. Baumrin, ed., *Philosophy of Science: The Delaware Seminar*, vol. 2. New York: Wiley, 1963.
19. GRÜNBAUM, ADOLF. *Philosophical Problems of Space and Time*. New York: Knopf, 1963.
20. HEMPEL, CARL G. *Aspects of Scientific Explanation*. New York: Free Press, 1965.
21. ———. "Deductive-Nomological vs. Statistical Explanation," in H. Feigl and G. Maxwell, eds., *Minnesota Studies in the Philosophy of Science*, vol. III. Minneapolis: University of Minnesota Press, 1962.
22. ———. *Fundamentals of Concept Formation in Empirical Science*. Chicago: University of Chicago Press, 1952.
23. HULL, CLARK L., et al. *Mathematico-Deductive Theory of Rote Learning*. New Haven, Conn.: Yale University Press, 1940.
24. KÖRNER, STEPHAN. *Experience and Theory*. New York: Humanities, 1966.
25. LENZEN, V. F. *The Nature of Physical Theory*. New York: Wiley, 1931.
26. MARGENAU, HENRY. *The Nature of Physical Reality*. New York: McGraw-Hill, 1950.
27. MEHLBORG, HENRY K. *The Reach of Science*. Toronto: University of Toronto Press, 1958.

28. NAGEL, ERNEST. *The Structure of Science*. New York: Harcourt, Brace and World, 1961.
29. NORTHROP, F. S. C. *The Logic of the Sciences and the Humanities*. New York: Macmillan, 1947.
30. PAP, ARTHUR. *An Introduction to the Philosophy of Science*. New York: Free Press, 1962.
31. POINCARÉ, HENRI. *Science and Hypothesis*. New York: Dover, 1952.
32. ————. *Science and Method*. New York: Dover, 1952.
33. POPPER, KARL R. *Conjectures and Refutations*. New York: Basic Books, 1962.
34. ————. *The Logic of Scientific Discovery*. New York: Harper, 1959.
35. REICHENBACH, HANS. *Axiomatik der relativistischen Raum-Zeit-Lehre*. Braunschweig: Vieweg, 1924.
36. ————. *Experience and Prediction*. Chicago: University of Chicago Press, 1938.
37. SCHEFFLER, ISRAEL. *The Anatomy of Inquiry*. New York: Knopf, 1963.
38. SCHLICK, MORTIZ. *Algemeine Erkenntnislehre*. 2nd ed. Berlin: Springer, 1925 (1st ed. 1918).
39. SMART, J. J. C. *Between Science and Philosophy*. New York: Random House, 1968.
40. WOODGER, JOSEPH HENRY. *The Techniques of Theory Construction*. Chicago: University of Chicago Press, 1939.

14

DEFENSE OF ANARCHY

PAUL K. FEYERABEND

What is all this commotion good for? The most it can achieve is to ruin one's peace of mind. There one has one's little rooms. Everything in them is known, has been added, one item after another, has become loved, and well esteemed. Need I fear that the clock will breathe fire into my face or that the bird will emerge from its cage and greedily attack the dog? No. The clock strikes six when it is six like it has been six for three thousand years. This is what I call *order*. This is what one loves, this is what one can identify with. CARL STERN-HEIM, *Die Hose*

FROM P. K. Feyerabend, Against method: Outline of an anarchistic theory of knowledge, in M. Radner and S. Winokur (Eds.), *Minnesota Studies in the Philosophy of Science*, Vol. 4 (Minneapolis: University of Minnesota Press, 1970). Pages 17–26, 91, 92. Reprinted by permission of the author and the University of Minnesota Press.

Preface

THE following essay has been written in the conviction that *anarchism,* while perhaps not the most attractive *political* philosophy, is certainly an excellent foundation for *epistemology,* and for the *philosophy of science.*
The reason is not difficult to find.

"History generally, and the history of revolutions in particular, is always richer in content, more varied, more manysided, more lively and 'subtle' than even" the best historian and the best methodologist can imagine (1). "Accidents and conjunctions, and curious juxtapositions of events" (2) are the very substance of history, and the "complexity of human change and the unpredictable character of the ultimate consequences of any given act or decision of men" (3) its most conspicuous feature. Are we really to believe that a bunch of rather naive and simple-minded rules will be capable of explaining such a "maze of interactions" (4)? And is it not clear that a person who *participates* in a complex process of this kind will succeed only if he is a ruthless *opportunist,* and capable of quickly changing from one method to another?

This is indeed the lesson that has been drawn by intelligent and thoughtful observers. "From this [character of the historical process]," writes Lenin, continuing the passage just quoted, "follow two very important practical conclusions: first, that in order to fulfill its task, the revolutionary class [i.e., the class of those who want to change either a part of society, such as science, or society as a whole] must be able to master *all* forms and sides of social activity [it must be able to understand, and to apply not only one particular methodology, but any methodology, and any variation thereof it can imagine], without exception; second, [it] must be ready to pass from one to another in the quickest and most unexpected manner" (5). "The external conditions," writes Einstein, "which are set for [the scientist] by the facts of experience do not permit him to let himself be too much restricted in the construction of his conceptual world by the adherence to an epistemological system. He therefore must appear to the systematic epistemologist as a type of unscrupulous opportunist . . ." (6).

The difference between epistemological (political, theological) *theory* and scientific (political, religious) *practice* that emerges from these quotations is usually formulated as a difference between "certain and infallible" (or, at any rate, clear, systematic, and objective) *rules,* or *standards,* and "our fallible and uncertain faculties [which] depart from them and fall into error (7). Science as it should be, third-world science (8), agrees with the proscribed rules. Science as we actually find it in history is a combination of such rules and of *error.* It follows that the scientist who works in a particular historical situation must learn how to recognize error and how to live with it, always keeping in mind that he himself is liable to add fresh error at any stage of the investigation. He needs a *theory of error* in addition to the "certain and infallible" rules which define the "approach to the truth."

Now error, being an expression of idiosyncrasies of an individual thinker, observer, even of an individual measuring instrument, *depends on* circumstances, on the particular phenomena or theories one wants to analyze, and it *develops* in highly unexpected ways. *Error is itself a historical phenomenon.* A theory of error will therefore contain rules of thumb, useful hints, heuristic suggestions rather than general laws, and it will relate these hints and these suggestions to historical episodes so that one sees in detail how some of them have led some people to success in some situations. It will develop the imagination of the student without ever providing him with cut-and-dried prescriptions and procedures. It will be more a collection of stories than a theory in the proper sense and it will contain a sizable amount of aimless gossip from which everyone may choose what fits in with his intentions. Good books on the art of recognizing and avoiding error will have much in common with good books on the art of singing, or boxing, or making love. Such books consider the great variety of character, of vocal (muscular, glandular, emotional) equipment, of personal idiosyncrasies, and they pay attention to the fact that each element of this variety may develop in most unexpected directions (a woman's voice may bloom forth after her first abortion). They contain numerous rules of thumb, useful hints, and they leave it to the reader to choose what fits his case. Clearly the reader will not be able to make the correct choice unless he has already *some* knowledge of vocal (muscular, emotional) matters and this knowledge he can acquire only by throwing himself into the process of learning and hoping for the best. In the case of singing he must start using his organs, his throat, his brain, his diaphragm, his buttocks before he really knows how to use them, and he must learn from their reactions the way of learning most appropriate to him. And this is true of all learning: choosing a certain way the student, or the "mature scientist," creates a situation as yet unknown to him from which he must learn how best to approach situations of this kind. This is not as paradoxical as it sounds as long as we keep our options open and as long as we refuse to settle for a particular method, including a particular set of rules, without having examined alternatives. "Let people emancipate themselves," says Bakunin, "and they will instruct themselves of their own accord" (9). In the case of *science* the necessary tact can be developed only by *direct participation* (where "participation" means something different for different individuals) or, if such direct participation cannot be had, or seems undesirable, from a study of past episodes in the *history* of the subject. *Considering their great and difficult complexity these episodes must be approached with a novelist's love for character and for detail,* or with a gossip columnist's love for scandal and for surprising turns; they must be approached with insight into the positive function of strength as well as of weakness, of intelligence as well as of stupidity, of love for truth as well as of the will to deceive, of modesty as well as of conceit, rather than with the crude and laughably inadequate instruments of the logician. For nobody can say in abstract terms, without paying attention to idiosyncrasies of person and circumstance, what precisely it was that led to progress in the past, and nobody can say what moves will succeed in the future.

Now it is of course possible to simplify the historical medium in which a scientist works by simplifying its main actors. The history of science, after all, consists not only of facts and conclusions drawn therefrom. It consists also of ideas, interpretations of facts, problems created by a clash of interpretations, actions of scientists, and so on. On closer analysis we even find that there are no "bare facts" at all but that the facts that enter our knowledge are already viewed in a certain way and are therefore essentially ideational. This being the case the history of science will be as complex, as chaotic, as full of error, and as entertaining as the ideas it contains and these ideas in turn will be as complex, as chaotic, as full of error, and as entertaining as are the minds of those who invented them. Conversely, a little brainwashing will go a long way in making the history of science more simple, more uniform, more dull, more "objective," and more accessible to treatment by "certain and infallible" rules: a theory of errors is superfluous when we are dealing with well-trained scientists who are kept in place by an internal slave master called "professional conscience" and who have been convinced that it is good and rewarding to attain, and then to forever keep, one's "professional integrity" (10).

Scientific education as we know it today has precisely this purpose. It has the purpose of carrying out a rationalistic simplification of the process "science" by simplifying its participants. One proceeds as follows. First, a domain of research is defined. Next, the domain is separated from the remainder of history (physics, for example, is separated from metaphysics and from theology) and receives a "logic" of its own (11). A thorough training in such a logic then conditions those working in the domain so that they may not unwittingly disturb the purity (read: the sterility) that has already been achieved. An essential part of the training is the inhibition of intuitions that might lead to a blurring of boundaries. A person's religion, for example, or his metaphysics, or his sense of humor must not have the slightest connection with his scientific activity. His imagination is restrained (12) and even his language will cease to be his own (13).

It is obvious that such an education, such a cutting up of domains and of consciousness, cannot be easily reconciled with a humanitarian attitude. It is in conflict "with the cultivation of individuality which [alone] produces, or can produce well developed human beings" (14); it "maim[s] by compression, like a Chinese lady's foot, every part of human nature which stands out prominently, and tends to make a person markedly dissimilar in outline" (15) from the ideal of rationality that happens to be fashionable with the methodologists.

Now it is precisely such an ideal that finds expression either in "certain and infallible rules" or else in *standards* which separate what is correct, or rational, or reasonable, or "objective" from what is incorrect, or irrational, or unreasonable, or "subjective." Abandoning the ideal as being unworthy of a free man means abandoning standards and relying on theories of error entirely. Only these theories, these hints, these rules of thumb must now be renamed. Without universally enforced standards of truth and rationality we can no longer speak of universal error. We can only speak of what does, or does not, seem appropriate when viewed from a particular and restricted point of view, different views, temperaments, attitudes giving rise to different judgments and different methods of approach. Such an *anarchistic epistemology*—for this is what our theories of error now turn out to be—is not only a better means for improving knowledge, or of understanding history. It is also more appropriate for a free man to use than are its rigorous and "scientific" alternatives.

We need not fear that the diminished concern for law and order in science and society that is entailed by the use of anarchistic philosophies will lead to chaos. The human nervous system is too well organized for that (16). Of course, there may arrive an epoch when it becomes necessary to give reason a temporary advantage and when it is wise to defend *its* rules to the exclusion of everything else. I do not think we are living in such an epoch today.

When we see that we have arrived at the utmost extent of human [understanding] we sit down contented. HUME (17)

The more solid, well defined, and splendid the edifice erected by the understanding, the more restless the urge of life . . . to escape from it into freedom. [Appearing as] reason it is negative and dialectical, for it dissolves into nothing the detailed determinations of the understanding. HEGEL (18)

Although science taken as whole is a nuisance, one can still learn from it. BENN (19)

Introduction; The Limits of Argument

The idea of a method that contains firm, unchanging, and absolutely binding principles for conducting the business of science gets into considerable difficulty when confronted with the results of historical research. We find, then, that there is not a single rule, however plausible, and however firmly grounded in epistemology, that is not violated at some time or other. It becomes evident that such violations are not accidental events, they are not the results of insufficient knowledge or of inattention which might have been avoided. On the contrary, we see that they are necessary for progress. Indeed, one of the most striking features of recent discussions in the history and philosophy of science is the realization that developments such as the Copernican Revolutions, or the rise of atomism in antiquity and recently (kinetic theory; dispersion theory; stereochemistry; quantum theory), or the gradual emergence of the wave theory of light occurred either because some thinkers *decided* not to be bound by certain "obvious" methodological rules or because they *unwittingly broke* them (20).

This liberal practice, I repeat, is not just a *fact* of the history of science. It is not merely a manifestation of human inconstancy and ignorance. It is reasonable *and absolutely necessary* for the growth of knowledge. More specifically, the following can be shown: considering any rule, however "fundamental," there are always circumstances when it is advisable not only to ignore the rule, but to adopt its opposite. For example, there are circumstances when it is advisable to introduce, elaborate, and defend ad hoc hypotheses, or hypotheses which contradict well-established and generally accepted experimental results, or hypotheses whose content is smaller than the content of the existing and empirically adequate alternatives, or self-inconsistent hypotheses, and so on (21).

There are even circumstances—and they occur rather frequently—when *argument* loses its forward-looking aspect and becomes a hindrance to progress. Nobody wants to assert (22) that the teaching of *small children* is exclusively a matter of argument (though argument may enter into it and should enter into it to a larger extent than is customary) (23), and almost everyone now agrees that what looks like a result of reason— the mastery of a language, the existence of a richly articulated perceptual world (24), logical ability—is due partly to indoctrination, partly to a process of *growth* that proceeds with the force of natural law. And where arguments *do* seem to have an effect this must often be ascribed to their *physical repetition* rather than to their *semantic content* (25). This much having been admitted, we must also concede the possibility of non-argumentative growth in the *adult* as well as in (the theoretical parts of) *institutions* such as science, religion, and prostitution. We certainly cannot take it for granted that what is possible for a small child—to acquire new modes of behavior on the slightest provocation, to slide into them without any noticeable effort—is beyond the reach of his elders. One should expect that catastrophic changes of the physical environment, wars, the breakdown of encompassing systems of morality, political revolutions, will transform adult reaction patterns, too, including important patterns of argumentation (26). This may again be an entirely natural process and rational argument may but increase the mental tension that precedes and causes the behavioral outburst.

Now, if there are events, not necessarily arguments, which *cause* us to adopt new standards, including new and more complex forms of argumentation, will it then not be up to the defenders of the status quo to provide, not just arguments, but also contrary *causes*? (Virtue without terror is ineffective, says Robespierre.) And if the old forms of argumentation turn out to be too weak a cause, must not these defenders either give up or resort to stronger and more "irrational" means? (It is very difficult, and perhaps entirely impossible, to combat the effects of brainwashing by argument.) Even the most puritanical rationalist will then be forced to stop reasoning and to use, say, *propaganda* and *coercion*, not because some of his *reasons* have ceased to be valid, but because the *psychological conditions* which make them effective, and capable of influencing others, have disappeared. And what is the use of an argument that leaves people unmoved (27)?

Of course, the problem never arises quite in this form. The teaching of standards never consists in merely putting them before the mind of the student and making them as *clear* as possible. The standards are supposed to have maximal *cause efficacy* as well. This makes it very difficult to distinguish between the *logical force* and the *material effect* of an argument. Just as a well-trained pet will obey his master no matter how great the confusion he finds himself in and no matter how urgent the need to adopt new patterns of behavior, in the very same way a well-trained rationalist will obey the mental image of *his* master, he will conform to the standards of argumentation he has learned, he will adhere to these standards no matter how great the difficulty he finds himself in, and he will be quite unable to discover that what he regards as the "voice of reason" is but *a causal aftereffect* of the training he has received. We see here very clearly how the appeal to "reason" works. At first sight this appeal seems to be to some *ideas* which *convince* a man instead of *pushing* him. But conviction cannot remain an ethereal state; it is supposed to lead to *action*. It is supposed to lead to the *appropriate* action, and it is supposed to *sustain* this action as long as necessary. What is the force that upholds such a development? It is the causal efficacy of the standards to which appeal was made and this causal efficacy in turn is but an effect of training, as we have seen. It follows that appeal to argument either has no content at all, and can be made to agree with any procedure (28), or else will often have a conservative function: it will set limits to what is about to become a natural way of behavior (29). In the latter case, however, the appeal is nothing but a concealed *political maneuver*. This becomes very clear when a rationalist wants to restore an earlier point of view. Basing his argument on natural habits of reasoning which either have become extinct or have no point of attack in the new situation, such a champion of "rationality" must first restore the earlier material and psychological conditions. This, however, involves him in "a struggle of interests and forces, not of argument" (30).

That interests, forces, propaganda, brainwashing techniques play a much greater role in the growth of our knowledge and, a fortiori, of science than is commonly believed can also be seen from an analysis of the *relation between idea and action.* One often takes it for granted that a clear and distinct understanding of new ideas precedes and should precede any formulation and any institutional expression of them. (An investigation starts with a problem, says Popper.) *First,* we have an idea, or a problem; *then* we act, i.e., either speak, or build, or destroy (31). This is certainly not the way in which small children develop. They use words, they combine them, they play with them until they grasp a meaning that so far has been beyond their reach. And the initial playful activity is an essential presupposition of the final act of understanding (32). There is no reason why this mechanism should cease to function in the adult. On the contrary, we must expect, for example, that the *idea* of liberty could be made clear only by means of the very same actions which were supposed to *create* liberty. Creation of a *thing,* and creation plus full understanding of a *correct idea* of the thing, *very often are parts of one and the same indivisible process* and they cannot be separated without bringing the process to a standstill. The process itself is not guided by a well-defined program; it cannot be guided by such a program for it contains the conditions of the realization of programs. It is rather guided by a vague urge, by a "passion" (Kierkegaard). The passion gives rise to specific behavior which in turn creates the circumstances and the ideas necessary for analyzing and explaining the whole development, for making it "rational" (33).

The development of the Copernican point of view, from Galileo up to the twentieth century, is a perfect example of the situation we want to describe. We start with a strong belief that runs counter to contemporary reason. The belief spreads and finds support from other beliefs which are equally unreasonable, if not more so (law of inertia; telescope). Research now gets deflected in new directions, new kinds of instruments are built, "evidence" is related to theories in new ways until there arises a new ideology that is rich enough to provide independent arguments for any particular part of it and mobile enough to find such arguments whenever they seem to be required. *Today* we can say that Galileo was on the right track, for his persistent pursuit of what once seemed to be a silly cosmology created the material needed for the defense of this cosmology against those of us who accept a view only if it is told in a certain way and who trust it only if it contains certain magical phrases, called "observational reports" (34). And this is not an exception—it is the normal case: theories become clear and "reasonable" only *after* incoherent parts of them have been used for a long time. Such unreasonable, nonsensical, unmethodical foreplay thus turns out to be an unavoidable precondition of clarity and of empirical success (35).

Trying to describe developments of this kind in a general way, we are of course obliged to appeal to the existing forms of speech which do not take them into account and which must be distorted, misused, and beaten into new patterns in order to fit unforeseen situations (without a constant misuse of language there cannot be any discovery and any progress). "Moreover, since the traditional categories are the gospel of everyday thinking (including ordinary scientific thinking) and of everyday practice, [such an attempt at understanding] in effect presents rules and forms of false thinking and action—false, that is, from the standpoint of [scientific] commonsense" (36). This is how *dialectical thinking* arises as a form of thought that "dissolves into nothing the detailed determinations of the understanding" (37).

It is clear, then, that the idea of a fixed method, or of a fixed (theory of) rationality, arises from too naive a view of man and of his social surroundings. To those who look at the rich material provided by history, and who are not intent on impoverishing it in order to please their lower instincts, their craving for intellectual security as it is provided, for example, by clarity and precision, to such people it will seem that there is only *one* principle that can be defended under all circumstances, and in *all* stages of human development. It is the principle: *anything goes* (38).

This abstract principle (which is the one and only principle of our anarchistic methodology) must now be elucidated, and explained in concrete detail.

Counterinduction I: Theories

It was said that when considering any rule, however fundamental or "necessary for science," one can imagine circumstances when it is advisable not only to ignore the rule, but to adopt its opposite. Let us apply this claim to the rule that "experience," or "the facts," or "experimental results," or whatever words are being used to describe the "hard" elements of our testing procedures, measure the success of a theory, so that agreement between the theory and "the data" is regarded as favoring the theory (or as leaving the situation unchanged), while disagreement endangers or perhaps even eliminates it. This rule is an essential part of all theories of induction, including even some theories of corroboration. Taking the opposite view, I suggest introducing, elaborating, and propagating hypotheses which are inconsistent either with well-established *theories* or with well-established *facts*. Or, as I shall express myself: *I suggest proceeding counterinductively in addition to proceeding inductively.*

There is no need to discuss the first part of the suggestion which favors hypotheses inconsistent with well-established *theories*. The main argument has already been published elsewhere (39). It may be summarized by saying that evidence that is relevant for the test of a theory T can often be unearthed only with the help of an incompatible alternative theory T'. Thus, the advice to postpone alternatives until the first refutation has occurred means putting the cart before the horse. In this connection, I also advised increasing empirical contents with the help of a *principle of proliferation:* invent and elaborate theories which are inconsistent with the accepted point of view, even if the latter should happen to be highly confirmed and generally accepted. Considering the arguments just summarized, such a principle would seem to be an essential part of any critical empiricism (40).

The principle of proliferation is also an essential part of a humanitarian outlook. Progressive educators have always tried to develop the individuality of their pupils, and to bring to fruition the particular and sometimes quite unique talents and beliefs that each child possesses. But such an education very often seemed to be a futile exercise in daydreaming. For is it not necessary to prepare the young for life? Does this not mean that they must learn *one particular set of views* to the exclusion of everything else? And, if there should still remain a trace of their youthful gift of imagination, will it not find its proper application in the arts, that is, in a thin domain of dreams that has but little to do with the world we live in? Will this procedure not finally lead to a split between a hated reality and welcome fantasies, science and the arts, careful description and unrestrained self-expression (41)? The argument for proliferation shows that this need not be the case. It is possible to *retain* what one might call the freedom of artistic creation *and to use it to the full,* not just as a road of escape, but as a necessary means for discovering and perhaps even changing the properties of the world we live in. For me this coincidence of the part (individual man) with the whole (the world we live in), of the purely subjective and arbitrary with the objective and lawful, is one of the most important arguments in favor of a pluralistic methodology (42). . . .

Conclusion

The idea that science can and should be run according to some fixed rules, and that its rationality consists in agreement with such rules, is both unrealistic and vicious. It is *unrealistic,* since it takes too simple a view of the talents of men and of the circumstances which encourage, or cause, their development. And it is *vicious,* since the attempt to enforce the rules will undoubtedly erect barriers to what men might have been, and will reduce our humanity by increasing our professional qualifications. We can *free* ourselves from the idea and from the power it may possess over us (i) by a detailed study of the work of revolutionaries such as Galileo, Luther, Marx, or Lenin; (ii) by some acquaintance with the Hegelian philosophy and with the alternative provided by Kierkegaard; (iii) by remembering that the existing separation between the sciences and the arts is artificial, that it is a side effect of an idea of professionalism one should eliminate, that a poem or a play can be intelligent as well as informative (Aristophanes, Hochhuth, Brecht), and a scientific theory pleasant to behold (Galileo, Dirac), and that we can change science and make it agree with our wishes. We can turn science from a stern and demanding mistress into an attractive and yielding courtesan who tries to anticipate every wish of her lover. Of course, it is up to us to choose either a dragon or a pussycat as our companion. So far mankind seems to have preferred the latter alternative: "The more solid, well defined, and splendid the edifice erected by the understanding, the more restless the urge of life . . . to escape from it into freedom." We must take care that we do not lose our ability to make such a choice.

NOTES

1. V. I. Lenin, 'Left Wing' Communism, an Infantile Disorder (Peking: Foreign Language Press, 1965), p. 100 (the book was first published in 1919 in order to criticize certain puritanical elements in German communism). Lenin speaks of parties and the revolutionary vanguard rather than of scientists and methodologists. The lesson is, however, the same.

2. H. Butterfield, The Whig Interpretation of History (New York: Norton, 1965), p. 66.

3. Ibid., p. 21.

4. Ibid., p. 25.

5. Lenin, 'Left Wing' Communism, p. 100. It is interesting to see how a few substitutions can turn a political lesson into a lesson for methodology which, after all, is part of the process by means of which we move from one historical stage to another. We also see how an individual who is not intimidated by traditional boundaries can give useful advice to everyone, philosophers of science included. Cf. notes 27 and 33, 35, 38.

6. P. A. Schilpp, ed., Albert Einstein, Philosopher-Scientist (Evanston, Ill.: Tudor, 1948), p. 683.

7. D. Hume, A Treatise of Human Nature (Oxford: Oxford University Press, 1888), p. 180.

8. Popper and his followers distinguish between the socio-psychological process of science where errors abound and rules are constantly broken and a "third world" where knowledge is changed in a rational manner, and without interference from "mob psychology," as Lakatos expresses himself. For details and a criticism of this poor man's Platonism, see the text to note 194 below.

9. E. H. Carr, Michael Bakunin (London: Macmillan, 1937), pp. 8–9.

10. Thus external pressure is replaced by bad conscience, and freedom remains restricted as before. Marx describes a similar development in the case of Luther in the following words: ". . . Luther eliminates external religiousness and turns religiousness into the inner essence of man . . . he negates the raving parish-priest outside the layman, for he puts him right into his heart." Nationaloekonomie und Philosophie; quoted from Marx, die Frühschriften, ed. S. Landshut (Stuttgart: Kroner, 1953), p. 228.

Whatever remains of irrationality in history is suppressed by the quasi-historical and indeed quite mythological manner in which scientists describe the genesis of their discoveries, or of the discoveries of others. ". . . history is wholly subordinated to the needs of the present, and indeed only survives to such an extent, and in such form, as serves present needs." Among the present needs, however, the propagation of what is thought to be good science is the most important one. Hence, history is replaced by myths "which are to be consonant with what [one thinks] to be good physics, and they are to be internally consistent." Paul Forman, "The Discovery of the Diffraction of X-Rays by Crystals: A Critique of the Myths," *Archive for the History of the Exact Sciences*, 6 (1969), 68–69. Forman's paper presents an interesting example to illustrate this statement. Another example is the myths which have been invented to explain the origin of the special theory of relativity. For an excellent account with plentiful sources see G. Holton, "Einstein, Michelson, and the 'Crucial' Experiment," *Isis*, 60 (1969), 133–197.

11. "This unique prevalence of the *inner* logic of a subject over and above the *outer* influences is not . . . to be found at the beginning of modern science." H. Blumenberg, *Die Kopernikanische Wende* (Frankfurt: Suhrkamp, 1965), p. 8.

12. "Nothing is more dangerous to reason than the flights of the imagination. . . ." Hume, *A Treatise of Human Nature*, p. 267.

13. An expert is a man or a woman who has decided to achieve excellence in a narrow field at the expense of a balanced development. He has decided to subject himself to standards which restrict him in many ways, his style of writing and the patterns of his speech included, and he is prepared to conduct most of his waking life in accordance with these standards (this being the case, it is likely that his dreams will be governed by these standards, too). He is not averse to occasionally venturing into different fields, to listen to fashionable music, to adopt fashionable ways of dressing (though the business suit still seems to be his favorite uniform, in this country and abroad), or to seduce his students. However, these activities are aberrations of his *private* life; they have no relation whatever to what he is doing as an expert. A love for Mozart, or for *Hair*, will not make his physics more melodious, or give it a better rhythm. Nor will an affair make his chemistry more colorful.

This separation of domains has very unfortunate consequences. Not only are special subjects voided of ingredients which make a human life beautiful and worth living, but these ingredients are impoverished, too, emotions become crude and thoughtless, just as thought becomes cold and inhumane. Indeed, the private parts of one's existence suffer much more than does one's official capacity. Every aspect of professionalism has its watchdogs; the slightest change, or threat of a change, is examined, broadcast, warnings are issued, and the whole depressing machinery moves at once in order to restore the status quo. Who takes care of the quality of our emotions? Who watches those parts of our language which are supposed to bring people together more closely, which have the function of giving comfort, understanding, and perhaps a little personal criticism and encouragement? There are no such agencies. As a result professionalism takes over even here.

To mention some examples:

In 1610 Galileo reported for the first time his invention of the telescope and the observations he made with it. This was a scientific event of the first magnitude, far more important than anything we have achieved in our megalomaniac twentieth century. Not only was here a new and very mysterious instrument introduced to the learned world (it was introduced to the *learned* world, for the essay was written in Latin), but this instrument was at once put to a very unusual use: it was directed toward the sky; and the results, the astonishing results, quite definitely seemed to support the new theory which Copernicus had suggested over sixty years earlier, and which was still very far from being generally accepted. How does Galileo introduce his subject? Let us hear.

"About 10 months ago a report reached my ears that a certain Dutchman had constructed a spyglass by means of which visible objects, though very distant from the eye of the observer, were distinctly seen, as if nearby. Of this truly remarkable effect several experiences were related, to which some persons gave credence while others denied them. A few days later the report was confirmed to me in a letter from a noble Frenchman in Paris, Jacques Badovere, which caused me to apply myself wholeheartedly to enquire into the means by which I might arrive at the invention of a similar instrument. . . ." Quoted from Stillman Drake, ed., *Discoveries and Opinions of Galileo* (New York: Doubleday Anchor Books, 1957), pp. 28–29.

We start with a personal story, a very charming story, which slowly leads us to the discoveries, and these are reported in the same clear, concrete, and colorful way: "There is another thing," writes Galileo, describing the face of the moon, "which I must not omit, for I beheld it not without a certain wonder; this is that almost in the center of the moon there is a cavity larger than all the rest, and perfectly round in shape. I have observed it near both the first and last quarters, and have tried to represent it as correctly as possible in the second of the above figures. . . ." Quoted from Drake, ed., *Discoveries and Opinions of Galileo,* p. 36. Galileo's drawing attracts the attention of Kepler who was one of the first to read Galileo's essay. He comments: "I cannot help wondering about the meaning of that large circular cavity in what I usually call the left corner of the mouth. Is it a work of nature, or of a trained hand? Suppose that there are living beings on the moon (following the footsteps of Pythagoras and Plutarch I enjoyed toying with this idea, long ago . . .). It surely stands to reason that the inhabitants express the character of their dwelling place, which has much bigger mountains and valleys than our earth has. Consequently, being endowed with very massive bodies, they also construct gigantic projects. . . ." Quoted from *Kepler's Conversations with Galileo's Sidereal Messenger,* trans. Edward Rosen (New York: Johnson Reprint Corporation, 1965), pp. 27–28.

"I have observed"; "I have seen"; "I have been surprised"; "I cannot help wondering"; "I was delighted"—this is how one speaks to a friend or, at any rate, to a live human being.

The awful Newton who more than anyone else is responsible for the plague of professionalism from which we suffer today starts his first paper on colors in a very similar style: ". . . in the beginning of the year 1666 . . . I procured me a triangular glass prisme, to try therewith the celebrated phenomena of colours. And in order thereto having darkened my chamber, and made a small hole in my window shuts, to let in a convenient quantity of the sun's light, I placed my prisme at its entrance, that it might be thereby refracted to the opposite wall. It was at first a very pleasing divertisement, to view the vivid and intense colours produced thereby; but after a while applying myself to consider them more circumspectly, I became surprised to see them in an oblonge form. . . ." Quoted from *The Correspondence of Isaac Newton,* vol. I (Cambridge: Cambridge University Press, 1959), p. 92.

Remember that all these reports are about cold, objective, "inhuman" *inanimate* nature, they are about stars, prisms, lenses, the moon, and yet these are described in a most lively and fascinating manner, communicating to the reader an interest and an excitement which the discoverer felt when first venturing into strange new worlds.

Now compare with this the introduction to a recent book, a best seller even, *Human Sexual Response* by W. H. Masters and V. E. Johnson (Boston: Little, Brown, 1966). I have chosen the book for two reasons. First, because it is of general interest. It removes prejudices which influence not only the members of some profession, but the everyday behavior of a good many apparently "normal" people. Second, because it deals with a subject that is new and without special terminology. Also, it is about man rather than about stones and prisms. So one would expect a beginning even more lively and interesting than that of Galileo, or Kepler, or Newton. What do we read instead? Behold, oh patient reader: "In view of the pervicacious gonadal urge in human beings, it is not a little curious that science develops its sole timidity about the pivotal point of the physiology of sex. Perhaps this avoidance. . . ." and so on. This is human speech no more. This is the language of the expert. Note that the subject has completely left the picture. Not "I was very surprised to find" or, since there are two authors, "We were very surprised to find," but "It is surprising to find"—only not expressed in these simple terms. Note also to what extent irrelevant technical terms intrude and fill the sentences with antediluvian barks, grunts, squeaks, belches. A wall is erected between the writers and their readers not because of some lack of knowledge, not because the writers do not know their readers, but in order to make utterances conform to some curious professional ideal of objectivity. And this ugly, inarticulate, and inhuman idiom turns up everywhere, and takes over the function of the most simple and the most straightforward description.

Thus on page 65 of the book we hear that the female, being capable of multiple orgasm, must often masturbate after her partner has withdrawn in order to complete the physiological process that is characteristic for her. And, so the authors want to say, she will stop only when she gets tired. This is what they *want* to say. What they actually say is: "usually physical exhaustion alone terminates such an active masturbatory session." You don't just masturbate; you have an "active masturbatory session." On the next page the male is advised to *ask* the female what she wants or does not want rather than try to guess it on his own. "He should ask her"—this is what our authors want to convey. What is the sentence that actually lies there in the book? Listen: "The male will be infinitely more effective if he encourages vocalization on her part." "Encourages vocalization" instead of "asks her"—well, one might want to say, the authors want to be *precise*, and they want to address their *fellow professionals* rather than the general public and, naturally, they have to use a special lingo in order to make themselves understood. Now as regards the first point, precision, remember that they also say that the male will be "*infinitely* more effective" which, considering the circumstances, is not a very precise statement of the facts. And as regards the second point we must say that we are not dealing with the structure of organs, or with special physiological processes which might have a special name in medicine, but with an ordinary affair such as *asking*. Besides, Galileo and Newton could do *without* a special lingo although the physics of their time was highly specialized and contained many technical terms. They could do without a special lingo because they wanted to start afresh and because they were sufficiently free and inventive not to be dominated by words, but to be able to dominate them. Masters and Johnson find themselves in the same position, but they cannot speak straight any more, their linguistic talents and sensibilities have been distorted to such an extent that one asks oneself whether they will ever be able to speak normal English again.

The answer to *this* question is contained in a little pamphlet which came into my hands and which contains the report of an ad hoc committee formed for the purpose of examining rumors of police brutality during some rather restless weeks in Berkeley (winter 1968–69). The members of the committee were all people of good will. They were interested not only in the *academic* quality of life on campus; they were even more interested in bringing about an atmosphere of understanding and of compassion. Most of them came from sociology and from related fields, that is, they came from fields which deal not with lenses, stones, stars, as did Galileo in his beautiful little book, but with humans. There was a mathematician among them who had devoted considerable time to setting up and defending student-run courses and who finally gave up in disgust—he could not change the "established academic procedures." How do these nice and decent people write? How do they address those to whose cause they have devoted their spare time and whose lives they want to improve? Are they able to overcome the boundaries of professionalism at least on this occasion? Are they able to *speak*? They are not.

The authors want to say that policemen often make arrests in circumstances when people are bound to get angry. They say: "When *arousal* of those present is the inevitable consequence." "Arousal"; "inevitable consequence"—this is the lingo of the laboratory, this is the language of people who habitually mistreat rats, mice, dogs, rabbits, and carefully notice the effects of their mistreatment, but the language they use is now applied to humans, too, to humans, moreover, with whom one sympathizes, or says one sympathizes, and whose aims one supports. They want to say that policemen and strikers hardly talk to each other. They say: *"Communication* between strikers and policemen is nonexistent." Not the strikers, not the police, not people are at the center of attention, but an abstract process, "communication," about which one has learned a thing or two and with which one feels more at ease than with living human beings. They want to say that more than 80 people took part in the venture, and that the report contains the common elements of what about 30 of them have written. They say: "This report tries to reflect a consensus from the 30 reports submitted by the 80 plus faculty observers who participated." Need I continue? Or is it not already clear that the effects, the miserable effects, of professionalism are much deeper and much more vicious than one would expect at first sight? That some professionals have even lost the ability to *speak* in a civilized manner, that they have returned to a state of mind more primitive than that of an eighteen-year-old who is still able to adapt his language to the situation in which he finds himself, talking the lingo of physics in his physics class and quite a different language with his friends in the street (or in bed)?

Many colleagues who agree with my general criticism of science find this emphasis on language farfetched and exaggerated. Language, they say, is an *instrument* of thought that does not influence it to the extent I surmise. This is true as long as a person has different languages at his disposal, and as long as he is still able to switch from one to another as the situation demands. But this is not the case here. Here a single and rather impoverished idiom takes over all functions and is used under all circumstances. Does one want to insist that the thought that hides behind *this* ugly exterior has remained nimble and humane? Or must he not rather agree with V. Klemperer and others who have analyzed the determination of language in fascistic societies that "words are like small doses of arsenic: they are swallowed unawares, they do not seem to have any noticeable effect, and yet the poisonous influence will be there after some time. If someone frequently enough replaces words such as 'heroic' and 'virtuous' by 'fanatical' he will believe in the end that without fanaticism, there is no heroism and no virtue." *Die Unbewaeltigte Sprache* (Munich: Deutscher Taschenbuch Verlag, 1969), p. 23. Similarly the frequent use of abstract terms from abstract disciplines ("communication"; "arousal") in subjects dealing with humans is bound to make people believe that a human being can be dissolved into a few bland processes and that things such as emotion and understanding are just disturbing elements, or, rather, misconceptions belonging to a more primitive stage of knowledge.

In their search for a bland and standardized language with uniform spelling, punctuation, standardized references, and so on experts receive increasing support from *publishers.* Idiosyncrasies of style and expression that have been overlooked by a referee will certainly be noticed by printers or editors, and much energy is wasted in quarrels over a phrase, or the position of a comma. It seems that language has ceased to be the property of writers and readers and has been purchased by publishing houses, so that authors are no longer allowed to express themselves as they see fit to make their contribution to the growth of English.

14. John Stuart Mill, *On Liberty,* quoted from *The Philosophy of John Stuart Mill,* ed. Marshall Cohen (New York: Modern Library, 1961), p. 258.

15. Ibid., p. 265.

16. Even in undetermined and ambiguous situations uniformity of action is soon achieved, and adhered to tenaciously. Cf. M. Sherif, *The Psychology of Social Norms* (New York: Harper Torchbooks, 1964).

17. *A Treatise of Human Nature*, p. xxii. The word "reason" has been replaced by "understanding" in order to establish coherence with the terminology of the German idealists.

18. The first part of the quotation, up to "appearing as," is taken from *Differenz des Fichte-schen und Schelling'schen Systems der Philosophie*, ed. G. Lasson (Hamburg: Felix Meiner, 1962), p. 13. The second part is from the *Wissenschaft der Logik*, vol. I (Hamburg: Felix Meiner, 1965), p. 6.

19. Letter to Gert Micha Simon of October 11, 1949. Quoted from *Gottfried Benn, Lyrik und Prosa, Briefe und Dokuments* (Wiesbaden: Limes Verlag, 1962), p. 235.

20. For details and further literature see "Problems of Empiricism, Part II," in *The Nature and Function of Science Theory*, ed. R. G. Colodny (Pittsburgh: University of Pittsburg Press, 1970).

21. One of the few physicists to see and to understand this feature of the development of scientific knowledge was Niels Bohr: ". . . he would never try to outline any finished picture, but would patiently go through all the phases of the development of a problem, starting from some apparent paradox, and gradually leading to its elucidation. In fact, he never regarded achieved results in any other light than as starting points for further exploration. In speculating about the prospects of some line of investigation, he would dismiss the usual considerations of simplicity, elegance or even consistency with the remark that such qualities can only be properly judged *after* [my italics] the event. . . ." L. Rosenfeld in S. Rozental, ed., *Niels Bohr, His Life and Work as Seen by His Friends and Colleagues* (New York: Interscience, 1967), p. 117.

One must of course realize that science does not achieve final results and that it is therefore always "before" the event, never "after" it. Simplicity, elegance, consistency are therefore *never* a *conditio sine qua non* of scientific knowledge.

Considerations like these are usually criticized by the childish remark that a contradiction entails every statement and that self-inconsistent views are therefore useless for science. I call the remark childish because it assumes that a self-consistent science is a realistic possibility, that the rule which leads to the result just mentioned is the only possible rule, and that the scientist is obliged to play the thinking games of the logician. There is of course no such obligation. Quite the contrary, the scientist can criticize the logician for providing him with inadequate instruments that make nonsense of the complex, delicate, and often self-inconsistent theories he uses.

For further information concerning Bohr's philosophy see my essay "On a Recent Critique of Complementarity," *Philosophy of Science*, 35 (1968), 309–331, and 36 (1969), 82–105. The essay also cites relevant literature.

22. Children "learn to imitate others . . . and so learn to look upon standards of behavior as if they consisted of fixed, 'given' rules . . . and such things as sympathy and imagination may play an important role in this development. . . ." K. R. Popper, *The Open Society and Its Enemies* (New York: Harper Torchbooks, 1967), II, 390. One should also compare the remainder of appendix i/15 which gives a clear account of the irrational elements in our knowledge.

23. In one of his numerous lucubrations in praise of Ordinary English ("Moore and Ordinary Language," in *The Philosophy of G. E. Moore*, ed. P. A. Schilpp, New York: Tudor, 1952, pp. 354ff) Malcolm makes the following comment: ". . . if a child who was learning the language were to say, in a situation where we were sitting in a room with chairs about, that it was 'highly probable' that there were chairs there, we should smile, *and correct his language*" (italics in the original). One can only hope that the children whom Malcolm addresses in this manner are not as gullible as are most of his students and that they will retain their intelligence, their

imagination, and especially their sense of humor in the face of this and other "methods" of education.

24. Cf. below, text to note 208.

25. Commenting on his early education by his father, and especially on the explanations he received on matters of logic, J. S. Mill made the following observations: "The explanations did not make the matter at all clear to me at the time; but they were not therefore useless; they remained as a nucleus for my observations and reflections to crystallize upon; the import of his general remarks being interpreted to me, by the particular instances which came under my notice afterwards." *Autobiography* (London: Oxford University Press, 1963), p. 16. In "Problems of Empiricism, Part II" I have argued that the development of science exhibits phase differences of precisely this kind. A strange and incomprehensible new principle often serves as a "nucleus for observations and reflections to crystallize upon" until we obtain a theory that is understood even by the most uneducated empiricist. For a general discussion of the problem touched upon in this remark, see Hegel, *Wissenschaft der Logik*, I, 51–64. See also St. Augustine, *De doctrina Christiana*, 11/9: "The first . . . case is to know these books [i.e., the books of the old and of the new testament]. Altogether, we may not yet understand them, but by reading we can either memorise them, or become somehow acquainted with them." The way in which apparently aimless talk may lead to new ideas and to a new state of consciousness has been described, briefly, but exquisitely, by Heinrich von Kleist, "Ueber die allmaehliche Verfertigung der Gedanken beim Reden," in Hans Meyer, ed., *Meisterwerke Deutscher Literaturkritik* (Stuttgart: Goverts, Neue Bibliotek der Weltliteratur, 1962), 741–747.

26. "Recourse to direct action changed the whole tenor of the struggle, for the workers' self-confidence is enormously increased (and their knowledge transformed) once they act without delegating any of their power to political parties or trade unions. 'The factory is ours so do we need to start working for the bosses again?' This idea arose quite spontaneously, not by command, or under the aegis of the so-called vanguard of the proletariat [with its special methods, rules, prescriptions, and its special idea of rationality], but simply as a *natural response to a concrete situation*." D. Cohn-Bendit, *Obsolete Communism: The Left Wing Alternative*, trans. A. Pomerans (London: André Deutsch, 1968), p. 67. Cohn-Bendit's emphasis on "spontaneity. . . . The chief enemy of all bureaucrats" (p. 154) agrees with the tenor of the present paper which wants to eliminate excessive bureaucracy not only from *government, but also from the administration of knowledge* (where it appears as an appeal to rationality). For the formation of natural responses to ambiguous situations, see also Sherif, *The Psychology of Social Norms*.

27. (A) K. R. Popper, whose views I have in mind when criticizing the omnipresence of argument, has admitted that "rationalism is necessarily far from comprehensive or self-contained." *The Open Society and Its Enemies*, II, 231. But the question I am asking is not whether *there are* limits to our reason. The question is *where* these limits are situated. Are they outside the sciences, so that science itself remains entirely rational (though the decision to become scientific may be an irrational decision); or are irrational changes an essential part of even the most national enterprise that has been invented by man? Does the historical phenomenon 'science' contain ingredients which defy a rational analysis? Can the abstract goal of coming closer to the truth be reached in an entirely rational fashion, or is it perhaps inaccessible to those who decide to rely on argument only? These are the questions to which I want to address myself in the present essay.

(B) Surprising insights into the limitations of methodological rules as well as into their dependence on a certain developmental stage of mankind are found in Lenin's and Mao's political writings and, of course, in Hegel's philosophy. It needs only a little imagination to turn the positive advice contained in these writings into advice for the scientist, or the philosopher of science.

Thus, we read on pp. 40ff of Lenin's 'Left Wing' Communism (a book that is very useful as a theoretical basis for the criticism of contemporary left radicalism, campus radicals, leftist puritans, and other leftovers from the undialectical political stone age): "we can (and must) begin to build socialism, not with imaginary human material [as does the doctrine of critical rationalism], nor with human material specially prepared by us [as do all Stalinists, in politics as well as in the philosophy of science], but with the [quite specific] human material bequeathed to us by capitalism. True, that is very 'difficult,' but no other approach to this task is serious enough to warrant discussion." Replace "socialism" by "rationality of the future," "capitalism" by "critical rationalism," and our case is stated with perfect clarity.

It seems to me that such attention to the wider political context will free the philosopher of science from the Nagel-Carnap-Popper-Kuhn carrousel. The only philosopher who secretly imbibes the forbidden brew of Leninism is Lakatos—and the results are evident in his magnificent work. All that is required now is that he confess his vices openly so that others may learn to delight and enlighten us in a similar way.

(C) An excellent example of the need for moving forces in addition to argument is provided by the history of witchcraft in the thirteenth to seventeenth centuries. "No mere skepticism, no mere 'rationalism,' could have driven out the old cosmology," writes H. Trevor-Roper in his analysis (The European Witch Craze, New York: Harper Torchbooks, 1969, p. 181). "A rival faith had been needed. . . ." Despite all the arguments against it "the intellectual basis of the witch craze remained firm all through the seventeenth century. No critic had improved on the arguments of Weyer; none had attacked the substance of the myth . . ." (pp. 160–161). Such attacks did not occur, and they could not have been effective. They could not have been effective, because the science of the schools was "empirically confirmed" (p. 191), because it "created its own evidence" (p. 166), because it was firmly rooted in common belief (p. 124), leading to strong experiences, to "illusions" which were "centralised . . . around" the main characters of the dominating myth such as for example "the devil" (p. 125), and because strong emotional forces were expressed by the myth as well. The existence of the empirical evidence made it difficult to argue against witchcraft in a "scientific" manner. The existence of the emotional force would have neutralized even an effective scientific counterargument. What was needed was not simply a formal criticism, or an empirical criticism; what was needed was a change of consciousness, a "rival faith" as Trevor-Roper expresses himself, and this rival faith had to be introduced against tremendous odds, and even in the face of reason. Now it is of course correct that a general and forceful education in the rules of rationalism, dogmatic, critical, or otherwise, will make it more easy for arguments to win the day—well-trained dogs heel more promptly than do their anarchistic counterparts—but the discussion of the value of argument will now be considerably more difficult, and perhaps entirely impossible. Besides, man was not meant to be a rational animal. At any rate he was not meant to be castrated and cut apart. But whatever our position on that head, we shall have to admit that rational argument works with rational people only and that an appeal to rational argument is therefore discriminatory. Rational people are specially prepared, they have been conditioned in special ways, their freedom of action and of thought has been considerably restricted. If we oppose discrimination and mental restriction, then the omnipresence of reason can no longer be guaranteed and our assertion in the text holds. Cf. also Burr's letter to A. D. White, quoted from George Lincoln Burr, His Life and Selected Writings (Ithaca, N.Y.: Cornell University Press, 1943), p. 56, my italics: "To my thought—and here I differ widely from both Buckle and

Lecky . . . —it was not science, not reason that put an end to inhumanity in so many fields: *the pedants were as cruel as the bigots.* Reason came in only to sanction here reforms which had been wrought in spite of her. *The real antagonist of theology and of rationalism alike* [and it does not make any difference whether we speak here of dogmatic rationalists, or of skeptics, or of critical rationalists as is shown by the example of Glanville] *was the unreasoning impulse of human kindliness."*

(D) The example of witchcraft shows that the wider context we need in order to see science, or the "search for truth," in perspective need not be politics. It can be religion, metaphysics, theology, or what have you. In "Classical Empiricism" (in R. E. Butts, ed., *The Methodological Heritage of Newton*, Toronto: University of Toronto Press, 1970), I have linked developments of science with developments in theology and I have commented on the wider perspective of the theologians when compared with that of the scientists. Today, of course, politics are much more popular. Besides, Professor Imre Lakatos, the secretary general of the slowly disintegrating Popperian party, is a politician first, and a theologian only much much later, and he knows Lenin better than he knows St. Thomas. This is why I have taken my extrascientific quotations from revolutionary politics, and not from revolutionary theology (besides, everyone has by now forgotten that St. Thomas was a revolutionary, too).

28. According to Popper we do not "need any . . . definite frame of reference for our criticism"; we may revise even the most fundamental rules and drop the most fundamental demands if the need for different measures of excellence should arise. *The Open Society and Its Enemies*, II, 390.

29. "No new progressive epoch has ever defined itself by its own limitations. . . . In our case, however, watching the boundaries is regarded as more virtuous than transcending them." Speech of Milan Kundera at the IVth Congress of Czech Authors, Prague, June 1967. Quoted from *Reden Zum IV. Kongress des Tschchoslowakischen Schriftsellerverbandes* (Frankfurt: Suhrkamp, 1968), p. 17. "Our case" is of course also the case of revolutionary developments in science and methodology. In his introduction to the German translation of Burke's writings on the French Revolution, Gentz comments in a similar vein (quoted from P. G. Gooch, *Germany and the French Revolution*, London: Longmans, 1920, p. 95): ". . . the eulogist of new systems always finds opinion on his side [optimist], while the defender of the old must [read: will] appeal to reason." The "opinion" of today is, of course, the "reason" of tomorrow which is already present in a naive, immediate, undeveloped form.

30. Leon Trotsky, *The Revolution Betrayed*, trans. M. Eastman (Garden City, N.Y.: Doubleday, 1937), pp. 86–87.

31. The priority of idea over behavior, problem over physical adaptation, brain over body—these are other versions of the ideology I am criticizing, and all of them have been refuted by more recent research. Thus the discovery of the australopithecines confronted us with a being that combines the brain of an ape with nearly human dentition, posture, and (possibly), behavior. Such a combination "was not anticipated in earlier speculation" (George G. Simpson *et al.*, *Life: An Introduction to College Biology*, New York: Harcourt, Brace, 1957, p. 793) where it was assumed that it is the brain that is responsible for the remaining human features and not the other way around: man became erect, he started using his hands, because his brain told him so. Today, we must admit that a new posture leading to new tasks may "create" the brain needed for these tasks (this, essentially, was also Engels's conjecture in his little essay about the function of the band in the humanization of our apelike ancestors).

It also seems that certain comprehensive features of early civilization such as domestication or agriculture did not arise as attempts to solve problems. Rather "man at play inadvertently discovered their practical use." F. Alexander, *Funda-*

mentals of Psychoanalysis (New York: International Universities Press, 1948), p. 113; cf. also G. Róheim, *The Origin and Function of Culture* (New York: Nervous and Mental Disease Monographs, 1943), pp. 40–47, on the origin of the economic activity of mankind, and *Psychoanalysis and Anthropology* (New York: International University Press, 1950), p. 437, on the reasons why parents take care of their children. This is most easily proved by the fact that wool in sheep, a surplus of milk in cows, an abundant amount of eggs laid by fowls are all a *consequence* of domestication and cannot have acted as a *reason* for it. Hahn (*Die haustiere in ihrer Beziehung zur Gesellschaft des Menschen*, Leipzig: Johann Ambrosius Barth, 1896, pp. 79, 154, 300, paraphrased after R. H. Lowie, *The History of Ethnological Theory*, New York: Farrar and Reinhart, 1937, pp. 112ff.) suggests that people kept poultry originally as alarm clocks, or for cockfights—both noneconomic motives. He also suggests that early man was an idler, doing useful labor as, a pastime, rather than with serious and problem-conscious intent. Q. H. Schultz ("Some Factors Influencing the Social Life of Primates in General and of Early Man in Particular," in S. L. Washburn, ed., *Social Life of Early Man*, Chicago: Aldine, 1961, p. 63) says: "It was no radical innovation for Dawn man to use their hands for picking up rocks or clubs as ready defence to overcome the lack of large teeth. Nearly every captive macaque delights in carrying new objects around its cage, and apes are *entertained for hours* by a blanket, or a bucket which they will not let out of their hands without a fight" (my italics).

Wherever we look we see a happy and playful activity leading to accidental solutions of unrealized problems. We do not *see* serious problem-conscious thinkers engaged in the attempt to intellectually discuss and then properly solve the problems they have set up. Later on the sequence is of course inverted by postulating either a divine inventor or a problem situation to which the minds of the contemporaries are supposed to have found the appropriate solution. Such an intellectualistic account is neither correct nor helpful for it prevents us from improving unknown faults of our situation in a spontaneous way and it also prevents us from recognizing such faults in retrospect, after their removal has made their substance clear. By all means, let us be rational: But let us not make the mistake of believing that man can and should improve his lot by reasoned planning only.

32. Cf. notes 22 and 25.

33. I cannot believe that a revolution such as the French Revolution occurred "*in the full consciousness* of [the] rights [which people possess] as men and citizens" as Wilhelm von Humboldt expresses himelf (quoted from Gooch, *Germany and the French Revolution*, p. 109), or that a revolution such as the Copernican Revolution proceeded in the full consciousness of the ideas and methods, and with a full understanding of the instruments about (i.e., within the next 300 years) to be invented. In all these cases the element of action—unreasonable, nonsensical, mad, immoral action when seen from the point of view of a contemporary—is a necessary presupposition of whatever clarity one would like to possess, but can achieve only *after the event*, as the *result* of the actions performed. For material from the history of science see my "Problems of Empiricism, Part II," especially sections 7, 8, 11.

In *politics* and *religion* the point just made implies the need for (mass) action in addition to (party) doctrine, even if the doctrine should happen to contain definite and absolutely clear rules of procedure. *For such rules, while clear and complete when compared with other rules, are aways woefully inadequate vis-à-vis the ever changing multitude of social conditions.* (In physics the situation is exactly the same: the *formalism* of the elementary quantum theory is a monster of beauty and precision. But it is very difficult to exactly specify experimental arrangements capable of *measuring* even the simplest observable. Here we must still rely on the correspondence principle.) But it is just to such conditions that their content must be referred and in the process 'anarchistic' action, i.e., action that is directly related neither to theory nor to the existing institutions, plays an essential part: "We cannot tell . . . *what* immediate cause will most serve to rouse [a revolution], kindle it, and impel very wide masses [of scientists, for example] who are at present dormant into the struggle. . . . History generally, and the history of revolutions in particular, is always richer in content, more varied, more many-sided, more lively and 'subtle' than even the best parties and the most class conscious vanguards of the most advanced classes imagine. . . . From this follow two very important conclusions: first, that in order to fulfil its task the revolutionary class must be able to master *all* forms, or sides of social activity without exception . . . second, that the revolutionary class must be ready to pass from one form to another in the quickest and most unexpected manner." Lenin, '*Left Wing*' *Communism*, p. 100. Cf. also the text to note 5. The application to science is quite straightforward if we keep the proper rules of translation [note 27(B)] in mind. Cohn-Bendit, *Obsolete Communism*, gives a vivid account of an anarchism of the kind. "Problems of Empiricism, Part II" applies the lesson to science. Cf. also notes 35 and 38.

[Addition in fall 1969: I now prefer the label of *Dadaism* to that of *anarchism.* There is not much difference between the two procedures *theoretically* (for partial argument see my essay "The Theatre as an Instrument of the Criticism of Ideologies," *Inquiry*, 10 (1967), 298–310, especially footnote 12 and text). But an anarchist is *prepared to kill while a Dadaist would not hurt a fly.* The only thing he does hurt is the "professional conscience" of the defenders of the status quo which at any rate must be exposed to discomfort if one wants to find its limits and if one wants to move beyond them. The necessity for mass action (interruption of "professional meetings," for example) is not denied—*but it must be restricted by a dogmatic respect for human lives and by a somewhat less dogmatic respect for the views of the opposition.*]

In *philosophy* this point implies the dependence of theoretical structure on individual action and individual decision: Kierkegaard's analysis of the Ethical applies to the sciences as well. See note 35.

34. The phrase "magical" is quite appropriate, for the inclusion of well-formed observational reports was demanded in books on magic, down to Agrippa's *De occulta philosophia.*

35. Our understanding of ideas and concepts, says Hegel (*Gymnasialreden;* quoted from K. Loewith and J. Riedel, eds., *Hegel, Studienausgabe*, vol. I, Frankfurt: Fischer Bücherei, 1968, p. 54), starts with "an uncomprehended knowledge of them" ("Es ist damit derselbe Fall wie mit anderen Vorstellungen und Begriffen, deren Verstehen gleichfalls mit einer unverstandenen Kenntnis anfaengt . . ."). Cf. also *Logik*, I, 39–40. "It sometimes happens that at a new turning point of a movement, theoretical absurdities cover up some practical truth." Lenin, diary note at the Stuttgart Conference of the Second International, quoted from Bertram D. Wolfe, *Three Who Made Revolution* (Boston: Beacon, 1948), p. 599.

The ideas which are needed in order to explain and to justify a certain procedure in the sciences are often created only by the procedure itself and remain unavailable if the procedure is not carried out. This shows that the element of action and faith which some believe has been eliminated from the sciences is absolutely essential for it: "Even intellectual history, we now admit, is relative, and cannot be dissociated from the wider social context with which it is in constant interaction." Trevor-Roper, *The European Witch Craze*, p. 100. "We are here up against an extremely interesting historical and philosophical phenomenon," writes Ronchi in his discussion of Galileo and the telescope ("Complexities, Advances, and Misconceptions in the Development of the Science of Vision: What Is Being Discovered?" in A. C. Crombie, ed., *Scientific Change*, London: Heinemann, 1963, p. 552), "which illustrates the possible harm that can be caused by logic and reason [i.e., by the exclusive use of well-established ideas and rational methods] while pure faith—for all its unreasonable-ness—may bring about the most fruitful results."

It is also interesting to note to what extent Kierkegaard's ideas about the role of faith, passion, subjectivity apply to our scientific life (provided, of course, we are in-terested in fundamental discoveries, and not just in the preservation of the status quo, in methodology, and elsewhere). Cf. *Concluding Unscientific Postscript*, trans. David F. Swensen and Walter Lowrie (Princeton, N.J.: Princeton University Press, 1941), especially chapter II: "Truth as Subjectivity." Kierkegard emphasizes the *process* over the result. "While objective thought translates everything into results and helps all mankind to cheat, by copying these off and reciting them by rote, subjective thought puts everything in process and omits the result; partly, because this belongs to him who has the way, partly because as an existing individual he is constantly in process of coming to be which holds true of every human being who has not per-mitted himself to be deceived into becoming objective, inhumanly identifying him-self with speculative philosophy in the abstract [for example, with the rules of critical rationalism]" (p. 68). One might add that the results of objective thought which are supposed to give reason to everything emerge only at the end of a long *process* which therefore will have to occur without reason and will have to be passed through on faith only: The "rationality" of the early Royal Society, to take but one example, was entirely a matter of faith.

Kierkegaard's thought has had a decisive influence on Bohr (for material see M. Jammer, *The Conceptual Development of Quantum Mechanics*, New York: Mc-Graw-Hill, 1966, pp. 172ff). It could be used, in conjunction with material from the history of science, to help us construct a new methodology which takes into con-sideration the role of the individual thinker, not just because he is there, and be-cause his fate should be of interest to us, but because even the most dehumanized and "objective" form of science could not exist without his unreasonable and humor-less passionate efforts. Cf. also note 27.

36. H. Marcuse, *Reason and Revolution* (London: Oxford University Press, 1941), p. 130. The quotation is about Hegel's logic.

37. Cf. note 18.

38. "It would be absurd to formulate a recipe or general rule . . . to serve all cases. One must use one's own brains and be able to find one's bearings in each separate case." Lenin, 'Left Wing' Communism, p. 64. Cf. also note 27(B).

The reader should remember that despite all my praise for Marxism and its various proponents I am defending its *anarchistic* elements only and that I am defending those elements only insofar as they can be used for a criticism of epistemological and moral rules. I quote Lenin because of his insight into the complexity of historical conditions (which is incomparably superior to the insight of scientists and of philosophers of science) and because he recommends an appropriately complex method. I recommend Luxemburg because in elaborating her method she has always seen the individual before her eyes (one cannot say the same about Sir Karl Popper). I quote Mao because he is prepared to abandon doctrine, to experiment, even in quite fundamental matters. However, I do *not* quote these authors because of their defense of a uniform society of the future, or because of their belief in inexorable laws of history (in the case of Lenin the latter belief is present in a more critical form, for it is connected with *po-tentialities* rather than with actual developments). Such a society, such laws, it seems to me, would be even less attractive than the "system" of today whose dogmatism has the advantage of being tempered by dishonesty, doubt, cowardice, and indolence.

Some of my friends have chided me for elevating a statement such as "anything goes" into a fundamental principle of epistemology. They did not notice that I was joking. Theories of knowledge as I conceive them develop, like everything else. We find new principles, we abandon old ones. Now there are some people who will ac-cept an epistemology only if it has some stability, or "rationality" as they are pleased to express themselves. Well, they can have such an epistemology, and "anything goes" will be its only principle.

39. "Problems of Empiricism," in *Beyond the Edge of Certainty*, ed. R. G. Colodny (Englewood Cliffs, N.J.: Prentice-Hall, 1965), sections IVff, especially section VI. (The relevant material has been reprinted in P. H. Nidditch, ed., *The Philosophy of Science*, London: Oxford University Press, 1969, pp. 12ff, especially pp. 25–33.) "Realism and Instrumentalism," in *The Critical Approach to Science and Philosophy*, ed. M. Bunge (Glencoe, Ill.: Free Press, 1964). "Reply to Criticism," in *Boston Studies in the Philosophy of Science*, vol. II, ed. R. S. Cohen and M. W. Wartofsky (New York: Humanities, 1965).

40. Looking back into history we see that progress, or what is regarded as progress today, has almost always been achieved by counterinduction. Thales' principle according to which there is unity behind the variety of appearances lies at the bottom of all science, ancient and modern. Yet it is contradicted by observations of the most primitive kind (change; the difference between air and iron, for example). The same applies, and to an even larger extent, to Parmenides' principle of the impossibility of all motion. (Even a rationalist like Popper now feels inclined to attack Parmenides on empirical grounds.) The modern interpretation of mental illness as being due not to the action of some external spiritual principle but to autonomous disturbances of the sick organism ran counter to numerous instances where the action of such a principle was *felt* (split personality, hearing voices, forced movement, objective appearance of emotions and dreams, nightmares, etc.) and *objectively observed* (phantom pregnancy, disintegration of speech patterns). Denying the power of the devil in these times was almost as foolish as (or, considering the threat of hellfire, much more foolish than) denying the existence of material objects is regarded today. Then, Copernicus put forth his magnificent hypothesis and upheld it in the face of plain and indubitable experience (for literature see the reference in note 20). Even Newton, who explicitly advises against the use of alternatives for hypotheses which are not yet contradicted by experience and who invites the scientist not merely to *guess*, but to *deduce* his laws from "phenomena" (cf. his famous rule IV), can do so only by using as "phenomena" *laws which are inconsistent with the observations at his disposal*. (As he says himself: "In laying down . . . Phenomena, I neglect those small and inconsiderable errors." *Sir Isaac Newton's Mathematical Principles of Natural Philosophy and His System of the World*, trans. A Motte, rev. F. Cajori, Berkeley: University of California Press, 1953, p. 405.) For a more detailed analysis of Newton's dogmatic philosophy and of his dialectical method see my paper "Classical Empiricism."

Yet all these lessons are in vain. Now as ever counterinduction is ruled out by methodology. "The Counterinductive rule," says W. Salmon in his essay "The Foundation of Scientific Inference" (*Mind and Cosmos*, ed. R. G. Colodny, Pittsburgh: University of Pittsburgh Press, 1966, p. 185), is "demonstrably unsatisfactory." He fails to explain how the application of a "demonstrably unsatisfactory" rule can lead to so many satisfactory results which could not have been obtained in any other way.

41. "Fantasy as encountered in many people today is split off from what the person regards as his mature, sane, rational, adult experience. We do not then see fantasy in its true function, but experienced merely as an intrusive, sabotaging, infantile nuisance." R. D. Laing, *The Politics of Experience* (New York: Ballantine, 1967), p. 31.

Laing restricts his discussion of experience and of fantasy to their effect upon interpersonal relations (p. 23: "here, however, I am concentrating upon what we do to ourselves and to each other"). Fantasy, for him, is "a particular way of relating to the [social] world" (p. 31), telling us of problems, abilities, wishes which have become suppressed. The domain of natural science, the physical universe, remains unaffected.

But why should we restrict ourselves to rebuilding man's perception of *society* and of his *fellow men?* Why should we be interested in social reform alone and consider only new pictures of *society?* Is the structure of our *physical world* to be taken for granted? Are we expected to meekly accept the fact that we are living in a lousy material universe, that we are alone in a great ocean of lifeless matters? Or should we not try to change our vision of this universe, too, by leaving the domain of orthodox physics and considering more charming cosmologies? (The only alternative is to become mechanical oneself—this is the path chosen by some scientists, astronauts, and other strange beings.) Proliferation (revival of astrology, witchcraft, magic, alchemy, elaboration of Leibnitz's *Monadology*, and so on) will be a powerful guide in these matters. Psychiatrists and sociologists, however, must not rest content with changing perception and society. They must interfere with the *physical* world and contemplate *its* reform in terms of our fantasies.

42. Those who want to consider the psychological consequences of proliferation will have to distinguish between intraindividual proliferation (plurality of world views within one and the same individual) and interindividual proliferation (plurality of world views in society, each individual holding only a single view and developing it according to his talents and his drive).

Intraindividual proliferation may in extreme cases lead to multiple personality. If we believe the teaching of psychoanalysis then there are always at least two elements present, the ego and the ego ideal, and the latter is ambivalent, being the result of the Oedipus complex. Freud, *Das Ich und das Es* (Leipzig-Vienna-Zurich: Internationaler Psychoanalytischer Verlag, 1923), p. 40. It is this ambivalence which turns the elements *against each other*, contributes to the *development* of both, and creates the dynamics of the individual. (In an animal which is also guided by different principles, for example by different instincts, the principles are not in competition *but work peacefully side by side*, each becoming active in specific circumstances only: G. Róheim, *Psychoanalysis and Anthropology*, p. 430.) The participation of various elements *in any particular human action* explains the "increase of flexibility, as compared to the animal world"; it explains why man "is the only organism normally and inevitably subjected to psychological conflict" (J. Huxley, *The Uniqueness of Man*, London: The Mall, 1941, p. 22); but it also explains why human behavior always presents "a mild case of insanity" (Róheim, *Psychoanalysis and Anthropology*, p. 442). The situation is further complicated by teachers, deans, bosses, and other authorities "who perpetuate the role of the father, whose demands and restrictions have remained active in the ego-ideal, and now act as moral censors in the form of our conscience" (Freud, *Das Ich und das Es*, p. 44). Imposing such a multiplicity of demands with merciless insistence, with a great amount of moralistic grumbling, threatening, headshaking, is bound to lead to crises in the life of the individual so treated and to extreme actions. "There are . . . disastrous choices [such] as those which confronted young people who felt that the service of God demanded forswearing the world forever, as in the Middle Ages, or cutting off one's finger as a religious offering, as among the Plains Indians." M. Mead, *Coming of Age in Samoa* (New York: Morrow, 1961), p. 200. Are we forced to renounce pluralism in favor of happiness and a balanced development?

I do not think we are driven to those extremes. Proliferation produces crises only if the chosen alternatives are played against each other with a vengeance. "The organization of science," writes R. K. Merton ("Behavior Patterns of Scientists," *American Scholar*, 38 (Spring 1969), 220), "operates as a system of institutionalized vigilance, involving competitive cooperation. It affords both commitment and reward for finding where others have erred or have stopped before tracking down the implications of their results, or have passed over in their work what is there to be seen by the fresh eye of another. In such a system, scientists are at the ready to pick apart and appraise each new claim to knowledge. This unending exchange of critical judgment, of praise and punishment, is developed in science to a degree that makes the monitoring of children's behavior by their parents seem little more than child's play." In a warlike community of this kind proliferation will certainly lead to tension and nastiness (and there exists a good deal of nastiness in science, as well as in other critically rationalistic enterprises) but there is no need to combine proliferation with a war of all against all. All that is needed is less moralism, *less seriousness,* less concern for the truth, a vastly deflated "professional conscience," a more playful attitude, conventionalization of "a lack of deep feeling" (Mead, *Coming of Age in Samoa,* p. 7; cf. also p. 35: "and with this goes the continual demand that [one] should not be too efficient, too outstanding, too precocious. [One] *must never excel his fellows by more than a little,"* my italics)—and a good deal of laziness—and we shall be able to have our cake: to have freedom of choice in practical as well as in intellectual matters—and to eat it: to have this freedom without too much mental or emotional strain. This is one of the reasons why I regard the moralism of today, whether it is now found on the right, with the defenders of "The System," or on the left, with the "New Revolutionaries," whether it carries with itself the invitation to "search for the truth," or the admonition to pursue some practical aim, as one of the most vicious ideologies invented by man.

15

DOES THE MIND MATTER?*

KENNETH S. WAGONER *and* FELIX E. GOODSON

Wagoner. In your writing you have defended the view that experiential components play an active role in both thought and behavior: That experience plays a functional role.

Goodson. Yes, that is true. And you I take it accept the view, frequently called epiphenomenalism, that experience is simply a nonfunctional derivative of certain physiological processes taking place in the nervous system.

Wagoner. I suspect so. It is my position that experience is not necessary for behavioral adjustment. It seems to me that if an experiential component plays some role that would not be completely accomplished by the physiological process, it must to that extent exist apart or be manifested separate from the physiological process. If so where and how? To me such a view implies a "spiritual, mental," substance, call it what you will, that is immaterial and yet has the remarkable capacity to influence material substance. Shades of Descartes.

---

* Written for this volume.

Goodson. I do not hold that experiential components exist apart from, or act separate from, physiological changes. Rather I hold that they are a fundamental aspect of certain remarkable, and as yet unknown, events that I call, for want of a better name, physioexperiential events.

Wagoner. This seems to beg the question. You are pleading the function of an event that you admit is as yet unknown.

Goodson. Well, the specific physioexperiential character of the event is unknown but the experiential aspect is well known. It is given directly in the various categories of experience, such as red, pain, thirst, and sweet, to mention but a few.

Wagoner. I still feel that you are begging the question, that you have simply given expression to the old identity hypothesis that has been around in various guises since Aristotle. If the experiential component is centered in, a derivative of, or whatever, the physical, how does it function apart from the physical? If it does not, it remains contained within the physical. If it does, it must exist apart from the physical and you are back in the old dilemma, of the human being as a split system.

Goodson. It perhaps seems that way but I hold a different view. There are many transformations in nature. Take a flashlight, for instance. There are a number of remarkable transformations as we turn it on, from battery to activation of the filament to the emission of light. In biological systems there are likewise many transformations, all natural outcomes of organismic changes, and I believe that experience can be so considered. The experiential aspect of this physioexperiential event is a natural and functional outcome of biological happenings in the nervous system.

Wagoner. No one I know would disagree with your last sentence. Let us assume for the sake of argument that we someday locate, analyze, and completely understand this so-called physioexperiential event of yours. Surely its presence will be demonstrated in terms of certain physiochemical changes, and our knowledge of these changes will surely be given in terms of recording units or some other experimental observation. What will the experiential aspect provide that is more than this? We will have the necessary information as given in measures of physiological change. What more will a knowledge of the experience provide? Nothing, I submit.

Goodson. That is an interesting point. Even when we know the precise nature of the physioexperiential event there may still appear to be two events, depending upon perspective. From the standpoint of the observer it will appear as your instrument readings, but from the standpoint of the individual within whom it is occurring it will appear as the familiar components of experience.

Wagoner. Well, then it seems to me that you have once again segmented the system into two different kinds of substance, mental and physical.

Goodson. I do not think so. In every process one can always look at the before and the after. One can look at the activity of a flashlight either in terms of the processes in the filament or the light emitted, but there is still only one process.

Wagoner. Perhaps, but to extend your analogy, you are pleading that the light somehow has a function on its own, a function that is somehow "more than" the processes in the filament.

Goodson. I am pleading the function of the total event. In the case of the physioexperiential event the experiential aspect is the only part we know; it is given directly. May I point out that you are pleading the function of an aspect of the event, the physical aspect, about which we know nothing at all, while I am pleading the function of the aspect that is given to us directly. It is known as given. Which of us then is begging the question more?

Wagoner. Yes, but I base my conjecture upon the well-documented position that various processes of the body, if they are to be understood, must be based upon something measurable and objective, something physical rather than something ephemeral, perhaps even mystical.

Goodson. I do not think that experience is mystical; indeed it is the form in which all knowledge is given, objective or otherwise. To doubt the function of experience is to defend the position that the human being could adapt to his environment without such inputs as pain, light, sound, taste, to mention but a few of the experiential categories. Adaptation can be made perhaps, as Helen Keller demonstrated, but it is accomplished only with great effort and persistence.

Wagoner. I can imagine a robot that could adapt just as well as any human being and that would operate completely without the experiential components you talk about. By the time subjective experience occurs, everything necessary in the nervous system for adaptive behavior is already occurring or has already occurred.

Goodson. Yes, I can imagine your robot too. But it would be a robot. Humans are made of different materials, and the principles of their adaptive processes are likewise different.

Wagoner. Not necessarily; with sufficient knowledge that we may well have later on, the proper physiochemical processes could be made to occur and my robot would have experience. Experience would be added and the robot would "think" it was great, but it wouldn't add anything to its behavioral adjustment.

Goodson. You attacked me for some of the statements made in my writing; now let me make a somewhat similar accusation about some of the assumptions implicit in your research. As I recall it, you published an article in which experienced pressure was correlated with the systematic depression of the skin. Doesn't this suggest that, at least in your active research, you accept experience, i.e., that of pressure, as more than epiphenomenal.

Wagoner. It might appear that way, but I don't think so. It is implicit in the notion of epiphenomenalism that experience is a nonfunctional derivative of physiological change. By *nonfunctional* we mean that it does not in itself enter into action, or affect or change behavior, but this does not necessarily imply that it may not be important as a source of information about the process from which it is derived. I notice my shadow moving with me as I walk along. Certainly as far as my behavior is concerned that shadow is epiphenomenal, yet someone could observe it and infer from its movement a great deal about my own movement.

Goodson. An excellent answer. I think I agree with you that epiphenomenalism does not rule out the use of experience and the method of introspection as both the source and technique of important information. But we are not in agreement on the central issue, whether experiential components enter into action. The argument, I think, centers on the issue of what to call the component. You construe it as primarily physical, with the experiential aspect as epiphenomenal. But you do admit to an experiential aspect?

Wagoner. I do not deny that. I have used it in research as an indicator of change, as you have pointed out.

Goodson. But if you admit it, whether as epiphenomenon or something else, haven't you admitted the existence of the very kind of substance you visualize as "spiritual or mystical?"

Wagoner. Go on; this is getting interesting.

Goodson. Wouldn't it stretch our capacity for credulity less to view experience as a natural manifestation of certain biological events, which enter directly into action? We can call them physioexperiential events. They are not some kind of spiritual, mystical intrusion but simply a natural manifestation of the direction in which protoplasm has evolved to resolve the input problem efficiently in a complex organism.

Wagoner. Well, I will admit to one thing, that there is a resurgence of interest in "mental" events, as suggested by a number of the articles that are coming in response to your letters. It seems to me that the burden of proof rests upon those who would give such events a functional role in behavior. Because we can explain the actions of a robot in simpler terms, let us explain the human being in like terms, at least until there is some evidence to the contrary.

Goodson. Well, at least we are in agreement that there is such an physioexperiential event; we simply take different views toward it. Perhaps we are not so far apart after all.

Wagoner. Perhaps.

16

A DEBATE ON MIND

B. Blanshard *and* B. F. Skinner

Opening Remarks by Professor Blanshard

Behaviorism is the view that mind can be adequately studied through the behavior of the body. Sometimes it is offered as a method only, implying nothing as to whether a distinct realm of consciousness exists. But it clearly cannot stop there. If there are in fact conscious events distinct from bodily events, a method that disregards them and confines itself to the body cannot be adequate to the study of mind. If behaviorism is to be adequate as a method, it must also be sound as a philosophy; it will give us an adequate science of mind only if mental behavior *is* bodily behavior. And this bold conclusion is one that both Watson and Professor Skinner have had the courage to draw.

What is the difference between the older and the newer behaviorism? It is not a difference in philosophy; it is a difference in policy over what it is in behavior that may be most profitably studied. Watson held that the events to be studied under such heads as sensation, perception, and imagination were events within the body, and particularly in the nervous system; he held what Lovejoy called a hypodermic theory of consciousness. Professor Skinner's approach is different. Without denying that events in the nervous system do largely determine behavior, he is not much interested in them, for he holds that they are all themselves conditioned by stimuli from the outside. The best course for the psychologist, therefore, is to bypass these minute and often conjectural nervous changes and to correlate observable stimuli directly with observable bodily responses. This is the new program for psychology, which is offered with the promise that if it could be carried through, it would explain every kind of human behavior.

The layman will at once have a question. Is he to understand that conscious motives, feelings and ideas have no part in determining conduct or therefore in explaining it? To this question Professor Skinner's answer is essentially the same as Watson's: ideas, motives, feelings in the traditional sense are not, even in principle, observable events, and science can take no account of them. Does this mean that they may be real events, though beyond scientific range? No. There are no events

from B. Blanshard and B. F. Skinner. The problem of consciousness—a debate. *Philosophy and Phenomenological Research*, 1967, 27, 317–337. Reprinted by permission of the authors, *Philosophy and Phenomenological Research*, and the University of Buffalo Foundation, Inc.

that, if factual at all, are beyond the interest of science. Are we then to dismiss distinctively conscious events altogether? Watson said Yes, on the ground that he could find no such events in his testtubes. Professor Skinner would put it less crudely, but I think his conclusion is in substance the same. He says that to resort to "nonphysical events" is to offer a "fictional explanation" (Skinner, 1953, references at end); the belief in a mind or consciousness irreducible to any form of bodily change seems to him an anachronism, a last lingering survival of primitive animism (Skinner, 1953).

I believe this view to be radically mistaken. I shall urge three points against it: (1) that there *is* such a thing as consciousness, irreducible to physical change; (2) that its denial, instead of according with modern science, is in conflict with it; and (3) that to reject the efficacy of consciousness makes nonsense of practical life (Blanshard, 1939).

First, then, there *is* such a thing as consciousness, distinct from bodily change. For a philosopher to be called upon to prove this is a strange sort of challenge. Modern philosophy began with what I think is the valid insight that consciousness is the most certain thing in the world. Descartes showed that you can doubt with some plausibility the existence of rocks and rivers; you can doubt the existence, at least when unobserved, of your own hands and feet. But you cannot coherently doubt that you are conscious, for to doubt it *is* to be conscious; you establish the fact of consciousness in the very act of doubting it. The behaviorist may reply that by "doubting" Descartes must have meant some physical response, and in taking it for a form of consciousness he was merely deluded. But this will not do either, for a delusion is clearly a fact of consciousness; matter in motion cannot be deluded.

But the behaviorist has persuaded himself that matter in motion is all there is. And if you talk about sensing or perceiving or thinking, he is commonly prepared to tell you *what* movements of matter you ought to mean by these words. For Watson, a toothache was a change in a dental nerve. What is a toothache for Professor Skinner? He says that when a person reports "my tooth aches," he is making a verbal response to an event within his body. What sort of event? Though Professor Skinner adheres to his policy of saying little about such events, this much seems to be clear: the event is a physical event, a movement of matter, since it can be investigated by science, and this is the only kind of event that science recognizes. On the point of greatest interest, Professor Skinner's behaviorism is thus at one with Watson's.

And its major difficulties are the same. The most obvious one is that the experience of pain, for example, is self-evidently *not* the same thing as a physical movement of any kind. That their identification is a confusion can be shown in various ways. First their properties are different. If a pain were any kind of physical motion, we could ask what its direction and velocity were, whereas it makes no sense to talk of the direction or velocity of a toothache. On the other hand, we speak of the pain as dull or excruciating, while a dull or excruciating motion is meaningless again.

Secondly, no behaviorist behaves as if his theory were true. For example, he has occasionally, like the rest of us, had to visit his dentist. The dentist says, "Mr. B., this may be pretty painful; shall I use a little cocaine?" "Yes, by all means," says Mr. B. He clearly wants to avert something; *what?* On his theory, it is a particular physical event, about whose nature he is not very clear. But why should he select this event for his aversion? There is nothing in it as a physical change to make it more objectionable than a million others. What makes it objectionable is plainly just one thing: it happens to carry with it, no one knows why, an excruciating pain, which is as different from the physical change that conditions it as are any two things in the world. If the behaviorist admits that it is this he is trying to avert, he has broken out of his behaviorism; if he denies it, his own conduct refutes him.

Thirdly, he continually deserts his program in his experimental practice. He agrees that, as a psychologist, he is concerned with such events as feeling rage or sorrow, as seeing colors and hearing sounds. What he insists on is that these names be now given not to conscious experiences, which cannot be scientifically studied, but to physical responses that can. But *what* responses are these old names now to mean? It would be ridiculous to give the name "rage" to the limp and drooping behavior of sorrow; one must give it to the kind of behavior that we know as the normal expression of rage. But what that implies is that even in assigning the new terms, we must fall back on the old meanings. "Rage" is now to mean the kind of behavior that we can link uniquely to the *emotion* of rage. We must resort to the conscious state as our only reliable index to the behavior that is supposed to supplant it. Perhaps the oddest achievement of this kind is the Watsonian physiological psychology. Watson would identify seeing blue with the response of the optic nerve to a definite kind of stimulation, namely that of light waves about seven microns long, and seeing red with the response to waves about four microns long. But how did he know which of these minutely different responses to call "seeing blue" and which "seeing red"? It was by starting with the conscious sensation and then looking for its nervous correlate— which meant, of course, that at every step of his experimental inquiry he assumed the very difference between sensation and nervous event which it was his main purpose to deny.

Behaviorists, old and new, have been forced into inconsistency in another way. They are concerned to explain why some responses are acquired and others stamped out. A child, if it tastes sugar, will take it readily in the future, and if given quinine will in the future avoid it. Why? Common sense and traditional psychology answer, because it finds one pleasant and the other disagreeable. The behaviorist must profess not to know the meaning of such words. " 'Pleasant' or 'satisfying'," writes Professor Skinner, "apparently do not refer to physical properties of reinforcing events, since the physical sciences use neither these terms nor any equivalents" (Skinner, 1953). The business of science is simply to report that the sugar response is "reinforced" and the quinine response "extinguished." But *why* should sugar reinforce a response and quinine inhibit it? There is nothing in the physical properties of either, taken alone, that throws the least light on this. Hence even behaviorists as skilful as Professor Skinner in excluding reference to conscious experience find themselves willy-nilly using terms that mean such experience— or else mean nothing at all. Professor Skinner writes, for example, "though we have been reinforced with an excellent meal in a new restaurant, a bad meal may reduce our patronage to zero"; and on the next page, that in extinguishing a response, "the current preferred technique is punishment" (Skinner, 1953). Now do such terms as "excellent," "bad," and "punishment" refer to pleasure and pain or not? If not, they are wholly irrelevant in explaining why one response is maintained and another dropped. If they do help in explaining this, as Professor Skinner here implies that they do, it is because they are drawing their force from an interpretation that behaviorism denies them.

Why should behaviorists reject this interpretation? They answer, as we have seen, that it is because it is vetoed by science, and they want above all things to be scientific. "The methods of science," writes Professor Skinner, "have been enormously successful wherever they have been tried. Let us then apply them to human affairs." What Professor Skinner seems here to be saying is that he is moved by the desire to explain things scientifically, though he cannot mean by this what most people mean. The behaviorists of the sixties, like the positivists of the thirties, dismiss as meaningless all references that go beyond physical things and events, entities that at least in principle can be publicly observed. If there was anything purely psychical about us, like old-fashioned desires and sensations, no one else could ever hope to observe them, or therefore meaningfully speak of them.

This curious "physicalism" of the early positivists has now been abandoned by the positivists themselves; Ayer, Feigl, Hempel and Carnap have all renounced it. Behaviorists apparently still cling to it. They still think it demanded by science, though in fact it is deeply at odds with science. That is my second thesis. It will be enough to support it with a single instance.

Consider the behaviorist treatment of images. Watson took the heroic course of denying that there were such things, thereby, as someone remarked, exalting a personal defect into an ontological principle. I shall not pause to argue whether images exist; I shall assume that they do. No one among us who is a fair visualizer will have any trouble in summoning up, for example, the face of Einstein, with its cloud of white hair, its moustache and wrinkles, and its sad, dark eyes. What is the behaviorist to do with such images? He cannot say that when we talk of them, we mean only certain motions among the particles in the brain, for we know too well that we do not. Nor can he say, with common sense and traditional psychology, that they exist in the realm of consciousness, for now there is no such realm. Professor Skinner struggles manfully with the problem, admitting that "perhaps the most difficult problem in the analysis of behavior is raised by responses beginning 'I see . . . ,' 'I hear . . . ,' and so on, *when customary stimuli are lacking*" (Skinner, 1953). He recognizes that such reports may be true; he has read the famous chapter of Galton in which a portrait painter is described whose imagery was so vivid that he could paint from it after his sitter was gone. Professor Skinner's explanation of such performances is that seeing is a response which may be conditioned to occur in the absence of its normal stimulus, like the salivating of Pavlov's dog. This is no doubt true, but it leaves the critical question untouched. What is the status of the imaginary or hallucinatory object that the subject admittedly "sees"? It is in the physical world for on the behaviorist account, there is nowhere else for it to be. But it is not in the subject's head, for no surgeon, nor the subject himself with the help of mirrors, will ever find it there. And of course it is not in consciousness; Professor Skinner avoids using the word "imagine" and insists on using "see," even in cases of hallucination. Now if the object thus admittedly seen is not in consciousness and not in the head, where is it? One can only conclude that it is out there in nature. But if this conclusion is offered as consistent with modern physics, it is not hard to predict the comment of the physicist. It would certainly be eloquent, but it might not be quotable.

Images have always offered special difficulty for the behaviorists, and I do not want to exploit that difficulty unduly. So perhaps I should add that precisely the same difficulty is occasioned by ordinary perception. Professor Skinner uses the example of seeing a rainbow in the sky. What is it that we are here responding to? He does not, as Watson did, develop the fact of light waves impinging on nerve ends. He holds, and rightly, that these are not what we see; what we are seeing is the reds, greens and yellows of the bow in the sky. But then these reds, greens and yellows are not really there at all. Would any responsible physicist admit for a moment that they are? He would admit, of course, that the vibrations are there, but that is a quite different matter. The whole modern tradition of physics from Newton down has relegated the reds, greens, and yellows to sensations, sense-data in our minds, caused indeed by outer vibrations, but utterly different from them. Bertrand Russell did attempt fifty years ago to work out a philosophy of science that would place even colors, tastes, and smells out there in nature, but in his last important book in philosophy (Russell, 1948), he comes full circle. He holds that *everything* we directly perceive exists in consciousness, and that the entire world of physical science is a speculative construction built on that foundation. And about the secondary qualities such as colors, sounds and smells, physics would surely agree with him. Regarding these qualities, Professor Skinner seems to me caught in a dilemma. If he puts them in physical nature, he is at odds with science. If he puts them in consciousness, he abandons behaviorism. And I doubt if he can find an ontological purgatory between these two.

My third thesis is that behaviorism leaves a vacuum at the heart of our moral and practical life. It makes us out to be hollow men in a wasteland. It tells us that we are machines—enormously complicated machines, but in the end nothing more. Let us assume for the moment that this is true, and ask what would be the value of a world in which only such machines existed and that unscientific embarrassment, consciousness, did not exist. The answer I suggest is simple: it would have no value at all. Consciousness, however frail and evanescent, is the seat of all goods and evils, of all values of all kinds, and they would go out with it like a candle.

Run down the list of things which, in the opinion of major thinkers, make life worth living. What are they? They are such things as pleasure or happiness, wisdom or understanding, friendship, the sense of beauty, the sense of duty. All of them, you will note, are forms of consciousness. The wisdom prized by Spinoza was not that of a computer, even the giant one pictured by the *New Yorker* which, to the dismay of its mechanics, is issuing from its depths a slip reading "Cogito ergo sum." What Spinoza meant was conscious insight, the *experience* of understanding. The pleasure stressed by Bentham and Mill, the friendship prized by Epicurus, the beauty prized by Schopenhauer, were the *experience* of these things; and when Kant put good will at the top of them, he meant the *conscious* recognition and choice of duty. These men would all have been bewildered by the suggestion that the goods they spoke of lay in the play of nerves or limbs; they would have said that if by some miracle an unconscious robot were to duplicate the story of St. Francis or Casanova, there would be no good or evil about it. With that judgment I agree. In an account of human conduct that confines itself to physical change, everything of intrinsic value has been left out.

Nor is that all. The behaviorist is committed to ignoring not only the goods that give life value, but also the motives that make men seek them.* For him the only causes of human behavior lie in its physical conditions. Professor Skinner points out and deplores that it is a "common practice to explain behavior in terms of an inner agent which lacks physical dimensions and is called 'mental' or 'psychic'"; he gives as an instance of this mistake the remark about a lecturer that "what he says

* The criticism has been developed in three recent books, Joseph Wood Krutch's *The Measure of Man*, Floyd W. Matson's *The Broken Image*, and Jacques Barzun's *Science the Glorious Entertainment*.

is often disorganized because his *ideas* are confused" (Skinner, 1953). There can be "no violation," he says "of the fundamental principle of science which rules out 'final causes'" (Skinner, 1953). Conscious purposes and intentions, even if they existed, could not affect bodily behavior; "since mental or psychic events are asserted to lack the dimensions of physical science, we have an additional reason for rejecting them" (Skinner, 1953).

Put abstractly in this way, the doctrine seems not implausible. But consider what it means in the concrete. Here are a few of the things that strictly and literally follow: Your conscious interest or desire to hear a discussion of behaviorism today had no part in making you come here. St. Francis's love for his fellows, if that means a feeling as distinct from physical conditions, had no influence on how he treated them. Hitler's hatred of the Jews contributed nothing toward his orders to have them exterminated. No gourmet has ever chosen one item on a menu rather than another because of his desire for a pleasanter food. Newton's theoretical interest had no part in keeping him at his desk, nor did his ideas of gravitation ever affect in the slightest what he said or put down on paper. No one has ever done anything because he saw it to be his duty, or even because he mistakenly thought it to be his duty. The novelists, dramatists, and historians of the world have been governed by a unanimous illusion. They have represented Othello as moved to action by feelings of jealousy, and Romeo by his love of Juliet, and Silas Marner by his love of money, and Napoleon by his love of power, and Churchill by his love of England. A psychologist with full understanding would have freed himself from such delusions. He would see that all these "mental states" are equally irrelevant in explaining how people behave.

Of course this disparity between the judgment of the world and that of the behaviorist does not *prove* the behaviorist wrong. But it does show who must assume the burden of proof. And if one asks which is the more probable: that every major moralist, historian, and man of letters has been talking nonsense about human life, or that a set of brilliant young psychologists should have been carried away by excess of zeal, one cannot hesitate long.

REFERENCES

1. SKINNER, B. F., *Science and Human Behavior* (Macmillan, 1953), pp. 278, 29, 81, 70, 71, 265–6, 30, 31.
2. RUSSELL, BERTRAND, *Human Knowledge, Its Scope, and Limits* (London: Allen and Unwin), 1948.
3. BLANSHARD, BRAND, *The Nature of Thought* (London: Allen and Unwin; N.Y. Humanities Press, 1939); Chapter IX is an examination of the older behaviorism.

Reply by Professor Skinner

Professor Blanshard correctly paraphrases the behavioristic principle that ideas, motives, and feelings have no part in determining conduct and therefore no part in explaining it, but he is wrong in saying that it is because these things are not observable. No major behaviorist has ever argued that science must limit itself to public events. The physicalism of the logical positivist has never been good behaviorism, as I pointed out twenty years ago (Skinner, 1945).[1] In an adequate science of behavior nothing that determines conduct can be overlooked no matter how difficult of access it may be. To make inferences about private events is not to abandon or destroy an "objective" position. As a behaviorist, however, I question the nature of such events and their role in the prediction and control of behavior.

I do not expect to find answers in any "'hypodermic" theory of consciousness. It is the introspective psychologist who would escape from dualism through physiology. The organism is not empty, and it is important to study what goes on inside it, but most physiologists are looking for the wrong things. No matter how much they may improve their techniques, they will never find sensations, thoughts, or acts of will. On that point Professor Blanshard and I agree, but I do not agree that mental events are thereby shown to be irreducible to physical change.

Behaviorism begins with the assumption that the world is made of only one kind of stuff—dealt with most successfully by physics but well enough for most purposes by common sense. Organisms are part of that world, and their processes are therefore physical processes. In studying behavior, especially the behavior of men, we exhibit further instances of the thing we are studying. In thus behaving about behaving we may raise some tricky problems, but they have their counterparts in "thinking about thinking."

A special problem arises from the inescapable fact that a small part of the universe is enclosed within the skin of each of us. It is not different in kind from the rest of the universe, but because our contact with it is intimate and in some ways exclusive, it receives special consideration. It is said to be known in a special way, to contain the immediately given, to be the first thing a man knows and according to some the only thing he can really know. Philosophers, following Descartes, begin with it in their analysis of mind. Almost everyone seems to begin with it in explaining his own behavior. There is, however, another possible starting point—the behavior of what Max Meyer used to call the Other-One. As a scientific analysis grows more effective, we no longer explain that behavior in terms of inner events. The world within the skin of the

---

1 Skinner, B. F., "The Operational Analysis of Psychological Terms," *Psychology Review*, 1945.

Other-One loses its preferred status. But what about the so-called introspective evidence?

Let us consider a few examples. The so-called *conative* aspects of consciousness have to do with the initiation and direction of action. A man is said to act when he wills to do so and to act in a given way to fulfill a purpose. A competing, external explanation is suggested by the concept of the stimulus. In determining which response will occur and when, a stimulus usurps some conative functions. But a great deal of behavior is not simply elicited by stimuli. It is true that stimulus-response theorists still try to leave the initiation and selection of behavior to a "total stimulating situation," but we often know that such a situation has acted as a stimulus only after the fact. In the concept of operant behavior, not to be confused with stimulus-response theories, the stimulus is merely the occasion for action. The initiation and selection of a response are matters concerning its probability, and probability of response is determined by other variables—in particular, by the contingencies of reinforcement. I have suggested that operant reinforcement is simply a more effective formulation of purpose (Skinner, 1963).[2] To the extent that an analysis of contingencies of reinforcement permits us to predict and control when and how a man will act, we have nothing to gain by speaking of a purposive act of will.

So-called *cognitive* functions of consciousness are also displaced by an adequate analysis of the Other-One. A hungry pigeon will repeatedly peck a colored disk if reinforced with food when it does so, but it adds nothing to say that it pecks because it knows that it will get food. Similarly, if it has been reinforced for pecking a red disk, it will also peck a yellow one, though not so rapidly, but it adds nothing to say that it has seen some similarity in the two disks and has mentally generalized from one to the other. Observable contingencies of reinforcement also account for discrimination, abstraction, and concept formation, as well as for other kinds of changes in behavior said to show cognitive processes. To the extent that they do so adequately, no explanatory role survives to be played by mental processes as such.

But the question is, do we not *see* conative and cognitive activities? Before answering it, we should ask what it means to see anything. Here the mentalist has almost succeeded in sealing off a behavioristic analysis. It has long been supposed that sensing or perceiving is something man does to the environment; we are only beginning to discover what the environment does to man. The modern concept of stimulus control reverses the very direction of action and, for that and other reasons, is not readily seen to be equivalent to "direct experience." A convenient account of stimulus control has been written by Herbert Terrace (1965).[3]

2 Skinner, B. F., "Operant Behavior," *American Psychologist*, 1963.
3 Terrace, Herbert, "Stimulus Control" to appear in W. K. Honig, ed., *Behavior: Areas of Research and Application*.

Instead of asking our subject to describe "what he sees," using his everyday vocabulary supplemented by a few technical terms, we can bring his behavior under the control of explicit stimuli. The subject can be an animal as well as a man. A nonverbal psychophysics, with either animals or men, is proving to be much more feasible than early critics of behaviorism foresaw. The mentalist will say that we are still getting our subject to tell us what he sees—even when he is an animal. But nothing comparable to experience enters into the formulation, although the same contingencies of reinforcement account for the same behavior, including behavior said to report the content of consciousness.

If the mentalist insists that we have still left out "seeing" itself, we must ask him what he means. What has been left out? What *is* seeing? What does a perceiver do—either to, or about, or in response to the world he perceives? "To experience" often seems to mean simply "to be in contact with." We know the world in the social sense of having been introduced to it. Knowledge is a form of "acquaintance" (the word comes from the same root as cognition). But the action is often more positive. The perceiver apprehends the world almost as one apprehends a criminal. He makes it his own almost as if he were ingesting it, as one ingests the body of a god in the rites of Mithra. He knows the world almost in the biblical sense of possessing it sexually.

Contact and possession are important elements in the concept of experience because they are related to the physical privacy of the world within one's skin. They have led to the view that the world *beyond* one's skin can be known only from copies. When the copies are discovered to be bad, it is concluded that the world can never be known as it really is. Richard Held has described the search for copies of reality and for an explanation of their shortcomings in his paper *Object and Effigy* (1965).[4] Physiologists and neurologists have tried to support the notion of inner copies by tracing the stimulus into the nervous system, where it can be more intimately possessed, but their facts seem to show that the organism begins at once to analyze stimuli and to respond to them in ways which cannot be regarded as the construction of effigies. The behaviorist has no interest in experience as contact or possession, and he quite sensibly leaves the environment where it is. And even if private copies of it existed in the external world, they would not answer the question we are asking. Put the thing you see wherever you like— the surface of the organism, in the heart of the nervous system, or in the mind—what does it mean to say that you see it?

The behaviorist must give his own answer, and like everyone else he finds it difficult. The study of operant behavior suggests that we look to the contingencies of reinforcement. How are responses brought under stimulus control? What responses are involved? A pigeon may learn to

4 Held, Richard, "Object and Effigy," in Gyorgy Kepes, ed., *Structure in Art and in Science*, Braziller, N.Y., 1965.

discriminate between colors in pecking at disks for food, but surely there is nothing about seeing color which involves pecking disks. Usually, however, an enormous number of responses come under the same kind of stimulus control, and it is possible that seeing color is something common to them. Precurrent responses of observing or attending to stimuli may be important. In verbal behavior certain generalized contingencies maximize control by stimuli and minimize control by other variables, producing the kind of response I have called a tact—and may be especially relevant. Naming a color is no closer to seeing a color than pecking a colored key, but the psychophysicist usually accepts it as an equivalent activity. A similar analysis of contingencies may eventually explain why a subject responds to one feature of a stimulus rather than to another or sees one thing as if it were something else.

All these issues, together with their uncertainties, arise when we are said to see our acts of will, our thoughts, our sensations, our images. Things of this sort *should* be seen with special clarity. They are inside our bodies; we are in contact with them; we possess them; there is no need for copies. But the fact is, they are not seen clearly at all. Two people rarely agree about them, and for good reason. A private event may be close to the perceiver, but it is remote from the environment which teaches him to perceive. We learn to tell the difference between colors when people reinforce our behavior appropriately while manipulating colored objects. We cannot learn the difference between a resolution and a wish, or between guessing and believing, in the same way. Certain techniques permit the verbal environment to circumvent the fact of privacy, but only to a limited extent (Skinner, 1945; 1957).[5] In particular, we describe our past and present behavior, even when it is not visible to others, and we appear to describe our future behavior when we announce an intention. We often do so simply because we are in a favorable position to observe the variables of which our behavior is a function, and many of these are public, but whether public or private, all the events described are physical.

Professor Blanshard must deny this. "The experience of pain . . . ," he says, "is self-evidently not the same thing as a physical movement of any kind." His example is as nearly self-evident as possible, but I am afraid it does not quite make the grade. Painful stimuli, being inside the body, are both particularly strong and hard to observe in other ways, and they do not need to be copied. The experience of an external object would serve Professor Blanshard less well as an example. The expression "physical movement," taken from a contemporary analysis of matter, also contributes to the plausibility, for a *motion* is not likely to be dull or excruciating. But *things* are. Indeed, these two adjectives are applied to pain just because they apply to the things which cause pain. A dull pain is the kind of pain caused by a dull object, as a sharp pain is caused

5 Skinner, B. F., *Verbal Behavior*, Appleton-Century-Crofts, 1957.

by a sharp object. The term "excruciating" is taken from the practice of crucifixion.

Ideas, motives, and feelings are more important to Professor Blanshard's argument than pain, and they are by no means so self-evidently perceived. The processes or states which such terms describe acquire control very slowly. Only a long and complicated history of reinforcement leads one to speak of sensations, images, and thoughts. Such a history is characteristic only of certain cultures. Our own culture shows wide variations—it produces the thoroughgoing extravert on the one hand and the introspective psychologist and philosopher on the other. Some sort of history of reinforcement is essential. Descartes could not begin, as he thought he could, by saying "Cogito ergo sum." He had to begin as a baby—a baby whose subsequent verbal environment eventually generated in him (though not, I am sure, in millions of his contemporaries) certain subtle responses, one of which was "cogito." It is a loose term, not because the events it is said to describe are necessarily vague, but because they are almost inaccessible to the verbal community which builds all descriptive verbal repertoires.

Professor Blanshard seizes upon my admission that the problem of images is difficult. It is difficult for the mentalist too. What do you see when what you see is not really there—as in a memory, a fantasy, or a dream? But first, what do you see when what you see *is* there? Someone shows you a picture of a group of scientists, among them Einstein. He asks, "Is Einstein there?" and you say, "Yes," as you have been taught to do in thousands of comparable cases. But suppose he asks, "Do you *see* Einstein?" and you say, "Yes." What have you reported? Did you, in response to his question, simply look at Einstein a second time? If so, how do you distinguish between "seeing Einstein" and "seeing that you are seeing Einstein"?

A possibility which needs to be considered is that in reporting that you see Einstein, you are reporting a *response* rather than a *stimulus*. No matter how obscure its dimensions, the behavior called seeing must be involved, and you must be reporting *it*, rather than the presence of the thing seen, when you report that you see something. *You may be reporting the same thing when you report that you see something which "isn't really there"—when you are merely "imagining how Einstein looked."* Seeing something in memory is not necessarily seeing a copy. The whole concept of "stored data structures"—supported without warrant by the analogy of the computer—may be quite wrong. What is stored may be responses—in this case the responses involved in seeing. *When I recall how something looked, I may simply be recalling how I once looked at something.* There was no copy inside me when I first looked at it, and there is none now. I am simply doing again what I once did when I looked at something, and I can tell you that I am doing so.

In another criticism of behaviorism, Professor Blanshard[6] has written, "The bats' heads taken by the toper to be emerging from the wallpaper are clearly not physical objects—what in the world would physics do with them? They are not processes in the nervous system; they are not muscular responses; and it is absurd to turn one's back on them and insist that they are nothing at all." But why is it absurd? We have no more reason to assume the existence of imaginary or hallucinatory objects than of memories as sense data. The toper is quite literally "seeing things." His behavior would be most readily evoked by actual bats' heads emerging from wallpaper, but it can occur, especially after toping, in the absence of any such stimuli. Physiologists may someday find the precursors or mediators of that behavior, but they will never find anything that looks like a bat, for there is nothing of that sort inside the skin *at any time*—whether external stimuli are present or not.

The same explanation may hold for seeing something which does not closely correspond with an external stimulus. Under certain conditions, analyzed in the study of perception, the response of seeing a straight line may be evoked by a curved line. We do not need to say that the straight line is in "the world as it appears to be" and the curved line in "the world as it really is." There is no world as it "appears to be"; there are simply various ways of seeing the world as it is—in this case, a way of seeing a straight line in response to a curved line as a stimulus.

Professor Blanshard feels that I am forced into another absurd position in having to assert that "Hitler's hatred of the Jews contributed nothing toward his orders to have them exterminated" and that Newton's ideas of gravitation never "affected in the slightest degree what he said or put down on paper." But again, why are these statements absurd? If we are to speak of Hitler's hatred, it is necessarily as an inference from a long series of verbal and nonverbal actions. Hitler himself undoubtedly had other information, for he must have observed small-scale actions of the same sort not seen by anyone else, as well as responses of his autonomic nervous system. But no one part of this complex was the cause of any other part—unless, indeed, following William James, we could say that the action caused the feelings. A much more reasonable view is that the whole pattern was caused by environmental events in Hitler's personal history. It is too late to discover enough of these to make a convincing case (only historians and psychoanalysts explain individual behavior that way), but it is important to emphasize that the real causes lay in the environment, because if we want to do anything about genocide, it is to the environment we must turn. We cannot make men stop killing each other by changing their feelings. Whatever UNESCO may say to the contrary, wars do not begin in the minds of men. The situation is much more hopeful. To prevent war we must change the environment. In

[6] Blanshard, Brand, "Critical Reflections on Behaviorism," *Proceedings of the American Philosophical Society*, 1965.

doing so we may well reduce the so-called mental tensions which accompany, and are erroneously said to foster, war-like acts.

And so with Newton. We infer his ideas from the things he said and wrote. Newton himself knew about things he almost said and wrote, as well as things he said or wrote, and revoked, but the ideas he did not quite express were not the causes of the ideas he expressed (in behavioristic terms, his covert responses were not the causes of his overt). The point is important if we are to induce young people to have ideas. For more than two thousand years teachers have been trying to stimulate minds, exercise rational powers, and implant or tease our ideas, and they have very little to show for it. A much more promising program is to construct an educational environment, verbal and nonverbal, in which certain kinds of verbal responses, some of them original, will be emitted. We are closer to such an environment than most educators know.

Did Shakespeare actually represent Othello as moved to action by feelings of jealousy? We should quite justly complain that he had not motivated his character if he had done so. He paints a detailed picture of jealous behavior ending in the smothering of the innocent Desdemona. Most of that behavior, as one should expect in a play, is verbal. Othello tells us about his actions past, present, and future, and his emotional states. Some of this is public and some private, but no one part is the cause of any other part. If he had had time, he might have described the wound he inflicts upon himself, but the felt pain was no more responsible for his death than his feelings of jealousy were responsible for his jealous acts. A common cause was involved in each case. We must turn to the machinations of "honest Iago" to understand Othello's behavior, and it is a standard criticism of the play that Iago's motives are *not* clear. Certainly it will not do for Professor Blanshard to tell us that he was moved to action by his "villainy."

I am surprised that Professor Blanshard cites the contrary judgment of the world. Philosophers seldom enjoy the support of that judgment, and it seems dangerous to value it too highly. When physicists began to assert that fantastic amounts of energy could be extracted from a lump of mud, I doubt that they were much disturbed by the fact that "every major moralist, historian, and man of letters" would have called it nonsense. Against the judgment of the world, the behaviorist may set the opportunity to discover comparable sources of energy making it possible at long last to deal effectively with human behavior. I continue to argue the behavioristic position because I believe it has vast implications. Current education supplies a useful example. Powerful techniques of teaching, derived from an experimental analysis of behavior, are being widely opposed in the name of traditional philosophies of education— philosophies which are avowedly mentalistic and which receive substantial support from mentalistic, particularly cognitive, psychologists. Those who subscribe to them have no really effective new techniques to offer, but their discussions of education are warmly received because they frequently allude to the mysteries of mind. Millions of school children are being sacrificed on the altar of cognitive theory. Men have suffered long enough from that strange quirk in their behavior which keeps them from applying the methods of natural science to their own lives.

Concluding Remarks by Professor Blanshard

In my opening paper, I made three criticisms of Professor Skinner's behaviorism. Has he answered them?

The first point was that a conscious event such as a toothache is not the same as a physical event—that is, a motion of particles—because its properties are self-evidently different. A motion has velocity, but not a pain; a pain may be dull or excruciating, while it is meaningless to say this of a motion. Professor Skinner replies that though a motion cannot be dull or excruciating, a physical object can be, and "these two adjectives are applied to pain just because they apply to the things which cause pain. A dull pain is the kind of pain caused by a dull object, as a sharp pain is caused by a sharp object." On this there are three comments to be made.

First, it seems to be untrue. Dull toothaches or headaches are not normally caused by dull objects, or sharp ones by sharp objects. Secondly, granting that a pain may be caused by a physical thing, that does not show that the pain itself is a physical thing; cause and effect are not necessarily alike. Thirdly, even if the term "dull" is ascribable to a physical thing as well as to a pain, it is ascribed in a wholly different sense. The dullness or sharpness of a thing is a matter of its shape; that of a pain is not, for a pain has no shape. This reply can be extended to other cases. The fact that we describe mental events in terms of metaphors drawn from the physical is not evidence that the mental *is* physical and that we are not using metaphors at all.

In maintaining that there are distinct conscious events, I pointed out, further, that philosophers from Descartes to Russell have found their own consciousness the most certain thing in the world. I am still not clear how Professor Skinner would answer them. He seems to take several lines. One is that they would not have had this certainty if their psychology had been of the right kind and had based itself on the behavior of the Other-One. This of course is true, for we never observe the consciousness of other persons, but only their bodily behavior, and hence if we were confined to this sort of psychology, all talk of consciousness would be ruled out from the beginning. But the question is whether this sort of psychology does not itself leave something out. We all talk with confidence about our own desires and purposes, and the burden of proof is clearly on anyone who would ignore them.

So Professor Skinner offers a second line of reply: we do not need them in explaining behavior. The purpose by which we explain a given action has, if it exists at all, certain conditions of a physical kind. Why not, then, bypass the purpose and connect our behavior directly with these prior conditions? If *a* causes *b*, and *b* causes *c*, then *a* causes *c*, and if we can link these two directly, we shall not need to introduce anything inner or mental whatever. The chief novelty of Professor Skinner's behaviorism lies, I suppose, in this attempt to bypass inner events, whether mental or physical, by correlating their causes directly with their effects and ignoring these events themselves. But surely you do not abolish the intermediate link in the chain by ignoring it. Every chug of the engine in your car has prior causes which are therefore the remoter causes of the car's running, but that does not mean that the engine can be eliminated. Even if you did succeed in linking event 3 with event 1 in your explanation without mentioning 2, that does not prove that there is no 2.

Furthermore, we have the most impressive positive evidence that 2 does exist, the evidence of direct awareness. I am aware that I am now thinking about behaviorism with the purpose of criticizing it. Here we meet with Professor Skinner's third line of reply: he questions this awareness. He says that we never see these inner processes. I agree, for I hold that they are not, like physical processes, the sort of events that can be seen. I can say this, but I am puzzled as to how Professor Skinner can say it. On his theory these processes are as truly physical events in space as the rolling of billiard balls, and such events *can* normally be seen. It is one of the paradoxes about behaviorists that they first tell us that pains and thoughts are just physical movements in space, and then when we draw the conclusion that we should be able to see them like other such movements, they draw back in dismay. Surely they should either give up the theory that these processes are physical movements—that is, give up behaviorism—or else go courageously forward to the view that we may hope, with a new electronic microscope, to see someone's toothache or concept of liberty lurking or scurrying about in his head. This the behaviorist feels, with the rest of us, to be absurd. On his premises, I do not see why.

Still, consistently or not, Professor Skinner does deny that pains and thoughts can be seen, and, on that ground apparently, questions whether there really are such things. But surely seeing is not the only kind of awareness. We may be vividly aware not only of shapes and sizes, but also of our activity of thinking, of our being hot, of being in doubt what should be done about Viet Nam, of the last time we saw Paris, of the funniness of a joke, or of 2-and-2's making 4. I should not for a moment deny that there are difficulties in analyzing these kinds of awareness. I should only maintain that no argument by which people have sought to analyze them away is half so certain as their own disclosures to us. If any behavioristic or Christian Scientist tells me that my consciousness of an intense pain is an illusion, I can only say, No, thank you; if that is science, I prefer to stay with common sense or (heaven help me) philosophy.

The second thesis of my paper was that behaviorism, for all its desire to be scientific, is really in conflict with science. Only physical things and events exist, says Professor Skinner. Images, hallucinations and sensations of blue, if anything at all, must therefore be physical things or events. But no physicist would accept this. No natural scientist would introduce the bats' heads seen by the toper, or our images of Einstein, or the hues we see in the rainbow, into physical space. The behaviorist is here ranging himself not against philosophy only, which he would do with equanimity, but against physics also, which he respects. What is Professor Skinner's reply?

I have had some difficulty in following it, but apparently it is this. The image of Einstein is not an object seen or imagined at all, and hence the problem of finding a place for it does not arise. At some time in the past we have seen Einstein in person or in a picture, and when we now have an image of him, we are repeating the response or activity of seeing. "No matter how obscure its dimensions, the behavior called seeing must be involved, and you may be reporting *it* rather than the presence of the thing seen when you report that you see something." That is, the seeing occurs, but without an object. To have an image is to engage in an activity of seeing into which the alleged object is telescoped or dissolved. And this activity of seeing is of course bodily activity.

What is most striking about this theory, to my mind, is its appeal from experienced fact to a materialist metaphysics; it could hardly have been suggested by the facts themselves. I report that I have an image of Einstein, so clear that I can see the fluffy hair and some of the wrinkles; I am told that in fact I am seeing nothing at all. I report that in my own experience seeing is always a seeing of something or other, that to see and yet see nothing is impossible. I am told that the impossible is perfectly possible, and this must be regarded as a case of it. I report that in my own experience there is a sharp difference between the object of a response and the response itself; I am told that here the object has been absorbed in the response in a way to which nothing in the facts seems to correspond. I report that in my own experience there is a difference between contemplating and acting, that I can envisage a face or a scene without doing anything about it. I am told that there is no such distinction, that contemplating *is* behaving. I report that seeing Einstein in imagination, even if it is in a sense behaving, seems at the farthest possible remove from the making of a bodily adjustment. I am assured that my having an image *is* a bodily adjustment and nothing more.

Now I believe in philosophy, but in a philosophy that starts from facts as given, not as moulded to suit the interest of a materialist or any other metaphysics. The behaviorist is committed to an antecedent philosophical theory which requires him to regard images, like everything else, as physical. But he meets with so stout a resistance from the physicist that he feels compelled to change his tactics and to say that the image is not a physical thing; it is really the physical activity of seeing. But this does not remove the difficulty; it doubles it; for now in addition to calling an image physical, he is trying to dissolve an object into the process of responding to it. It cannot be done. If my image of Einstein is not a physical thing, neither is it a physical process.

My third thesis was that in denying consciousness, behaviorism makes us robots or hollow men, since consciousness is the seat of all values and all motives. Regarding values, Professor Skinner says nothing, and I remain in the dark as to how values of any kind can exist in a world of matter in motion. Regarding motives, however, he is gratefully clear. He accepts my reading of behaviorism as implying that Hitler's hatred had nothing causally to do with his acts of genocide, and adds that mental tensions are "erroneously said to foster war-like acts." Newton's "ideas" made no difference to what he wrote, and Othello's feelings of jealousy were no more responsible for his jealous acts than his feelings of pain were responsible for his death. To the comment that here he would have against him "every major moralist, historian, and man of letters" Professor Skinner replies that these men would also have opposed modern science when it said you could extract vast energy from a lump of mud.

Now I do not think they would; humanists are more likely to be helplessly credulous when scientists speak in their own field. But even if they did, the testimony of humanists when in turn they speak in their own field can hardly thus be brushed aside. They feel threatened by a rising wave of computerized philistinism, which seems bent on liquidating the world they live in. They are coming to learn with bewilderment that the new science of mind rules out as an antiquated delusion the entire realm of mind once occupied by the humanities. It says that in the traditional humanistic sense the poetry of Keats, the thought of Kant, the music of Mozart, the morality of Schweitzer, the religion of Tillich, even the scientific reflection of Newton and Darwin, literally never existed at all, and that there was really nothing about these men except their bodily complexity to distinguish them from an IBM computer. And the theory not only destroys the humanities in principle; it makes education in them or any other field pointless, for there is nothing about a complex robot to make it more worth being than a simple robot. "We cannot make men stop killing each other," says Professor Skinner, "by changing their feelings." Why educate their feelings at all, one wonders, if not even the hatred of a Hitler or the jealousy of an Othello can make the slightest difference in what they do? It seems equally pointless to educate men to reflect, for the foresight of the consequences of their conduct can never affect that conduct. Indeed it is hard to see why, in a behaviorist world, any consequences should be better than any others. Why should I not impose suffering on others if it is only a mentalistic unreality? Fortunately Professor Skinner is so unreasonable a behaviorist as to be a very kindly and considerate man.

He has quoted a name we both revere, and may I do so too in closing? William James, our greatest psychologist, was a man who believed in science thoroughly, but also believed in the existence, the importance, and the efficacy of consciousness. He concluded his Lowell Lectures with this sentence: "I, for one, as a scientist and practical man alike, deny utterly that science compels me to believe that my conscience is an ignis fatuus or outcast, and I trust that you too . . . will go away strengthened in the natural faith that your delights and sorrows, your loves and hates, your aspirations and efforts are real combatants in life's arena, and not impotent, paralytic spectators of the game."

17

REDUCTION AND
THE MIND–BODY PROBLEM*

Terry Horgan

This paper will discuss recent work in the philosophy of mind concerning the mind–body problem, and recent work in the philosophy of science concerning intertheoretic reduction. I hope to bring into focus the ways in which the philosopher's perspective concerning problems of the mind supplements the psychologist's perspective, and to highlight the points at which the two perspectives meet.

The mind–body problem is the problem of the relation between the mental and the physical, in humans and in other higher animals. A classic formulation of the problem, as well as a classic proposal for solving it, was given by Descartes. He contended that mind and body are separate substances: the body consists of unthinking matter, which has physical location and extension; the mind is a nonphysical entity with no precise location in space and no extension, whose essence is consciousness. Descartes' proposal has largely fallen out of favor in contemporary

---

* Written for this volume.

philosophy of mind and philosophy of science, largely because there is no real scientific evidence for the existence of nonextended, nonlocalizable mental substances. Accordingly, recent discussions of the mind–body problem have tended to formulate the problem in terms of *events:* How are mental events related to physical events?

A currently popular answer, much debated in the contemporary literature, is the psychophysical identity thesis, which asserts that every mental event involving a given person is identical to some physical event involving the person's body. Standard rivals to the identity thesis are epiphenomenalism, interactionism, and parallelism. Each of the latter views asserts that mental events are not identical to physical events but they differ in their claims about causation. An epiphenomenalist asserts that physical events cause mental events, but that mental events have no effects whatever. (Mental events are "epiphenomena," because they have no effects.) An interactionist claims that physical events cause mental events, and also the converse. A parallelist maintains that mental and physical events occur "in parallel," without causally interacting with one another.

What is at stake regarding these different conceptions of the mental–physical relation? When this question is posed, the subject of inter-theoretic reduction comes into play. The identity thesis is generally thought to be closely related to the Unity of Science hypothesis. This hypothesis asserts that a unified system of microreduction is obtainable, in principle, among the various domains of science. The system would establish a reductive hierarchy among the sciences in accordance with the hierarchy of composition of the entities with which each science deals. Social groups are composed of multicellular living things, which are composed of cells, which are composed of molecules, which are composed of atoms, which are composed of elementary particles. Accordingly, the social sciences would be ranked high in the reductive hierarchy, the biological sciences would occupy a middle position, and the physics of elementary particles would be the final reductive stage. Because the reducibility relation among theories is transitive, this envisioned reductive system would microreduce all of science to elementary-particle physics, thereby establishing the unity of science.[1]

Both advocates and opponents of the psychophysical identity thesis are often found to agree on these two points: (1) that a successful microreduction of mentalistic psychology to natural science would be at least highly relevant to the truth or falsity of the identity thesis and (2) that one argument for the identity thesis is that its truth would enable just such a reduction of psychology to physical theory. Agreement on these

1 For a discussion of evidence in favor of the Unity of Science hypothesis, see P. Oppenheim and H. Putnam, "Unity of Science as a Working Hypothesis," in H. Feigl, M. Scriven, and G. Maxwell (Eds.), *Minnesota Studies in the Philosophy of Science,* Vol. 2 (Minnesota: University of Minnesota Press, 1958).

contentions by both parties to the dispute establishes the putative connection between the identity thesis and the Unity of Science hypothesis. The belief that the identity thesis is related to the hypothesis of reducibility of psychology, and thus to the more general Unity of Science hypothesis, is a natural one. It is not difficult to understand why many philosophers are at least tacitly inclined to hold this view. At first glance, it seems that the reduction of psychology to physical science would consist simply in showing that persons are identical to their bodies and that every psychological event is identical to some physical event. (The word *event* is used in a broad sense here, to include states and processes.) If the matter is viewed this way, of course, then the identity thesis is part and parcel of the microreduction of psychology. But if we consider the most prominent account of reduction in the philosophy of science, we find that the relation between the identity thesis and the microreducibility of psychology is far more tenuous than it originally appeared.[2]

The most prominent account of reduction is due to Ernest Nagel.[3] Its essentials are as follows. Let T_2 be the theory to be reduced, and let T_1 be the theory serving as the reduction base. We assume that T_2 and T_1 are axiomatic theories with their distinctive primitive predicates and postulates. Now according to Nagel, T_2 is reducible to T_1 just in case the following conditions are met:

1. T_2 contains terms not in T_1.
2. There is a set B of established T_2–T_1 "bridge laws"—laws systematically linking concepts of T_2 to concepts of T_1.
3. Each T_2 postulate is logically derivable from the T_1 postulates and B.
4. For each primitive predicate of T_2 there is a predicate of T_1 such that their biconditional is a bridge law in B.

These conditions characterize reduction in terms of the logical relation of deducibility. T_2 reduces to T_1 just in case T_2 is a logical consequence of $(T_1 \cup B)$, where B is a set of empirically established bridge laws that link the concepts of T_2 to those of T_1. These bridge laws must be biconditionals; that is, they must specify, in terms of the concepts of T_1 alone, necessary and sufficient conditions for applying each concept of T_2.

An example will serve to clarify this description of reduction. Consider the well-known reduction of classical thermodynamics to molecular statistical mechanics. The Boyle–Charles law for ideal gases can be deduced from the principles of statistical mechanics as applied to the molecular theory of gases. The key bridge law required for the reduction is the principle that the temperature of a gas is proportional to the mean kinetic energy of its component molecules. This principle specifies that

---

[2] Jaegwon Kim explores the question of the relationship between the psychophysical identity thesis and several prominent reduction theses, in "Reduction, Correspondence, and Identity," *The Monist*, 3 (1968): 424–38.

[3] See Ernest Nagel, *The Structure of Science* (New York: Harcourt Brace Jovanovich, 1961), ch. 11.

a necessary and sufficient condition for a gas to have any given temperature is that the component molecules of the gas have the appropriate corresponding mean kinetic energy. Once the concept of temperature is thus linked to the concept of mean molecular kinetic energy, the Boyle–Charles law for gases is derivable by logic alone from molecular statistical mechanics together with this bridge law.

We return now to the question of the relation between the psychophysical identity thesis and the thesis that psychology is reducible to physical science. (I will call the latter the *reducibility thesis*.) Reduction, as characterized by Nagel, makes no mention of event identity or attribute identity. The reducibility thesis does not imply that mental events and attributes are identical to physical events and attributes. So the thesis may well be true, even if no mental event or attribute is identical to any physical event or attribute.

The upshot of our discussion, then, is that the psychophysical identity thesis does not have the close connection to the reducibility thesis, and thus to the Unity of Science thesis, that it is often thought to have. The reducibility thesis could equally well be maintained by advocates of any of the nonidentity views: epiphenomenalism, interactionism, and parallelism. Reducibility requires the establishing of systematic bridge laws linking psychological attributes and events to physicochemical attributes and events, but it does not require that these bridge laws be identity statements.

II

In light of this result, we must ask again what is at stake between these various competing mind–body theories. This question will be my central concern for the remainder of the paper. We can begin to develop an answer by first posing another question: What is the relevance of empirical scientific results to the dispute? That is, to what extent can empirical discovery lend confirmation or disconfirmation to (1) the reducibility thesis and (2) the various competing theories of the mental–physical relation? The answer to part (1) of this question is clear: The reducibility thesis can only be established on the basis of *empirically discovered* bridge laws. Whether or not such laws exist, and what they are if they do exist, can only be determined by means of extensive empirical study. The reducibility thesis is an empirical hypothesis, subject to the same sorts of empirical confirmation or disconfirmation as other scientific hypotheses.

Part (2) of our question is more difficult. It is not at all clear how the potential results of empirical inquiry could affect the dispute between the identity thesis and its rival theories. Let us assume, for subsequent discussion, that the reducibility thesis will eventually receive strong empirical confirmation.[4] What would this tell us about the relation of the mental to the physical? Only that mental attributes and events are systematically *correlated* with physical attributes and events. This result appears to be compatible with all four of the standard philosophical theories of the mental–physical relation.

So we have at least reached a negative answer regarding the question of the nature of the dispute between these various theories. That is, we have found that empirical findings cannot provide a basis for choosing one of them over another. How then can the dispute be adjudicated? What is at issue if empirical inquiry is irrelevant to the dispute? One answer—the answer that would be given at this point by a logical positivist—is that nothing whatever is at issue between the competing mind–body theories. A strict logical positivist would insist that the sole cognitive meaning of any statement is contained in its empirical, observationally ascertainable consequences. Hence, because there is no empirical difference between the identity thesis, epiphenomenalism, interactionism, and parallelism, we should conclude that these competing views are really pseudotheses, devoid of all cognitive content. They are metaphysical statements, and all such statements were alleged by logical positivists to be meaningless.

This is not the place to enter into the demise of logical positivism. Suffice it to say that few contemporary philosophers consider themselves strict logical positivists, largely because it has proved extraordinarily difficult to state a precise and unobjectionable formulation of the positivist criterion of cognitive meaning.[5] Furthermore, contemporary philosophers are inclined to admit that certain kinds of meaningful statements —for example, the fundamental assumptions of scientific theories such as quantum mechanics—are incapable of direct translation into purely observational terms. The relation of such assertions to observation is far more indirect than the logical positivists believed it to be.[6]

"But even in the case of quantum mechanics," a sympathizer of logical positivism might say, "there is *some* ultimate connection between theory

[4] Lack of space prevents me from considering the question whether the *falsity* of the reducibility thesis would establish the falsity of certain mind–body theories. If a particular mind–body theory is understood to presuppose the existence of systematic psychophysical correlation laws, then the falsity of the reducibility thesis would establish the falsity of the given mind–body theory. But it is a controversial question whether certain mind–body theories (in particular, the identity theory) *do* presuppose psychophysical correlation laws. For a discussion of this issue, see J. Kim, "On the Psycho-Physical Identity Theory," *American Philosophical Quarterly* 3 (1966): 227–35.

[5] See C. G. Hempel, "Problems and Changes in the Empiricist Criterion of Meaning," *Revue Internationale de Philosophie* 4 (1951): 41–63.

[6] See C. G. Hempel, "A Logical Appraisal of Operationism," *Scientific Monthly* 1 (1954): 251–20. Also W. V. Quine, "Two Dogmas of Empiricism," *Philosophical Review* 60 (1951): 20–43.

and observation. Yet in the case of the various mind–body theories we are considering, it has been claimed that no conceivable empirical finding could favor one thesis over another." This reply seems reasonable: There is indeed an inclination to say that a mind–body thesis must make some difference observationally if it is to possess cognitive content. Perhaps we should stop here and declare, in the spirit of logical positivism, that the mind–body problem is really a meaningless pseudoissue.

Contemporary philosophy of mind has not taken this course, however. Debate over the psychophysical identity thesis and its rivals has continued unabated. Philosophers act as though some sense can be made of the dispute, despite its apparent lack of empirical consequences. So we return to our still unanswered question: What exactly is the import of the mind–body problem, in light of the lack of empirical consequences to differentiate among the competing proposed solutions?

We can come to grips with this question, I suggest, by focusing on the nonempirical aspects of scientific theory construction. Scientists are generally agreed that theory construction involves a vaguely defined but crucially important nonempirical component—simplicity. Two theories, both of which are compatible with all known data and both of which are equally powerful in predictive capability, nonetheless might differ on the score of simplicity. If so, we would choose the simpler of the two.[7]

Certainly many current arguments in favor of the mental–physical identity thesis can be read as attempts to show that the thesis is simpler than its rivals, and that therefore it ought to be adopted. Because of this frequent emphasis on simplicity considerations, philosophical discussions of the mind–body problem are really continuous with—and supplementary to—scientific theory construction. Both enterprises seek to increase our understanding of the world by constructing a maximally parsimonious account of its fundamental features. With respect to this goal of maximum possible simplicity, some philosophical theories of the mind–body relation may be substantially better than others, even though the competing theories do not differ in empirical import. If so, then the dispute begins to make sense and the means for resolving it begin to become apparent.

III

Let me give these considerations some flesh by describing a specific argument frequently propounded by advocates of the psychophysical identity thesis. The argument is due to Herbert Feigl and J. J. C. Smart.[8]

---

[7] On the various types of simplicity involved in scientific theory construction, see R. Rudner, "An Introduction to Simplicity," *Philosophy of Science* 23 (1961): 109–115.

[8] Herbert Feigl, *The "Mental" and the "Physical": The Essay and a Postscript* (Minneapolis: University of Minnesota Press, 1967); J. J. C. Smart, "Sensations and

They claim that the identity thesis significantly simplifies the overall structure of scientific theory, because it enables us to eliminate what they call "nomological danglers," irreducible and unexplainable psychophysical laws. They appear to be arguing as follows: We adopt the Unity of Science hypothesis. In particular, we assume that mentalistic psychology is reducible to physical science (to neurophysiology, perhaps, and ultimately to microphysics). Now suppose that we discover a set of systematic psychophysical correlation laws. The laws of psychology could then perhaps be explained on the basis of the laws of neurophysiology in conjunction with these psychophysical laws. But how are the correlations *themselves* to be explained? They cannot be taken as irreducible and unexplainable, because then it would not be strictly true that psychology is reducible to neurophysiology; it would be more accurate to say that psychology is reducible to neurophysiology *cum* correlation laws. Psychophysical laws would "dangle" outside the domain of the reducing science, because they contain psychological concepts. On the other hand, it is not clear how these correlation laws could be explained on the basis of the reducing theory, because the laws of neurophysiology and the other natural sciences make no reference to mental or psychological concepts at all. So psychophysical correlations pose a dilemma: they are neither explainable nor acceptable as part of the reducing theory.

Feigl and Smart contend that the way out of this dilemma is to *identify* the entities and properties that are connected by psychophysical correlation laws. If we discover a lawlike correlation between experiences of pain and occurrences of a particular pattern of neural stimulation, then we should identify pain with this type of neural stimulation. A correlation that is based on an identity requires no further explanation, because the identity tells us that the "correlated" entities or properties are really one and the same. Moreover, the identity itself is simply not the sort of fact that requires explanation; we don't ask *why* the morning star is the evening star or why water is H_2O. Similarly, if the property pain *is* the associated brain property, we don't need to ask why this is so. Thus if we can derive the laws of psychology from the laws of natural science in conjunction with psychophysical identity statements, then the reduction to natural science will be complete. Identity statements, unlike mere psychophysical correlation laws, are not "nomological danglers" that themselves require explanation.

Considerations of this sort motivate the following passage from Smart:

Certainly we are pretty sure in the future to come across new ultimate laws of a novel type, but I expect them to relate simple constituents: for example, whatever ultimate particles are then in vogue. I cannot believe that ultimate laws of nature could relate simple constituents to configurations consisting of

---

Brain Processes," *Philosophical Review* **68** (1959): 141–50; J. J. C. Smart, *Philosophy and Scientific Realism* (New York: Humanities Press, 1963).

perhaps billions of neurons (and goodness knows how many billion billions of ultimate particles) all put together for all the world as though their main purpose in life was to be a complicated negative feedback mechanism of a complicated sort. Such ultimate laws would be like nothing so far known in science. They have a queer "smell" to them.[9]

It is beyond the scope of this paper to assess the merits of the Feigl–Smart argument.[10] Rather, let me emphasize the *nature* of the argument, in connection with the remarks of section II. Feigl and Smart appeal to simplicity considerations. They contend that a theory that identifies psychological attributes and events with their physicochemical correlates is simpler than one that does not. Reducibility of psychology to natural science would still be possible without such identification, but such reducibility would leave us with irreducible and unexplainable psychophysical bridge laws. It is simpler, they contend, to keep the number of irreducible scientific laws to a minimum, by assuming that the only irreducible laws are to be found in natural science (ultimately, perhaps, in microphysics). They admit that this assumption has no empirical consequences over and above the consequences of the reducibility thesis itself. Nonetheless, they claim that simplicity considerations give us decisive reason to accept the psychophysical identity thesis over rival mind–body theories.

To summarize: I have tried to isolate the major point of overlap between contemporary psychology and contemporary philosophical discussion of the mind–body problem, and I have described a way in which philosophical work can supplement psychological theorizing. The main point of overlap, I suggest, concerns the reducibility thesis. Many philosophers and scientists are inclined to accept this thesis, as well as the more general Unity of Science hypothesis. Their inclination is based not only upon the success of reductions and partial reductions in the past, but also upon the belief that scientific theory as a whole would be notably simpler if the reducibility thesis, and the Unity of Science hypothesis, were true. Still, the question of the truth or falsity of these views is an empirical matter. It is the task of psychologists and other empirical researchers to determine whether there exist systematic intertheoretic bridge laws that would reduce psychology to natural science. Philosophers cannot decide the question in advance.

Philosophical work on the mind–body problem does have a legitimate role to play, however, supplementary to the work of psychologists. This role involves the nonempirical elements that inevitably must enter our

---

9 Smart, "Sensations and Brain Processes," p. 143.

10 I discuss the argument at length in my doctoral dissertation, *Microreduction and the Mind-Body Problem* (The University of Michigan, 1974). I contend there that although the argument does contain an important element of truth, it does not really support the psychophysical identity thesis at all. I argue against the identity thesis, and I adopt a version of mental–physical interactionism.

overall theoretical account of the world—elements of simplicity. If we adopt the reducibility thesis and the Unity of Science thesis as plausible working hypotheses, then the question of the metaphysical status of intertheoretic bridge laws must inevitably be faced. Are such laws to count as irreducible laws within our envisioned unified science, or not? Unified science would evidently be simpler if bridge laws were not among the irreducible, unexplained laws of nature, and this fact compels us to give serious attention to the Feigl–Smart contention that such laws really involve identities. Thus philosophical discussion of the mind–body problem supplements theory construction in psychology: both enterprises aim at the goal of achieving a maximally simple account of our complex world.

Part II
THEORY CONSTRUCTION

T H E three sections of this second division of the book focus directly on the nature and function of theory. Throughout Part II an effort is made to describe theory in a manner that appreciates both the shifting character of our techniques and subject matter and the inescapable requirement that science wherever practiced brings with it a demand for precision and orderly procedures.

The first section, "Nature of Theory," considers both formal and informal kinds of theoretical effort (the latter labeled theorizing) and the problem theory criticism. The section on "Logical Perspectives" then offers a sampling of ways in which formal logical analysis can contribute to theory. The final section, "Procedural Issues," contains a variety of problems relating to theory construction (e.g., an influential treatment of intuition, and the growing concern with implementation of intellectual functions, as by sensuous or experiential factors).

NATURE OF THEORY

This section opens with a selection by Marx on formal theory. Formal theory is defined as interpretive efforts in which hypotheses and similar explanatory devices are publicly announced, as in written reports.

In the second selection Marx considers more informal modes of theory construction—called theorizing—which may be regarded as the important underlying bulk of that iceberg of which formal theory constitutes the peak. A major intent of this paper is to help correct the imbalance that typically exists with regard to the attention that these two types of theory construction receive, and to give more credit than is commonly afforded the crucial role of theorizing in science.

In the final paper of this section Goodson and Morgan review the important problem of evaluating theories. They analyze the more crucial characteristics of good and bad theories and provide guidelines for theory criticism.

18

FORMAL THEORY

Melvin H. Marx

ALTHOUGH the distinction between formal and informal modes of theory construction is sometimes blurred, there is nonetheless one basic characteristic of formal theory that clearly justifies the distinction. This is the fact that formal theory is, generally, the ultimate objective of the scientist and is most likely to be published and scrutinized, in more or less final and reasonably well-polished form. It is the version that tends to be reproduced and described in secondary sources, such as textbooks, as well as, more importantly, the form that is often tested in the laboratory. But it is by no means the same theory that is actually used, in a working form, by the scientists who do the research and the theoretical development. That is, as we shall see in more detail later, it would be a serious mistake to identify this developed product with the *developing* theory

This selection is a revised version of Marx (1970), Chapter 1. © Copyright, Melvin H. Marx, 1970.
Glossary and references for this selection are provided at the end of Selection 19.

as it is spawned and nurtured in the laboratory and/or the scientist's study (or whatever kind of workshop is involved). The latter form is much more likely to be untidy and inelegant, but it is the form that is most important to science, because without it the final polished version is not produced. These less publicized modes of theories, and the related processes that may be labeled *theorizing*, to denote their more informal nature, are considered in Selection 19.

In order to provide a framework for the present situation in psychology with regard to formal theory construction, this chapter begins with a historical overview. The section on theory construction then follows, with discussions of definition, raw materials and building blocks for theories, the role of theory, and modes of theory construction. The chapter is concluded by a discussion of theory evaluation.

Historical Overlook

The first efforts at a formal psychology are generally credited to the Greek philosophers. Their methods were essentially rational, or interpretive in the absence of planned data, although Aristotle had a distinctly more empirical point of view and apparently made a number of astute observations in various fields (see Boring, 1950). Throughout the medieval period empirical science generally languished and the almost purely rational approach of the theologians and philosophers predominated in Western society. The advent of important changes during the Renaissance affected mainly the physical and strictly biological sciences, with such behavioral science as there was still largely tied to philosophy.

The birth of a scientific psychology during the latter half of the nineteenth century was marked by an attempt to make observations of the sort that had come to be characteristic of the natural sciences. The empirical methodology that was used mainly developed from sensory physiology, which with traditional philosophy provided the parentage of the new discipline. Thus Fechner was concerned primarily with the mind–body problem, a classical philosophical legacy, and Wundt and Titchener were concerned with the analysis of consciousness, another ancient philosophical problem. But their techniques were new. They were attempting, for the first time on a large and systematic scale, to make factual observations rather than merely to build interpretations on the basis of some rational scheme.

The emergence of a functional psychology, as a direct by-product of the Darwinian evolutionary theory, offered a less obviously theoretical effort than had the earlier structuralism. As we shall see, however, the functional approach did not deny interpretation. As a matter of fact it laid the basis for a continuing and viable type of theory construction. In the meantime, special interpretations were being developed by the various psychoanalytic and associationistic systems, stimulated initially by Freud and Pavlov, respectively. Nevertheless, in spite of the predominance within psychology of the major "schools," little developed in the way of highly formalized theory until the late 1930's, when the so-called Age of Theory (Koch, 1959) emerged.

Although it was Tolman (1932) who introduced into psychology the intervening-variable concept—a distinctly "theoretical" technique—it was Hull (1943) and later Spence (1956) who developed the most highly formalized (deductive) type of theory. As a matter of fact, the Hull–Spence approach was undoubtedly the major force evident in general behavior theory within psychology throughout the late 1940's and the early 1950's.

Recently, the positivistic (inductive) mode of theory construction has flourished. Its rise is partly a consequence of the disillusionment with the highly formalized theoretical procedure represented by the Hull–Spence tradition; their grand approach was unable to live up to the overly high ambitions of many of its early proponents. This is really a kind of atheoretical procedure, as Skinner (1950, 1961) has emphasized, although it certainly represents a systematic effort as well as a minimal type of theory building.

With regard to the contemporary picture, in terms of avowed efforts at theory building, there now exists a much healthier situation than obtained during the peak of the Hull–Tolman opposition. Far from exclusive concern with one of the two theoretical foci, there are multiple theoretical foci, or perhaps subfoci, with varied interrelationships. The original Hullian theory, first developed into the Hull–Spence theory, has now proliferated into a number of offshoots, such as those represented by the work of Miller (1959), Logan (1960), and Amsel (1958, 1962). On the cognitive side, there has been the development of positions like the well-known Festinger (1957) cognitive-dissonance theory and the more generalized schema of Miller, Galanter, and Pribram (1960). Then there are theoretical "mavericks" (in that they spring from no well-developed prior theoretical source), such as Mowrer (1960a, 1960b), with his concentration upon "hope-disappointment" and "fear-relief" as critical variables in behavior.

Recently there have been many less pretentious theoretical efforts, sometimes called miniature systems, which have neither a relationship with any other focal system nor any large-scale theoretical ambitions of their own. They have developed, and are developing, in close relationship to experimental *problems,* with such theoretical work as now occurs being mainly of the functional mode, as described below.

In addition to their concentration upon behavioral problems, rather than behavior theories, the contemporary theoretical efforts emphasize support *for,* rather than merely evidence *against,* theory. This characteristic serves to distinguish them from the typical experimental-theoretical efforts of the 1940's and 1950's, when the major objective was to disconfirm some implication of an opposing account. These contemporary efforts, although primarily concerned with the building of theory, do show some concern for alternative theoretical accounts. Massive pieces of evidence directly contradictory to one or another of the various major theoretical positions are accorded theoretical weight more or less commensurate with their judged importance. Nevertheless, the bias is positive, and this methodological characteristic is certainly to be strongly encouraged.

An additional encouraging characteristic of contemporary theorizing is its growing eclecticism. Good examples are the Miller's (1959) "liberalized" S-R reinforcement position and the increasing tendency of the operant conditioners, for whom certain concepts (for example, motivation) were once strictly forbidden, not only to introduce such concepts but also to engage in at least a limited amount of explicit theorizing (for example, Honig, 1966, which contains a number of chapters with theoretical content, and the more recent Schoenfeld, 1969). Also, the very recent effort of Goodson (1973) to integrate much of the data of psychology into a unified theory based upon evolutionary principles should be mentioned.

Theory Construction

DEFINITION OF THEORY

Like many concepts in science, theory is not readily definable to the satisfaction of all interested persons. For the present purposes, however, the following definition may be advanced. *A theory is a provisional explanatory proposition, or set of propositions, concerning some natural phenomena and consisting of symbolic representations of (1) the observed relationships among (measured) events, (2) the mechanisms or structures presumed to underlie such relationships, or (3) inferred relationships and underlying mechanisms intended to account for observed data in the absence of any direct empirical manifestation of the relationships.*

Some comments on the three explanatory levels included in this definition are required. For one thing, it is evident that level 2 can be reduced to level 1, the least abstract, by means of empirical demonstration. For example, before the invention of the microscope made it possible to see capillaries in an animal body, the existence of such structures, as bridges between the venules and arterioles, which could be directly seen, was predicted on the basis of a theoretical assumption. Similarly, to take an example on the other end of the size dimension, the existence of the planets Pluto and Neptune was predicted, in the absence of direct empirical evidence, on the basis of logical deductions from other data.

Although psychology has not been so outstandingly successful in such predictions as yet, the fundamental procedure that it uses is the same as that used in the examples mentioned.

Most interest in theory construction attaches to the third, and most abstract, level of conceptualization. Here the relationship between the data, based upon direct empirical observations, and the theory is not so obvious. Consider, for example, the cognitive-dissonance notion (Festinger, 1957). This theoretical proposition holds that there is a very strong tendency toward the maintenance of a consonant relationship among cognitions. An important implication of this theory is that when a decision has been reached with difficulty, an S tends to regard the chosen alternative as relatively more attractive and the rejected alternative as relatively less attractive. The cognitive-dissonance theory has been extremely successful in that it has stimulated a great deal of research not only on human Ss (for example, Abelson et al., 1968; Brehm and Cohen, 1962; Festinger, 1964; Glass, 1968; Zajonc, 1968; Zimbardo, 1969), but also on lower animals (for example, Lawrence and Festinger, 1962; Mowrer, 1963). It is quite apparent that, whatever the initial source of this construct, cognitive dissonance is not something that is directly implicated by the objective relationships among the data, but is rather an invention and intrusion of the theorist. In this respect it is like the great majority of psychological theoretical constructs that have been devised to help account for the great variety of behavioral data.

RAW MATERIALS: FACTS

Before proceeding to the detailed consideration of the various modes of theory development it will be necessary to look a little more closely at the basic raw materials from which theories are constructed. The primary scientific effort is at the empirical level and is expressed in terms of what is often called data language. Because the more or less direct sensory observations that are made at this level are likely to be agreed upon by all observers, they tend to become *facts*, or symbolic representations, usually verbal in nature, of such sensory observations.

"Facts" are deceptively simple. Although there are a number of various logical (philosophical) meanings of the term (see Hanson, 1969), for our present purposes the one outlined in the preceding paragraph is the most useful. It closely represents the actual usage of the term *fact* in ordinary discourse as well as in science. As Guthrie (1946) has aptly observed, it is this meaning—the socially accepted verbalized proposition —that we are actually using when we make such statements as, "Let's get down to the facts." And it is this kind of generally accepted proposition that is at the heart of the scientific enterprise.

As thus used, the term *fact* has several distinguishing characteristics. First, there is the matter of *social consensus*. It is this consensus that produces the factualness in propositions. Second, all facts are *relative*, both in time and place and, especially, in respect to the population of acceptors of the propositions. For instance, it was a fact several centuries ago that the world is flat even though we no longer accept such a statement as a fact. This simply means that it was at the time generally accepted as true by most, if not all, of the various classes or populations of people, including scientists. Thus, facts are not hard and immutable truisms, but are in actuality quite flexible, as indeed they must be if science is to progress.

Third, the relationship of facts to direct sensory observation is not always apparent. This is so because of the critical element of *belief*, or trust, that enters into all facts. Although most facts in science are closely tied to sensory observations, all are not. Consider, for example, the proposition that the world is flat. Few of us would accept that as fact today, but how many of us, scientists included, can point to direct sensory observation of our own that disconfirms this proposition? Or consider the evidence for the principle of evolution. Few people are in a position to offer observations in support of this proposition, or set of propositions, but to most of us the evolutionary principle has a high degree of factualness. This situation exists because of the fact (for most of us!) that we readily defer to authority, in which we place trust. Although these facts may be labeled beliefs, there is no hard-and-fast line that separates such propositions from those for which we do have direct evidence of observation (such as, "the rat turned right at the choice point," "the client wept for five minutes," and so on). As we shall see later, even such apparently simple observations are subject to error—and so there is necessarily a high degree of trust always involved in facts. In this respect scientific facts are on the same continuum as political, economic, and religious dogma—although admittedly at somewhat opposite ends in terms of the degree to which sensory observations are involved. In science, data are generally facts that do involve such sensory observations. So when we speak of the data language we typically mean the language of empirical observation, as contrasted with reasoning or speculation.

BUILDING BLOCKS

Primitive Terms. Primitive terms are thus labeled because it is not the role of the theory itself to define them; rather, they are simply taken from extratheoretical sources, even extrascientific sources, and their ordinary meaning is assumed to apply within the theory. Although there are certain obvious risks involved in this procedure, mainly relating to the variety of meanings and ambiguities that ordinary terms acquire in scientific, let alone lay, usage, it does appear to be fundamentally a reasonable procedure. When there are serious differences of meaning in such ordinary terms, however, it is quite apparent that the efficiency with which the theory is communicated will be improved if the theoretician does make some effort to indicate the precise nature of the meanings that he intends, especially for key terms.

To illustrate the nature of primitive terms let us review briefly one prominent usage. Clark Hull, who developed in the late 1930's and the 1940's the most elaborately formalized learning theory that psychology has yet seen, included extremely detailed primitive terms within his theoretical system itself. For example, in describing the role of the incentive, he specified the weight of the food in grams. Thus, his definition of reaction potential, a key construct in the system, includes the specification of reward as consisting of "a 2.5-gram pellet of the usual dry dog food" (Hull, 1951, p. 100).

This high degree of particularity does have the virtue of being readily understood, even by the least theoretically sophisticated of readers: who does not understand what Hull meant by the terms *food, weight,* and *grams?* Nevertheless, such particularity does tend to circumscribe by definition the generality of the theory which Hull intended to apply to all mammalian behavior—and it has been criticized on this score (for example, Marx and Hillix, 1963, p. 251).

Constructs. Constructs are the heart of theories. Constructs are a special kind of concept. Like all concepts, they represent a categorization or classification of things or events, so that by a single symbol a host of concrete observations can be represented. Simple concepts—such as *chair, circle, automobile, child*—can be identified for the naïve observer by the pointing out of specific examples. This property of being identifiable by direct pointing is not so readily applied to constructs, because they are symbolic representations of a more complex sort. Constructs represent relationships or processes assumed to occur among or in objects or events. Some constructs can still be pointed at, as *events*—for example, *accident* when two automobiles collide. But the kinds of constructs that are used in most theories are somewhat more difficult to identify because they involve more complex relationships, such as the relationships among events. Thus, to take some common examples, although it is relatively easy to identify the behavior *weeping* in a person, the construct *grief* requires more elaborate description (of antecedent events, other persons, and the like). Similarly, although it is relatively easy to identify eating behavior in an infrahuman organism, it is a little more difficult to identify hunger, which involves again both antecedent stimulus events, such as deprivation of food, as well as contemporary behaviors. Because it is this more complex type of concept, the construct, that is typically involved in theories, the difficulties of communication are necessarily greater, apart from the question of the validity of the relationships described in the theory. (The problem of communication will be treated at more length in the later section on operationism under theory evaluation, pp. 17 ff.)

When constructs are related to variables, as they are in most psychological theories, the problems of identification, in an empirical sense, are magnified. Most psychological research is aimed at determining the relationships among variables. Experiments, as even the beginning student of a scientific subject should know, are essentially attempts to relate independent (manipulated) variables to dependent (measured) variables, with unwanted variation eliminated by control (holding constant) of other variables. Now, the experiment and its *immediate* interpretation is often difficult enough, but it is quite apparent that again the difficulties are compounded when a more ultimate type of interpretation is attempted, as by subsuming a number of often diverse experimental results under a single unifying principle—that is, a theory. Small wonder that so many behavioral scientists have turned away from the more formal types of theory construction and followed Skinner and other positivists along the safer path of dealing only with directly observable values. Nonetheless, some theoretical progress has been made, even in psychology, with its inordinately complex subject matter, and there does not seem to be any reason why continued progress cannot be made along the path to more effective behavioral theory.

Before leaving the topic of constructs, one special warning should be sounded concerning their relationship to theory. Use of the more operational types of constructs, such as the intervening variable (discussed below), has often been criticized on the ground that such highly operational constructs are "sterile" (see Benjamin, 1955). I do not think that this criticism is well taken. It is not the construct per se, but rather the theoretical proposition, or set of propositions, in which it is embedded, for which sterility or fertility is at issue. Thus, when critics attack a construct as sterile, what they are really saying, and would be more accurate in so saying, is that they question its *use within a theory*. Although this distinction may seem like a thin one to some, it is basically important because we have enough problems in criticizing theoretical work even if we keep the grounds of our criticism straight. Confusion of functions among the various elements of the theory is an unnecessary muddying of already disturbed waters.

OTHER COMMON TERMS

Although there are of course a number of other terms commonly used in relation to theories, only a limited attempt will be made here to show such relationships. A very brief description will be presented of only the three most important of these other terms—law, hypothesis, and postulate. The decision to limit this discussion is based partly on space restrictions but also on the assumption that, for the present purposes, in critically presenting the fundamental elements of formal theories it is not necessary to consider the logical interrelationships of these other terms at any length.

A *law* is a relatively well-established relationship among variables, usually empirical variables rather than theoretical (abstract) constructs. Being thus close to the empirical level and concrete observations, most laws are composed of primitive terms. However, sometimes the term *law* is used to refer to a more theoretical type of proposition, particularly if it enjoys a high degree of confidence in the scientific community.

The term *hypothesis* is often used to refer to a more tentative or provisional type of theoretical proposition, and specifically to an experimental or statistical prediction in a study. Apart from this relatively limited use, *hypothesis* when used in an explanatory sense suggests less formality and less empirical support than *theory*.

A *postulate* is either a proposition that is part of a more comprehensive theory, and so is directly or indirectly subjected to test (thus being really a kind of hypothesis), or an assumption that is simply made by the theory and is not intended to be tested. In any case the term *postulate* tends to suggest a more singular and specific type of proposition, whether consisting of primitive terms or constructs or some combination thereof, than does the term *theory*.

THE ROLE OF THEORY

Tool and Goal Functions. Generally speaking, all theory may be viewed as having two major and complementary functions: it serves as a *tool*, to guide observation and so produce new and firmer facts, and it is a *goal* of science in that our ultimate objective is as complete an understanding as possible of the natural world, including of course man and his artifacts.

There is some argument as to the utility of theory as a tool, as discussed in more detail below in connection with the inductive, or positivistic, mode of theory construction. Nevertheless, most of us will admit that theory has some utility in this respect. The role of theory as an objective is dual. It (1) summarizes, or describes, and (2) explains.

The summarizing function of theory is valuable because it provides economy of expression. Thus it is simpler to state the "law of gravity" as a kind of general proposition than to state separately the host of discrete observations with regard to falling bodies. Similarly, it is more economical (if sometimes riskier) to use some personality attribute, such as anxiety, to summarize a variety of separate behaviors shown by an individual. Few will argue with this kind of summarizing function, although there is often danger in premature and overextended summarizing.

The explanatory function of theory takes us one step further. Now we must assume that the ultimate objective of our scientific enterprise is the understanding of the order of nature—and that by use of theoretical constructs and propositions (hypotheses, or guesses at relationships among variables) we are not merely summarizing nature but are in addition probing, symbolically, its structure. Obviously such probing, by symbolic representations more or less firmly anchored on an empirical basis, entails even greater risks than the use of theory in its summarizing functions. Some explication of these risks is attempted in later parts of this chapter.

Search for Realities: Discovery or Creativity? There have been many questions raised as to the role of "truth" as an objective of theory. To put the matter a different way, is the major role of the scientist that of a discoverer, of natural phenomena, or a creator, of explanatory propositions concerning nature? Although various authorities have adopted one or the other side of this issue, it seems to me that we need to recognize that the scientist is both a discoverer and a creator. There is no question but that (1) his probes of nature are designed to uncover such order as he can find in nature, and that at the same time (2) he is always to some extent, and frequently to a very great extent, creative. Sometimes, to be sure, his creativity of order is so far ahead of his uncovering order that critics refuse to accept it as valid. But such occasional excesses should not be allowed to obscure the fact that fundamentally, theory construction is an act of creation and that the scientist is in one way or another attempting to create a picture of the world as it really is.

The tempering of the creative aspect of theory construction by the empirical restraints imposed by observation and experiment is perhaps the major problem facing the scientific theorist. The various modes of theory construction represent different kinds of attempts by scientists to solve this problem. To this issue we now turn.

PRIMARY MODES OF THEORY CONSTRUCTION

Following the classification and terminology introduced previously, we may categorize theories into one of four paradigmatic classes: model, deductive theory, functional theory, and inductive theory. These four modes are shown schematically in Figure 1, which is a modification of the earlier version (Marx, 1963, p. 14).

The primary dimension in Figure 1 is the direction of the relationship between theory and data; it is this dimension, with directionality indicated by arrows, that fundamentally differentiates the major modes. Straight vertical lines represent a relatively static, summarizing relation-

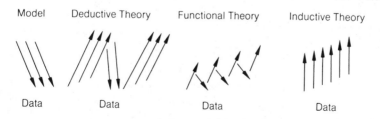

FIGURE 1. *Direction of interaction between theory and data in four modes of theory construction.*

ship between data and theory (characteristic of the inductive mode). Slanted lines represent a more dynamic relationship, in which data, theory, or both play a more active role. The length of the lines represents the scope of the theory, that is, the extent to which it is removed from data. The horizontal dimension represents the passage of time.

No interaction between the empirical and theoretical level is indicated in Figure 1 for either the model or the inductive theory. In the model there is no interaction, because no feedback is planned from data to model. Exactly the contrary relationship is evident in inductive theory, with no feedback intended to operate from theory to data. True interactions are evident in both deductive and functional modes, with feedback from data to theory emphasized in each case.

Although these paradigmatic modes of theory construction are not always exactly exemplified, in actual theoretical efforts, they do tend to be more or less closely approximated. What is most important is that they represent focal types of theory construction and illustrate the major types of interactions between empirical and theoretical levels of discourse.

The Model. As originally intended, in its early applications, a model is a conceptual analogue that is used to suggest how empirical research on a problem might best be pursued. That is, the model is a conceptual framework or structure that has been successfully developed in one field and is now applied, primarily as a guide to research and thinking, in some other, usually less well-developed field. An illustration from the history of psychology would be the use of the telephone switchboard as a model for interpretation of the central nervous system, or from an even earlier era, the hydraulic system as a model for the nervous system generally. Neither of these two physical models is seriously entertained today with reference to the nervous system because now we know enough about its functions to see that they are not particularly appropriate; at the time of their initial proposal, however, our ignorance was sufficient to permit their serious consideration. It may also be mentioned that this consideration was more evident with regard to the interpretation of empirical research on the nervous system than to the suggestion of such research, and in this respect the value of these models was something less than optimal.

The important feature of the model from the present point of view relates to the one-way direction of the relationship between theory and data. When a model is used in the manner described, *essentially as a guide to research,* there is no intention that it be modified as a consequence of the results of that research, as is indicated by the direction of the arrows shown in Figure 1. The lack of interest in revising the model itself—or its strictly heuristic role, to put it another way—is reflected in the statement that it represents an "as if" type of thinking (Boring, 1957).

That is to say, the investigator proceeds "as if" such and such were the case, and is not directly concerned with the validity of his assumptions, but only with their practical value in leading him to useful research and interpretation.

Two serious qualifications need to be made to the preceding description. First, perhaps largely as a function of what Koch (1959) has called the shift in confidence with regard to formal theorizing, an increasing number of investigators have developed what once might have been called theories but now appear in the guise of "models." In other words, the term *model* is more and more coming to replace the term *theory*, mainly perhaps because its use relieves the investigator—or at least may be intended to relieve the investigator—of responsibility for checking the adequacy of any substantive theoretical propositions. Although there is certainly some justification for much of the current usage of the term *model*, it is nevertheless disturbing that the usage has been carried to such an extreme. In addition to erasing what looks like a quite legitimate distinction between the model and the other types of theory construction, the indiscriminate use of what is really theory (at least in our present meaning) in the guise of "model" can too often give the investigator a false sense of security. Ultimately he is going to be called upon to take some responsibility for establishing relationships among the consequences of his interpretative thinking; a good case can be made for the proposition that taking such responsibility should not be too long put off.

Second, there are a number of theoretical endeavors in which a model is used in combination with some other type of theory construction. The best examples here are the recently popular mathematical models in learning theory (Estes, 1959). In these cases a mathematical model, usually fairly simple in form, is taken as an initial framework from which a behavioral theory can be developed. In most cases the theoretical development within the framework of the model is of a more or less deductive mode, in that a formal set of propositions is set up and modified in accordance with empirical results. This usage does involve in part what might be called a true use of the model ("true," that is, to our present definition) because (1) the conceptual structure is taken from another discipline, in this case mathematics, and (2) there is no intention to modify that conceptual framework, insofar as it applies to mathematics. It is the addition of the behavioral theory, which is intended for empirical test and modification, that complicates this particular use of the model and so can lead to some confusion unless the separation of the total theoretical effort into two or more stages is made.

It must be said that by no means everyone will adhere to this distinction, whereby the mathematical models are described as theories, functional or deductive, rather than "true" models. But if it, or some similar distinction, is not maintained, there would seem to be no place to put the strict model within the framework of theory. A good illustration of the viability of the model, so defined, may be found in Spear's (1967) application of the interference theory of verbal associations (developed entirely upon the basis of research on verbal learning with human Ss) to the problem of retention of incentive magnitude—an area of research that has predominantly if not exclusively utilized infrahuman Ss, mainly laboratory rats. This theoretical effort was clearly motivated by an attempt to apply a relatively well-developed theoretical structure to a problem area in need of conceptualization and theoretical structuring, and no intention to look for feedback to the verbal-learning area was evident.

Deductive Theory. As indicated by the diagram in Figure 1, deductive theory involves a distinctly two-way relationship with data. It is marked by a more or less formalized set of logically interwined propositions, well exemplified by the behavior system developed by Hull (1943, 1951, 1952), which are deliberately subjected to a thoroughgoing empirical attack.

This kind of theoretical effort clearly combines the tool (heuristic) function of theory with the goal (theory as an objective) function. Although this is in some ways an advantage, it is also a weakness of deductive theory, in that once a formal set of propositions is developed there are certain disadvantages inherent in it. These are well illustrated by the fate of the Hullian system once serious criticism was directed at it (for example, Koch, 1954; Seward, 1954; Cotton, 1955). For one thing, there is a strong tendency toward personal involvement, which may often interfere with the strictly factual evaluation of the theory itself that is called for, as Skinner (1961) has maintained. Much of the polemic associated with the Hull-Tolman opposition mentioned previously may be attributed to this personal involvement.

Also, and fundamentally more important, once a theory is formalized and propagated it tends to become invested with more authority than the factual underpinnings merit. The inertia of theory so established may well become a serious detriment to the development of more effective interpretations. In spite of these difficulties, and others that will be discussed in connection with functional theory, there is a certain attraction associated with deductive-type theorizing. Part of this is due to its greater elegance—especially in contrast to functional theory, which tends to be messy, like the research to which it is very closely related. All ongoing research is necessarily more untidy in its development than the subsequent account of it. But mostly the attraction of deductive theory is probably due to the fact that it takes the form that we like to think our theory should have—a nicely interrelated network of explanatory propositions all logically tied together. Whether or not the deliberate use of this ultimate type of theory is in practice the best way to *develop* such a theory is an open question. The proponents of functional theory, which we next consider, say no, for reasons which we shall now examine.

Functional Theory. The major distinction between functional theory construction and the deductive mode is that the functional mode entails interpretation that is much more short term. That is, nothing as elaborate as the Hullian system is attempted; rather, the emphasis is on relatively modest and restricted explanatory propositions, whose development is closely related to a particular experimental problem and the data that can be produced to bear upon this problem. Thus the functional type of theory is not only closer to the data, and therefore much more readily modified, but also of considerably less scope than the typical deductive theory. This quicker responsiveness to data is indicated in Figure 1 by use of single short arrows, rather than sets of longer arrows, for both directions of the interaction.

These differences, although important, are nonetheless differences of degree rather than kind, because both types of theory utilize deductive (as well as, less overtly, inductive) reasoning and both types emphasize feedback from research data. Most of the examples of functional theorizing can be drawn, historically, from the functionalism school in psychology (see Hilgard and Bower, 1966, Ch. 10; Marx and Hillix, 1973, Ch. 10). Contemporary illustrations are less easy to identify, mainly because by its very nature this kind of modest theorizing is less conspicuous than the other modes. However, it does seem safe to assert that, in various guises, most contemporary theoretical-experimental work may be placed in this classification, because the emphasis more and more tends to be on the problem rather than on the theory per se.

The major criticism that has been generally directed against the functional type of theory concerns its lack of distinctiveness. Much as eclectism has been attacked for being nondescript and vapid, as compared with more distinctive forms of theoretical doctrine, so functionalism has been accused of a lack of clearcut theoretical substance. Most of this kind of criticism has come from proponents of formal deductive theory, such as Hullian. On the other hand, functional theory is sometimes also attacked from the opposite side, by positivistic psychologists expounding the virtues of inductive theory or no theory at all, for being too theoretical. This amenability to attack from either side of the theoretical spectrum reflects the central position of functional theory and its problems.

Inductive Theory. As the least overtly "theoretical" mode of interpretation of data, inductive theory is best illustrated in contemporary psychology by the operant-conditioning movement spearheaded by Skinner (1938, 1956, 1961, 1966a, 1966b). This variety of positivism (or ultrapositivism) is marked by an aversion to explicit interpretation of a theoretical sort and by the belief that once sufficient facts, or data, are accumulated they will speak for themselves. In other words, summary statements of empirical relationships will be gradually accumulated and will eventually become the kind of generalized explanatory principles that we need. No logical inferences or deductive conclusions are necessary. The strictly inductive procedure (working from individual instances to general conclusions, rather than from hypothesized general conclusions as premises to particular instances, as in the case of the deductive mode) is indicated in Figure 1, where the inductive mode is shown to involve a strictly one-way relationship: data to theory. Moreover, the strictly summarizing function of inductive theory is indicated by the vertical, as compared to sloping, lines; this characteristic is intended to suggest the absence of any directive influence (tool function) by theory.

Most of the criticisms of the deductive mode of theory construction, the major ones of which have been mentioned, have come from the proponents of inductive theory. Besides Skinner himself these have included Brunswik (1955a, 1955b) and Sidman (1960).

Critics of the strictly inductive mode of theory construction have pointed to the older, and better-established, sciences, in which logical (deductive) inferences have consistently played a major role in their development (*in addition to* the primarily inductive activities, or fact accumulation, the importance of which is not denied). Another argument against the Skinnerian approach is that the positivist is actually using some kind of inference, as in designing his experiments. This activity constitutes in practice a kind of interpretation of prior data, and it is better by far that his logic be explicated than that it remain hidden in his own covert (thinking) behavior, or be restricted to those to whom he speaks informally, as in his laboratory. It is held that the social corrective function of science, by means of which errors of individuals in experiment or theory are corrected when others attempt to repeat observations and interpretations, is best served if such public exposure of the logic behind the data collection is expressly planned and produced.

From the present point of view, it is not necessary to decide which of these various procedures is best or to attempt to decide which of the various criticisms has the most merit. There does not seem to be an inherent weakness in any of the theoretical modes described, although different sorts of weaknesses may of course develop in the various ways in which the procedures are implemented. All of the modes of theory construction may therefore be said to have their place in psychology; those we use will be determined partly by our own experiential background, accounting for our own individual styles of research, and partly by the problems we are attacking. But there is plenty of room for each of these procedures and there is greater likelihood of eventual scientific advance if all are used.

Theory Evaluation

CHARACTERISTICS OF THEORIES

There is one prime characteristic that a theory must have if it is to be scientifically useful, and that characteristic is testability. This criterion is therefore discussed first in this section, followed by the intimately related problem of fitting the theory to the data, which many will see as the fundamental characteristic but which is always dependent upon the testability factor. Certain other important but less critical considerations are then treated.

Testability. If there is no way of testing a theory it is scientifically worthless, no matter how plausible, imaginative, or innovative it may be. This proposition is sometimes hard for the layman to swallow. As a matter of fact, it may also sometimes be hard for the scientist to accept. But there does not seem to be any alternative to its acceptance.

The major obstacle to acceptance of the priority of the testability criterion is probably the feeling that a theory which successfully predicts natural events is the most valuable theory, and that therefore successful prediction—or, put another way, a close fit with the data—is the most important criterion of a good theory. As suggested, this argument overlooks the simple fact that only a testable theory can be a successful theory in this sense, so that we have not really overturned our primary criterion, but have rather elaborated or implemented it. Furthermore, in real scientific life theories typically contribute not by being right but *by being wrong.* In other words, scientific advance in theory as well as experiment tends to be built upon the successive correction of many errors, both small and large. Thus the popular notion that a theory must be right to be useful is incorrect. As the following selection spells out in detail, this notion is based upon the fallacious assumption that effective theories are produced, full blown, by some sort of insight rather than by a succession of less effective approximations. But the latter process is actually the more common one. Indeed, the scientist alone among men not only admits the probability of his being wrong, but in a sense earnestly endeavors to be wrong, so as to be able to pinpoint not only the direction but also the amount of his error. Upon a succession of such "errors" the correct interpretation is ultimately developed. The success of this process obviously depends at all times upon the testability of the theories that are actually advanced and used.

It is important to note that testability does not always need to be direct and immediate. Many illustrations of this fact may be found in astronomy, where experiments in the sense of active manipulation of variables are generally not feasible. Consider also the theory of evolution, as propounded by Darwin. Here experiments as well as field observations can be performed and the theory can be tested in a wide variety of ways. But it is not tested directly, in the sense that new animals or species are produced through natural selection. Rather, the multiple implications of the theory—in such widely separated fields as paleontology, comparative anatomy, and biochemistry—are tested. A major factor in the nearly universal scientific acceptance of the Darwinian theory has been its great success in producing such testable implications, and the very high degree of confirmation that they have enjoyed.

The only qualification to this general position concerns *potential* testability. That is, a particular theory may be at the present time untestable, but should new techniques or devices be developed it may well become testable. Potential testability may therefore be accepted, although grudgingly, because if this door is opened too wide it may well turn out to have opened a Pandora's box. Perhaps the best way to resolve this dilemma is to advise the petitioner that he should return when the necessary techniques have been developed, that is, when the theory has become testable. In the meantime if he or others wish to hold on to the theory, that is their business, but it must not be misrepresented as scientifically valuable until its testability is assured.

Significance. The criterion of significance, which obviously concerns the "payoff" of a theory and so tends to be emphasized as most critical by the layman, must take second place to testability, for reasons already stressed. Nonetheless the various ways in which theories can be significant should be explicated. The most important question in this regard is, "Does the theory contain relevant explanatory mechanisms for observed events?" Here the key word is probably *relevant,* because this characteristic is best expressed by means of successful prediction. From a somewhat more abstract point of view, another question is, "Does the theory contain ordered conceptualizations of natural phenomena?" These conceptualizations may be either *consolidative,* in that they tend to summarize prior empirical data, or *innovative,* in that they break new ground for future research. The relationship of these two characteristics to the inductive theory mode and the other interactive modes is apparent.

It is extremely difficult to pinpoint significance in scientific affairs because of varying standards and objectives. Ultimately the only jury is the judgment of the relevant scientific community. (This observation tends to underscore the creativity aspect of scientific theory, because there does not seem to be any very good, sure way to identify "discoveries.") The problem of significance will be discussed again, in Selection 19, with regard to the individual scientist and the questions that he sometimes asks himself concerning his own work.

Parsimony. The principle of parsimony, often called William of Occam's razor or Lloyd Morgan's canon, from early proponents, is a rough guideline to the acceptability of hypotheses and principles. It says that when one selects a proposition as an explanation of some set of events it is safer to choose the alternative that is simpler, in terms of assumptions needed, among those which satisfy *all* the data. Its primary function is thus to guide acceptance, not testing, of ideas. In this respect it is often unfairly maligned, as has been pointed out elsewhere (Marx, 1963, pp. 20 ff.). If anything, parsimony should serve as a spur, not a deterrent, to the creation and testing of new ideas, especially when the proponents of more complex accounts are not satisfied with the simpler accounts.

As hinted previously, the applicability of the principle of parsimony is more important in applied science than in pure science. When practitioners or policy makers in government, education, industry, or the military must select a new program, there may be enormous practical consequences, for better or worse. In addition, there may not be time for extended testing before the decision must be made. Thus it is of critical importance that parsimonious thinking be judiciously applied within these areas.

The basis for the principle of parsimony is partly historical, in terms of our experience in the various sciences, and partly logical. Historically, scientists have learned that the more assumptions there are involved— or the more complex a theory is—the greater likelihood there is of error. And once a serious error creeps in, the whole theoretical superstructure may be fatally weakened. The situation is something like that which is obtained when a lie is told; one needs to continue fabrication in order to support the original misstatement, until a whole network of falsehood may be developed.

Logically, the reason for the greater effectiveness of the simple solution is, in large part, that science mainly consists of a more or less feeble groping toward "truth," or factualness, and that most of our original ideas are doomed to extinction. On a probability basis alone, therefore, the fewer the links in the chain, the less the likelihood of serious error.

Apart from practical consequences, such as those mentioned, the failure to respect the principle of parsimony results in the overloading of relatively untested, and therefore unconfirmed, ideas. Differences of opinion as to the value of such ideas tend to separate experimentally oriented scientists from others, such as some personality theorists within psychology, who have basically different interests. The student should keep in mind, however, that the argument for parsimony revolves around the present acceptability of relatively untested ideas and not their potential utility.

Like the notion of "fact," the principle of parsimony is deceptively simple. However, there are a number of different ways in which parsimony can be applied. The number of premises is perhaps the most prominent of these and perhaps the most important, but one can also consider the degree of abstractness (the more abstract notions being generally considered the less parsimonious) or, as in the case of animal behavior, the level of function (that is, reasoning presumed in a dog which shows the trick of returning with a newspaper as compared with a more "mechanistic," or S-R, type of conditioning presumed). But however it may be implemented, the basic proposition remains the same: one accepts and implements the simpler principle, *of the principles that are consistent with all of the available data,* because it provides the least risk of eventual error.

KEY PROBLEMS

Operationism. Initially expressed by the physicist Bridgman (1927), the principle of operationism is simply a formal statement of a very basic rule in scientific communication: that the empirical basis for each term used, and especially for each theoretical construct, be clear. Fundamentally this principle merely asks for clarity in communication: "Tell me what you mean, in terms of operations I can make or observe, by your language." Thus viewed, it is logically unassailable. Moreover, it obviously has its greatest impact in those areas of psychology where it is most difficult to apply, for example, in clinical and personality theory.

If the principle of operationism is fundamantally so secure, why then has there been so much dispute concerning it, especially in psychology? One answer to this question is suggested by the comment concerning the difficulty in certain areas of psychology. Proponents of theoretical propositions that are not based upon operationally clear concepts have consistently argued against the principle, largely on the ground that it discourages creativity. More basically, however, the resistance to operationism has come very largely from the fact that in practice this fundamentally simple rule quickly becomes more complicated. That is, its implementation is far more difficult than its fundamental expression. No attempt will be made to deal with the variety of objections that have been raised; however, one can point out that, whatever merit these have (and some of course do have considerable merit), it is more important that we recognize the principle of operationism as an objective in scientific communication, as an *ultimate* requirement rather than as one that needs to be perfectly satisfied here and now, in every facet of scientific communication. But it is also important that progress in intelligibility be made and that each investigator attempt to improve the operational clarity of his language. It is the failure to do this that can very legitimately be criticized, particularly when it is evidenced most clearly in those who themselves vehemently oppose the fundamental principle.

It is instructive to pit communicability, stressed in the operational criterion, against truth-value, as in the simple 2 by 2 chart shown in Table 1. The four resulting types of theories may be separately considered.

Type 1 theory, which is both clearly communicated and "true," is obviously the most desirable objective, and the type upon which scientific advance ultimately depends. Type 2 theory, for which empirical support

TABLE 1
Theories Dichotomized on the Communication
(Operationism) and Truth (Predictability)
Dimensions

		Operational	
		Yes	No
True	Yes	1	2
	No	3	4

is claimed but in the absence of operational definitions, is clearly a troublemaker. From one point of view, it is a contradiction, for if one does not understand the meaning of the terms (and perhaps the operations), how can one ever know if the data fit the theory? At best, viewed more generously and giving proponents the benefit of considerable doubt, this kind of theory tends to generate much heat and light. Until improved communicability occurs, argumentation without clear specification of the issues is encouraged. Zeroing in on basic issues can only be achieved after some degree of operational clarification is achieved.

Type 3 and 4 theories are of the sort that lead to the kind of paradigm clash described by Kuhn (1962) as productive of scientific revolutions. This is particularly true, perhaps, of type 4, where neither criterion is met. Type 3 theory is a kind of scientific workhorse, in that operationally clear but empirically unsupported notions are not only very frequent but also, as described, scientifically very useful. By narrowing the margin of error over a succession of stages they pave the way for the ultimately successful type I theory. Thus, both types of operationally clear theories are useful, whereas neither of the other types is, in any immediate, positive sense.

The Intervening Variable. As a special case of the dispute concerning operationism in psychological theory construction, the role of the intervening variable may be more closely examined. Initially proposed by Tolman (1932) but developed most extensively by Hull (1943) and Spence (1956, 1960), the intervening variable was intended to permit the formal representation of intraorganismic processes. The introduction of the operational issue was made by MacCorquodale and Meehl (1948; selection 2 in this volume) when they distinguished between two types of theoretical constructs. What they called the hypothetical construct was essentially nonoperational, whereas their "true intervening variable" was an operational, purely descriptive representation of some particular stimulus-response relationship.

Although the intervening-variable technique has certainly not led to the immediate success in theoretical endeavors that some of its early proponents may have expected, it is by the same token hardly the complete failure that some have assumed (for example, Koch, 1959). As in the case of operationism generally, it is necessary to recognize that the intervening variables which have been proposed vary in the degree to which they satisfy the operational requirement and that continuing attempts to improve them in this regard are necessary.

What has elsewhere (Marx, 1951; 1963, Ch. 10) been called the E/C *type* of intervening variable may be cited as an illustration of the kind of use in theory construction that is possible with this technique. Essentially, this kind of construct relates directly to the independent variable that differentiates the experimental (E) from the control (C) group. It is assumed to represent *whatever intraorganismic functions are necessary to account for the observed S-R relationship* (the responses observed to occur in a particular stimulus situation).

As an illustration of the possibilities inherent in this kind of theoretical procedure the interesting experiment by Mowrer and Viek (1948) and the conceptually similar experiment by Marx and Van Spanckeren (1952) were offered (Marx, 1951). In the former experiment, food-deprived rats were trained to eat mash from a stick presented through the metal bars of a shock-grid floor. All animals were shocked 10 sec. after they started to eat (or following a set time interval if no eating occurred). The experimental/control (E/C) difference concerned whether or not the rat was able to influence the shock himself. Experimental Ss were able to turn the shock off immediately by jumping off the grid; each control S received exactly the same amount of shock on each trial as its matched experimental partner but was unable to influence the duration of the shock by anything it did. An important behavioral difference emerged under these conditions: experimental Ss ate reliably more quickly and more often than control Ss.

In the Marx and Van Spanckeren (1952) study an experimental group of audiogenic-seizure sensitive Ss was allowed to turn off the noxious, seizure-producing stimulus (high-intensity, high-frequency sound) and showed reliably less seizures than matched controls which received exactly the same amount of noxious stimulation but were unable to affect it by their behavior.

In each of these experiments the behavioral difference may be attributed to some difference, within the two groups of Ss, that is directly attributable to the difference between the experimental and control treatments—hence is labeled an E/C intervening variable. Several comments may be made concerning this kind of informal usage.

First, the E/C intervening variable is not a spectacular, attention-attracting construct. Rather, it represents the kind of workaday procedure that is commonly used, without fanfare, mostly in the functional type of theory construction.

Second, a major advantage it offers is that it permits E to strike a balance between two extreme positions, the emphasis on highly formal theory (as represented by Tolman, Hull, Spence) and the ultrapositivistic rejection of all or most overt theory (as advocated by Skinner and his adherents).

Third, the E/C technique has the further advantage of opening up to public scrutiny the critical but too often ignored problem of identification of variables. There has been an unfortunate tendency to gloss over this important and necessary process and emphasize instead either theoretical solutions, often in the absence of adequate empirical implementation, or empirical procedures per se. The E/C procedure forces attention on the interfacing problem, the relationship between empirical and theoretical procedures—and so goes to the heart of the problem of theory construction.

Individual vs. Group Functions. Traditionally, in psychological research and theorizing, groups of Ss have been used and conclusions about individuals have been drawn on this basis. Assaults on this practice have been made with increasing vigor within recent years. There have been two major sources of this criticism of group research.

Certain personality theorists, led by Gordon Allport (1937), have criticized research and theory on the ground that it is nomothetic (directed at general laws) rather than idiographic (tailored to the individual person). The rationale for this criticism is that each individual is unique and that he can therefore be understood only through a study of himself, and not by means of nomothetic principles. This has been an influential criticism and has had a particularly strong impact upon psychologists who are concerned with the "whole person" as opposed to the specific behavior mechanisms.

Without denying in any way the importance of studying individual Ss, as emphasized in the idiographic approach, it can nevertheless be maintained that a clear distinction needs to be drawn between such study as it is used in clinical practice—where ideographic procedures may well be essential—and in strictly scientific research and theory—where idiographic procedures may still be useful but only as one *means* of attaining nomothetic principles. That is to say, if one is primarily interested in science as opposed to practice, then one is necessarily concerned with nomothetic principles. It may be necessary, for certain purposes, to use single individuals, but when this is done it is done because of technical considerations rather than because of the absence of a nomothetic objective. Thus it is possible to accept the basic merits of the stress upon individual study and at the same time deny the main thrust of the Allport argument, his premise that nomothetic principles are entirely separate from idiographic study.

The second source of attack upon group studies has come from the Skinnerian camp. Here the leader has been Murray Sidman. The early attack centered upon the distinction between individual and group curves (Bakan, 1954; Estes, 1956; Sidman, 1952). It is now generally agreed that in terms of mathematical functions representing behavioral processes, data obtained from groups cannot be freely used for individual function.

VALIDATION OF THEORIES

Empirical vs. Logical Tests. Theories can be tested both logically and empirically. Logical tests, although to some extent critical within the formulation of all theories and both necessary and sufficient for certain types of propositions (notably those within strictly logical and mathematical frameworks), are of limited utility with regard to the primarily empirical propositions of natural science, including psychology.

There are some interesting facts concerning the kinds of restrictions that operate within these two types of theoretical tests. First, if one accepts the logical system used by the theorist, then it is possible completely to confirm *and* disconfirm propositions by means of deductive logical procedures. But to do this means that one must operate within an essentially closed logical system, without direct empirical implications. Second, when empirical tests of theories are used, in the more characteristic scientific fashion, an important distinction between confirmation and disconfirmation of propositions emerges. This is that propositions are more readily disconfirmed by failures of empirically derived data to fit the predictions made than they are supported by successful predictions. (Again, we must assume that all the various conditions of both the experiment, or other kind of observation, and the logic are acceptable; although this may not often be the case, we will assume that it is for purposes of advancing the exposition.) The reason for this logical inability to guarantee absolute certainty for even the most securely supported theoretical propositions is that it is always conceivable that some other theoretical proposition can be advanced which will be able to make the same empirical predictions. Because it is impossible, on the basis of either formal logic or scientific common sense, to guarantee the uniqueness of any particular theory, this important restriction on positive support for theory has been generally accepted by scientists.

Within logic, the formal reasoning that permits rejection of a proposition on the basis of demonstration of the falsity of an implication of it is called *modus tollens,* and the acceptance of the truth of a proposition on the basis of the demonstration of an implication of it is called the *fallacy of affirming the consequent.*

The limitation imposed by avoiding the latter fallacy is evident in the simplest of purely inductive procedures. For example, if we are examining specimens of some newly discovered species for the appearance of some particular characteristic *x,* then each successive occurrence of *x* without exception certainly helps to build up our confidence in the probability that *all* members of this species enjoy this characteristic. But it is always possible that an exception will occur, and perfect assurance of the correlation can never be obtained on a strictly empirical basis, no matter how many individual confirmations are accumulated. On the other hand, a *single* well-established exception or negative instance is sufficient to destroy the proposition, at least in its bald and unqualified form.

The consequence of this situation is that scientists are limited to *probability statements* in the validation of theories with empirical import. In practice this is not a very severe limitation, although perhaps unpleasing to those who have logically compulsive or perfectionist tendencies. Each bit of confirming evidence then tends to strengthen our confidence in the empirical relevance of a theory, and the wider the *range* as well as the *depth* of such confirmations, the greater the confidence in the theory. New experimental evidence, especially if it has been produced by theory, is particularly impressive, as is also the demonstration of relevance of the theory to whole new sets of established data.

Another consequence of this limitation is that even the best-supported scientific principles, whether called theories or laws, are not beyond question. Historically, even within the most natural of the natural sciences (for example, physics), there have been many instances where principles once believed to be indestructible, or as nearly final as they could be, have been overturned. Scientists therefore keep an open mind on all their theories and laws, although as a practical matter some of them are so well established as to be treated as though they were really sacrosanct. But it is always necessary to keep a small amount of humility in reserve, just in case. Psychologists, as one might expect, should have an ample supply of humility on hand at all times, because of the relatively low probability levels with which most of our theoretical propositions are presently endowed.

Auxiliary Conditions. Auxiliary conditions are those particular conditions that are essential to the successful application of some theory to a set of data. Such conditions, unfortunately, are not always explicated and, as a matter of fact, may not even be recognized. Nonetheless, they are among the most important aspects of the data-theory relationship. They play an especially critical role in a subject matter such as psychology where many complexly interacting variables typically are involved. Indeed, the effective explication and manipulation of auxiliary conditions may well be as important a determiner of the success of a theory, or a theorist, as explanatory ideas per se.

The term *condition* is preferable to the terms *assumption* or *hypothesis*, which are used by Hempel (1966) in his excellent exposition of this problem, because of its neutrality. That is to say, it is a broader concept than either *assumption*, which suggests somewhat more knowledge of the situation than frequently occurs, or *hypothesis*, which suggests even more strongly not only knowledge but also theoretical specification to some degree.

There have been in the history of psychology, and of learning theory, many illustrations of the failure to take all the essential facets of the situation into account. Consider the early Hullian learning theory. In developing it, Hull had made the auxiliary but tacit assumption that a given amount of incentive had a fixed effect upon performance. However,

Crespi (1942) first showed that rats shifted up from less incentive or down from more incentive tend to perform at a higher or lower level, respectively, than control Ss which are maintained throughout the experiment on the same incentive value as that used after shifting in the other cases. This demonstration of incentive contrast effects, or the relative rather than the absolute role of an incentive, was among the experimental results that influenced Hull in his modification of the interplay of constructs in his system.

Consider also the fact that Pavlov in his interpretation of the basic conditioning paradigm he developed did not emphasize his use of motivated Ss; yet if his Ss had not been motivated, as by the deprivation of food, his conditioning results would have been markedly different. Thus there is a necessity for this condition, in addition to those involved in the theory per se, in order that the proper supporting data be obtained.

Whether such auxiliary assumptions are ultimately incorporated into the theoretical structure itself or are merely maintained as essential environmental conditions will of course vary with both the intent of the theorist and the degree to which they can be abstracted. But in any event they play a profound role in interpretations of data and need to be actively searched for by the theorist. Moreover, they may be recognized as relating very closely to the kind of experimental specificity which operates in learning (and other) research to increase the diversity of results even when identical designs and procedures are used but unspecified and usually unidentified variations in the local application of these presumably operate. Failures to replicate experimental results would thus generally be due to this kind of variation, and its importance in behavioral research would be very difficult to exaggerate.

Relation of Theory to Experimental Prediction: A Paradox. Paul Meehl has called attention to an interesting paradox in regard to theory testing in psychology and physics. Although all the details of his provocative exposition cannot be presented here, his own wording of the paradox will be quoted, followed by a brief presentation of the gist of the argument and a discussion of how the paradox can be resolved. Meehl states,

In the physical sciences, the usual result of an improvement in experimental design, instrumentation, or numerical mass of data, is to increase the difficulty of the "observational hurdle" which the physical theory of interest must successfully surmount; whereas, in psychology and some of the allied behavior sciences, the usual effect of such improvement in experimental precision is to provide an easier hurdle for the theory to surmount [Meehl, 1967, p. 103].

The basis for this argument is the fact that so often in psychological research we seek a simple yes/no decision from our data. (For example, do boys or girls excel on some test at this age or that? Will rats learn faster when given spaced trials or massed trials?) Improving the sensitivity of the empirical test in the ways indicated increases the probability that the null hypothesis (the presumption that there is no difference) will be rejected, on statistical grounds. According to Meehl's argument, this improvement in sensitivity should actually weaken our confidence in theoretical propositions so supported because of the fact that we have "a prior probability approaching ½ of finding a significant difference" (Meehl, 1967, p. 103). A positive result (that is, one in accord with theory) is under such conditions not really a very impressive one. Nevertheless, many Es not only accept it gratefully but also, Meehl argues, tend to treat the theory as though it deserved the confidence accorded the empirical result on the basis of the very low p-value made possible by the high-powered statistical test! Meehl calls this a "subtle-tendency" among even "investigators who would never make an explicit identification of the one probability number with the complement of the other" (1967, pp. 107–108).

This situation in psychology, where progressively more powerful statistical testing of a theory can produce progressively more spurious support for it, contrasts with the situation in physics, where specific point predictions are customarily made. There the more powerful the supporting evidence, the greater the legitimate theoretical support.

An additional stricture that Meehl levels against the psychologist concerns the positive and negative tests of hypotheses mentioned in a previous section of this chapter. On the misuses of such tests, Meehl says,

The writing of behavior scientists often reads as though they assumed—what it is hard to believe anyone would explicitly assert if challenged—that successful and unsuccessful predictions are practically on all fours in arguing for and against a substantive theory. Many experimental articles in behavioral sciences, and, even more strangely, review articles which purport to survey the current status of a particular theory in the light of all available evidence, treat the confirming instances and the disconfirming instances with equal methodological respect, as if one could, so to speak, "count noses," so that if a theory has somewhat more confirming than disconfirming instances, it is in pretty good shape evidentially. Since we know that this is already grossly incorrect on purely formal grounds, it is a mistake a fortiori when the so-called "confirming instances" have themselves a prior probability, as argued above, somewhere in the neighborhood of ½, quite apart from any theoretical considerations [Meehl, 1967, p. 112].

Meehl points out that the basic "methodological paradox [but not the error of interpretation just mentioned] would exist for the psychologist even if he played his own statistical game fairly . . . [because] most psychological theories, especially in the so-called 'soft' fields such as social and personality psychology, are not quantitatively developed to the extent of being able to generate point-prediction" (1967, p. 113). He then solicits from logicians and philosophers of science helpful suggestions for improving the situation without the psychologist "making unrealistic attempts at the premature construction of theories" (1967, p. 113).

Although not able to speak to this point for the logician or the philosopher of science, the writer nonetheless feels that this stimulating critique can be answered on psychological grounds, at least up to an important point. Fundamentally, the major weakness in Meehl's argument seems to lie not in his formal exposition, but in one major (unspecified but implicit) presumption. This presumption is that psychology can and should have formal theoretical structures of a formalized sort in the absence of anything like a solid data base. If one rejects this argument and accepts instead the position emphasizing the continuity of informal theoretical efforts called theorizing, then there is less need to worry much about transferring confidence levels from empirical results to theoretical structures at the relatively immature stages of research. Of course, this solution does not modify the basic situation Meehl describes; rather, it ameliorates it by reducing its impact upon theory construction in psychology. It will still be necessary to watch for the kind of excesses that Meehl criticizes, but it will certainly not be necessary to make them.

To extend this argument a bit, we may note that parametric experiments (and their counterpart in correlational psychology, multivariance analysis) are becoming increasingly common in psychological research. Moreover, there does not seem to be any a priori reason why they cannot be applied to all kinds of problems, regardless of their degree of "softness." Surely one does not need to adopt an ultrapositivistic position to hold that such experiments can be designed and performed in the absence of the sort of formal theory about which Meehl is concerned.

Finally, it should be noted that the deleterious effects upon psychology of the paradox noted by Meehl depend not only upon the statistical situation itself, but also (and actually more so) upon the way in which psychologists behave in it. In other words, unless one is unduly impressed by the kind of empirical support involved in the paradox, little harm will be done. Sophisticated theorists are unlikely to put much weight on the results of a single dichotomous test of the sort he describes. This kind of result is valuable as a guide to theorizing, but is hardly sufficient for formal theory. Theoretical propositions are tested not only under directly replicated conditions but also under a variety of different conditions, and it is only after a considerable amount of empirical support has been amassed that very serious attention can be accorded a theoretical proposition. The implication of these notions is that perhaps we had as well continue to attempt to improve the theoretical and scientific sophistication of our students (if not our colleagues) as ask the logician for aid.

19
THEORIZING

Melvin H. Marx

The Significance of Theorizing

Psychology is not generally in such an advanced state of scientific development as to enjoy the applicability of full-scale formal theoretical processes. For this reason it is particularly important that full attention be paid to the more informal aspects of interpretation of data here lumped together under the rubric *theorizing* and certain related problems that the scientist needs to face in his attempts to build his science.

It must not be inferred from this, however, that only the relatively unadvanced sciences utilize such informal modes. On the contrary, theorizing, in the sense of forming tentative interpretative notions about data, is a continuous and critical function of all scientific work. Formal theories by no means appear full-blown, as though incubated somehow in the scientist's unconscious, but rather develop, usually more or less haphazardly, by means of a myriad of trials and errors and out of many more informal hunches and discarded theories. There is an intimate and continuous relationship between observation and reasoning in all science, and this relationship begins long before formal theory is intended or at all appropriate.

Put another way, theories in the formal sense are the ultimate of the scientist's theorizing. It is important to realize that the latter process consists of many more activities than are evident in the final product. Theorizing, as the activity of development of theories, merits at least as much attention as the theories themselves, especially if one is interested in the manner of development of the theories. Hence the present chapter.

This selection starts with an elaboration of the general principle just described, in the form of correcting a number of common fallacies concerning scientific theories. The related problems of training one to theorize and to be creative are considered in the next two sections. A section on personal factors in research and theorizing follows. The selection is concluded by a short section on recent trends in theorizing.

Correcting Some Common Fallacies

Because of the prominence, among students as well as laymen, of certain fallacious notions concerning formal theory building it is im-

---

This selection is a revised version of Marx (1970), Chapter 2. © Copyright, Melvin H. Marx, 1970.

portant to dispose of some of these more common fallacies before proceeding to other problems that beset the theorist. Our discussion will state a number of these, in corrected form, and then in each case indicate why the correction is needed.

Science does not proceed in a more or less direct line to laws and theories. Nothing could better describe the real situation. In point of fact, science is an extremely messy and untidy business, with errors and false starts much more common than successes. This all-important point, already made, will be elaborated later in the discussion.

Science is not strictly logical, in a formal sense, or straightforward. In fact, formal logic, although potentially useful in some respects, is seldom explicitly used in theory building. Its prominence in descriptions and explanations of theories is therefore quite misleading. Deductive logic may be used in a very informal and quite unplanned manner, as suggested. Watson's (1968) recent account of the "breaking" of the genetic code is a realistic, if unusually frank, account of the kind of work that actually goes into scientific successes. Merton's (1969) essay, moreover, indicates quite clearly that this sort of striving for recognition, via "priority" in research and theory, is by no means unique to science in this century.

A *particular method or theory is fruitful and should be retained even if relatively complete success is not attained by it.* Approximation—and very incomplete success—is characteristic of all science, and the spectacular theoretical successes described in the popular press and the textbooks are mostly the product of hindsight. That is to say, if one could look more closely at the actual development of an ultimately successful theory he would find that its course was erratic and irregular, with the final success resulting from the cumulative advances made possible by a good number of partial successes and approximations. These are customarily ignored or minimized in later accounts. With the zigs and zags thus eliminated the straight line appears, but it is not truly representative of the actual work.

This point has many ramifications. To mention but one illustration, Israel and Goldstein's (1944) early rejection of operationism in psychology was largely (and in the writer's opinion, erroneously) based on their conviction that it was a procedure that could not be applied perfectly and completely to scientific work from the very beginning.

Single and generally simple theories may not account for all data of a certain class (say, learning). Although this is a much more arguable and uncertain point than the preceding ones, it does seem quite probable that as more is learned about the interactions of variables (commonly ignored in the early theoretical efforts), complexities will develop even in the simple theories. And although certain monolithic theories, such as Hull's behavior system, can be strongly defended on heuristic grounds alone—that is, in terms of their vigorous promotion of research and their throughgoing test of a particular principle or set of principles—

there is nonetheless a clear theoretical danger involved. This is the risk that more effective principles will be overlooked when zealous attention to one's own ideas overrides the ideal of scientific impartiality.

Many proponents of the simple theory do not propose it in the belief that it will account for all the data of a certain class but rather on the grounds (again, heuristic) that an effective procedure is to push a simple account as far as one can. Although this is a popular and quite defensible notion, it may also be pointed out that it is equally feasible to attempt to work toward simple and monolithic theory in the other direction: that is, to start with the assumption that, say, the various diverse phenomena of learning are explicable on *different* principles, in accordance with their different empirical bases, rather than being expressions of a single principle, and then see how closely these different principles can be brought together through successive researches. This procedure would have the important advantage of letting research success, rather than initial inferences, dictate the direction of the theory development.

Laws and theories do not need to be directly tested, as in crucial experiments where alternative accounts are clearly contradicted. Although this procedure may be valuable, it is by no means the only, or even the most commonly effective, procedure by which scientific laws and theories are developed. An alternative procedure is to attack specific problems, or experimental-theoretical issues, rather than directly test specific theories. The data can then be used to throw light on theories. The problem rather than the theory is thus the central objective of the research. This procedure will be recognized as a form of the functional mode of theory construction described in Selection 18.

A good example of the limitations of the direct-test procedure occurred during the 1940's and 1950's, when Hullian and Tolmanian learning theories were being opposed. The net result of many (almost countless) experiments directed toward determining which of these two theories is correct is that there is not only no clear resolution of this question but also little concern with the issue. Inconsistent data (that is, data inconsistent with one or the other of the two theories as initially posed) forced such changes and compromises as to leave little of the original accounts intact. The use of such constructs as r_g-s_g (a Hull–Spence mechanism referring to implicit goal responses, and one that is close to Tolman's expectancy construct) helps to close the gap between the central notions of what were once apparently quite distinct theoretical positions.

Can Theorizing Be Taught?

The question as to whether or not it is possible to train students to be effective theorizers is one of such obvious significance, in psychology as well as elsewhere in the scientific enterprise, that one wonders why it has not received much more attention. This wonderment is especially relevant with regard to psychology, which has generally tended to be more self-conscious of its scientific status and more concerned about formal training especially than the older and better-established sciences.

THEORIZING AS AN ART

To what extent is theorizing an art, in the sense that it is difficult to pin down the exact manner in which it is developed or should be trained? In a thoughtful paper Polanyi has recently summarized the positive answer: "Science is grounded, and is firmly grounded, on the kind of indefinable insights which the current view of science regards as mere psychological phenomena, incapable of producing rational inferences" (1968, p. 27; selection 28.) Leeper (personal communication) has aptly compared theorizing with certain other skills, pointing out the lack of clearcut guidelines. Thus,

On complex things, a person commonly is not able to verbalize adequately what he does. If he is a photographer, for instance, he may be a great one, judged by his works, or if a woman is a skillful nursery-school teacher, she may be a great one, but that does not mean either that such a person would say much abstractly about what he does and why, or that he has developed his skill through such aids. . . . With reference to theory building and evaluation, we ought to make it clear that our abstract formulations are likely to be very incomplete, and we ought to stress that "learning to theorize" in science comes, as it were, through an apprenticeship business, or with the help of one's peers, because otherwise there will be just the simpler things that will have to be learned with the aid of formulations and the more subtle things won't be there. It might be compared with the learning of a language. If Chomsky and the like are right, any language is going to have a lot of features in it that aren't in the books on grammar and rhetoric. So, if a person tried to learn a language merely by working from a dictionary, giving him the basic elements, and a grammar book, giving him the rules of combination, the resulting language-functioning he would show would be a queer, sort of lifeless thing. People would be able to say, "Well, that just isn't the way that one should do that," but if he asked what was wrong and where the rule was that covered it, they couldn't say.

Leeper's comment suggests that the best way to teach one to theorize is to expose him to this kind of activity in practice, in what is generally called the apprentice system. Within such a system the student is exposed not only to precept and observation, much of which he can get in standard course work, but is himself permitted to practice doing the kinds of things that are involved in theorizing. For this function to be served, full participation in all the important research functions is required. This means giving as much responsibility to the participating student as he can reasonably accept.

The fundamental problem seems to be in large part motivational. The trick is somehow to impart to the student some of what has often been called "the excitement and fascination of science." Nowhere is this characteristic more evident than in relating theory and experiment. Attempting to devise new experimental tests of some theoretical principle or to understand how some new set of data is related to such a principle can be as intellectually challenging as any of the creative enterprises of man.

Orthodox academic procedures are not likely to have these important characteristics. Rote learning of facts or working through of "canned experiments" in the laboratory are much more likely to extinguish than to spark excitement. On the other hand, exposing students to current theoretical-experimental issues and live experiments often ignites the spark that persists throughout a lifetime of intellectual achievement in science. Moreover, this kind of creative activity—and it is important to stress to laymen and new students especially that theoretical-experimental work in science, is really as creative as artistic expression—can be, in the current vernacular, "fun." Note what one of the more successful theoreticians in psychology has to say about his career. E. C. Tolman, surveying that career, testified as follows,

I started out . . . with considerable uneasiness. I felt that my so-called system was outdated and that it was a waste of time to try to rehash it and that it would be pretentious now to seek to make it fit any accepted set of prescriptions laid down by the philosophy of science. I have to confess, however, that as I have gone along I have become again more and more involved in it, though I still realize its many weak points. The system may well not stand up to any final canons of scientific procedure. But I do not much care. I have liked to think about psychology in ways that have proved congenial to me. Since all the sciences, and especially psychology, are still immersed in such tremendous realms of the uncertain and the unknown, the best that any individual scientist, especially any psychologist, can do seems to be to follow his own gleam and his own bent, however inadequate they may be. In fact I suppose that actually this is what we all do. In the end, the only sure criterion is to have fun. And I have had fun [Tolman, 1959, p. 152].

The problems involved in training one to theorize are basically similar to those involved in one special facet of such activity—the stimulation of originality, or creativity—and that subject is intensively treated in the next major section of this chapter.

EXPERIMENTIZING

One last point remains to be made concerning training in the present context. Just as theorizing is basic to formal theory construction, so what might be called, analogously, *experimentizing* may be seen as basic to more formal experimentation. In other words, one formal experiment is often preceded by a series of informal observations. Generally these are not reported. (As a matter of fact, they are typically excised from reports by space-conscious editors if included.) Although the parallel may not be perfect, particularly in that experimentizing is probably much less essential to the formal experiment than theorizing is to the formal theory, nevertheless the two processes do seem to have a great deal in common. One important implication for training should be noted. This is that it may be almost as difficult to determine how the experiment was actually developed from the final account as it is to determine the course of the theoretical development from the final theory. Steps to counteract this condition are obviously necessary in training the student to be an E; exposure to research reports of the usual sort is certainly not sufficient. Again, there is no substitute for the actual experience, as obtained in something like the apprentice system. In this respect it is unfortunate indeed that more experimentizing is not encouraged in psychology. A special need for this kind of training exists in psychology because of the nature of much of the experimentation that is done. Unlike most other biological research, psychological problems typically do not encourage, and literally may not even permit, preliminary and informal investigation. As an example, consider the fruitful series of experiments of "bystander apathy" recently reported by Latané and Darley (1969). These experiments necessarily entail radical deception of the Ss, who in one way or another must be led to believe that they are experiencing some kind of emergency situation. Such deception cannot be readily or lightly employed by Es. The situation is in this important respect quite unlike that faced by any of the biological scientists whose use of microscopes or surgical tools is relatively unrestricted, except where human Ss are concerned.

Other examples closer to the problems of psychological theory, may also be cited. To learn very much about certain of the more refined theoretical issues in, say, verbal learning, one must "run" a considerable number of Ss under reasonably tight controls and subject the resulting data to sophisticated statistical analyses. Such problems simply do not lend themselves to the same kind of informal approach that is so often possible with, say, a microscope and a few drops of pond water. As a result, psychologists need to be much more concerned about training their students to do as much as they can in the way of informal experimentation as well as informal theory construction.

Can Creativity Be Taught?

THE CONTEXTS OF DISCOVERY AND CONFIRMATION

Recognition of two rather different types of scientific activity—the discovery of relevant variables and solutions to problems on the one hand, and the testing of the validity of such solutions, on the other hand—will help to clarify the nature of much argumentation both inside and outside scientific circles. Take Freud, for a classic example. Was he a scientist? There seems to be little question that he was not only an extremely astute observer but also a most insightful thinker, and that he produced ideas as stimulating and provocative as any concerned with personality develop-ment. But all of these achievements properly belong within the sphere of discovery; when confirmation is involved, Freud's scientific weakness quickly appears. Not only was he himself not engaged in what most of us would consider to be adequate scientific testing of his notions, he did not seem to recognize the need for such confirmation. What is generally called *clinical validation*—repeated observations, made generally under the same (relatively or completely uncontrolled) conditions as stimulated the original ideas—was apparently all that Freud felt necessary for verification.

Now whether Freud is to be classified as a scientist, on the basis of his great contributions within the context of discovery, or not so classified on the ground that he did not act on or perhaps even appreciate the key necessity for adequate confirmation, is entirely a matter of semantics and one that certainly should be avoided here. Which decision is made is much less important than recognizing the essentially semantic nature of the question, and consequently of the answer.

The complementary character of these two activities, neither of which is sufficient unto itself for science to proceed, should be evident. But this very fact presents us with one of the fundamental dilemmas within psy-chology: how to maintain scientific rigor, mainly with regard to the adequate testing of hypotheses, and at the same time encourage freshness and innovation in thinking. This dilemma is most critical at the time of research training. It is obvious that most of our graduate training, at least in experimental psychology, consists of procedures that deal with tech-niques of confirmation. A major reason for this relative neglect of dis-covery and creativity is that we simply do not know very well to teach them, if indeed they can be taught.

CREATIVITY TRAINING

Most critics agree that more originality is needed not only in students but also in professionals. As a matter of fact, there has been too little originality in American science generally, at least up to recent times. Most of the major contributions to pure science have come from Europe, or from European-trained scientists who have emigrated to the United States (for example, Einstein, Fermi, Lewin), while we have excelled in technology.

Our research-training procedures in psychology have generally been unrealistic in that they have been disproportionately concentrated on confirmation-type practice (for example, statistical techniques) at the expense of the encouragement of independent, original thinking (which in the typical American student is unfortunately not likely to be very much encouraged at *any* state of his education).

The Apprentice System. The Estes Park conference of a special com-mittee on research training of the American Psychological Association

(1959) emphasized the neglect of creativity and opted strongly for the previously mentioned apprentice system, whereby the student works in close coordination with a senior reseacher and his staff, participating in all the phases of on-going research projects. There is no question that this is the best over-all solution to the problem. However, even this solution has some problems, such as the following:

1. There are probably not enough senior researchers with sufficiently active and vigorous programs, especially at some of the smaller doctoral-training institutions. Furthermore, some of those who do have appropriate projects may themselves be inhibiting rather than encouraging individuals and may be more concerned with the efficient completion of their research than with the more time-consuming, and often superficially inefficient, problem of training graduate students to think and act for themselves. Also some of the researchers who do have vigorous projects and who would be interested in this kind of training are not in a position to undertake it. (For example, many are in governmental laboratories.) The increasing popularity of postdoctoral training helps to take care of this problem.

2. Many local problems may intervene to complicate the proper placement of students—for example, politics and jealousies within the department, lack of adequate familiarization devices, premature commitments (such as to clinical or counseling curricula by students who turn out to be better bets for experimental-theoretical work but who cannot readily shift without serious loss of time and credit once they are well started on the initial program).

3. Even under ideal conditions, some question may be raised about overconcentration by the student in a single area or laboratory, especially when he starts early in his career (perhaps as an advanced undergraduate) even though this is the best time from the point of view of taking optimal advantage of opportunities. An antidote to this problem is the deliberate effort to force at least small research ties in graduate training in other areas and laboratories, such as by formal requirements in the program.

4. Encouragement of creativity is hindered, throughout our educational system, by two factors that are generally disturbing to teachers: (a) allowing students to express original and creative ideas is time-consuming and necessarily produces a great deal of chaff and a relatively small amount of wheat and (b) many such ideas, and especially perhaps the better ones, are threatening to the teacher, both personally and professionally, and so are not always encouraged. Recognition of these problems should help the interested teacher to take steps to overcome them and so facilitate his stimulation of creativity in the student.

Some Reservations. With regard to any attempts to train creativity, two general reservations may be mentioned in advance of the discussion.

First, not all scientists need to be equally creative. Much steady, careful work needs to be done in science with a minimum creative component. The consolidation that is necessary after a spate of new ideas is not well or graciously done by those who are interested in what seem to them to be bigger and better ideas. Here a practical problem is the overstimulation of ambition concerning originality and creativity in too many students who are not themselves prime candidates for such achievements, and the consequent ruining of what might otherwise be more modest but nonetheless important careers in science.

Second, it is not possible to force creativity, particularly in many students whose entire background, educational and otherwise, has encouraged conformity rather than independence of thinking. Our educational system, with its dedication to stereotyped problems, solutions, and procedures, simply does not prepare many for a creative career in science.

Some Generalizations. In spite of these cautions, it is important that more emphasis be placed in training on creativity and originality. The following comments are based upon over two decades of laboratory experience and graduate-student advising. (The interested reader should also see Mackworth [1965] for an especially provocative discussion, emphasizing the discussion between problem *solving* and problem *finding;* also, Price and Bass [1969] have treated the relationship between science and technology with regard to the innovative process.)

First, it is important to recognize that creative and original ideas typically come unpredictably, but often in spurts. They mostly come after hard work, much preparation, and more or less complete immersion in a problem. Because there is a clear danger that such immersion in a problem tends to fixate sets and rigidify thinking, so as to reduce the likelihood of effective solutions, it is at the same time important for the investigator to take "breaks" from his work and do what he can to encourage fresh points of view. Bringing in naïve but otherwise qualified consultants for making suggestions as to new starts is a commonly used and often helpful procedure.

Second, new ideas typically look great at first, but more sober second thoughts and more critical evaluation (by others, if not by oneself) usually reduce the perceived value of them. Some constraints are therefore needed for early screening of ideas but these should not be so severe as to discourage their production. Critical checking of new ideas against reality—preferably experimental data, old or newly obtained—is the ideal procedure. Unfortunately, however, this means hard and detailed work of the kind that is most often put off and avoided.

Third, productive ideas seem most often to be the result of a combination of dreaming and doing, of intuition and observation. They must be close enough to reality to permit testing but enough removed from the ordinary to get out of the ruts of normal thought. Fads and highly developed systems in psychology seem thus to be among the worst enemies of creativity, because they so clearly tie one down to preconceived notions and well-established patterns of interpretation.

Fourth, productive scientific thinking may be analyzed into two related but empirically separable processes: "inspiration" and "perspiration." Although much more is said of inspiration, or the initial conception of an idea, the development of the idea, involving perspiration, is probably the more important process. This is so because few people have no potentially good ideas, and some people have great numbers of such ideas, but most such ideas are simply not adequately checked out. As suggested, much more effort is needed to develop an idea than simply to initiate it. Moreover, it is impossible to determine in advance which ideas are the most promising (assuming a reasonable degree of feasibility). The bigness in the idea thus tends to come in the process of development of the idea. Furthermore, new inspirations are much more likely to occur after this kind of perspiration.

Lest the preceding discussion seem to downgrade inspiration too severely, let it be said that it plays an obviously essential function in scientific thinking. It seems to depend upon a kind of mental alertness, a readiness to see relationships in a new light and to abstract new variables. It is thus the key factor in the much-emphasized "serendipity," or accidental discovery. It is not the accident per se but rather one's alert noting and interpretation of it that makes the difference.

Helpful in this respect is the ability to notice discrepancies or gaps in raw observations and data as well as theories. An outstanding illustration of this ability is afforded by the discovery, in 1955, of radio signals from the planet Jupiter by two young American astronomers. This is an especially interesting and instructive incident because it involves their recognition of the significance of what had apparently been a more or less commonplace event. As Smith (1969) has commented, in his recent fascinating account of this story, "the Jovian signals can be detected with quite modest short-wave equipment; the author has even heard them on a small transistor radio with a two-foot 'whip' antenna. It seems inevitable that the bursts must have been heard, but gone unrecognized, countless times before their 'discovery' in 1955" (p. 180). Smith introduces his report with the conclusion that, "Throughout the history of science men have become famous simply by refusing to ignore small nuisances that most of us would have brushed aside" (1969, p. 177). One wonders how many similar "recognitions" await "discovery" in psychology.

It is of course best if E can take an active role in the process of closing the gaps, that is, make "accidents" occur rather than merely wait for them. But whether active or passive, this ability seems to be dependent upon one's carrying around a number of continuing (persistent, if sometimes dormant) problems close to the threshold of thinking. And these, in turn, are dependent upon a high degree of persistent motivation as well as a good fund of information. Great achievements rarely occur in the absence of this kind of strong and persistent motivation and dedication to problems. Kuhn's (1962) influential volume has emphasized the role of revolutionary changes—in so-called scientific "paradigms"—in the advance of science, and this kind of development is obviously closely related to the problem of creativity and its encouragement. (Cf. selections 3 and 4).

Some Positive Suggestions. Finally, a small number of positive suggestions may be mentioned in the hope that creativity can be encouraged by implementation of them in training. Fundamentally, and most important of all, the student must do research, as often as possible and as soon as possible in his training. The student as E must be free to make his own mistakes, to try out his own ideas. Designing experiments is fine, but doing them is better. "Pilot experiments" are especially valuable. The best kind of experience is probably that previously described as apprenticeship, where the student participates, as actively as his level of training and local conditions permit, in all phases of an ongoing program, under supervision of a more experienced E. Beyond this, the student should

1. Read with research ideas in mind, use research ideas wherever possible in examination papers, term papers, and so on.
2. Utilize literature reviews and integrative papers fully (rather than mechanically in response to course requirements); these often contain much food for effective thought.
3. Participate as fully as possible in active research discussions—"bull sessions"—as well as more formal research staff meetings and individual conferences.

In addition to these more or less apparent suggestions, there are other particular ways in which the student in training (and the professional psychologist also) can actively search for innovations:

1. He can study and evaluate the particular steps important theorists have taken in the production of their systems.
2. He can look for new ways to analyze data, especially when the data have been collected in a routine manner (for example, the goaltime measure that only recently has been included as a separate time in runaway studies). Most data analysis tends to be stereotyped and data are seldom sufficiently "milked."
3. He can devise new empirical indicants of critical variables, for example, anxiety, motivation, implicit goal responses, and so on. Only recently, after many years of theorizing, has the first direct, if partial, measure of the latter (r_g-s_g) appeared (Deaux and Patten, 1964). The multiplicity of meanings, most without empirical underpinnings, for such gross constructs cannot be properly reduced without this kind of innovation.

Personal Factors in Research and Theorizing

This section considers some of the major conditions that operate, via more direct effects upon the person himself, to influence productivity in experimentation and theorizing.

Delayed Knowledge of Experimental Results. Ordinarily, in behavioral research there are many sources of delay not only between the initial design of an experiment and the final interpretation, but also simply between the initiation of the experiment and the knowledge of its results. For example, there are often interposed elaborate statistical analyses and sometimes complex processing of the data. Even with rapid computer techniques for these purposes, in which the most complicated data processing and statistical analysis may take merely seconds, there are still delays, for example, in preparing the appropriate computer programs, obtaining computer time, and so on. (The situation may be compared to the problem of getting to and from the airports of large cities, where such preparatory times are often equal to or greater than the actual inflight times between the cities themselves.)

Viewing preliminary data, which has the advantage of giving some initial knowledge of results, has the disadvantage of possible biasing later results, as described in detail by Rosenthal (1966). That is, if one sees some trend in the early data, the expectations thus produced may well bias him in the collection of further data. The safest procedure generally is to complete the collection of the data, once the experiment is formally initiated, before attempting to look at any results, even though this does aggravate the problem of feedback to E.

Indirect Data. Unlike most biological data, as has already been noted, behavioral data need to be viewed abstractly. That is, they cannot ordinarily be looked at directly in the way that one can look through a microscope or observe the growth of a plant. In these situations not only are the data directly obtainable but failure or success is to some degree also immediately evident.

In psychology, operant conditioning has something of an advantage over competing methodologies in that the E can watch a cumulative recorder or observe shaping of behavior directly. In clinical research, especially, behavior modification techniques have these advantages compared with orthodox clinical procedures, such as traditional psychotherapy.

Although there does not seem to be any generally applicable ultimate solution to these problems of delayed and indirect behavioral data, they can be alleviated by some of the newer techniques available (for example, libraries of ready computer programs, use of X by Y computer plotters). Basically, however, behavioral researchers will need to learn to be more patient and more tolerant of delay and ambiguity than many other scientists. This kind of tolerance needs to be instilled in them, as far as is possible, in their professional training.

Remoteness from Data. It is important that E stay close to his data—that is, that he himself directly observe, as far as feasible, the behavior that makes possible the data. Here there is a very real risk that success will corrupt as more and more high-powered technical aids (such as automated controlling and recording devices) are added and various kinds of assistants are employed (made possible by, say, federal largesse in the form of research grants). In such a situation E tends to spend more time in planning and reporting and less time in actual observations of the kind that probably initiated the research project and that are to some degree necessary for its continued development.

This problem is aggravated by the fact that, in addition to the essential tasks of interpreting and reporting data and planning further observations, E is increasingly committed to various ancillary disciplines. For example, as the scope of his research grows, he may be called upon to be something of an engineer (to understand and make decisions about his equipment, not to mention building or modifying it himself), a mathematician or statistician or computer programmer (especially as data reduction becomes more dependent upon sophisticated computerized procedures), a veterinarian (if he uses animals, in which case he is inevitably faced with problems of disease control), a physicist, chemist, sociologist (for special knowledge many times in research, such as the role of sucrose as a reinforcer, personal interactions in small groups), and finally a personnel expert (for employee selection) and counselor (for employee satisfaction when a research and a research-support staff is assembled).

The increasing use of automated devices poses a special problem for graduate research training. This problem occurs whenever graduate students work with staff members who have succeeded in obtaining such equipment for their own research programs. If the graduate student is trained exclusively, or nearly so, on such equipment, then he is poorly equipped to make do with simpler devices when he moves into his own career, where initially he will probably lack the advantages he enjoyed in the established laboratory where he was trained. One partial solution to this special problem is for the sponsor to make express provisions for at least some training with simpler devices. This procedure has the added advantage of probably insuring some experience with direct behavioral observations as well as with the simpler equipment.

Faddishness and Conformity in Research. Although there are promising signs of a much-improved situation, the problem of faddishness has been especially acute within psychology. Currently "hot" research topics—whether Hullian theory, as in the 1940's, problems associated with intracranial brain stimulation, as was true in the 1960's, or biofeedback, as is the case today—seem to receive all too much attention from professional psychologists, as well as from graduate students. Any E is likely to have the problem of adapting and modifying both his experimental procedures and his theoretical guidelines to the needs of his research, rather than sticking blindly to a single experimental procedure or theoretical account (either or both of which he may have learned in graduate training). Against the need for adaptation one must always of course weigh the value of continued single-minded investigation—both procedures have merit and utility—but on balance the need for adaptation seems best to fit the kind of problems that science faces.

There are many illustrations of situations where some stagnation in research has occurred and seems to have been at least partly produced by the failure to broaden the range of experimental and theoretical attacks upon critical problems. To take one example, Thorndike's (1933) spread-of-effect technique—having S guess numbers to match words or nonsense-syllable stimuli in a serial multiple-choice learning task—came to be fixed as *the* procedure used (see Marx, 1956; Postman, 1962) and has only occasionally been varied. (More recent developments on this problem are available in Greenwald [1966], who attempted to reopen these issues by stimulating reconsideration of Nuttin's [1949] important variation in procedure and theory, and in retorts by Postman [1966] and Marx [1967], as well as the more recent and complete account by Nuttin and Greenwald [1968]. This sticking so closely to a single procedure probably accounts in part for the paucity of recent effective data on this particular problem. Underwood (1964) provides an extensive treatment of this general point in a survey of the field of rote learning.

The recent modifications of Skinner's free-response operant-conditioning technique to apply to discrete-trial (or controlled-operant) methodology (Gonzales, Brainbridge, and Bitterman, 1966; Atkinson and Calfee, 1964; Marx et al., 1965) provide an encouraging sign that experimental procedures are becoming freer.

Emotional Involvements. With regard to theoretical issues, we have already discussed some of the problems associated with monolithic theories, such as Hull's, or systems, such as Skinner's. One special problem should be elaborated. This is the emotional reaction, and counterreaction, that is so often associated with overly zealous attachment to or reaction against some particular systematic position. Just as the most extreme anticommunist is likely to have been at one time an avid communist or the most outspoken atheist at one time a religious devotee, so the polemicist in psychology may swing from one emotional extreme to the other. Two illustrations from the recent history of psychology suggest how this phenomenon, albeit in somewhat milder form, may operate to influence attitudes.

Consider these two contrasting views of Hull's theoretical efforts:

If the earlier publications gave any reason for doubting the fruitfulness of Hull's constructs, *Principles of Behavior* should go far toward dissipating such doubt. Hull's previous work left no room for questioning the methodological maturity of his *general* approach; the present work makes it no longer possible to question the value and richness of his *specific* theoretical assumptions.

and

Under close scrutiny, not a single member of a single class of such [Hull's] theoretical components satisfied the requirements for rigorous scientific theory of the sort envisaged within the theorist's explicit objectives. More importantly, many of the detailed solutions embodied in the theory of major problems in the methodology of psychological theory construction—e.g., the techniques employed for the "measurement" of independent and dependent variables, the techniques for the construction of quantitative, or even qualitative function forms—proved to have little merit within their concrete theoretical context, however suggestive certain of them may be in defining the problems that behavior theorists must face.

Unlikely as it may seem, at least at first glance, these two excerpts were written by the same critic (Koch, 1944, p. 270; and Koch, 1954, pp. 159–160). What a difference a decade makes! It is quite apparent that the "close scrutiny" that intervened between the two statements produced a marked turnabout in evaluation, and it also seems quite possible that the extremely negative tone of the second evaluation might be in part a function of the overly optimistic tone of the initial evaluation.

Another illustration of this kind of phenomenon may be seen in the present situation regarding the mechanism of language and language development. Stimulated by Skinner's (1957) interpretation of language, behavioristically inclined psychologists have for some time tended to regard language as a prime example of operant behavior that can be nicely incorporated within an empirical conditioning framework. This view, however, has come under increasing attack from the new linguists, spearheaded by Chomsky (1959), and as a result has been slowly giving way. For example, Bem and Bem (1968, p. 498) commented as follows:

It is not biological considerations which are prompting an increasing number of psychologists to accept some of the extraordinary conclusions about the innate character of linguistic competence, but the apparent failure of any current notions about learning to account for the new linguistic observations in even a remotely satisfying way. Some well-known psychologists (for example, Jenkins, 1968) have made public "mea culpa's" as mediational models of language have withered under the attack, while others more discreetly, are privately following suit. And, even though one of us has found Skinner's approach to verbal behavior heuristically valuable for illuminating certain non-linguistic phenomena (Bem, 1965), we, too, are among the persuaded.

Again, it is highly probable that such defections would be much less radical had the early acceptance of the learning viewpoint been less enthusiastic and unguarded. As Bem and Bem point out, this acceptance was often on a strictly programmatic basis, in the absence of empirical data.

A dangerous consequence of this kind of phenomenon, and one that needs to be carefully guarded against, is that once the prematurely accepted point of view is discarded there will not be an adequate effort to salvage potentially valuable parts of it. Thus there has been a tendency to reject all of Hull's system, because it has not lived up to its early promise, and there may well be a similar tendency to disregard the potentially significant role that learning may well play in language development, even granted that nativistic factors are also critical, and perhaps even more so than learning. Adoption of more qualified endorsements of theoretical positions from their inception may help to prevent the occurrence of these kinds of situations in the future.

The Publication Explosion. The E today, and increasingly in the future, has the problem of absorbing a tremendous mass of literature, mostly periodically but also consisting of a mass of books. This publication explosion raises the question of the meaning of scholarship: for example, what does *know one's field* mean in the light of all this information? A plausible answer to this question is that one must know guidelines to the literature, and the major principles and procedures; specialization is possible only in a progressively narrowing area of knowledge and field of research. While some recent advances in information storage and retrieval may be noted (for example, use of computer, special indexing systems), these can at best alleviate rather than resolve the fundamental problem, and it is certain that future scholars and researchers will be faced with an increasingly different situation.

As the boundaries of knowledge are enlarged, and the mass of detail within them increased, and as one's specialty becomes relatively more restricted, it becomes increasingly necessary that one learn general principles. But at the same time these principles may be more difficult to learn. Increased concern with the delineation and promulgation of principles and unifying propositions therefore becomes more important, and indicates the significance of theory development as well as the necessity of more effective publication devices (especially with regard to research reviews and the like).

Significance. Each E sooner or later must face up to the problem of the *significance* of his work. To continue to ignore this issue completely becomes increasingly difficult. This issue can be evaluated either with regard to real-life or theoretical-interpretative objectives, the former more often emphasized to the neglect of the latter (pure science pursuit).

In the face of questionable significance on either count, which is by far the most typical situation unless very low standards of significance are used, the scientific E must have a strong intrinsic motivation to sustain him through months and years of investigation. Experienced Es need to reflect upon the common opinion (for example, Kuhn, 1962) that it is so often the young novice who contributes the significant innovative ideas. Breaking out of old and established patterns of thought, emphasized elsewhere in this selection, is the major means by which more seasoned Es can make this kind of contribution.

The ability to tackle the "right" problems as well as tackle them effectively is part of the profile of the successful scientist. This is partly the ability to seize upon techniques that "work," either serendiptiously, as in the case of the ICS technique accidentally discovered by Olds and Milner (1954), or purposely, as in the development of the cannula-implantation technique for chemical treatment of the brain by Grossman (1960). How to develop such skills is obviously within the province of creativity training, discussed earlier.

Summary: Recent Trends

By way of a summary and a concluding statement, some of the trends in theory that have been discussed in this and the preceding selection and that are represented throughout other parts of this book may now be briefly characterized.

1. The most prominent substantive trend during the past decade, and one that has provided the atmosphere and direction for numerous other changes now in process, has been a lessening involvement with a strictly behavioristic orientation and a contrasting resurgence of interest in "mental" problems and perspectives.

2. Among the less prominent but perhaps equally significant substantive trends has been a reduced interest in certain aspects of traditionally emphasized topics such as learning (particularly those aspects related to some of the orthodox theories of an earlier era) and comparative psychology. These traditional problems have been largely replaced by a refocusing of both experimental and theoretical efforts. In the case of learning, contemporary interest centers on information processing and memory, and the related problems of attention, cognition, and linguistics. In the case of comparative psychology, contemporary interest has shifted to ethological work, stimulated initially by biologically trained animal behaviorists, and to behavior genetics.

3. The most prominent methodological trend of the past decade or so has been the de-emphasis of "grand" or systematic theories of broad scope (for example, Hull and Tolman). In their place have been developed an increasing number of so-called miniature theories, concentrating on problem areas of much smaller scope. The major difference, methodologically, is that researchers now seem to be working *toward* larger and more systematic theories rather than *from* them. There has also been a renewed concern with fundamental problems, such as necessary assumptions underlying theories, and the beginnings of new appreciation for integrative theories.

4. Theories and theorizing (in the sense of constructing more provisional sorts of propositions) have been marked by an increasingly *eclectic* flavor. Moreover, certain of the originally quite distinct theoretical systems have converged to where the differences in some cases have practically disappeared (for example, Hullian and Tolmanian theory, in certain respects).

5. With regard to empirical relationships, there has been a most encouraging shift from an emphasis on *disconfirmation* (typically of some one else's position) to *confirmation* of theories. Although, as we have seen, theories are more readily disconfirmed than confirmed by empirical results, it may be considered a thoroughly wholesome shift in attitude to have researchers more concerned with support for than evidence against theories. This is particularly true if such concern motivates Es to devise new means of investigating old problems.

6. Finally, theoretical distinctions among investigators in learning as well as in other areas of psychology have come to revolve more and more around particular *mechanisms* and *methodological* details, rather than around basic methodological assumptions and biases. Although these latter may still differ markedly, they no longer monopolize the center of the stage and no longer produce the excessive amounts of heat, often obscuring the more important substantive matters at issue, that were once evident.

7. All of these changes may be regarded as signs of increasing scientific maturity on the part of behavioral investigators and theorists. The shift of attention from systematic differences, with which psychology had seemed to be especially obsessed, to more specific experimental and theoretical questions of the sort that most other sciences are typically concerned with is an especially encouraging sign. More stress on *theorizing*, as the process of theory construction, is needed, in contrast to the kind of nearly exclusive attention devoted in training and in much of the professional literature to formal theory, as the ultimate product of theorizing.

Whatever the ultimate fate of these various new movements and forces, the ferment they have produced within psychology can only be regarded as a healthy sign and a mark of growing maturity.

GLOSSARY

Apprentice System. Training of student in actual research setting, in which he is permitted active participation in all or most phases of research under the supervision of an established investigator.

Auxiliary Condition. A factor that is essential to the demonstration of an empirical implication from a theory but that is not formally incorporated within the theory per se.

Cognitive Dissonance (Festinger). Theoretical proposition that there is a strong tendency to maintain consonance among cognitions and that dissonance will therefore be resisted.

Concept. A generalized class name which represents certain abstracted properties of the class.

Consolidative. The property (as in a theory) of summarizing and ordering prior data.

Construct. A concept that represents relationships among things and/or events and their properties.

Context of Confirmation. Emphasis on testing of hypotheses, as by experimentation and statistical analysis.

Context of Discovery. Emphasis on creation of hypotheses, mainly of an innovative sort, and identification of key problems.

Data. Recorded results of observations, preferably of an experimental (controlled) nature.

Data Language. Verbal representation of the direct ("raw") observations of the scientist.

Deduction. A formal logic in which specific conclusions are drawn from generalized premises.

Deductive Theory. A logically organized (deductively related) cluster of laws and postulates.

E. Abbreviation for experimenter.

E/C Intervening Variable (Marx). Construct directly related to the independent variable that differentiates the experimental (E) from the control (C) condition.

Empirical. Relating to sensory experience; denotes reliance on observation.

Experiment. A contrived situation in which the effects of one or more independent (manipulated) variables are assessed on dependent (measured) variables with extraneous variability minimized by the holding constant of controlled (eliminated) variables.

Experimentizing. The process of *in-*

formal and preliminary researching whereby more formal experimentation can be developed.

Fact. A symbolic proposition, usually a verbal statement, that is generally agreed upon by some particular group of persons.

Fallacy of Affirming the Consequent. In logic, the error of accepting the truth of a general proposition on the basis of the demonstration of a particular implication of it.

Formal Theory. Explicit explanatory proposition that is produced for public scrutiny and testing.

Functionalism. The psychological system that stresses adapting to the environment as a fundamental factor in behavior and experience.

Functional Theory. Less formalized explanatory propositions that are closely related to data (empirical propositions) and without fixed logical form.

Hypothesis. A relatively tentative and specific type of theoretical proposition.

Idiographic. Relating to the description of the particular conditions of an individual.

Induction. A logic in which specific propositions are accumulated to produce generalized conclusions.

Inductive Theory. Descriptive statements summarizing clusters of empirical propositions with minimal inferential commitment.

Informal Theory. Explanatory proposition that is typically incomplete and usually not fully explicated; intended to be used as working tool in preliminary research and theory development.

Innovative. The property (as in a theory, or in one's researching or theorizing) of breaking new ground for future research and theory construction.

Intervening Variable. An intraorganismic construct that abstracts the relationship between antecedent (stimulus) and consequent (response) conditions, with no meaning beyond this relationship.

Law. A relatively well-established relationship among empirical variables; or, a particularly well-established theoretical proposition.

Mathematical Model. A form of theory construction in which a mathematical formulation (model) is used as a starting point for the development of a theory (often a learning theory).

Model. A conceptual analogue, generally brought in from some other field, whose function is to direct empirical research.

Modus Tollens. In logic, rejection of a proposition on the basis of the demonstrated falsity of an implication.

Nomothetic. Relating to the development of general scientific laws.

Operant Conditioning (Skinner). A learning situation in which S emits responses (rather than elicits them, as in classical conditioning) and is typically permitted to respond freely.

Operationism (Bridgman). The guiding principle that in scientific communication the empirical basis of each term be explicitly provided.

Paradigm Clash (Kuhn). An inconsistency between opposing scientific frameworks, often leading to scientific revolution.

Parametric Experiment. An experiment in which several values of a variable are empirically assessed rather than merely one or two, so that a functional relationship can be more satisfactorily developed.

Parsimony. The scientific rule of thumb that says one should accept the simpler of theoretical alternatives when all fit the data equally well; especially relevant to the practical implementation of theories, rather than their development or testing.

Pilot Experiment. A preliminary type of experimental research designed to train an E and/or to determine the most feasible conditions for later, more formal experiments.

Positivism. A metatheoretical and general scientific position that emphasizes parsimony and operationism in data language and eschews theorizing and inferential commitment.

Postulate. A part of a theory, or a working assumption not intended for test.

Primitive Term. A verbal symbol whose meaning is not given by the theory in which it is used.

S. Abbreviation for subject.

Serendipity. Accidental discovery and recognition of some fact or principle.

Significance. The value (as of a theory or one's professional work) either in terms of practical utility (applied science criterion) or development of scientific understanding (pure science criterion).

Structuralism. The system that stresses the analysis of consciousness into elements through the method of introspection.

Testability. The characteristic of being open to (empirical) evaluation, the primary criterion of theoretical utility.

Theorizing. The process of informal development of explanatory propositions.

Theory. A provisional explanatory proposition concerning natural phenomena and consisting of symbolic representations of observed relationships, presumed underlying mechanisms, or inferred relationships.

Variable. A class of objects or events,

or properties thereof; a factor or condition that is conceptualized and/or empirically manipulated for scientific purposes.

REFERENCES

ABELSON, R. P., ARONSON, E., McGRUIRE, W. J., NEWCOMB, T. M., ROSEN-BERG, M. J., & TANNENBAUM, P. H. (Eds.) *Theories of cognitive consistency: A sourcebook.* Chicago: Rand McNally, 1968.

ALLPORT, G. W. *Personality: A psychological interpretation.* New York: Holt, 1937.

AMSEL, A. The role of frustrative non-reward in noncontinuous reward situation. *Psychol. Bull.,* 1958, **55,** 102–119.

———. Frustrative non-reward in partial reinforcement and discrimination learning. *Psychol. Rev.,* 1962, **69,** 306–328.

ATKINSON, R. C., & CALFEE, R. C. An automated system for discrete-trial research with animals. *Psychol. Rep.,* 1964, **14,** 424–426.

BAKAN, D. A generalization of Sidman's results on group and individual functions, and a criterion. *Psychol. Bull.,* 1954, **51,** 63–64.

BEM, D. J. An experimental analysis of self-persuasion, *J. exp. Soc. Behav.,* 1965, **1,** 199–218.

BEM, D. J., & BEM, S. L. Nativism revisited. A review of Eric H. Lenneberg's *Biological foundations of language. J. exp. anal. Behav.,* 1968, **11,** 497–501.

BENJAMIN, A. C. *Operationism.* Springfield, Ill.: Charles C Thomas, 1955.

BORING, E. G. *A history of experimental psychology.* 2nd Ed. New York: Appleton-Century-Crofts, 1950.

———. When is human behavior predetermined? *Scientific Monthly,* 1957, **84,** 189–196.

BREHM, J. W., & COHEN, A. R. *Exploration in cognitive dissonance.* New York: Wiley, 1962.

BRIDGMAN, P. W. *The logic of modern physics.* New York: Macmillan, 1927.

BRUNSWIK, E. Representative design and probabilistic theory in a functional psychology. *Psychol. Rev.,* 1955a, **62,** 193–217.

———. In defense of probabilistic functionalism: A reply. *Psychol. Rev.,* 1955b, **62,** 236–242.

CHOMSKY, N. Review of B. F. Skinner's *Verbal behavior. Language,* 1959, **35,** 26–58.

COHEN, M. R., & NAGEL, E. *Introduction to logic and scientific method.* New York: Harcourt, Brace, 1934.

COTTON, J. W. On making predictions from Hull's theory. *Psychol. Rev.,* 1955, **62,** 303–314.

CRESPI, L. P. Quantitative variation in incentive and performance in the white rat. *Amer. J. Psychol.,* 1942, **55,** 467–517.

DEAUX, E. B., & PATTEN, R. L. Measurement of the anticipatory goal response in instrumental runway conditioning. *Psychon. Sci.,* 1964, **1,** 357–358.

ESTES, W. K. Learning. In P. R. Farnsworth (Ed.), *Annual review of psychology.* Stanford, Calif.: Annual Reviews, 1956. Pp. 1–38.

———. The statistical approach to learning theory. In S. Koch (Ed.), *Psychology: A study of a science.* New York: McGraw-Hill, 1959.

FESTINGER, L. A theory of cognitive dissonance. New York: Harper & Row, 1957.

———. Conflict, decision and dissonance. Stanford, Calif.: Stanford Univer. Press, 1964.

GLASS, D. C. Theories of consistency and the study of personality. In E. F. Borgatta and W. W. Lambert (Eds.), Handbook of personality theory and research. Chicago: Rand McNally, 1968. Pp. 788–854.

GONZALES, R. C., BAINBRIDGE, P., & BITTERMAN, M. E. Discrete-trials lever-pressing in the rat as a function of pattern of reinforcement, effortfulness of response, and amount of reward. J. comp. physiol. Psychol., 1966, 61, 110–112.

GOODSON, F. E. The evolutionary foundations of psychology: A unified theory. New York: Holt, Rinehart & Winston, 1973.

GREENWALD, A. G. Nuttin's neglected critique of the law of effort. Psychol. Bull., 1966, 65, 199–205.

GROSSMAN, S. P. Eating or drinking elicited by direct adrenergic or choliner-gic stimulation of hypothalmus. Sci., 1960, 132, 301–302.

HANSON, N. R. Perception and discovery: An introduction to scientific inquiry. San Francisco: Freeman, Cooper & Co., 1969.

HEMPEL, C. G. Philosophy of natural science. Englewood Cliffs, N.J.: Pren-tice-Hall, 1966.

HILGARD, E. R., & BOWER, G. H. Theories of learning. 3rd ed. New York: Ap-pleton-Century-Crofts, 1966.

HONIG, W. K. (Ed.), Operant behavior: Areas of research and application. New York: Appleton-Century-Crofts, 1966.

HULL, C. L. Principles of behavior. New York: Appleton-Century-Crofts, 1943.

———. Essentials of behavior. New Haven: Yale Univer. Press, 1951.

———. A behavior system. New Haven: Yale Univer. Press, 1952.

ISRAEL, H. E., & GOLDSTEIN, B. Operationism in psychology. Psychol. Rev., 1944, 51, 177–188.

JENKINS, J. J. The challenge to psychological theorists. In T. R. Dixon and D. L. Horton (Eds.), Verbal behavior and general behavior theory. Engle-wood Cliffs, N.J.: Prentice-Hall, 1968. Pp. 538–549.

KOCH, S. Review of Hull's Principles of behavior. Psychol. Bull., 1944, 269–286.

KOCH, S., CLARK L. HULL. In W. K. Estes et al., Modern learning theory. New York: Appleton-Century-Crofts, 1954. Pp. 1–176.

KOCH, S. Epilogue. In S. Koch (Ed.), Psychology: A study of a science. Vol. 3. New York: McGraw-Hill, 1959. Pp. 729–788.

KUHN, T. S. The structure of scientific revolutions. Chicago: Univer. of Chicago Press, 1962.

LATANÉ, B., & DARLEY, J. M. Bystander "apathy." Amer. Sci., 1969, 57, 244–268.

LAWRENCE, D. H., and FESTINGER, L. Deterrents and reinforcement: The psy-chology of insufficient reward. Stanford, Calif.: Stanford Univer. Press, 1962.

LOGAN, F. A. Incentive. New Haven: Yale Univer. Press, 1960.

MACCORQUODALE, K., & Meehl, P. E. On a distinction between hypothetical constructs and intervening variables. Psychol. Rev., 1948, 55, 95–107.

MACKWORTH, N. H. Originality. *Amer. Psychol.*, 1965, **20**, 51–66.

MARX, M. H. Intervening variable or hypothetical construct. *Psychol. Rev.*, 1951, **58**, 235–247.

———. Spread of effect: A critical review. *Genet. Psychol. Monogr.* 1956, **53**, 119–186.

———. Analysis of the spread of effect: A comparison of Thorndike and Nuttin. *Psychol. Bull.*, 1967, **67**, 413–415.

——— (Ed.). *Theories in contemporary psychology.* New York: Macmillan, 1963.

——— (Ed.). *Learning: Theories.* New York: Macmillan, 1970.

MARX, M. H., & HILLIX, W. A. *Systems and theories in psychology.* New York: McGraw-Hill, 1973.

MARX, M. H., TOMBAUGH, T. N., HATCH, R. S., & TOMBAUGH, J. W. Controlled conditioning boxes with discrete-trial programming for multiple experimental use. *Percept. Mot. Skills*, 1965, **21**, 247–254.

MARX, M. H., & VAN SPANCKEREN, W. J. Control of the audiogenic seizure by the rat. *J. comp. physiol. Psychol.*, 1952, **45**, 170–179.

MEEHL, P. E. Theory-testing in psychology and physics: A methodological paradox. *Philos. Sci.*, 1967, **34**, 103–115.

MERTON, R. K. Behavior patterns of scientists. *Amer. Sci.*, 1969, **57**, 1–23.

MILLER, G. A., GALANTER, E., & PRIBRAM, K. H. *Plans and the structure of behavior.* New York: Holt, 1960.

MILLER, N. E. Liberalizatioin of basic S-R concepts: Extensions to conflict behavior, motivation, and social learning. In S. Koch (Ed.), *Psychology: A study of a science.* Vol. 2. New York: McGraw-Hill, 1959.

MOWRER, O. H. *Learning theory and behavior.* New York: Wiley, 1960a.

———. *Learning theory and the symbolic behavior.* New York: Wiley, 1960b.

———. Cognitive dissonance or counterconditioning: A reappraisal of certain behavioral 'paradoxes.' *Psychol. Record*, 1963, **13**, 197–211.

MOWRER, O. H., & VIEK, P. An experimental analogue of fear from a sense of helplessness. *J. abnorm. soc. Psychol.*, 1948, **43**, 193–200.

NUTTIN, J. "Spread" in recalling failure and success. *J. exp. Psychol.*, 1949, **39**, 690–699.

NUTTIN, J., & GREENWALD, A. G. *Reward and punishment in human learning.* New York: Academic Press, 1968.

OLDS, J., & MILNER, P. Positive reinforcement produced by electrical stimulation of septal regions and other regions of the rat brain. *J. comp. physiol. Psychol.*, 1954, **47**, 419–427.

POLANYI, M. Logic and psychology. *Amer. Psychol.*, 1968, **23**, 27–43.

POSTMAN, L. Rewards and punishments in human learning. In L. Postman (Ed.), *Psychology in the making.* New York: Knopf, 1962.

———. Reply to Greenwald. *Psychol. Bull.*, 1966, **65**, 383–388.

PRICE, W. L., & BASS, L. W. Scientific research and the innovative process. *Sci.*, 1969, **164**, 802–806.

ROSENTHAL, R. *Experimenter effects in behavioral research.* New York: Appleton-Century-Crofts, 1966.

SCHOENFELD, W. N. (Ed.) *Theory of reinforcement schedules.* New York: Appleton-Century-Crofts, 1969.

SEWARD, J. P. Hull's system of behavior: An evaluation. *Psychol. Rev.*, 1954, 61, 145–159.

SIDMAN, M. A note on functional relations obtained from group data. *Psychol. Bull.*, 1952, 49, 263–269.

SKINNER, B. F. *The behavior of organisms: An experimental analysis.* New York: Appleton-Century-Crofts, 1938.

————. Are theories of learning necessary? *Psychol. Rev.*, 1950, 57, 193–216.

————. A case history in scientific method. *Amer. Psychol.*, 1956, 11, 221–233.

————. *Verbal behavior.* New York: Appleton-Century-Crofts, 1957.

————. *Cumulative record.* Rev. ed. New York: Appleton-Century-Crofts, 1961.

————. Operant behavior. In W. K. Honig (Ed.), *Operant behavior: Areas of research and application.* New York: Appleton-Century-Crofts, 1966a.

————. What is the experimental analysis of behavior? *J. exp. anal. Behav.*, 1966b, 9, 213–218.

SMITH, A. G. Jupiter: The radio-active planet. *Amer. Sci.*, 1969, 177–192.

SPEAR, N. E. Retention of reinforcer magnitude. *Psychol. Rev.*, 1967, 74, 216–234.

SPENCE, K. W. *Behavior theory and conditioning.* New Haven: Yale Univer. Press, 1956.

————. *Behavior theory and learning.* Englewood Cliffs, N.J.: Prentice-Hall, 1960.

THORNDIKE, E. L. An experimental study of rewards. *Teach. Coll. Contr. Educ.*, 1933, No. 580.

TOLMAN, E. C. *Purposive behavior in animals and man.* New York: Appleton-Century-Crofts, 1932.

————. Principles of purposive behavior. In S. Koch (Ed.), *Psychology: A study of a science.* New York: McGraw-Hill, 1959. Pp. 92–157.

UNDERWOOD, B. J. The representativeness of rote learning. In A. W. Melton (Ed.), *Categories of human learning.* New York: Academic Press, 1964.

WATSON, J. *Double helix.* New York: Atheneum Press, 1968.

ZAJONC, R. B. Cognitive theories in social psychology. In G. Lindzey and E. Aronson (Ed.), *The handbook of social psychology.* Reading, Mass.: Addison-Wesley, 1968.

ZIMBARDO, P. G. *The cognitive control of motivation.* Glenview, Ill.: Scott, Foresman, 1969.

SUGGESTED READINGS

BERGMANN, G. *Philosophy of science.* Madison: Univer. of Wisconsin Press, 1957. As one of the more psychologically sophisticated philosophers of science, Bergmann has been a long-time contributor to the psychological literature (mainly in collaboration with the late Kenneth Spence). This book represents his treatment of the standard problems of theory construction from a highly advanced vantage point (more or less the theoretical status of physics, in which field the author is also highly competent).

ESTES, W. K., KOCH, S., MacCORQUODALE, K., MEEHL, P. E., MUELLER, C. G., JR., SCHOENFELD, W. N., & VERPLANCK, W. S. *Modern learning theory.* New York: Appleton-Century-Crofts, 1954. This book represents the fruits of a summer conference during which several young psychologists made an extensive critical evaluation of five classical learning theories: *Hull*, by S. Koch; *Tolman*, by K. MacCorquodale and P. Meehl; *Skinner*, by W. Verplank; *Lewin*, by W. K. Estes; and *Guthrie*, by C. Mueller and W. N. Schoenfeld. Although now necessarily somewhat dated, the volume remains a valuable example of theoretical criticism.

The excitement and fascination of science. Palo Alto, Calif.: Annual Reviews, 1965. Consisting of personalized accounts that originally appeared as prefaces within four of the *Annual Review* series (biochemistry, pharmacology, physical chemistry, and physiology), this book is intended to impart some of the flavor of science suggested in the title. Although behavioral science is not represented, there is nevertheless a great deal of generally interesting material on the process of research and theorizing.

GOODSON, F. E. *The evolutionary foundations of psychology: A unified theory.* New York: Holt, Rinehart & Winston, 1973. A contemporary example of broad-scale and integrative theory development. An effort to integrate the multitude of psychological findings and problems within an evolutionary frame.

HEMPEL, C. C. *Philosophy of natural science.* Englewood Cliffs, N.J.: Prentice-Hall, 1966. This little book provides an especially lucid and useful introduction to basic problems of theory construction and evaluation. The author succeeds in simplifying many of the more intricate complexities by unusually clear and straightforward exposition.

HILGARD, E. R., & BOWER, G. H. *Theories of learning.* (3rd Ed.) New York: Appleton-Century-Crofts, 1966. This third edition of a standard source on learning theory contains much up-to-date and penetrating description and evaluation of contemporary research problems.

KOCH, S. (Ed.) *Psychology: A study of a science.* Vols. I–III. New York: McGraw-Hill, 1959. These volumes represent an ambitious attempt to portray the science of psychology, with special emphasis upon theoretical developments, as it was in the late 1950's.

KUHN, T. S. *The Structure of scientific revolutions.* Chicago: Univer. of Chicago Press, 1962. Enormously influential in stimulating consideration of "paradigm clashes" as sources of advance in science, Kuhn's monograph stands as a landmark in the field and should be consulted by all students concerned with the problems of how changes in scientific thinking occur.

MANDLER, G., & KESSEN, W. *The language of psychology.* New York: Wiley, 1959. This plainly written book covers all the standard problems involving theory construction in psychology, with special attention to language per se.

MARX, M. H. (Ed.). *Theories in contemporary psychology.* New York: Macmillan, 1963. This book, a collection of both reprinted papers and expressly written essays, emphasizes learning theories as well as general theoretical methodology.

MARX, M. H., & HILLIX, W. A. *Systems and theories in psychology.* New York: McGraw-Hill, 1973. The systematic and historical approach here adopted provides basic information on the major figures in the development of learning theories.

McCain, G., & Segal, E. M. *The game of science.* Belmont, Calif.: Wadsworth, 1969. Although primarily written "for the intelligent student or layman whose acquaintance with science is superficial," in the words of the authors, this surprisingly fresh and down-to-earth account of the "game" of science has nonetheless something to say to many professionals and can, moreover, be strongly recommended as required reading for those who tend to think of science in terms of any of the various inappropriate stereotypes.

Michalos, A. C. *Philosophical problems of science and technology.* Boston: Allyn & Bacon, Inc., 1974. An examination of the classic problems in the philosophy of science by a number of the outstanding contemporary writers in the field.

Roe, Anne. *The making of a scientist.* New York: Dodd, Mead, 1953. Personal factors in the development of constructs are emphasized in this well-known treatment by a professional psychologist.

Sidman, M. *Tactics of scientific research.* New York: Basic Books, 1960. This is an able exposition of research strategy with illustrative materials drawn from laboratory experiences utilizing operant conditioning methodology.

20
EVALUATION OF THEORY*

Felix E. Goodson *and* George A. Morgan

Science is comprised of methods for investigating man and his world, data derived from the utilization of these methods, and theories developed to make these data understandable. In this paper we will focus on scientific theories, briefly examining their nature and function and then describing a set of criteria by which they can be evaluated.

The Nature and Function of Theories[1]

The term *theory* has many meanings, even among scientists. One popular usage contrasts theory with practice. We do not want to use

[1] There are a number of useful sources on this topic. Within psychology, see, for example, Allport (1955), Baldwin (1967), and Marx and Hillix (1973). In the philosophy of science, see, for example, Bergmann (1957); Feigl, Scriven, and Maxwell (1958); and Braithewaite (1955).

---

* Written for this volume.

theory in this sense, noting that even the applications of science may well be based on theoretical principles of the type described below.

A second meaning, found among both the public and some scientists, contrasts theory with certainty, emphasizing the untested or partially verified nature of theory. Although it is true that many theories, perhaps especially those in psychology, lack adequate empirical support, this is not a necessary property of a scientific theory. The contemporary version of Newton's theory of universal gravitation, for example, is well grounded in data, its principles having been verified or corroborated in many experiments. A related usage, which likewise is not the one we will use, is that of theory as a hypothetical entity, process, or condition such as "electron," "cell assembly" or "the unconscious." Such constructs may be components of a theory, but we feel that theory should have a broader meaning.

The more general scientific usage, which we will follow in this paper, is that a theory is a set of statements (definitions, assumptions, laws, hypotheses, and so on) used to explain the facts or data in a given area. Philosophers of science have usually emphasized the logical, deductive connections between the component statements of a theory. At the top are said to be the general principles, assumptions, premises, and postulates. Below these, and deducible from them, are middle-level laws and hypotheses. At the base of the theory lie the empirical laws and hypotheses that rest upon the particular data in the area under consideration. In an ideal theory, one should be able to move following the rules of logic from the top levels of the theory down through the laws and hypotheses to the empirical data.[2]

In our usage a middle-level law is a well-established theoretical proposition. It is based upon and subsumes lower-level laws, which are well-established empirical relationships. A hypothesis is a less well-established statement or one that is newly deduced from higher-level principles, or hypotheses. In this usage hypotheses are generated by the theory and after adequate verification become laws. Although some laws are arrived at through this deduction and verification process, in actuality many scientific laws are developed inductively. They are summaries of disparate, empirical data that may not have been generated to test the theory in question.

The preceding paragraph hints at two points to which we will return in our discussion of criteria for evaluating theories. First, a theory deductively generates new hypotheses and, thus, new data, which in turn reflect back on its adequacy. Second, a theory attempts to subsume and integrate a set of facts that would otherwise be uninterpretable. Following

---

2 Note that in selection 18, Marx has described four types of theory construction: the model, deductive, functional, and inductive. Although the present description of theory most closely resembles Marx's deductive, the criteria discussed in the next section are intended to apply to all four types.

this argument one step further, a theory has two basic functions, which correspond to Marx's (selection 18) labels of "tool" and "goal." A theory serves as a tool or guide to research by generating testable hypotheses and it serves the goal of helping man understand the world. Later in the paper we will argue that aiding understanding is the primary function of scientific theories and the ultimate criterion by which they must be evaluated.

Theories differ from one another and from this idealized form in many ways. This is perhaps especially the case in the social sciences and psychology where few if any theories approximate the sophistication implied above. A number of dimensions along which theories vary have evaluative connotations that will be discussed in the next section.

Criteria for Evaluating Theories[3]

We feel that the following list of criteria provides a relatively complete treatment of the issues surrounding the evaluation of theories. The labeling and ordering of the criteria are, of course, somewhat arbitrary. There were also problems of how to group related points and reduce the overlap between them. Nevertheless we feel that this discussion is quite systematic and should be helpful, especially since few such detailed treatments are available.

1. TESTABILITY

In this section we will consider two major interrelated considerations by which theories can be judged. The first is the extent to which the contingent statements of the theory are in a form such that they have empirical consequences that can be tested, at least in principle.[4] The second general consideration is intertwined with the first. It has to do with the extent to which the theory is actually able to deductively generate new hypotheses and, thus, previously unknown data.

Testability, in the sense of empirical verifiability, is often cited as *the* basic, minimal necessary criteria for all scientifically meaningful statements. Allport (1955) uses the phrase, "immediate experimental availability," to indicate that the terms in contingent theoretical state-

3 Brief discussions of criteria for evaluating psychological theories can be found in Allport (1955), Baldwin (1967), Estes et al. (1954), and Marx and Hillix (1973). More philosophically oriented treatments are found in, for example, Braithewaite (1955) and Popper (1968). Kuhn (1970) and O'Neil (1969) provide historical examples, largely from the natural sciences, of the evolutions and revolutions in scientific theories as a result of the inadequacies found in earlier theories. Several of the examples mentioned in this section are discussed in more detail in these books.

4 Baldwin (1967) distinguishes between contingent statements, such as the theoretical principles, laws, and hypotheses, which are empirically testable, and noncontingent statements, such as definitions and rules of operation, which cannot be tested. The latter, however, must be explicit, clear, and used consistently. More discussion of this topic is presented under the criteria of internal consistency.

ments should be sufficiently operationalized for the statement to be verified. Although higher-level theoretical statements are not themselves testable, they should lead to deductions that are. The verification or refutation of these deductions reflects on the adequacy of the theory.

Unfortunately, a number of the most important scientific theories have been relatively difficult to test in a direct way. As an example, consider Darwin's theory of evolution, which is one of the most widely accepted integrative systems in the life sciences. It could be argued that this theory is nothing more than a series of global pronouncements that cannot generate hypotheses to test its most basic assumptions because the time necessary for new species to evolve is much too long. On the other hand, one could maintain that a confirmation of the position can be derived from the many natural observations and experiments that provide indirect evidence. In any case, evolutionary theory has had unusual scientific importance because with a few simple principles it subsumes an unusual amount of the diversity of nature and helps man understand, at least in a general way, much that would otherwise remain incomprehensible.[5] In spite of this qualification, it seems necessary to insist that the terms used must be open to operational definition and the statements must be at least potentially testable.

Several aspects of testability that are often overlooked should be mentioned at this point. One is that the *process* by which hypotheses are generated by a particular theory is always inferential. In ideal form, it should adhere strictly to the rules of logic and should be executed with such careful attention to the deductive steps involved that there can be little disagreement that the hypothesis is logically derived from the theory in question. In actuality, the structure of most theories in psychology makes the process of deduction very difficult and subjective. The result is that many so-called testable hypotheses are at best loosely stated propositions that relate only in a general way to the conceptual system.

When an attempt is made to *apply* the results of the test of a given hypothesis to the evaluation of a particular theory, the problem becomes even more complex. One scientist may conclude that a particular experimental result is clearly consistent with a given theory, while another may honestly maintain that the results are at best peripheral to the position in question. Generally speaking, the clearer the deductive steps involved in the derivation of the hypothesis, the easier it will be to determine the appropriateness of the finding to the particular theory.

[5] This is a preliminary statement of the argument, which will be expounded in the section on explanatory power and understanding, that aiding understanding is the ultimate criterion for a theory and that this is accomplished when a theory can organize and simplify a mass of previously uncoordinated data. Goodson (1973) shows how evolutionary theory can be extended to help make psychological data understandable.

Those theories whose hypotheses can be tested in a scientifically rigorous fashion are generally felt to be more adequate. However, there is considerable disagreement about what constitutes an adequate test. Some psychologists insist on a strict application of the experimental method with manipulation of the independent variables and precise control over other variables. Others accept correlational methods and careful naturalistic observations. Still others would de-emphasize controls, instead focusing on the breadth or the "real-life" nature of the observations. The demand for test precision is laudable but, unfortunately, in psychology it has frequently led investigators to emphasize theories and research problems that are peripheral to important issues. There often seems to be an inverse relationship between the importance of a problem and its amenability to rigorous, experimental test. In striving for objectivity and precision, we have often tended to emphasize theories that have contributed little to the search for a real understanding of human behavior because the technical considerations of theory construction have been at least partially fulfilled. We may admire Hull's theory, yet it is difficult to show that it greatly advanced our understanding of the human being or even the rat.

Although the impulse toward precision may lead us to emphasize both theories and research with trivial implications, it has helped stifle what is probably an even more dangerous predilection: the preoccupation with orientations that, because of their extreme generality and ambiguity, are impervious to logical analysis and/or empirical test.

Now to return to the second major consideration. It is desirable for a theory to be able to predict new facts, but this is not essential if the theory is consistent with and helps explain the known facts. Indeed, theories that lead to really new predictions are quite rare in psychology. In general, psychologists have all they can do to test the theories they have developed to handle the available observations. Of course, any empirical test of a theory will yield data that is at least technically new. However, in psychology these data are seldom of the nature of the discovery of the planet Neptune, whose existence had been predicted earlier on the basis of Newton's theory of planetary motion.

To what extent is a theory only an instrument for producing testable hypotheses and to what extent should it be considered representational of the empirical domain? Although there has been much argument on this point, it seems obvious that any theory generating empirically testable hypotheses that *are confirmed* (assuming, of course, that both inferential process and testing techniques are adequate) must to *that* degree be representational. Thus, to the extent that the Ptolemaic and Copernican views of the solar system both generated testable hypotheses that were confirmed, they were both, at least to that extent, representational. They seem contradictory simply because we have emphasized those features that are ostensibly opposite rather than those that are similar or even in some cases overlapping. An effective theory has two general character-istics: (1) it is a utilitarian instrument to the degree that it generates testable hypotheses, and (2) it becomes representational of the empirical domain to the extent that such hypotheses are confirmed.

It is important to note that to enhance the status of the *theory*, the predictions of new facts should be derived logically from the theoretical principles themselves. Many creative hypotheses proposed by psycholo-gists are related in a general way to some theory, but that is not the same thing as being deduced from the theory. We shall return to this topic under the discussion of criterion 7, stimulation value.

In summary, it is necessary that the terms of a theory have empirical referents and that the statements be testable, at least in principle. A theory will be more useful if it can generate many testable hypotheses, especially ones that lead to the discovery of new facts. These hypotheses should be derived in a logical manner, appropriate to the theoretical position, tested in a rigorous fashion, and pertinent to the resolution of basic problems.

2. RESPONSIVENESS

It is desirable that a theory be responsive to new evidence. Two related questions enter into the discussion. *Can* the theory be modified without becoming too unwieldy or unparsimonious? And to what extent is it so insulated from empirical data that its proponents are *unwilling* to change it?

Here we touch upon an interesting dilemma. The more inclusive a theory, the more useful it is, if it has empirical reference and subsumes the pertinent data with precision. Yet the more abstract the theoretical principles, the further it is removed, in terms of logical steps, from the facts themselves, and the greater is the likelihood that some error may be made in the inferential process. Thus there is a tendency for the more inclusive theory to be less responsive to empirical data than one more limited in scope.

The more widely disseminated and generally accepted the theory, the less likely it is to be changed as a function of new and even compelling evidence. In extreme cases, tradition and authority can be so influential that even the most conscientious investigator may make faulty observa-tions or draw distorted inferences. Thus da Vinci, when doing an autopsy on the human heart, drew into his otherwise very accurate sketches the holes in the septum that were essential to Galen's theory of blood circula-tion, even though he could not find them.

The responsivity of a theory is also affected by the number and quality of competing positions. Hull's learning theory, for instance, was altered a great deal because of repeated controversy with Tolman. In a field where there are few competing positions, there may be a greater reluctance by scientists in the area to question a given theory.

Not only should a theory be modifiable or responsive to new data, ideally it should be open to destruction or refutation by a critical empirical test. A theory that remains impervious to the possibility of refutation is suspect. If there is no potential for refutation, either directly or through its derivatives, we are dealing with metaphysics or theology, and not science. Nevertheless, a theory seldom falls as a result of a crucial experiment; more often it is diminished by the slow attrition of many partial failures and the added burden of the qualifications required when it is modified to fit the new data. Once a theory is firmly held it is seldom abandoned, even when the weight of empirical evidence is against it, unless there is a simpler theory that fits the data at least as well ready to take its place.[6]

The individual scientist's commitment to his theoretical position may well affect the responsiveness of the position. Although a scientist is presumably trained to view his subject matter in an unbiased manner, some degree of emotional attachment to the conceptual system that serves to integrate his personal scientific efforts is inevitable. Thus certain scientists have had a great, even grave, personal commitment to the adequacy of a given theoretical position. Examples of this sort of involvement have been common in the history of psychology, ranging from Titchener's commitment to structuralism to the contemporary behavior therapist's insistence on the principle of operant conditioning. When such an adherence is coupled with an ambiguously stated theory and a complex subject matter area, the relative unresponsivity of the position is markedly increased. Not only does the individual tend to select data that conform to the theory, but it may be difficult to know when a particular empirical finding supports the theory and when it does not. For example, the psychoanalyst may accept the view that this theory is indeed the ultimate explanation of human behavior and personality. Given the nature of his training and the ambiguity and complexity of the human being, it is no wonder that in many cases the theory provides the perceptual coercion that in turn produces the validating evidence.

Thus emotional commitment adds to the unresponsivity of a theory by introducing bias into the selection of evidence. The error is probably more pronounced when the subject matter is complex, the theory is widely accepted, and there are fewer competing theories.

3. INTERNAL CONSISTENCY

In an adequate theory, the propositions or statements should be related to each other in accordance with established or explicitly described rules of logic and syntax. Terms should be defined clearly and used consistently

---

[6] Thus, there is obviously overlap between this criterion and parsimony (number 5 below). Ptolemaic "earth-centered" theory of the universe was weighted down by so many modifications that it was finally, albeit reluctantly, replaced by Copernican theory. O'Neill (1969) and Kuhn (1970) discuss this and other changes in scientific paradigms.

throughout. Similarly, any special rules of operation should be explicit and consistent. Although not conventially accepted as a scientific theory, the contemporary statement of Euclidian geometry fulfills most of the requirements and its format provides an ideal of internal consistency with each term precisely defined, each postulate stated with exceptional clarity, and each theorem derived with unimpeachable logic.

All widely held scientific theories probably meet some minimal standard on this criterion, but, unfortunately, there is considerable variability and this is particularly the case within psychology. Hull's theory and many of the recent microtheories of learning and perception are good examples of internally consistent positions. On the other hand, many personality theories, perhaps because of complexity of subject matter, seem loosely stated with apparent contradictions in some of their statements.

Although internal consistency is an important and basic criterion, a theory may be the model of logical consistency and still be trivial when it comes to aiding man's understanding.

4. SUBSUMPTIVE POWER

This dimension refers to the extent that the system in question integrates the available empirical data. This integration process has three facets. First, theories may vary in the *completeness* with which the data within the particular area of concern are subsumed. Thus even in a well-delimited area, a theory may deal effectively with certain relevant facts and leave other vitally important empirical findings untouched. For instance, research into the nature of light energy has produced such divergent and apparently contradictory empirical findings that it has been necessary for physicists to resort to both corpuscular and wave conceptions to make the data meaningful. The Young–Helmholtz theory of color vision is another example; it handles the data on after-images and complementaries effectively, but fails to deal adequately with the phenomenon of color blindness.

Second, theories may vary in subsumptive power relative to the *sheer amount* or breadth of information they integrate. Newton's theory of universal gravitation applies to a great variety of seemingly disparate data, whereas Lotze's theory of the generation of tactual spatiality is extremely specific and limited in its scope.

Third, theories may vary relative to the *logical clarity* of the subsumptive process. Thus in certain positions the various steps involved in the inductive movement from empirical data to theoretical generalization are stated with succinctness and precision, whereas in others this inferential process is ambiguous and incomplete. Although there may be disagreement concerning the degree to which inferential precision was achieved, Hull was cognizant of this problem and endeavored to demonstrate the applicability of particular empirical findings to his learning theory. Most theories in psychology have paid little attention to this problem, however, with the result that it is at times difficult to determine when a given empirical finding is encompassed by a position and when it is not.

In summary, there are at least three aspects of subsumptive power: (a) the exhaustiveness or completeness with which the data in a specific area is integrated, (b) the generality or total amount of data subsumed, and (c) the inferential precision or logical clarity of the subsumption process.

5. PARSIMONY

Theories may also vary in terms of the number of their assumptions or postulates. Because science strives for the greatest possible economy in the process of explanation, the simplest theory becomes the most acceptable under those conditions where other factors are equal.

In its effort to reduce the complexity of nature, science accepts the theory that explains the "most with the least." A scientist should always ask the following question about a given theory: Is there a *simpler* conceptual system that will integrate and make explicable the data of the area? If the answer is affirmative, the old system, all other factors being equal, should be abandoned in favor of the new. However, other factors are rarely, if ever, equal and thus parsimony alone is not enough. One should always ask whether the simplicity obscures rather than clarifies, and whether the theory really handles the complexity of the subject.

Guthrie subsumed both learning and forgetting with the single principle of prior contiguous association; likewise, Skinner suggested that the principle of reinforcement is the key to understanding changes in behavior. However, many psychologists now feel that both of these theories achieved parsimony by oversimplifying the subject matter.

6. COMMUNICABILITY

This criterion involves the extent to which a given theory can be transmitted between two or more individuals without distortion or loss of information. Its importance becomes evident when we consider that science is a cumulative social phenomenon and cannot by definition be limited to the logic or insights of one person.

A major factor in communicability involves the type of concept used. If the terms of the theory are poorly defined (i.e., unduly abstruse, ambiguously stated, or replete with emotional loading), loss and distortion of information during transmission are bound to occur. In general, the greater the complexity and the lower the coherence of a theory the more distortion will be introduced into the communication process. The relative novelty and difficulty of the concepts must also be considered. For example, there can be little doubt that much of the distortion that took place in Einstein's theory of relativity during the first decades after its publication was due to the novelty of its orientation and the abstractness of its terms.

Thus, four dimensions along which theories can be evaluated emerge from our discussion of communicability: (a) the clarity with which the terms are defined, (b) the complexity or difficulty of the formulation, (c) the coherency of the principles comprising the theory, and (d) the novelty of its orientation and mode of presentation.

7. STIMULATION VALUE

What has been the general heuristic value of the theory? That is, to what extent has it provided a general framework within which scientific research and controversy have taken place?

The primary scientific significance of the stimulation value of a theory is, of course, whether it generates scientific research. Yet it is historically apparent that general public interest is often related to scientific activity. The public supplies both the funds and personnel necessary for science to proceed, and if interest is present concerning an area, both of these essential ingredients will be more easily obtained.

No necessary relationship exists, however, between a theory's scientific usefulness and the extent of its public impact. In some instances, as in the case of Gall's phrenology, theories have generated wide public interest and concern but provided little integration and even less insight.

A number of factors influence the extent to which a theory will have human impact. Its general timeliness, for instance, is of prime importance. Darwin's theory probably would have had little immediate effect if it had been published in 1759 rather than 1859. In the mid-eighteenth century the problem of species variation was of little concern, whereas a century later it had become a vital issue because of the findings in botany and physical anthropology. Thus the utilization of a theory must wait upon the Zeitgeist, as Boring said, and must depend for its general impact upon the previous existence of a question and a concern.

If a theory is too highly specialized or too difficult for more than a very small group of specialists, it will probably not have a broad impact. On the other hand, Freud's psychoanalytic theory and Darwin's theory of evolution have not only served as effective stimuli for scientific activity, but have also produced repercussions of great magnitude in general society. Why such a public storm was created by these two theories gives further insight into those factors that propel a theory beyond the strict confines of science into the domain of public concern. Freud's theory stirred the world because it promised to make explicable areas that are of vital interest to every human being—sex, the unconscious, abnormal behavior, and so on. Darwin's theory produced wide public concern because it threatened an area of intense emotional commitment, that of religion.

In summary, there are at least two aspects of stimulation value: (a) the extent of public interest and concern, and (b) the amount of scientific activity generated.

Problems with Relying on the Criteria

There seem to be at least two major difficulties in evaluating the adequacy of a scientific theory based on the preceding criteria. First, there is some degree of overlap and interaction between the dimensions. For example, there is clearly a close relationship between a theory's responsiveness and its testability; the communicability of a position is affected by its internal consistency; and stimulation value is to some extent a function of communicability. Although mutually exclusive independent categories would have been preferable, the multiple functions and characteristics of theories make such categories impossible to achieve.

Second, as noted in each section, the criteria have limitations and/or major exceptions that in real life make them, even as a group, less than adequate yardsticks for measuring the value of a theory. Each is important, and a scientifically viable theory should rate highly on at least most of these dimensions. However, it is our contention that unless a theory significantly aids the scientist in his struggle to order and understand his subject matter, it will be a sterile academic edifice no matter how carefully constructed and how highly it rates on the preceding seven traditional criteria. The situation may be somewhat analogous to the problems implicit in achieving reliability and validity. That is, in order for a theory to be useful, it must obtain relatively high marks on each of the seven criteria, but although that is necessary, it is not sufficient.

An even more heretical proposition that we shall propose, but not specifically endorse, is that it may be possible for a theory to help man somehow in his struggle for understanding even though it rates poorly on most of the preceding criteria. Psychoanalytic theory is the obvious example. Many psychotherapists, even those who are not committed analysts, feel that their reading of Freud provides them with more insights about the functioning and problems of their patients than other, perhaps more organized and rigorous, theories. Likewise, many psychology textbooks, dealing with topics in abnormal psychology, personality, or developmental psychology, fall back on Freudian notions to explain the behavior under consideration or to tie things together. Perhaps this is merely deference to a historically important figure, or perhaps these areas are so weak in competing positions that there is little choice but to present Freud's concepts. However, it may be that this less than exemplary theory according to the listed criteria does, in fact, rate quite well on the ultimate criterion of helping the scientist understand man.

Explanatory Power and Understanding[7]

Because many definitions of understanding have been given, it is important to clarify its meaning in the context of this paper. As a first approximation we can say that understanding is a subjective feeling of satisfaction with the adequacy of an explanation. A theory that provides a good explanation of some phenomenon can be said to rate highly on explanatory power because it produces a feeling of understanding in those who study it. Of course, a firm feeling is not enough—it could be a misunderstanding. Such feeling must match reality. A definition that allows at least potential empirical check on the accuracy of understanding proposes that understanding is a state or condition in a person that enables him to respond adaptively in a certain situation. Thus, the extent of the understanding would be judged by the degree to which effective behavior was demonstrated. Unfortunately, such a checking process would be difficult to achieve. It would be difficult to define what we mean by adaptive behavior and to determine when we had sufficiently sampled the situations pertinent to the validating process. Such an empirical demonstration of understanding would usually involve a check upon the accuracy of a prediction made by the subject, meaning that the degree of understanding would be determined by the relative accuracy of prediction.

This leads to the common, but we feel erroneous, practice of equating understanding with prediction and to the affirmation that prediction rather than understanding should be the basic goal of science. Thus, it is maintained that the goal of science should be a complete statement of the variables in nature and of their relationships so that given any one factor, its covariation with any other could be accurately predicted. There is nothing wrong with such a formal statement, but it leaves the essential human element out of the picture. Although understanding may only be empirically demonstrated through the success or failure of prediction, the two concepts should not be equated. Understanding is a subjective, experiential condition, whereas prediction takes the form of a statement of the relationship presumed to exist between two or more variables. Predictions are typically stated in terms of logical or mathematical symbols, but these would have neither meaning nor significance unless understood. Thus in the representation of the data of science there are always two components: the formal statement in terms of verbal declaration

[7] There are many discussions of scientific explanation both within psychology (e.g., Allport, 1955) and among philosophers of science (e.g., Braithewaite, 1955; Feigl and Maxwell (Eds.), 1962; and Nagel, 1961). Unfortunately, there is much less written about the goal of explanation, namely, human understanding. Furthermore, many treatments of explanation seem to get lost in philosophical intricacies.

or mathematical equation and the subjective experiential aspect comprised of some person's comprehension of the meaning of such verbal or mathematical statement.

It is important to note that one may have a relatively thorough and complete understanding of something, and yet be unable to make predictions with anything approaching precision. We can give a fair explanation of what causes volcanoes, but our ability to predict, much less control, when one will erupt is limited. Another reason for distinguishing between predictability and understanding is that certain relationships are more basic than others to the understanding of a given phenomena. Such basic relationships need not be more predictable than others that are relatively inconsequential. For example, the relationship between the explosion of gas in the cylinder of an engine and the movement of the pistons is fundamental to the understanding of how a car works. It is, however, no more consistent than the relationship between the output of exhaust and the speed with which the wheels turn. In endeavoring to understand how a car or an organism works, we should not only look for consistent relationships, but concentrate on discovering relationships that are fundamental in the organism's operation.

How, then, does theory aid in the process of understanding? Although it may seem complex and incomprehensible, a theory should be a simplifying statement. Man, faced with the diversities and complexities of the world, seeks understanding and the consequent control of his environment that this understanding gains for him. Facts not represented in a manner that makes them meaningful are fruitless. An adequate theory aids in understanding by emphasizing, and in many cases representing, those features that a large number of apparently different events have in common. Newton's theory of universal gravitation is exemplary in this respect. His basic principles were so general in their application that they subsumed a large number of more restricted laws, thus organizing and greatly simplifying a vast number of previously uncoordinated observations.

It may seem paradoxical that the ultimate criterion for scientific research, with its insistence upon control of variables and clarity of concepts, should reside in something as subjective and as difficult to define as that which is implied by the term *understanding*. Yet because the process of science must culminate in some fashion, it seems not only reasonable but necessary that it terminate in the context that gave it motivation: man's subjective experience.

REFERENCES

ALLPORT, F. *Theories of perception and the concept of structure.* New York: Wiley, 1955.

BALDWIN, A. *Theories of child development.* New York: Wiley, 1967.

BERGMANN, G. *Philosophy of science*. Madison: University of Wisconsin Press, 1957.

BRAITHEWAITE, R. B. *Scientific explanation: A study of the function of theory, probability and law in science*. Cambridge, England: Cambridge University Press, 1955.

ESTES, W. K., KOCH, S., MACCORQUODALE, D., MEEHL, P. E., MUELLER, C. G., JR., SCHOENFELD, W. N., & VERPLANCK, W. S. *Modern learning theory*. New York: Appleton-Century-Crofts, 1954.

FEIGL, H., & MAXWELL, G. (Eds.). *Minnesota studies in the philosophy of science. Volume III: Scientific explanation, space and time*. Minneapolis: University of Minnesota Press, 1962.

FEIGL, H., SCRIVEN, M., & MAXWELL, G. (Eds.). *Minnesota studies in the philosophy of science. Volume II: Concepts, theories, and the mind-body problem*. Minneapolis: University of Minnesota Press, 1958.

GOODSON, F. E. *The evolutionary foundations of psychology*. New York: Holt, 1973.

KUHN, T. S. *The structure of scientific revolutions* (revised). Chicago: University of Chicago Press, 1970.

MARX, M. H., & HILLIX, W. A. *Systems and theories in psychology* (2nd edition). New York: McGraw-Hill, 1973.

NAGEL, E. *The structure of science: Problems in the logic of scientific explanation*. New York: Harcourt Brace Jovanovich, 1961.

O'NEILL, W. M. *Fact and theory: An aspect of the philosophy of science*. Sidney: University of Sidney Press, 1969.

POPPER, K. R. *The logic of scientific discovery* (revised English edition). London: Hutchinson, 1968.

LOGICAL PERSPECTIVES

NOBLE's *essay concerns the logical triumvirate of induction, deduction, and the less commonly appearing* abduction (*meaning the "formulation and testing of hypotheses"*). *The use of psychological illustrations, focusing on Skinner and Spence, renders the logical information in the essay especially useful.*

The paper by Krantz concerns measurement and lawfulness in psychology. It is a comprehensive treatment of the focal problems that psychologists face in their continuing efforts to develop quantitative expressions for behavioral and experimental relationships.

The excerpt from Polanyi's essay concerns the manner in which the scientist, using essentially universal human intellectual processes, actually proceeds to make decisions. The selection represents Polanyi's much-cited emphasis on intuitive functions, such as tacit knowing, in contrast to formal logical deductions.

21

INDUCTION, DEDUCTION, ABDUCTION

CLYDE E. NOBLE

AN experimental psychologist, in his or her professional capacity as a natural scientist who studies the laboratory behavior of organisms, has three principal tasks. Indeed, I shall argue that all behavioral scientists spend most of their time (or should do so) in the following activities: (1) performing inductions, (2) deriving deductions, and (3) formulating and testing hypotheses in the domain of psychology. For convenience, let me adopt the term C. S. Peirce (1839–1914) employed for the third mission; he called it *abduction*. Now we have three concise words: induction, deduction, abduction. More emphasis upon that Peircean trilogy would have desirable pragmatic consequences for our science. Let us now try to justify this opinion with a bit of behavioral philosophy.

Philosophers of psychology do not, *qua* professionals, induce or deduce

FROM C. E. Noble, Philosophy of science in contemporary psychology, *Psychological Reports*, 1974, 35, 1239–1246. Reprinted by permission of the author and *Psychological Reports*.

or abduce. Rather, they analyze the roles that induction, deduction, and abduction play in the science of behavior. Such behavioral philosophers (sometimes called methodologists of psychology) engage in the critique of psychological procedures, concepts, and principles. They will be found analyzing the empirical operations, the systematic terminology, and the techniques of theory construction used by professional psychologists. Persons who philosophize about the science of psychology (not to be confused with all "philosophers of mind") are specialists who examine and reflect upon the technical work of psychologists, and who participate in a continuing dialectic about the philosophical problems and issues of behavioral science. Expressed differently, their mission is a progressive analysis and review of the knowledge claims, observational assumptions, inferential processes, criticisms, alternative interpretations, clarifications, and conceptual strategies associated with psychological methods, terms, and theories. For example, it is often said that inductivism (e.g., Skinner, 1969) and deductivism (e.g., Spence, 1956) are somehow antithetical or dichotomous. On the contrary, analysis of induction and deduction reveals them to be complexly interwoven processes, certainly not substitutes for one another, nor even structurally (i.e., formally) distinct as is commonly believed. However opposite and complementary they may be when considered from an epistemological view, there is no logical reason why inductive generalizations cannot be arranged into a systematic conceptual scheme whose ordering relations are deductive (Lee, 1973). Science is a progressive enterprise, and we are prone to forget the interdependence of facts, hypotheses, and generalizations as scientific knowledge advances (Nagel, 1961). Our theories integrate our laws in a manner analogous to the way our laws integrate our data (Bergmann, 1957). In short, a theory unsupported by data is without foundation; data unorganized by theory are without relevance.

Induction

This is the process of acquiring abstract, general knowledge about the concrete particulars of experience. The latter provide the perceptual evidence from which empirical inductions are formed, and the conclusion or concept always manifests a greater degree of generality than does the evidence on which it is based. A host of separate observations (percepts) in the psychology of learning led to the rational conclusion that contiguity of stimuli and responses is a necessary (though not sufficient) condition for association formation. Similarly, on the evidence of many experimental coordinates relating previous massed practice and current resting time to sudden performance gains without further practice, the concept of reminiscence was introduced. In the above instances the conclusion (principle of contiguity) and the concept (reminiscence) both represent generalizations derived from individual percepts; the numerous specific percepts are connected by those generalizations. So generalizations arise from percepts. Percepts characterize the empirical aspect of knowledge whereas generalizations characterize the rational aspect. In science these two aspects are interrelated, and it serves no useful purpose to draw honorific distinctions between them. Nevertheless, one should not forget that the *validity* of deductive generalizations is certain provided the rules of logic are obeyed, whereas the *truth* of inductions is only probable on the evidence.

Validity and invalidity are characteristics of arguments; this is a question of logical *form* (organization, relations, structure) independent of space and time. Truth and falsity are characteristics of propositions; this is a question of empirical *content*—of matters of fact present in experience (at particular loci in space and points in time) and which are judged to be veridical perceptions. Of course, all perception is fallible, but within the larger context of scientific theory perceptual knowledge is, in principle, self-correcting, i.e., corrigible at a later time. This explicit reference to subsequent observations is a defining quality of empiricism. Indeed, the relevance of future evidence implies that inductive generalizations cannot yield perfect universality. The census is never complete so knowledge must be progressively confirmed by new data. Induction cannot provide certainty or necessity. These arguments that appear to do so are camouflaged deductions.

I have said that empirical generalizations depend upon perceptual facts. Yet percepts are not equivalent to concepts, even though they have the same source in the continuum of experience. Examples of percepts are events named by proper nouns; examples of concepts are ideas named by common nouns. Percepts are concrete, specific events having spatio-temporal location; concepts are not so localized for they are abstract and general. We may say that percepts *are* instances whereas concepts *have* instances (Lee, 1973). Whatever is abstract and general is conceptual, not perceptual, so there is a theoretic theme operating in the formation of concepts from percepts. Scientific description, explanation, interpretation, and understanding all require development of conceptual schemes. Science, therefore, is fundamentally a theoretical enterprise even at the level of low-order empirical laws.

Skinner professes to conduct research "in a rather Baconian fashion" (1969, p. 82); he asserts, for instance, that "a smooth curve showing a change in probability of a response as a function of a controlled variable is a fact in the bag, and there is no need to worry about it as one goes in search of others" (p. 84). The picture of a Grand Anti-theoretician in action evoked by this passage may be comforting to radical empiricists, but it does not take account of the highly abstract nature of functional relationships obtained in psychology laboratories. A discovery that $R = f(S)$ is, from my point of view, no mere "fact." It is considerably more general than a percept because several concepts are being interrelated in a proposition involving the quantitative dependency of R upon S in a "causal" setting. If nothing else, a consideration of the unexamined instances of $R = f(S)$ render this so-called "fact in the bag" a frankly hypothetical statement. Parametric variations often require us to alter the mathematical forms of our inductive generalizations.

Many great scientists have, apparently without following any canons of induction, been intuitively gifted at formulating significant concepts and working these into replicable functions of broad applicability. Some of them contend that analyses of scientific method misrepresent how scientists think. Skinner is one of these. But I suggest that it does not follow from the insightful properties of a given scientist's problem-solving behavior that data should be gathered without the aid of hypotheses or that laws should be de-classified as facts, or that most theories are unnecessary, misleading, and wasteful. The present analysis is based not on psychology but on logic and epistemology. I believe that it is crucial to the understanding of scientific method in psychology. I hope that it will also be applicable to scientific behavior.

Earlier I referred to validity and truth as characteristics of arguments and propositions, respectively. Now concepts, e.g., terms, symbols, words, have neither truth nor validity, but if they are going to enter pragmatically into laws and theories they must be significant, i.e., both operationally meaningful and systematically interrelated (Bergmann, 1957). The infamous Bergmann Coefficient $[BC = (Wbc \times Wt)/No. \text{ leg hairs}]$ has some of the former properties but none of the latter. Although it is precisely defined and even indicates a replicable measurement procedure, the concept appears in no scientific laws. On the other hand, the ubiquitous Intelligence Quotient $[IQ = 100 (MA/CA)]$ has a number of properties that qualify it as a significant concept—perhaps entirely too many for the taste of certain sociologists. IQs, unlike BC scores, are interrelated as well as meaningful. Experimental psychologists are powerfully reinforced when they formulate significant concepts because their quest for economical descriptions and explanations of behavior is thereby facilitated. To discover a law is one of life's greatest rewards.

Deduction

This is the process of inferring necessary conclusions from a combination of premises whose truth is either given or assumed. To say that a conclusion is deducible from its premises is to say that the latter imply the former. Although deduction by itself cannot yield any empirical knowledge, a logically correct deductive argument leads to a valid conclusion because the conclusion is contained implicitly within the premises. Whether the conclusion is also true depends on the premises. Since any valid conclusion is a logical consequence of its premises, it cannot be false if the premises are true. Their factual status can be determined directly by observation and experimentation. Alternatively, the truth or falsity of a proposition may be deduced from other propositions whose truth has already been established, i.e., verification may be indirect as well as direct. There are no concepts in a valid conclusion whose grounds are not already in the premises, and these concepts' extension is determined by the joint extensions of those in the premises. In other words, premises and conclusion must be relevant to each other. The logical relation (operation) permitting the inference is that of implication.

A familiar example of deductive logic is the categorical syllogism. In schematic form: (1) All As are Bs; (2) a' is an A; (3) ∴ a' is a B. This conclusion is necessary because special instances are contained within a general rule, i.e., the relation of inclusion is transitive. Categorical syllogisms are unconditional arguments; they make statements absolutely, with no strings attached. A less familiar example of deduction is the hypothetical syllogism. One mood is the following: (1) If A is B, then C is D; (2) A is B; (3) ∴ C is D. The form of this argument contains one or more if-then relations connecting an antecedent clause, called the *protasis*, with a consequent clause, called the *apodosis*, such that the truth of the apodosis is contingent upon the truth of the protasis. The if-then contingency is a factual matter; there is no necessary connection between antecedent and consequent. Using the customary symbols 'p' for the protasis, 'q' for the apodosis, and '⊃' for the so-called material conditional (or relation of implication), this syllogism reduces to: (1) $p \supset q$; (2) p; (3) ∴ q. By thus affirming the antecedent of the major premise in the minor premise, we must draw an affirmative conclusion (*modus ponens*), i.e., '$p \supset q$' means that 'p true and q false' is disallowed. Of course, even granted that the proposition '$p \supset q$' is materially true, there are three remaining possibilities: (1) both p and q may be true, or (2) p may be false and q true, or (3) both p and q may be false. The other mood of hypothetical syllogisms occurs when the minor premise denies the consequent of the major premise; in that case the conclusion we draw must be a denial (*modus tollens*). Thus: (1) $p \supset q$; (2) not-q; (3) ∴ not-p. Incidentally, the presence of negative clauses in either premise has no effect on the mood of the syllogism, however much psychological confusion it may produce.

There are four possible inferences resulting from the combination of two moods and two conditions of validity, but only the paradigms shown above are valid. It is fallacious in the minor premise either to affirm the consequent or to deny the antecedent. Once again, valid implication alone does not provide sufficient grounds for true inferences about matters of fact. A scientist must determine empirically the material truth (or falsity) of p or q. Merely to entertain the hypothesis that p or q is true (or false) is not enough; there must be an assertion based on the appeal to evidence. Hypothetical syllogisms are conditional arguments; they contain "iffy" propositions, and their conclusions are logically contingent upon these.

The utility of such hypothetical deductive arguments in behavioral science is much greater than that of categorical deductive arguments because psychologists may be able first to determine the joint truth and validity of major premises from theoretical sources. Then for the minor premises either (1) demonstrate the truth of their antecedents more easily than the falsity of their consequents or (2) demonstrate the falsity of their consequents more easily than the truth of their antecedents. Thus the task of establishing the truth of the consequent (q) or the falsity of the antecedent (not-p) may be accomplished indirectly and more quickly, or at less cost, than proving or disproving them directly. The phrase *scientific proof* is used advisedly; it refers to the conjunction of true propositions and valid arguments.

Abduction

I have referred to this as the process of formulating and testing hypotheses. Peirce limited abduction to the making of hypothetical inferences of the if-then form, but I should like to broaden the meaning of his term to include the whole schema of formation and confirmation.[1] So I shall say that scientists *abduce* whenever they perform a deduction from a set of generalities and subsequently test one or more implicates by empirical methods. If the logical relation between protasis and apodosis in the complete paradigm holds in fact, then one concludes that the hypothesis is to that extent verified, i.e., there is an increment to its credibility or evidential support. Should the rational connection not be sustained empirically, then the hypothesis must be altered or abandoned. By the *hypothesis* I refer to the entire theorematic schema, not to the protasis or conceptual model alone.

Most general concepts and principles are developed inductively, as we have seen, but induction does not always proceed according to the neat canons of Mill and Dewey. Instead, careful observation, insightful hunches, and thorough acquaintance with the phenomena of one's field somehow combine in creative imagination to produce significant concepts and unifying principles. Whatever the behavioral problem-solving mechanisms may be, the most abstract, universal aspects of the protasis have to be obtained from induction because there is no other source of generalities acceptable to the natural sciences. One's deductive, observational, and experimental skills are also integral parts of this complex

[1] In *The Collected Papers of Charles Sanders Peirce* (Ed. by Hartshorne, Weiss, & Burks, Harvard University Press, 1931–1958), one finds several meanings of abduction. Those closest to the present usage are, in Peirce's words: (1) "the operation of adopting an explanatory hypothesis," (2) "studying facts and devising a theory to explain them," (3) "the provisional adoption of a hypothesis," and (4) "the form of inference that originates wholly new ideas, that plays a distinctive role in the advancement of knowledge." Scientific cognition, he maintained, involves the interaction of all three types of inference: induction, deduction, and abduction.

abductive process. Assuming, then, that we have a verifiable hypothesis let us ask what other criteria must be satisfied in order for it to be maximally useful.

The four principal ones are consistency, precision, fertility, and simplicity (Hempel, 1966; Lee, 1973; Nagel, 1961). An acceptable hypothesis should be: (1) logical and compatible with other established hypotheses, (2) clearly and precisely stated, (3) fruitful in the dual sense of generating empirical data and implying other hypotheses, and (4) expressed as simply as possible while adhering to the data. The fourth criterion is typically less crucial than the first three, and none of them take precedence over the verifiability of the hypothesis. Some have recommended the criterion of falsifiability as an index of empiricalness (Popper, 1959); thus, before entertaining any hypothesis as genuine one should attempt to overthrow it by resorting to observation, or preferably to experiment (Johnson, 1940). For an hypothesis to be materially true is more important than to be acceptable in terms of consistency, precision, fertility, or simplicity. In short, utility is secondary to probability. Inductive hypotheses in natural science are either confirmed or disconfirmed but not "proved" in a logical or mathematical sense. Synonyms of *confirmed* are verified, corroborated, and substantiated. Synonyms of *disconfirmed* are disverified, overthrown, and falsified. To speak of "validating" hypotheses is misleading.

It is important to note that even when a given inductive hypothesis is confirmed by particular data this does not establish the independent truth of its antecedent generalization, e.g., the law $R = m \, [1 - e^{-kS}]$, i.e., the protasis of the hypothesis under examination is not thereby separately proved. To believe so is fallacious reasoning. Instead, what verification does is to establish that the entire conditional relation between protasis and apodosis holds true in nature. To repeat, both terms are conditions of the whole hypothesis (Noble, 1975). From the pragmatic epistemological point of view (Lee, 1973), all knowledge is relative not absolute, and scientific laws are contingent upon the instances to which they apply. Experience, i.e., observation and experimentation, alone must determine that such generalizations are the laws by which our facts can be ordered. An empirical law has no material status except in terms of the facts of which it is a generalization. This doctrine of verification is based on relative frequency of confirmation. It is consistent with the frequency theory of probability (von Mises, 1957; von Wright, 1965).

The final topic to engage our attention is a brief logical analysis of the process of abduction in the context of theoretical psychology. I shall schematize a valid deduction derived from the inductive generalizations of a behavior theory and applied hypothetically to an experimental situation thus:

$$\text{'}(T \cap C)\text{' log. imp. '}(p \supset q)\text{'}$$

where T = theory or hypothetico-deductive system, C = specific initial and boundary conditions, '∩' = sign denoting conjunction of classes, p = experimental stimulus operations (e.g., S above), q = behavioral effects (e.g., R above), '⊃'= sign denoting material implication. The paradigm says that the conjunct of T and C logically implies that if p is the treatment given to a group of subjects, then the observed result will be q. We can conceive of T as an explicit, quantitative theory of learning and performance; of C as the apparatus and task factors, organismic constraints, technical parameters, bridge principles, etc. required to connect the theoretical system with the local situation; of p as a standard classical-conditioning stimulus treatment (S) administered repetitively to the subjects; and of q as the consequent conditioned responses (R) observed and measured in the subjects' behavior. In short, the schema asserts hypothetically that from T and C jointly it follows that p should result in q.

The sign of logical implication between the two parentheses indicates that an experimental psychologist performs the deduction by considering the meanings and relationships among concepts within the abstract theory as they are applied to an actual laboratory situation when precise initial and boundary conditions are stipulated. My use of material implication in the right-hand expression denotes that q is empirically contingent upon p. If we find that whenever we deliver p we get q, then the hypothesis is supported. Either q occurs or q fails; that is a matter of fact. The test of '$p \supset q$' is not, however, the whole scheme of verification, i.e., the causal sequence of '$p \supset q$' being observed does not establish the "truth" of T. This cannot be done, nor does it need to be done. Verification establishes that the entire deduction holds in fact; consequently, our laboratory experience is ordered and made understandable by this theory. One may entertain all such hypotheses that have survived empirical tests, but when rival hypotheses have equal probability a careful scientist will wish to consider secondary criteria, e.g., an hypothesis displaying greater consistency or precision may be more acceptable.

This concludes our brief treatment of induction, deduction, and abduction.[2] By paying closer attention to the logic of these activities we psychologists could, in my judgment, advance our science more rapidly than is the case at present. During the past decade there has been a palpable deemphasis upon attempts to systematize psychology. Many of us are content to work in an empiricistic frame of reference with little concern about developing conceptual schemes. Theory is the key to renewed growth because all three processes outlined here manifest a common theme; the factor which unifies induction, deduction, and abduction is the hypothetical nature of scientific knowledge. Theory construction,

---

[2] More extensive comparisons of induction and deduction may be found in Braithwaite (1968), Hempel (1966), Lee (1973), Nagel (1961), Noble (1975), Popper (1959), and von Wright (1965).

let us acknowledge, is no simple task. Scientific theories must not only be testable in principle, they should also have explanatory power, they ought to clarify and coordinate our empirical laws, and they are expected to provide us with predictive and postdictive capabilities (Braithwaite, 1968, Hempel, 1966, Nagel, 1961). This is a tall order for a young science, but as we continue the age-old quest for psychological theory we may rest assured that there is no loftier scientific enterprise.

REFERENCES

BERGMANN, G. *Philosophy of science.* Madison: Univer. of Wisconsin Press, 1957.

BRAITHWAITE, R. B. *Scientific explanation.* London: Cambridge Univer. Press, 1968.

HEMPEL, C. G. *Philosophy of natural science.* Englewood Cliffs: Prentice-Hall, 1966.

JOHNSON, H. M. Pre-experimental assumptions as determiners of experimental results. *Psychological Review,* 1940, **47,** 338–346.

LEE, H. N. *Percepts, concepts and theoretic knowledge.* Memphis: State Univer. Press, 1973.

NAGEL, E. *The structure of science.* New York: Harcourt, Brace, & World, 1961.

NOBLE, C. E. On Johnson's paradox: hypothesis verification. *American Journal of Psychology,* 1975, in press.

POPPER, K. R. *The logic of scientific discovery.* New York: Basic Books, 1959.

SKINNER, B. F. *Cumulative record.* (Enlgd. ed.) New York: Appleton-Century-Crofts, 1961.

———. *Contingencies of reinforcement.* New York: Appleton-Century-Crofts, 1969.

SPENCE, K. W. *Behavior theory and conditioning.* New Haven: Yale Univer. Press, 1956.

VON MISES, R. *Probability, statistics and truth.* (2nd rev. ed.) London: Allen & Unwin, 1957.

VON WRIGHT, G. H. *The logical problem of induction.* (2nd rev. ed.) Oxford: Blackwell, 1965.

22

MEASUREMENT AND LAWFULNESS IN PSYCHOLOGY

David H. Krantz

Measurement is employed in two quite different ways in scientific research. Usually, the investigator searches for quantitative laws, relying on previously established physical measurement. This is what chemists do, for example, in weighing various products of reactions. Such weight measurements led ultimately to the periodic table and to the chemical theories suggested by it. Similarly, physiologists and psychologists measure variables such as pupil diameter in order to discover laws of functioning of the visual system and the brain.

The second use for measurement is to represent an empirical structure by an analogous or homomorphic numerical structure. It is this second use that leads to construction of measurement scales de novo. For example, the weight measure was originally introduced because the properties of numerical weights gave a convenient representation to qualitative empirical observations. Objects can be compared qualitatively in a pan balance and the resulting empirical ordering is represented by the numerical ordering of the scale values (weights) assigned to them. Similarly, putting two objects together is represented by adding their weights. A set of empirical relations that leads to construction of measurement scales in this fashion is called a measurement structure.

In physics, measurement structures are very common. In most other sciences, previous physical measurement is used to generate new empirical relations. The laws satisfied by these latter relations lead to formulation of theories, but they do not lead to introduction of new measurement, that is, the empirical relations do not constitute measurement structures, even though they were generated by use of previously established physical measures. In psychology, however, the program of introducing new numerical functions, to measure such variables as intelligence, utility, or sensation magnitude, has long been attractive. In some cases, appropriate qualitative psychological laws do lead to such new, nonphysical measurement.

In this article I review some kinds of lawful structures that lead to measurement, briefly first in physics, then more thoroughly in psychology. I conclude by emphasizing that many areas of psychology should and

from D. H. Krantz, Measurement structures and psychological laws, *Science*, 1972, **175**, 1427–1435. Copyright 1972 by the American Association for the Advancement of Science.

do operate in the same way as biology or chemistry, so that previously established physical measures are used to discover new psychological theory, but not to establish new measurement scales. In still other areas, psychological measurement structures seem quite promising.

Measurement Structures in Physics

In some cases, physical measurement is based on quantitative laws and their importance for measurement is generally recognized. For example, interval-scale measurement of temperature is based on the law of linear expansion of a thermometric substance; while measurement of temperature ratios (Kelvin scale) depends on the third law of thermodynamics. Another sort of example is provided by measurement of density, which depends on the fact that the ratio of the mass to the volume of a homogeneous substance is independent of the volume.

The measurement of physical quantities such as length, mass, and duration is logically prior to the formulation of the quantitative laws of physics. Nevertheless, philosophers and physicists investigating the foundations of physics have long understood that even these so-called fundamental measurements are based on certain qualitative physical laws. For example, suppose that two straight rods, a and b, are laid side by side (Fig. 1) and that b extends beyond a at both ends (that is, b

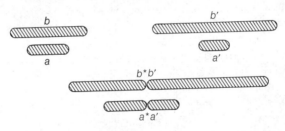

FIGURE 1. *Illustration of qualitative law underlying additive measurement of length. If rod b is longer than rod a and b′ is longer than a′, then the end-to-end concatenation of b and b′ is longer than the concatenation of a and a′.*

is longer than a, denoted $b > a$). Similarly, suppose that $b' > a'$. If now b and b' are concatenated by laying them end to end, and if, alongside them, a and a' are concatenated similarly, then the combination of b and b' is longer than the combination of a and a'. Denoting the operation of end-to-end concatenation by $*$, we have the following simple law:

If $b > a$ and $b' > a'$, then $b * b' > a * a'$ (1)

In the fundamental measurement of length, two qualitative (that is, nonnumerical) empirical relations are used, the comparison relation $>$

and the concatenation operation *. These empirical relations satisfy various qualitative laws, such as that shown in Eq. 1. It can be proved (1) that the qualitative laws satisfied by > and * imply that a real-valued function, or length measure, can be constructed, such that larger function values correspond to longer rods and such that the length of a * b is the sum of the lengths of a and b.

Fundamental measurement of mass and duration also requires qualitative comparison relations and concatenation operations, and these empirical relations satisfy the same abstract laws, like the one in Eq. 1, that hold in the case of length. From a formal standpoint, the procedures for assigning numbers as measures of objects are identical for length, mass, and duration: one concatenates many identical objects (for example, centimeter-lengths, gram-masses, or pendulum periods) and counts how many such identical objects are needed to match approximately the object to be measured. Such measurement, based on concatenation, is called extensive measurement (1). (Some of the most interesting lengths, masses, and times are those occurring on cosmic or molecular scales, and these, of course, are measured indirectly by using the much more elaborate quantitative laws of physics to relate them to quantities on a laboratory scale, such as the length of a photographic track or the arc length along a meter scale.)

Measurement Structures in Social Science

Extensive measurement has had few applications to fundamental measurement of psychological variables, because no concatenation operations are known for variables such as loudness, utility, intelligence, thirst, or anxiety, which satisfy appropriate qualitative laws. In particular, Eq. 1 can be shown to fail for many natural concatenation operations. Comparison relations which resemble > abound, but in the absence of additional structure, such as that provided by *, they lead only to ordinal measurement. However, concatenation is not the only possible source of additional structure; various other kinds of structure can combine with a comparison relation and if appropriate qualitative laws are satisfied, interval- or ratio-scale fundamental measurement results.

The possibility that nonextensive structures may lead to satisfactory measurement was first widely recognized after the publication by von Neumann and Morgenstern (2) of a set of qualitative axioms leading to interval-scale measurement of utility. They assumed a comparison relation >, where a > b is interpreted as "a is preferred to b," and a family of combining operations for options a, b: for any probability p, 0 < p < 1, and any a, b, they assumed that a combined option [pa, (1 − p)b] exists, where this is interpreted as a lottery in which option a (which may itself be a lottery) is obtained with probability p and option b with probability 1 − p. Their axioms for this structure constitute a set of qualitative laws for "rational" decisions among risky options. These qualitative laws imply the existence of a real-valued (utility) function u over the set of all options, such that $a > b$ if and only if $u(a) > u(b)$ and

$$u[pa, (1 - p)b] = pu(a) + (1 - p)u(b)$$

In recent years, a great many nonextensive structures, with corresponding systems of qualitative laws leading to interval- or ratio-scale measurement, have been studied mathematically (3–5). Most of these structures (including von Neumann and Morgenstern's) reduce to, or are closely related to, one particular class of structures, in which there is a comparison relation, $>$, and the objects compared can be regarded as elements of a Cartesian product. That is, the ordinal position of any object, with respect to $>$, depends on the levels of two or more independently controllable (or at least identifiable) factors. Measurement based on such structures requires the simultaneous development of scales for the ordered variable and for the contributions of each factor, and so it has been called simultaneous conjoint measurement (6); the empirical relational structures may be termed conjoint structures.

Qualitative Laws in Conjoint Structures: Independence

To illustrate a conjoint structure, let us consider the psychological variable "response strength" and its dependence on three independently controllable factors, amount of food deprivation (a), quality of food reward (b), and degree of previous experience (c). To be even more concrete, consider rats traversing a long straight alley. Assume that the response strengths of the rats are ordered (inversely) by observing the total times required to traverse the alley (7). Deprivation (a) may be indexed by percentage of normal body weight, reward (b) by concentration of sucrose solution offered at the end of the alley, and previous experience (c) by number of previous runs through the alley (say, with no deprivation but with sucrose available). The word "indexed" is used because, for purposes of conjoint measurement, only a nominal scale on each factor is required a priori; in the present example, the effect of reduction in body weight on running speed might well be nonmonotonic.

The simplest types of qualitative laws that can be tested in a conjoint structure are independence laws. To illustrate, suppose that four groups of rats are tested in conditions abc, $a'b'c$, abc', and $a'b'c'$, shown in Fig. 2. Assume that a represents more deprivation than a' (in a range where increasing deprivation increases running speed), but b represents less reward than b'. Therefore there will be doubt, a priori, as to whether treatment combination ab or $a'b'$ produces more response strength. Let c, c' be any two different levels of the experience factor. Let the four experimental groups be matched by taking sets of four littermates and randomly assigning them to distinct groups. Now suppose the following

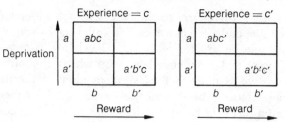

FIGURE 2. *Illustration of experimental design to test whether the ordering of the joint effect of deprivation and reward is independent of experience. Independence holds when the ordering of* ab *relative to* a'b' *is the same at* c *as at* c'.

results are obtained: most of the rats in group *abc* traverse the alley in less time than do their littermates in group *a'b'c;* and most in group *abc'* are faster than their littermates in group *a'b'c'.* We conclude that the combination *ab* produces more response strength than *a'b',* independent of the choice of a fixed level of experience factor, *c* or *c'.* If the result were replicated for enough different levels of *a, b, c, a', b', and c',* one would conclude that the ordering of combined deprivation-reward effects, at constant experience, is independent of the level of experience. This qualitative law is formally expressed as follows:

$$abc > a'b'c \text{ if and only if } abc' > a'b'c' \quad (2)$$

The experimental situation of comparing concatenations of rods (Fig. 1) yields the first qualitative law (see Eq. 1), which is the key to construction of an additive length measure. Likewise, the second qualitative law (Eq. 2), tested in conjoint structures by the experimental design of Fig. 2, is the key to additive (or multiplicative) conjoint measurement. In fact, if the second law is valid for a three-factor conjoint structure, and if the two symmetric independence laws hold, by which the ordering of *ac, a'c'* combinations is independent of the fixed level of *b,* and the ordering of *bc, b'c'* combinations is independent of the fixed level of *a,* then, with the addition of one or two technical assumptions (for example, continuity), one can prove (8) that there exists a monotonic transformation of the ordinal dependent variable that decomposes into the sum of the three scales, one for the contribution of each factor. This monotone transformation is unique up to linear transformations (changes of origin and units); so we obtain interval-scale measurement, over the objects compared, and over each factor as well. Sometimes the exponentials of these various scales are used, resulting in a multiplicative combination of the factor effects.

There are other kinds of qualitative laws for conjoint structures, corresponding to more complicated rules of combination of the factor effects. But independence laws are so important that it pays to dwell on them a bit more, and to present a few somewhat disguised examples.

First, note that there are really two sorts of independence laws: single-factor independence, in which the ordering of the effects of one factor is the same, no matter what fixed levels are chosen in all other factors; and joint-factor independence, in which the ordering of the joint effects of two or more factors is independent of the fixed levels of the remaining factors. The second law illustrated joint-factor independence: the ordering of the factor combinations ab, $a'b'$ was considered, for different levels of the remaining factor. Single-factor independence is quite a weak condition: it means only that each factor can be ordered in such a way as to contribute monotonically to the overall effect. In other words, scales can be constructed such that the rule of combination of the factors is monotone in each variable, but no other constraint on the rule is imposed. Often the orderings on single factors are given in advance, by the very operations that define the factors. For example, suppose we compare the momenta of objects that move in a fixed direction. The two relevant factors are mass and speed. But the very operation that defines a nominal scale of mass also defines an ordering, consistent with the ordering obtained by observing momenta, holding speed fixed.

One striking class of violations of single-factor independence is suggestive of multiplicative combination of factors, with positive, zero, and negative multipliers. A reversal in the sign of a multiplier reverses totally the ordering of the products. A zero multiplier produces a degenerate ordering. For an example, consider an experiment in which subjects rate the moral connotation of adverb-adjective combinations, such as "slightly evil." Not surprisingly, "slightly evil" is rated higher than "very evil" but "slightly pleasant" is rated lower than "very pleasant" (9). This suggests that scale values of adjectives are both positive and negative and multiply the adverb scale values. When the only violations of independence involve total reversals of ordering or degenerate ordering, we speak of sign dependence; this generalizes the notion of independence (10, 11).

In contrast to single-factor independence, joint-factor independence is a very strong condition. As remarked above, when all possible joint-factor independence laws hold, we obtain additive measurement. Note that in the two-factor case, the only possible independence laws are single-factor ones; so other kinds of laws, of a kind mentioned below, must be studied to determine whether additive measurement is possible.

Examples of Independence Laws

The first example is a fairly transparent one: the theory of consumer choice, in economics. The objects compared are commodity vectors $(x_1, \ldots, x_n)$, where x_i is the amount of the ith commodity. The comparison relation is defined by the consumer's choice or preference between competing commodity vectors available to him. Single-factor independence merely means that amounts of each commodity can be ordered so that it is a good: values higher in the ordering are always preferred to lower ones, the amounts of other commodities being held constant. Joint-factor independence means lack of complementarity between commodities (12). Suppose, for example, that the second law (Eq. 2) is violated, with $abc > a'b'c$ and $a'b'c' > abc'$. If a is ordered above a', b' above b, and c above c' (by single-factor independence) then the first and third commodities are complementary, since with more of the third, the consumer also wants more of the first, and is willing to sacrifice some of the second commodity for that end.

The second example concerns a reformulation of the von Neumann and Morgenstern utility theory in terms of conjoint structures (13, 14). A risky operation can be regarded as a vector $(x_1, \ldots, x_n)$ where the outcome x_i is obtained if event E_i occurs, and $E_1, \ldots, E_n$ is a set of events, exactly one of which will occur. Joint-factor independence now states that if the result x_i is the same for two risky options, then the value of x_i—good or bad—is disregarded in choosing between the options; the decision-maker focuses on the events E_j, $j \neq i$ and chooses as though one of those events were bound to occur.

This principle is regarded as a normative law of rational decision-making, and is often known as the extended sure-thing principle. It was emphasized by Savage (13). As a descriptive law of human choice, it often fails (15), but there is little doubt about its value as a normative principle, and it is therefore valuable to teach people to act in accordance with it. For example, contract-bridge teachers tell students that in choosing between two plays, they should treat as irrelevant distributions of opponents' cards for which the two plays will have the same outcome, and attend only to the consequences for card distributions where the two plays may have different outcomes.

A third example arises in testing for linearity of an input-output transformation, where the input may be measurable only on a nominal scale and the output only on an ordinal scale (16). For an example, the input $x(\tau)$ could be light intensity, as a function of time τ, and the output $y(t)$ could be neural-firing rate of some visual-system unit, as a function of time t. Usually, linearity is defined by the superposition law: if $x'(\tau) = x(\tau) + \bar{x}(\tau)$, then the corresponding output functions satisfy $y'(t) = y(t) + \bar{y}(t)$. If, however, the input is subject to an arbitrary distortion and the output to a monotone distortion, we can define linearity by a generalized superposition law. Let x_1 and x_2 be two input functions that coincide for some values of τ (see Fig. 3, where x_1, x_2 are periodic inputs that coincide in the second half, designated $-A$, of each period). Let x_1' and x_2' be modifications of x_1 and x_2, where only the common part is modified (see lower half of Fig. 3). The generalized superposition law affirms that for any t, the outputs y_1 and y_2 are ordered in the same way as the modified outputs of y_1' and y_2'; that is,

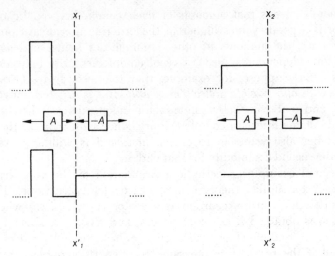

FIGURE 3. *Inputs* x_1 *and* x_2 *coincide in the second half of each period* $(-A)$. *Inputs* x'_1, x'_2 *are formed from* x_1, x_2 *by adding a common input that is zero except in* $-A$. *According to the generalized superposition law, the output ordering of* x_1 *and* x_2 *is the same as that of* x'_1 *and* x'_2.

$$y_1'(t) \geqslant y_2'(t) \text{ if and only if } y_1(t) \geqslant y_2(t) \quad (3)$$

This generalizes the usual superposition principle, because modifying x_1 and x_2 to obtain x_1' and x_2' is like adding a "difference input" $\bar{x}$ to both x_1 and x_2, where $\bar{x}$ is restricted to being zero except for values of τ where the original inputs coincide.

To understand why the generalized superposition law is an instance of joint-factor independence, note that each τ defines a factor. Input function x is a vector, with factor-level $x(\tau)$ on the τ factor. The ordering of outputs $y_1(t)$ and $y_2(t)$ depends on the joint effects of all factor-levels $x_1(\tau)$ and $x_2(\tau)$, where these do not coincide. The ordering of $y_1'(t)$ and $y_2'(t)$ depends on exactly the same joint effects. Hence Eq. 3 follows from joint independence.

This formulation leads, for example, to methods for testing linearity of neural processing, where neural-firing rate is taken as only an ordinal measure of the output of a hypothesized linear process.

For a final example, I turn to the psychological literature on impression formation (17) and multidimensional psychophysics (18). In general, several different factors may contribute to a percept or an impression. The example of adjective and adverb factors contributing to the impression produced by the phrases such as "slightly pleasant" was cited above; other examples include impressions of job candidates produced by test scores for intelligence and motivation, and perception of size as a function of visual angle and perceived distance. In each of these cases, one has a fairly obvious conjoint structure, and independence laws may be examined.

Slightly more disguised is the application of qualitative independence laws to multidimensional geometric models of proximity or dissimilarity. In these models (18), one tries to represent stimuli by vectors $x = (x_1, \ldots, x_n)$, $y = (y_1, \ldots, y_n)$, for example, in such a way that stimulus dissimilarities vary monotonically with (Euclidean) distance, that is, with

$$d(xy) = [\sum_{i=1}^{n} (x_i - y_i)^2]^{1/2}$$

This model postulates, among other things, that an impression of dissimilarity varies monotonically with an additive combination of contributions from the differences along each of several dimensions. This postulate can be studied in isolation, that is, in the context of the much more general model

$$d(x,y) = F[\sum_{i=1}^{n} \varphi_i (x_i, y_i)] \quad (4)$$

where F is an arbitrary monotone function and each φ_i is a function of two (nominal-scale) variables x_i, y_i. This, and other generations of the Euclidean model have been studied by conjoint-measurement method (19). Equation 4 leads immediately to joint-factor independence laws: if the dissimilarity produced by some combination of differences on $n - 1$ dimensions exceeds that produced by some other combination on those same dimensions (the difference on the nth dimension remaining constant), then that same ordering holds, as the constant difference on the nth dimension is varied.

In a study of dissimilarities of schematic faces, by Tversky and Krantz (20), the independence laws were well supported. The stimuli, shown in Fig. 4, were made up with two levels of each of three attributes: long

FIGURE 4. *Eight faces varying on three binary attributes, used to test whether the contributions of the differences on the three attributes contribute additively to overall dissimilarity.*

versus wide face, empty versus filled eyes, straight versus curved mouth. Each pair of faces could have either a large difference or zero difference, on each of the three attributes. Fig. 5 exhibits a typical test of joint-

if and only if

FIGURE 5. *A test of joint-factor independence for the stimuli of Fig. 3. The comparison of the joint effect of (large mouth difference, zero eye difference) with the joint effect of (zero mouth difference, large eye difference) should yield the same results, regardless of the kind of shape difference (zero or large) that is present.*

factor independence. The top two pairs of faces compare the joint effect of large mouth and zero eye difference to the joint effect of zero mouth and large eye difference, at a fixed (zero) level of shape difference; the bottom two pairs compare the same two joint effects, at a different fixed level of shape difference.

Many other examples of conjoint structures and independence laws could be cited; but these four, together with the example for strength of response in the preceding section, may give something of a feeling for the variety of different situations subsumed under the same formal structure.

Other Qualitative Laws in Conjoint Structures

Qualitative laws more complicated than independence laws have been used in the analysis of two-factor conjoint structures (6), where independence does not suffice for additive measurement, and in the analysis of nonadditive combination rules for conjoint structures with three or more factors (11). Here I present a single example with a very common nonadditive rule, in which the effects of two variables are added and then the sum is multiplied by the effect of the third variable. That is, we have scales φ_1, φ_2, φ_3, such that the scale

$$\varphi(a,b,c) = [\varphi_1(a) + \varphi_2(b)]\varphi_3(c)$$

preserves the ordering of comparisons $>$. In other words,

$abc > a'b'c'$ if and only if $[\varphi_1(a) + \varphi_2(b)]\varphi_3(c)$
$$> [\varphi_1(a') + \varphi_2(b')]\varphi_3(c') \quad (5)$$

Note that this hypothesis implies one of the three possible joint-factor independence laws: if we assume that the φ_3 values are all positive, then the ordering of joint effects of the a and b factors is independent of the fixed level in the c factor (Eq. 2). However, it is easy to show that the other two joint-factor independence laws fail.

Consider the experimental design shown in Fig. 6, where there are eight

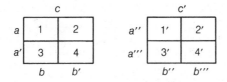

FIGURE 6. *Experimental design to test a qualitative law that is necessary in a measurement structure where scale values of* a *and* b *factors are added, and their sum is multiplied by the* c *scale value. The law states that if one diagonal of the unprimed* (c) *matrix dominates one diagonal of the primed* (c') *matrix, then the other pair of diagonals cannot have reversed dominance* (c' *dominating* c).

conditions, a 2×2 factorial design at level c of the third factor and another 2×2 factorial at level c'. Suppose that cells 1, 2, 3, 4 in the first 2×2 design are, respectively, compared with cells $1'$, $2'$, $3'$, $4'$ in the second one, with the results $1 > 1'$, $2 > 2'$, but $3' > 3$ and $4' > 4$. If we use Eq. 5 these comparisons translate into the following inequalities in φ_i values:

$$[\varphi_1(a) + \varphi_2(b)]\varphi_3(c) > [\varphi_1(a'') + \varphi_2(b'')]\varphi_3(c')$$

$$[\varphi_1(a') + \varphi_2(b')]\varphi_3(c) > [\varphi_1(a''') + \varphi_2(b''')]\varphi_3(c')$$

$$[\varphi_1(a''') + \varphi_2(b''')]\varphi_3(c') > [\varphi_1(a') + \varphi_2(b)]\varphi_3(c)$$

$$[\varphi_1(a'') + \varphi_2(b'')]\varphi_3(c') > [\varphi_1(a) + \varphi_2(b')]\varphi_3(c)$$

By adding the first two inequalities we obtain

$$[\varphi_1(a) + \varphi_2(b) + \varphi_1(a') + \varphi_2(b')]\varphi_3(c) > [\varphi_1(a'') + \varphi_2(b'') + \varphi_1(a''') + \varphi_2(b''')]\varphi_3(c')]$$

But by adding the second pair of inequalities we produce the contradictory inequality. This shows that Eq. 5 implies a new qualitative law: if $1 > 1'$ and $2 > 2'$, then $3' > 3$ and $4' > 4$ cannot both hold. A similar argument would apply if we started with $1 > 2'$ and $2 > 1'$, or even with $1 > 3'$, $2 > 4'$. Thus we have the following generalization:

If one diagonal of a 2×2 factorial design, at a fixed level of the third factor, dominates one diagonal of another 2×2 factorial at a different fixed level of the third factor, then the other diagonals cannot have reversed dominance. (6)

The laws shown in Eqs. 2 and 6 are both necessary if scale values satisfying Eq. 5 are to be constructed; however, they are not sufficient to guarantee that such scale values exist. A more complete discussion of these kinds of laws can be found in (11) and (5). For an empirical example in which Eq. 5 seems to hold, and where Eqs. 2 and 6 were tested to infer this, see Coombs and Huang (21). They studied perceived riskiness of games consisting of multiple plays of even-chance two-outcome gambles; the additive factors were the regret or disparity between the two outcomes (a) and the expected value per single play (b); the multiplicative factor (c) was the number of plays per game.

Direct Estimates of Sensation

One of the most impressive bodies of experimental results in psychology has been amassed by S. S. Stevens' technique, which requires observers to assign numbers "in proportion to" their sensations. Particularly important is the consistent prediction of cross-modality matches (22), cross-context matches (23), and heterochromatic matches (23, 24) from such numerical assignments.

What has not been done is to set forth explicitly the empirical relational structure generated by these experiments and the qualitative laws that lead to measurement. Stevens' claim (25) that the sone scale of loudness is a prime example of ratio-scale measurement in psychology seems to be based on a mere pun: the instruction to assign numbers "in proportion" to sensation.

To justify Stevens' claim that his "proportion" instructions lead to a ratio scale, note that the requirement to assign numbers "in proportion" demands that the observer judge the presented stimulus relative to previous stimuli. One may hypothesize that the observer orders pair (a,b) of stimuli with respect to some perceived quality of such pairs. The perceived quality may be called the sensation "ratio" of the pair. The quotation marks indicate that this quality is not actually a ratio, rather, it is a perceptual attribute of stimulus pairs within a single modality. Thus, the assumed relational structure is simply a comparison relation > over pairs of stimuli:

(a,b) > (c,d) if the sensation "ratio" produced by a relative to b is at least as great as the sensation "ratio" produced by c relative to d.

This hypothesis leads, therefore, to a two-factor conjoint structure, in which the first factor is the stimulus that is judged and the second one is the standard relative to which it is judged. This formulation is not too different from others that have been given in connection with direct estimation of sensation (26), and it was, in essence, suggested by Stevens (27), who rejected it on the grounds that it leads only to a logarithmic interval scale, rather than a ratio scale, for sensation measurement.

The conjoint structure for a single sensory modality can be extended, however, to include cross-modality comparisons of sensation ratios, for example, $(a,b) > (a',b')$ where a,b come from one modality and a',b' from another. Elsewhere (28), I have shown that this extended structure is capable of subsuming Stevens' major results, including the results of numerical estimation and cross-modality experiments, provided that appropriate qualitative laws are assumed. The key qualitative law is the following:

$$\text{If } (a,b) > (a',b') \text{ and } (b,c) > (b',c'), \text{ then} (a,c) > (a',c') \quad (7)$$

[The law shown in Eq. 7 was discussed by Hölder in his 1901 analysis of interval measurement on a line (1).] From this law, and some technical assumptions, it can be shown that a measurement scale exists for each modality, such that the order of ratios of scale values predicts within- and cross-modality comparisons of sensation "ratios." With an additional law, one can prove that the measurement scales are correctly given by numerical estimation. Moreover, the scales are indeed ratio scales (unique except for choice of units), except for the possibility of transforming all of them by a fixed power transformation (in effect, changing the numerical response scale by raising it to a power).

The theory just sketched provides an example of the way in which a sufficiently rich body of empirical results can sometimes be recast as a measurement structure, satisfying appropriate qualitative laws. Once this has been done, some of the focus of attention changes. The empirical question, "What is the form of the numerical estimation function as stimulus energy varies?" loses some importance; instead, we ask what is the nature of the underlying quality of pairs that is judged, and what is the relation of such a perceived quality of pairs to sensory processing.

Measurement Structures in Color Perception

Color perception provides the best examples of measurement structures in psychology. In classical trichromatic color measurement, as well as in the empirical observations underlying both the Young-Helmholtz theory of color blindness and the Hurvich-Jameson theory of opponent colors, the structures that arise are not conjoint structures at all, but a quite different sort, which I term Grassmann structures. Other aspects of color perception give rise to a variety of conjoint structures: the attempt to represent color discrimination or similarity in uniform color spaces requires multidimensional scaling structures; the scaling of hue and brightness requires sensation "ratio" structures; the relation of saturation to hue and whiteness exemplifies the $(\varphi_1 + \varphi_2)\varphi_3$ structure discussed above;

and there are yet other examples. Furthermore, color perception provides a kind of microcosm of psychology. The empirical relational structure of color mixture and color matching, with its qualitative laws (Grassmann's laws) leading to trichromatic color measurement, is extremely well established; modern measurement analysis just formalizes what Thomas Young knew. The Grassmann structures involved in color blindness and opponent-color perception are very natural and probably correct, but more detailed investigation of their qualitative laws is still needed. In the area of color discrimination and color similarity, there is a great mass of empirical relations, but the appropriateness of measurement analysis is quite uncertain. The idea of representing saturation comparisons by a three-factor composition rule [red-or-green + yellow-or-blue] × [white-or-black]$^{-1}$, is a bit speculative; we do not really know what the best way of making saturation comparisons is, nor what qualitative laws to expect. Finally, areas such as color memory or esthetics are still preparadigm: there are some good studies, but we have no clear idea what sorts of empirical structures may eventually appear, nor whether they will be measurement structures.

I will now give a brief sketch of the (Grassmann) structures that arise in color matching and in opponent-colors theory.

Trichromatic color measurement is based on metameric matching of lights and on two operations on lights, additive color mixture and scalar multiplication. A light is identified by a curve giving its energy density as a function of wavelength, for wavelengths in the visible electromagnetic spectrum. Two lights a,b are metameric (denoted $a \equiv b$) if they look exactly alike in color hue, saturation, and brightness). For example, a light with a broad spectrum, such as the output of a tungsten-filament lamp, can be matched exactly by a light with energy concentrated at just two wavelengths (for example, 470 and 580 mm). Two lights a,b can be mixed to form $a \oplus b$, the light that has at each wavelength the sum of the energies of a and b; and a light a can have its energy at each wavelength multiplied by a fixed nonnegative constant t, to form $t * a$. The empirical relational structure consists of the set of lights and the relations $\equiv$, $\oplus$, and $*$; $\equiv$ depends on a human observer, while $\oplus$ and $*$ depend only on physics.

The qualitative laws that involve only $\oplus$ and $*$ are physical laws, for example, $t * (a \oplus b) = (t * a) \oplus (t * b)$. The qualitative laws that also involve $\equiv$ were first stated by Grassmann (29). They can be reformulated as follows:

$$\equiv \text{ is transitive, reflexive, and symmetric} \quad (8)$$

$$a \equiv b \text{ if and only if } a \oplus c \equiv b \oplus c; \text{ and if } a \equiv b, \text{ then } t * a \equiv t * b \quad (9)$$

For any four lights, a positive linear combination of two of them or three of them matches a positive linear combination of the remaining two or one, respectively; and there are three lights such that no positive linear combination of any two of them matches the remaining one. (10)

In Eq. 10 we define a positive linear combination of lights, $a_1, \ldots,$ a_m to be an additive mixture of scalar multiples $(t_1 \; {}^{\circ} \; a_1) \; \oplus \; \ldots \; \oplus$ $(t_m \; {}^{\circ} \; a_m)$, where $t_i \gtreqqless 0$ and at least one t_i is strictly positive.

A structure that satisfies both Eqs. 8 and 9 may be termed a Grassmann structure; if Eq. 10 also holds, it is a trichromatic Grassmann structure.

The law shown in Eq. 8 is usually considered to be a test of the adequacy of the empirical operations defining $\equiv$; the law shown by Eq. 9 is interpreted as implying that $\equiv$ is determined at the level of retinal cones, before any nonlinearities in the sensory transduction process; and the law shown by Eq. 10, trichromacy, restricts the number of independent channels, at the level of the cones and above, to three. For a discussion of those empirical laws, see Brindley (30).

The measurement consequences of these laws are embodied in the standard systems of color measurement (31). There exists a vector-valued measure, $\varphi = (\varphi_1, \varphi_2, \varphi_3)$, defined over lights, such that metameric lights correspond to equal vectors $[a \equiv b$ if and only if $\varphi(a) = \varphi(b)]$ and additive mixture and scalar multiplication of lights correspond to ordinary addition of vectors and multiplication by scalars. The measure φ is determined only up to arbitrary changes of linear coordinates, that is, it can be transformed by an arbitrary 3×3 matrix with a nonzero determinant.

Much of color theory can be regarded as attempting to consider additional empirical relations, besides $\equiv$, $\oplus$, ${}^{\circ}$, and on the basis of the qualitative laws satisfied by such additional empirical structure, to find a more tightly defined coordinate system that gives a simple representation of all the empirical relations. For example, the empirical structures defined by color-discriminability data have been used for such purposes since Helmholtz (32). Such use of color discriminability has only been partially successful, mainly because of our lack of knowledge of the qualitative laws by which small differences on different dimensions or channels combine to determine overall discriminability.

Differences among color theories lie mainly in different choices of which additional empirical relations should be given first consideration. The Hurvich-Jameson opponent-colors theory emphasizes observations that certain lights, viewed under achromatic adaptation and surround conditions, appear neutral with respect to one of the main hue attributes. For example, some lights appear reddish, others greenish, but some are neither reddish nor greenish. This last neutral set includes the "unique" yellows, the "unique" blues, and the achromatic lights. Denote it by C_1. Likewise, there is a set C_2 of unique reds-greens, which are neutral on the yellow-blue attribute. Lights that are in both C_1 and C_2 are achromatic.

Jameson and Hurvich measured the "redness" of a light by the intensity of a standard green needed to just cancel out the red, that is, such that the mixture is in C_1. That is, two lights are equally red (or green) if admixture of the same third light brings them to neutrality. This defines an equivalence relation $\equiv_1$ on lights:

$$a \equiv_1 b \text{ if and only if for some } c, \text{ both } a \oplus c \text{ and } b \oplus c \text{ are in } C_1$$

A yellowness-blueness equivalence relation, $\equiv_2$, may be defined similarly. Their first main empirical result (33) is that the measures of redness-greenness and yellowness-blueness obtained by cancellation to C_1 and C_2 neutrality are linear combinations of the trichromatic color-matching functions. It can be shown that this is the same as the assertion that the empirical relations $\equiv_1$, $\oplus$, * and $\equiv_2$, $\oplus$, * yield 1-chromatic Grassmann structures (Eqs. 8, 9, and 10, with 1-chromacy replacing trichromacy) compatible with the trichromatic structure $\equiv$, $\oplus$, *. In particular, this requires that the following two qualitative laws hold:

If $a \equiv b$ and a is in C_1, then b is in C_1 (and likewise for C_2)   (11)

If a is in C_1, t * a is in C_1, and b is in C_1 if and only if
$a \oplus b$ is in C_1 (and likewise for C_2)   (12)

The law shown in Eq. 11 is surely correct. Their results give indirect support to Eq. 12 and there is some direct evidence for it, but a more careful test is needed. It should be remarked in this connection that C_1 and C_2 (like the set of lights that appear chromatic) vary as a function of adaptation and surround color, and that these sets may not satisfy Eq. 12 except with achromatic or near achromatic conditions, such as those used by Jameson and Hurvich.

When these laws hold, it is possible to get a tightly constrained measurement representation $\varphi = (\varphi_1, \varphi_2, \varphi_3)$, where φ gives trichromatic color measurement, φ_1 measures redness-greenness, and φ_2 measures yellowness-blueness. Here, φ_1 and φ_2 are ratio scales. Under conditions where whiteness-matching also yields a .1-chromatic Grassmann structure, φ_3 can be required to measure whiteness on a ratio scale. These measures are based on cancellation and matching, or both, and will not coincide numerically with the results of direct-estimation experiments; the qualitative laws linking direct estimation of hue to cancellation measures remain to be elucidated.

Discussion

The above examples all indicate that measurement of psychological variables is a consequence, rather than a forerunner, of lawfulness. In many experiments, one collects quantitative data, relying on counting, on physical measurement, or on some well established method of psychological measurement. In such cases, one does not have new measurement of a new psychological variable; one simply has a count, or a measure of a well-known physical or psychological quantity, which is often hypothesized to be correlated with the new psychological variable under investigation. New measurement—that is, a new numerical function—is introduced only to provide a simpler representation of the results of such experiments. When such new measurement has been possible, the data (quantitative or qualitative) have yielded a measurement structure.

For example, consider the Hurvich-Jameson method of measuring redness by canceling via admixture of a standard green light. Their procedure was bound to lead to a number—the mean intensity of the green light at which their observers were satisfied with the adjustment to neutrality. This number is a physical measure of the intensity of the green cancellation light. One can, by fiat, identify this physical measure, as an operational definition of "redness," but to do so would be foolish. Suppose some other green cancellation light led to results that were not proportional to those obtained by the first light; which, then, would measure "redness?" Once one determines that the results are unaffected by the choice of the green cancellation light, one already has lawfulness; indeed, this invariance result is essentially equivalent to the law shown in Eq. 12. Jameson and Hurvich derived their confidence in the measurements from a different manifestation of Eq. 12: the fact that the results were lawfully, indeed linearly, related to color-matching functions. If one were to have no such lawfulness, then blindly stating that one particular set of measurements constitutes the operational definition of "redness" would merely conceal the fact that one had really only measured the physical intensities of some particular green light.

Moreover, once new functions have been introduced, giving a simple representation of lawful empirical relations, intuitive names like "redness" may give way to new names that describe better the nature of the functions introduced. These sharper names correspond to new empirical distinctions, which might never have been discovered if one were content merely to identify a count or a physical measure as an operational measure of a psychological variable.

How much lawfulness is sufficient for psychological measurement? This question has no general answer, of course, but recent theoretical studies in measurement foundations go some way toward answering it. If the empirical observations can be cast in the form of a conjoint structure with three or more factors, then the independence laws are essentially sufficient for additive measurement; or other sufficient sets of laws are known for some kinds of nonadditive measurement. Similarly, Stevens' instructions for "proportional judgment" suggested a generalization of two-factor conjoint structures with the law shown in Eq. 7 as the sufficient condition of ratio-scale measurement. Likewise, knowledge of

Grassmann structures permits one to recognize the laws that must hold for the Hurvich-Jameson cancellation procedure to yield a linear transformation of color-matching functions, which measures redness-greenness, and so on. In short, research on measurement structures (3–5) has amassed a collection of abstract measurement structures; if data can be made to fit some variant or some extension of these known structures, then various measurement representations with convenient properties can be constructed.

The known abstract measurement structures provide a tool that can be powerful, but also perhaps dangerous. The power comes from the discovery of experiments that really should have been done before but were not done. For example, there have been a number of papers in which investigators have attempted to test whether, in the response-strength example given earlier, drive, incentive, and habit combine by $\varphi_1 + \varphi_2 + \varphi_3$ or $(\varphi_1 + \varphi_2)\varphi_3$; one now sees how to do much more decisive experiments (11) by testing joint-factor independence and other laws, such as Eq. 6. In general, tests of joint-factor independence are likely to be scientifically fruitful: when they fail, they may fail systematically, in highly interesting ways (the examples of complementary or substitutable commodities were cited above). Likewise, Eq. 7 for relative judgments of stimulus pairs and Eq. 12 for color appearance deserve direct investigation.

The danger of this tool, however, lies in the fact that for many substantive areas of psychology, there is absolutely no reason to expect qualitative laws leading to measurement structures. The goal of scientific psychology is not measurement, but theory. And theory comes in various and unexpected forms.

To take an example from another science: one of the seminal qualitative laws of chemistry was the law of stoichiometric proportions. This law might at first seem to suggest a sort of chemical measure, that is, valence. But the fact that valence is a multivalued and partially periodic function of atomic number leads in a quite different theoretical direction: to the periodic table, and ultimately, to the electron-shell theory.

In fact, biology and chemistry have not produced measurement structures. In these sciences, physical measurement is employed extensively, and qualitative and quantitative laws abound; these laws have, in turn, led to various sorts of theories. One might well expect that many areas of psychology should proceed similarly; and indeed, many of the best established and most lawful areas do so. The idea of measuring psychological variables such as loudness, utility, and intelligence is still very attractive, and in some cases, successful; but a focus that is devoted exclusively to measurement may be sterile. It would seem much more fruitful to look for any kinds of regularities and laws, using known abstract measurement structures merely as a sometimes useful heuristic tool. Occasionally, newly discovered laws may generate novel measurement structures, but more often, other kinds of theory may result.

I have not yet discussed what is actually the largest and best known body of literature on psychological measurement: psychometrics. In all of the various areas of psychometrics, measurement still depends critically on lawfulness. The laws that are involved, however, are mostly much more complicated than any of the ones described above. One postulates a geometric and a statistical model, or both; the law that holds is simply that the model fits the data (with a sufficiently low number of dimensions in the case of geometric models); and the measures are coordinates in the geometric model, or parameters of the hypothetical probability distributions. In other words, the laws in question usually do not have simple statements directly in terms of observable empirical relations; they cannot be summarized in any better way than by saying that such-and-such a model fits the data, in so many dimensions.

When a psychometric model does give a spectacular fit in a low dimensionality, with measurement parameters that make sense and vary appropriately under psychological manipulations of various sorts, the scientific value of the results can scarcely be doubted. The main disadvantages of such an approach are:

1. Because the laws are so complex, failures to fit are both harder to detect (violations may be hidden in random error) and less informative when detected, as compared with tests of the sort of qualitative laws described here.

2. The approach presupposes measurement as the goal, and is therefore even more subject to the dangers of inappropriate theorizing that I have just described above.

The first point can be met, in some cases, by reducing the complex model to a series of simpler qualitative or quantitative laws. This has been partially accomplished for Thurstonian scaling (34) and for multidimensional scaling (19).

Conclusions

Empirical laws in psychology may be based on physical measurements (for example, voltages, times), counting, ordering, or just classifying. It is a pointless, though widespread practice to use a physical measure or a count as a "definition" of a psychological variable; this practice obscures the fact that all one has done is measured a physical variable, or counted. What is important are the empirical laws that are established by use of such quantitative or qualitative observations. Some kinds of empirical relations and laws yield measurement structures, akin to the qualitative structures underlying fundamental measurement in physics. Measurement structures are empirical structures that can be described most simply by introduction of a new numerical function; such a function is a new measure, and is typically interpreted as measuring some particular psychological variable.

Measurement structures, formulated abstractly, sometimes provide valuable tools for formulating new empirical hypotheses to be tested; but in many instances, other kinds of theory may be more appropriate. The main focus of research ought always to be the discovery of simple laws; these may or may not lead to new measures.

REFERENCES AND NOTES

1. O. Hölder, *Ber. Verh. Saechs. Gesell. Wiss. Math. Phys. Kl.* 53, 1 (1901); P. Suppes, *Port. Math.* 10, 163 (1951); D. H. Krantz, *Phil. Sci.* 34, 348 (1967); F. Roberts and R. D. Luce, *Synthese* 18, 311 (1968); E. Holman, *J. Math. Psychol.* 6, 286 (1969); R. D. Luce and A. A. J. Marley, in *Philosophy, Science, and Method: Essays in Honor of Ernest Nagel*, S. Morgenbesser, P. Suppes, M. G. White, Eds. (St. Martin's, New York, 1969).

2. J. von Neumann and O. Morgenstern, *Theory of Games and Economic Behavior* (Princeton Univ. Press, Princeton, N.J., ed. 3, 1953).

3. J. Pfanzagl, *Theory of Measurement* (Wiley, New York, 1968).

4. P. C. Fishburn, *Utility Theory for Decision Making* (Wiley, New York, 1970).

5. D. H. Krantz, R. D. Luce, P. Suppes, A. Tversky, *Foundations of Measurement* (Academic Press, New York, 1971), vol. 1.

6. R. D. Luce and J. W. Tukey, *J. Math. Psychol.* 1, 1 (1964).

7. One sometimes hears the argument that duration is a physical, ratio-scale measure, therefore, the performance of the rat is measured on a ratio, rather than an ordinal scale. This is wrong. Ratio-scale measurement of duration is based on qualitative laws such as that shown in Eq. 1, in which there is concatenation of time intervals. The observations on the rats compare only total durations; no intervals are concatenated. Therefore only the physical comparison relation for duration, and its qualitative laws (for example, transitivity) are used, and only ordinal measurement of duration is involved.

8. G. Debreu, in *Mathematical Methods in the Social Sciences*, K. J. Arrow, S. Karlin, P. Suppes, Eds. (Stanford Univ. Press, Stanford, Calif., 1960). See also chap. 6 in (5).

9. N. Cliff, *Psychol. Rev.* 66, 27 (1959); H. F. Gollob, *J. Pers. Soc. Psychol.* 10, 341 (1968).

10. R. Roskies, *J. Math. Psychol.* 2, 266 (1965).

11. D. H. Krantz and A. Tversky, *Psychol. Rev.* 78, 151 (1971).

12. J. R. Hicks, *Value and Capital* (Clarendon, Oxford, ed. 2, 1946).

13. L. J. Savage, *The Foundations of Statistics* (Wiley, New York, 1954).

14. R. D. Luce and D. H. Krantz, *Econometrica* 39, 253 (1971).

15. M. Allais, *ibid.* 21, 503 (1953); K. R. MacCrimmon, in *Risk and Uncertainty*, K. Borch and J. Mossin, Eds. (Macmillan, New York, 1968).

16. Closely related work is found in V. J. Mizel, *Can. J. Math.* **22**, 449 (1970).
17. N. R. ANDERSON, *Science* **138**, 817 (1962).
18. R. N. SHEPARD, J. *Math. Psychol.* **3**, 287 (1966).
19. R. BEALS, D. H. KRANTZ, A. TVERSKY, *Psychol. Rev.* **75**, 127 (1968); A. Tversky and D. H. Krantz, *J. Math. Psychol.* **7**, 572 (1970).
20. A. TVERSKY and D. H. KRANTZ, *Percept. Psychophys.* **5**, 124 (1969).
21. C. H. COOMBS and L. C. HUANG, *J. Math. Psychol.* **7**, 317 (1970).
22. J. C. STEVENS, J. D. MACK, S. S. STEVENS, *J. Exp. Psychol.* **59**, 60 (1960); S. S. Stevens, *Percept. Psychophys.* **1**, 5 (1966).
23. D. JAMESON, in *International Colour Meeting Stockholm 1969* (Musterschmidt, Göttingen, 1970), p. 377.
24. B. C. WILSON, thesis, New York University (1964), and University Microfilms, Ann Arbor, Mich.; T. Indow and S. S. Stevens, *Percept. Psychophys.* **1**, 253 (1966).
25. S. S. STEVENS, *Science* **161**, 849 (1968).
26. I have seen three excellent papers along this line, which, however, their authors seemingly do not intend to publish. I would be happy to concede to R. N. Shepard priority for the particular formulation presented here. Relevant published items are H. Helson, *Adaptation-Level Theory* (Harper & Row, New York, 1964); and J. Pfanzagl (3).
27. S. S. STEVENS, *Psychol. Rev.* **64**, 153 (1957).
28. D. H. KRANTZ, *J. Math. Psychol.*, in press.
29. H. GRASSMANN, *Phil. Mag.-IV* **7**, 254 (1853).
30. G. S. BRINDLEY, *Physiology of the Retina and the Visual Pathway* (Arnold, London, ed. 2, 1970).
31. Y. LE GRAND, *Light, Colour, and Vision* (Chapman and Hall, London, 1968).
32. H. L. F. VON HELMHOLTZ, *Handbuch der Physiologischen Optik* (Voss, Hamburg and Leipzig, 1896); W. S. Stiles, *Proc. Phys. Soc. London* **58**, 41 (1946); D. B. Judd and G. Wyszecki, *Color in Business, Science, and Industry* (Wiley, New York, ed. 2, 1963).
33. D. JAMESON and L. M. HURVICH, *J. Opt. Soc. Am.* **45**, 546 (1955).
34. G. DEBREU, *Econometrica* **26**, 440 (1958); R. D. Luce, *Individual Choice Behavior* (Wiley, New York, 1959); H. D. Block and J. Marschak, in *Contributions to Probability and Statistics*, I. Olkin, S. Ghurye, W. Hoeffding, W. Madow, H. Mann, Eds. (Stanford Univ. Press, Stanford, Calif., 1960).
35. Supported by NSF grant GB 8181 to the University of Michigan. I wish to thank R. D. Luce and A. Tversky for their critical comments on several previous drafts.

23

TACIT KNOWING

MICHAEL POLANYI

I AM happy to have this opportunity to put before you thoughts about the nature of scientific knowledge which I have pursued for some time past. My starting point dates back to my book, *Science, Faith and Society* (Polanyi, 1946). Upon examining the grounds on which science is pursued, I saw that its progress is determined at every stage by indefinable powers of thought. No rules can account for the way a good idea is found for starting an inquiry, and there are no firm rules either for the verification or the refutation of the proposed solution of a problem.

This speculation may sound similar to much of what is often heard today. We are told that the teachings of science claim only to be probable but also to be merely tentative, ever open to refutation by adverse evidence. But this is not true. We bet our lives on the certainy of science every day, be it in medicine or engineering; in fact, nothing is more certain in our world than the established results of science. My point is that the *absence of strict criteria* on which to base our acceptance of science merely shows that our confidence in scientific knowledge *is based on nonstrict criteria*. Science is grounded, and is firmly grounded, on the kind of indefinable insights which the current view of science regards as mere psychological phenomena, incapable of producing rational inferences.

I believe, therefore, that any attempt to eliminate nonstrict modes of inference—or even to reduce them to insignificance—must be misleading. Such attempts have hampered philosophy and damaged our scientific methods. Later I shall give some examples of such cases.

My main task will be to survey the nonstrict rules of inference—in other words, the informal logic—on which science rests. This nonstrict logic will be seen to rest to some extent on psychological observations not hitherto accepted as the foundations of scientific inference. In these informal elements of science we shall recognize the *indeterminacy of scientific knowledge,* and I shall start by describing *three closely linked kinds of such indeterminacy.* The *first* indeterminacy lies in the *indeterminate content* of scientific knowledge. We shall find a *second* indeterminacy in the fact that the *coherence* which makes us accept a discovery to be true can be only *vaguely defined,* and a third indeter-

FROM M. Polanyi, Logic and psychology, *American Psychologist,* 23 (1), 1968, 27–43. Copyright 1968 by the American Psychological Association. Reprinted by permission.

minacy will be seen when we find that the *data* on which a discovery ultimately rests *are not fully identifiable*.

Three Indeterminacies of Knowledge

All knowledge has an indeterminate content whenever it bears on reality. I shall show this to be scientific knowledge. It was Copernicus who claimed for the first time that science can discover new knowledge about fundamental reality, and this claim triumphed in the Copernican revolution. But recently—for the past 80 years or so—the claim of science to know reality has been shaken by a positivist critique which condemned such claims as metaphysical. But I myself agree with Copernicus. In my opinion it is impossible to pursue science without believing that it can discover reality, and I want to reestablish here this belief in reality, although the resurrected idea of reality will, admittedly, look different from its departed ancestor.

It is not easy, of course, to say exactly what Copernicus believed when he persistently maintained, against heavy opposition, that his system was not merely a new computing device, but was a true image of the planets circling the sun. But it will become clear what he meant if we first look at the way the successors of Copernicus—for example, Kepler—relied on the reality of the heliocentric system. The three laws discovered by Kepler were based on the reality of the Copernican system: He was able to discover these laws only because he accepted it *as a fact* that the earth goes round the sun.

Whenever we believe in the reality of a thing, we expect that the thing will manifest itself in yet unknown ways in the future. But notice also that the laws by which Kepler confirmed the reality of the heliocentric system were very different from anything Copernicus himself might have expected. The elliptic planetary paths of Kepler conflicted sharply with the basic beliefs of Copernicus. Yet it remains true that Kepler's discoveries confirmed Copernicus' claim that his system was real, which shows that a claim to reality is essentially indeterminate. Affirmations of reality in nature always have a widely indeterminate content.

This fact brings us to our next point, which is the indefinable character of the signs by which we recognize reality in nature. The vagueness of the signs pointing to reality can be seen in the work of Copernicus. Copernicus claimed that his theory was an image of reality because it had a coherence that was lacking in the Ptolemaic system, and the principle of this argument was sound because it is the coherence of a thing that makes us attribute reality to it. We commonly recognize its coherence at a glance by merely looking at a real thing. I look at my right hand as I move it about in front of me, and I see a thousand rapidly changing clues as one single, unchanging object moving about at changing distances, presenting different sides at variable angles and in variable light. The integration of innumerable, rapidly changing particulars makes us see a real object in front of us.

Solid objects are deemed to be real inasmuch as they suggest another side not visible at the moment and also a hidden interior—and, moreover, they promise to last for some time, possibly colliding with other things and affecting them in one of an infinite number of possible ways. Such are the typical indeterminacies of a real thing.

By pointing at coherence as a token of reality, Copernicus made an essential contribution to the method on which empirical science was to be established. Science was to him (like perception) a way of seeing reality, and was what the theory of Copernicus meant to his successors who developed it further up to Newton's day. It is indeed what the body of science is to the scientist to this day: He sees in science an aspect of reality which as such is an inexhaustible source of new and promising problems. Natural science continues to bear fruit, because it offers us an insight into external reality.

These views of science and of its belief in reality were put forward about 20 years ago in my *Science, Faith and Society* (Polanyi, 1946). Since then I found welcome support for regarding science as an extension of perception when I became acquainted with the great work of Whewell (1890), written nearly a century before. Speaking of Kepler's discovery of the elliptic path of the planet Mars, Whewell wrote:

To hit upon the right conception is a difficult step; and when the step is once made, the facts assume a different aspect from what they had before: that done, they are seen in a new point of view; and the catching of this point of view is a special mental operation, requiring special endowments and habits of thought. Before this, the facts are seen as detached, separate, regular; as parts of a general fact, and thereby possessing new relations, before unseen [p. 254].

Whewell knew well that he was dissenting here from the Baconian theory of induction; he fiercely attacked Mill's development of this theory, which was nevertheless to dominate the conception of scientific theory for many years afterward. Whewell held that Baconian enquiry can succeed only when guided by dawning insight. And in describing the act of insight, he reveals its kinship to the way our eyes, sharpened by native gifts and by special training, make out the true nature of a puzzling spectacle before us.

In the passage here quoted, Whewell also anticipates another part of my theory. He says that, by becoming parts of a comprehensive entity, the facts acquire new relations, hitherto unseen. I think he speaks here of a true coherence in nature, the inexhaustible implications of which are felt in its bearing on reality.

My view of coherence in science owes much to Gestalt psychology, but I go beyond Gestalt when speaking of *true* coherence in nature. A tendency to good closure is only a *clue to coherence;* it does not establish *true coherence.* Take the famous ambiguous picture representing either a vase or two opposing profiles. As we shift from one way of seeing it to the other, we either see the vase as a real body and the rest of the picture as empty background, or we see, on the contrary, the profiles as real bodies and the space between them as empty. We can observe here a sensory quality indicating coherence as well as the reality of coherence. But since this sensory quality can be shifted at will between two mutually exclusive alternatives, it does not *establish* a true coherence.

The way a judgment of true coherence is arrived at can be seen when a jury faces a serious and difficult decision. The jurors may see a pattern of circumstances pointing to the accused. But it is always conceivable that this pattern may be due to chance. How unlikely a chance should they admit to be possible? Or what degree of coincidence should be considered not to be reasonably believable? No rule can decide this. The decision must be arrived at under the discipline of a grim personal responsibility. It must rely on an ultimate power of the mind, on which the scientist too must ultimately rely for establishing a true coherence in nature.

This concludes my sketch of two major indeterminacies introduced by Copernicus into the foundation of science. I pass now to a third kind of indeterminacy that is intrinsic to all empirical knowledge, and hence also to science.

I have spoken of the numberless items that contribute to my seeing my hand in front of me. They are known to us mainly by observing the various deficiencies caused by cutting out these several items. I can cut out marginal clues by looking at my hand through a blackened tube and observing that this makes my hand appear to swell up when brought nearer to my eyes. We can observe that the action of our eye muscles contributes clues to our vision by the application of drugs which increase the effort of contracting the muscles, and hence makes objects look smaller. Afflictions of the inner ear cause the whole spectacle before us to lose its balance; and there is ample evidence that past experiences, which we can hardly recall, affect the way we see things.

Perception thus establishes an observation of external facts without formal argument and even without explicitly stating the result; I hope to eventually show that science, too, is based on such nonexplicit knowing. But first I must set out the general structure of such knowing and expose the new indeterminacies introduced by it into empirical knowledge.

Consider the act of viewing a pair of stereoscopic pictures in the usual way, with one eye on each of the pictures. Their joint image might be regarded as a whole, composed of the two pictures as its parts. But we can get closer to understanding what is going on here if we note that, when looking through a stereo viewer, we see a stereo image at the focus of our attention while we are aware of the two stereo pictures in some peculiar nonfocal way. We seem to look through these two pictures, or past them, while we look straight at their joint image. We are indeed aware of them only as guides to the image on which we focus our attention. I can describe this relationship of the two pictures to the stereo image by saying that the two pictures function as *subsidiaries* to our seeing their *joint* image which is their joint meaning. This is the typical structure of tacit knowing which I shall now describe in some detail.

The grounds of all tacit knowing are items—or particulars—like the stereo pictures of which we are aware in the act of focusing our attention on something else, away from them. This I call the *functional relation* of subsidiaries to the focal target, and we may also call it a *from-to relation*. Moreover, I can say that this relation establishes a *from-to knowledge* of the subsidiaries, as linked to their focus. Tacit knowing is a from-to knowing. Sometimes it will also be called a from-at knowing, but this variation will be only a matter of convenience.

It will not be difficult to demonstrate the indeterminacies inherent in from-to knowledge, but I want first to add some other features to the structure of from-to knowledge. A characteristic aspect of from-to knowledge is exemplified by the change of appearance which occurs when the viewing of a pair of stereo pictures transforms these into a stereo image. A stereo image has a marked depth and also shows firmly shaped objects not present as such in the original stereo pictures. It therefore shows a novel sensory experience created by tacit knowing. Such *phenomenal transformation* is a characteristic feature of from-to knowing. I have already actually mentioned such a case when I spoke of the sensory quality of coherence in nature.

A moment ago I anticipated another feature of from-to knowing when I said that the stereo image is the *joint* meaning of the stereo pictures. The subsidiaries of from-to knowing bear on a focal target; in my view, whatever a thing bears on may be called its meaning. Thus the focal target on which they bear is the meaning of the subsidiaries. We may call this an act of sense giving and recognize it as the *semantic aspect* of from-to knowing.

A few examples will help to make us familiar with these three aspects of tacit knowing: the functional, the phenomenal, and the semantic. I could cite here the cases of visual perception and of scientific discovery, which are my main interests in this exposition, but they have complications which I wish to avoid for a time.

Take, as a simpler case, the from-to structure of the act of reading a printed sentence. The sight of the printed words guides our focal attention away from the print to a focal target that is its meaning. We have here both the *functions* of from-to knowing and its *semantic* aspect. Its *phenomenal* aspect is also easy to recognize; it lies in the fact that a word in use *looks different* from what it would be like to someone who met it as a totally foreign word. The familiar use of a word, which is our subsidiary awareness of it, renders it, in a way, bodiless, or, as it is sometimes described, transparent.

Another example—and one that will help us later to understand visual perception—is the case of tactile cognition: of using a probe to explore a cavity, or a stick to feel one's way in the dark. Such exploration is a from-to knowing, for we attend subsidiarily to the feeling of holding the probe in the hand, while the focus of our attention is fixed on the far end of the probe, where it touches an obstacle in its path. This perception is the function of tacit knowing and is accompanied by particularly interesting *phenomenal transformation*. The sensation of the probe pressing on fingers and palm, and of the muscles guiding the probe, is lost, and instead we feel the point of the probe as it touches an object. And, in addition to the functional and the phenomenal, the probing has, of course, a *semantic* aspect. For the information we get by feeling the point of the instrument is its meaning to us: It tells us what it is that we are observing by the use of the probe.

This use of probes may remind us of the fact that all sensation is assisted by some, however slight, skillful performance, the motions of which are performed with our attention focused on the intended action so that our awareness of the motions is subsidiary to the performance. From-to structure includes all skillful performances, from tying a knot to playing a piano. More about this later.

We now have enough material to uncover the indeterminacies inherent in from-to knowing. We have a very obvious indeterminacy before us in the case of stereo vision. The three-dimensional depth of the stereo image has its basis in the differences between the two stereo pictures, that is to say, the differences due to the fact that the pictures are taken at points a few inches apart. These tiny differences are not noticeable by simple inspection, and even if we used powerful methods for measuring them, we would find them difficult to itemize since they extend all over the surface. We see, then, how readily our subsidiary awareness picks up and embodies in the focus of our attention items of evidence that we should never notice directly and might indeed find difficult to identify even if we searched for them. This demonstration should suffice to make it clear that the *grounds* of from-to knowledge may often be *unspecifiable*.

Let me stop here for a moment and recall the indeterminacy of all knowledge bearing on reality and the indeterminacy due to the impossibility of giving a precise rule for establishing true coherence in nature. We have now added, as a third indeterminacy of empirical knowledge, the fact that we may not know on what grounds we hold our knowledge to be true.

But let us realize that we could turn this deficiency into a flourish. Instead of deploring that a statement about external reality has an indeterminate content, we could take pride in the fact that we can thus *see beyond established facts;* instead of regretting that we cannot define the quality of coherence in nature, we could be gratified at the capability of *feeling* such subtle, virtually invisible, signs of reality. Far from being embarrassed by our incapacity to state all the grounds on which empirical knowledge rests, we could insist on the recognition of our powers to *know far more than we can tell.* These faculties are indeed those that we *shall* claim once we have accepted tacit knowing as a legitimate and, in fact, indispensable source of all empirical knowledge. But we must realize the whole depth of our tacit commitments before we can make them so firmly our own. For this, let me show yet further aspects of our tacit knowledge.

The Tacit Triad

The structure of tacit knowing includes a conjoint pair of constituents. Subsidiaries exist as such by bearing on the focus to which we are attending from them. In other words, the functional structure of from-to knowing includes jointly a subsidiary "from" and a focal "to" (or "at"). But this pair is not linked together of its own accord. The relation of a subsidiary to a focus is formed by the act of a person who integrates one to the other. And so the from-to relation lasts only so long as a person, the knower, sustains this integration.

This is not merely to say that if we no longer look at a thing, we shall cease to see it. There is a specific action involved in dissolving the integration of tacit knowing. Let me describe this action.

We have now seen three centers of tacit knowledge: first, the subsidiary particulars; second, the focal target; and third, the knower who links the first to the second. We can place these three things in the three corners of a triangle. Or we can think of them as forming a triad, controlled by a person, the knower, who causes the subsidiaries to bear on the focus of his attention.

We can then say that the knower integrates the subsidiaries to a focal target—or that the subsidiaries have a meaning to the knower which fills the center of his focal attention, and that hence the knower can dissolve the triad by merely looking differently at the subsidiaries. The triad will disappear if the knower shifts his focal attention away from the focus of the triad and fixes it on the subsidiaries.

For example, if, instead of looking at the stereo pictures through the viewer, we take them out and look at them directly, we lose sight of their joint appearance on which we had focused before. Or if we focus our attention on a spoken word and thus see it as a sequence of sounds, the word loses the meaning to which we had attended before. Or again, we can paralyze the performance of a skill by turning our attention away from its performance and concentrating instead on the several motions that compose the performance.

These facts are common knowledge, but their consequences for the theory of tacit knowledge are remarkable. For the facts confirm our view that we can be aware of certain things in a way that is quite different from focusing our attention on them. They prove the existence of two kinds of awareness that are mutually exclusive, a *from-awareness* and a *focal awareness*. They also confirm that in the from-awareness of a thing we see a meaning of it, a meaning which is wiped out by focusing our attention *on* the thing, which will face us then in itself, in its raw bodily nature. The dual nature of awareness is made manifest here as the sense deprivation involved in substituting one kind of awareness for another.

Suppose, then, that it is possible, at least in principle, to identify all the subsidiaries of a triad; however elusive they may be we would still face the fact that anything serving as a subsidiary ceases to do so when focal attention is directed on it. It turns into a different kind of thing, deprived of the meaning it had in the triad. Thus subsidiaries are—in this important sense—essentially unspecifiable. We must distinguish, then, between two types of the unspecifiability of subsidiaries. One type is due to the difficulty of tracing the subsidiaries—a condition that is widespread but not universal—and the other type is due to a sense deprivation which is logically necessary and in principle absolute. This adds a fourth, and quite fundamental, indeterminacy to the grounds on which empirical knowledge rests.

I hope that if this analysis convinces us of the presence of two very different kinds of awareness in tacit knowing, it will also prevent us from identifying these two different kinds of awareness with a difference between conscious and unconscious awareness. Focal awareness is, of course, always conscious, but subsidiary awareness, or from-awareness, can have all levels of consciousness; it can range from a subliminal level to a fully conscious level. What makes awareness subsidiary is its functional character, and I shall therefore claim the presence of subsidiary awareness even for functions inside our body at levels completely inaccessible to experience by the subject. This claim will be particularly important for the theory of visual perception.[1]

Tacit Inference

Subsidiaries function as such by being integrated to a focus on which they bear. This integration is the tacit act of a person and can be valid or mistaken. Perception can be true or mistaken and so can our judgment of coherence, whether in deciding on the facts of a legal case or when

---

[1] What I call "subsidiaries" include "subceived stimuli" (see Polanyi, 1966, pp. 7–9). Wall and Guthrie (1959, pp. 205–210) have shown that conditioning to shock syllables persists without reinforcement for subliminal presentation, but is extinguished for subliminal presentation when extinguished for supraliminal presentation. They note the parallelism between the subceived stimulus and the Freudian unconscious.

perceiving coherence in nature. To arrive at such conclusions may be called an *act of tacit inference,* but such inferences differ sharply from drawing conclusions by an explicit deduction.

Piaget (1950) has described the contrasts between a sensorimotor act like perception and a process of explicit inference. Explicit inference is reversible: We can go back to its premises and go forward again to its conclusions, and we can rehearse this process as often as we like. This is not true for perception. For example, once we have seen through a visual puzzle, we cannot return to an ignorance of its solution. This holds, with some variations, for all acts of tacit knowing. We can go back to the two pictures of a stereo image by taking them out of the viewer and looking at them directly, but this completely destroys the stereo image. When flying by airplane first started, the traces of ancient sites were revealed in fields over which generations of country folk had walked without noticing them. But once he had landed the airman could no longer see them either.

In some cases deprivation is incomplete. Thus we can concentrate on the sound and the action of our lips and tongue in producing a word, and this will cause us to lose the meaning of the word although the loss can be instantly made good by casting the mind forward for using the word once more in saying something. The same is true for a pianist who paralyzes his performance by intensely watching his own fingers: He can promptly recover their skillful use by attending once more to his music. In these instances the path to the integrated relation—which may have originally taken months of labor to establish—is restored from its abeyance in a trice, while at the same moment the sight of the sense-deprived particulars is lost.

Explicit inference is very different; no such breaking up and rediscovery takes place when we recapitulate the deduction of the theorem of Pythagoras. Once this basic distinction between explicit inference and tacit integration is clear, it throws new light on a 100-year-old controversy. In 1867 Helmholtz offered to intepret perception as a process of unconscious inference, but this theory was generally rejected by psychologists, who pointed out that optical illusions are not destroyed by demonstrating their falsity. Psychologists had assumed, quite reasonably, that "unconscious inference" had the same structure as a conscious explicit inference. But if we identify "unconscious inference" with tacit integration, we have a kind of inference that is not damaged by adverse evidence, as explicit inference is. This difference between a deduction and an integration lies in the fact that deduction connects two focal items, the premises and consequents, while integration makes subsidiaries bear on a focus. Admittedly there is a purposive movement in a deduction—which is its essential tacit coefficient—but the deductive operation can be mechanically performed while a tacit integration is intentional throughout and, as such, can be carried out only by a conscious act of the mind. Brentano (1942, orig. publ. 1874) has taught that consciousness necessarily attends to an object, and that *only* a conscious mental act can attend to an object. My analysis of tacit knowing has amplified this view of consciousness. It tells us not only that consciousness is intentional, but also that it always has roots *from which* it attends to its object. It includes a tacit awareness of its subsidiaries.

Such integration cannot be replaced by any explicit mechanical procedure. In the first place, even though one can paraphrase the cognitive content of an integration, the sensory quality which conveys this content cannot be made explicit. I have already illustrated this fact much earlier by pointing to the quality of coherence in nature, but all of my examples of tacit knowing can be used to demonstrate it.

The irreducibility of tacit integration can be observed more fully for practical knowing. I could point to our incapacity to control directly the several motions contributing to a skillful performance—even such a familiar act as using our limbs. But these cases are perhaps too common to impress the imagination. So I shall take instead the example of finding one's way with inverting spectacles. It is virtually impossible to get about while wearing inverting spectacles by following the instruction that what —in the case of right-left inversion—is seen on the right is actually on the left, while, conversely, things seen on the left are on the right. The Austrian psychologist, Heinrich Kottenhoff (1961), however, has shown that continued efforts to move about while wearing inverted spectacles produce a novel quality of feeling and action by integrating the inverted sights to appropriate sensorimotor responses, so that the subject again finds his way about. This reintegration can be performed only subsidiarily; any explicit instruction to reintegrate sights and sensorimotor responses would be quite meaningless.

I have often quoted the case of the cyclist, but it still teaches its lesson here. We cannot learn to keep our balance on a bicycle by taking to heart that, to compensate for an imbalance, we must take a curve of which a radius is proportional to the square of the bicycle's velocity over the angle of imbalance. Such knowledge is totally ineffectual unless it is known tacitly.

The way in which particulars are picked up and assimilated as subsidiaries will be extensively dealt with in the section on discovery. But we may anticipate one of its aspects, pointed out by Konrad Lorenz (1967) who arrived independently at the view that science is based on a gestaltlike integration of particulars. He demonstrated that the speed and complexity of tacit integration far exceeds the operations of any explicit selection of supporting evidence. I have recently (Polanyi, 1967b) developed this idea further by showing that the serial behavior demonstrated by Lashley (1951) in the production of a spoken sentence can be understood by considering that tacit knowing can pick up simultaneously a whole set of data and combine them in a meaningful spoken sequence.

An integration established in this summary manner will often override single items of contrary evidence. It can only be damaged by new contradictory facts if these items are absorbed in an alternative integration which disrupts the one previously established. In Ames's skew-room experiment the illusion of a boy taller than the man persists so long as the evidence of the room's skew shape is slight, but the illusion is instantly destroyed if a shift of the observer's position or a tapping of the ceiling makes the skewness of the room more manifest. This fact effectively competes, then, with the hitherto established integration and destroys it.

David Hume has taught that, when in doubt, we must suspend judgment. This theory might apply to conclusions derived on paper which can be manipulated at will—at least on paper. Our eyes continue to see a little boy taller than a grown man although we know this to be false, so long as no feasible alternative integration is presented to the imagination. But if an alternative is presented, and this perception happens to be true, a new perception will take place and correct our errors. Helmholtz could have answered his opponents on this score, but he would have had to admit that his "unconscious inferences" were very different from conscious inferences.

Indwelling

There is yet another important aspect of tacit knowing which should be included here. In all examples of tacit knowing that I have given, the focal target which forms the meaning of the subsidiaries is placed some distance away from them. Most striking, perhaps, was the displacement of meaning when the sensations of hand and muscles holding a probe were displaced to the far end of the probe. The displacement of the focal target invariably went in the same direction, namely, away from us. And if one tries to construct a triad, the focus of which points in the opposite direction—so that the meaning of the subsidiaries would lie on our side of them—this proves impossible.

The most important displacement of meaning is found in visual perception; I mention perception here only to explain why meaning produced by tacit knowing is always displaced outward. Our senses point into external space and our actions, too, are, as a rule, projected outward; so the objects of our conscious attention lie predominantly outward from us. Our muscles, our sense organs, our nervous system, are experienced as they perform their functions of noticing and interpreting things outside and manipulating them for our own purposes. One is aware of the body subsidiarily as it performs these functions, while focal observation of one's own body is only superficial. We may look focally at our hands and feet, but even so our subsidiary awareness of them predominates: One still feels them to be part of the body. This is what the from-knowledge of the body feels like to us: It amounts to awareness of living in one's own body.

Having identified the feeling of being in one's body with from-knowledge of the body, one can look upon all from-knowledge as akin to the sense of being in one's body's. *In this sense, then, to make something function subsidiarily is to interiorize it, or else to pour one's body into it.* The fact that we do feel probes and tools to be part of the body bears out this parallelism. Any integration of things which makes them bear on our focal interest can be regarded as an indwelling of these things.

We may say that our own existence, which we experience, and the world that we observe are interwoven here. Bodily being, by participating subsidiarily in one's perceptions and actions, becomes a being in the world, while external observations and projects subsidiarily involving one's own bodily feelings become, up to a point, a self-transformation, an existential choice. And this involves our cultural framework. Every time we rely on our traditional grounds in forming a judgment, we somewhat modify their meaning, and on these lines a creative act can renew our grounds extensively. Copernicus, for example, radically changed the grounds of empirical judgment, and since then the grounds of scientific judgment have been further modified repeatedly.

This adds yet another indeterminacy to the four I have previously mentioned. Applied to science, our fifth indeterminacy consists of the existential choices involved in modifying the grounds of scientific judgment.

But something even more vital follows from formulating tacit knowing as an act of indwelling. It deepens our knowledge of living things. Biology studies the shapes of living things and the way they grow into these shapes from germ cells; it describes the organs of plants and animals and explains the way they function; it explores the motor and sensory capacities of animals and their intelligent performances. These aspects of life are controlled by biological principles. Morphology, embryology, physiology, psychology all study the principles by which living beings form and sustain their coherence and respond in ever new ways to an immense variety of novel circumstances. The ways in which animals, such as cattle or dogs or men, coherently control their bodies form a comprehensively functioning system. Any chemical or physical study of living things that is irrelevant to these workings of the organism forms no part of biology.

We therefore recognize and study the coherence of living things by integrating their motions—and any other normal changes occurring in their parts—into our comprehension of their functions. *We integrate mentally what living beings integrate practically.* Chess players rehearse a master's game to discover what he had in mind. Generally we share the purpose of a mind by indwelling its actions. This is my answer to the great question: How do we know another mind? . . .

When the imagination goes into action to start a scientific enquiry, it not only becomes more intense, but also more concrete, more specific. Although the target toward which it thrusts is yet empty, it is seen to lie in a definite direction. It represents a particular problem vaguely pointing but still always pointing to a hidden feature of reality. Once the problem is adopted, its pursuit will rely on a particular range of resources that are felt to be available in a particular direction. These resources will include the amount of labor and money needed for the quest. No problem may be undertaken unless we feel that its possible solution would be worth the probable expense.

These strangely perceptive anticipations are not arrived at either by following rules, or by relying on chance; nor are they guaranteed by a wealth of learning. Yet their practice is common and indeed indispensable; no scientist can survive in his profession unless he can make such anticipations with a reasonable degree of success. For this goal he needs exceptional gifts. But his gifts, although exceptional, are of the same kind as underlie the mere use of speech, and are actually found at work in every deliberate human action. They are intrinsic to the dynamics of all from-to knowledge, down to the simplest acts of tacit knowing.

In science the path from problem to discovery can be lengthy. The enquiry having been launched, the imagination will continue to thrust forward, guided by a sense of potential resources. It batters its path by mobilizing these resources, occasionally consolidating some of them in specific surmises. These surmises will then tentatively fill, up to a point, the hitherto empty frame of the problem.

It is a mistake to think of heuristic surmises as well-defined hypothetical statements which the scientist proceeds to test in a neutral and indeed critical spirit. Hunches often consist essentially in narrowing down the originally wider program of the enquiry. They may be most exciting, and may indeed turn out later to have been crucial, yet they are mostly far more indeterminate than the final discovery will be. The range of indeterminacy lies at some point between that of the original problem and of its eventual solution.

Besides, the relation of the scientist to his surmises is one of passionate personal commitment. The effort that led to a surmise committed every fiber of his being to the quest; his surmises embody all his hopes.

The current theory that ignores the mechanism of tacit knowing must ignore and indeed deny such commitments. The tentativeness of the scientist's every step is then taken to show that he is uncommitted. But every step made in the pursuit of science is *definitive*, definitive in the vital sense that it definitely disposes of the time, the effort, and the material resources used in making that step. Such investments add up with frightening speed to the whole professional life of the scientist. To think of scientific workers cheerfully trying this and trying that, calmly changing course at each failure, is a caricature of a pursuit consuming a man's whole person. Any questing surmise necessarily seeks its own confirmation.

You might expect me to conclude by showing how a problem is eventually resolved by the discovery of a coherence in nature, the hidden existence of which had first been sighted in a problem and which had become increasingly manifest by its pursuit. I must, however, first introduce another factor, the identification of which we owe to Henri Poincaré. In a classic essay included in *Science et Méthode* (1908) he described two stages in the way we hit upon an idea that promises to solve a scientific problem. The first stage consists in racking one's brains by successive sallies of the imagination, while the second, which may be delayed for hours after one has ceased one's efforts, is the spontaneous appearance of the idea one has struggled for. Poincaré says that this spontaneous process consists in the integration of some of the material mobilized by thrusts of the imagination; he also tells us that these thrusts would be useless but for the fact that they are guided by special anticipatory gifts of the scientist.

It seems plausible to assume, then, that two faculties of the mind are at work jointly from the beginning to the end of the enquiry. One is the deliberately active powers of the imagination, and the other a spontaneous process of integration, which we may call *intuition*. It is intuition that senses the presence of hidden resources for solving a problem and which launches the imagination in its pursuit. And it is intuition that forms there our surmises and which eventually selects from the material mobilized by the imagination the relevant pieces of evidence and integrates them into the solution of the problem.

But, you may ask, what about the measurements, computations, and algebraic formulae used in the pursuit and formulation of science? These are, of course, essential, but I have dealt with them when showing that the use of language is a tacit operation, both in our spoken language and in our understanding of it when spoken by others. The same applies to all other explicit thought; it can be developed and understood only by a tacit operation and it is thus based throughout on tacit knowing. All knowledge is either tacit or rooted in tacit knowing.

To sum up, I call "logic" the rules for reaching valid conclusions from premises assumed to be true. Currently logic seems to be defined instead as the rules for reaching strict conclusions from strict premises. I think we should reject this definition. No strict rules can exist for establishing empirical knowledge. Most people know this, but would urge us to accept strictness as an unattainable ideal for which to strive. But this is to turn a blind eye on tacit knowing, in which alone lies our capacity for acquiring empirical knowledge.

Our age prides itself on its unflinching frankness in calling a spade a spade and worse than that. But for all this bluntness, we are strictly Victorian when it comes to mentioning the mind, acknowledging its autonomous actions and its indeterminate range of knowing—even though all the power and beauty of thought relies on these tacit faculties.

I think we should drop these intellectual fictions, for there are reasonable alternatives that are much nearer the truth.

REFERENCES

BRENTANO, F. *Psychologie vom empirischem Standpunkt.* (Reprint of 1874 ed.) Leipzig: Oskar Kraus, 1942.

KOTTENHOFF, H. Was ist richtiges Sehen mit Umkehrbrillen und in welchem Sinne stellt sich das Sehen um? In, *Psychologia Universalis,* Vol. 5. Meisenheim am Glan: A. Hain, 1961.

LORENZ, K. Gestalt perception as fundamental to scientific knowledge. *General Systems,* 1967, 7, 37–56.

PIAGET, J. *Psychology of intelligence.* New York: Harcourt, Brace, 1950.

POLANYI, M. *Science, faith and society.* London: Oxford University Press, 1946. (Reprinted: Chicago: University of Chicago Press, 1964).

———. Sense-giving and sense reading. *Philosophy,* 1967, 42, 301. (b)

WHEWELL, W. *Philosophy and discovery.* (Quoted text written in 1856) London: John W. Parker, 1890.

PROCEDURAL ISSUES

In the first selection Blackburn presents a powerful argument for the opening of both scientific eyes—for the complementarity of the orthodox quantitative ("intellectual") look and an equally emphasized qualitative ("sensuous") look.

In his review of Ghiselin's book on Darwin, Staddon describes a style of scientific problem solving that zeroes in on the actual problem, using whatever techniques seem appropriate to get the job done. The illustrations from Darwin's work that Staddon describes are useful reminders that the most successful scientific problem solvers operate in this way, rather than blindly following the procedures laid down by their teachers or models (and all too often reported in secondary sources, such as textbooks, as "gospel").

Underwood's article on individual differences as they relate to theory construction touches on a long-overdue correction of the tendency of psychologists to be too much concerned with relatively simple (main) effects, in their theorizing as well as their experimentation. Increased recognition of the great variety of interactions among variables in psychological data, of which individual differences variables constitute simply one type, should greatly improve the effectiveness of our theory construction in the future.

Dunnette's appeal for forsaking trivia ("fads, fashions and folderol") in psychology and concentrating on fundamental problems is one that each of us needs to take seriously. There are few research programs that could not benefit from a careful screening of the type that is recommended in the essay.

The last selection, by Goodson, examines in depth the slippery problem of intercommunication. Failure to recognize the many pitfalls in communication that await the unwary accounts for much of the difficulty in effective evaluation of theories, and more concern with these problems should help to improve this situation.

24

SENSUOUS–INTELLECTUAL COMPLEMENTARITY

Thomas R. Blackburn

WE LIVE in a technological culture, and that culture is in trouble. Recent essays (1–3), that have explored the relationship between modern science and the history and psychology of technological man, have generally concluded that the scientist's quantifying, value-free orientation has left him helpless to avoid (and often a willing partner in) the use of science for exploitative and destructive ends.

The past few years have seen the rapid growth of a counter-technological culture in which science, as we know it, plays no role in the contemplation of nature. The counterculture, because it is still in the process of growth and formulation and because of its very nature, is no single philosophical system. For our purposes, the salient feature of the counterculture is its epistemology of direct sensuous experience (4), subjectivity, and respect for intuition—especially intuitive knowledge based on a "naïve" openness to nature and to other people. Both on its own merits and as a reaction to the abuses of technology, the movement has attracted increasing numbers of intelligent and creative students and professional people. I believe that science as a creative endeavor cannot survive the loss of these people; nor, without them, can science contribute to the solution of the staggering social and ecological problems that we face.

More fundamentally, much of the criticism directed at the current scientific model of nature is quite valid. If society is to begin to enjoy the promise of the "scientific revolution," or even to survive in a tolerable form, science must change. In its own terms, the logical-experimental structure of science that has evolved since Galileo's lifetime is magnificent. It has, in Lewis and Randall's phrase (5), its cathedrals. To demolish these, to reject what has been achieved, would be barbaric and pointless, since the very amorality of science makes it not wrong, but incomplete. The claims of science as such (as opposed to, say, "defense" research), as well as the claims of its critics, while contradictory, are not incompatible.

Niels Bohr's concept of complementarity arose when apparently con-

FROM T. R. Blackburn, Sensuous-intellectual complementarity in science, *Science,* 1971, **172,** 1003–1007. Copyright 1971 by the American Association for the Advancement of Science.

flicting results in elementary particle physics forced an expansion of the frame of reference of classical physics (6). Bohr himself came increasingly to believe that complementarity was a concept that could be applied to far more than just the purely physical systems that had led him to its formulation (7, pp. 3–22). It is conceivable, then, that the notion of complementarity offers a method of including both sensuous and intellectual knowledge of nature in a common frame of reference. The result, far more than a mere compromise or amalgamation of the two viewpoints, could be a richer science, in which esthetic and quantitative valuations, each retaining its own integrity, would contribute equally to the description of nature that science long ago took for its province. Further, it may produce a scientific ethic that is less destructive toward nature.

Complementarity in Modern Physics

Phenomena on the atomic level present the investigator with a wealth of seemingly contradictory observations. Light undergoes diffraction, which can only be explained by adopting the classical wave model. Yet, in the photoelectric effect and in photon-scattering experiments, the predictions of the wave model are not realized, and the actual observations can only be rationalized by postulating quanta of light that carry momentum and have a relatively definite location (subject to the restrictions of the Heisenberg uncertainty principle). Again, negative electricity is first found to be quantized in electrolysis and the oil-drop experiment, and each unit of negative electricity behaves in a cathode-ray tube like a little lump, with a mass of 9×10^{-28} gram, and a charge of 4.8×10^{-10} electrostatic unit. Yet, direct a stream of these "particles" onto a crystal, and diffraction phenomena take place; to explain these phenomena requires that the "electrons" be treated as a train of waves. Attempts to measure the position and momentum of a particle, or the energy and duration of a state of a dynamic system, may be perfectly successful in separate experiments, but never in the same experiment on the same system.

All of these familiar results of quantum physics are given a quantitative expression in the Heisenberg uncertainty principle, and a general philosophical basis in Bohr's principle of complementarity. Viewing these phenomena from the standpoint of deterministic descriptions of events in space and time (the goal of classical physics) Bohr says:

Within the scope of classical physics, all characteristic properties of a given object can in principle be ascertained by a single experimental arrangement, though in practice various arrangements are often convenient. . . . In quantum physics, however, evidence about atomic objects obtained by different experimental arrangements exhibits a novel kind of complementary relationship. . . . Far from restricting our efforts to put questions to nature in the form of experiments, the notion of *complementarity* simply characterizes the answers we can receive by such inquiry, whenever the interaction between the measuring instruments and the objects forms an integral part of the phenomena [8].

And again,

Indeed the ascertaining of the presence of an atomic particle in a limited space-time domain demands an experimental arrangement involving a transfer of momentum and energy to bodies such as fixed scales and synchronized clocks, which cannot be included in the description of their functioning, if these bodies are to fulfill the role of defining the reference frame. Conversely, any strict application of the laws of conservation of momentum and energy [that is, any causality] implies, in principle, a renunciation of detailed space-time coordination of the particles [8].

After complementarity in physics had been accepted, it was realized that observations which give conflicting (complementary) views of phenomena cannot, when taken by themselves, be accepted as complete *nor, therefore, as totally correct* descriptions of nature. Electrons behave in ways that can be accounted for by thinking of them as particles; but they are *not* particles, since they also (under different conditions of observation) behave in ways that can be accounted for by thinking of them as waves. Only the complementary description is complete and, to the best of our knowledge, correct. However, to say this is not to impugn the accuracy of the different experimental measurements that give, respectively, the one-sided wave or particle results.

Bohr made it very clear that, in the context of quantum physics, the idea of complementarity had nothing to do with any renunciation of rational objectivity in science. Yet the very idea of an objective description of phenomena (for example, in unambiguously reporting the results of an experiment) requires that macroscopic (that is, classical) equipment and observations be described in ordinary language, no matter how much that language could be refined and specialized for technical usage. The duality of light's behavior arises not from the light "itself" (if such an idea even has any meaning), but from the observation of light as it interacts with experimental equipment and in the description of such observations in language that only contains the classical terms "wave" and "particle" as models for the phenomenon.

Although it was the phenomena of quantum physics that forced Bohr to the idea of complementarity as a mode of knowledge, he quickly realized that other apparent contradictions in the description of nature also admitted of a similar resolution. In a series of essays, he considered its application to biology and psychology (8) and, finally, to the whole range of human intellectual experience (7, pp. 67–82). Since the extension to wider problems of an idea that is valid in a clearly limited context is dangerous to the integrity of that idea, the present attempt at even further extension requires a list, as complete as possible, of the characteristics both of the idea of complementarity, and of the situations to which it may be fruitfully applied. It will then remain to discover to what extent the conflict between the analytical and intuitive understandings of nature satisfies those criteria. I intend to use only the physical application of complementarity as a model, since it seems the least ambiguous and is generally accepted as a necessary interpretation of phenomena by workers in the field.

On this basis, then, the following characteristics defining complementary realities may be listed:

1. A single phenomenon (for example, "light" or "matter") manifests itself to an observer in conflicting modes (for example, as "waves" or "particles").

2. The description or model that fits the phenomenon depends on the mode of observation. (In this way, the idea of objectivity is somewhat broadened, but not eliminated.)

3. Each description is "rational"; that is, language (including mathematics if necessary) is used according to the same consistent logic in either description, with no appeal to revealed truth or mystical insight.

4. Neither model can be subsumed into the other. Thus, for example, classical and statistical thermodynamics do not constitute complementary formulations, even though they can be developed from apparently independent axiomatic bases.

5. Because they refer to a (presumably) single reality, complementary descriptions are not independent of each other. For example, the differential equation of wave motion used in the description of an electron in an atom must be "normalized"; that is, its integral over all space must correspond to the quantity of mass and electrical charge carried by one electron (measurable only in experiments in which particle behavior is manifested).

6. Complementarity is not mere contradiction. The alternate modes of description never lead to incompatible predictions for a given experiment, since they arise from different kinds of experience. Thus, Newtonian and relativistic mechanics are not complementarities, since it can be shown experimentally that the former leads to incorrect predictions of phenomena that are correctly predicted by the latter.

7. It follows from number 6 that neither complementary model of a given phenomenon is complete. A full account of the phenomenon is achieved only by enlarging the frame of reference to include both models as alternative truths, however irreconcilable their abstract contradictions may seem.

Quantitative Science and the Sensuous Alternative

The importance of quantitative modeling in the creation of the scientific world view is an old story, and there is no need to belabor it here.

Critics and apologists of science alike have recognized that the cyclic coupling of experimental observation with mathematical theorizing has been the driving force behind the huge advances achieved since the time of Descartes in understanding the complex of phenomena that we call nature. Where critics and apologists have parted, however, is on the moral consequences of such an approach to nature. Some, like C. P. Snow (9) and J. Bronowski (10), find in the scientist's rigorous adherence to verifiability, and in his humility in the face of evidence contradictory to his theories, the best hope of salvation that mankind has. To others (2, p. 205), the alleged objective consciousness of the scientist is not only a myth, but a vicious one, behind which men may perpetrate monstrous crimes against nature without acknowledging personal involvement and, therefore, guilt. Most recently, Lewis Mumford (3) has found in the mechanical world view the fatal metaphor for a society of machine-like repression of human feelings and human freedom. It is not my purpose to evaluate Mumford's critique of science [which is sometimes too condemnatory even for the generally antitechnological *New York Review of Books* (11)]. It seems to me, however, that some undeniably dangerous attitudes do exist in science's present stance toward nature; and, to the extent that these attitudes exist, they represent dangers to the integrity of human freedom and of the terrestrial environment.

In his everyday experience, man finds the world chaotic and, in the perhaps revealing word of the scientific theorist, "messy." Complex brown and black mixtures prevail over pure substances. It is no wonder, then, that mankind, in reaction to this chaos, is inclined to bring the phenomena indoors to calm, well-lighted laboratories in which they can be studied one at a time, or in well-defined combinations. Nor is it any wonder that he often chooses to understand nature in terms of mental models (which include scientific theories and "laws" as well as pictorial or tactile models) that are understandable just because they are the creation of his own mind. These mental models serve as maps or blueprints of reality. Like maps and blueprints (and like shadows), they simplify complex systems by projecting them onto a simpler space that has a smaller number of dimensions than are required for a complete description of the original system. A complex part of nature (such as a coral reef, a cell, or a city) is, metaphorically, many-dimensional. It is brought under scientific scrutiny by projecting it onto a simpler, under-dimensioned space, within which it can be grasped and quantified.

Then, depending on its appearance within that space, generalizations are drawn according to the logical and mathematical rules appropriate to the quantification space. Physical implications of the mathematical model are subjected to quantitative test under controlled conditions. To the extent that experiment confirms theory and suggests new theoretical steps, science progresses.

The pure intellectual excitement of science, its success in illuminating some of the darkness that threatened to engulf us with the fall of religious world views, and the social benefits of its technological consequences are beyond serious question. There are those who are chafing to get on with the extension of mankind's intellectual hegemony to the understanding and complete control of our natural environment, our societies, our heredity, and our fellow man. Yet the potential and actual evils that have already come from the "ethically neutral" pursuit of knowledge for its own sake, and the alienation of science and scientists from the rest of the culture, are also beyond question. To take credit for the successes of science and the blessings of technology, but to blame the abuses on the incompetence or venality, or both, of planners, politicians, and businessmen, seems fatuous in the extreme. Nor, knowing what we do now of the momentous social consequences of the "purest" science, can we seek forgiveness for the next social or ecological disaster. Our understanding of really complex systems (organisms, societies, ecosystems, the mind) is rudimentary, and our ways of investigating such systems and communicating about them, primitive. The danger of a scientific-technological disaster arises when practitioners of the quantifying art forget about the philosophical foundations of their enterprise. It is easy to ignore the too-messy world outside the laboratory door: to mistake domains and functions in quantification space for nature, and the manipulation of these for the only method of understanding nature. (As a physicist once remarked to me in the course of a seminar on group theory, "The matrices are all there is.")

I realize that the connection I have just made between scientific practice and ethics is a tenuous and controversial one, though Roszak and Mumford make it with great force. In fact, Alfred North Whitehead made just these points over 40 years ago in his widely admired and little heeded series of lectures, Science and the Modern World (12). However, by relying lopsidedly on abstract quantification as a method of knowing, scientists have been looking at the world with one eye closed. There is other knowledge besides quantitative knowledge, and there are other ways of knowing besides reading the position of a pointer on a scale. The human mind and body process information with staggering sophistication and sensitivity by the direct sensuous experience of their surroundings. We have, in fact, in our very selves, "instruments" that are capable of confronting and understanding the blooming, buzzing, messy world outside the laboratory. If that were not so, Homo sapiens would never have survived the competitive pressure from predators who are also so equipped. There are three tenets of countercultural thought that, it seems to me, hold great promise for the enrichment of scientific practice and, perhaps, for the improvement of scientific morality.

1. The most reliable and effective knowing follows from direct and open confrontation with phenomena, no matter how complicated they are. Nature can be trusted to behave reliably without suppression of the

manifold details of a natural environment, and nature's ways are open to direct, intuitive, sensuous knowledge.

2. It follows from the first point that, to know nature well, the human body is to be trusted, cherished, and made sensitive to its natural and human environment. Since the self and the environment are inextricable (contrary to the philosophical stance of classical science), one can understand his surroundings by being sensitive to his own reactions to them.

3. Because knowledge of nature is, in this way, equally open to all, the "expert" is highly suspect. His expertise is likely to be confined to abstractions, and there is a danger that he will project sensitive and complex problems onto some underdimensioned space where he feels less involved and more in control of phenomena. (This threatening aspect is generally confined to the psychological and social sciences, but it can also be seen in the attitude of the ecology movement toward the Army Corps of Engineers.)

In sum, it seems to me that there is much of value in the mind-set that includes these ideas. It is certainly not confined to hippies and "eco-freaks." Thoughtful and respectable writers on educational theory (13) hold much the same view of learning and have much the same criticism of conventional knowledge, which is based on quantification. Furthermore, for very different reasons, industrial scientists have been telling academic scientists this for years. Industrial scientists have attacked what they see as a ludicrous overemphasis on abstract theory in science education. In fact, it may be just the academic scientist's self-imposed isolation from the complexities of the "real" world that has made him so helpless to curb the ecological abuses of his profit-motivated colleagues.

A Complete Natural Science

I now consider whether abstract-quantitative and direct sensuous information meet the requirements of a complementary description of nature.

1. The language, the epistemology, and the models of the two approaches all present us with conflicting pictures of nature; yet the phenomena are consistent and repeatable in each mode.

2. Which description of nature one gives depends entirely on one's method of knowing. For example, one can predict rain by reading the barometer or by going outdoors and sniffing the air, with about equal reliability. The explanations of the prediction, though, will differ, depending on the manner in which the experiment was performed on the atmosphere.

3. Though it may be difficult to convince partisans of either viewpoint, both approaches are "rational." That is, both use a consistent logic, based clearly on the observation of phenomena, in such a way as to ensure

that another observer in the same situation would come to the same conclusion. (Before conventional scientists rush in with cries of "subjectivity"
in criticism of the sensuous approach, they might stop to consider whether
or not a person selected at random off the street could be asked to repeat
their highly sophisticated observations. "With the proper training he
could," they reply; and the reply of the sensuous observer of nature
would be exactly the same for *his* method.)

4. It goes without saying that neither approach to nature can be
subsumed into the other. A number is not an experience, nor is an equation the same thing as intuition. These things are projections of nature into
separate (disjunct) mental spaces.

5. Sensuous information is not independent of quantitative knowledge,
since they both have their referent in the same system of nature. Of
course, abuses of both methods are possible: drug- or wish-induced distortion of the senses, and politically or economically motivated suppression of contrary data for the quantifier. [The controversies in Russia over
genetics and those in the United States over the carcinogenicity of
smoking have been fought entirely on traditional, theory-experiment
grounds. They recall the happiness of Watson and Crick when a colleague
guessed the *wrong* structure for DNA (14).] Yet in the long run, such
distortions are corrected or at least forgotten, since both the sensuous
and experimental investigator share humility in the face of nature.

6. By the same reasoning, both sensuous and quantitative descriptions
of nature may be true; they lead, by the process of continuous self-
correction, to reliable models of nature. The woodsman or farmer knows
when to expect rain or frost, or where to find a given animal, without
quite knowing *how* he knows these things. Reasonably accurate descriptions of weather patterns and animal behavior may also emerge from the
tabulation and correlation of quantitative data.

7. Finally, neither sensuous nor quantitative knowledge of nature is
complete. In fact, it should be clear from the examples I have chosen
that each is really an undernourished view of nature, because each lacks
the information available through the other mode. Indeed, it is difficult to
think of single problems that have been attacked by both modes of
knowing, so different are the mind-sets of the two classes of investigators.

The theoretical-experimental mode has built its grand structure by
confining the phenomena investigated to the kind that can be brought
into a laboratory. Worse, because such laboratories and their operation
are very expensive, the phenomena investigated have largely been confined to those in which a source of wealth has a vested interest—however broadly that interest has been expressed, and however apparent has
been the freedom of the investigator to follow knowledge for its own
sake.

On the other hand, the sensuous investigation of nature has generally
been confined to "naturalists." Their undoubted and often sublime

understanding of nature, and the integrity they have preserved by being poorly funded, have been undercut by their concomitant (in fact, complementary) weakness in rigorous quantitative formulation of what they know. Competition for funds and recognition has made naturalists and scientists rivals, mutually indulgent at best, contemptuous at worst, rather than colleagues in the process of learning about nature. The two groups are, in fact, comparable to two groups of physicists, one of which insists on regarding light as particles, and the other of which treats light only as waves. Such a situation would be ludicrous in modern physics, yet it is exactly what we now confront in science as a whole.

Having said these things, I am now in the position of having to supply a positive model for science. I will try by suggesting that, just as in quantum physics, the truth about nature is to be found only by expanding the frame of discourse to include both of these complementary models of reality.

Two successful models of complementarity in serious scientific investigation may show what I mean. First, there is what began (and, as far as I know, is still regarded) as a dispute between Goethe and Newton over the nature of color. Both men developed theories of color: Newton's was purely quantitative; Goethe's dealt with the sensuous perception of color, including such phenomena as complementary colors and clashing colors. In a speech before the Society for Cultural Collaboration in Budapest in 1941, the German physicist Werner Heisenberg [who played a central role in the formulation of complementarity in quantum physics (6)] reviewed these two theories, especially the less familiar one of Goethe. Heisenberg clearly saw that the two are complementary, in that they are addressed to the same phenomenon from entirely different points of view. Yet, even for Heisenberg, Goethe's view had to be seen as in *opposition* to Newton's, and his verdict is rendered in language that is unfortunately characteristic of our approach to complementary realities (15).

[The] battle is over. The decision on "right" and "wrong" in all questions of detail has long since been taken. Goethe's color theory has in many ways borne fruit in art, physiology, and esthetics. But victory, and hence influence on the research of the following century, has been Newton's.

Yet, if one asks himself "What is color?" the complete answer to such a question can be found only in the complementary descriptions from physics and art. To insist on projecting the question into one or the other of those separate worlds may be a good way to initiate research, but, at the same time, it distorts the original intention of the question.

The second area of nature in which complementary modes of learning have been applied, this time often by the same investigators, is in the study of animal behavior. Of many examples, the finest of which I am aware is George Schaller's study of gorillas (16). Here, in a beautiful whole, are a "serious" and straightforward account of the nature of the gorilla, and an account of Schaller's own presence in the forest—how he interacted with the gorillas and what he learned by observing the effects of this interaction. [In fact, Schaller's method was so far from the observation, by concealed experiments, of captive animals in drab and sensuously meaningless mazes, cages, and boxes that it is inconceivable that his understanding of gorilla behavior is at all accessible to the orthodox animal psychologist (17).]

Implications for the Future of Science

At this writing, it seems beyond dispute that, for at least the next decade, the most important, active, and heavily funded field of science will be ecology—in its broadest sense. Unless we reach a full and effective understanding of human society and its place in the biosphere, there will be no science worth speaking of in the 21st century. It is lucky indeed that the generation born since 1950 is, as a group, deeply interested in all aspects of ecology. Yet this group will not use its energy and intelligence to seek scientific approaches to ecological problems until they are convinced that science is not "irrelevant" or, in fact, demonic.

What is urgently needed is a science that can comprehend complex systems without, or with a minimum of, abstractions. To "see" a complex system as an organic whole requires an act of trained intuition, just as seeing order in a welter of numerical data does. The conditions for achieving such perceptions have been discussed at length among scientists (with little discernible impact on the way we train scientists). The consensus, if any, is that they follow only after long periods of total immersion in the problem. The implication for the present discussion is that the intuitive knowledge essential to a full understanding of complex systems can be encouraged and prepared for by: (i) training scientists to be aware of sensuous clues about their surroundings; (ii) insisting on sensuous knowledge as part of the intellectual structure of science, not as an afterthought; and (iii) approaching complex systems openly, respecting their organic complexity before choosing an abstract quantification space into which to project them.

Because of the primitive, and even repressed, attitudes we now have (and pass on to our students) about intuitive knowledge and its transmission from one person to another, it is difficult to be more precise. Perhaps science has much to learn along this line from the disciplines, as distinct from the mystical content, of Oriental religions. If we do learn to know complexities through the complementary modes of sensuous intuition and logical abstraction, and if we can transmit and discuss the former as reliably as we do the latter, then there is hope for a renaissance in science as a whole comparable to that which occurred in physics between 1900 and 1930.

As usual, the bulk of the active and creative work in any such renaissance will fall to younger people: that is, to just those who, as a group, view the present posture of science as most suspect. Because the recruitment of each new generation of scientists takes place in the undergraduate colleges, I believe that the time is far overdue for a thorough restructuring of the way we educate scientists. Because higher education in Europe and the United States flourished along with the scientific revolution, its assumptions are largely those of science: that knowledge abstracted and codified into lectures and textbooks will stand for full knowledge (18).

In ex post facto response to the demands of our students (who may be only dimly aware of what is bothering them), we "inject" relevance into our teaching by means of examples that have been wrenched from their organic context and used to exemplify the abstractions that are the real matter of serious courses in science. I have gone so far, in my own teaching, as to sacrifice a few laboratory afternoons for my students to contemplate—without "lab sheets," ill-concealed hints about procedure, or even a demand that they keep and turn in a notebook—the colors, smells, textures, and changes of some substances on which they would do a rigorous and abstractly interpreted experiment the following week. In many instances, students have seen the connection and have become really excited about their dual insights into chemical systems. But even this is only a feeble fluctuation in the normal curriculum. Most of the students who go through it on their way to a degree are, at best, tolerant of my efforts to let them really know something about equilibria in aqueous solutions. At the risk of judging them too harshly, I cannot but feel that, by the time I see them, their natural curiosity about the physical world has been corrupted by too many years of rules, abstractions, and quickie true-false tests. And their fellows, who have awakened to the one-sidedness of the abstract worlds of scholarship in general and of science in particular, and have summarily rejected them, I never see at all.

I might address these remarks primarily to those who teach undergraduates. Yet there is no teacher of science who is not himself a scientist, and science as it is taught is allegedly a representation of science as it is practiced. If the practice of science continues its present one-sided and underdimensioned course, new scientists will be recruited predominately from among those people to whom such a view of the world is most congenial. Yet such people are least fitted, by temperament and training, to hold in mind the complementary truths about nature that our looming tasks will require. Indeed, one may seriously question whether even an underdimensioned science can be maintained as a creative enterprise by scientists recruited from among those of lesser imagination, sympathy, and humanity. Neils Bohr's vision of the unity of human knowledge only echoes, a half-century later, that of Walt Whitman: "I swear the earth shall surely be complete to him/or her who shall be complete. The earth remains jagged and broken to him/or her who remains jagged and broken."

REFERENCES AND NOTES

1. L. WHITE, JR., Science 155, 1203 (1967); L. W. Moncrief, ibid. 170, 508 (1970); N. O. Brown, Life Against Death: The Psychoanalytical Meaning of History (Wesleyan Univ. Press, Middletown, Conn., 1959), chap. 16.
2. T. ROSZAK, The Making of a Counter Culture (Doubleday, Garden City, N.Y., 1969).
3. L. MUMFORD, The Myth of the Machine: The Pentagon of Power (Harcourt Brace Jovanovich, New York, 1970).
4. To some readers, "sensuous" may suggest genital sexuality. Although "unconventional" sexual morality is a feature of the counterculture (as it is of the technological one), I use the word in a more general sense: that is, the response of the whole body, including the senses, to phenomena. Usually, such a response is, of course, not susceptible to quantification. It is also dependent on subjective factors such as mood and attention, but it is undeniably a source of information about the world around us.
5. G. N. LEWIS and M. RANDALL, Thermodynamics and the Free Energy of Chemical Substances (McGraw-Hill, New York, 1923).
6. W. HEISENBERG, "Quantum theory and its interpretation," in Neils Bohr: His Life and Work as Seen by His Friends and Colleagues, S. Rozental, Ed. (Wiley, New York, 1967).
7. N. BOHR, Atomic Physics and Human Knowledge (Wiley, New York, 1958).
8. N. BOHR, in Essays, 1958–1962, on Atomic Physics and Human Knowledge (Wiley, New York, 1963).
9. C. P. SNOW, The Two Cultures and the Scientific Revolution (Cambridge Univ. Press, New York, 1959).
10. J. BRONOWSKI, Science and Human Values (Harper, New York, 1956).
11. E. HOBSBAWN, "Is science evil?," in New York Review of Books, 19 November 1970.
12. A. N. WHITEHEAD, Science and the Modern World (Macmillan, New York, 1925).
13. J. BRUNER, On Knowing: Essays for the Left Hand (Harvard Univ. Press, Cambridge, Mass., 1962); J. Holt, How Children Learn (Pitman, New York, 1967); R. Jones, Ed., Contemporary Educational Psychology: Selected Readings (Harper, New York, 1967).
14. J. WATSON, The Double Helix (Atheneum, New York, 1968).
15. W. HEISENBERG, Philosophic Problems of Nuclear Science (Pantheon, New York, 1952).
16. G. SCHALLER, The Year of the Gorilla (Ballantine, New York, 1965).
17. For a single research paper that nicely combines sensuous and mathemati-

cal descriptions of a phenomenon, see C. W. McCutchen [*Science* 170, 61 (1970)].

18. Of course, we know that that isn't really true; we just act as if it were. And it takes no great perception on my teacher's part to see that most of his class don't really understand what they write back to us on examinations; perhaps that's why we are careful to set such examinations as soon as possible after the material is "learned."

25
EXPLANATION AND PROOF[1]

J. E. R. Staddon

The work and methods of Charles Darwin are yet to have their full impact on psychology. Michael Ghiselin's excellent book is valuable to psychologists because he provides the best extant account of these methods and of the highly sophisticated style of thinking that underlies them. There are two areas where Darwin's work seems to be especially relevant to psychology: the nature of explanation and proof in a historical science, and the role of definitions in the development of a science.

The flavor of Darwin's explanatory method can readily be illustrated by example. Ghiselin begins his account with a description of Darwin's first great synthesis: the theory of coral reefs. The theory deals with the occurrence of three types of coral formation in the Pacific Ocean: fringing reefs, barrier reefs, and coral atolls. The most puzzling of these are the coral atolls, which are composed entirely of coral, often consist of a ring-like formation enclosing a central lagoon, and frequently occur in deep water far from any land mass. Since the coral of which they are composed had been shown not to grow below a certain depth, their origin posed a difficult question. By realizing that these three kinds of formation are all instances of the same process, Darwin was able both to explain atolls and to organize a large number of observations. Ghiselin summarizes his theory as follows: "Fringing reefs occur adjacent to a body of land. Darwin held that they form when coral grows outward from the

1 A review of Michael T. Ghiselin's *The Triumph of the Darwinian Method* (Berkeley, Calif.: University of California Press, 1969).

FROM J. E. R. Staddon, Darwin explained: An object lesson in theory construction, *Contemporary Psychology*, 1971, 16 (11), 689–691. Copyright 1971 by the American Psychological Association. Reprinted by permission.

land, in the direction of the water. Barrier reefs are a kind of submerged coral wall, at some distance from land and separated from the shore by a lagoon channel. They would arise if the land were to sink and the coral on the outer edge of a fringing reef were to grow upward. If, say, a volcanic island were partially to sink, the coral would grow upward at the outer rim of any fringing reef that surrounded it and would have a lagoon channel separating a barrier reef from the shore. Should sinking continue, the island itself would ultimately disappear from view. Yet if the coral continued to grow upward on the barrier reef, the circle of coral would be maintained, and the result would be an atoll." The distinctive thing about this explanation is that it accounts for an observed phenomenon by the opposed action of two independent processes: sinkage of the substrate, on the one hand, opposed by coral growth, on the other. Ghiselen, following D. T. Campbell and Karl Popper, describes this as a selective-retention model. Evolution by means of natural selection is, of course, the most famous example of this kind of theory: 'blind' variation is here opposed by the selective retention of beneficial variations. Ghiselin shows that this approach is characteristic of Darwin and can be seen in most of his theoretical contributions.

A more psychological example is provided by Darwin's work on climbing plants. He attributes the climbing action of vines to the combined action of two factors: a tendency for the growing tip of all plants, but especially climbing plants, to move continuously in a circular fashion (circumnutation), opposed by an encountered obstacle, such as the stem of another plant; the outcome is that the turning, growing tip twines about the obstacle and thus climbs up it. Stimulus-response components, such as phototropism, are easily accommodated within such a system if the speed of movement of the growing plant becomes dependent on factors such as light intensity. The elegant work of Kühn, Fraenkel and Gunn, and others, on orientation in animals provides a modern extension of these ideas, although the relationship between Kühn's concept of kinesis and Darwin's ideas is rarely remarked.

More explicitly psychological, and better known (although still not fully incorporated into the contemporary mainstream of thinking on the subject), is Darwin's analysis of emotional expression in terms of three principles of action. Once again, a phenomenon is interpreted as an interaction between two or more independent processes. However, the clearest example I have found of this kind of thinking in a psychological context is a speculation on the behavior of ants, which Darwin made in a letter to August Forel. The phenomenon in question was the removal by ants (to a surprisingly great distance) of empty cocoons from their nests. Darwin wrote as follows:

The ants carrying the cocoons did not appear to be emigrating. . . . But when I looked closely I found that all the cocoons were empty cases. . . . Now here I think we have one instinct in contest with another and mistaken one.

The first instinct being to carry the empty cocoons out of the nest. . . . And then came the contest with the other very powerful instinct of preserving and carrying their cocoons as long as possible; and this they could not help doing although the cocoons were empty. According as the one or other instinct was the stronger in each individual ant, so did it carry the empty cocoon to a greater or less distance.

If one is not thrown into a fit of the vapors by the term 'instinct,' this account must impress by its subtlety, its probable correctness, and its similarity to contemporary ethological theories (the disinhibition inter- pretation of displacement activities, for example).

The way in which Darwin sought to prove his theories bears little re- semblance to what is often taught as standard scientific method. No crucial experiments, no statistical tests, no quantitative predictions. In- stead his method was to establish the probable truth of a proposition by means of converging, independent lines of evidence, some from his own experiments (carried out to test the hypothesis), some from the observa- tions of others: "The line of argument often pursued throughout my theory is to establish a point as a probability by induction and to apply it as hypotheses to other points and see whether it will solve them." The role of experiment was not—as in the prototypical 'crucial' experiment— to provide the keystone to an arch of deductive reasoning, but simply to generate additional evidence, to find some more pieces of the jigsaw puzzle. Thus, his conjecture concerning coral reefs was supported by distributional evidence—there was evidence for subsidence in just those areas where atolls and barrier reefs are found; by structural evidence— the sides of atolls are very steep and consist of coral and not rock; by evidence for subsidence on the atolls themselves; and by details of the relationships between the topography of reefs and the topography of adjacent land masses. Ghiselin truly remarks that an interlinked argu- ment of this sort compels assent: ". . . those who disagree with the con- clusions do so because they do not understand the argument [p. 158]."

It can easily be seen that the power of Darwin's theories lay not so much in their mathematical, or even logical, precision, or in their con- formation to philosophically derived canons of methodological rigor, but in the wealth of empirical consequences that flowed from them. As Ghiselin puts it (perhaps a little strongly): ". . . the crudest approxima- tion, if it provides hints for the solution of a broad range of problems, has every advantage over the most elegant mathematical law, which asserts nothing of interest [p. 236]."

Darwin's attitude toward the problem of definition was very different from that advocated in most methodological texts in psychology. Far from being careful about definitions, operational or otherwise, ". . . he does not bother to define his terms any more than is necessary to allow his readers to make the distinction he has in mind [p. 201]." It would be wrong to attribute this apparently cavalier attitude either to lack of philosophical sophistication, or to a primitive stage of scientific development. On the contrary, a relative neglect of definitions can easily be justified on logical grounds: (1) grant that the aim of scientific investigation is the discovery of sets of axioms (i.e., theories) that will allow us to deduce as many empirical consequences as possible: (2) and given that in any formal system (such as Euclidean geometry), the definitions follow the axioms, i.e., are simply restatements of the axioms in a way that appeals to common experience: (3) then it follows that terms cannot be defined until the axioms have been discovered. Hence Darwin's reluctance to put much emphasis on definition. Once the theoretical system of which the terms are a part is well understood, of course the definitions become obvious. Thus, it would have been senseless for Newton to have been exact in his use of the term "force" before he discovered the laws of motion; afterwards the proper definition was obvious. The point is that the laws come first, definitions afterwards.

This way of thinking about definition and classification has important implications for taxonomy. As Ghiselin points out, the meaning of the term "species," for example, derives from the mechanism whereby different species came about, which involves genealogy (Darwin's "propinquity of descent"), geographical distribution and isolation, common selection pressures, etc. Morphology, the original criterion for species identification, can be seen as merely a by-product of these forces and, therefore, is not a necessary part of the definition of the term.

The implication of this point of view for psychology is that the prevalent emphasis on operational definition of theoretical concepts is excessive and possibly self-defeating. The objective should be to find the pattern which underlies the empirical observations; once that is found the proper meaning of terms like "learning," "memory," "reinforcement," and so on will presumably be obvious. In the absence of such an understanding, efforts to advance by honing our definitions are mere scholasticism. . . .

26

INDIVIDUAL DIFFERENCES AND THEORY CONSTRUCTION*

BENTON J. UNDERWOOD

MY PROPOSAL is that we should formulate our nomothetic theories in a way that will allow an immediate individual-differences test. I am proposing this because, among other benefits, I believe this approach will make individual differences a crucible in theory construction. The argument I advance is applicable to theory construction in all areas of experimental psychology, but my illustrations come largely from the areas of learning and memory. I feel impelled initially to reconstruct as best I can the reasons that led me to compose an article dealing with theory construction. It has resulted from a professional uneasiness that has grown over the past few years. These pinpricks of uneasiness seemed to say that our profession needed to open a discussion of theory construction in psychology, a discussion led by psychologists, for psychologists. When the uneasy feelings were articulated in this manner, I was able to identify three developments that had been responsible for the pinpricks. And then a fourth development took place which led me to presume I might have something to say that could just possibly initiate the discussion.

The first source of uneasiness was quite an unlikely one, namely, *the undergraduate student.* On occasion, a perceptive one will ask me, "How do you get a theory?" How does one answer this question? I found myself answering with a few pieces of trivia of the kind that any experienced teacher has ready for such moments. My lack of a guiding answer was demonstrated most blatantly when I found myself turning to anecdotes to shunt the question aside. Thus, I would tell the student that one great theoretical insight in the history of science is alleged to have occurred during a bath. So, perhaps, taking a bath would be a way to get a theory. But, of course (I told him), if you really want to develop a majestic theory,

* This article was a Distinguished Scientific Contribution Award address presented at the meeting of the American Psychological Association, New Orleans, August 1974. It was supported by the Psychological Sciences Division, Office of Naval Research under Contract N00014-67-A-0356-0010, Contract Authority Identification NR 154-321. Reproduction in whole or in part is permitted for any purpose of the U.S. Government.

FROM B. J. Underwood, Individual differences as a crucible in theory construction, *American Psychologist,* 1975, 30 (2), 128–134. Copyright 1975 by the American Psychological Association. Reprinted by permission.

the only avenue open is to learn to play the violin and go to Princeton. The question remained unanswered, but I did set about to see if I could put something down on paper of a systematic nature that might be given to a student who would be so brazen as to ask such a question. To some extent, what I say here was prepared for such a student.

The second stimulus I can identify as being involved in my uneasiness relates to developments in the area of memory, including the offshoot now called information processing. In particular, I refer to *structural model building*. Certainly, in the last dozen years, the favorite after-class occupation of many college professors has been that of building models of memory. Just what is responsible for this furious activity is not entirely apparent to me. One might guess that the flow diagram presented by our English colleague, Donald Broadbent, in his 1958 book *Perception and Communication* was involved, but I choose not to saddle him with this reverse lend-lease if he doesn't want to take the responsibility for it. The fact remains that we have models running out of our ears, and there seems to be no surcease.

This may be quite healthy; at least lots of people are getting skilled in drawing boxes, arrows, and circular nodes. But all of these models cannot be right, or even useful or believable, and evaluation seems to be rather low on the priority list. It seems to be easier to formulate a new model than to test an old one, and one never gets pinned down that way. I am being unfair, of course, and this is particularly troublesome because the model builders are very friendly people; many are my friends. All I ask of the builders is please, sooner or later, come up for breath and see what you have wrought. Is this really the way we want theory development to occur?

A third stimulus was a book published in 1967 called *Learning and Individual Differences*. It represents the thinking of a number of investigators brought together by Robert Gagné for a conference at the University of Pittsburgh. Reading this book gave me a small intellectual abrasion that has continued to fester over the years. I was unable to get rid of it by saying to myself that the problem of individual differences is someone else's responsibility. I finally came to accept the notion that individual differences ought to be considered central in theory construction, not peripheral. How can we make individual differences of central focus in our theories? This volume contains ideas, and I suspect that if one were to juxtapose what was said at that conference with some of my later comments, the similarity would be found to be more than coincidental.

And finally, certain events which occurred in our laboratory served as the catalyst for the final step, namely, that of *trying to bring individual differences into the mainstream of theory construction*. Some background is necessary. In 1966 an article was published (Ekstrand, Wallace, & Underwood) which proposed that verbal-discrimination learning (which is a special kind of a recognition task) is mediated by the subject discriminating the apparent frequency differences between the right and wrong words in each pair. The idea was subsequently extended to the more classical recognition procedures. The theory, commonly called *frequency theory*, has had some success in predicting the consequences of manipulating a number of independent variables. A severe critic might argue about the use of the word "success," but that is unimportant for the present paper. But it is important to understand the basic nature of the theory.

As I understand the strict use of the term *model*, it means that a set of empirical relationships developed in one area of discourse is applied to another area of research as a possible explanatory system. As an extreme case, if the laws and relationships among the functions of the organs of the digestive system were applied to memory as an explanatory system, this would be an illustration of the true meaning of the word *model*. This transfer from one area to another need not be across disciplines; it can be within a discipline. If the laws of learning are used to try to account for bizarre behaviors, it would be a form of modeling. Frequency theory, in the language of modeling, is a within-discipline model of an unusual kind. The theory asserts that the laws and relationships that hold for frequency discrimination (as viewed, perhaps, in the classical psychophysical sense) will determine the performance in the usual recognition-memory study. The unusual nature of the theory lies in the fact that when the theory was formulated there wasn't a body of laws and relationships concerning frequency discriminations. It has been necessary, therefore, to develop both areas simultaneously. Nevertheless, the theory is quite explicit on the central point; the facts of frequency discrimination must hold for the recognition situation or the theory is in trouble.

The theory as stated is a nomothetic theory, since the thinking was geared entirely to mean performances and mean frequency discriminations. This form of thinking can be blinding. But finally (and there were a number of developments that were responsible but that will not be set down here) the time came when a now obvious implication forced itself into our thinking. The whole fabric of the theory, quite by accident, rests on a postulate that is in fact an individual-differences postulate. However we might have stirred uncomfortably when we realized this and however we might have tried to find some escape, the implication would not go away. A subject who demonstrated fine or precise frequency discriminations must show good recognition memory; a subject who demonstrated poor or imprecise frequency discriminations must show poor recognition memory. What a devastating relationship to contemplate so late in the development of the theory, particularly so since we knew that both frequency discriminations and recognition memory yielded quite reliable scores. In this case, when the belated tests were made, the outcomes showed the prerequisite relationships. But suppose this had not been the outcome? Suppose we had found a zero correlation between measures of frequency discrimination and measures of recognition memory? The theory would simply have to be dropped. That we had demonstrated the necessary relationships on the fiftieth study, was, perhaps, a stroke of luck. The point is that, had we been so wise as to perceive it, the fiftieth study should have been the first study. If the data from this first study did not approve of the individual-differences relationship inherent in the theory, there would have been no theory, no 50 studies.

Let me now state the generalized case. If we include in our nomothetic theories a process or mechanism that can be measured reliably outside of the situation for which it is serving its theoretical purpose, we have an immediate test of the validity of the theoretical formulation, at least a test of this aspect of the formulation. The assumed theoretical process will necessarily have a tie with performance which reflects (in theory) the magnitude of the process. Individuals will vary in the amount of this characteristic or skill they "possess." A prediction concerning differences in the performance of the individuals must follow. A test of this prediction can yield two outcomes. If the correlation is substantial, the theory has a go-ahead signal, that and no more; the usual positive correlations across subjects on various skills and aptitudes allow no conclusion concerning the validity of the theory per se. If the relationship between the individual-differences measurements and the performance is essentially zero, there is no alternative but to drop the line of theoretical thinking. It is this form of reasoning that has led to the title of this article; individual differences may indeed be used as a crucible in nomothetic theory construction. The approach, I believe, provides a critical test of theories as they are being born; if they fail to pass the test, they should neither see the light of day nor the pages of the *Psychological Review*.

I now must turn to a broader perspective of theory construction and show how the individual-differences approach fits into this perspective. In effect, I am going to try to give the student an answer to his inquiry, albeit an indirect and an incomplete one. What I want to tell the student is that there seems to be a common way in which theoretical thinking gets started, and then I will provide him with some guidelines with which he should be concerned if he wants his theory to be disciplined in the sense that it can be discredited as well as affirmed.

A behavioral phenomenon is defined by the relationship between some independent variable and measured behavior. As research develops, certain key phenomena are identified and a body of empirical knowledge builds up around them. Thus, we have such key phenomena as extinction, retroactive inhibition, altruism, motivation, space perception, and so on. Now, even in the definition of such phenomena we may tend to allow an internalization of a process. It is not a great leap to recognize that the independent variable produces an influence only because it did something to the "workings" of the subject. When, over successive trials, we observe an increase in the number of correct responses given by a subject, we say that learning has occurred, although learning is neither the number of correct responses nor the trials. Learning is a term we use to represent the relationship between the two, and frequently also to represent the implicit belief that something has "gone on" in the subject. It is almost impossible to think of a term such as *motivation* without thinking of it at the same time as being changes in the organism.

The above illustrations suggest that it is difficult to avoid thinking about intervening processes even when thinking about the definition of so-called empirical phenomena. Theoretical efforts merely make the thinking about intervening processes more formal and more deliberate. The basis of theorizing is that of proposing intervening processes (some prefer the term *mechanisms*) that will mediate the observed empirical relationships between various independent variables and the key phenomenon of interest. I will not entertain the question of whether we should or should not be theorizing; not many can avoid it. But it is reasonable to ask what we propose to achieve by a theory. From one point of view, theorizing is simply one of the later steps along the chain of steps known as data reduction. We try to comprehend the scores of 100 subjects by getting a statistical description of the scores. We try to comprehend the scores of five groups given different levels of an independent variable by plotting the mean scores above the five levels of the variable. We try to summarize a number of different experiments in any area by trying to extract the commonalities and stating the empirical generalizations. We try, by theorizing, to state basic processes that could underlie the behavior and produce the several laws within the area of interest. Theorizing is always reductive in the sense that we try to propose processes more elementary (but more general) or basic than the phenomena for which we are trying to account. In all of the steps of data reduction, including theoretical speculation, we are trying to produce the ultimate in economy of thought.

Now (still speaking to the student), what guidelines can be used in proposing the intervening process? There are many obvious ones, such as explicitness and testability, but these are generally necessary consequences of others. I propose three guidelines.

The first guideline is a compound one: The theory must assume at least two intervening processes, and these processes must interact in some way to relate the independent variables to the dependent variable. This statement needs to be unpacked. Why must we have two processes? A single-process theory must always be isomorphic to empirical relationships. If I assume that interference as a theoretical process is responsible for forgetting, assuming that and no more, the empirical relationships give the complete story, since interference must vary in magnitude as forgetting varies in magnitude. As a theoretical concept, it is superfluous and has no predictive power. It can also be seen that if two intervening processes are assumed, but which vary in magnitude in exactly the same way for all independent variables, it reduces essentially to a single-process theory.

The moment we propose two intervening processes that, for at least one independent variable, have different functions and hence interact, we begin to get predictive power. This guideline seems to have been followed for many years, as witness the many different theoretical approaches including an excitatory and an inhibitory process (by whatever names) which are assigned differential functions for certain independent variables. The interaction can be "inserted" at two different points. It is probably most common to provide the interaction by having different functional relationships between the two assumed processes and the independent variables. But it would be quite possible to have the theoretical relationships be the same for the independent variable but differ with regard to their influence on the dependent variable.

I emphasize the necessity of the interaction between the intervening processes for at least one independent variable because I do not believe it has been clearly enunciated in recent years. I emphasize it also for quite a different reason. Those of us who teach undergraduates know that teaching them how to see, verbalize, and become generally facile in thinking about empirical interactions in data is adventurous, to say the least. But it seems necessary for them to develop this skill if we want them also to grasp the nature of predictive theory.

In the statement of this guideline it was indicated that there must be at least two intervening processes. The complexity of a theory increases directly as the number of postulated processes increase. Obviously we try to keep the number of processes to a minimum, but if it becomes necessary to add, we must add. In so doing we recognize that a problem in understanding will necessarily arise. Some idea of the magnitude of the problem of understanding can be obtained by trying to comprehend, for example, an empirical interaction among four variables. The complexity may be necessary and, if it is necessary, I believe we will find it imperative to represent the theoretical processes in strict mathematical terms so that the derivations can be unambiguous.

A second guideline I would suggest to my student is implicit in a number of previous statements. It is that any assumed process must be tied to at least one independent variable. I would point out to the student that not all would agree with this guideline, but also I would feel impelled to tell him that if he doesn't abide by this guideline he is likely to find himself in a pack of trouble. Nothing is more conducive to the infection of a theory by ploglies and homunculi than a free-floating intervening process. I read or heard (from a source that I have not been able to identify) that the idea that an intervening process must be tied to at least one independent variable is no longer considered essential and should be abandoned as an unnecessary stricture on the imagination needed for theorizing. It seems to me that it doesn't take much imagination to realize that to abandon this rule is to invite chaos.

The third guideline is concerned with the nature of the intervening processes to be postulated. I think we must allow great latitude, perhaps along several different dimensions, in proposed intervening processes. At one extreme, they may be strictly abstract mathematical propositions that disclaim any correspondence or relationship to a psychological process with which we might identify intuitively. Although we might not be able to resonate personally to such abstract, impalpable processes, they do have the very distinct advantage of avoiding misinterpretations that may occur when common psychological terms are used for identifying the processes. In any event, some of my subsequent comments cannot, it will be seen, be germane to the completely abstract intervening process.

At the other extreme, we may assume an intervening process that is more or less given by an empirical relationship in another area of psychological inquiry. Earlier I described the basic idea of frequency theory; it is a good illustration of this low-level form of theorizing. In between the two extremes there are various steps, and in fact many theories represent a mixed bag with regard to placement along the dimension of abstractness.

Now obviously, under this guideline, I have one specific proposal in mind, namely, that in choosing theoretical processes if at all possible choose at least one which has some possibility of yielding an individual-differences interpretation, as has been described. The illustration I gave from frequency theory may seem obvious and atypical. In fact, however, after I worked on the matter with other theoretical notions, I began to form the opinion that the individual-differences approach could in principle be implemented with any but the more abstract propositions. Let me give three illustrations.

If a free-recall list includes words occurring more than once, the recall of the words given spaced repetition will be superior to those given massed repetitions. Our theoretical thinking emphasized a reduced processing of the items when they were massed. Some indirect tests showed this to have some support. In thinking about this theory in light of the guideline under discussion, it seemed beyond doubt that subjects must differ in their propensity to attenuate processing. Now, if we could measure this tendency independently, and if it is a reliable individual-differences variable, we could make a test to tell us whether the theory should be dropped or whether we had a license to continue its development. Such a test now seems possible, and we will undertake it in the fall. My only regret is that we did not formulate this approach several years ago when the theory first came into being.

Assume that a theory is proposed for serial learning which includes a process identified as generalization along a spatial dimension. We have the techniques for measuring generalization outside the serial learning task. The role that generalization is assigned in serial learning must surely be in some way predictably different for subjects having different generalization gradients.

My skimming of abstracts has suggested that some investigators studying the skills involved very early in the process of learning to read are suggesting that the subject's ability to develop an internal schemata of each of the letters is important. The schemata will allow a "match" even though some distortion is present in the visually presented letters. At the same time, the schemata should not be too broad or it will accept wrong letters as a match. Would it be possible to get an independent measure of the characteristics of the schemata without visual inputs of letters? Adults can identify very accurately individual letters when "printed" on the skin of the back with the index finger (wielded by another person, of course). Would this be useful for measuring schemata in pure form in children? And, then, would this predict errors in identification of visually presented letters?

These three illustrations are sufficient to see the direction I think this approach might take. By this time, objections may be cropping up. I hope these can be anticipated in the three possible objections I will now discuss. Two of the objections can be handled quite satisfactorily, I believe; one is a little more difficult. We will start with the difficult one.

I used frequency theory to illustrate a basic application of the individual-differences approach. The theory, in addition to assuming that a frequency discrimination is critical, also assumes that the subject applies a rule to cover all pairs in a verbal-discrimination task, namely, the rule to choose the word with the highest apparent frequency in each pair. Suppose that frequency discrimination and the rapidity of rule discovery are correlated. That subjects with good frequency discrimination are also good verbal-discrimination learners might then be due to the fact that they learn rules quickly and that some rule other than the frequency rule is mediating the performance. In this particular case, there are several auxiliary facts (which will not be detailed here) that rule out this possibility, but it may not be possible to do this in other situations. The generalized issue concerns the correlative relationship between the performance produced by the intervening process being evaluated as an individual-differences variable, and the performance produced by other processes in the theory. The solution is to make sure that only the symptoms of the individual-differences variable are being measured in the case in which the other processes may also be operating to influence performance. If this cannot be done it may produce a positive conclusion concerning the individual-differences variable when in fact the evidence producing the positive conclusion results from a correlation with the consequences of the other theoretical process. To avoid this, we must in some way neutralize the effects of the other variable. Experimental ingenuity should find a way to accomplish this. But even if a solution is not found, it should be clear that we are no worse off than we are at present when this approach is not used. However, the most important function of the individual-differences approach is that of nipping an inappropriate theoretical notion in the bud, and this is indicated when a zero correlation is found. So, the first objection is by no means a lethal one.

The second objection is quite a different one. I think it a certainty that the individual-differences approach described here will be most applicable when the process used theoretically has more or less empirical status in another area of research within psychology. What constitutes another or different area? Behavior is behavior, some might say. I can illustrate the question in as stark a manner as possible. Suppose there is an empirical relationship derived from the learning of two-syllable words. Now, we say, we are going to use this relationship theoretically as a part of a theoretical system to explain the learning of three-syllable words. We go through the individual-difference routine and find a high positive correlation that, according to the argument which has been advanced, gives us license to proceed with the development of the theory. There isn't a good name for such thinking; around our laboratory we speak of this by the rather crude but descriptive word *incest*. We must be sure that when we use the approach I am advocating we are dealing with no more than kissin' cousins. I suppose that good judgment must be imposed, or that the union is acceptable when it is not intuitively obvious that they should be related. And further, we are always transferring what appears to be a simple process for use as a theoretical concept (along with the use of at least one other) in attempting to account for performance on a more complex task than the one used to measure the simple process directly.

A third objection that may be raised is not directed necessarily toward the individual-differences approach but toward the use of a relationship discovered in one area as an explanatory concept in another. It might be insisted that this approach doesn't explain anything. As an illustration: if frequency discrimination can be used to account for recognition memory, it is fine and good, but what has been gained? It merely means that to understand recognition memory, we must understand the processes involved in frequency discriminations. This objection is without validity and can be raised about any theoretical approach using behavioral constructs (as opposed to the use of physiological constructs). The whole idea behind behavioral theory is to reduce the number of independent processes to a minimum; to find that performance on two apparently diverse tasks is mediated at least in part by a single, more elementary, process is a step toward this long-range goal.

There is one further point that should be made, relative to the third guideline, the discussion of which has largely consisted of trumpets being blown in support of the individual-differences approach. There is nothing in this approach that prevents the use of mathematical expressions for the theoretical processes. Indeed, they should be used by all who have the skills and the wills. All that is being proposed is that when possible, one of the theoretical processes be identified in such a way that it is at least remotely feasible that it could be measured as an individual-differences variable.

It should be apparent that the more traditional attempts to relate nomothetic theories to individual differences by using standardized tests, for example, paper-and-pencil tests, are quite in line with the approach proposed here. Thus, tests of manifest anxiety, introversion-extroversion, ego strength, and so on, have been used to identify individual differences that are in turn said to be identifiable with assumed processes in nomothetic theories. If there are differences in the approaches, they lie in the indirectness of the measurements and the types of conclusions drawn when the theoretical tests are made. A positive correlation is to be responded to in the way discussed earlier. A zero correlation, however, is frequently not used in a critical, decisive manner. The investigator far too frequently puts the blame on the paper-and-pencil test for not measuring what it is said to measure, rather than putting the blame on the assumed theoretical relationship. Under these circumstances, the individual-differences variable is not a crucible in theory construction. Rather, it is an interesting adjunct of theoretical development.

As a final point, I would like to suggest an implication of the approach advocated here for the understanding of individual differences in general. As many have pointed out in the past, we cannot deal constructively with individual differences when we identify the important variables as age, sex, grade, IQ, social status, and so on. The critical variables are process variables. The approach proposed here, the approach which makes individual-differences variables crucibles in theory construction, will identify the process variables as a fallout from nomothetic theory construction if, of course, the nomothetic theories are dealing with fundamental processes of behavior.

Now that the article is completed, I find that I have exorcised the uneasy feelings that led to it. I had not hoped merely for therapy, but rather for a discussion of theory construction in the coming years. But even if this discussion does not ensue, you may be sure that the next student who asks me that question is likely to be severely imprinted.

REFERENCES

BROADBENT, D. E. *Perception and communication.* New York: Pergamon Press, 1958.

EKSTRAND, B. R., WALLACE, W. P., & UNDERWOOD, B. J. A frequency theory of verbal-discrimination learning. *Psychological Review*, 1966, *73*, 566–578.

GAGNÉ, R. M. (Ed.). *Learning and individual differences*. Columbus, Ohio: Charles E. Merrill, 1967.

27

THE RETURN TO ESSENTIALS

MARVIN D. DUNNETTE

The Questions We Ask

THERE are many titles that might be appropriate for this last game that I shall discuss. One might be, "Who's on First?"—or better yet, "What Game Are We In?"—or a rather common version in these days of large Federal support for research, "While You're Up, Get Me a Grant." My major point here is quite simply that the other games we play, the pets we keep, our delusions, our secrets, and the Great Name Game interact to cause us to lose sight of the essence of the problems that need to be solved and the questions that need answers. The questions that get asked are dictated—all too often—by investigators' pet theories or methods, or by the need to gain "visibility" among one's colleagues. One of my respondents—a younger but undoubtedly wiser head than I—summed it up nicely.[1] He said:

Psychologists seem to be afraid to ask really important questions. The whole Zeitgeist seems to encourage research efforts that earn big grants, crank out publications frequently and regularly, self-perpetuate themselves, don't entail much difficulty in getting subjects, don't require the researchers to move from behind their desks or out of their laboratories except to accept speaking engagements, and serve to protect the scientist from all the forces that can knock him out of the secure "visible circle."

Another of my respondents, a verbal behavior researcher, illustrated the dilemma by mentioning a fellow researcher who phrased his research question as: "How do the principles of classical and instrumental conditioning explain the learning of language?" This sort of question is clearly

[1] J. P. Campbell, personal communications, 1965.

FROM M. D. Dunnette, Fads, fashions, and folderol in psychology, *American Psychologist*, 1966, *21* (4), 343–352. Copyright 1966 by the American Psychological Association. Reprinted by permission.

illustrative of the tendency to defer too readily to existing popular points of view and to allow them to distort the direction of research activities. It would be better simply to ask "What is learned?" rather than making the premature assumptions that (a) language is learned in the sense that the term *learning* is usually used or (b) *all* learning is of only two types.

An even more serious and, unfortunately, probably more common form of the question-asking game is the game of "Ha! Sure Slipped That One Past You, Didn't I?" Here, the investigator shrewdly fails to state the question he is trying to answer, gathers data to provide answers to simpler questions, and then behaves as if his research has been relevant to other unstated but more important and more interesting problems. The vast majority of studies devoted to measuring employee attitudes have committed this error. It is no trick to develop questionnaires to gather systematically the opinions of workers about their jobs. It is quite something else, however, suddenly to begin talking about measures of employee *motivation* and to suggest that the employee responses have direct relevance to what they may actually do on the job. The literature on response set and response style is another clear case of new questions being designed to fit existing answers. Showing high correlations between scores on empirically developed scoring keys and the numbers of items keyed *True* or some other item index should not be taken as having any bearing on the empirical validities of these keys. Yet for over a decade, our literature has been burdened with all sorts of set and style studies characterized by seemingly endless factor analyses and silly arguments between persons committed to acquiescence and those committed to social desirability.

Thus, we all are far too eager to ask such questions as: "What problems can be *easily* answered?" "What else can I do with my test?" "What problems or questions does my theory lead to?" "What aspects of behavior can I study with my computer or with my apparatus?" or "What problems can I find that I can fit this method to?"

Certainly, as psychologists—as scientists presumably interested in the subject matter of human behavior—we should be able to do better than this!

The Causes

You may have inferred by now that I feel some sense of pessimism about the current state of psychology. Based on what you have heard so far, such an inference is probably appropriate. I *do* believe that the games I have described offer little that can be beneficial for psychology in the long run. The behaviors underlying the games represent enormous and essentially wasteful expenditures of our own research energy.

Even so, my mood is not basically pessimistic. In fact, we should be able to emerge from this soul searching with a constructive sense of discontent rather than one of destructive despair. The description of our condition carries with it a number of implications for corrective action. Moreover, we may infer from the condition some possible causes, and listing them should also suggest possible correctives.

To this end, let me consider briefly what I believe to be the major causes of psychology's fads, fashions, and folderol.

The most important, I believe, is related quite directly to the relative insecurity of being a scientist, a problem that is particularly acute in psychology where we must cope with such complex phenomena as those involved in the study of human behavior. The scientist's stance includes the constant need to doubt his own work. Moreover, the long-range significance of his work cannot often be forecast, and rarely can the scientist —least of all, perhaps, the psychologist—preplan his inspirations and his ideas. It is little wonder, then, that many seek, through their theories, methodologies, or other of the games we have discussed, to organize, systematize, and regularize their creative output. When viewed against the backdrop of publication pressures prevailing in academia, the lure of large-scale support from Federal agencies, and the presumed necessity to become "visible" among one's colleagues, the insecurities of undertaking research on important questions in possibly untapped and unfamiliar areas become even more apparent. Stern (1964) has recently very effectively stated the case for the desirability of moving from research into equally fulfilling careers of teaching and administration. But we cannot forget that the value system of science places research and publication at the peak, and it should, therefore, be no surprise that the less able researchers in psychology—learning early that no great breakthrough is in the offing—simply seek to eat their cake and have it too, by playing the games and the song and dance of scientific research, usually convincing even themselves that the games are "for real" and that their activities really "make a difference."

The perpetuation of this state of affairs is related to our present system of graduate education. Many psychology graduate students today find themselves under the tutelage of a faculty member who has bought the system wholeheartedly. Such students live for a period of from 3 to 8 years in an environment that enforces and reinforces the learning of a particular approach, a narrow point of view or a set of pet methodologies which come to define for them the things they will pursue as psychologists.

The Remedy

But here I am—sounding pessimistic and noxious again, and getting farther out on the limb than I really want to be.

In order to convince you of my good intentions and my hope for the future, I had better get on with some constructive suggestions. My suggested remedy—if it can be called that, for indeed it may be more painful than the disease—can be summarized in five imperative statements:

1. Give up constraining commitments to theories, methods, and apparatus!
2. Adopt methods of multiple working hypotheses!
3. Put more eclecticism into graduate education!
4. Press for new values and less *pretense* in the academic environments of our universities!
5. Get to the editors of our psychological journals!

Let me elaborate briefly on each of these recommendations.

First, I advocate a more careful and studied choice of research questions. As should be apparent, I believe research energy should be directed toward questions that contain as few as possible of any prior unproven assumptions about the nature of man. We must be constantly alert to the narrowing of research perspectives due to prior theoretical or methodological commitments. I am calling for less premature theorizing—particularly that which leads to vaguely stated "wide-band" theories that are often essentially incapable of disproof.

I am not advocating the abandonment of deduction in psychology; in fact, psychology needs stronger and more specific deductions rather than the weak and fuzzy ones so typical of so many current theories. What I am advocating is the more systematic study of lawful relationships *before* interpretations are attempted. When explanation *is* attempted, the data should be sufficient to allow hypotheses to be stated with the clarity and precision to render them directly capable of disproof. As the philosopher Karl Popper has said, there is no such thing as proof in science; science advances only by disproofs.

This leads directly to my second recommendation which is to state and systematically test multiple hypotheses. Platt recently advocated this approach which he calls *Strong Inference* (Platt, 1965). The approach entails devising multiple hypotheses to explain observed phenomena, devising crucial experiments each of which may exclude or disprove one or more of the hypotheses, and continuing with the retained hypotheses to develop further subtests or sequential hypotheses to refine the possibilities that remain. This process does not seem new; in fact it is not. It simply entails developing ideas or leads, stating alternative possibilities, testing their plausibility, and proceeding to develop predictive and explanatory evidence concerning the phenomena under investigation. One might say that the research emphasis is one of "studying hypotheses" as opposed to "substantiating theories." The difference seems slight, but it is really quite important. However, in psychology, the approach is little used, for, as we have said, the commitments are more often to *a* theory than to the process of *finding out*.

The method of multiple hypotheses takes on greatly added power when combined with greater care in the analysis and reporting of research results. Instead of serving as the sole statistical test of hypotheses, the statistical null hypothesis should always be supplemented by estimates of strength of association. The psychologist owes it to himself to determine not only whether an association exists between two variables—an association which may often be so small as to be trivial—but also to determine the probable magnitude of the association. As Hays (1964) has suggested, if psychologists are content to adopt conventions (such as .05 or .01) for deciding on statistical significance, they should also adopt conventions concerning the strength of association which may be sufficiently large to regard as worthy of further investigation. Obviously, such conventions cannot be the same for all areas and for all research questions, but it should be clear that an emphasis on magnitude estimation will demand that researchers give much more careful thought than they now do to defining ahead of time the actual magnitudes that will be regarded as possessing either theoretical or practical consequence.

By now, it is apparent why my fifth recommendation has to do with our journals. It will require a new kind of surveillance from both the editors and their consultants if we are to implement the greater care in research conception and in data analysis and reporting that I am advocating. When and if null-hypothesis testing is accorded a lower position in the status hierarchy and comes to be supplemented by emphases on Strong Inference and magnitude estimation, I would predict that the bulk of published material will, for a time, greatly diminish. That which does appear, however, will be guaranteed to be of considerably greater consequence for furthering our understanding of behavior.

One of the possible loopholes in the method of Strong Inference, it should be clear, is the great difficulty of designing and carrying out crucial experiments. Recently Hafner and Presswood (1965) described how faulty experiments had led physicists astray for several decades as they sought to explain the phenomenon of beta decay. We must broaden our conception of multiple hypotheses to include as one quite plausible hypothesis the possibility of poorly conceived or poorly conducted experiments. This, of course, simply speaks to the need for more replication in psychology of crucial experiments, a practice which undoubtedly would become more widespread if psychologists possessed fewer of their own theoretical pets and stronger motivation to examine systematically whole sets of contending hypotheses and alternative explanations.

My third and fourth recommendations need not be elaborated extensively. Both are intended to foster less pretense in the conduct of psychological research by enabling those scholars who may be ill fitted for the research enterprise to gain rewards in other endeavors. The change in the academic atmosphere would need to take the form of according more status to good teaching and to good administration. Perhaps this change would be most rapidly fostered if the scientific games I have described would be more readily recognized for what they are and appropriately devalued in the scheme of things within academia.

Obviously, greater eclecticism in graduate education is crucial to the successful outcome of my other suggestions. It is difficult to know how this can be implemented. But, at least, the goals seem clear. We desire to teach the core of psychology's knowledge and methods, its subject matter and its questions, the statistical methods and their appropriate applications—but most of all, through selection or training or both, we should seek to turn out persons with intense curiosity about the vast array of psychological questions and problems occurring everywhere in the world around us, with a willingness to ask *open* questions unhampered by the prior constraints of a particular point of view or method. Let us hope that graduate education, in the years ahead, will become more eclectic and that even the Great Men in our field may adopt a sense of humility when transmitting knowledge to the fledglings of our science.

The Outcome: Utopia

How do I envision the eventual outcome if all these recommendations were to come to pass? What would the psychologizing of the future look like and what would psychologists be up to?

Chief among the outcomes, I expect, would be a marked lessening of tensions and disputes among the Great Men of our field. I would hope that we might once again witness the emergence of an honest community of scholars all engaged in the zestful enterprise of trying to describe, understand, predict, and control human behavior.

Certainly our journals would be more meaty and less burdensome. There would be more honesty in publishing the fruits of one's labors. Negative results—the disproof of theoretical formulations and the casting aside of working hypotheses—would be a more important part of the journals' contents. In consequence, the journals would contribute more meaningfully to the broad effort to achieve understanding, and we should expect to witness a sharp decline in the number of disconnected little studies bearing little or no relation to each other.

Moreover, I expect that many present schisms in psychology would be welded. The academic-professional bipolarity described by Tryon (1963) would be lessened, for the advantages to both of close assocation between basic researchers and those practicing the art of psychology should become more apparent. The researchers would thereby establish and maintain contact with the real world and real problems of human behavior, and the professional practitioners would be more fully alert to the need for assessing their methods by generating and testing alternate deductions and hypotheses growing out of them.

Thus, in the long run we might hope for fewer disputes, a spirit of more open cooperation, greater innovation in the generation and testing of working hypotheses, greater care and precision in the development of theoretical formulations, and increased rigor in specifying the magnitude of outcome such that they have both practical and theoretical importance. Does this sound like Utopia? Indeed it does. But is it too much to expect of a science now well into its second 100 years? I think not. Let us get on then with the process of change and of reconsolidation.

REFERENCES

ASTIN, A. W. The functional autonomy of psychotherapy. *American Psychologist*, 1961, **16**, 75–78.

BERNE, E. *Games people play*. New York: Grove Press, 1964.

BINDER, A. Further considerations on testing the null hypothesis and the strategy and tactics of investigating theoretical models. *Psychological Review*, 1963, **70**, 107–115.

BRODY, N. Anxiety and the variability of word associates. *Journal of Abnormal and Social Psychology*, 1964, **68**, 331–334.

CHAMBERLIN, T. C. The method of multiple working hypotheses. *Science*, 1965, **148**, 754–759.

CHAPANIS, N., & CHAPANIS, A. Cognitive dissonance: Five years later. *Psychological Bulletin*, 1964, **61**, 1–22.

CRONBACH, L. J. The two disciplines of scientific psychology. *American Psychologist*, 1957, **12**, 671–684.

FEIGEL, H. Philosophical embarrassments of psychology. *Psychologishe Beitrage*, 1962, **6**, 340–364.

FRIEDLANDER, F. Type I and Type II bias. *American Psychologist*, 1964, **19**, 198–199.

GANZER, V. J., & SARASON, I. G. Interrelationhsips among hostility, experimental conditions, and verbal behavior. *Journal of Abnormal and Social Psychology*, 1964, **68**, 79–84.

GRANT, D. A. Testing the null hypothesis and the strategy and tactics of investigating theoretical models. *Psychological Review*, 1962, **69**, 54–61.

GUILFORD, J. P. Psychological measurement a hundred and twenty-five years later. Invited address presented at American Psychological Association, Chicago, September 1960.

HAFNER, E. M., & PRESSWOOD, S. Strong inference and weak interactions. *Science*, 1965, **149**, 503–510.

HAYS, W. L. *Statistics for psychologists*. New York: Holt, Rinehart & Winston, 1964.

HERZBERG, F., MAUSNER, B., & SNYDERMAN, B. *The motivation to work*. New York: Wiley, 1959.

MADDEN, J. M., & BOURDON, R. D. Effects of variations in rating scale format on judgment. *Journal of Applied Psychology*, 1964, **48**, 147–151.

MAIER, N. R. F. Maier's law. *American Psychologist*, 1960, **15**, 208–212.

McNEMAR, Q. Lost our intelligence? Why? *American Psychologist*, 1964, **19**, 871–882.

MEDNICK, M., MEDNICK, S. A., & JUNG, C. C. Continual association as a function of level of creativity and type of verbal stimulus. *Journal of Abnormal and Social Psychology*, 1964, **69**, 511–515.

MEEHL, P. E., & HATHAWAY, S. R. The K factor as a suppressor variable in the MMPI. *Journal of Applied Psychology*, 1946, **30**, 525–564.

NUNNALLY, J. The place of statistics in psychology. *Educational and Psychological Measurement*, 1960, **20**, 641–650.

PLATT, J. R. Strong inference. *Science*, 1964, **146**, 347–352.

ROZEBOOM, W. W. The fallacy of the null-hypothesis significance test. *Psychological Bulletin*, 1960, **57**, 416–428.

SOMMER, R. On writing little papers. *American Psychologist*, 1959, **14**, 235–237.

STERN, C. Thoughts on research. *Science*, 1964, **148**, 772–773.

TRYON, R. C., Psychology in flux: The academic-professional bipolarity. *American Psychologist*, 1963, **18**, 134–143.

WOLINS, L. Responsibility for raw data. *American Psychologist*, 1962, **17**, 657–658.

28

THE PROBLEM OF INTERCOMMUNICATION*

FELIX E. GOODSON

THE year 1879, only twenty years following the publication of Charles Darwin's great book, is the date generally accepted by most psychologists as natal for their discipline. On that date William Wundt established our first formal laboratory at Leipzig and with due ceremony cut the umbilical cord, freeing the babe from its mother Philosophy. Psychology has surely prospered but one may wonder if the parental separation has been as complete as initially supposed. We believe that one of the oldest and muddiest issues of philosophy, the problem of the nature of man's reality, still confounds our view of both our subject matter and our conceptual systems. This issue and its effects upon certain assumptions foundational to theory development will be explored in this paper. It will be suggested that many of our most scholarly and productive thinkers have, knowingly or not, fallen victim to one or the other

---

* Written for this volume.

extremes of an ancient dilemma, subjective idealism or naive realism. The manner in which these positions have intruded into our discipline, particularly into considerations of methodology and theory development, will be investigated. An effort will then be made to offer a resolution of some of the difficulties these positions bring with them by positing a view of scientific reality we believe to be implicit in evolutionary theory.

Subjective Idealism and Its Repercussions

Bishop Berkeley (1709), as every student of philosophy knows, gave the most widely disseminated version of subjective idealism. In essence Berkeley denied the existence of physical matter and posited mind as the immediate reality of all human beings. How can we know there is something out there more than the ways we have of knowing? We cannot, affirmed Berkeley. Because we can only know through experience, and experience is mental, then everything is mental. This remarkable, if extreme, position is apparently incapable of disproof. It is typically rejected in terms of the implications, that is, that it leads to solipsism, the view that each individual creates his own reality and in turn is encapsulated within it. In our view, it is this very solipsism that contaminates both the arguments and conclusions of some of our most articulate psychologists. It comes to us not from Berkeley but from Hume (1739) both directly and by way of his influence on Mach and Bridgman.

Boring (1950) maintained that to Mach "the stick in the water is bent and that if there be any illusion it is that the stick is still straight." In his great book *The Analysis of Sensation*, Mach (1914) defined his real world, as he lay on his sofa, as "parts of the room, framed above by an eye-brow and below by a mustache." Thus for him, reality is restricted to the immediate perception, uncorrupted by inferences from past experience or assumptions of a world existing apart from the experiencer. A particular science could have remarkably clear constructs in such a truncated world, each unimpeachably defined by Mach pointing to some item populating his room; but it would be a science for Mach only, and each time he looked at his room he would have to develop a new set of constructs that would have reference only in its particular slice of Mach's experience.

Bridgman (1936), the operationist, fell victim to this same kind of phenomenalistic encapsulation. "In the last analysis science is only my private science." Indeed! One might wonder why Bridgman spent so much time trying to communicate with others if all of science is restricted to that which is solely and uniquely his.

Hume's version of subjective idealism (1739) not only undermined the prevailing concept of causality and the corollary belief in the uniformity of nature, it also undercut man's faith in the representational character of mathematics. If reality consists of nothing more than a succession of awarenesses constituting the experience of each individual observer, causality can exist only as a level of expectancy; laws are reduced to probability statements with the level of probability based upon the number of observed conjunctions, and mathematics is transformed into a kind of postulational scheme having reference only to such contingencies, if at all. It certainly could not have reference to an external physical world, there was no demonstrable external physical world; it became simply a game played by a set of standard rules made up by some gamesman. The tendency to deny representational status to mathematics and to prescribe only postulational credentials to it has had long-persisting repercussions for theory development.

Little children in the development of language and certain scientists in the development of theory have both on occasion confused the symbolic system with the stratum it is supposed to represent. A given scientist may indeed develop a refined and impressive symbolic structure to represent some segment of his subject matter, then explore the ramifications of the symbolic system without realizing that little, if any, relationship actually exists between the symbols and the subject matter they are supposed to represent. Herbart (1850), for example, developed an ingenious, and in our view inadequately recognized, explanation of the process whereby items of memory come to focus. But he fell victim to this confusion. His theory was perceptive, his mathematics unimpeachable, but the relationships stated to hold among his symbols were not those actually describing the process under investigation. Exploring the ramifications of his symbolic system could only lead him further and further astray. This example points out an obvious feature of symbolic systems, both mathematical and verbal. They may not represent anything within the empirical domain, and even when reference does exist, it may only be partial. To represent some process with a formula smacks of objectivity but often involves a case of precision overkill, of seeming objectivity which can often be mistaken for adequate description.

Subjective idealism as expressed in Hume's empiricism and Mach's positivism helped emphasize the difference between the symbol (or symbol system) and the item (or process) it was supposed to represent, and thus helped provide the basis for the discipline of semantics leading into logical positivism and operationism. Scientists became wary of semantic confusion and re-emphasized the importance of objectivity in the definition of constructs.

But when carried over into theory construction, this movement laid the foundation for an erroneous interpretation of the nature and function of theory. What is the major function of theory? To certain scientists, including many psychologists, a given theory regardless of its acceptability is viewed as having postulational status only, without relation or reference to the physical environment. A theory is seen simply as a set of constructs, integrated according to the rules of logic and syntax: a kind of postulational sausage grinder which has the utilitarian function of generating testable hypotheses.

No one would disagree with the notion that a scientifically viable theory should generate hypotheses that can be tested in a manner allowing confirmation or disconfirmation. But such tests are not made by exploring the ramifications of a set of rules within the vacuum of a postulational scheme; they are not purely logical or syntactical. Such tests have empirical reference; confirmation signifies that to some degree the symbolic system is representational of something beyond its own structure. (See Goodson and Morgan, selection 20 in this volume.) "Yes," our protagonists might say, "it refers to the experience of the scientist, both as encompassing the theoretical system and the experimental test." If this is all there is to science, then both theory and research remain encapsulated within the knowing process of one person, the scientist in his dual role as theorist and observer. In such a scheme a theory is doubly encapsulated; a test has no reference beyond the ramifications of the symbolic structure, and *even if it did* it could have reference only to some segment of the scientist's restricted and isolated world. This kind of solipsism not only encapsulates each person's science within his own private world, it seems to equate discovery with creation. Accordingly, there could be no such thing as X rays, genes, the opposite side of the moon, or the vermiform appendix before their appearance within the sensing apparatus of some individual made them both a thing of science and anything at all. Few would agree with such a gross conclusion, yet subjective idealism as represented in the solipsisms of Mach and Bridgman leads us toward such a bizarre interpretation.

One might wonder how something as scientifically restrictive as subjective idealism could provide the atmosphere that helped generate logical positivism and operationism. We think it is because Mach's positivism forced us to admit the relativity implicit in our every observation; our experience of a stick varies, depending upon the position of the observer and the condition under which the observation is made.

A realization of the contingent nature of man's experience has moved into science on another and perhaps even more impressive tangent. Bessel (1823) probably began it with his writings on the personal equation inspired by the unfortunate (fortunate for science) experience of Kinnebrooke at the Greenwich observatory. It was given further expression and expansion by Helmholtz (1924), who insisted that there is a personal equation in every observation. We find it in Einstein's theory of relativity (it is not without significance that Einstein read Helmholtz extensively while a student at Zurich), which suggests that the measurement of anything must always be considered in terms of both the position and the velocity of the observer, and these in turn evaluated relative to the only factor that is not relative, the speed of light. Both

Mach and Einstein emphasized the importance of external variables, whereas Berkeley, Hume, Helmholtz, and many others emphasized internal variables, those implicit in the knowing processes themselves. But the contingent character of man's experience is central in both approaches: A relativity is obvious whether the effective variables be internally contributed or externally imposed.

Thus two tangents, one arising out of the subjective idealism of Berkeley, Hume, and Mach, the other out of astronomy and physics as represented in the writings of Bessel, Helmholtz, and Einstein, led to an appreciation of the importance of context variables upon each observation. This in turn led to a realization of the contingent status of our observations and/or measurements and the need for clarity and specificity in the definitions of our terms. Subjective idealism not only imposed a psychological interpretation upon the perception of three-dimensional space, it also led us to realize that the words we use are not absolute in their reference but limited in meaning to the experiences of people.

But the same tangent that inspired exciting and functional usages in perception and language has at another level led us terribly astray, into a kind of conceptual isolation. Small wonder that the problem of generalizability has been crucial for operationists. How can there be generalizability at all if each individual scientist is limited to his own personal view of reality? Language too must be restricted and have meaning only within the limited confines of each speaker's world.

We do not object to Bridgman's (1928) operationism. It has served as a much needed purifier of scientific concepts, first in physics and later in psychology where the need for decontamination was surely even greater. But we do object to Bridgman's view of reality, the notion that all science is restricted to the immediate sensing of each individual. We also object to the implication, drawn by many, that a theory is simply a set of logically related constructs that functions primarily as a generator of hypotheses. To assume an externally existing reality may go beyond immediate experience and may introduce an element of ambiguity into the meaning of our constructs, but without such reality the possibility of science as it is actually practiced would have to cease. Feigl (1960) has perhaps stated the issue best: "Doubts about the existence of physical objects are illegitimate not because the beliefs in question are incapable of confirmation or disconfirmation, but because doubts of this pervasive character would call into question the very principles of confirmation and disconfirmation that underlie all empirical inquiry."

Naive Realism and Its Implications

Realism in its simplest and most naive form is demonstrated in the notions of the small child. To him a real world exists, and he sees and hears (i.e., senses) this real world as it actually is. There is no argument about the nature of external reality, it is as directly experienced. He has no problem at all with the issue of intercommunication; that is, other people exist as separate entities who perceive exactly the same world he perceives: To him language has to do with these shared items existing independently in an external world. An impassioned defense for this version of realism is expressed in the writings of the Scottish philosopher Thomas Reid (1764): "The accumulated experience of all men every-where and at all times conjoins to argue for an independently existing external reality." This begs the question perhaps, but at least Reid, having read Hume, realized that there was a question. The antiquity of naive realism and one of the first statements of the manner in which humans apprehend external reality is represented in the writings of Lucretius in 100 B.C. To him there was an externally existing world filled with items such as houses and people and trees. How do we know this external reality? Everything in nature, according to him, is perpetually sloughing off thin replicas, films of atoms, which enter the eye and interact with the atoms of the mind, and suddenly we perceive the item. A more sophisticated version of realism and one that also acknowledges the importance of organism process in the determination of experience was given by John Locke (1690). In defending an external reality as the source of knowledge he submitted that there are two different kinds of experience—one type directly represents the nature of the external world (primary qualities) and the other, although activated by external phe-nomena, is entirely contributed by the organism (secondary qualities). "But all experience is purely mental," Bishop Berkeley might have said. "Is there really something more out there than the experience?" "If so, what is it?" "That something I know not what," replied Locke resolutely. A bit lame perhaps but in Locke we find one of the earliest and clearest expressions of the notion that man's reality is largely contributed by the knowing processes rather than being a direct expression of an external physical environment. To Locke, and incidentally to most modern thinkers on the subject, such attributes as colors, sounds, and pain, to mention but a few, exist only in the experiencer activated by stimuli in the external world, and in no way resemble any aspect of that external world.

With the writings of Johannes Müller (1837), physiology as well as philosophy came to the position that the external environment is given only indirectly: Some condition of the nerves intervenes between the experience and the stimulating circumstance, a condition that gives each experience its characteristic quality. Müller thus believed that all human reality reflects some aspect of the nervous system, and that knowledge can only be conversant about such private and inaccessible experiential qualities. But Müller was not an idealist. He held that each sense modality was peculiarly although not exclusively responsive to a certain type of stimulation; that is, the retina is most responsive to light stimulation but can be activated by pressure. This notion, almost identical to Sherrington's (1906) concept of adequate stimulation, at least provided a base for inferring the existence of an external world—an external world that presents itself through various kinds of stimuli peculiarly appropriate for the different kinds of receptor systems.

Thus the realist, at least in terms of the examples offered, has become almost as encapsulated in his own private and inaccessible world as the idealist. An external reality is assumed to exist but its existence rests primarily on the principle of adequate stimulation. It is an external reality that can never be known directly but must be inferred. The realist even as the idealist seems to have little basis for intercommunication knowing only the condition of his own nerves, and "that something I know not what" that gives rise to adequate stimulation.

Evolutionary Theory and the Scientist's Reality

Since 1859, in spite of periods of retrogression like the one in which many members of the life sciences became unduly impressed with gross mutations as the major arbiter and species fluctuation, Charles Darwin's theory has become more and more widely accepted. It is no longer just a speculative frame of reference or simply one of a number of equally viable alternatives. It pervades our thinking about all living organisms, both as they presently exist and as an explanation of their coming into being. It constitutes the most widely accepted rationale for our own emergence as a species and inevitably provides the basis for any theory presuming to make sense of the attributes we presently possess. We believe that contemporary psychology is rooted in evolutionary theory (see Goodson, 1973). It is here that we as theorists must begin and it is on this base that our structures ultimately must rest. If these affirmations are correct, an important question immediately arises. Does a consideration of the scientist as an evolved entity, as an evolutionary product, tell us anything about the kind of "reality" with which the scientist must cope and the theoretical structures he shall develop? We are convinced that such an examination will offer much toward an understanding of the kind of "reality" with which the scientist must deal, and in process will provide a base for inferring one of the most important functions of scientific theory.

Evolutionary theory implies that the progenitors of all living organisms, including scientists, came slowly into being through the workings of natural selection: an inexorable process involving the testing of countless variabilities in the crucible of the environment. *Contemporary organisms came into being out of an environmental context.* This statement implies the existence of both organisms *and* a physical environment. This rather unremarkable inference indicates that a realistic position is implicit in evolutionary theory. We would not give such emphasis to this seeming truism were it not for the fact that subjective idealism under the guise of the kind of positivism represented by Hume and Mach has had such a prolonged and we believe debilitating effect upon psychology's consideration of both scientific reality and scientific theory.

Subjective idealism and its sundry derivatives are simply incompatible with an evolutionary perspective. Even a brief examination of evolutionary theory suggests that a physical environment does exist, that scientists as living organisms exist separately from it, and that a profitable, in terms of a growing body of knowledge, commerce is in continuing process between such scientists and environment. How do we know about this physical environment? Through our sense organs, of course. But this does not mean that any organism perceives the environment as it actually is; indeed quite the opposite conclusion must be drawn. The segment of the environment that an organism perceives and that comprises its "personal reality" must necessarily be that which was significant in the evolutionary development of the species it represents. Thus the "reality" of any creature, and this includes psychologists, is limited to those extremely narrow bands of energy fluctuation to which, for survival and evolutionary development, it was necessary for the evolutionary ancestors of that creature to respond. But an organism does not perceive the environment "as it actually is" even in those energy ranges to which it is responsive. Different types of instruments may respond to the same energy changes in completely different ways. Which instrument provides the "true" picture? Obviously, none of them. Each simply records, in its characteristic fashion, the manner in which given energies fluctuate. *Yet, insofar as a given instrument responds differentially to energy fluctuations, it is representational of the environment and provides information about it.* The subjective idealists would lead us to think that the reading on the instrument was the only reality, that this reading automatically happened on its own and had no reference to anything beyond itself. The naive realist in turn would dispose us to think that the environment exists exactly as given by the instrument.

As in the case of instruments, we may assume that the sensory input of organisms (although it does not portray the actual nature of physical reality) is representational of at least certain limited segments and characteristics of physical reality. Further, even as we assume that instruments that are constructed alike give much the same recordings to similar energies, we may also assume that the sensory input of organisms is similar to the degree that they are constructed in like fashion and activated by similar energies. Members of the same species, within the limits of species variability, having the same evolutionary history, are constructed alike and when exposed to the same energies will have similar experiences. Thus although it may not directly portray the circumstances that bring about its introduction, experience is representational of the environment, and is the only way we can know about it.

Implications for Psychological Data

One of the contemporary illusions of many psychologists hinges on the view (which seems akin to naive realism) that certain types of sensory input are somehow more objective than other types. Thus for some a rat turning right in a maze is less subjective than such experiential components as "pain" or "red" or "sweet." The "rat," even as the "pain" and the "red" and the "sweet," is an experiential derivative occasioned when certain receptors are stimulated in particular ways. But, it might be objected, we perceive the "rat" as a phenomenon whereas such components as "pain" and "red" are not so perceived. Nevertheless, the rat as given in our experience is just as subjective as any other experiential component, and a rat turning right in a maze is no more public than the input component termed *red*.

We do not intend here to deny the objective existence of rats. Indeed, we affirm that such is the case. However, it is readily admitted that the rat of my experience would be quite different from what it now is were I to have receptors sensitive to other energy emanations (such as infrared) that mark its presence. Further it may be readily admitted that we cannot be sure that my experiential input termed *red* is the same as that which you affirm to be red; but neither can we be sure that your rat is the *same* as my rat. However, because the "organism shaping" of natural selection has determined that our physiology is much alike, we may infer that our experiential components are essentially similar. We affirm that my rat is similar to your rat and my red to your red, and where such is not found to be the case, there must be a defect in one or both of us. It is true that some people, those who are color blind, do not see the same red as most of us, but a careful examination of the pertinent receptors of such individuals will reveal a defect. It is also true that a different history with different experiential components may markedly affect their general character and meaning, but the raw sensory input of most humans is markedly similar. Instruments (such as altimeters) that are constructed alike will give much the same readings when the energy changes to which they are peculiarly responsive are imposed, and so will the sensory mechanisms of human beings.

From this analysis distinctions often made by psychologists between objective and subjective and between public and private break down. All human experience is subjective and private; but all of it, insofar as it is occasioned by externally imposed energy shifts, may be viewed as representational of changes in the environment and as such may be accepted as public information about the characteristics of the objective world.

But surely, one is almost forced to insist, certain types of sensory input are more amenable to scientific consideration than others. This is indeed the case. In general, it may be said that the input derived from exteroceptors is more reliable than that arising from the receptors located on the inside of the body. Such input is no more subjective than the information gained from the exteroceptors; it is simply that the receptors on the inside of the body are more diffuse, much less known, and more difficult to stimulate in a precise and systematic fashion. Thus, although we can infer that one person's rat or one person's red is essentially similar to another person's rat or red, it is much more difficult to assume that one person's anxiety or fear is similar to another's. In the prior case precise control of the stimulating circumstance is possible, whereas in the latter it is much more difficult to achieve. The problem of fear, and other emotional responses, has another complication that lends further difficulty to its study: Learning enters in to alter the manner in which different organisms may respond to the same stimulus. So even though the same stimulus may be applied, the internal receptors and consequent experiential input may be quite different. Most people love dogs but an individual who has been bitten by one may hate and fear them.

Certain aspects of the environment affect a greater number of sense modalities, in more complex ways, than do others. The input accounting for the presence of a rat may arise from a number of different receptor systems such as those that account for the experiences of light, sound, temperature, pressure, odor, and even taste if one were so disposed. And even within a single modality the input characteristics occasioning the experience of a rat may be much more complex than those that produce red. Thus the experiential complex designating the rat may be more reliable and consistent than that designating the stimulus 680 millimicrons (i.e., red). The rat, as well as many "things" in the environment, is represented by a number of indicators, whereas 680 millimicrons is represented by only one, the experience red. This greater number of shared indicators suggests that intercommunication may be more reliable about certain aspects of the environment than others. A person may be color blind, indeed completely blind, and still apprehend the presence of the rat, but the presence of 680 millimicrons would remain unknown to him. Does this not mean that rats are somehow less "private" than reds? No. Indeed, the rat, at least in one sense, is more private than the red. The process that organizes the multiplicity of sensory inputs (whether this process be totally innate or partially learned) so that the *phenomenon* rat is experienced is *contributed by the organism!* So, when we affirm that my rat is the same as your rat, we are not only assuming a similarity of raw sensory input, we are assuming a similarity of organization as well.

In the preceding argument, I have not intended to undercut the legitimacy of rat psychology; rather I am suggesting that intercommunication rests upon an assumption of shared indicators (i.e., experiences) and these in turn are a function of a similarity of structure and process in investigators. Indeed such an assumption is implicit if we take an evolutionary point of view. This approach allows us to bring under scientific scrutiny much data that certain psychologists have tended to relegate into the realm of the private and the inaccessible. All experience moves into the public domain because similarity of structure will occasion similarity of experience when like receptors are stimulated.

This analysis immediately raises a question about research methodology. What about introspection? Since the advent of the behaviorists led by the manifesto of John Watson (1913) and reinforced by the writings of numerous others from Guthrie to Skinner, introspection has been anathema to many psychologists. We believe that the rejection of this vital avenue to information about the human organism is unjustified for both methodological and practical reasons.

A logical anomaly seems implicit in behaviorism. Those who agree that psychology should be restricted to a study of "the behavior of the other one," as the pioneer behaviorist Max Meyer (1921) once proposed, are caught up in a curious paradox. In the name of an empirical objective science of the organism the very processes implicit in the word *empirical* must be rejected. The behaviorists insist that only data arrived at through experience is legitimate but deny that the process itself, that is, the nature and function of experience, is of sufficient importance to be of legitimate concern.

If the human being is a product of evolution, every attribute, whether physical (such as fingers and eyes) or psychological (such as pain and red), can be understood in terms of its adaptive contribution. A behaviorist can catalogue the physical characteristics and reactions of another organism, but the only way we can categorize the psychological attributes is through introspection. What are the psychological attributes? What contribution do they make to the workings of the organism? These are legitimate questions but ones that must be neglected completely if we reject the legitimacy of introspection. We hold (see Goodson and Morgan, Selection 29 in this volume) that the job of psychology is to understand how the organism works in the same sense that an automobile specialist understands how a car works. In the effort to gain this understanding the contribution of psychological attributes must be considered and, at least at the present time, their variety and character can only be arrived at through introspection.

Actually psychologists have not relinquished either introspection or the data derived therefrom. Although many psychologists have given lip-service to the tenets of behaviorism down through these past fifty years, most introductory psychology texts have continued to include material on such psychological attributes as vision, audition, pain, anxiety, and the like. At this most basic level, when we talk about "red," "pain," or "anxiety" we are not simply referring to a "verbal report" or to some other overt manifestation of response but to the experience itself. Further, it should be emphasized that many (perhaps most) psychologists were never caught up in this schizoid separation between theoretical pronouncement and practical use. The Gestalt psychologists, the psychoanalysts, the existentialists, and others have continued to make contributions with the method and data of introspection central to their approaches. The inclusion of an "experiential level" section in this volume both as a legitimate base for data and as interacting with other levels testifies not only to the durability of the method and data of introspection, but to the fact that there is a resurgence of interest and commitment to an understanding of the psychological attributes of man and to their contribution to the workings of the dynamic system he is.

The work of scientists may be viewed as efforts to explain the nature of the environment and/or living organisms. Because scientists are human beings who, even as other organisms, reflect in their processes and structure the environment in which they evolved, their external reality is restricted to the effects of those energy shifts that were significant in their evolutionary emergence. Some may disagree with this assertion and point out that the development of instruments allows an ever-expanding apprehension of the environment and thus effectively extends the "reality" of the scientist. Instruments do effectively extend man's *knowledge* of the environment, but regardless of their range and sensitivity they do not alter the sense organs or expand the categories of experience. Rather they transform characteristics of the environment so that man's sensory equipment can be responsive to them. A microscope or a magnetometer does not alter the nature of man's experience but transforms certain events or conditions in the objective world so that man can apprehend them.

Implications for Psychological Theory

If, as is postulated by evolutionary theory (Goodson, 1973), organisms evolved as a function of the development of more facile techniques for differential response and if cue utilization marks one of the crucial manifestations of increasing adaptive efficiency, an interesting inference is made possible concerning the environment. Not only does such a context exist, but certain regularities obtain within it. The existence of cue utilization as an adaptation attribute makes this inference necessary—for a cue could not function as a cue without being related with some invariance to some other event. Thus we may assume the existence of not only an external environment but one that is lawful, with both the context and its lawfulness being requirements for the evolutionary development of organisms as we know them.

These inferences pertaining to an objective environment and its lawfulness have some interesting implications for science. Certain statements and theories are simply more valid than others. They are valid to the extent that they represent *what actually obtains in the physical environment*. If certain relationships do exist in the objective world, a given theory is true to the extent that it represents these relationships. This suggests that a theory is not just an instrument for grinding out testable hypotheses, it is also representational to the extent that such hypotheses are confirmed. From this frame of reference the oft-quoted statement that "a theory is never true or false, it either works or does not work" is both misleading and confounded. It is misleading because it implies that a theory is only a hypothesis-generating instrument, without truth value. If a hypothesis is legitimately derived from a theoretical structure and is then adequately tested and confirmed, it is to that degree strengthened in its representational function. It is confounded because workability refers to its capacity to generate *confirmable* hypotheses, so to the extent that it works *it is* a true statement about the external environment.

Man was testing hypotheses about the external environment for millions of years—if we can believe the findings from physical anthropology, before the advent of formal science. Man's ability to survive in good measure reflects the extent that his symbolic systems validly represent critical segments of an ever-changing, perpetually hazardous environment. Perhaps the oldest analogue was a sort of pictorial memory, later buttressed by symbols, both spoken and written. But where man's representative systems (whether vague memory or highly structured theory) failed to portray accurately the variables and relationships of the external environment, his capacity for adjustment and survival has been correspondingly reduced. So it should not be surprising that theories, whether vague conjectures or highly integrated conceptual systems, should demonstrate their ultimate utility or lack of it in terms of the extent to which they represent valid statements about some aspect of the physical world.

We psychologists, as organisms, do exist and other human beings also exist. And as existing organisms we, even as does the context, work in certain definitive ways. Thus certain statements as to how human beings work, even as statements as to how a car works, *are true* and others *are false*.

What, then, is a scientific fact? It is a statement about some condition or process that actually characterizes the physical environment or other organisms. Certain regularities existed (call them laws of nature or what you will) during the slow evolutionary emergence of the human species and still exist to provide the context in which we and other organisms move precariously from life until death. A scientific fact has to do with some condition of the physical environment or organisms that actually does exist and that manifests itself in some particular definitive way. Scientific statements (whether fact, law, or theory) can be absolutely true to the extent that they describe the way that nature, whether physical environment or organisms, works. If uncertainty exists in science it lies in the techniques of observation and communication, not in the workings of the physical environment or living organisms.

REFERENCES

BERKELEY, G. An essay toward a new theory of vision. Dublin, 1709.

BESSEL, W. F. Astronomische Beobachtungen. Konigsberg; 1823.

BORING, EDWIN G. A history of experimental psychology (2nd ed.). New York: Appleton-Century-Crofts, 1950.

BRIDGMAN, P. W. The logic of modern physics. New York: Macmillan, 1928.

———. The nature of physical theory. Princeton, N.J.: Princeton University Press, 1936.

DARWIN, CHARLES. On the origin of species by means of natural selection. London, 1859.

FEIGL, HERBERT. Mind-body, not a pseudoproblem. Dimensions of mind. Edited by Sidney Hook. New York: New York University Press, 1960.

GOODSON, FELIX E. The evolutionary foundations of psychology: a unified theory. New York: Holt, Rinehart and Winston, 1973.

HELMHOLTZ, H. Psysiological optics (translated by J. P. C. Southall). New York: Optical Society of America, 1924.

HERBART, J. F. Psychologie als Wissenschaft. Leipzig: Werke, 1850.

HUME, DAVID. A treatise of human nature. London: Printed for John Noon, at the White-Hart, near Mercer's-Chapel in Cheapside, 1739.

LOCKE, JOHN. Essay on the human understanding. London: T. Basset, 1690.

MACH, ERNST. The analysis of sensations (5th ed.) (translated by S. Waterlow). LaSalle, Ill.: Open Court, 1914.

MEYER, M. F. The psychology of the other one. Columbia, Mo.: Missouri Book Co., 1921.

MÜLLER, JOHANNES. Handuch der physiologie des menschen (translated by William Baly). London, 1837–1842.

REID, THOMAS. An inquiry into the human mind, on the principles of common sense. Edinburgh, 1764.

SHERRINGTON, C. S. The integrative action of the nervous system. New Haven: Yale University Press, 1906.

WATSON, J. B. Psychology as the behaviorist views it. Psychol. Rev., 1913, 10, 421–428.

Part III
LEVELS OF ANALYSIS

PSYCHOLOGISTS *have been and still remain concerned with three types of data: (1) experiential, that is, relating to consciousness or "mind"; (2) physiological; and (3) behavioral. The history of psychology has been filled with controversy over which of these types or levels is most appropriate for the discipline. This debate has sometimes been so bitter that investigators who have gathered one type of data have ignored research utilizing another type as irrelevant to the true direction of psychology. There has been, however, increasing acceptance of the position that all three types provide appropriate subject matter for psychology and that the investigation of relationships across levels is desirable and perhaps necessary. The last section in this final unit of the book contains several papers that do, in fact, cross levels.*

After an introductory section, the major portion of this part of the book is comprised of contemporary expressions of psychologists' involvement with the three levels of data, grouped in accordance with those levels. Thus in the first of these sections the return to mind is catalogued and defended, in the second a forum is provided for the expression of some physiological positions, and in the third various interpretations and implications of the behavioral approach are offered. Finally, there is a concluding section presenting various efforts to define and to cope with psychology's tripartite subject matter.

OVERVIEW

THE *paper by Goodson and Morgan introduces this section with an informal discussion of several important topics. The paper begins with a brief overview of the history of psychology, highlighting the controversy over whether mind or behavior constituted the appropriate subject matter of psychology. As psychology matured, it progressed from primary concern with taxonomic problems to the determination of relationships. The major theme of the paper is that all types of data are to be investigated in the pursuit of relationships that underlie the behavior of the organism.*

The second paper in this section, by Silverstein, offers a further defense of the independence of the various levels of analysis. It rebuts the argument for any necessity of reduction of data or principles, as from the behavioral to the physiological level.

29

ON LEVELS OF PSYCHOLOGICAL DATA[*]

FELIX E. GOODSON *and* GEORGE A. MORGAN

PSYCHOLOGY has roots in both philosophy and physiology.[1] Early psychologists drew heavily on the principles of association developed by the eighteenth- and nineteenth-century British empiricists. From Locke to Bain philosophers struggled to understand how ideas become associated. What was the glue that held ideas together, enabling one to recall them in some order? The philosophers' most widely accepted answer, contiguous previous occurrence, was absorbed into the assumptions and biases of early psychologists as the law of association.

The scientific antecedents of psychology came primarily from continental Europe where, in the nineteenth century, physiologists and physicists made great strides in areas related to psychology. Müller's

---

1 The student who is unfamiliar with the history of psychology and its principal characters may want to consult one of the several thorough texts on this topic, e.g., Boring (1950) and Marx and Hillix (1973). Kuhn's (1970) important book about the nature of scientific revolutions would provide helpful background reading for this paper (cf. also selections 3 and 4).

---

[*] Written for this volume.

doctrine, that each quality of sensation has nerves specific to it was, according to Helmholtz, as important to psychology as the principle of the conservation of energy was to physics. Finding the locus of such mental functions as seeing, hearing, and thinking was a very ancient quest. During the 1800's there was marked scientific progress in understanding the extent to which such mental functions are localizable in the brain. The work of these early physiologists overlapped the domain of what was to become psychology, because their research naturally led them to look for relationships between physiological variables and both behavior (speech, reflexes, and so on) and experience (seeing, hearing, and so on). This approach has continued throughout the history of psychology, not much affected by the prevailing dogmas of the major theoretical systems described below.

Although Wundt called his newly established science *physiological psychology,* he grew disinterested in the body and concentrated his efforts on understanding the structure and content of the normal, adult human mind. Thus at the time of its formal beginning in 1879, and indeed for many years thereafter, the subject matter of psychology was the mind. Emphasis on the method of scientific introspection, to the exclusion of all else, was a predominant feature of the psychologist's commitment before the turn of the century. Even partial defections seemed to occasion sufficient guilt to require immediate expiation by a reaffirmation of the principle.

Although Wundt and his structuralist colleagues used the psychophysical methods to establish relationships between environmental change and experiential shift, they were much less interested in the relationships obtained than in the elements of experience thus exposed. In their compulsive attempt to break the mind into categories, the just noticeable difference became the ultimate element, the smallest brick in the total structure. What could be smaller than a jnd of experience derived from a single modality? It seems ironic that the isolation of this "smallest element" should be both the crowning achievement of structuralism and the revelation of its essential sterility.

Before 1900 the basic schism in the field was whether investigators should study the *content* of the mind, as the structuralists did, or the *process* (acts) by which such content comes into consciousness. Act psychology, involved as it was with these experiential will-o'-the-wisps that changed even as the examination was being made, did not fare even as well as structuralism, which had, at least, compiled a remarkable amount of consistent data. The act psychologists ended up with hardly any data at all. Kulpe and his Wurzburg school, in its zealous effort to find the contents of acts, demonstrated the ultimate futility of an orientation that had data as impalpable as its method was ephemeral. In so doing, it set the stage for the demise of both act and content schools.

At first the new, primarily American, school of functionalism gave lip-service to the notion that the proper subject matter of psychology was mind. However, they allowed into the field such an array of heretics and unauthorized methods that Titchener, that redoubtable defender of orthodox Wundtian structuralism, withdrew into self-imposed and somewhat petulant isolation at Cornell.

As the twentieth century began, psychologists became less enamored with minds, and soundings of defection became the rule rather than the exception. The seeds for this movement from orthodoxy had long been planted and were coming into bloom. The study of animal behavior based on Darwinian theory and given expression and technique by Thorndike and Yerkes, among others, became a major orientation for many psychologists. The testing movement, fathered by Darwin's cousin Galton, gained adherents and practical application, looking to Cattell in America and to Binet in France. Abnormal psychology, sloughing off demonism, was given studied consideration by some of the great minds of the century, including Kraepelin and Freud. The physiologists amassed remarkable amounts of data on the relations between cortical centers and both behavior and experience. Even the child and educational psychologists, led by Stanley Hall, achieved some respectability. It is small wonder, then, that Titchener, who insisted that psychologists should study the content of consciousness in trained, normal, adult human beings, was dismayed; it is difficult to get reliable introspective reports from rats, psychotics, or children.

For a while, functionalism provided a benign and accepting refuge for many of these disparate approaches. But eclecticism has a habit of being uninspiring and typically enlists few disciples in its behalf. Functionalism as a movement was too diffuse and too uncertain. It was stated that mind was the subject matter of psychology, but the functionalists acted as if they weren't convinced.

The scene was set. Psychologists, especially in America, had gone their sundry ways while still vaguely adhering to the notion that the proper subject matter was mind. Then along came Watson, and almost overnight in 1912 the mind ceased to be a serious subject for study, or at least it seemed so for a while. Watson's message was simple and direct: Because the only thing we can know about any organism is its behavior, psychology should center its attention on this knowable. It was, as Boring the great historian of psychology said, as if Watson had touched a match to all the disparate orientations, producing an explosion that left nothing but his own position. His method had an imperative ring. Psychologists should vary the environment and observe the changes in behavior occasioned by such variation. With the advent of behaviorism, psychology shifted from a primary emphasis upon taxonomy, as had been the case with the structuralists, to a concern with relationships. It is remarkable how little classification is required before relationships can be determined. All that is necessary is the isolation of a few relevant variables, utilizing the categories that have emerged in everyday language for such purposes. This is the approach the behaviorists took, with considerable success. The structuralists had stated the goals of psychology to be the isolation of the components of the mind and the determination of the laws of their relationship. Unfortunately, they became so enamored with the first half of the task they had only enough energy left to borrow *en masse* associationistic principles from the English philosophers.

Thus perhaps the great contribution of behaviorism was to redirect psychology from primarily taxonomic endeavors to a concentration on relationship determination. Even if there were few laws in psychology and their probability value low, at least they were laws and not mere designations of categories.

In spite of their vociferous differences, behaviorism had some things in common with structuralism. Both were concerned with finding basic elements, except that instead of elements of experience, behaviorists looked for elements of stimulation and response. The behaviorists also continued the search for the "cement" that hooked the elements together.

Even as psychology relaxed for a moment in the security of its new objectivism, another movement, both theoretically and personally disturbing, was slowly gaining the attention of the world. The stream of thought arising from Freud's intricate but obscure theory had burgeoned into a movement of unprecedented dimensions, always lurking on the periphery of scientific respectability but, nevertheless, virile and articulate. The structuralist's approach, the experimental study of the conscious mind, was almost incidental to psychoanalytic theory. Freud argued that most of man's motivation comes not from consciousness, but from the subterranean realm, that part of the iceberg beneath the water, the unconscious. He was, likewise, unimpressed by the simplistic environmentalism of the behaviorists. Freud insisted that most important human actions are caused by a tangled intermixture of biological urges and unconscious reverberations from childhood events.

Psychology has often vacillated between simple positions that include too little and complex ones that attempt to subsume too much. The former achieve their simplicity and clarity largely through the exclusion of important issues; the latter through their vagueness and generality allow problems to become lost in the morass the position represents. A contemporary psychologist in search of intellectual security can identify with neobehaviorism, as expressed by Skinner and his disciples, because practically everybody understands it; or, on the other hand, with neo-Freudianism because hardly anyone does.

At mid-century behaviorism and psychoanalysis were the dominant theories in America, but other positions were still in competition. Gestalt psychology had won points by showing that the whole is more than (or at least different from) the sum of its parts, a fact that both behaviorism and structuralism overlooked in their search for basic elements and the cement that holds them together. The contribution of Gestalt psychology was acknowledged by most psychologists, but new disciples were few and its vitality was gradually usurped by other orientations. The testing movement continued to run intercorrelations between its ofttimes unvalidated instruments. The descendants of Husserl, the existential psychologists, found meaning in "lived categories." In the background, the brain searchers—those zealous electrode sinkers, wave analyzers, and tissue cutters—continued their endeavors, almost unmindful of the theoretical clamor that burst around them on every side.

Following the period of the great "systems" (structuralism, functionalism, psychoanalysis, Gestalt, and the giants of neobehaviorism) psychology entered the age of microtheory. As in behavioristic simplicity and psychoanalytic diffuseness, there is security in specialization. It is better to have a small peace than a grand despair. Instead of a general behavior theory or even a theory of learning, there are now separate theories of reinforcement, extinction, generalization, and even eyelid conditioning.

Another recent but fading development is the use of models. Surely man will fit some analogue, symbolic or mechanical. Certain thinkers derive mathematical systems and endeavor to fix man with a formula; whereas others build a machine and then perceive that they, the builders, are constructed in its image.

Like the fabled blind men of Hindustani who once appraised an elephant, psychologists have been at odds with one another. Some remain fixated on the elephant's eyes and ears, some are concerned with what is beneath the massive skull. Many are fascinated with what happens as peanuts are doled out one by one, and still others remain entranced with the trunk, to which they ascribe grave, though somewhat mistaken, properties.

Most psychologists would acknowledge that their ultimate goal is a complete understanding of how the human being really works. However, we have seen that this goal has been approached in many ways. Some order can be brought to the confusion and controversy by describing a few key distinctions that run throughout.

In the preceding historical overview, we hinted at a difference between two kinds of facts. *Taxonomic facts* are arrived at by sorting some segment of experience into categories according to agreed-upon criteria. Although quite demanding and complex, as evidenced by the magnitude of the task facing botanists and ethnologists, taxonomy is propaedeutic to the central aim of science.

The second kind, *relational facts,* involve a precise statement of what follows what else. Their determination is the major task in all disciplines of science. Although taxonomy is less central, it is crucial because both the "what" and the "what else" must be defined before the relationship existing between them can be established. Since the inception of psychology, both taxonomy and relationship determination have been continuing corollary operations. Previously we pointed out that the structuralists seemed to become fixated on taxonomic problems while the behaviorists were able to proceed quickly to the important issue of determining relationships. Likewise, physiological psychologists have usually left the taxonomy to the anatomists, going on to look for relationships between physiological variables and both behavior and experience.

This last point brings up a second distinction in the history of psychology. There have been three different levels or types of data on which psychologists have focused: the experiential, the behavioral, and the physiological. The structuralists and the act psychologists were both primarily interested in conscious experience. The psychoanalysts were concerned with the unconscious. Because it is not directly accessible, they developed methods (e.g., free association and dream analysis) that they felt enabled them to get glimpses at the unconscious by way of verbal reports of experience. In general, the theoretical positions that have remained closer to their philosophical antecedents (e.g., phenomenology and existentialism) are still principally based on the experience of the psychologist himself. Other orientations, such as functionalism and Gestalt, have accepted as appropriate data both observations of behavior and the reports of feelings, thoughts, and perceptions. Behaviorism, we have seen, tried hard to exclude experience, both conscious and unconscious, from psychology. Thinking was permitted to the extent that it could be represented by objective indicators. Feelings and attitudes eventually sneaked into psychology as the verbal report of subjects, which is, after all, behavior. In spite of these sometimes grudging admissions, psychologists influenced by Watson still tend to feel that there is something less public and less objective about verbal or written reports than about behaviors such as right turns and key presses.

Somewhat surprisingly, almost all psychologists have accepted the results of those who work at the physiological level. Thus one finds chapters on the nervous system and the sense organs in most current introductory texts just as there were in the texts of Titchener and Watson. Often these descriptions seem quite unrelated to the remainder of the text, but they survive undisturbed from edition to edition.

An Allegory

Let us now consider a story intended to place our discussion of the three types of psychological data and several other issues in sharper perspective. It may also provide some further insight into the relatively recent history of psychology, the time when behaviorism, as represented by Skinner's operant learning theory, was the dominant position.[2]

Once upon a time, a few years ago, a ship arrived from a world so alien that the travelers aboard had not the slightest basis for comprehending the scene before them. Three travelers, so different as to defy description, stood before the visiplates that, even as they watched, cleared of the misty effusion that inevitably develops in hyperspace, and "looked" and "speculated" and "hypothesized."

"There's life down there," said Lim, his chromicles alternately changing from blue to green, indicating the extent of his excitement. "After a million parsecs and a billion planets, finally life."

"Well, at least there is movement," agreed Niks, his chromicles flickering alternately from gray to black, denoting the somber mood that almost always possessed this doughty traveler. "Change the magnification, Wom."

Wom's chromicles typically registered a nondescript yellow, evidence to anyone schooled in the art of chromicle interpretation, of a sense of inferiority. He turned a dial, and suddenly the scene became clearer. The outline of what they didn't realize were buildings and the shiny perpetual rhythm of what they didn't realize was automobile traffic became unmistakably represented.

"I told you there was life," Lim said, his chromicles pulsing.

The three aliens stood and gazed with rapt wonder at the scene below. They saw the cars moving to and fro, weaving in and out, starting and stopping. They concluded simultaneously that here, indeed, was another form of life. They did not "see" the people inside the cars because one mark of their alienness was that they were completely devoid of any receptors that would give even the slightest evidence of living protoplasm as we humans know it.

"Shall we land and make proximity observations?" asked Wom. The frequency of his chromicle pulses registered doubt and indecision.

"Of course not, you 'idiot,'" Niks said, more furiously than the simple question would seem to have occasioned. "I am in command of this expedition. The orientation for alien study that I gained from the Great Taw will determine the approach we shall take. It seems I must recapitulate. Remember that all life is a lawful extrusion of the interaction of the variables within a given environmental complex. The basic task of all science is to ascertain the relationships that exist among determinant events. We must observe these creatures and catalogue the consistencies in their behavior. Whenever possible we must systematically alter the conditions to which they are responsive and observe how their behavior changes as a function of such manipulations."

2 A basic presentation of Skinner's behavioristic position during this period can be found in his *Science and human behavior* (1953).

The other two members of the expedition were subdued by the cogency of this onslaught. The pulsing of their chromicles decreased in both frequency and intensity.

"First, we must determine the energy shifts to which they respond, and second, we must vary these energy dimensions and relate such changes to the behavior of the organism in question. Third, we must represent the relationships thus determined by mathematical equations." Niks looked about him. "Any disagreements?"

The other two nodded, but the dark glooming of their chromicles gave evidence of reservations. Niks chose not to notice and busied himself with focusing the observation apparatus and setting the recorders.

"Now there is nothing to do but wait," he said with a note of satisfaction as he clicked the delayer switch on the last recorder.

Much later they were interrupted by the ringing of the analyzer.

"Give us a summary," Niks ordered. The other two moved quickly to the machine; their "fingers" darted rhythmically over a series of buttons. The machine hummed, whined, emitted a series of undulating clicks, and then fell silent. Suddenly, the large screen was flooded with symbols, which could be translated:

The organisms in question are extremely insensitive. They respond differentially to but one energy dimension, the electromagnetic continuum, and to only two narrow bands within this dimension, one around 540 and the other at 680 Mu. The impact of energy around 540 Mu is correlated with the starting of said organisms, while the response to 680 is that of halting. There is also a relationship between general environmental alteration and the movement of such organisms. As light is removed because of the interposition of their planet between them and their sun, they tend to move to the edges and stop. But, with the return of their sun and the electromagnetic energy therefrom derived, the beings move back into the center of the area. Although they almost invariably avoid each other by remaining on one side of the path, they sometimes collide at great speed. The result in certain cases is the relative destruction of the organism involved. End of report.

"They must be simple creatures," said Niks with a puzzled look on his "face."

"I assume that the energy shifts account for the starting and stopping of the organisms," said Wom. "Such changes always precede the reactions so we can infer that the one causes the other."

"Not necessarily," broke in Lim. "Both changes may be due to some other as yet undetermined factor or factors. I think that these results show the limitations of the peripheral approach." Lim surprised everyone, including himself, with his forthrightness.

There was a long silence during which the chromicles along Niks' "back" put on a kaleidoscopic display, with angry red predominating.

"You are being more ridiculous than you are stupid, which indeed is a supreme negative accomplishment. We haven't even begun environmental manipulation and you—I know your prejudices—jump to the conclusion that there is something wrong with the method."

"Not with the method," said Lim.

"No, not with the method," echoed Wom, "but with the level you think is the only one worthy of observation. There are other data that should be considered as well."

"Like what data?" said Niks, somewhat subdued. "Aren't we trying to establish relationships so that we can predict one event from another? I already have a testable hypothesis derived from the analyzer report. I predict that when we change the electromagnetic continuum we will get differential behavior on the part of these organisms. If this is true, not only will we be able to predict, but we will also be able to control their behavior by a simple manipulation of the energy dimension. Let us prepare for the experiment."

He pressed a series of buttons and suddenly the ship came to rest on the corner of a building directly above a busy intersection.

"Now we'll find out," said Niks. "I've established control over the energy emanation source. The light would turn green any second, but I will keep it red. See, eight of them stopped. Now let's see what happens when I change it to green. There's no doubt about it, the energy emanations do control their behavior—540 makes them go, 680 makes them stop," said Niks with satisfaction. "Now, all that is necessary is to vary each emanation along all possible parameters and record the corresponding behavioral changes. Of course, our automatic equipment can do that."

So, a large number of parametric studies were run: The intensity of each energy dimension was varied systematically, and changes in behavior were noted; the temporal interval between the red and green energies was varied systematically and changes in behavior were noted; and all possible interactions between intensity and the temporal interval were studied and the behavioral effects were determined. In the process it was discovered that the behavior of the organisms varied in many ways, from the speed at which the light source was approached to the frequency with which they had collisions. Each of these variables was studied systematically, and the interaction between each one and all other variables was determined. Time passed and weeks became months before the analyzer finally projected a large number of equations on the screen.

"Ah!" said Niks with satisfaction. "We have the basic behavior equations of these organisms. Now we can make perfect predictions."

They tested a number of hypotheses and found, indeed, that their predictions were almost perfect.

"But," said Lim, "we still don't understand these organisms. Isn't there something more to scientific knowledge than sheer ability to predict? I would like to know, for instance, what kind of energy the organism utilizes in order to move, and how it utilizes this energy. I would like to look into its interior and determine the relationship between its internal mechanism and its overt behavior. Then, perhaps, we would truly understand this organism."

Lim was astonished at the vehemence of his own outburst. Both Niks and Wom looked at him with surprise flickering on their chromicles. After a long silence, Niks astonished the others by saying:

"Very well. I don't see what good it will do, but go ahead. I've finished my calculations. I've demonstrated the ability to make predictions and yet you insist that there is something more that can be gained by emphasizing a level of data that actually belongs to physiology. But I need a rest, so have a try at it." Niks turned and disappeared into a sleep cubicle.

"How about that!" said Wom.

"Yeah, how about that," echoed Lim. Both sets of chromicles were suffused with a new excitement.

So they reset the observation devices and focused them to explore the central recesses of the organisms in question. They also did something that Niks would have scorned. They set the analyzer to abstract from the mass of data the basic or fundamental process in the activation and functioning of their subjects.

Time passed, and the observation apparatus observed and the analyzer analyzed and many a relationship was determined. There was a consistent relationship between how far down the gas pedal was depressed and how fast the wheels turned, how much the brake was depressed and how rapidly the car decelerated, and how rapidly the wheels turned and the charge indicated by the ampmeter. These and a hundred more relationships, some pertinent and some adventitious for an understanding of an automobile, were observed, duly recorded, and systematically rejected by the analyzer because they were not the fundamental process. Lim and Wom pressed the report button again and again, but always the same information was projected on the screen.

The process fundamental to understanding of this mechanism cannot be determined from data derived from the present level of instrument setting. Suggest you use setting code-67.

Each time this information was flashed on the screen both aliens would gaze in unbelieving silence before ordering the machine to recalculate.

Finally Wom said, almost happily, "It's not a mistake, but you know that code-67 is forbidden. The data derived from that level are pure figment, tainted with the spirit, soul substance, and mind matter. Surely, the basic relationship, the fundamental process, can't reside at that level. Or can it?"

"Let's try it," said Lim. "Niks is asleep and nobody will ever know but you and me."

His chromicles waveling in anticipation, Wom said, "You set the dials, and I'll focus on the next one that stops."

So they set the observation equipment on code-67 and the analyzer on fundamental principle and then peered at the scanner.

Suddenly both aliens were gazing at a pulsing fire. There was no mistaking it. And, to make matters more complex, there were eight different loci for its appearance. The fire bursts followed one another in rhythmic succession.

"Maybe it's epiphenomenal," suggested Lim. Just as each cylinder produced maximal compression, the fire appeared as if by magic and completely filled the chamber.

"No," said Wom. "I believe we are looking at the fundamental process. I believe that the expansion of the fire causes the plunger to move outward and that this movement is finally, after numerous intermediate steps, transmitted to the wheels."

"Do you think the fire substance is some mysterious force?" asked Lim, somewhat awed.

"Not at all. I feel it is simply another natural manifestation and as lawful in its effects as any other."

"But what about the transformation? Is it possible for a fire substance to affect material substance? Maybe they simply run parallel. I mean, maybe the piston simply moves outward, and the fire expands simultaneously, but they do so independently," queried Lim.

"It is possible," frowned Wom doubtfully. "Yet, I do not believe that nature would manifest itself so unparsimoniously. You will note," and again he changed the focus of the apparatus, "that the small fire emanating from that pronged apparatus in the top of the cylinder seems to initiate the larger fire and that just prior to its initiation there is always an injection of fluid. I feel that the fire substance on the prongs transforms the liquid into more fire substance, and that this sudden transformation causes the plunger to move outward.

"I can't accept it," said Lim abstractly. "It's completely impossible for something spiritual to affect something material, and here you postulate a dual process. It's impossible."

"Yes, it does seem impossible, but maybe that's because of the preconceptions we have toward spiritual fire substance. Perhaps such fire substance is as lawful a manifestation of the physical universe as the movement of the cylinder. Perhaps, we project our own preconceptions—"

Wom stopped, suddenly aware of Niks standing at the doorway. He had apparently been observing them for some time. Quietly, he went to the observation apparatus and reset the dials for "behavioral level." Finally, turning to his stricken comrades, he said, "The less said about your defection and subsequent contamination, the better. As far as I'm concerned, we have all the data we need for near perfect prediction of the behavior of this organism. In science, we aspire to nothing more than this, simply because there is nothing more." And then, confident that his analysis of the situation was not only correct but complete, he activated a mechanism in the center of the major control panel, and the ship flew away home.

Conclusions

This allegory suggests some of the dilemmas that have bedeviled our fledgling science. Many psychologists have held and many still affirm the view that the proper subject matter of psychology is the study of behavior, especially the relationships between stimulus variation and behavioral change. For example, behavioristic psychologists have spent many hours studying the relationship between hours of deprivation and running speed in rats. Because the relationship is fairly reliable, reasonably accurate predictions can be made. Should we stop there or should we look for more basic mechanisms underlying the behavior? The Niks of the world, who have been in predominance, say that we should stop. The Lims and the Woms tentatively, almost guiltily it seems, suggest that we search for other relationships, perhaps on other levels or across levels.

Even as certain relationships are more fundamental than others in the understanding of how an automobile works, certain relationships are more fundamental for an understanding of how a rat or a human works. Does a rat run faster because it has been deprived a certain number of hours or because there are physiological changes like stomach contractions or because the experiential input of hunger constitutes a spur to action? Although the experience of hunger may be based on the amount of deprivation and the stomach contractions, a full understanding of the rat's motivation seems to require the inclusion of data of all three types.[3]

The allegory points to another issue that certain psychologists have been prone to forget; namely, organisms do not function as a series of relationships between elements, but as dynamically integrated *processes*. The behaviorists in their zeal to emulate physics tended to overlook a critical difference between the two subject matters. The variables of physics are deployed; they are not dynamically interlocked as is the case with organisms. In physics, variables can often be isolated and their relationships determined without the continuing reverberations and repercussions that variable change inevitably introduces where organisms are involved. But variable isolation, manipulation, and relationship determination are intrinsic to the analytical method of science! Yes, this is true and psychologists must continue in this process. But we should be

[3] During the last decade there has been increasing acceptance of the position that cognitive and experiential factors are necessary to understand the functioning of the human being. See, for example, Dember (1974), Goodson (1973), Radford (1974), and the selections in the next section.

sensitive to the limitations and restrictions of our techniques. Typically we dissect the organism into artificial components and then find to our occasional satisfaction that such components are interrelated. Although categorization is intrinsic to the analytical method, the "organism" that emerges from our endeavors is inevitably partial and incomplete.

Another issue hinted at in the allegory is that, contrary to some recent dogma, there are important differences between prediction and understanding. Niks may, indeed, have been able to make almost perfect predictions, but, even so, his understanding of how a car works was limited, to say the least. Furthermore, one may have a relatively complete understanding of a phenomenon and, nevertheless, be unable to make accurate predictions about it. For example, many high school students can give a fairly good explanation of what causes volcanoes, but their ability to predict when one will erupt is practically nil.

Even though certain relationships are much more basic than others for understanding a phenomena, they are not necessarily more consistent than ones that are relatively inconsequential. The relationship between the explosion of gas in the cylinder of an engine and the movement of the piston is fundamental to the understanding of how a car works, but it is not any more consistent than the relationship that exists between the output of exhaust and the rapidity with which the wheels turn. No relationship should be ignored, but our prime endeavor should be to find the fundamental principles by which organisms function. Once these principles have been discovered, the myriad relationships that can inevitably be established between the components of a dynamically integrated entity can be evaluated in terms of their contribution to the total process.

In summary, the contention of this paper is that psychology should be concerned with determining how living organisms work in the same sense that a watch specialist is concerned with how a watch works, or an automobile specialist is concerned with how an automobile works. Special efforts should be made to determine the principles that are most basic in the operation of the total organism. In this endeavor, psychologists have the advantage, or some have said the complication, that they can directly experience their subject matter as well as observe the behavior and physiological functioning of others. None of these types of data is the exclusively appropriate one for psychology. Data of all three types and particularly that from across levels should be emphasized. The papers presented in the various sections of this book attest that psychology is maturing to the point where these admonitions are, in fact, taking form.

REFERENCES

BORING, E. G. A history of experimental psychology. New York: Appleton-Century-Crofts, 1950.

DEMBER, W. N. Motivation and the cognitive revolution. *American Psychologist*, 1974, **29**, 161–168.

GOODSON, F. E. *The evolutionary foundations of psychology: A unified theory.* New York: Holt, Rinehart and Winston, 1973.

KUHN, T. S. *The structure of scientific revolutions* (2nd ed.). Chicago: University of Chicago Press, 1970.

MARX, M. H., and HILLIX, W. A. *Systems and theories in psychology* (2nd ed.). New York: McGraw-Hill, 1973.

RADFORD, J. Reflections on introspection. *American Psychologist*, 1974, **29**, 245–250.

SKINNER, B. F. *Science and human behavior.* New York: Macmillan, 1953.

30

ON REDUCTIONISM

ALBERT SILVERSTEIN

RAZRAN'S (1965) recent and stimulating article in this journal, though "designed to offer a summary and an analysis, both historical and contemporary, of the relation of Russian physiologists' psychology to American experimental psychology," clearly contains a major statement of strategy for the science of behavior which invites serious attention. Basically, Razran's contention is that "brain behavior conditioning," the Pavlovian approach to psychology, is the only approach. Unless a science of behavior rests on neurophysiological data, it is an incomplete science, "leading to illusory self-containment and self-contentment and would-be autochthony unenjoyed by other sciences: mere linguistic lifting-by-one's-bootstraps' solution of problems." As Razran compared American behavior theorists to Pavlovian reflexology, he carefully noted the degree of error of the former in missing the mark of the latter.

I must object to this approach to strategy, and my objections can be made most clearly by citing another recent example of it. Esper (1964) concluded his thoughtful *A History of Psychology* by admiringly quoting an excerpt of a speech made by von Dechterew at the Third International Congress of Psychology in 1896.

I could hope that the future Fourth Congress will be able to present itself as a purely physiological one. It is therefore . . . disagreeable to hear . . . voices of

F R O M A. Silverstein, The *"grubo"* psychology: Or can a science over 95 be happy without reductionism?" *Psychological Bulletin*, 1966, **66** (3), 207–210. Copyright 1966 by the American Psychological Association. Reprinted by permission.

the learned world which would drag psychology down again into the sphere of scholasticism and dogmatics. . . . Whoever has not completed serious professional studies in physiology and psychiatry will be looked upon by serious persons in the coming century, if he calls himself a psychologist, like someone who calls himself an architect without having attended a technical school or academy of architecture [pp. 339–340].

Such a point of view has been championed continuously by Russian reflexology for over 60 years. Razran told us that any contemporary Russian report of conditioning which is not accompanied by analysis of correlative neurophysiological changes is called *"grubo"*—coarse or incomplete. In this country, too, the pendulum has begun to swing back toward physiologizing, but this is a quite recent phenomenon, and von Dechterew's prophecy has been something less than completely fulfilled. Despite the fact that most of the founding of scientific psychology was done by men trained in physiology, it is positivism rather than reductionism that has been the guiding approach to our science. Despite lip service often given to the ideal that function must reduce to structure and that smaller units of analysis are more "scientific," the working rationale for psychology generally has been to isolate the relevant stimulus variables for behavior and to ignore what Brunswick (1943) called "artificially isolated proximal or peripheral technicalities of mediation [p. 262]." Even our theories of behavior have tended to use mediating mechanisms only to aid in systematic development of sets of coordinated functional relations between environmental and behavioral variables which are experimentally known.

Esper (1964) ascribed this rationale to the influence of extrascientific concerns; partly as reaction to the misleading brain-localization movement and partly as a social reform concern for socially significant behavior. He also admitted that, until recently, neurophysiology has not been adequately instrumented to meet the challenge of psychophysiological correlation. However, this is not the entire story, and two major points must be carefully weighed in understanding why psychologists have not chosen to make their science a subdivision of physiology.

To begin with, the problems of psychology are not those of physiology. The problems of psychology have their origin in the philosophy of the mind—in the classic mind-body, epistemology, ethical, and aesthetic questions. That is, psychological questions began with a curiosity about the behavior of the total, intact organism and its interaction with the environment. To be sure, there are aspects of these philosophical questions which have always been and may always be nonempirical. For this reason, contemporary psychology has altered the mode of approach to these questions and has radically rephrased them to meet the criteria of a natural science. But this does not mean that the conceptual focus of the questions has been changed, nor does it mean we must ignore the historical origins of our present-day concerns. For example, the problem of perceptual constancy is certainly a part of the empirical side of "what are the origins of knowledge?" and keeping the connection in mind makes it clearer what sort of curiosity prompted the investigation of the constancies and what sort of answers will satisfy the curiosity.

Sometimes the empirical questions which grew out of these classic queries were psychophysiological, but more often they were psychophysical (in the broadest sense of the term). By inquiring into the causes for size-constancy, we show as much interest in the effect of relations between distal stimulus variables as in the effects of proximal sensory factors. In asking whether cognitions as well as S-R connections are learned, we are not merely asking whether there are synaptic links between receptor processes and other receptor processes, we are also asking whether experience which involves no movements of the organism can produce changes in its response-dispositions, and, if so, whether such acquisition follows different functional laws than that which does involve movements. The issue of what constitutes reinforcement requires knowledge of the common denominators of stimulus events and organisms' reactions as much as it requires knowledge of the anatomy of the "pleasure centers." It seems to me that those psychological questions which are derived from specific observations of ourselves and discoveries in the laboratory rather than from our philosophic past also are most often formulated in completely empirico-behavioral terms.

I do not mean to imply that one should use historical criteria for evaluating theoretical formulations. Rather, I want to insist that there is more than ample historical justification for selecting psychological problems, and hence a "level of analysis," which make no reference to organisms' structural apparatus. Most of us have the faith that every stimulus event in the history of the organism has a neurophysiological counterpart. But the answers are *different* when we look to one or to the other as an explanation of behavior. The correlative identification of a phenomenon at a different data level makes it a different phenomenon. Conditioning is not a reflex arc or cortical excitation; it is the behavioral outcome of CS-US pairings (Pavlov's mistake here notwithstanding). The gradient of textural density of the perceived terrain (Gibson, 1950) again refers to a stimulus and not a neural event. I believe this is what Brunswick (1963) meant when he said that

Psychology must focus its descriptions on what organisms have become focused on (and on the gross correlations of these foci, per se), not on events located at the interstices between these foci. . . . Otherwise there would remain a white spot on the landmap of possible scientific knowledge [p. 231].

Analogically, we may note that all sentences are composed of sound groupings, but that the rules governing the combination of phonemes are not intertranslatable with the rules by which sentences are generated.

My second point is that I cannot understand why it has been asserted that having a cause for behavior from the stimulus realm is more *grubo* than having one at the neurophysiological realm—although it is clear that having *either* is more *grubo* than having both. What I am objecting to is not the vigorous attempt to find means of translating one type of variable into the language of the other, but the attitude that answers in terms of physiological variables are somehow more valuable. For while I have no doubt that psychology can be happy (i.e., favored by prosperity) with reductionism, I would contest the assertion that it cannot be happy without it. There seems to be an incurable vagueness of the term "basic" as used in this context. Operationally, it refers to a smaller unit of analysis; but it seems also to have carried surplus evaluative meaning which cannot be pinpointed. It certainly cannot mean that explanations from physiology comprise more complete knowledge of the same sort than are obtained from stimulus explanations. While we do have faith that there is complete intertranslatability from the behavioral to the physiological realms for the description of single events, we cannot have the same faith in the intertranslatability of lawful relations from the two realms. There is nothing like a guaranty that the effective interactions of environmental and practice variables will be isomorphic with the interaction of neurophysiological variables. Any one neural pattern may turn out to be produceable by a variety of antecedent environmental conditions, and any one antecedent condition of the environment may have the power to produce a variety of neural patterns. It seems wiser to be concerned with improving the adequacy of those functional relations that we hope eventually to translate into brain behavior than to worry prematurely about being *grubo* because we don't yet have the translations. It strikes me as doubtful that many neurophysiologists consider their theories coarse because they cannot relate them to the variables of physical chemistry or to the first cause of creation. Certainly one would never seriously call a physiologist "nonbasic" because he failed to spell out all the behavioral implications of his views.

It is sometimes implied that recent advances in psychopharmacology and intracranial stimulation will soon allow more effective practical control over behavior than that which is possible with environmental manipulations, and that this constitutes the grounds for calling physiology more basic. This is, however, no criterion of basic behavior-science, which seeks to understand things as they are, as well as how they might be under unusual laboratory arrangements. Finally, the claim for the greater basicness of physiology because of its more sophisticated instrumentation may also be dismissed. Superior instrumentation simply produces more precise and reliable answers, it does not make better questions. No psychologist has ever used such a criterion to suggest that our explanations are more basic because of our more sophisticated methodology.

The core of my second point is that the Pavlov, Razran, Esper, et al., viewpoint reveals a basic misunderstanding of the positivistic attitude. Razran likened positivism to the "'wisdom of Sirach who counselled not to want to investigate what is beyond one's strength as one has no need for things that are hidden.'" The essence of positivism is not a fear of investigatorial inadequacy. Rather, it is a suspicion of analogic explanations from data-realms other than one's own, and a desire to be certain that the phenomena observed are saved by a theory at their own "level" before trying to accommodate that theory to others from different scientific levels. Despite the fact that positivists are mainly concerned with the formal specification of terms and the criteria for evaluating propositions rather than with "levels" of explanation, it is no historical accident that most positivists have not argued for reductionism. An insistence upon explanations for phenomena that are based upon phenomena at a different level is certain to muddy those specifications that positivists insist on. According to Burtt (1955) it was the absence of such positivism that was partly responsible for the great delay before the acceptance of Copernican theory. Though this theory was a far simpler and more harmonious mathematical scheme than Ptolemy's, it upset the basic physics of the time. Similarly, in psychology, ignorance about behavior has been concealed, on occasion, by a retreat into the brain, as Esper himself documented.

It may be as Razran said, that brain-behavior conditioning has become an area of almost elite research in both experimental psychology and neurophysiology; but we can understand best the meaning of this phenomenon by relating it to environmental rather than internal variables. It is the *Zeitgeist* that has pushed the pendulum in that direction, a purely behavioral force.

REFERENCES

BRUNSWICK, E. Organismic achievement and environmental probability. *Psychological Review*, 1943, **50**, 255–272.

BRUNSWICK, E. The conceptual focus of systems. In M. H. Marx (Ed.), *Theories in contemporary psychology*. New York: Macmillan, 1963.

BURTT, E. A. *The metaphysical foundations of modern science*. Garden City, N.Y.: Anchor Books, 1955.

GIBSON, J. J. *The perception of the visual world*. Boston: Houghton Mifflin, 1950.

ESPER, E. A. *A history of psychology*. Philadelphia: Saunders, 1964.

RAZRAN, G. H. S. Russian physiologists' psychology and American experimental psychology: A historical and a systematic collation and a look into the future. *Psychological Bulletin*, 1965, **63**, 42–64.

THE EXPERIENTIAL LEVEL

THIS *section contains selections that document and defend psychology's return to an active concern with mind. Much of the objection to the concept of mind has to do with the fact that notions of a theological spirit or soul, with all their implications for vitalism and mysticism, have retained a tenacious hold upon our thinking about mind or consciousness or experience. We have tended to reject these concepts, but many believe— and this conviction has been gaining momentum—that in psychology's efforts to exorcise the mystical demon we have tended to reject what is perhaps the central factor in man's nature. This section demonstrates a renewed interest in mind or consciousness, not as a spiritual, transcendental intrusion but as a natural expression of the manner in which information about man's environment and processes are represented.*

In the first paper, one which early signaled the beginning of a new involvement with the experiential level, Zener evaluates the role of experience in contemporary psychology. The role of experience is further considered in the following three articles.

Radford reviews some of the problems central to the study of mental phenomena. Shallice offers an information-processing model for cognitive variables. Finally, Sperry presents an unusual and provocative theory, based upon his own pioneering split-brain research, in which consciousness is assumed to play a superordinating role in brain physiology.

31
THE SIGNIFICANCE OF EXPERIENCE

KARL ZENER

THE present essay consists substantially of a paper presented as part of a symposium on current behavioristic theory and methodology. It was expected that my contribution might approach the subject from the contrasting point of view of Gestalt theory. Initially, the two theories

FROM K. Zener, The significance of experience of the individual for the science of psychology. In H. Feigl, M. Scriven, and B. Maxwell (Eds.), *Minnesota Studies in the Philosophy of Science*, Vol. 2. (Minneapolis: University of Minnesota Press, 1958). Pages 354–369. Reprinted by permission of University of Minnesota Press.

differed in a number of basic ways. Central among these differences were these: at the methodological level, their systematic treatments of conscious experience, at the empirical level, their differential stress upon the factor of organization; at the theoretical level, their differing stresses upon "peripheral" factors vs. "brain" processes, and the general properties of those central brain processes—i.e., their atomistic vs. field character. On the one hand, Gestalt psychologists have, within the last twenty-five years, failed to increase markedly the specificity of their statements concerning the detailed properties of Gestalt processes and their determining conditions. Certain neo-behavioristic theories, on the other hand, have incorporated into their systems functional equivalents of such processes (cf. Hull's afferent neural interaction, 10). Others have so modified their original stresses as to obscure any general differences between theirs and the Gestalt position. Only the first-mentioned difference still remains fundamental—namely, the difference accorded, at least in practice, to the scientific status of experience. It is this difference that I propose to examine, in its relation to the potential content of the science of psychology. The word "experience" will here be used to refer in a general way to what has variously been termed awareness, conscious or direct experience, the phenomenal world, or, though I dislike the term, simply consciousness.

I shall contend that the difference in point of view involved still remains of the greatest importance, and that, if maintained, the long-range consequences of the dominant behavioristic emphasis will prove crippling for the development of psychology. Let us assume that psychology aims toward an understanding of all, including the most valued and most specifically human levels, of behavior and experience. Let us also assume that psychology as a science attempts, in an increasingly adequate fashion, to characterize the most significant features, at all levels, of the events we regard as psychological; to identify their determining conditions; and, most essentially, to state with increasing specificity the interrelations between such events and their conditions—that is, to formulate psychological laws.

We shall not be concerned with problems of the logical characteristics of the linguistic structure of science but rather with the basis in observation which is presupposed by any such analysis. The question which I propose to consider is the following: How is the actual and potential achievement of the aims of science just mentioned influenced by the practicing scientist's formal view of the role of experience in science? To restate the problem: What is the relation that may obtain at a stage of development of a science comparable to the present state of psychology between the breadth of its observation base and the character of its content in terms of functional relationships? In particular, we shall consider the limitations which a marked restriction of the range of experience regarded as scientifically unable or legitimate may have both upon the further development of psychology as a science and also upon the interrelationships between scientific psychology and other branches of knowledge concerning human behavior, such as the humanities.

What I have to say has little direct bearing upon the hygienic analyses of previous improprieties in the use of language in science which have been vigorously furthered by the philosophers of science in recent decades. I wish to point out, however, some of the unfortunate consequences which have resulted from acceptance by psychologists of these methodological emphases without viewing them in proper perspective to the psychologist's total task as a scientist. As a scientist, his total task involves the discovery, as well as the ordering and the verification of relevant knowledge. The psychologists' methodology of verification indeed needed re-analysis. Here I am convinced chiefly to inquire into the consequences for psychology of the quasi-emotionally based rejection of direct experience for other aspects of his scientific task.

Although the historical development of the behavioristic view of the status of conscious or direct experience in the science of psychology is well known, reference here to certain aspects of it is instructive. Titchener envisaged the primary tasks of psychology as the analytical description of conscious experience and the specification of its determining conditions. Watson reacted against this exclusive interest in the analysis of experience rather than of behavior. In itself this was a healthy reaction to Titchener's radical restriction of the subject matter of psychology. Unfortunately Watson's own initial denial of the existence of conscious experience constituted just as drastic an amputation upon the body of psychology—one which in its practical consequences was not reversed by his later formal admission of its existence. For the "ontological" status of conscious experience as a vital aspect of many of the events constituting the referents of psychological constructs was still implicitly denied, as was its "functional" status as a direct observation base of psychology. However complex his own reasons for this rejection of experience, his most valid scientific one was the failure of the refined Titchenerian "introspective" method to yield consistent results especially when applied to the analysis of complex experiences.

Clearly, consistency or inter-individual agreement in observation is, in *some* sense, a central and irreducible requirement of scientific method, and the full force of Watson's criticism has never been adequately dealt with by his theoretical opponents. There has been too much of a tendency to insist upon the desirability, and even in *general* terms the necessity, of recognizing phenomenal reality or direct experience; not enough of a detailed spelling out of a convincing methodological rationale. Such a rationale must adequately recognize and analyze the potential sources of error and discriminate the conditions of observation under which the experiential aspects of reality as reported can and cannot be assimilated into the interrelated system of functional relationships constituting psychological science. Only thus can the hard core of the Watsonian critique be satisfactorily met. The extent to which it can be met is after all not an a priori matter or one to be decided autistically, however great the felt urgency to make science "meaningful," but one which must be decided empirically, and with full recognition of its difficulties. The *extent* to which experiential variables may be assimilated into the body of psychological science *might* in practice have proven to be limited to the necessary but qualitatively trivial role of perceived pointer readings in physics. The argument in favor of this possibility is on its face persuasive. How can any event, such as a particular experience of an individual, directly accessible only to one person and thus absolutely private, and, as a unique event, uncheckable, serve as a basis for the establishment of scientific laws? Such a possibility appears in principle incompatible with the accepted supra-individual or public character of science. It has thus been frequently assumed that only those events which in principle can be simultaneously observed by multiple observers whose independent reports in turn may be observed and compared, also by multiple observers termed exeprimenters—only such events may be accepted as constituting a legitimate observational basis for science.

In general methodological discussions, the original observational basis is often almost taken for granted without any detailed specification of assumed conditions. Thus, it is assumed that, under so-called standard, but frequently unspecified conditions, any normal person will see a green field as green, and the oaks on its edges as spreading out in three-dimensional space. Or, it may be proposed—if reports on green fields or oaks on their edges are not in complete agreement "let us get back to the pointer readings of the physical scientist—where agreement is assured." Psychologists, however, perhaps shocked by such an epistemologically uncritical position, and impressed by the possible lacks in correspondence between one's experience and one's report of it, have frequently taken a radically opposed position. They have insisted that only verbal reports by the observing subject of his own experience, including that of another's behavior, or perhaps better, written statements concerning experience or behavior, or, even better, graphic records of the consequences of such behavior are public and, therefore, safe starting points for the science of psychology. Thus, observable written words or sentences have become acceptable scientific data, but the individual's experiences to which they may refer, that is, the experiential referents of those words, are disenfranchised as private and, therefore, illegitimate.

Let us examine in more detail whether such an intransigent insistence upon the criterion of interobserver agreement with respect to the particular observations upon which science rests is either necessary or desirable.

Let us also examine the conditions under which the criterion may be applied without hampering scientific advance. Unfortunately for us, philosophers of science have discussed this problem chiefly in terms of physical science. It is therefore worthwhile to consider briefly the differential consequences for physics and for psychology of the two just suggested restricted observational bases (i.e., pointer readings and verbal reports).

In physics, it has gradually become possible to make many data-yielding experimental observations by reading the dials of scientific instruments, the so-called pointer readings. This is a type of perceptual situation specifically designed to maximize accuracy of observation and thus also interobserver agreement in the report of observation. Physics has achieved primary reliance upon such a type of observational situation only after a long period of development. At present, this type has definite advantages and sets only minor restrictions on the investigation of a wide range of physical events. This present state of affairs depends, however, upon several basic facts. The specificity of inferences permitted by the detailed character of current physical knowledge makes it possible to connect physically and deductively that part of the situation observed (the instrument dial) with the actual events in the physical systems being studied in such a way that almost any process may be determinately related to standard physical instruments (the character of whose internal structure and processes is of course known in complete detail). Secondly, the perceptual experience involved is reduced to that of displacement of a pointer on the dial or scale of a measuring instrument. Apparently, for such perceptions to yield inter-individual consistency of report, the only important preconditions within the observer are adequate visual acuity, attention, and a minimal level of verbal articulateness. Finally, the physicist uses perceptual experiences in any case solely as *indifferent indicators* of the events in which he is directly interested. Accuracy and consistency of report are his only concerns and he can and does ignore the particular phenomenal properties on which the report is based. They are mere epistemological handles necessary for the check of his theory against reality, but the *locus of his scientific concern* is elsewhere. As Pratt (15) points out, the present physicist leaves the level of observation almost immediately, further descriptive analysis of the experienced world would profit him little if at all, and the experiences against which he does check his scientific inferences have no intimate or intrinsic relationship or correspondence with his scientific (explanatory) constructs.

With regard to each of these considerations, current psychology differs radically from current physics. The first and most vital difference consists in the content of the two sciences. In contrast to physics, psychology is interested in the experience and behavior of, and events within, the human organism, not in external events per se. The processes intervening between external stimulus conditions and reactive behavior are certainly complex. No human behavior can be adequately explained without reference to them. And in the vastly important class of primarily endogenously regulated actions, they provide the major key to understanding and prediction of behavior. (Furthermore, one of the currently most misleading practices in psychology is that of assuming that an explanation is provided by functional relationships between external independent and dependent variables affecting a system, itself consisting of a complex set of variables which are merely kept constant in the experimental situation.) Experience or awareness is presumably more directly dependent upon these intervening processes than is overt behavior, including verbal report. This remains true even though we have difficulty in specifying any basic postulate, such as that of isomorphism, expressing in detail the form of this dependence. And it is extremely likely that clues as to the properties of these intermediate processes may be yielded by sensitive phenomenal description. However, *wholly aside from this heuristic consideration, the phenomenal characteristics of our perceptual and other behavior in themselves constitute an aspect of the universe with which it is the peculiar task of psychology to deal scientifically.*

Secondly, the lack of specificity in the functional relations constituting present psychology does not permit us to construct observational situations in which important features of complex human activities are unambiguously linked via recording apparatus to simple pointer readings characterizable only in terms of a physical-thing language. To take aspects of peripheral behavior as indicators of central events with the same specificity as pointer readings are taken by physics would require that our knowledge of the effector processes intervening between them and these central processes (i.e., those underlying the experience or constituting the implicit behavior) be as detailed and determinate as that of the processes of the interior of the physical measuring instruments connecting its moving pointer to the relevant properties of the physical event in which the physicist is interested. In such cases these effector processes (or these *plus* the recording instrument) *are* for the psychologist or the physiologist the equivalent of the measuring instrument alone for the physicist. They mediate between the events observed and the events constituting, in the particular experiment, the locus of concern of the scientist. In the case of psychology as in physics, the experimenter's *locus of concern* is operationally determinable by the terms of the hypothesis he proposes to test and by the type of generalization he makes of his experimental findings (i.e., of the *laws* they are taken to define). If we are interested in relating to their determining conditions the significant features of human and animal behavior, including the perceptual activity of experiencing, we cannot limit ourselves to observations determined primarily by external conditions. All psychologically relevant experience is in some degree, and most of it is in a marked degree, conditioned by internal states and processes of the individual. Therefore, restriction of observational situations to those in which the role of internal determinants is minimized, as in the observations of physics, disastrously limits the range of psychological events that can be directly reported.

It is true that psychology has gained by utilizing observational situations similar to those of physics. Concentration of experimental attention on kinds or aspects of behavior especially of animals capable of being connected to physical measuring instruments has permitted the determination of quantitative and quasi-quantitative relationships of great interest. We are concerned here, however, with the consequences of too exclusive a utilization of such situations. Carried to the extreme to which much methodological discussion would indicate as desirable, it would result in the exclusion, in principle, of all experience in the production of which differences in past experience, in special capacities, in present motivation, or in personality, would play a significant role, as well as those differences in receptor equipment and attention affecting observation in standard physical situations. Thus would be excluded all the more complex experiences of everyday life, all those constituting the working data of the clinical psychologist, and the whole range of artistically creative experiences as well as those which constitute the subject matter of the humanistic disciplines. In other words, in the interest of achieving scientific objectivity, description of all most characteristically human experience is avoided as failing to achieve the criterion of general inter-observer agreement so frequently insisted upon as scientifically necessary. (See Spence, 16, for a forceful recent restatement of this point.)

I should like to suggest that this *criterion*, as generally stated, is *not a necessary one for scientific observation*. Rather, developments in our knowledge of perception provide the *possibility, in principle, of transcending the difficulties raised by inter-individual variability in reports on experience*. Since science seeks to formulate systems of functional interrelationships (laws) between certain characteristics of events and their relevant conditions, the "objectivity" required by science means only that *under given specifiable and manipulable conditions, repeatable events* (in the present context, repeatable experiences) *can be shown to recur*. Whether or not we can directly check the individual occurrence of a particular experience becomes therefore of only minor importance if the experience uniformly recurs under adequately specified conditions. Furthermore, specification of the conditions need not, as in physics, be primarily in terms of the external situation. It may require, in addition, a detailed and even elaborate specification of personal, or organismic, conditions. Adequate specification of the relevant personal variables will at present often not be possible without further research. However, present technical difficulties should not obscure the matter of the methodological principle here involved. Techniques of experimental manipulation and control of internal variables will increase in adequacy with increasing knowledge both of perceptual and effector processes (just as with physics the development of precision of laws and measuring instruments has been a circular process). Manipulation of the conditions under which, for instance, occurrence of musical experiences of specified characteristics may be predicted, may involve years of training of a person of defined musical abilities. The number of such persons available for experimental subjection to controlled auditory stimulus events might not be large. However, this would not, in principle, invalidate the scientific objectivity or repeatability of the functional relationships that might be obtained with this limited number of observers possessing specified characteristics. Again an observation need not be repeatable by any given person picked randomly from the street, or from the classroom, in order for it to serve as an adequate basis for establishment of psychological laws. It is required only that it be repeatable under specifiable external and internal conditions, even though, practically, this may limit its repetition to a very restricted set of persons. I am, therefore, suggesting that the *more general* and, to me, acceptable, objective intended by the current criterion of "public character of individual observations" or of inter-observer agreement would be better and more flexibly served by the substitution of the *criterion of repeatability of obtained functional relationships between specified experiences and specified conditions* (external and internal).

The importance of specification of hitherto unstressed internal conditions may be illustrated by reference to the recent work of one of my colleagues, Dr. M. Gaffron. Her observations on the effect of right-left mirror-image reversals in painting and etchings provide striking phenomenal indications of processes which may enter in a very basic way into the perception of three-dimensional space (3, 4). Individual subjects are variously sensitive toward the various components of the complex phenomenal effects of right-left reversal. Such effects include shifts in the left location of the observer within the picture space, the direction from which individuals within the picture space are felt to be perceived, the internal groupings of such individuals as determined by spatial arrangement or by their personal inter-relationships. Such felt differences indicate the necessity of investigating laterality and the complexities of brain dominances in human observers. The effects of hitherto neglected factors of laterality may not only explain variations in the results of such perceptual experiments but, upon more adequate specification, may lead to the discovery of new dimensions of human experience.

Paradoxically, considering Titchener's position, the possibility of incorporating phenomenal observations of complex experiences into lawful relationships (i.e., into science) will depend upon the developments of techniques of diagnosis (projective and other techniques of so-called clinical or individual difference psychology) of internal, personal variables, and upon techniques of controlling them, as much as upon the controls of external stimulus variables. It will also depend upon the development of a more adequate knowledge of the processes of perceptual learning.

We thus urge the advantage of a broadened range of phenomenal experiences upon which psychology may be based, and obversely, deny that they need be limited only to those upon which general intersubjective agreement can be obtained. A more extreme form of the position here rejected lies in the contention that the difficulties of phenomenal observation and report can best be avoided by recourse to so-called objective experimentation with animals.

It has been asserted that in objective experiments with rats Lashley has demonstrated the major facts concerning perceptual grouping, figure-ground differentiation and the like, originally reported by Wertheimer, Rubin, and Köhler in human "introspective" experiments. The implication that human reports on experience were therefore dispensable is incorrect. Science consists of far more than confirming already observed relationships. Strategically the important advance was the initial identification or discovery of these experiences at the human level. This constituted the pre-condition for their subsequent check at the animal level. As the original human observations in the history of the psychology of simple perceptual forms have historically preceded confirmation of similar functional relationships at the animal level, so we may expect that identification of the characteristics of more complex experiences of greater human significance will be made by observers sensitized to such features of their own experience. The work of Michotte and his co-workers on the phenomenal characteristics of the perception of "mechanical causality," "reality," and "permanence" provide illustrations (14). Furthermore, such observations will not be invalidated if they are never confirmed at the animal level.

An examination of some of the ways in which useful descriptive categories have originated would be relevant to the present argument. The standard sensory attributes such as pitch or loudness distinguished within the Wundtian-Titchenerian tradition arose out of a tendency to identify the simplest dimensions of uncomplicated experience. Doubtless, knowledge of the dimensions of physical stimuli played a certain role in their initial identification. But such a phenomenal dimension as tonal volume scarcely arose in this way. Contrariwise, the initial specification of the phenomenal characteristics of such experiences as figure-ground by Rubin or the varieties of apparent movement by Wertheimer arose from a free unrestricted description of their experiences. Later, general acceptance of these phenomenal categories came after sufficient determination of their stimulus conditions and formulation of adequate instructions enabled other observers consistently to identify and report these features in their own experiences. I suggest that twentieth-century sensory psychophysics has exploited the capital of phenomenological distinctions made in the nineteenth century—and am apprehensive that no new comparable wealth of phenomenal distinctions relevant to more complex perceptions is being presently accumulated.

At times mixtures of physiological theory, of physical conceptions of the stimulus, and of properly naive phenomenal description have yielded valuable new distinctions. One illustration is that of perceptual segregation, introduced by Wertheimer and Köhler. It was probably derived in part from speculations as to brain functioning. The more recent suggestions by Gibson that surfaces, edges, and texture gradients constitute the basic phenomenal dimensions of three-dimensional space doubtless derive in part from a geometrical and physical analysis of the characteristics of the optical stimulus (5, 6).

There is no reason why the constructive role of phenomenological description should be confined to the area of perception as traditionally conceived. Quite to the contrary, I would urge that its more systematic extension to other areas would provide a powerful tool to initial identification of significant variables, and, in the idiom of my colleague S. Koch, further the pre-conditions for incipient theory. MacLeod (12, 13) and Asch (1) have strongly argued this point with regard to social psychology. Fritz Heider (8, 9) has shown the possibilities of identification of different action attributes. Koch has recently illustrated the forcefulness with which a set of personal phenomenal observations may be brought to bear upon the general mode of thinking about motivational processes (11). That certain central systematic motivational concepts (e.g., Lewin's *Aufforderungscharacter*, Murray's press) have had phenomenal overtones may have been neither wholly unintentional nor without virtue.

A further potential empirical gain stemming from the present argument is the factual contribution which would result from more systematic phenomenal characterizations of the less usual kinds of experience; that is, those kinds traditionally regarded as scientifically unusable because of lack of sufficient intersubjective agreement in reporting them. Such experiences would typically occur in situations in which some type of internal factor plays an unusually predominant role, or in which the total situation is one which for practical and humanitarian reasons would not be experimentally instituted. Acute situations of great danger, of great stress, of unusual deprivation, of drug addiction or administration, are examples of one type. Psychiatrically or neuropathologically abnormal individuals, both in chronic and in acute situations such as that of brain operation, provide further examples. Observations under such conditions are by no means lacking but their systematic utilization has been. The point to be made here is that the potential advantage to be gained by more systematic use of those unusual situations is, in principle, the same as that widely recognized in the area of complex motivation. There, discovery of important features of the interplay of motives in normal situations has been gained by attention to their exaggerated manifestations under abnormal conditions. In the present context, it is suggested that phenomenal dimensions, as for instance that of reality-unreality, which in usual experience may not vary enough to be noticed, may exhibit themselves more clearly under unusual conditions. Further examples of the same point are provided by instances of experience dependent upon rare characteristics of the observer such as exceptional training or special talent, particularly as combined in the creative artist or thinker of high capacity.

Psychology need not fall prey to the common attitude that genuine values in a democratic framework are limited only to those achievable by all men. It has much to gain by consciously seeking to identify and determine the conditions of the more rarely occurring experiences even if they only occur with more differentiated human beings. We may expect that their identification will be followed, if more slowly, by a specification of their conditions, which would constitute the occasion of their assimilation by psychological science. This is not to suggest that there are no limitations to such scientific assimilation. There well may be inherent limitations derived from the special attitudes under which some types of experience occur and those necessary for adequate observation and verbal report. Here, I have been more concerned to point out that such limitations may be far more closely approximated than to attempt to determine their exact character. For fuller exploitation of phenomenal experiences under usual conditions, it is clear that fuller knowledge of the interrelationships between experience and the report on it is required.

A few remarks may be made as to general conditions which would be favorable to the discovery of new phenomenal characteristics. It is quite probable that individuals vary considerably in their awareness of the phenomenal dimensions or characteristics of experience. Such awareness may well be decreased by the inevitable emphasis developed in scientific activity upon conceptual categorization and enhanced by a certain reluctance immediately to categorize experience in terms of the characteristics traditionally recognized in the language of technical psychology or of everyday language. Let us refer to individuals capable of freeing themselves from traditional categorization, as experientially sensitive observers. Certainly an increased number of such among psychologists would be desirable.

Another precondition for progress in phenomenal observation is a more general trust in one's own experience. Recent generations of psychology students are extraordinarily reluctant to trust any of their own descriptions of their own experience not immediately confirmed by the reports of any happenstance bystander quite without reference to whether certain conditions of training, attitude, motivation, and the like are required for occurrence of the phenomenal characteristic in question. This is apt to be accompanied by a corresponding uncritical acceptance of the significance of verbal reports of others provided considerable agreement is exhibited among them, often without even raising the question of the character of the relationship between the words of the report and their referents in the experience of the individual. This is reflected also in the frequent uncritical acceptance of graphic records without adequate consideration of their relation to the underlying events. All of these features stem from the neglect of experience of the individual as having direct scientific status in current psychology.

One of the most urgent technical questions involves the relationship between experience and its various indicators. A major source of confusion stems from the identification of a property of experience with its most frequent indicator—the verbal report—that is, of identifying a red experience with the report "it is red," or of the felt experience of the plastic character of a piece of sculpture with the report "it is plastic." Explicit justification of this practice on operational grounds (see Stevens, 17) seems not to be currently maintained (2, 15, 16) and yet, in practice, as Boring has recently indicated (2), actual concern is apt to be deflected from the experiential referent to its operational index, the report. And, since the "report" is publicly observable and is a "response," it tends to be regarded as the significant end term of the functional relationship being established. It is also frequently treated as a sheer response, with neglect of its referent, phenomenal experience. However one may protest that this constitutes an unnecessary distortion of the essentials of the behavioristic analysis, there remains the incontrovertible historical fact of pragmatic significance that, within the last thirty years, no new phenomenological distinctions have arisen out of investigations by any behavioristically oriented psychologists.

Furthermore, since the behavioristic formulation shifts the burden of scientific responsibility from the report of the subject to the report of the experimenter, no incentive exists for a more adequate analysis of the process intervening between occurrence of and report on experience. Fortunately for the behaviorist, there exists no need within his formulations to search for le mot juste—to adequately characterize any of his experiences. The current attitude is that it is the behavior that counts—and that means the report, not its forgotten referent, the experience.

Yet, obviously, a more intensive analysis of the interrelation of language and experience is required. Even a more central and general problem, however, lies in the analysis of meaning in behavior, not only linguistic behavior. Thus, it is often strictly irrelevant whether an observer reports in verbal terms the presence of a phenomenal characteristic, or presses a key after an appropriate verbal instruction from the experimenter. There is thus a functional equivalence of the role of verbal instruction and of verbal report. The meaning of the key-pressing behavior may be identical with that of a verbal characterization. And, under certain conditions often achieved only with laborious effort, this meaning may be established by non-verbal training methods. A specification of these conditions would be equivalent to a statement of the conditions under which language develops. But these problems cannot be further pursued here.

One final comment concerning the current devaluation of free unrestricted description in experimental phenomenal analysis. Graham has characterized free description as being on the level of casual conversation and recognizes only reports highly restricted by instructions as of scientific value (7). This ignores the role played by free description of experience in the essential developmental stage of identification of new phenomenal categories. Initially, the individual psychological observer need not be able by himself to specify a particular phenomenal dimension which nevertheless he may be perfectly capable of reporting if requested by the experimenter to do so through appropriate instructions. But before the determining conditions of an experience can be established, at any level of parametric detail, the significant phenomenal characteristics of the experience must first be identified. And this is in a sense a creative task. I am by no means identifying this task with the whole task of science. But in the early stages, it may constitute a very critical phase of scientific advance, and psychology in most of its fields is in such an early stage of development.

To recapitulate, I have stressed the significance of our conscious experiences for the science of psychology in respect to the development of new knowledge and to the character of the content of psychology. Discussions of scientific method, particularly in the context of behavioristic psychology, have tended to stress problems of testability, of concepts and of functional relations, relatively neglecting the extent to which either the concepts or functional relations investigated correspond to those aspects of the universe which in some sense are most central and significant for the area of reality with which the science deals. I have contended that an acceptance of the necessity, in principle, of general intersubjective agreement on individual observations, and a too exclusive concern with verbal reports as such rather than with the experiences to which they refer, have together enormously narrowed the range of experiences regarded as legitimately accessible to psychological science. Among other consequences, this has resulted in an unfortunate and unnecessarily wide gap between psychological science and the humanities as branches of knowledge; it has limited advances in areas of scientific psychology itself even outside that of perception, notably in those of motivation and social psychology.

Great technical difficulties in specifying the relations between experience and report still remain. It is my conviction that these technical difficulties are soluble with sufficient insight and experimental effort, but that a general precondition of their solution resides in a change in the climate of opinion in which psychologists work. Such a change would involve a more general trust in observation of one's own experience, and an increased recognition of the scientific legitimacy of the observation of more rarely occurring experiences provided that the conditions of such experiences are specifiable. Finally, and this I cannot overstress, such a change would involve clearer recognition that full development of psychology as a science requires that a sufficient number of its scientific observers and experimenters must themselves be highly developed in those characteristics which are most essentially and significantly human.

REFERENCES

1. ASCH, S. E. Social Psychology. New York: Prentice-Hall, 1952.
2. BORING, E. G. "A History of Introspection," Psychological Bulletin, 50:169–189 (1953).
3. GAFFRON, M. "Right and Left in Pictures," Art Quarterly, 13:312–331 (1950).
4. ———. "Some New Dimensions in the Phenomenal Analysis of Visual Experience," Journal of Personality, 24:285–307 (1956).
5. GIBSON, J. J. The Perception of the Visual World. Cambridge, Mass.: Riverside Press, 1950.
6. GIBSON, J. J. "The Perception of Visual Surfaces," American Journal of Psychology, 63:367–384 (1950).
7. GRAHAM, C. H. "Visual Perception" in S. S. Stevens (ed.), Handbook of Experimental Psychology, pp. 868–920. New York: Wiley, 1951.
8. HEIDER, F. "Social Perception and Phenomenal Causality," Psychological Review, 51:358–374 (1944).
9. HEIDER, F., and M. SIMMEL. "An Experimental Study of Apparent Behavior," American Journal of Psychology, 57:243–259 (1944).
10. HULL, C. L. Principles of Behavior. New York: D. Appleton-Century Co., 1943.
11. KOCH, S. "Behavior as 'Intrinsically' Regulated: Work Notes Towards a Pretheory of Phenomena called 'Motivational,'" in M. R. Jones (ed.), Nebraska Symposium on Motivation. Lincoln: Univ. of Nebraska Press, 1956.
12. MacLEOD, R. B. "The Phenomenological Approach to Social Psychology," Psychological Review, 54:193–210 (1947).
13. ———. "The Place of Phenomenological Analysis in Social Psychological Theory," in J. H. Rohrer and M. Sherif (eds.), Social Psychology at the Crossroads, pp. 215–241. New York: Harper, 1951.
14. MICHOTTE, A. La Perception de la Causalité. Louvain: l'Institut superieur de Philosophie, 1946.
15. PRATT, C. C. The Logic of Modern Psychology. New York: Macmillan, 1948.

16. SPENCE, K. W. "The Empirical Basis and Theoretical Structure of Psychology," *Philosophy of Science*, 24:97–108 (1957).
17. STEVENS, S. S. "Psychology: The Propaedeutic Science," *Philosophy of Science*, 3:90–103 (1936).

32
THE ROLE OF INTROSPECTION

JOHN RADFORD

JOYNSON (1970, 1972) has argued for the use of introspection in opposition to what he regards as the "generally accepted doctrine" (Broadbent, 1961) of objective experiment. This view "defines the subject matter of psychology as behavior rather than mental life; it rejects the view that psychology investigates conscious experience through introspection [Joynson, 1972, p. 1]." Now this view, as Joynson allowed, has perhaps never been "generally" accepted, though it has been extremely influential. As an example of a phenomenon that ought to interest psychologists, but that might have no behavioral counterpart, C. A. Mace used to give an *unfulfilled intention:* "He thought of going out by one door, but actually went out of another." Mace (1965) observed that "psychology is regaining consciousness [p. 1]." Burt (1962, 1968) put a forceful case for the study of consciousness.

On the other hand, some writers, imbued with the "accepted doctrine," have gone to considerable lengths to incorporate some of the phenomena of consciousness within a respectable behaviorist framework. Hebb (1968) presented a somewhat tortuous argument with respect to mental imagery. He wished to "dispose of what seems to be a misconception, that reporting imagery, or describing it, is necessarily introspective [p. 466]." His argument is, first of all, that experiences may give rise to reactions: experiences, that is, in the sense of stimulus conditions that can be specified by an observer. Among the reactions may be vocal sounds or indeed verbal reports. But these are simply objectively recordable instances of behavior: "It is obvious that in such reactivity—when I burn my fingers and say 'Ouch'—no question of looking inward arises. My verbal response is no more dependent on introspection than a dog's

FROM J. Radford, Reflections on introspection, *American Psychologist*, 1974, 29 (4), 245–250. Copyright 1974 by the American Psychological Association. Reprinted by permission.

yelp when his tail is trod on [p. 467]." The processes involved can, in principle, be reduced to a physiological chain of cause and effect. In the case of imagery, much the same chain is called into play, except that the initial stimulus is absent. To make his point, Hebb (1968) quoted the case of a *phantom limb:* Above the level of the amputation the same nervous mechanisms may operate as before the limb was lost. The same argument applies to *memory imagery:*

Though there is now no sensory input, the same central process, more or less, is exciting the same motor response—more or less. . . . It is the same outward-looking mechanism that is operative, not introspection. . . . At least, it is not introspection in the sense of a special inward-looking mechanism of self-knowledge [p. 467].

This led Hebb to suggest that "the mechanism of imagery is an aberrant mechanism of exteroception." This is an odd view, for why should imagery be in any sense "aberrant"? Imagery is presumably a form of internal representation of the environment, and there is no reason to think such mechanisms anything other than natural. The view arises, however, from Hebb's determination to abide by what he regards as "the rules of objective psychology, in which mental processes are examined by inference, and not by direct observation [p. 468]." This is interesting, for Hebb seems here to adopt the exact opposite of the view of the classical introspectionists. "One does not perceive one's perceptions," said Hebb, "nor describe them; one describes the object that is perceived, from which one may draw inferences about the nature of the perceptual process [p. 467]." Now this view of perception itself can certainly be questioned. Piaget and Inhelder (1966), for example, held that even when one makes a copy of a drawing, it is not the drawing that is copied directly, but a mediating image of the drawing. However, even if the mechanism of perception were of a stimulus–response kind and even if the mechanism of imagery were similar, it would not follow that the reporting of the image was not introspective. It might not be systematic, as in some of the classical studies (I suspect that is part of what Hebb meant by a "special" mechanism). And, of course, the *statements* about the image can be treated as behavior. But that is not the same thing as saying that no introspection is involved, as I hope to show.

Let me quote another attempt to bring some of these awkward phenomena within the behaviorist fold. Bourne, Ekstrand, and Dominowski (1971) presented a textbook, *The Psychology of Thinking*. But thinking must be treated in a certain way: "Thinking is purely and simply a behaviour concept . . . thinking is a simple noncommittal way to describe a behaviour which, like all behaviour, is completely observable [p. 7]." With this view, it is not surprising that introspection finds no place in the book, nor indeed that "thinking" is restricted to concepts, problems, and language. This view is interesting, because it is almost identical, in essence, with that of J. B. Watson. The latter, as is well known, wished to reduce thinking to subvocal language, that is, a particular aspect of observable behavior. It might be felt that in 50 years little has changed. All the behaviorists we have quoted have been happy to include speech in their objective studies, and Boring (1953) suggested that this meant that introspection was being allowed to carry on its business under a new name, that of *verbal reports*. But this, it seems to me, is unfair to the behaviorists.

It seems to me that we can distinguish between introspections as data and introspection as a method. By "data" I mean here the statements of introspection, not the objects of introspection. Introspections as data in this sense can, I think, always be treated as verbal reports, if that is what we wish to do. They can be recorded in the same way that we record "the subject pressed the lever," or "the subject scored x on the test." What is recorded is "the subject says that . . ." he has an image, a feeling, etc. Such records must, of course, be subject to the usual checks used for all experimental data and in particular must yield satisfactory levels of significance. It may also be argued that records of this type need a special sort of check, analogous to that used for personality questionnaire responses. Essentially, this is not to take the response at its face value, but to establish empirically its relationship to some other variable. This might be an aspect of the stimulus conditions, and/or other behavior.[1] Some examples are provided by Woodworth (1938). If this can be done then, it may be argued, statements of introspections can be considered acceptable in the same sense as other widely accepted sorts of psychological data.

But is there, in fact, no difference between Hebb saying "Ouch" and a dog yelping? The real issue must lie in whether there is another class of data, distinguished by being accessible only by a particular method, that of introspection. This question has a number of aspects. Philosophically, it is a version of the body–mind problem. Historically in the behavioral sciences, there has been the change from regarding consciousness as a reservoir of experience to be investigated directly, to regarding it as a construct, inferred from other observations (Boring, 1953). As we noted, that is Hebb's view. But there are also more strictly psychological aspects.

The first of these is that "the method of introspection" covers several different, though related, methods. McKellar (1962) offered a classification of these. He made six sorts of distinctions:

We may first contrast the systematic methods of "classical introspection" with those of a relatively unsystematic kind. Secondly, the use of trained introspectionists differs from the work of the Gestalt psychologists and others who

---

1 I owe this point to E. Valentine.

sought, by introspection, to study the phenomena of naive human experience. Thirdly, introspections may be classified by the circumstances in which they are obtained: the laboratory, the clinic, the analytic situation, and daily life. Fourthly, some introspection is carried out mainly for communication to the experimenter, while in other cases it is carried out partly or largely to extend the investigator's own empathic understanding. Fifthly, introspection under normal circumstances may be contrasted with the use of the method in special, experimentally produced circumstances: those produced by drugs, sensory deprivation, hypnosis, etc. Sixthly, we may contrast introspections made or elicited by trained psychologists from those made or elicited by others [p. 628].

This is the only classification of introspective methods I have come across in the recent literature. Clearly, McKellar's distinctions do exist, though perhaps they are not all of equal theoretical importance. For example, introspections when the subject is or is not under the influence of a drug would not appear to be different *methods*, though the *results* will very likely be different in the two cases—as would the results of any observation. It seems to me, considering the range of activities that have been referred to as "introspection," that three groups can be distinguished, in terms of what it is that the subject is to do. There are, first, cases of self-observation. The individual reports on his own experience: He aims to observe his own mental events, in the same way that an astronomer observes stars or a behaviorist observes responses. Second, there are self-reports: By this I mean cases in which the person tells of his experiences, but without trying to be objective—for example, experiences under unusual conditions. Third, there are cases of thinking aloud: the technique used, for example, in Duncker's (1945) well-known experiments on problem solving. These distinctions are not absolutely clear-cut, but they do, I think, refer to three different activities. Wundt distinguished between introspection and self-perception (Boring, 1953). By the latter I take it he meant what I have called self-reports. For introspection proper, trained observers were required. The distinctions are confused by several factors. First, all the activities can, in principle, be more or less systematic. That is to say, the experimenter (who may also be the observer) can exercise a greater or lesser degree of selection. This feature, however, has in practice been an issue mainly in the first case. Watt (1904; quoted by Humphrey, 1963) developed the method of fractionation in an attempt to get at thought processes by systematic self-observation. Second, the activities have in use sometimes been confounded. A good example here is psychoanalysis. The only point about the analytic use of introspection that is clear is that it comes at the extreme end of the nonselective range, because the prime rule for the patient is to hold nothing back. Now there is a sense in which psychoanalysis could be said to use what I have called thinking aloud: The patient simply says out loud what is passing through his head. He does not have to observe himself; that is the analyst's job. In this respect psychoanalysis takes on a curiously behavioristic air, for the analyst deals with what is objectively observable: the patient's behavior and speech. (A patient might make a remark and add: "I meant . . ."; and the analyst might reply: "Let us look, not at what you meant, but at what you said.") Since the rule is to hold nothing back, however, the patient will inevitably also engage in self-observation. And since the aim of analysis is to give the patient more control over his own behavior, he will, if the analysis is successful, become more objective about what he says (and does). He moves, in a sense, from being subject to being experimenter. The analyst *also* makes inferences about the patient's internal experiences, and the patient learns to do this too. A third confusing factor, though of less importance here, is that it is difficult to be sure that introspection is not always in fact retrospection (Bakan, 1954).

It will be seen that the data resulting from all three methods can, if desired, be treated as verbal behavior, in the way we have already discussed. A further step can be taken, and mental events can be inferred from this behavior. The first method, however, that of introspection proper, is distinguished in that its essential aim is to make direct observations of a particular class—observations of events not otherwise accessible. The distinction between these and other events is expressed by Bakan (1954) as that between experience and that of which the experience is. It is brought out by the example of the *stimulus error*. The phrase was coined by Titchener (Boring, 1957) to refer to the "error" of an observer in lapsing from the psychological viewpoint, in reporting on phenomena, to some other viewpoint. The psychologist should report on what he experiences. It is for the physicist, or some other scientist, to report on the external stimuli that bring about the experience. Boring instances a two-point threshold: The Titchenerian psychologist's task was to report when he experienced the two points as one, regardless of the fact that he knew there were two.

This brings out another aspect: the question of trustworthiness. As Boring (1953) pointed out, in classical psychophysics controls are not used; the control lies in the training of the subject. Psychophysical experiments can, of course, be done with animals using methods of discrimination training. Titchener ruled out of psychology animals (and children and clinical patients) because they could not be trained to observe their mental events and to distinguish between these and physical events.

Thus, it seems important to know whether there is a unique method; and if so, whether this should be used by psychologists, either among other methods or, as Titchener demanded, exclusively. Classical German psychology, as established by Wundt, defined psychology as the science of experience: immediate experience, not inner experience, because there is no valid distinction between inner and outer experience. As Boring (1957) put it: "The data of experience are merely themselves; a perception does not have to be perceived in order to be a perception; it has only to occur [p. 332]." This is interesting in view of Hebb's objection to introspection, quoted earlier. However, it follows from this definition that the method of psychology is that of self-observation. For Wundt, "having an experience is the same as observing it [Boring, 1957, p. 332]." Boring spoke with great authority, yet a glance at the simplest form of Wundtian experiment casts doubt on this. For example, Wundt (1924) himself gave as an introductory and basic experiment listening to a metronome and observing the way in which we perceive the beats falling into a rhythmic pattern. The attempt to be more systematic led the followers of Wundt, notably Külpe and Titchener, to emphasize the training necessary for such self-observation.

A number of departures from, and reactions against, these views took place in psychology. They include Gestalt psychology and psychoanalysis. The most extreme, as far as method is concerned, was behaviorism. It was on this point that Watson took his stand. He wrote in 1930:

> Behaviourism, as I tried to develop it in my lectures in Columbia in 1912 and in my earliest writings, was an attempt to do one thing—to apply to the experimental study of man the same kind of procedure and the same language of description that many research men had found useful for so many years in the study of animals lower than man [p. IX].

Watson seems to have had several reasons for this view. One was his interest in the study of animal behavior itself. Another appears to have been an intense dislike of any suggestion of mysticism, such as he felt was involved in the study of consciousness. The only point of theoretical interest, however, is that of objectivity. Watson (1930) equated behaviorism with objective psychology, and introspective psychology, with subjectivity. He does not, however, present any arguments in support of this.

Thus, Watson agreed with the classical psychologists in insisting on a particular method, necessitated by a particular subject matter. Some attempts have been made, on the other hand, to resolve the opposition. Thus, Boring (1953) argued:

> Operational logic, in my opinion, now fuses this single dichotomy because it shows that human consciousness is an inferred construct, a concept as inferential as any of the other psychologists' realities, and that literally immediate observation, the introspection that cannot lie, does not exist. All observation is a process that takes some time and is subject to error, in the course of its occurrence [p. 187].

But the dichotomy is not fused here, for if consciousness is inferred, it presumably cannot be observed directly. Thus, Boring comes down on the side of the physicist and not the (Titchenerian) psychologist. It is, besides, not satisfactory to reject a method merely because it can lie. Infallibility of method does not exist in science.

A more sophisticated attempt is due to Burt (1962). He argued that the early objection to introspection, that two observers would disagree, was merely the result of failing to realize the importance of individual differences. The behaviorist insistence that data be public is unhelpful, because certainty in science is unobtainable. This objection, argued Burt, rests on the distinction between what is "public" and what is "private." Thus, it is said that language is inadequate to convey the experience of one person to another. But, in general, we do understand what is meant. Then it is said that only one person can observe the events of consciousness. But strictly speaking, this applies to every firsthand observation. The behaviorist attempt to make introspections respectable by treating them as verbal reports merely misdirects our attention, for it is precisely the subject's experience, not his verbal behavior, in which we are interested. Burt next argued that the model of the physical sciences adopted by Watson was a crude and oversimplified one, which would not be accepted now. It is not clear, however, what in Burt's view would be accepted; nor whether he thinks this presumably more sophisticated model appropriate for psychology. Finally, Burt attacked the newer behaviorists' argument from the principle of parsimony. A system such as that of Hull, Burt claimed, is far from parsimonious. And parsimony can only be achieved, in any case, when a science has reached a highly developed stage. Here again Burt's arguments are open to objection. Given that behaviorism is not parsimonious, it could still be more so than introspection. And by what criterion are we to tell if a science is highly developed, other than its degree of parsimony? If the principle of parsimony is accepted, then it is for each side to show that it is more parsimonious than the other. Burt concluded that introspection should be among the methods of psychology, though it should certainly not be the only one.

Introspection is necessary, not only because it brings new questions to the fore, but also because it alone can supply much of the observational data needed to answer them. . . . We need to know what intervenes between the stimulus and the subsequent response; and here, so I have argued, introspection yields the most important clues [p. 238].

Burt's (1962) argument, then, seems to be that introspection as a method is not unique, but that the data it yields cannot be obtained in any other way. This implies a contradiction. Burt rests his case, first of all, on the notion of the probabilistic nature of science, arguing that no scientist in any field would insist on absolute certainty before accepting a datum. But, as he goes on to say, the crux lies in the distinction between what is "public" and what is "private." Burt (1962) seems here to wish to deny any such distinction: "Strictly speaking, *every* first-hand observation is necessarily 'private.' Whether certain observations are treated as 'public' turns not on their specific or intrinsic nature, but merely on the context [p. 231]."

I think Burt's argument is open to objection, but in practice, the objections may not matter much. First of all, it may well be that whether observations are *treated* as public depends on the context, but that does not answer the question whether they *are* public. Now, in what sense is every firsthand observation "private"? This seems true in the sense that each individual experience is unique. First, each individual is unique, by virtue of different makeup, different history, etc. But even if an exact facsimile of an individual were produced, there must logically be two experiences, since to qualify as individuals the beings must at least be distinct in time and place. The experiences might be identical in content, but there would be no way of proving this with absolute certainty. But it does not follow that because there are always two experiences, there are always two things of which the experience is. The question as to whether there is a reality independent of observers has, of course, a long philosophical history. It seems to me that science, if it is to operate at all, must assume that this is so. But we could, in fact, rest the argument at the point of saying that there is a distinction between events that we may suppose to exist independently and those of which we cannot suppose this. The first are "public"; the second "private." In the second class we put experiences; in the first, stimuli and responses. In practice, the distinction is often not very important. On the "private" side, the difficulties of communicating experience have been exaggerated, as Burt pointed out. On the "public" side, exact replications are rather infrequent.

R. S. Peters (1953) pointed out that both Titchener and Watson were part of the "observationalist" tradition of science. Titchener held that we directly observe experience; Watson, that all we can observe is behavior. Later behaviorists such as Hebb say that we infer our knowledge of private events from the behavior we see. In the case of adult human beings, this behavior is usually verbal; but in the case of nonverbal beings, it may be, for example, discrimination learning. This, however, raises the question of what it is that we infer. To say that a child, an animal, or another adult has "an image" seems a curiously artificial statement, unless we have from our own experience some notion of what sort of a thing an image might be. It seems odd, in other words, to suppose that "image" has exactly the same sort of intervening variable status as, say, "filter."

I am aware, of course, that a forceful movement, represented by writers such as Lacan, denies the whole possibility of applying to human beings principles of objective observation that derive from the physical sciences. (See, for example, Caws, 1968.) But this argument would lead us too far afield. Within the observationalist tradition, Peters criticized the insistence on method which was characteristic of both Titchener and Watson. Science is not such that there is any one method that guarantees success. Nor, indeed, are there methods that must be utterly proscribed. Rather, there are criteria for assessing any method as more or less useful. To put it another way, scientific "method" is a much broader concept than the "methods" of introspection or behavioral analysis. These are better regarded as techniques, being two of those in the scientist's repertoire. As Peters (1953) put it: "All that is required for an inquiry to be a theoretical science is that conscious attempts should be made to overthrow hypotheses [p. 719]." There seems no reason, in practice, why introspections cannot be used for this purpose, even though they be held to be logically distinct from other sorts of observation. If introspection conflicts with itself or with other data, this is no different from any conflict of results.

It might be argued that it is simply a matter of what we are interested in. Presumably both Titchener and Watson were happy for the other to pursue his own path, but each insisted that "you must not call it psychology." But to define a science by its subject matter or by its techniques seems unhelpful. There is no way of saying in advance what will turn out to be relevant or useful. Rather, science as a whole is the enterprise of establishing statements that correspond with reality, and any one science is simply a group of loosely related enquiries, put together for convenience or because of demonstrable connections. Psychologists, it seems to me, are people who are interested in the behavior and experience of men and animals. Like every scientist, the psychologist says with Molière "je prends mon bien où je le trouve." Introspection gives us information about experience. It yields some data otherwise inaccessible. It may besides bring to light facts that might otherwise be overlooked, or stimulate us to ask new questions. Like any technique, it has peculiar difficulties, especially when used in odd circumstances. These, however, are the natural hazards of science. I would suggest that the battle that began over 60 years ago, and which some are apparently still fighting, might now be amicably concluded.

REFERENCES

BAKAN, D. A reconsideration of the problem of introspection. *Psychological Bulletin*, 1954, **51**, 105–118.

BORING, E. G. A history of introspection. *Psychological Bulletin*, 1953, **50**, 169–189.

———. *History of experimental psychology.* (2nd ed.) New York: Appleton-Century-Crofts, 1957.

BOURNE, L. E., EKSTRAND, B. R., & DOMINOWSKI, R. L. *The psychology of thinking.* Englewood Cliffs, N.J.: Prentice-Hall, 1971.

BROADBENT, D. E. *Behaviour.* London: Eyre & Spottiswoode, 1961.

BURT, C. The concept of consciousness. *British Journal of Psychology*, 1962, **53**, 229–242.

————. Brain and consciousness. *British Journal of Psychology*, 1968, **59**, 55–69.

CAWS, P. What is structuralism? *Partisan Review*, 1968, **35**, 75–91.

DUNCKER, K. On problem-solving. *Psychological Monographs*, 1945, **58**(5, Whole No. 270).

HEBB, D. O. Concerning imagery. *Psychological Review*, 1968, **75**, 466–477.

HUMPHREY, G. *Thinking: An introduction to its experimental psychology*. New York: Wiley, 1963.

JOYNSON, R. B. The breakdown of modern psychology. *Bulletin of the British Psychological Society*, 1970, **23**, 261–269.

————. The return of mind. *Bulletin of the British Psychological Society*, 1972, **25**, 1–10.

MACE, C. A. Causal explanations in psychology. In C. Banks & P. L. Broadhurst (Eds.), *STEPHANOS: Studies in psychology: Essays presented to Sir Cyril Burt*. London: University of London Press, 1965.

McKELLAR, P. The method of introspection. In J. Scher (Ed.), *Theories of the mind*. New York: Free Press of Glencoe, 1962.

NATSOULAS, T. Concerning introspective "knowledge." *Psychological Bulletin*, 1970, **73**, 89–111.

PETERS, R. S. *Brett's history of psychology*. London: Allen & Unwin, 1953.

PIAGET, J., & INHELDER, B. *Mental imagery in the child*. New York: Routledge & Kegan Paul, 1971.

WATSON, J. B. *Behaviorism*. London: Kegan Paul, Trench, Trubner, 1930.

WOODWORTH, R. S. *Experimental psychology*. New York: Holt, 1938.

WUNDT, W. *An introduction to psychology*. London: Allen & Unwin, 1924.

33

THE FUNCTIONS OF CONSCIOUSNESS

TIM SHALLICE

IN THIS paper it is argued that the basic phenomenological concept—consciousness—can be mapped onto an information-processing concept. In arguing for this mapping, the paper has two aims. The major aim is to remove an anomaly in information-processing theory, namely, that while many aspects of mental life have been modeled, theorists have avoided direct consideration of conscious awareness, although this is vital if cognitive psychology is to have a satisfactory theoretical base.

FROM T. Shallice, Dual functions of consciousness, *Psychological Review*, 1972, **79** (5), 383–393. Copyright 1972 by the American Psychological Association. Reprinted by permission.

The minor aim is to facilitate the interpretation of experiments which involve the subject in complex introspections, judgments, or strategies.

In the development of models, cognitive psychologists have approached the problem of consciousness indirectly as in work on attention (e.g., Deutsch & Deutsch, 1963; Posner & Boies, 1971) or have used it as an unexplained component as, say, in Waugh and Norman's (1965) requirement that transfer from primary to secondary memory requires conscious rehearsal. There has been no explanation of how such a phenomenological concept can be related to ideas about mechanism. One possibility is to reject the need for such an explanation, to argue that consciousness is a pseudoconcept. Yet, increasingly, concepts such as strategy and rehearsal are being used as explanatory concepts. Such concepts depend on the theorist reflecting on his conscious experience and are very different from a concept like primary memory whose roots lie in physiology and computer technology. Even a concept like eidetic imagery is not understood by a person lacking it as he would a mechanistic concept, but through descriptions by other people. Hence, if consciousness is to be rejected as a pseudoconcept, to be consistent such concepts must be rejected too.

This would much restrict the present explanatory repertoire, but it would also have other repercussions. Subjective reports are increasingly used, if on occasion slightly disguised under the label "protocols." Also more use is being made of instructions which require subjects to monitor their conscious experience in complex ways as for Sperling's (1967) subjects who had to adjust the time of occurrence of a click so that it coincided subjectively with the termination of a visual image. If consciousness is a concept as unrelated to reality as a concept like "ghost," how such experiments produce scientifically useful results becomes very mysterious and unexplained. It thus seems that the problem of consciousness occupies an analogous position for cognitive psychology as the problem of language behavior does for behaviorism, namely, an unsolved anomaly within the domain of the approach.

Turning to the second aim, phenomenological evidence remained acceptable, at least in perception, even when psychology was at its most behaviorist. Judgments required of subjects would be of standard sorts, for example, psychophysical ones, and the theoretical explanations given for the results could normally be in terms of mechanisms clearly distinct from the judgment process itself. For instance, the results of color-matching experiments are interpretable in terms of retinal mechanisms, while the matching process itself is central. Moreover, the assets and pitfalls of particular judgmental procedures became known (see Woodworth & Schlosberg, 1954), alternative judgment procedures could be used to cross-check inferences, and potential judgmental artifacts can be investigated by hypothesis testing—the converging operations of Garner, Hake, and Eriksen (1956). In effect, the judgmental procedures become almost as objective a source of data as a physical measuring instrument such as an electrode (see Attneave, 1962, for a related view). However, the more central the mechanism under investigation, or to use Miller, Galanter, and Pribram's (1960) term, the less it belongs in the Image, the more difficult do such cross-checking operations become. The introspection or judgment process will be intimately involved with the mechanisms under investigation so the two stages will not be separable as measuring instrument and phenomenon. As an illustration, consider the difficulty of demonstrating that De Groot's (1965) protocols of chess thinking are free of artifacts. His main results depend on obtaining verbalizations from chess masters, as they analyze difficult positions, a procedure that cannot be simulated at present and only in a very general way, repeated. His findings provide some of the best support for the primarily serial-processing nature of complex thought, but they depend on the uncritical acceptance of introspective evidence—one of the best learned dangers in psychology.

One means of avoiding this danger is to develop theories of the introspective process so that one can assess theoretically what should or should not be subjectively reportable. This assumes that the introspective process can be split into two parts—the production of conscious experience and the reporting of the experience. The primary evidence for making this split is the way in which experimenters, for example, in perceptual experiments, utilize their own experience in the experimental situation in order to interpret the subjects' reports (Natsoulas, 1967; Rosner, 1962). The extremely complex problems relating to the second stage have been interestingly discussed by Natsoulas (1967, 1970); they will not be considered in this paper.

Two linked assumptions are made in attacking the problem of the relation between conscious experience and mechanism. First, the identity theory of the relation between mind and brain will be assumed correct. This is that mental processes are identical with certain physical processes in the brain in the sense of "identity," by which a gene is identical with a section of a deoxyribonucleic acid (DNA) molecule. Following from this, the problem of relating information-processing theories to phenomenological generalizations is assumed analogous to that of relating two neighboring fields of science. "Phenomenological generalizations" refers to hypotheses ranging from ones based on simple introspection such as that conscious experience can be of various types, percepts, images, intentions, etc., to more obscure philosophical ones such as that a defining characteristic of a mental state is its property of intentionality.

With respect to the second assumption, it is clear that one technique in science for relating two fields is by constructing isomorphic correspondences between the concepts and operations of one field and those of another. Numerous examples of such constructions exist in the history of science, the most famous recent one being that of molecular biology linking biology and chemistry. As Beckner (1959) showed, using this example, it is not necessary to construct isomorphisms between all the concepts and operations of one paradigm and those of another (i.e., reduction of the first to the second) for the linking to be successful. He argues that the concept of a kidney cannot be reduced to its physical and chemical properties, since it can only be understood in terms of its function within a whole system, and function cannot be related to existing physical and chemical concepts.

This becomes clearer if one uses the analogy of a scientific theory as a map of the world. Two perfectly correct maps of the same area cannot necessarily be totally reduced one to the other, as they may be concerned with different aspects of the area, for example, ancient monuments and geological structure. This approach avoids one claimed difficulty for identity theory (Shaffer, 1961); while conscious experience does not have the property of being spatially localized, brain states do.

In general, it seems that the philosophical objections to the identity theory can be answered (Armstrong, 1968; Borst, 1970). Probably the strongest objections are linked to Wittgenstein's (1953) succinct but opaque claim: "An 'inner process' stands in need of outward criteria [p. 153]." Wittgenstein's approach has frequently been interpreted (e.g., Smart, 1963) to mean that insofar as mental states can be communicated, they can be reduced to observables. It follows that any attempt to use phenomenological information in science which does not just rephrase behavioral information would be vacuous. As pointed out earlier, the practice of current research appears to be proving this claim false. It is likely that Wittgenstein did not hold such a neobehaviorist position (see Malcolm, 1963) and that his arguments are more relevant to the problems surrounding the second stage of the introspective process—the reporting—which are not considered in this paper. His actual argument depends on showing that phenomenological terms do not describe a private world unrelated to action. Therefore, it seems compatible with the present approach in which consciousness is to be related to action.

Proponents of the identity theory have argued for it on the ground of parsimony, given present scientific knowledge. By contrast, Gray (1971) has argued that it offers no guides to what properties of the brain give rise to consciousness, and that it limits the scientific questions one can ask about consciousness. Identity theorists do tend to view consciousness as a property dependent, at least in part, on the nerve cell composition of the brain and not just on its system of organization (e.g., Armstrong, 1968). However, the present theory demonstrates that the identity theory can relate to system level properties of the brain and that it can form a basis for theorizing on questions which Gray considered important, such as the survival value of consciousness.

As no presently existing model seems to provide a basis for constructing an isomorphism, one is developed in this paper. It is not conceived as a finished model—other models might well be constructed to account for the limited empirical evidence considered—but the development of a model enables answers to the metalevel questions to be made concrete. Since the argument on the proposed isomorphic relation between phenomenological and information-processing concepts moves over a number of different considerations, a brief summary of the isomorphism is presented here. The brain is conceived of as containing, among other units, a large set of action systems (similar to Miller et al.'s, 1960, TOTE units), only one of which can be maximally activated at any given time. A certain sort of input to each action system has two functions. It determines first whether that action system will become dominant, that is, maximally activated. If so, it then sets the goal of the action system until either the goal is achieved or the action system is reactivated with a different goal. It is this input (the *selector input*) that is identified with the content of consciousness. A flow diagram of the model is shown in Figure 1.

Since direct empirical testing of multiaxiomatic theories is notoriously complex (see Broadbent, 1958), the model is constructed on the basis of cybernetic considerations so as to provide another form of support. It is argued that the model satisfies constraints necessary for any mechanism which would function like a human organism. The cybernetic section is followed by a brief review of the empirical evidence which is itself followed by more detailed phenomenological considerations.

One claimed characteristic of a conscious state is that it has an object. One is thinking of X, perceiving Y, or intending Z, and only one of these at once. This unitary nature of consciousness is mirrored in psychology by limited-capacity ideas. Evidence, particularly that of Posner and Boies (1971), discussed later, indicates that there is a limited capacity for the programming of motor responses, which suggests developing the model from consideration of the control of actions.

Cybernetic Considerations and Model Assumptions

A common assumption of theorists is that the infinite variety of one's potential actions is produced by the operation of a finite number of internal control systems (e.g., Piaget's, 1970, schemes; Miller et al.'s, 1960, TOTE units). It has been widely argued that human control systems operate hierarchically in an analogous way to computer programs where the main program may call in routines which may themselves call in other routines and so on (Miller et al., 1960; Newall, Shaw, & Simon, 1958). Miller et al. were primarily concerned with the way particular control systems operated. Instead, in this section, while their general approach is accepted, the problem of how to control passes from one system to another is tackled. The unit of control—the action system—is

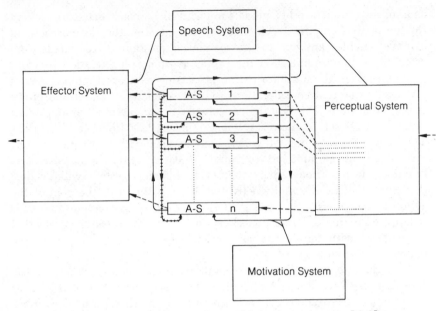

FIGURE 1. *Information flow in the model (*n *action system [A-S] version). Solid lines represent selector input. (Speech output via the effector system is included in this category as, on the model, it has the function of providing selector input for other people.) Hatched lines represent inhibitory interactions between action-systems. (To avoid complicating the diagram, the only inhibitory output shown is that from Action System 1.) The dotted lines in the perceptual system represent the partial autonomy required for particular specific input processing. For simplicity, certain interconnections not considered in the models have been left out, e.g., sensory-effector ones. As no arguments have been presented on whether or not a functionally separate memory unit is required, the memory aspects of the model are not represented.*

treated as a black box whose properties, stated in later assumptions, are similar to those of programs, except for Assumptions 3 and 4. (The program analogy is not intended to refer to the internal operation of action systems, which are probably most easily conceived in analogue terms following the work on simulation of motor skills; e.g., Bernstein, 1967; Gibbs, 1970; Wiener, 1948.)

Using the program analogy, the basic problem of this section is how a mechanism simulating a human could have the following three properties: (a) a very large number of individual programs; (b) the routine facility, that is, hierarchical changes of control; and (c) rapid access to and realization of the most vital program. Throughout, the effects of learning are ignored so that only asymptotic performance will strictly be relevant to the model. The assumptions of the model are the following:

1. In addition to perceptual, motivational, and effector systems, the brain contains a set of action systems.

2. Action systems operate so as to attain a goal, by means of output to effector units or to other action systems. Each action system may have a finite number of variables set as a goal when it is initiated.

If more than one action system has a subsystem in common, then it becomes a separate action system or an effector unit. The setting of variables, discussed in Assumption 6, and the separation of common subsystems are both necessary to enable the system to operate in an analogous fashion to a computer program. The separation between action systems and effector units will be dealt with after Assumption 5.

3. The speed and accuracy with which an action system operates depends on its level of activation, which can continuously vary. The minimum level of activation necessary for normal functioning differs between action systems depending on their complexity and the extent to which they have been learned.

4. No more than one action system may be strongly activated (i.e., become dominant) at any given time. This results from the activation of each action system being inhibited by every other action system by an amount which increases monotonically with the other's activation.

The two last assumptions are put forward as a solution to the potential cybernetic problem that an organism has many goals which it needs to achieve at any one time and has only a limited number of effector units available.

It would be possible to arrange that each effector unit is controlled by the most important action system requiring it, by either serial or nonserial means. Serially, a relatively simple program could list the action systems in order of performance. Given the large number of action systems a human would need to possess and the need to make continual changes in priority with the changing stimulus situation, such a system would prove very slow given the relative slowness of neural as opposed to electronic processing. For example, if 2^n action systems existed, to reassess the priority of one action system would require n successive activation comparison operations.

On a simple parallel model operating according to Assumption 3, it would seem possible for each effector unit to be controlled by the action system which activates it most strongly, inputs from other action systems being inhibited. However, consider the situation in which two action systems are roughly equally activated. An example would be changing gear and signaling to go right in an English car. In such a car, changing gear involves movements with the left hand and foot while holding the steering wheel with the right hand; signaling right involves holding the steering wheel with the left hand while using the right arm for signaling. Thus the effector units for both arms receive conflicting input from the two action systems. If the motivating circumstances for changing gear and signaling right are equally strong, then all four inputs to the motor control units will be equally strong (this presupposes that the outputs of an action system to each effector unit are equally strong; other assumptions are also disastrous). Given any noise in the system, there would be a 50% chance of the effector units being under the control of different action systems, if the stronger input to effector units inhibits the weaker. One consequence could be that both hands would leave the steering wheel, a somewhat dubious and unusual maneuver.

This example shows that a parallel system operating just according to Assumption 3 fails to ensure that at least one action system can control all the effector units it requires. Yet unless this condition is realized, no satisfactory action can ensue. Assumption 4 is added to solve this problem, as the input to an effector unit from the dominant action system will now be much stronger than other inputs. It would also avoid the potential cybernetic problem that some action systems might not be physically independent in the brain. The second part of Assumption 4 is derived from ideas on lateral inhibition in sensory systems (e.g., Ratliff, 1965) and those on inhibitory requirements of cell assembly theory (Milner, 1957). It also removes the necessity of having a separate system which selects which action system is to be dominant; the two functions of selection and operation can be performed by the same system. To prove that it is sufficient to produce the required property of always allowing one action system to be dominant clearly depends on a more precise formulation of the action system interactions. A very much simplified formalization of the interaction of action systems, which has the required property, is given in the Appendix.

It is now possible to differentiate between action systems and effector units, solely in terms of their interrelation with other units.

5. An action system has the capacity to inhibit all other action systems sufficiently to become dominant; an effector unit does not.

This would not require a dichotomy of amounts of inhibition that can be produced by systems. With a continuous range of amounts of inhibition, systems only producing a very small amount would never be capable of becoming dominant given normal activity in other systems.

6. An action system can have two excitatory types of input, that necessary for its ongoing operation (specific input) and that necessary to activate it and set its goal (selector input). The selector input can come from either perceptual or motivational systems or other action systems.

For a routine to be entered in programming, the main program must set a number of variables and then use an instruction which passes control to the routine. These variables will determine how the routine operates on that particular entry. For action systems to operate in an analogous way, other systems must activate it and set its goal; these are the functions of the selector input. By contrast, a routine can call for further input of data while operating; this corresponds to the specific input. The difference between these two types of input was noted for skills by Bernstein (1967). For instance, when reaching for an object, the visual and kinesthetic input which provides an estimate of the position and velocity of the hand has a different function from that input producing the initial object recognition which determines what action system will be most strongly activated and what its goal will be on that particular operation. The specific input, then, is required for the continual estimation of rapidly changing variables necessary for the operation of the action system; the selector input, for differentiating between this particular operation of the action system and others. The memory requirements for the specific input will normally be small, and insofar as the action system can be modeled by a linear system, it will be zero. The selector input, though, must clearly be stored in a memory for, if the goal and activation of an action system depended on continual input, then an animal could not even turn away from its goal to achieve it.

It would seem possible that only the amount of activating boost and the characteristics of the goal would need to be maintained in the memory; not the input that gives rise to them. However consider the example of braking to an emergency stop in a car. The goal of this action is at one level to have one's foot pressed as firmly down on the brake as possible. At another level, it is to stop the car as quickly as possible. Yet what is done after the car is stopped must depend on why the stop was initiated even if the perceptual input that initiated it is no longer present. Thus it seems necessary for the initial selector input to be stored in memory so that the goal of later action systems can be set. There would be no point in storing the specific input for this purpose, since it is specific to the action system.

7. When an action system becomes dominant, its selector input is stored in a memory, so that it, too, can act as a later selector input.

Finally, for humans, at least some action systems must be capable of being activated and having their goals set by speech input; otherwise speech could not influence action. Thus speech must produce one form of selector input. Similarly in order to have a need satisfied by another person, it must be possible to transmit by means of language what action system is dominant (at least for some action systems), and what is its goal.

8. A speech system exists with both input and output aspects. As input,

it can produce another form of selector input. As output, it acts as a nondominant action system symbolizing which action system is dominant and what is its goal.

Empirical Testing

It is difficult to test complex information-processing theories using input-output relations. Yet a test of the present theory involves a problem other than complexity. For most information-processing theories, the units are known in advance. For example, testing Morton's (1969) "logogen" theory depends on the reasonable assumption that to each word in the language there corresponds a logogen. Thus, Morton's theory can be tested with its units—the logogens known in advance from other sources. For the present theory, the units—the action systems—cannot be established in this way. No dictionary of action systems exists. Since skill or cognitive competence does not stabilize either over individuals or within an individual's life, unlike language competence, even the prospect of a dictionary seems remote.

The problem of empirical testing is approached in two ways. It is shown that the theory offers an answer to certain known difficulties for existing theories. Second, one situation is examined to show that the theory could be corroborated more closely, if appropriate assumptions about action systems are made.

Two widely held generalizations have been implicitly assumed in developing this theory. The first is that motor skills can be simulated in analogue fashion (e.g., Gibbs, 1970; Wiener, 1948). Bernstein (1967) produced evidence for the equivalent generalization that skilled performance can be fitted by a set of differential equations. The second is that thought can be partially simulated by serially organized computer programs (e.g., Arbib, 1969; Miller et al., 1960; Newall et al., 1958; and in essence, Selz, 1922).

The other widely held generalization about skill is the analogy between the nervous system and a limited-capacity information-transmitting channel. While no longer accepted in its strict mathematical sense, it remains a useful rough description of certain aspects of skilled behavior (Broadbent, 1971; Welford, 1968). On the present theory, this characteristic is deduced by considering how a system based on the first generalization, that is, motor skills being simulated in analogue fashion, could operate in practice, for the second generalization corresponds to Assumption 4—that only one action system can be strongly activated at any one time.

Similarly it is widely held that thought cannot just be a serial process under control of a master program (Neisser, 1963; Reitman, 1965; also Humphrey, 1951, for a criticism of Selz). On the present model, it is possible to deduce this nonserial characteristic from the way in which nondominant action systems can operate at the same time as a dominant one. In its simplest form, this corresponds to the way in which a simple task can be performed in parallel with a complex one. One can both walk and talk.

More interestingly, the theory is able to account for those changes in dominance which would be difficult to explain in terms of a totally serial program. De Groot's (1965) application of Selz's theory of thought to chess is possibly the most detailed examination of the application of a purely serial theory. He stated:

The more miscroscopically we examine the phase structure, the more we come across automatic processes and sequences that must be governed by an extensive series of fixed linkages. Calculating a variant and working out a plan are, in fact, operations which in any experienced player are completely controlled by routine [p. 274].

Yet even he is forced to postulate insightful advances:

In both thought processes [in two different protocols] we are concerned with "calculational serendipity," that is during routine calculations there may be a sudden coincidentally evoked means-abstraction with respect to the main goal [p. 278].

In the present approach, a chance perceptual configuration could so strongly activate another action system so as to make it dominant. Such a possibility would become more likely, if two additional assumptions hold. First, that selector input can be internally generated by inner speech or imagery; second, that if an action system has not attained its goal, it will remain submaximally activated even when not dominant. However, the major point is that the present approach has this potential; a purely serial approach does not.

As an illustration of the way in which the theory can be tested more directly, given assumptions about the action systems operating, consider the assumption from which the deductions about the two generalizations mentioned above flow; namely, that no more than one action system may be dominant at any given time. To test this, it is necessary to examine the effect of simultaneously combining two problems, each requiring a dominant action system for its solution, but which do not require the same effector units or lower level action systems.

One such situation appears to be that used by Posner and Keele (1969). Their subjects performed a reaction time task at varying stages of a task involving a motor movement to a target. The reaction time task is slowed by being performed at the same time as the movement task, which is itself relatively unaffected. This fits with the movement task being controlled by a dominant action system and the reaction time task by a nondominant one. As expected in the theory, the slowing is greatest and independent of target size in the initiation of the movement task, when its action system would need to take in selector input and must be dominant. This is not just a question of perceptual filtering, as shown by other experiments of Posner and Boies (1971) on probe reaction time in perceptual matching tasks where response selection but not perceptual encoding is found to produce slowing. To account for the other variations in slowing over the duration of the movement task would require more detailed assumptions about the change in activation over time of the dominant action system, and in particular the interaction of this with the requirements of the task.

Phenomenological Correspondences

Our mental concepts could not arise were it not for the structure of the human brain. "Smell" depends on the existence of an olfactory system; "image" depends on the possibility of internal input to the higher levels of the perceptual systems. It is held that similar considerations apply also for the concept "consciousness." In the present information-processing model, the brain, is a set of relatively independent systems, whose operations are coordinated at any moment by the selector input to the dominant action system. The selector input selects which action system is to be dominant, sets the goal of the action system, and is itself preserved in memory. It is suggested that this input corresponds to the concept consciousness, in the mental-state sense of the word. Thus, when one is conscious of X, a certain action system is receiving selector input, which represents X. The selector input has the dual functions of (a) providing the activation that enables the action system to become dominant and of (b) setting its goal. To mix levels of analysis, these functions can be said to be the dual functions of consciousness. Such a view of consciousness is related to the one held by Armstrong (1968), according to which it is "a mental state of a person apt for bringing about a certain sort of behaviour [p. 82]."

If consciousness is identical with the selector input to the dominant action system in the sense that a section of a DNA molecule is identical with a gene, then one should be able to demonstrate corresponding properties of the two concepts.

Mental states, with the possible exception of emotions like "free-floating" anxiety, have been held by philosophers since Brentano (1874) to have the property of intentionality, to point beyond themselves, to use Armstrong's (1968) expression; a percept, a memory, an intention are all of something. The selector input, too, points beyond itself, since being used to form the goal of an action system, it refers to only a part of the world.

The model can also explain the different types of conscious content. Some are obvious, for example, percepts would correspond to selector inputs from the perceptual system; intentions would be selector inputs from a previously dominant action system. The less obvious correspondences are those related to lack of conscious content. Since an action system only requires selector input at the beginning of its operation, it can operate with little or no selector input. As known to the Würzburg school (see Humphrey, 1951), the whole of the solution period of a problem is not necessarily filled with conscious content. Moreover, it explains why one is not conscious of processes connected with the lower levels of skills, as these would always be directly controlled by never-dominant effector units. It also helps to explain why skills, initially performed under conscious controls, can be performed later without conscious control. If one accepts the idea that learning a skill involves the formation of a neural system of increasing redundancy, then initially the corresponding action system would require maximum activation; with practice it would function satisfactorily with less.

The present approach requires that mental terms in phenomenal reports refer to conscious states. Since conscious states are unobservable, it might be argued that it would be impossible for a child to learn such terms. This would only be plausible if the unobservable events did not have a relatively consistent relationship with observables. Skinner (1957) gives a series of examples of how such learning could occur, if there is a consistent relationship; these examples are not critically dependent on his general behavior theory. In the model, relatively consistent relationships exist between conscious states and observables—the relation, determined by the perceptual system, between a stimulus and the selector input and, more importantly, the control relationship between selector input and action. While the detailed processes by which mental terms attain their complex context-dependent meanings are poorly understood, such meanings do not seem to provide difficulties in principle for the present approach.

Discussion

It has been argued in this paper that consciousness is a scientifically acceptable concept, as it refers to a particular type of brain process and can be mapped into an information-processing concept. This also applies to phenomenological terms such as "percept" and "intention," if used in the appropriate context. It has not been the aim of this paper to provide a complete account of consciousness, as the model besides being incomplete, is highly tentative, as the problem of empirical corroboration remains severe. Moreover, the cybernetic arguments depend on the acceptance of computer programming analogies and on the use of loose criteria such as the ease of neural construction. The incompleteness of the model is shown by no correspondence being given for many types of experience such as the consciousness of relation or doubt or expectation. Nor have aspects of consciousness such as the complexity of conscious perception been considered.

More serious, perhaps, is that the model appears to give no account of certain perceptual types of consciousness seemingly unrelated to action, such as noticing a color or seeing someone's face you half recognize. One possible explanation is that an action system exists which maximizes perceptual input from a part of the world determined by its selector input, combining both motor movements (e.g., eye movements) and resetting of the perceptual system. This process would fit with the orienting response and is analogous to Dixon's (1971) suggestion that when a stimulus comes into consciousness, the "gain" of those perceptual systems relevant to it are increased and of irrelevant ones inhibited. Here, a phenomenological fact could be accounted for by extensions to the model which are related to ideas already in the literature. It illustrates the way in which, if the general correspondence theory is correct, properties of phenomenal experience could be used to help develop information-processing ideas.

The major point of the paper, however, is not to argue for this specific model, but to attempt to demonstrate that a model can be developed with an element isomorphic to consciousness. Such an isomorphism makes comprehensible how consciousness, a concept so basic that it is impossible to define using ordinary language, or even to show, can be part of our scientific conceptual framework. The paper, thus, attempts to justify the increasing practice of using phenomenal reports and concepts in investigations primarily oriented toward the development of mechanistic theories. The mixing of these two types of explanation has been challenged by both behaviorists and phenomenologists (e.g., Giorgi, 1970), who would each accept only one type as legitimate. Eventually, if such a model is well supported empirically, it could provide a foundation for developing theoretical criteria for the interpretation of phenomenal reports in cognitive experiments, where at present only intuitive methods can be used.

Appendix

What is required is to show that mutual inhibition between action systems is sufficient to produce the desired dominance property. Since action systems are neural systems, the obvious mathematics to use is neural net theory. However, neural net theory is notoriously intractable if applied to complex networks (see Griffith, 1963).

A relatively simple mathematical formalization of the system can be obtained which is tractable and, for one isolated action system, approximates to Griffith's (1963) results for the behavior of a single purely excitatory net. This is to describe the behavior of a system of n action systems by the following set of equations:

$$\frac{dy_i}{dt} = \begin{cases} ax_i + by_i - c(\sum_{j \neq i} z_j) - e \\ \qquad \text{if } y_i > 0 \text{ or } \frac{dy_i}{dt} > 0 \\ \\ 0 \qquad \text{if } y_i = 0 \text{ and } \frac{dy_i}{dt} \ngtr 0 \end{cases}$$

where $z_i = \max (y_i - d; 0)$ and a, b, c, d, e are constant and positive.

In these equations, y_i (nonnegative) represents the activation level of the ith action system, x_i represents its selector input, and z_i represents its contribution to the inhibition of other systems. If one assumes that $c > b$ (i.e., inhibition is the more powerful at high levels of activation), and that if after a certain point in time the selector inputs are constant and at least one is greater than some critical level, then it follows that one and only one of the action systems will have an activation that will increase rapidly and continually. In fact this is a formalization of the mutually inhibitory interaction of a system of pure excitatory neural nets, but the dominance relation should be robust enough to survive complicating the operation of the individual interacting elements.

REFERENCES

ARBIB, M. A. Memory limitations of stimulus-response models. *Psychological Review*, 1969, 76, 507–510.

ARMSTRONG, D. M. *A materialist theory of mind*. London: Routledge, 1968.

ATTNEAVE, F. Perception and related areas. In S. Koch (Ed.), *Psychology: A study of a science*. Vol. 4. New York: McGraw-Hill, 1962.

BECKNER, M. *The biological way of thought*. New York: Columbia University Press, 1959.

BERNSTEIN, N. A. *The co-ordination and regulation of movements*. Oxford: Pergamon Press, 1967.

BORST, C. V. *The mind-brain identity theory*. London: Macmillan, 1970.

BRENTANO, F. *Psychologie vom empirischen Standpunkte*. Berlin: Duncker & Humboldt, 1874.

BROADBENT, D. E. *Perception and communication*. London: Pergamon Press, 1958.

———. *Decision and stress*. London: Academic Press, 1971.

DE GROOT, A. D. *Thought and choice in chess*. The Hague: Mouton, 1965.

DEUTSCH, J., & DEUTSCH, D. Attention: Some additional theoretical considerations. *Psychological Review*, 1963, 70, 80–90.

DIXON, N. F. *Subliminal perception: The nature of a controversy*. Maidenhead, England: McGraw-Hill, 1971.

GARNER, W. R., HAKE, H. W., & ERIKSEN, C. W. Operationism and the concept of perception. *Psychological Review*, 1956, **63**, 149–159.

GIBBS, C. B. Servo-control systems in organisms and the transfer of skill. In D. Legge (Ed.), *Skills*. London: Penguin, 1970.

GIORGI, A. *Psychology as a human science: A phenomenologically based approach*. New York: Harper & Row, 1970.

GRAY, J. A. The mind-brain identity theory as a scientific hypothesis. *Philosophical Quarterly*, 1971, **21**, 247–254.

GRIFFITH, J. S. On the stability of brain-like structures. *Biophysical Journal*, 1963, **3**, 299–308.

HUMPHREY, G. *Thinking: An introduction to its experimental psychology*. London: Methuen, 1951.

MALCOLM, N. *Knowledge and certainty: Essays and lectures*. Englewood Cliffs, N.J.: Prentice-Hall, 1963.

MILLER, G. A., GALANTER, E., & PRIBRAM, K. H. *Plans and the structure of behavior*. New York: Holt, Rinehart & Winston, 1960.

MILNER, P. The cell assembly: Mark II. *Psychological Review*, 1957, **64**, 242–252.

MORTON, J. Interaction of information in word recognition. *Psychological Review*, 1969, **76**, 165–178.

NATSOULAS, T. What are perceptual reports about? *Psychological Bulletin*, 1967, **67**, 249–262.

———. Concerning introspective knowledge. *Psychological Bulletin*, 1970, **73**, 89–111.

NEISSER, U. The multiplicity of thought. *British Journal of Psychology*, 1963, **54**, 1–14.

NEWELL, A., SHAW, J. C., & SIMON, H. A. Elements of a theory of human problem-solving. *Psychological Review*, 1958, **65**, 151–166.

PIAGET, J. Piaget's theory. In P. H. Mussen (Ed.), *Manual of child psychology*. (3rd ed.) New York: Wiley, 1970.

POSNER, M. I., & BOIES, S. J. Components of attention. *Psychological Review*, 1971, **78**, 391–408.

POSNER, M. I., & KEELE, S. W. Attention demands of movements. In *Proceedings of the 16th international congress of applied psychology*. Amsterdam: Swetts & Zeitlinger, 1969.

RATLIFF, F. *Mach bands: Quantitative studies on neural networks in the retina*. San Francisco: Holden-Day, 1965.

REITMAN, W. R. *Cognition and thought*. New York: Wiley, 1965.

ROSNER, B. S. Psychophysics and neurophysiology. In S. Koch (Ed.), *Psychology: A study of a science*. Vol. 4. New York: McGraw-Hill, 1962.

SELZ, O. *Zur Psychologie des produktiven Denken und des Irrtums*. Bonn, Germany: Cohen, 1922.

SHAFFER, J. Could mental states be brain processes? *Journal of Philosophy*, 1961, **58**, 813–822.

SKINNER, B. F. *Verbal behavior*. New York: Appleton-Century-Crofts, 1957.

SMART, J. J. C. Materialism. *Journal of Philosophy*, 1963, **60**, 651–662.

SPERLING, G. Successive approximations to a model for short-term memory. *Acta Psychologica*, 1967, **27**, 285–292.

WAUGH, N. C., & NORMAN, D. A. Primary memory. *Psychological Review,* 1965, 72, 89–104.

WELFORD, A. T. *Fundamentals of skill.* London: Methuen, 1968.

WIENER, N. *Cybernetics, or control and communication in the animal and the machine.* New York: Wiley, 1948.

WITTGENSTEIN, L. *Philosophical investigations.* Oxford, England: Blackwell, 1953.

WOODSWORTH, R. S., & SCHLOSBERG, H. *Experimental psychology.* New York: Holt, 1954.

34
AN EMERGENT THEORY OF CONSCIOUSNESS[1]

R. W. SPERRY

IN STUDIES involving surgical section of the cerebral commissures, we have been confronted repeatedly in recent years with questions concerning the quality and distribution of conscious awareness in the bisected brain, particularly in work with human patients (Sperry, 1968a, 1968b; Sperry, Gazzaniga, & Bogen, 1969). In the surgically separated state, the two hemispheres appear to be independently and often simultaneously conscious, each quite oblivious of the mental experiences of the opposite hemisphere and also of the incompleteness of its own awareness. Many problems are raised in regard to the seeming unity of conscious experience in both the normal and bisected condition and the relation of conscious unity to the neural process. How should we conceive the unifying role of the corpus callosum and the nature of the information it carries between the two domains of consciousness? Do the conscious qualities extend from grey matter into the corpus callosum? What is the nature of the interface between the conscious and unconscious processes?

One of the things to come out of these and related concerns, as a somewhat corollary development, has been a modified concept of the

[1] This article is based on a paper presented to the National Academy of Sciences, April 1969, in Washington, D.C. Work of the author and his associates is supported by Grant No. 03372 from the National Institute of Mental Health and by the F. P. Hixon Fund of the California Institute of Technology.

FROM R. W. Sperry, A modified concept of consciousness. *Psychological Review,* 1969, 76 (6), 532–536. Copyright 1969 by the American Psychological Association. Reprinted by permission.

nature of mind and its relation to brain activity. This revised view has continued to gain increasing support in the author's thinking over the past 5 years (Sperry, 1966, 1969a, 1969b) and is now favored over other alternatives. We deal here, of course, with the Number 1 problem in brain research, for which the evidence at hand still falls far short of providing any full or final answer. Nevertheless, the supreme importance of the problem for all kinds of human value, as well as scientific matters, prompts us to search ahead of the evidence from time to time as science advances, for any possible new insight. Even a partial solution that would enable us to decide between very broad and general alternatives—like whether consciousness is cosmic or individual, mortal or immortal, in possession of free will or subject to causal determinism, and the like—could have profound and far reaching ideological implications. In any search for meaning, identity, ultimate goals and values, or new ideologies, the nature of mind and its relation to physical reality becomes central and basic.

Most behavioral scientists today, brain researchers in particular, have little use for consciousness. For the objective experimental standpoint, it is difficult to see any place in the material brain process for the likes of conscious experience. Most investigators of cerebral function will violently resist any suggestion that the causal sequence of electro-physico-chemical events in the brain, that they work with and are trying to analyze, could in any way be influenced by conscious or mental forces. It is the working man's faith in the neurosciences—that goes back to near the turn of the century—that a complete objective explanation of brain function is possible in principle without any reference to the subjective mental phenomena. Whatever the stuff of consciousness, it is generally agreed in neuroscience that it does not interact back causally on the brain's electrophysiology or its biochemistry.

The current interpretation of consciousness takes issue with this prevailing view of twentieth century science. In the present scheme the author postulates that the conscious phenomena of subjective experience do interact on the brain process exerting an active causal influence. In this view consciousness is conceived to have a directive role in determining the flow pattern of cerebral excitation. It has long been the custom in brain research to dispense with consciousness as just an "inner aspect" of the brain process, or as some kind of parallel passive "epiphenomenon" or "paraphenomenon" or other impotent by-product, or even to regard it as merely an artifact of semantics, a pseudoproblem (Boring, 1942; Eccles, 1966; Hook, 1961).

The present interpretation by contrast would make consciousness an integral part of the brain process itself and an essential constituent of the action. Consciousness in the present scheme is put to work. It is given a use and a reason for being, and for having been evolved. On these terms subjective mental phenomena can no longer be written off and ignored in objective explanations and models of cerebral function, and mind and consciousness become reinstated into the domain of science from which they have been largely excluded since the advent of behaviorism and dialectic materialism. Without going through all the details, an attempt is made in the following to briefly outline the salient features of the hypothesis and some of the reasoning behind the foregoing statements.

First, conscious awareness, in the present view, is interpreted to be a dynamic emergent property of cerebral excitation. As such, conscious experience becomes inseparably tied to the material brain process with all its structural and physiological constraints. At the same time the conscious properties of brain excitation are conceived to be something distinct and special in their own right. They are "different from and more than" the collected sum of the neuro-physico-chemical events out of which they are built.

Compared to the elemental physiological and molecular properties, the conscious properties of the brain process are more molar and holistic in nature. They encompass and transcend the details of nerve impulse traffic in the cerebral networks in the same way that the properties of the organism transcend the properties of its cells, or the properties of the molecule transcend the properties of its atomic components, and so on. Just as the holistic properties of the organism have causal effects that determine the course and fate of its constituent cells and molecules, so in the same way, the conscious properties of cerebral activity are conceived to have analogous causal effects in brain function that control subset events in the flow pattern of neural excitation. In this holistic sense the present proposal may be said to place mind over matter, but not as any disembodied or supernatural agent.

When it is inferred that conscious forces shape the flow pattern of cerebral excitation, it is not meant to imply that the properties of consciousness intervene, interfere, or in any way disrupt the physiology of brain cell activation. The accepted biophysical laws for the generation and transmission of nerve impulses, for example, are in no way violated. The electrophysiologist, in other words, does not need to worry about any of this, provided that he restricts himself to analytic neurophysiology. He does need to be concerned, however, if he wishes to follow a sensory input to conscious levels and to explain how a sensation or a percept is produced, or how the subsequent volitional response is generated.

Although the mental properties in brain activity, as here conceived, do not directly intervene in neuronal physiology, they do *super*vene. This comes about as a result of higher level cerebral interactions that involve integration between large processes and whole patterns of activity. In the dynamics of these higher level interactions, the more molar conscious properties are seen to supersede the more elemental physio-chemical forces, just as the properties of the molecule supersede nuclear forces in chemical interactions.

To put this another way—the individual nerve impulses and associated elemental excitatory events are obliged to operate within larger circuit-system configurations of which they as individuals are only a part. These larger functional entities have their own dynamics in cerebral activity with their own qualities and properties. They interact causally with one another at their own level as entities. It is the emergent dynamic properties of certain of these higher specialized cerebral processes that are interpreted to be the substance of consciousness. It would be helpful if one could illustrate the foregoing with a few fluoroscopy-like film sequences of some of the higher cerebral activity patterns in action. As yet, however, the instrumentation in brain research remains entirely inadequate to record the pattern dynamics of brain activity. About the only instrument known at present by which one brain can plug into and read out directly the conscious experience of another brain, is the corpus callosum.

The subjective mental phenomena are conceived to influence and to govern the flow of nerve impulse traffic by virtue of their encompassing emergent properties. Individual nerve impulses and other excitatory components of a cerebral activity pattern are simply carried along or shunted this way and that by the prevailing overall dynamics of the whole active process (in principle—just as drops of water are carried along by a local eddy in a stream or the way the molecules and atoms of a wheel are carried along when it rolls down hill, regardless of whether the individual molecules and atoms happen to like it or not). Obviously, it also works the other way around, that is, the conscious properties of cerebral patterns are directly dependent on the action of the component neural elements. Thus, a mutual interdependence is recognized between the sustaining physico-chemical processes and the enveloping conscious qualities. The neurophysiology, in other words, controls the mental effects, and the mental properties in turn control the neurophysiology. One should remember in this connection, however, that the conscious phenomena are in a position of higher command, as it were, located at the top of the organizational hierarchy.

The present hypothesis represents a midway compromise between older extremes of mentalism on the one hand and materialism on the other. The present is mentalistic in accepting the existence of potent mental forces that transcend the material elements in cerebral function. It is materialistic in denying that these mental forces can exist apart from the brain process of which they are a direct property. This "emergent interactionism," or "idealistic materialism" as some would label the present compromise, permits proponents of both extremes to retain some of their more important concepts.

Whereas the older interpretations of consciousness as inner aspect, epiphenomenon, or semantic pseudoproblem have remained largely sterile, conceptually and experimentally (e.g., there is no place to go from an epiphenomenon), the emergent interaction scheme is by contrast potentially fruitful. It suggests new problems, possible approaches, and new leads to follow in working out the nature of the mental properties, their interactions, and their relations to the sustaining neurophysiology. For example, it follows directly from the foregoing that the brain process must be able to detect and to react to the pattern properties of its own excitation. It must detect the overall qualities of different kinds and different species of cerebral process and respond to these as entities rather than to their individual cellular components. There exists considerable indirect evidence, particularly from observations on perceptual and cognitive phenomena, that the brain does in fact do exactly this. One may include here the extensive evidence on perception collected during the 1920s and 1930s by the Gestalt school of psychology (Koffka, 1935; Kohler, 1929). The present view rests largely on an extension of some of the same holistic principles extrapolated now to cerebral physiology. Earlier experiments in which the author's findings had seemed to undermine Gestalt field theory, along with the related concept of psychoneural isomorphism (Sperry & Miner, 1955; Sperry, Miner, & Myers, 1955), do not apply to the present interpretation. The conscious properties are here conceived quite differently in terms of operational effects of specialized neural circuitry (Sperry, 1952) rather than in terms of isomorphic correspondence based on electric field effects or volume conduction.

Among other implications of the current view for brain research is the conclusion that a full explanation of the brain process at the conscious level will not be possible solely in terms of the biochemical and physiological data such as we are now perforce engaged in gathering. Important as these analytic data are for understanding cerebral activity, they must fall short of providing an account of mental phenomena like sensations, percepts, ideas, images, illusions, feelings, etc. For a full explanation of these gnostic functions, we are going to need, in addition, a further description and account of the higher order pattern activity in the cerebral process, the emergent properties of which are conceived to constitute the qualities of consciousness.

The foregoing points out also the specific problem of determining the nature of the unifying forces that cause a pattern of excitatory events to function as an entity in brain dynamics. It emphasizes further the need for new technology that will enable us to record the pattern aspects of cerebral function which at present can only be extrapolated from indirect or highly particulate sampling procedures.

To determine precisely how the more elemental physiological aspects of brain activity are used to build the emergent qualities of awareness becomes the central challenge for the future. At present even the general principles by which cerebral circuits produce conscious effects remain obscure. Very possibly these will become understandable, not in terms of isolated circuit principles, but only in terms of advances in cerebral design superimposed on the background of an already elaborately evolved central nervous system. There is reason to think that the critical organizational features of the neural circuitry for generating conscious awareness are mainly genetic or inherent and are activated through the brainstem arousal system, and once activated, become exquisitely responsive to changing sensory as well as centrally generated input.

This present interpretation implies some revision in traditional stimulus-response concepts of central nervous control. Any scheme, regardless of its complexity, in which sensory impulses are conceived to be routed through a central network system into a motor response becomes misleading. The present view suggests the presence of ongoing central processes specifically organized for conscious awareness around the different sensory modalities. These central mechanisms have their own intrinsic organization and special dynamics that in large part are determined centrally and autonomously. The sensory input becomes incorporated into the central process, altering the dynamics of the system and thereby its conscious properties. The initial train of sensory inflow is largely absorbed and transformed within the higher level central mechanism, and only indirectly through its perturbation of the holistic properties of the central process does the sensory input influence awareness or the volitional motor response. The present view places greater emphasis on the central processes and their specialized organizational features that create out of neural excitation the higher order phenomena of mental experience.

Returning to the primary thesis, it may be taken to imply something like the following: As we look around the room at different objects in various shapes, shades, and colors, the colors and shapes we experience, along with any associated smells and sounds, are not really out where they seem to be. They are not part of the physical qualities of the outside objects, but instead, like hallucinations or the sensations from an amputated phantom limb, they are entirely inside the brain itself. The perceived colors and sounds, etc., exist within the brain not as epiphenomena, but as real properties of the brain process. When the brain adjusts to these perceived colors and sounds, the adjustment is made not merely to an array of neural excitations correlated with the colors and sounds but rather to the colors and sounds themselves. Many uncertainties obviously remain and the foregoing is only proposed on a tentative and speculative basis for its consideration alongside the alternative theories for explaining mind and consciousness available to date.

REFERENCES

BORING, E. G. Sensation and perception in the history of experimental psychology. New York: Appleton-Century-Crofts, 1942.

ECCLES, J. C. (Ed.) *Brain and conscious experience.* New York: Springer-Verlag, 1966.

HOOK, S. (Ed.) *Dimensions of mind: A symposium.* New York: Collier Books, 1961.

KOFFKA, K. *Principles of Gestalt psychology.* New York: Harcourt, Brace, 1935.

KOHLER, W. *Gestalt psychology.* New York: Liveright, 1929.

SPERRY, R. W. Neurology and the mind-brain problem. *American Scientist,* 1952, **40**, 291-312.

————. Mind, brain and humanist values. *Bulletin of Atomic Science,* 1966, **22**(7), 2–6.

————. Hemisphere deconnection and unity in conscious awareness. *American Psychologist,* 1968, **23**, 723–733. (a)

————. Mental unity following surgical disconnection of the cerebral hemispheres. In, *The Harvey lectures.* Series 62. New York: Academic Press, 1968. (b)

————. Perception in the absence of the neocortical commissures. *Research Publications for the Association of Research in Nervous and Mental Disease,* 1969, in press. (a)

————. Toward a theory of mind. *Proceedings of the National Academy of Sciences,* 1969, **63**, 230–231. (b)

SPERRY, R. W., GAZZANIGA, M. S., & BOGEN, J. E. The neocortical commissures: Syndrome of hemisphere deconnection. In, *Handbook of clinical neurology.* Vol. 4. Amsterdam: North Holland, 1969, in press.

SPERRY, R. W., & MINER, N. Pattern perception following insertion of mica plates into visual cortex. *Journal of Comparative and Physiological Psychology,* 1955, **48**, 463–469.

SPERRY, R. W., MINER, N., & MYERS, R. E. Visual pattern perception following subpial slicing and tantalum wire implantation in the visual cortex. *Journal of Comparative and Physiological Psychology,* 1955, **48**, 50–58.

THE PHYSIOLOGICAL LEVEL

For many who would unravel the workings of the human mechanism the key must lie within the nervous system. Surely some center or some process must underlie man's rudest skill and subtlest thought. The search for neurophysiological solutions to actual psychological problems focuses on such monumental questions as, (1) How are memories encoded? (2) What are the neurophysiological processes involved in attention? (3) What is the nature of the physioexperiential process that accounts for mental events?

In the first paper of this section Webster outlines certain of the assumptions and conceptualizations involved in brain research. The neurophysiological limitations to the concept of mind are analyzed by Sinsheimer.

35

CONCEPTUALIZATIONS OF BRAIN FUNCTION[1]

WILLIAM G. WEBSTER

MUCH of the history and the contemporary concern of physiological psychology focuses upon the related issues of the identification of the functions of the brain and cerebral localization of those functions. These issues of brain-behavior relations are often identified with cortical functioning, perhaps in part because of the controversy which surrounded Lashley's concepts of equipotentiality and mass action, but the history of attempts to identify the functions of the subcortical neuroanatomical structures is certainly as real. It is reflected, for instance, in discussions of homeostatic feeding and satiety centers, centers for the regulation of water balance and body temperature, and neural substrates of maternal, sexual, and aggressive behaviors. It is reflected in such titles of contemporary literature of physiological psychology as "Functions of the

[1] Preparation of this manuscript was supported in part by Grant APA-0399 from the National Research Council of Canada.

FROM W. G. Webster, Assumptions, conceptualizations, and the search for the functions of the brain. *Physiological Psychology*, 1973, 1 (4), 346–350. Reprinted with permission from *Physiological Psychology*, the author, and Psychonomic Society.

amygdala" (Goddard, 1964), "Hippocampus and internal inhibition" (Kimble, 1968), "Septum and behavior: A review" (Fried, 1972), *Functions of the corpus callosum* (Ettlinger, 1965), or "Approach-avoidance dissociation in rat brain" (Olds, 1960), to name but a few, as well as in chapter and section headings of most contemporary textbooks of physiological psychology.

There are certain problems and issues of a conceptual nature which are implicit in attempts to specify brain function using the classical neuropsychological experimental method involving direct manipulation of the brain. These issues, which have profound implications for research methodology and data interpretation, can be seen in rather sharp focus when viewed against a historical backdrop of the development of this experimental method and of the parallel development of thought during the 19th century concerning cerebral localization of function.

A Historical Overview

There are several very adequate accounts of the modern history of cerebral localization of function (e.g., Boring, 1950; Walker, 1957; and especially, Young, 1968, 1970), and consequently only a few points concerning the basic logic of the experimental method as applied to the study of brain-behavior relations need be mentioned and commented upon.

The development of this experimental method is usually credited to Pierre Flourens (1794–1867) and was in part a reaction to the phrenological approach of Franz Joseph Gall (1758–1828). The conceptual and methodological framework of Gall's approach to the understanding of individual differences in behavior has been very elegantly and succinctly sketched by Young (1970, p. 36) as follows:

	implies		implies		implies	
	$\longrightarrow$		$\longrightarrow$		$\longleftarrow$	
Striking Behavior	Faculty		Cortical Organ		Cranial Prominence	
	$\longleftarrow$		$\longleftarrow$		$\longrightarrow$	
	causes		causes		causes	
(talent, propensity, mania)	(innate instinct)		(activity varies with size)		(size varies with underlying organ)	

For Gall, individual differences in behavior were to be accounted for in terms of innate or inborn faculties. These faculties of the mind were seen as being localized within the brain, and for each distinct faculty there was presumed to be a separate and distinct cerebral organ. It was the size of the cerebral organ that determined the strength of the associated faculty, and the relative strengths of the faculties were reflected in the form of talents or other outstanding behavioral attributes. Furthermore, the size of each cerebral organ was reflected in the size of the overlying cranium.

Within this framework, the study of individual differences had then two facets: first, the identification of the faculties of the mind, which were equated with the functions of the brain; and second, the localization of function in various parts or organs of the brain. It was in the first facet that Gall was, in fact, more concerned and interested, and he argued that the functions of the brain were ones of biological significance, specifically rejecting the view that these necessarily included the categories, derived from philosophy, of perception, attention, judgment, memory, imagination, and so on. Furthermore, he argued that they could be discovered only by observation and empirical study, in much the same way as could the functions of any part of the body be discovered. Basically, his methodology involved correlating the presence of cranial prominences (from which he inferred the size of the underlying cerebrum) of living individuals, skulls and head casts, with the manifestation of striking talents or propensities (from which he inferred the existence and relative strengths of faculties). From this, he ultimately concluded that there were some 37 separate, distinct, and highly localized human faculties.

It was against this emphasis on a high degree of localization of function that Pierre Flourens (1794–1867) argued on the basis of his experimental method of brain ablation. For Flourens, the problem of determining and localizing brain function was simply one of making inferences about faculties based on changes in behavior which followed the removal of cerebral tissue. The logic of this experimental method was deceptively simple: remove a part of the brain, observe what the organism ceases to do, and infer the normal function of the removed part. His most notable success within this orientation was in the study of the cerebellum of pigeons. The removal of successive slices of cerebellar tissue led to an increasing loss of motor control, and from this Flourens made the reasonable inference that the cerebellum was concerned with motor coordination and not with reproduction, as Gall had maintained.

At this point, it is instructive to contrast Flourens's observations of the behavioral changes which followed the removal of the cerebrum of a hen with the inferences he made on the basis of these:

I let this hen starve several times for as long as three days. Then I brought nourishment under her nose. I put her beak into grain. I put grain into her beak. I plunged her beak into water. I placed her on a shock of corn. She did not smell, she did not eat anything, she did not drink anything, she remained immobile on the shock of corn and she would certainly have died of hunger if I had not returned to the old process of making her eat by herself.

Twenty times, in lieu of grain, I put sand into her beak: and she ate this as she would have eaten grain.

Finally, when this hen encounters an obstacle in her path, she throws herself against it, and this collision stops her and disturbs her, but to collide with an object is not the same as to touch it. . . . She is collided with and she collides but she does not touch [Flourens, 1842, pp. 90–91; translated by Young, 1970].

Flourens made the intuitively reasonable inference that the bird had lost its senses, but then he proceeded to make the following inferences about the functions of the cerebrum:

An animal which really touches a body, judges it; an animal which does not judge anymore therefore does not touch anymore.

Animals deprived of their cerebral lobes have, therefore, neither perception, nor judgment, nor memory, nor will: because there is no volition when there is no judgment; no judgment when there is no memory; no memory when there is no perception. The cerebral lobes are therefore the exclusive set of all the perceptions and of all the intellectual faculties [Flourens, 1842, pp. 96–97; translated by Young, 1970].

It is evident from this quotation that Flourens not only rejected Gall's methodology, but also his ideas on the nature of the functions of the brain, and echoed the classical faculties of perception, will, volition, and memory. Furthermore, the quotation indicates the basis of his arguments against the doctrine of cerebral localization: his ablations did not result in changes in one behavior and not others, but produced graded deficits in all the behaviors, which he noted. However, it is important to appreciate that even if there were localization of function in the various parts of the cerebrum, an ablation method as neuroanatomically incongruent as that used by Flourens, a method involving slicing through the entire cerebrum, would likely produce the types of results that Flourens in fact obtained, that is, an increasing loss of all functions.

The basic logic of the experimental method as developed by Flourens still permeates much contemporary research in physiological psychology and has two partially interdependent facets that deserve attention. The first supposes that the functions of the brain can be inferred by observing what behavioral alterations follow direct neurological manipulation. The second supposes that function can be localized at least in the sense of that part of the brain which was manipulated being a component of a larger system mediating the function underlying the behavioral alteration.

Inferences from Behavioral Alteration

The fundamental problem encountered in relation to the first facet is which categories of behavior or which categories of experience, or, in more classical terms, which faculties of the mind, are appropriate for characterizing behavioral alterations. Following the logic of Flourens, if we plan to observe what an animal ceases to do or begins to do after a brain ablation or during electrical stimulation of the brain, we must decide at some point what it is we are going to observe and under what conditions we are going to observe it. Is the decision to be based upon the philosopher's categories of perception, memory, volition, imagination, and so on? Do we instead resort to the sensory-motor categories that developed in the late 19th century and classify behavioral alterations in sensory and motor terms? Do we use categories which have in some sense biological significance for the organism? Encountered occasionally is the notion that such questions need not be of concern, for the functions of the brain will become evident, even obvious, in the nature of the alterations which follow brain lesions or which accompany electrical stimulation of the brain. However, as Teuber (1959) has emphasized in reference to the study of penetrating brain wounds in humans, changes in behavior are "often subtle, elusive, require very special tasks for their discovery, and even then might go undiscovered [p. 158]." A striking example of the subtle nature of the behavioral alteration that can follow major neurological insult is the notable absence of observable effects which follow sectioning of the corpus callosum. Only with the use of special testing procedures (Gazzaniga, Bogen, & Sperry, 1962, 1963, 1965) does the role of the callosum in interhemispheric integration become evident. If special tests are required to detect behavioral change, then the importance of recognizing assumptions regarding functional categories and implicit conceptualizations concerning the organization of the nervous system becomes evident. Considerations such as the type of environment in which the organism is tested, the internal state of the organism at the time of testing, or the specific tasks employed to detect and measure behavioral change (and hence the manifestation of behavioral change), all depend upon the categories regarded by the E to be relevant and significant. Whether an organism is tested, following some treatment, for changes in sensory thresholds, or on a perceptual task, or in a situation involving social interaction or in one involving the assessment of a motivational state depends upon these conceptualizations. If, for example, the organization and functions of the hypothalamus are conceptualized in terms of homeostatic regulatory mechanisms, the effects of manipulation of hypothalamic functioning will tend to be assessed in those terms and not in terms of changes in, for instance, memory or perceptual functioning (see Marshall, Turner, & Teitelbaum, 1972). Hence, inferences about function based upon alterations in behavior produced by neurological manipulation will tend to be in terms of the original (explicit or more usually implicit) conceptualizations.

Functions of the Brain

The logic of Flourens's experimental method of ablation called for observing the effects of removing a part of the nervous system. For Flourens, the parts of the nervous system were sixfold: the cerebrum, cerebellum, corpora quadrigemina, medulla, spinal cord, and spinal nerves. Young (1970) has suggested that this conception of the cerebrum's being a unitary structure was probably based largely on the philosophical influence of Descartes and the concept of the unity of mind. The ablation methodology adopted in the study of cerebral functioning, that involving surgical slicing through the entire cerebrum, of course was congruent with this conceptualization of the cerebrum, but, as noted earlier, this methodology would most likely generate results that would support the conceptualization even if it were incorrect.

The issue of just what constitutes a part of the brain is obviously of central importance for the question of localization of function. Should the hippocampus be considered as a unitary structure or can cytoarchitectonic differentiation be interpreted to indicate functional differentiation? Under what conditions can nuclei making up the amygdaloid complex be considered homogeneous and under what conditions must they be regarded as functionally distinct? Should two nuclei closely associated through a major fiber tract be considered a single part of the nervous system in terms of function? Should regions of the nervous system whose electrophysiological activity appear to covary be considered a single part? It is not the purpose of this paper to explore the issue of what constitutes a "part of the brain," but it is simply to be pointed out in passing that, given cerebral localization of function, an underinclusive conceptualization could lead to no detectable behavioral effects of some neurological manipulation if there is equipotentiality. However, an overinclusive conceptualization may lead to bizarre and uninterpretable treatment effects and to the type of inference concerning localization of function made by Flourens.

It is basically neurological assumptions and conceptualizations of the type alluded to above which underlie one of the major criticisms of the study of brain-behavior relations through any form of direct manipulation of the brain. This stems from the brain's being regarded as functionally analogous to mechanical and, more recently, to electronic devices. The criticism is worthy of careful consideration, as it points clearly to how assumptions and conceptualizations can dictate methodology and as it points to the conditions under which it might be possible to, in some sense, localize function in specific brain structures.

The criticism can be exemplified with the argument of Gregory (1961), who has pointed out quite compellingly that there would be serious difficulty in attempting to deduce the functioning of an electronic circuit, such as a computer or television, by observing the effects on the circuit output of either "ablating" or removing component parts, or by "stimulating" the parts of the circuit with high-voltage probes. If a tube or a resistor is removed from a radio circuit and it is found that the radio begins to howl, it is unlikely that the function of the tube or resistor would be considered in terms of howling, that is, it is unlikely that it would be inferred that the normal function of the tube or resistor was to suppress or inhibit howling. Yet, as Gregory (1961) points out, this type of inference of some system's having the function of inhibiting some other system or some behavior is often encountered in physiological psychology. The reason for the difficulty is that in any complex serial processing circuit such as a radio or a television, the output is very dissimilar to the functioning of any of the component parts. The output of the system is described in terms different from those likely to be used to describe the function of the parts, and consequently it is unlikely that removing a part will indicate what the normal function of the part really is. Those who have paid for a television repairman need no reminding of the converse, that even when a circuit diagram is known and the principles of operation of each part are understood it can be very difficult to trace a malfunction given some abnormal output.

Part of the problem is that of distinguishing primary from secondary effects. In a complex circuit, seldom does the removal of a part produce an effect simply because the part is absent. Rather, the removal of the part disrupts the functioning of other components, and this induced malfunctioning itself produces some alteration in the output. Consequently, the alteration in the output of such a system might be due to the primary effects of the treatment and/or to secondary effects due to the alteration of the normal functioning of other parts of the system.

A second aspect of this problem is derived from the fact that, unlike most electronic circuits, biological organisms are adaptable and respond to changes in their behavior with other changes in their behavior. A minor facet of this is how to interpret transient behavioral change: has the organism adapted to the particular change, or was the change due to some psychologically trivial phenomenon such as brain edema? A second, and much more important, facet is concerned with the appearance of secondary effects which are an adaptation to or a response to the primary effects. In the context of brain ablations, it is possible to conceptualize the relationship between two behavioral alterations as being either independent or hierarchical. If they are related in a hierarchical manner, the organism shows a behavioral alteration. A. *because* of the existence of Behavioral Alteration B, a direct consequence of the lesion; or conversely, it shows B *because* of the existence of A. One could also imagine a double hierarchy of mutually reinforcing alterations. If the alterations are independent, they can be independent in one of at least two ways. Either the lesion or stimulation or other treatment produces the two alterations in behavior quite independently (as might be the case if there were a high degree of localization of function and the lesion invaded two different areas of the brain) or the two behavioral alterations are independent but are both secondary effects due to the treatment producing some underlying primary effect which causes both. Weiskrantz (1968b) has argued that it is possible, at least theoretically, to establish that behavioral alterations are independent within certain limits. He proposes that this can be done by producing Behavioral Alteration A by some means other than the original treatment and showing that Behavioral Alteration B does not occur, and conversely by showing that the induction of B by some means other than the original treatment does not produce Behavioral Alteration A. But, he maintains, it is logically impossible to establish the existence of a hierarchical relationship, that is, to distinguish between primary and secondary effects.

These problems, among others, obviously raise serious questions about the utility of any form of direct neurological manipulation in the study of brain-behavior relations. Gregory (1961) has, in fact, suggested that "to deduce the functioning of a part from the effect upon the output of removing or stimulating this part we must know at least in general terms how the machine works [p. 322]." Returning to the analogy of the television, he suggests that to interpret the effects of removing a part, it is necessary first to know the circuit diagram and, second, to understand the principles of operation of the circuit. Even as forceful an advocate of the use of direct manipulation of the brain as Weiskrantz (1968a) concedes that "we can make judgments about how some treatments affect the inner workings of the organism only if we already know something about the way they already work [p. 401]." However, Weiskrantz points out that the functioning of the brain is, in fact, not deduced in a logical manner, but that the neuroscientist works with sets of intuitive hunches and guesses and formulates hypotheses and models which he tests against reality and modifies. Furthermore, and more important for the present discussion, he argues that the brain is in fact not analogous to a television set or other electronic circuitry. First, the basic units of the nervous system, the neurons, are unlike electronic components in that they are digital and either fire or do not fire, and information presumably is encoded and processed partly in terms of the frequency and patternings of firing. However, since the processes which determine the digital output are the analogue processes of excitation and inhibition, Weiskrantz is much less skeptical of inferences about excitatory and inhibitory functioning based on dysfunction caused by ablation and stimulation than is Gregory. Indeed, he argues that this type of hypothesis has, in fact, been most fruitful in the past in generating research. A second reason for rejecting the electronic circuit analogy is that the mammalian nervous system is the product of multiple stages of evolution, with new sets of components and functional principles being superimposed upon previous sets, consequently maintaining the evolutionary history of the nervous system very much intact. In contrast, newer models of electronic devices are not the product of new components being added to old but often consist of entirely new types of integrated designs. In essence, then, Weiskrantz argues that because of its evolutionary development, the brain is not a serial information processing device made up of a large number of small and relatively independent processing units.

How the organization of the nervous system is conceptualized, then, has enormous implications for methodology. Given that Gregory's analogy of the brain and electronic circuits is valid, that is, given that the brain acts as serial information processor in which information is taken in bit by bit and processed bit by bit by the entire circuit, his analysis of the utility of any direct neurological manipulation for the study of brain function would seem valid and well founded. However, given the orientation of Weiskrantz, that the brain acts as a parallel information processing device, one which consists of a large number of independent processing units, then even Gregory would probably concede the utility of methods like ablation and stimulation for the study of these independent units.

It is, then, no coincidence that those parts of the nervous system which, through the use of such methods as ablation and stimulation, are *apparently* best understood in functional terms at present are those which seem to act as parallel information processors, the sensory, motor, and certain homeostatic regulatory systems. Double dissociation can be easily demonstrated in the study of these systems. However, the problem with these methods is that, while they are appropriate for the analysis and dissociation of parallel processing systems, they are simply not tuned for the detection and study of the serial processing aspects of the nervous system, if there are such aspects.

Conclusions

It has been emphasized that the types of behavioral change looked for after neurological manipulation, as well as the methods of neurological manipulation themselves, are greatly influenced by how the functions of the brain and the structure of the brain are conceptualized. A comparison of the position represented by Gregory (1961) with that represented by Weiskrantz (1968a) further suggests that if the organization of the brain with respect to the processing of information relevant to some behavior is serial in nature, such methods as ablation and stimulation are unlikely to be of utility in unraveling questions of brain-behavior relations and functional localization; if it is parallel in nature, however, they may be. One of the important consequences of conceptualizing the nervous system as being a parallel information processing system and then proceeding to study it with methods like ablation and stimulation is that the results of such study will tend to support the validity of the conceptualization and will tend not to provide evidence against it. This is precisely the problem pointed out earlier in reference to the methodology of Flourens.

Flourens (1842), himself, said, "Everything in experimental research depends upon the method, for it is the method which gives the results [p. 502]." This paper has attempted to point out that method is very much determined by the assumptions and conceptualizations of the experimenter. It is these which determine the conditions under which the dependent variables are assessed and, indeed, the choice of the dependent variables themselves, and it is these which determine the choice of the independent variables. To the extent that method is dictated by assumptions and conceptualizations, then, everything (to overstate it somewhat) in experimental research depends upon assumptions and conceptualizations. It must be emphasized, though, that it is impossible to work without some set of assumptions, and this paper has attempted to make evident the importance of explicitly recognizing them and of recognizing the implications for methodology and data interpretation of working within one conceptual framework or another.

REFERENCES

BORING, E. G. *A history of experimental psychology.* (2nd ed.) New York: Appleton-Century-Crofts, 1950.

ETTLINGER, E. G. (Ed.), *Functions of the corpus callosum.* London: Churchill, 1965.

FLOURENS, P. *Recherches expérimentales sur les propriétés et les fonctions du système nerveux dans les animaux vertébrés.* (2nd ed.) Paris: Ballière, 1842.

FRIED, P. A. Septum and behavior: A review. *Psychological Bulletin,* 1972, **78,** 292–310.

GAZZANIGA, M. S., BOGEN, J. E., & SPERRY, R. W. Some functional effects of sectioning the cerebral commissures in man. *Proceedings of the National Academy of Sciences,* 1962, **48,** 1765–1783.

————, BOGEN, J. E., & SPERRY, R. W. Laterality effects in somes-thesis following cerebral commissurotomy in man. *Neuropsychologia,* 1963, **1,** 209–215.

————, BOGEN, J. E., & SPERRY, R. W. Observations on visual perception after disconnexion of the cerebral hemispheres in man. *Brain,* 1965, **88,** 221–236.

GODDARD, G. V. Functions of the amygdala. *Psychological Bulletin,* 1964, **62,** 89–109.

GREGORY, R. L. The brain as an engineering problem. In W. H. Thorpe and O. L. Zangwill (Eds.), *Current problems in animal behaviour.* Cambridge: Cambridge University Press, 1961. Pp. 307–330.

KIMBLE, D. P. Hippocampus and internal inhibition. *Psychological Bulletin,* 1968, **70,** 285–295.

MARSHALL, J. F., TURNER, B. H., & TEITELBAUM, P. Sensory neglect produced by lateral hypothalamic damage. *Science,* 1971, **174,** 523–525.

OLDS, J. Approach-avoidance dissociation in rat brain. *American Journal of Physiology,* 1960, **199,** 965–968.

TEUBER, H.-L. Some alterations in behavior after cerebral lesions in man. In

A. D. Bass (Ed.), *Evolution of nervous control from primitive organisms to man.* Washington, D.C.: American Association for the Advancement of Science, 1959. Pp. 157–194.

WALKER, A. E. The development of the concept of cerebral localization in the nineteenth century. *Bulletin of the History of Medicine,* 1957, **31,** 99–121.

WEISKRANTZ, L. Treatments, inferences and brain function. In L. Weiskrantz (Ed.), *Analysis of behavioral change.* New York: Harper & Row, 1968a. Pp. 400–414.

————. Some traps and pontifications. In L. Weiskrantz (Ed.), *Analysis of behavioral change.* New York: Harper & Row, 1968b. Pp. 415–428.

YOUNG, R. M. The functions of the brain: Gall to Ferrier (1808–1886). *Isis,* 1968, **59,** 251–268.

————. *Mind, brain and adaptation in the nineteenth century.* London: Oxford University Press, 1970.

36

NEUROPHYSIOLOGICAL LIMITS OF MIND

ROBERT L. SINSHEIMER

THE inviolate principle of causality—that a precisely determined set of conditions will always produce precisely the same effects at a later time —underlies our entire scientific perception of the universe. And yet in the smoothly flowing channels of natural causality there has always been in our conception one seemingly irrational, unordered, swirling eddy—the human mind. Increasingly now we cannot avoid this vortex, nor can we continue to skirt around it, for herein is the ultimate perceiver and herein form the shapes of surmise. And so, as in our dreams where we are surprised by that which we ourselves have conjured, the perceiver must in wonder inquire, "How do I perceive?" and the mind ask, "What is thought?"

The great discoveries in genetics and our enlarged understanding of the biochemistry of heredity have led to increasing discussion of the possibility of the designed change of human beings—not only of the repair of overt genetic defects but also of the longer range enhancement of the capabilities of man. Naturally, much of this discussion has con-

FROM R. L. Sinsheimer, The brain of Pooh: An essay on the limits of mind, *Engineering and Science Magazine,* January, 1970, **33,** 8–13, 36–40. Reprinted by permission of the author and *Engineering and Science Magazine.*

cerned the improvement of man's finest and most precarious quality, his mind.

To consider this issue in any serious way one must first inquire as to what qualities of mind are considered to be genetic in origin (and are thus susceptible to genetic modification) and to what extent these qualities limit the performance of man—and what might be the consequence of their modification. In a philosophical sense such an endeavor —man trying to improve his own capacity—is clearly a boot-strap project, an adventure in positive feedback. And yet this is what we have done all the way from the jungle. What we consider now is but an extension, albeit in a new dimension. What can we honestly say about the mind from our present knowledge? I do believe that such a presentation can be useful in the same sense that the sixteenth-century maps of the world were useful, essentially as a rough chart of what it is we need now set out to learn, bearing in mind that the enterprise may well require as many years as were needed to fill in those ancient maps.

Further, in this *special* case there is special merit in such a projection of knowledge that we may hope to have concerning the human brain and thus concerning its, and our, future potential. For this effort to see how our brain came to be and how it might be advanced can serve to provide us a valuable perspective in which to view our present reality, in which to see more clearly our present limitations and, therein, the origins of some of our most basic dilemmas.

The very opening lines of *Winnie-the-Pooh* provide my theme.

Here is Edward Bear, coming downstairs now, bump, bump, bump, on the back of his head, behind Christopher Robin. It is, as far as he knows, the only way of coming downstairs, but sometimes he feels that there really is another way, if only he could stop bumping for a moment and think of it.

Now Edward Bear, or Winnie-the-Pooh as he was known to his friends, was of course a bear of very little brain. But nonetheless I often think that these lines constitute a splendid parable to man and his whole scientific enterprise—that we perforce go bump, bump, bump along the paths of scientific discovery when had we but the acumen, the brain power, we could immediately deduce from the known facts the one right and inherently logical solution. This seems particularly true in biology wherein all extant phenomena have for so long been subject to and ordered by the harsh disciplines of natural selection, and wherein the right answer, when we find it, always does seem so inevitably right.

And yet of course we don't have the acumen and we can't immediately deduce the right solution because, like Pooh, our brains too are really very limited compared to the complexity about us and the frequent immediacy of our tasks. And in simple fact what else can we sensibly expect when we are apparently the first creature with any significant capacity for abstract thought? Indeed, even that capacity developed primarily to cope with stronger predators or climatic shifts, not to probe the nature of matter or the molecular basis of heredity or the space-time parameters of the universe.

A physicist friend of mine frequently remarks on how much more difficult it seems to be to teach a 17-year-old a few laws of physics than it is to teach him to drive a car. He is always struck by the fact that he could program a computer to apply these laws of physics with great ease but to program a computer to drive a car in traffic would be an awesome task. It is quite the reverse for the 17-year-old, which is precisely the point. To drive a car, a 17-year-old makes use, with adaptation, of a set of routines long since programmed into the primate brain. To guage the speed of an approaching car and maneuver accordingly is not that different from the need to gauge the speed of an approaching branch and react accordingly as one swings through the trees. And so on. Whereas to solve a problem in diffraction imposes an intricate and entirely unfamiliar task upon a set of neurons.

I think the computers first made us aware of one of the more evident limitations of the biological brain, its millisecond or longer time scale. Computers flashing from circuit to circuit in microseconds can readily cope with the input and response time of dozens of human brains simultaneously or can perform computations in a brief period of time for which a human brain would need a whole lifetime.

Similarly I believe that we will come to see that our brains are limited in other dimensions as well—in the precision with which we can reconstruct the outside universe, in the nature and resolution of our concepts, in the content of information that may be brought to bear upon one problem at one time, in the intricacy of our thought and logic—and it will be a major contribution of the developing science of psychobiology to comprehend these limitations and to make us aware of them, to the extent that we have the capacity to be aware of them.

For I think it is only logical to suppose that the construction of our brains places very real limitations upon the concepts that we can formulate. Our brain, designed by evolution to cope with certain very real problems in the immediate external world of human scale, simply lacks the conceptual framework with which to encompass totally unfamiliar phenomena and processes. I suspect we may have reached this point in our analysis of the ultimate structure of matter, that in various circumstances we have to conceive of a photon as a wave *or* as a particle because these are the only approximations we can formulate. We, and I mean we in the evolutionary sense, have never encountered and had to cope with a phenomenon with the actual characteristics of a photon.

And likewise with the subnuclear particles. I was intrigued to learn that the latest attempt to formulate a theory of subnuclear particles is a bootstrap or self-consistent field theory, which as I understand it is a bit like saying it is there because it is there and it has to be there.

To my mind this is in effect a bold attempt to adapt the concepts available to the human mind to an intractable and perhaps unimaginable reality. As Einstein so well said, "The most incomprehensible thing about the universe is that it is comprehensible."

Similar problems of concept may well arise on the vast scale of the universe or, more to the point, in the intricate recesses of the mind. Our problem will be somehow to shape a mirror to the mind such that we can comprehend its reflection.

I have tried to think how we might approach this problem of the limits to thought inherent in the structure of our brain and therefore potentially extensible by genetic modification. One approach would be comparative or phylogenetic. If we could trace the detailed chemical and structural changes in the central nervous system as evolution has progressed through the vertebrate species, and if we could correlate these changes with the changes in the reactive and conceptual capacities of these species, we would have one basis for future extrapolation.

Now the comparative approach to phylogenetic evolution has been somewhat in disfavor in this recent era of biochemical ascendance, and for good reason. The biochemistry of all living creatures is really so similar. Hardly anyone would venture to suggest the differences between man and monkey are a consequence of a novel and major innovation in biochemistry. Indeed the biochemistry of man and a yeast cell are astonishingly similar. It is evident that almost all of the most basic processes of biochemistry must have been elaborated in some very remote time of evolution.

Rather, then, the differences between man and monkey must derive largely from some elaborations of structure, and thereby function on a cellular and multicellular level and primarily in the central nervous system. And these innovations must have arisen through the usual genetic mechanisms. How many genetic changes were there, literally? It's clear they did not require any major addition to the genome. The haploid DNA content of man and monkey is identical within the precision of measurement—a few percent.

Our abilities to compare and homologize or differentiate the DNA's of different species—say, man and monkey—are as yet very crude. The DNA–DNA hybridization experiments of Roy Britten and D. Kohne indicate that, on an average, the DNA sequences of man and monkey are highly homologous. Comparative measurements of the thermal stability of human DNA, chimpanzee DNA, and test-tube hybrids of these DNA's suggest that in the fifteen or so millions of years since these species have diverged there have developed about 1.6 nucleotide changes per 100 nucleotide pairs, or about 5 changes per 300 base pairs—which is equivalent to 100 amino acids of protein sequence. Since, because of redundance, about 20 percent of random nucleotide changes will not result in an amino acid change, we might expect a mean evolutionary distinction between these two species of about 4 amino acids per sequence of 100 in the absence of selective bias.

However, the interpretation of such homologies has since been complicated by the recognition that these experiments as they have been performed to date can only concern or involve certain fractions of the DNA, specifically those fractions that are made up of large families or molecules, or closely related sequences represented literally tens or hundreds of thousands of times in the genome. These represent about 40 percent of primate DNA. Under the conditions of these experiments, sequences represented less often simply never find a partner with which to hybridize in any reasonable time. The existence of these large families of closely related sequences, which may in total comprise some half of the genome, is both a surprise and a conundrum in itself, but in addition it does at present clearly limit the quantitative significance of statements about DNA homology between species, for we can say as yet very little about the possible homology of the less frequent DNA species.

Studies of the available rates of genetic mutation, as evidenced by changes in the amino acid sequences of particular proteins, suggest that the time of divergence of man and present-day monkeys from a presumed common ancestor *has been sufficient* to allow significant changes. The observable changes in amino acid sequence in any special protein are of course strongly biased by possible, and generally unknown, selective pressures that limit permissible change. Thus the alpha hemoglobin in the gorilla differs in only one amino acid from that of man. And that of the chimpanzee is identical to that of man. In an over-all sense, the rate of acceptable mutation in the globins is only about 1 amino acid per 100 residues per 6,000,000 years. For other proteins, such as cytochrome c, the allowable rate proves to be even less: 1 in 20,000,000 years. But a more accurate measure of the possible rate of amino acid replacement *may* be obtained from the fibrinopeptides which appear to serve no other function than to be excised from fibrinogen, when it is converted to fibrin in the formation of a blood clot, and then to be degraded. In these the apparent rate is 1 amino acid change per 100 residues per 1 million years. These numbers are in reasonable agreement with the averaged estimate from nucleotide change—approximately 4 replacements per 100 amino acids per 15,000,000 years.

It is thus possible to suggest that in the last several million years a considerable number of the proteins of man could have undergone mutational changes in one or two amino acids. But a *major* change in a particular protein would be highly unlikely—at least by the mutational processes leading to the changes so far studied.

Now of course the body undoubtedly has mechanisms whereby the consequences of even a single amino acid change in a strategic protein can be greatly amplified. But the conclusion I tend to draw from this admittedly loose argument is that the genetic distinction between a man

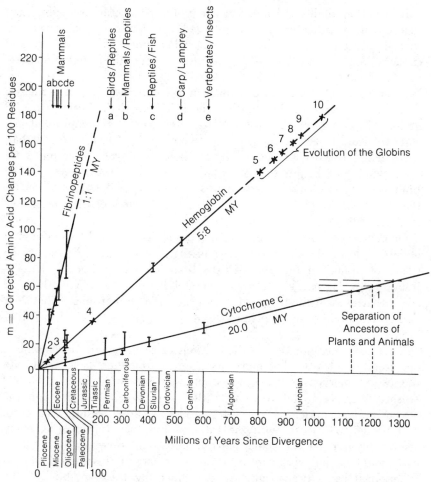

FIGURE 1. *The number of changes in amino acids between the same protein from two different species is plotted here against the time in the past at which the two species ancestors diverged. The unit evolutionary period is the average time required for one difference to show up per 100 residues. Molecules such as cytochrome c, which interact closely with other macromolecules, have longer unit evolutionary periods than such non-specific proteins as the fibrinopeptides. (Adapted from R. E. Dickerson and I. Geis, The Structure and Action of Proteins. New York: Harper & Row, 1969.)*

and a monkey is, in a quantitative sense, not a great one. Hence, there is a greater chance that in time we will be able to define and understand this change and conceivably recapitulate it in the laboratory. In this connection it would certainly be of great value to have phylogenetic comparisons of specific brain proteins as well as of hemoglobin.

In addition to his enhanced capacity for conceptual thought, man exceeds other primates in his enlarged consciousness, his power of speech, and undoubtedly in such underlying functions as memory and capacity for numeration. What changes provide the bases for these qualities?

If we compare the brain of a man and, let us say, that of a rat, we find the rat brain weighs a little over 1/1,000th that of the man: 1.6 grams vs. 1,450 grams. Yet the rat is a rather complex organism. It can learn intricate mazes; it can fight or defend itself; it reproduces; it has, particularly in the wild, quite intricate behavior. After observing a rat for a while, one begins to wonder what the other 99.9 percent of the brain is doing in man. If one compares the volume of the cerebral cortex, the ratio becomes even greater: 5,000 to 1 (500 cubic centimeters to 0.1 cubic centimeter).

Of course size of brain is a rather crude indicator. The brain of a chimpanzee weighs 450 grams, that of man 1,450 grams. A dog has 80 grams of brain, a rabbit 10. But the brain of man is not all that extraordinarily large. The brain of the dolphin weighs 1,700 grams. It rivals that of man in structural complexity and proportions. What is it doing? The brain of an elephant weighs 5 kilograms, a whale 6 to 7 kilograms.

If we examine animals at various levels of phylogenetic development, one trend is, clearly, that more and more information is brought into the central nervous system. Thus, in man somewhat over 2,000,000 sensory fibers bring information to the brain, about half through the cranial nerves (optic, auditory, etc.) and half through the spinal cord.

If we compare man with the rat, we find that 12 times as many sensory fibers enter the spinal cord and 10 to 12 times as many fibers carry auditory and visual information. But most of this increase in informational capacity has already developed by the evolution of the primate. The principal difference between the primate and man appears to be in the elaboration of structures for the analysis and integration of the sensory input. If we compare the number of cells in area 17 of the visual cortex in man and in the macaque, or of the areas 17, 18, and 19 of the visual cortex in man and the orangutan, or the number of cells in the auditory cortex in man and the chimpanzee, we find large increments in man over the primates. And, of course, even larger differences are found in the volumes of the frontal cortex, the functions of which are still disturbingly poorly understood. We are only now, in experiments such as those of David Hubel and T. Wiesel, beginning to learn some of the ways in which networks in these areas of the cortex analyze the sensory input in monkeys; we have no information yet as to how these means of handling sensory data may differ between the lower primates and man.

Table 1

A better indicator of brain capacity is the amount of information brought into the central nervous system. A comparison of man and the rat shows that 12 times as many sensory fibers enter the spinal cord and 10 to 12 times as many fibers carry auditory and visual information.

	SENSORY FIBERS INTO SPINAL CORD	AUDITORY FIBERS	OPTIC NERVE FIBERS
Man	1,000,000	30,000	1,000,000
Macaque	550,000	30,000	1,000,000
Rat	80,000	3,000	80,000

Table 2

The principal difference between the primate and man appears to be in the elaboration of structures for the analysis and integration of the sensory input. Large increments in man over the primates are shown in this comparison of the number of cells in area 17 of the visual cortex in man and in the macaque, or of the areas 17, 18, and 19 of the visual cortex in man and the orangutan, or of the number of cells in the auditory cortex in man and the chimpanzee.

	MAN	PRIMATE
Cells, area 17, visual cortex	540,000,000	150,000,000 (macaque)
Cortical surface, area 17	26 cm²	18.7 cm² (orangutan)
Cortical surface, area 18	39 cm²	14.5 cm² (orangutan)
Cortical surface, area 19	39 cm²	14.2 cm² (orangutan)
Cells, area 41, auditory cortex	100,000,000	10,000,000 (chimpanzee)

One of the most obvious distinctions between man and the lower animals is in the quality and quantity of his consciousness. Man can escape from the here and now; he can compare alternate responses and originate new actions by internal imagery. In the nature and origin of consciousness is one of the most profound of mysteries.

What determines the modality of consciousness? How do certain stimuli cause pain, others color, others tone or taste? What defines the spectrum of color sensation? Why are there no more colors or no other tones? Clearly there are structural and very likely chemical, and therefore, genetic, bases for these phenomena.

There are individuals, for instance, who are genetically insensitive to pain. In some instances this defect is peripheral. The nerve receptors in the skin which are usually considered to be the sensors of pain are lacking. In others the sensory cells and sensory fibers, at least as far as can be seen, appear to be intact, and the defect may be central—an indifference to pain. An interesting point is that these people, lacking a sensory modality, do not appear to know what pain is. It is absent from their consciousness, which thus seems, in part at least, discrete. It is of interest that such people often can distinguish temperature quite normally but there is no pain associated with hot or cold. This condition is most often disastrous to the individual. It is also of great interest that in two cases siblings from first-cousin marriages have shown this trait, suggesting that it may be a consequence of a fairly simple genetic alteration.

Now I personally rather doubt that we have the conceptual capacity to really comprehend the origin of consciousness; but I do expect that we will learn that consciousness of various modalities may be associated with circuits of the brain connected in diverse ways, possibly with diverse chemical transmitters and effecters, all programmed genetically, and that by modifying these programs we may indeed, in a true sense, expand consciousness into unknown sensations and into undreamt intensities. If this sounds absurd, consider that many vertebrates have no color vision at all. By changing their genetic program an entire new sense has been added. We might be able to build chemical switches into various sectors of consciousness so that pain specifically could be turned off for surgery or a widened sense of taste or color turned on for enjoyment. Conceivably, new receptors—for electric fields or radio waves, for ionizing radiation or what have you—could be developed to go with new modalities of consciousness.

Whatever may be the basis of conscious thought, it is clear that much of the operation of the brain cannot be brought to consciousness; it is, somehow, inaccessible or screened. There is very likely much merit in the automation of many activities. Yet, as we know, conflicts and distortions on the subconscious level can produce grave disturbances of the psyche and are most difficult to detect and analyze. If more of the unconscious could be made at least selectively accessible, it could be a very considerable boon.

Language

Of course one of the major distinctions of man is his ability to communicate, particularly through speech. Remarkable as this capacity is, it must be recognized that it is a limited device. There are very real limitations of language and communication. Can we truly express everything we experience or conceive in speech? There are problems of precision, of connotation, and of association. We frequently have to coin new words for new concepts, and still it is difficult to convey their meanings to others. The expression of feelings and emotions is particularly difficult and seems to interweave several dimensions of emotionality. One can sum up a whole complex of emotions by an analogy (such as an Oedipus complex or a messianic complex) which is extremely hard to decompose analytically in words.

The average person is said to know some 20,000 to 60,000 basic words (dependent upon the definition of "know") and perhaps 100,000 derivates of these. In ordinary speech he uses 2 to 3,000 basic words; in ordinary writing, maybe 10,000. (This difference between stored information and effective information is curious. It is of interest that there is a similar difference between the overall sensory input—2 to 3,000,000 fibers —and the overall motor output—about 350,000 fibers in man.)

The rate of direct communication is typically about 150 words per minute. These it may be estimated contain at most 2,000 bits of information. Of course that depends a little upon the speaker.

Speech is probably genetically one of the newest of nature's inventions and obviously one of major importance for the development of interindividual communication, the consequent development both of group behavior and properties, and the transmission of knowledge and culture from one generation to the next. Yet there is no reason to believe this relatively recent innovation is perfected. Indeed, as we have indicated, there is good reason to believe speech is a very imperfect device for communication.

If we could manage a significant improvement in the potential precision and speed of our vocal communication, this could be of major consequence. We could, for instance, use many more of the potential phonemes and thereby markedly increase the potential information density.

I think it is interesting that our friend Pooh, although of little brain, used language with considerable precision and economy—as in the time he was hanging onto a balloon suspended in the air and, wanting down, he asked Christopher to shoot the balloon. So Christopher aimed very carefully and fired.

"*Ow!*" said Pooh.
"Did I miss?" Christopher asked.
"You didn't exactly *miss*," said Pooh, "but you missed the *balloon*."

One well-known indicator of the limitations of our capacity for speech is our frequent inability to bring to mind the right word for an object or a person or a concept. Pooh also suffered from this all-too-human failing—as when Christopher says:

"What do you like doing best in the world, Pooh?"
"Well," said Pooh, "what I like best—" and then he had to stop and think.

Because although Eating Honey *was* a very good thing to do, there was a moment just before you began to eat it which was better than when you were, but he didn't know what it was called.

I am of course assuming here that our command of language and indeed the structure of language, whatever it is, are at least in large part a consequence of genetically determined neuronal structure. I think this is very reasonable. And along these lines I would like to return to the concept I developed earlier—that we can learn to do certain things rather easily because, in effect, approximate programs for these operations are built in.

Learning

Could we not extend this? Could we not build in through the proper circuitry certain packets of knowledge so that every generation need not learn these anew, such as a language, or the periodic table, the Krebs cycle, etc. Migratory birds evidently have genetic programs that enable them to recognize stellar constellations. Other birds innately recognize rather complex songs. It does not seem inconceivable.

This is only an extension, although certainly in another dimension, of the wise ideal so well expressed by Whitehead, who wrote: "It is a profoundly erroneous truism—that we should cultivate the habit of thinking what we are doing. The precise opposite is the case. Civilization advances by extending the number of important operations which we can perform without thinking about them."

Statistically at least it is clear that there are changes in the human brain with aging. There are times of optimum ease of learning such matters as language or mathematics. There are optimum periods for creative work, and these seem to differ in the different sciences. In early childhood there are critical periods for mastering certain skills, and if these are past, the effect may well be nearly irreversible. Also we know there are at various times in life irreversible hormonal influences on parts of the brain. We know the number of cells in the brain does not increase after six months or a year of age and, indeed, decreases after 30 to 40 years of age.

If we understood these matters, we could perhaps control these factors. We might keep open and extend critical periods of learning. We might learn to reverse untoward hormonal effects or even to increase the number of brain cells and thus permit continued increase of information and counteract senility.

Matters of learning clearly involve the intake of information and the storage of memory. We do not understand these matters well. Numerous studies of varied design indicate that the rate at which we can abstract information from our sensory presentation—visual, for example—is highly limited by a narrow channel capacity. Various studies have been made and, despite some variation of interpretation, there seems to be a general agreement that while some 40 to 50 bits of information may be taken in visually in a flash and held for somewhat less than a second, at the most 10 bits of information per second can be abstracted from a presentation and used to control an output or be relayed to a memory bank. This channel capacity is certainly a major parameter in the determination of the speed and quality of the working of the brain.

The limited capacity of the brain to abstract information from a visual display underlies the McLuhan fallacy and explains why people still read books. Could this rate of information-handling be markedly increased? If so, we could enter the McLuhan era.

Further, it seems likely that the limitation upon the bits of information we can process at one time is related to a deeper question. How many data can we hold in our mind at one time, how many can we bring to bear upon a particular conceptual problem? Surely this is limited, and this in turn restricts our ability to cope with problems of great complexity except by overabstraction and oversimplification. Conceivably we might be able to increase this quantity.

Memory

Now, of course, it is easy to list various qualities and suggest independently improving this or that one. But properly one needs to consider and needs to be able to consider the effect of changing any one facet of intellectual performance upon an individual's whole personality. Personality is like a network with more-or-less-balanced tensions and strains; modification anywhere can affect the whole. Consider what one might first think to be a purely mechanical element such as memory. Upon reflection, memory is easily seen to be a central element in the whole cerebral process. With a little reflection I think it becomes obvious that the quality of memory, its extent, its rapidity, its precision and acuity must influence the whole life pattern through our perception of and response to any situation.

We know all too little about memory. It has become known that there is a short-term memory for the relatively brief storage (on the order of seconds) of information, and a longer term, more enduring memory, of a qualitatively different nature. I suspect that we do not yet begin fully to grasp the significance and function of these distinct memories. As we learn more about the roles of these separate memory systems, we may find that the existence of erasable short-term memory provides an essential gap that permits a distinction between our internal and external worlds. It provides a transient recording that permits us to respond to the immediate yet not to be constantly overwhelmed by the immediate, so we may select from it the important and the general. Without such a buffer we could not plan, we could not withdraw sufficiently from immediate reality.

It is even possible that our sense of time and of time passing is related to the rate of decay of our short-term memory. In our subconscious and in our internal world there is little sense of time. A past event can seem as real as the present. Drugs which affect our sense of time may do so through their effects upon these processes.

If these speculations have any validity, then the ability to alter physiologically or genetically the rates and extent of these processes of memory could have profound effects upon our perception of the world.

I might insert at this point that to a biochemist one of the major impediments to research upon many of these questions is the existence of the so-called blood-brain barrier. This is a poorly understood physiological mechanism that stringently restricts the transport of foreign substances into the central nervous system. Presumably this was designed to provide a specific neuronal environment and to protect the brain against physiological vicissitudes and not just to frustrate biochemists. But certainly one major contribution that genetics could make would be to alter this barrier—optimally, perhaps, by incorporation of some biochemical switch whereby it could be opened or closed so as to permit biochemical investigation.

Human Genetic Variants

Another and different approach to the potentials inherent in further development of the brain is by a consideration of the attributes of individuals with special gifts of one character or another. It is clear that, presumably by genetic circumstances, individuals arise with marked asymmetries of talents. It is also clear that in accord with the concept of interdependence of various cerebral functions the hypertrophy of one talent is often accomplished by major, even disastrous, consequences to others, although we are at present unable to trace the causal connections.

The so-called idiot savants who have a general mental age of two or three years but can, with great rapidity, perform extraordinary numerical feats are an extreme example. One of these, given the series 2, 4, 16, immediately continued to square each successive number into the billions. Similarly, given the numbers 9-3, 16-4, he proceeded to do square roots of numbers into 3 and 4 digits. Another class of feeble-minded individuals is known to have extraordinary talents of mimicry.

Of a less drastic and more desirable nature are the special talents we associate with musical genius, such as a Mozart who composed significant works at the age of four, or artistic genius, or literary genius, or extraordinary skill at chess. There are individuals who are extraordinarily articulate; there are others with extraordinary ability in three-dimensional visualization and spatial orientation far beyond the corresponding talents of normal people.

The capacities of these individuals indicate levels of achievement that could become commonplace, beside which we may feel like Pooh who was somewhat weak in this matter of spatial orientation and symmetry.

"I *think* it's more to the right," said Piglet nervously. "What do *you* think, Pooh?"

Pooh looked at his two paws. He knew that one of them was the right, and knew that when you had decided which one of them was the right, then the other one was the left, but he could never remember how to begin.

"Well," he said slowly—

A particular case of an extraordinary development of the faculty of memory has recently been described in considerable detail by A. R. Luria in the book *The Mind of a Mnemonist*. This analysis is of particular interest because Luria is especially concerned not only with this unusual mnemonic talent but with its consequence for the whole personality of the man who had it. This man's memory in truth could not be saturated and was apparently imperishable. He could quickly, in two or three minutes, learn a table of 50 numbers of a list of 70 words which he could then repeat or just as easily present in reverse order, or, if given an intermediate word, go forward or back from this. He memorized a nonsensical formula

$$N \cdot \sqrt{d^2 \times \frac{85}{vx}} \cdot \sqrt[3]{\frac{276^2 \cdot 86x}{n^2v \cdot \pi264}} \cdot n^2b = sv\frac{1624}{32^2} \cdot r^2s$$

in a few minutes, and when asked 15 years later, without warning and with no intervening exposure, he was able to reproduce the earlier test situation and the formula without error. He literally never forgot or lost anything once committed to memory.

As Jerome Bruner suggests in his foreword to [Luria's] book, it is as though the metabolism responsible for short-term memory was defective in this man and everything experienced was transferred into the long-term memory. His world was one of intense visual imagery. He was never able to develop and grasp or project ideas and generalities. He was, in effect, overwhelmed by an endlessly increasing store of perceptions.

As another corollary, the man had significant difficulty in distinguishing between the internal and the external world. He had great difficulty in planning. He could not withdraw enough from the immediate reality. Furthermore, his sense of time was often faulty. For this man the past was as real as the present. He had no childhood amnesia and seemingly could remember impressions to very early childhood.

This man was also remarkable in another way. He had a strong synesthesia. As I have pointed out, to most of us our senses are quite distinct. Sight, sound, taste, smell, touch, pain are all uniquely stimulated, except when under the influence of certain drugs which appear to facilitate sensory interaction. In this man almost all the senses seemed fused. Every sound also had an image in color, often a taste and a touch and a smell as well. (It is conceivable that this effect is also related to a short-term memory defect. The persistence of a sensory input may permit it to spread and involve other perceptual centers.) He said:

I recognize a word not only by the images it evokes but by a complex of feelings the image arouses. It is not a matter of vision or hearing but some overall sense I get. Usually I experience a word's taste and weight, and I don't have to make an effort to remember it. But it is difficult to describe. What I sense is something oily slipping through my hand. Or I am aware of a slight tickling in my left hand caused by a mass of tiny lightweight points. When that happens I simply remember without having to make the attempt. . . . Even when I listen to works of music I feel the taste of them on my tongue. If I can't, I don't understand the music. This means I have to experience not only abstract ideas but even music through a physical sense of taste.

I think it is obvious that for such a person the world would be a very different place than it is for us.

His strongest reaction was imagery. He lived very much in a world of images. Obviously this could create very serious problems. For some words, for example, the images the sound of a word created would fit its meaning, but for others there would be a conflict and confusion. Many words we know have multiple meanings (fast, for example). This created great difficulty for him. He could not comprehend metaphors at all.

Take the word nothing. I read it and thought it must be very profound. I thought it would be best to call nothing something. I see this nothing and it is something. If I am to understand any meaning that is fairly deep I have to get an image of it right away. So I turned to my wife and asked her what nothing meant. But it was so clear to her that she simply said nothing means there is nothing. I understand it differently. I saw this nothing and thought she must be wrong. If nothing can appear to a person then it means it is something. That's where the trouble comes in.

It's interesting that Pooh had the same difficulty with abstractions—as when Christopher says:

". . . what I like *doing* best is Nothing."
"How do you do Nothing?" asked Pooh, after he had wondered for a long time.
"Well, it's when people call out at you just as you're going off to do it, What are you going to do, Christopher Robin, and you say, Oh, nothing, and then you go and do it."
"Oh, I see," said Pooh.
"This is a nothing sort of thing that we're doing now."
"Oh, I see," said Pooh again.

The Two Realities

There is one other aspect of this man's unusual mental and psychical structure that should be mentioned. His poor distinction between external and internal reality was perhaps reinforced by an extraordinary control over his autonomic functions. He could increase his pulse rate from 70 to 100 by imagining he was running and then reduce it to 64 by imagining he was lying quietly in bed. He could raise the temperature of his right hand by two degrees and then later lower that of his left hand by one degree. How did he do this? He said,

There is nothing to be amazed at. I saw myself put my right hand on a stove. Oh, it was so hot. So naturally the temperature of my hand increased. But I was holding a piece of ice in my left hand. I could see it there and began to squeeze it and of course my hand got colder.

He claimed also to be able to alter his sensitivity to pain at will.

Let's say I'm going to the dentist. You know how pleasant it is to sit there and let him drill your teeth. I used to be afraid to go but now it's all so simple. I sit there and when the pain starts I feel it. It's a tiny orange-red thread. I'm upset because I know that if this keeps up the thread will widen until it turns into a dense mass. So I cut the thread, make it smaller and smaller until it's just a tiny point and the pain disappears.

It was demonstrated that he could vary his eye adaptation by imagining himself to be in rooms of varying levels of illumination.

His strange memory and his synesthetic experience created in this man a critical difficulty in distinguishing between the world of his imagination and the external world. Lacking a clear distinction, such as we know is observed in certain drug states, his fantasies could be as real or more real to him than the external world.

This was a habit I had for quite some time. Perhaps even now I still do it. I look at a clock and for a long while continue to see the hands fixed just as they were and not realize time had passed. That's why I'm often late.

All of which may bear importantly on the major question of how we make this critical distinction between internal and external.

I have gone into detail because this individual provides such a powerful illustration of the interlocking and interdependent character of our various mental and psychological attributes, and thus of the extensive consequences of what are undoubtedly a few strategically placed genetic alterations. Conceivably, they might amount to little more than an altered metabolism leading to the localized endogenous synthesis of an unusual substance with certain LSD-like properties.

I have thus far been principally concerned with the more cerebral and operational aspects of central nervous system function. Another most important field for genetic intervention is our motivational and emotional states. It seems all too clear to me that we are the victims of a variety of emotional anachronisms, of internal drives no doubt essential to our survival in a primitive past, but quite unnecessary and undesirable in a civilized state. We have surely more than we need in aggression. Could we not lower aggressiveness, bearing in mind that we must be on guard for possible corollary consequences?

Pessimism and depression are perhaps necessary in a world that merits suspicion, but their exaggeration has little merit. This is illustrated splendidly in the Pooh stories, where Eeyore, the donkey, one of Pooh's friends, is the embodiment of depression. One day Eeyore finds his tail is missing.

"You must have left it somewhere," said Winnie-the-Pooh.
"Somebody must have taken it," said Eeyore. "How like Them," he added.

But in a more humane world such qualities might be of little use. We will undoubtedly continue to have need of compassion. There is in the Pooh stories another episode in which after a period of intense rain and general flooding of the premises Edward Bear and Christopher Robin are impelled to rescue their close friend Piglet, who is stranded on a tree branch not much above the rising water. But how to accomplish this? After both are stumped for some time, Pooh has an idea which certainly far exceeds his normal cortical limitations. He suggests that they invert Christopher Robin's umbrella and use it as a boat. Christopher is so awed by this unexpectedly brilliant and, I might add, successful invention that he later names this worthy craft *The Brain of Pooh*.

I like to think that driven by necessity or even better by compassion we too will learn to exceed our normal cortical limitations and we too may tap talents yet unseen.

So much of what we see, so much of what we perceive, so much of what we experience is in truth what we conceive. It is contributed by the mind of the beholder and thus must depend in detail upon the innate structures and functions of the mind, upon its accumulated experiences, upon its physiological state, and even in a regenerative manner upon how the mind conceives of itself. And our view of the mind, even the very concept that we may at some future time be able to augment and improve our capacities, may react upon our behavior long before we achieve these visions.

For a number of the most strategic and salient structural elements of the mind there is already evidence of significant genetic determination. These genetic factors, and they may not be so many in number, define our intellectual and conceptual limits. I propose that through phylogenetic studies and through studies of the rare human genetic variants we can learn much concerning their basic cerebral components, in preparation for the day when we wish to begin to move back their limits.

And so perhaps, when we've mutated the genes and integrated the neurons and refined the biochemistry, our descendants will come to see us rather as we see Pooh: frail and slow in logic, weak in memory and pale in abstraction, but usually warm-hearted, generally compassionate, and on occasion possessed of innate common sense and uncommon perception —as when Pooh and Piglet walked home thoughtfully together in the golden evening, and for a long time they were silent.

"When you wake in the morning, Pooh," said Piglet at last, "what's the first thing you say to yourself?"

"What's for breakfast?" said Pooh. "What do *you* say, Piglet?"

"I say, I wonder what's going to happen exciting *today*?" said Piglet.

Pooh nodded thoughtfully. "It's the same thing," he said.

THE BEHAVIORAL LEVEL

WATSONIAN *behaviorism inspired an unusual amount of experimental activity and ushered in an era of great intellectual ferment, resulting in such major theoretical efforts as Guthrie's contiguity theory of learning, Tolman's sign gestalt theory, and Hull's S-R theoretical system based upon interlocking intervening variables. The movement presently finds its most articulate expression in Skinner's atheoretical descriptive behaviorism, which has elevated the principle of reinforcement to remarkable prominence. The techniques of this movement have escaped the confines of psychology and have spilled out into contemporary society with far-reaching implications for behavior change. Through the application of differential reinforcement, behavior is being shaped: abnormal behavior to normal, ignorant behavior to educated, drunken behavior to sober, childlike behavior to mature—and the areas of application and the list of claims grow. The proponents of objective behaviorism are cognizant of the rising tide of dissent outlined in various sections of this book but they continue in their resolve to keep psychology descriptive and objective, a respectable member of the natural sciences, uncontaminated by mentalism and neurological speculation.*

The first paper, by Kantor, places behaviorism in historical context. Next Kendler and Spence outline the tenets of neobehaviorism as it is presently conceived. Then Skinner presents a summary of his own position, the behaviorist position, which still seems to find much acceptability among contemporary psychologists. This paper is a clear expression of his views on scientific method, as he has incorporated these concepts within the conceptual framework of the operant-conditioning approach to psychology.

These statements are followed by papers that try to place the movement in perspective. In the first, Day suggests that it is time for behaviorists to become more concerned about social issues and human concerns; specifically, they should turn their attention to an assessment of the contingencies involved in the fulfillment of people's lives as fully developed human beings. Next London pleads for an end to ideology and polemics and a concentration upon techniques as a viable approach to behavior modification. Finally, Powers presents a feedback model that he feels will allow stimulus-response laws to be predictable within a control system interpretation of behavioral organization.

37

BEHAVIORISM IN THE HISTORY OF PSYCHOLOGY

J. R. KANTOR

IN ENTERING upon a discussion of the place of behaviorism in the history of psychology I am strongly reminded, and I want to remind you, of Eddington's famous comparative description of the two tables.

The first table, you recall, is the substantial object of everyday life, an object that not only does not collapse when you lean upon it but is also made up of coherent solid substances, including enduring colors as well as tactile and other qualities. The second table, the scientific one, is entirely different. It consists mostly of emptiness teeming with electric charges moving about with great speed. But contrasted with the raw materials of the familiar table, the scientific table is based on such raw materials as ether, electrons, quanta, potentials, and Hamiltonian functions. We are so strongly reminded of Eddington's two tables because when we concern ourselves with behaviorism in psychology we are analogously called upon to distinguish two related but still different movements.

The first is the familiar so-called Watsonian behaviorism, whose origin goes back to several articles published by Watson in 1913. Watsonian behaviorism has been cultivated mostly by psychologists who have devoted themselves to the study of learning in animals, especially white rats. Its outstanding characteristic is the rejection of the introspective method of observation along with mental states which require such a method for their study. Watsonian behaviorism is also reductive; it dissolves the psychological event into neural, muscular, and glandular acts of the organism.

The second description of behaviorism, the one we may regard as the scientific one, is much more significant. It is not based upon a specific technique or department of study but upon the whole enterprise of investigation. Psychological behaviorism, when scientifically described, is rooted in many concrete events in the history of science. It is the product of a complex evolution through many centuries, an evolution influenced by the contingencies of diverse but interrelated societies. As we shall see, Watsonian behaviorism is only one incident in the long evolution of psychological behaviorism.

FROM J. R. Kantor, Behaviorism in the history of psychology, *The Psychological Record*, 1968, 18, 151–166. Reprinted by permission of the author and *The Psychological Record*.

As it is our task to describe and evaluate the place of behaviorism in the history of psychology, we must define behaviorism clearly. By behaviorism we understand the study of the behavior of some *confrontable* thing or process; thus the term "behaviorism" is equivalent to the term "science."

In astronomy, behaviorism is the study of the interaction of stars, suns, planets, galaxies and celestial radiation. In physics, behaviorism is the study of various activities, objects, or properties of objects; for example, moving bodies, energy, radiation, magnetic attraction, and atoms and their component electric charges. In biology, behaviorism signifies that the investigator observes the behavior of nucleic acids, cells, organs, and organisms, as well as various organic processes such as photosynthesis, metabolism, growth, reproduction, and disintegration. In psychology, behaviorism is the study of the interactions of organisms with other organisms or objects; in other words, the subject matter of the science of psychology consists of definite confrontable events just as do the subject matters of the other sciences. Psychological behaviorism is, then, the investigation of fields of action which occur in the same spatio-temporal framework as the subject matters studied by any of the other sciences and are in this respect identical with the data of the other sciences.

Now I propose the hypothesis that the evolution of behaviorism in the history of psychology is basically the record of that discipline's efforts to achieve scientific status, and so it becomes our task to trace the various steps in that evolution. I suggest that an examination of the evolution of psychological behaviorism reveals at least six interrelated periods, each of which has left its mark upon both the tradition and science of psychology. I say tradition and science because it is an unfortunate fact that psychology, unlike other sciences, has never completely separated itself from its non-naturalistic tradition. Psychology has not, like astronomy, left behind the astrological phase of its history.

Let us turn now to the six periods of psychological behaviorism; here are the names which we use to characterize them briefly.

1. Archaic or Naive Behaviorism.
2. Antibehaviorism.
3. Prebehaviorism.
4. Protobehaviorism.
5. Watsonian Behaviorism.
6. Authentic Behaviorism, Interbehaviorism, Field Behaviorism.

Archaic Behaviorism

To the question where and when authentic behaviorism or scientific psychology originated, we find a ready answer; it began with Aristotle and other ancients in the fourth century B.C. Of course, Aristotle had no intimation of a science called psychology, but in his biological work he inquired into the activities of organisms among which he included, besides the metabolic processes and reproduction, such psychological behavior as sensing, remembering, imagining, thinking, and dreaming. What is significant here is that he regarded those psychological activities as ways in which plants and animals interacted with the things constituting their environments. For example, in describing vision as a sensory phenomenon he specified the activity of each of the components, (a) the reacting organism with its sense organ, (b) the visible object with its color, and (c) a transparent medium between them, that is light.

At this point we must be sure to mention that Aristotle had no inkling of what has later been postulated as mental or psychic representatives of objects. In essence Aristotle's psychology was completely naturalistic though obviously it was bound to be naive and extremely simple. An acquaintance with the details of psychological history precludes the view that behaviorism was an invention of Watson or anyone in the twentieth century. At this point I want to add the suggestion that whatever failings may be attributed to the physics and other scientific studies of Aristotle, they do not count against his status as a psychologist.

Before we leave this first period it should be mentioned that the naturalistic viewpoint characteristic for Greek psychology is a definite reflection of the relatively safe and secure economic and political conditions which are about to be replaced by another and very different type of social life and science. The glorious civilization of Athens soon gave way to the culture of Alexandria of the Ptolemies. And it was in Alexandria that spirit and mentality had their first origins in Western European culture.

Antibehaviorism

Our next period, which we call antibehaviorism, and which is the longest in point of time, covers more than seventeen centuries, from the second century B.C. to the fifteenth century A.D. It may be regarded as an empty period from the standpoint of achievement. However, it is not merely a gap, but really a negative phase since what it lacks in the way of science is substituted for by religious speculations which have exerted a great influence upon scientific thought and have provided a general cultural background that has persisted from the second century B.C. to this very moment. It is antibehaviorism which is the basis and cause for the existence of behaviorism as a problem and a doctrine in the history of psychology and of science.

Such were the cultural conditions of the second period that science as the free investigation of confrontable events practically disappeared, while the civilization of the time became replete with religious and transcendental preoccupations. This is the era of theology and super-cosmic cogitation. Intellectual interests were deeply concerned with problems of a moral and religious type. Knowledge of the natural world had given way completely to an interest in the supermundane destiny of man. The primary pursuit of the age is the search for the best means of personal salvation. The problem of saving souls eclipsed all concern for the affairs of the actual world and current experience. This viewpoint is excellently illustrated by the comments of St. Augustine in his *Confessions*. He writes:

And men go abroad to wonder at the heights of mountains, the lofty billows of the sea, the long courses of rivers, the vast compass of the ocean, and the circular motions of the stars, and yet pass themselves by, nor wonder that while I spake of all these things I did not then see them with mine eyes; yet could I not have spoken of them, unless those mountains, and billows, and rivers, and stars which I have seen, and that ocean which I believed to be, I saw inwardly in my memory, yea, with such vast spaces between, as if I verily saw them abroad.

Yet did I not absorb them into me by seeing, when as with mine eyes I beheld them. Nor are the things themselves now within me, but the images of them only. And I distinctly know by what sense of the body each was impressed upon me.[1]

But not only was science cast aside in favor of religious preoccupations. There was outspoken hostility toward it. Science was regarded as stale and unprofitable in the face of the pressing demand for eternal security and perennial bliss.

During the course of all this preoccupation with the supernatural, with salvation, and with the relation of man to God, the foundation was laid for inclining psychology towards spirit and away from the concrete adjustments of organisms to each other and to other surrounding things. The spiritistic period is the source and origin of soul, inextensible thought, and myriads of invisible and intangible things and processes. Man himself was divided into a natural and a supernatural part, the latter of which is the basis for our present-day constructs of mentality, consciousness, experience, sensations, and other psychic processes.

It is melancholy to observe how little psychologists realize that the model they adopt for interpreting psychological events is directly derived from the antibehavioristic era. This is true not only of the mentalist, but also of the ordinary behaviorist, who does, however, exhibit antibehavioristic tendencies more in the case of sensory and perceptual processes than in the case of habits and learning. But both types of psychologists operate with descriptions that belong more to the traditions inherited by psychology than to its scientific aspect. There can be no doubt that the description of "seeing" or "experiencing" a color as something occurring when an impulse terminates in the brain is based upon the spiritistic ideas

1 See Augustine, *Confessions*, Book 10.

engendered in the antibehavioristic era. We shall deal further with this type of description later.

I believe it is clear that psychologists are reinforced in their use of antibehavioristic constructs by the fact that physicists and physiologists also use them. That other scientists besides psychologists have adopted transcendental postulates simply illustrates the coherence of culture. One branch of science influences another. Basic here is the fact that specialization in science is of recent origin. A close study of psychological development reveals that the current model of visual discrimination was built up by Newton in his *Optics*. This model was adopted by those philosophers who later developed psychology as a specialty.

One of the great values of the history of science is that, rightly studied, it will teach us a great deal concerning the origin of our constructs. It is impossible then, to overlook the straight path that leads back from all notions of mentality, private experience, sensations, and ideas to the spiritistic tradition of the antibehaviorism period. It was that religious period which has given rise to the bifurcation of the universe. The antibehavioristic period is the time when men sought for the nature of reality and could not find it in the confrontable events that could be observed with varying degrees of facility. Accordingly, they built up the notion that reality was a world behind the appearances. Reality was hidden and unseeable except through the medium of the spirit or the soul. From his dissatisfactions with the difficulties and troubles of the familiar world and from his hope of a better life to come, antibehavioristic man created the dichotomies of subjective and objective, of the internal and the external worlds, of mind and body, and of the primary and secondary qualities, in sum the whole idealistic or spiritistic philosophy.

What is of importance to us at this point is the continuity of history. Our different periods are not isolated entities. They are links in a chain. What the Greek and Latin church fathers wrought for social and religious purposes—the arguments of Tertullian, the parables of Philo, the cosmos of Plotinus—live on in the constructs of mind and introspective consciousness. The subjectivity and personalism of St. Augustine became the heritage of Descartes and his followers.

Though the spiritism of the antibehavioristic period lived and lives on, it did, of course, change in various ways. As early as the thirteenth century the thinkers who were exclusively professional or lay churchmen began to allow some place to non-theological subjects. They adopted the motto that nature could not be despised despite all the values that accrue to grace. Notable among the scholars of the day were the Franciscan friar Roger Bacon and the Dominican saints Albert and Thomas. All these showed a remarkable interest in once again studying natural things and events alongside theological wisdom; they thus helped to renew interest in behaviorism or science. St. Thomas, especially, deserves credit for reintroducing Aristotle's psychology to Western Europe, although both in language and doctrine he transmuted it to conform to the spiritistic culture of his time.

Prebehaviorism

Although authentic behaviorism does not again emerge until the twentieth century, there are two intervals which must be regarded as continuous with and in a genuine sense preparatory to authentic behaviorism. We have named these periods "Prebehaviorism" and "Protobehaviorism." Essentially they represent the traditional spiritistic doctrine as modified by attempts to reject and refute the overwhelming dominance of the mental. Thus these two periods lead forward to behaviorism.

In prebehaviorism we distinguish three separate but interrelated stages. The first stage represents an attempt to naturalize the spirit or soul. Here is one of the earliest arguments that science, the study of nature, must be enlarged to make room for what was presumed to be an aspect of reality additional to the usual observational one. This additional aspect was, of course, the spiritual. Outstanding here are the postulations of such thinkers as Descartes, Hobbes, Leibniz, and Spinoza, that the divergence between the natural and the supernatural could be overcome by verbally incorporating spirit into nature or verbally making it identical with nature. Thus was born the interactionism of Descartes, the identity doctrine of Spinoza, and the parallelism of Leibniz, as well as Hobbes' so-called materialism.

The second stage of prebehaviorism consists of a definite change from the cosmic and theological interests dominant earlier to human and epistemological concerns. Thus, in the seventeenth and eighteenth centuries such thinkers as Locke, Berkeley, and Hume turned psychological or mental problems in the direction of human understanding and knowledge. There is much to criticize in this movement to establish an empirical mode of knowledge; both Berkeley and Hume went so far as to absorb actual confrontable events in the mental process of human knowledge. On the other hand, the English empirical movement departed farther than the earlier prebehavioristic stage from purely cosmic principles by centering the knowledge process in the activities of man. This is true despite the fact that Berkeley did not entirely rely upon human mentality to guarantee knowledge, but resorted to the intervention of God.

The third stage of the prebehavioristic period we may designate as the age of man. This is the age of the social revolutions and the Enlightenment. At this time we have the convulsive social events of the American and French revolutions.

Now man as a social being became the focus of interest; though social communities are still as always dominated by rulers and the well-to-do, individual rights and privileges are stressed. The age of man is marked by the discovery of the worth and dignity of the human individual and the placing of high value upon his feelings and social needs.

The outstanding doctrinal result of the new humanistic thinking was the minimization of the transcendental features of man as compared with his materialistic or naturalistic aspects. The mental aspects of man were made subservient to those of his body. It is this materialistic phase of the prebehavioristic interval which exerted a strong influence on the later development of Watsonian behaviorism.

In summarizing the prebehavioristic period in the development of scientific psychology, we note in the first stage the attitude that spiritistic things can be brought into juxtaposition with natural things. Nature, it is thought, must be enlarged to accommodate spirit. This was a step away from the antibehavioristic attitude that had inevitably tied spirit to the theological realm. In the case of human beings Descartes asserted that the soul could interact with the pineal gland. Here, too, we must recall Spinoza's anticipation of the Jamesian view of the prominence of bodily action in emotional behavior, and also Hobbes' assertion that the mental is motion.

In the next stage, the soul was transformed from a mere supermundane entity into the mind and into the source and basis of human knowledge. This is a trend toward a naturalistic position.

Finally, in the third and humanistic phase this period reaches its peak with the emphasis on man as a social, political, and economic creature. Now psychological thinking is turned sharply toward the qualities of persons and a great impetus is given to the study of the affective traits. The ultimate outcome is to minimize the mental traits of man and to make them dependent upon the body. At this time the ground is prepared for the emergence of eighteenth-century French materialism.

Protobehaviorism

When we reach the period of protobehaviorism we come to a progressive link in the chain of psychological development. In this period we have a decided preparation for an authentic behavioristic evolution of psychology. One stage of the protobehavioristic period is the age of physiological and experimental psychology as connected with such well known figures as Weber, Fechner, Wundt, and Ebbinghaus. We call this the protobehavioristic period because, while there is no interruption in the continuity of the spiritistic tradition, psychology becomes involved with manipulations and experimental work. Despite their manipulations, however, the men of this period believed themselves to be working with the psychic aspects of human action. Consciousness and the mental were to be studied by means of bodily motions and processes. The view is formulated that psychology must follow the lead of physiology and study organic action as a clue to the nature and the workings of the mind.

What is unique and important about this stage of the protobehavioristic period is that operational techniques were exploited alongside the speculations concerning consciousness and mental contents. The performance of various operations or experiments cannot but have the potentiality of leading to the study of confrontable events despite the mentalistic interpretations made of the events observed.

We must note, however, that this first stage of protobehaviorism is decidedly characterized by a striking divergence between the postulations and the detailed operations performed. This divergence is an extremely effective barrier to a full-fledged scientific movement in which the hypotheses and interpretations must be fully integrated with the experimental operations performed on the events studied. In the particular case to be discussed, the experiments upon organisms were completely vitiated by transcendental interpretations, which stood at the opposite pole from the behavioristic ones.

For example, to interpret the operations and the results reached by Fechner as a relation between psychic processes and either (a) the nature of the organic excitation or (b) the traits of the stimuli as in the standard formula

$$S = k \log R$$

is to misconstrue the entire situation. Clearly, what is happening is that the subject is performing a response describable either as a judgment or a comparison or as a verbal reference to the reaction or to the stimulus object. Accordingly, the formula should be transformed into

$$R = k \log S, \text{ or } R = k S^n.$$

Now the R symbolizes a concrete action of the subject while the S represents some trait of the stimulus object.

A second distinctive stage of the protobehavioristic period we may call evolutional behaviorism. Basically, evolutional behaviorism is a result of the great movement known as biological or Darwinian evolution.

It is a matter of common knowledge that Darwinism has exerted a tremendous influence upon psychology as well as upon every other phase of our Western European culture. When we analyze its most important influence, we see that evolutionism demonstrated the possibility of treating geological, biological, and psychological events as definite naturalistic processes without invoking theological and supernatural factors. In biology especially, Darwinism demonstrated the interactions of observable and confrontable events whenever all sorts of changes and metamorphoses occurred.

In so far as psychology in particular is concerned, Darwin showed the definite interrelations of organic things so that the theological notion of man's difference from and superiority to the rest of creation was rendered null and void. The result for psychology was that animal behavior became a comparative study and the doctrine developed that human psychology could be enhanced by the study of animals in their normal and laboratory environments. It is impossible to overestimate the importance of this aid which psychology received from biological evolution. Suffice it to suggest the advantages of evolutionism for the emergence of psychological behaviorism. In detail, there is hardly a doubt that functionalism in psychology was greatly facilitated by the developments in organic evolution and it is likewise certain that Watsonian behaviorism had a definite basis in functional psychology.

Watsonian Behaviorism

If we have been reading the history of psychology correctly, it should be clear that protobehaviorism led more or less inevitably toward Watsonian behaviorism. The tradition of experimentation in psychology was well established and the same may be said of the animal studies which received so great an impulse from evolution theory. Indeed, it is no exaggeration to say that Watsonian behaviorism required little more to come into existence than a confluence of some of the factors that had been developing in previous periods of the history of psychology. Recall that eighteenth- and nineteenth-century materialism were also ways of misprizing the psychic.

All psychologists who appreciate the value of psychological behaviorism as a scientific movement will realize that it is impossible to minimize the great merit of Watson in promoting an objective and naturalistic view in the field of psychology. But this is not to overlook that Watson's dissatisfaction with consciousness and introspection had a basis in the opinions current in his day. It has been pointed out that "symptoms of Behaviorism are detectable in the writings of Cattell as early as 1904."

Much more telling evidence of an incipient anti-mentalism is the famous article of James entitled "Does Consciousness Exist" of 1904 and the writings of Singer on "Mind as an Observable Object" in 1911 and his paper on "Consciousness and Behavior" of the next year. To consult the pre-Watsonian writings of the philosophers Woodbridge, Bawden, Tawney, Bode, and others, and of the biologists such as Jennings and Loeb, is to conclude that behavioristic ideas were certainly in the air before Watson issued his manifesto.

Further evidence that Watsonian behaviorism is only one item in the evolution of an authentic behaviorism we find in the great influence upon Watson of the Russians Bechterev and Pavlov. The inadequacies of the introspective psychologies contributed only a negative attitude. When Watson became familiar with conditioning techniques the way was opened to a more self-sufficient naturalistic attitude and investigative program. The conditioning techniques reinforced the conviction that psychological data were confrontable events.

Watson's manifesto was then only an announcement of changes that were taking place in psychology. It would be a great mistake, however, to deprecate the importance of that manifesto, since in the processes of cultural change and revolutions of thought a great potency attaches to the formulations embodying attitudes and beliefs. Such formalizations can serve as catalysts bringing about changes in viewpoint. Thus it cannot be denied that Watsonian behaviorism was a powerful factor in moving psychology toward an objective and naturalistic position. Even though Watson based his manifesto on his revulsion against the structural and functional variations of the description of consciousness, his discontent with those specific forms of mentalism showed the way toward a complete emancipation of psychology from its mentalistic servitude. Watsonian behaviorism ultimately became a guide to a genuine and comprehensive view of naturalistic psychology.

In the history of psychology, then, the greatest value of Watsonian behaviorism is that it was a great step forward in the evolution of the subject toward the status of a natural science. However, Watsonian behaviorism can be considered only as a tentative and preliminary version of naturalistic psychology. Great changes were necessary before it could become authentic behaviorism. The nature of these changes is apparent when we compare the traits of Watsonian behaviorism with the more advanced form of anti-mentalism which we have called authentic behaviorism, interbehaviorism, or field behaviorism.

Interbehaviorism or Field Behaviorism

As stages in the evolution of naturalistic psychology, both Watsonian and field behaviorism are opposed to all forms of mentalism, but there is still a vast difference between them. Although Watsonian behaviorism objects to consciousness or mentality, it does so under the influence of the mind-body tradition. Watsonian behaviorism simply sets mentality aside as unnecessary and interfering. Even the strict version of Lashley simply denies the existence of consciousness or mentality. Moreover, when the Watsonian behaviorist asserts that he has transcended the sheer negative attitude of rejecting mentality and is cultivating a new science, that of behavioralism, he only approaches authentic behaviorism because the behavior he studies is strictly limited to the behavior of certain animals and particular techniques. Furthermore, the Watsonian behaviorist makes use of the same model of the sensory processes as the mentalist.

By contrast, field behaviorism starts in a completely different way. It approaches psychological studies from the standpoint of confrontable events in the same way as any natural science does. The field behaviorist becomes interested in the interbehavior of organisms under definite environing conditions and proceeds to investigate them in a manner suitable to the original events and in conformity with the technological means available. He does all this independently of the transcendental postulates which have dominated psychology since the extinction of the naive behaviorism of the Greeks.

Our next comparison between the different behaviorisms is concerned with the role assigned to biological elements and puts into bold relief the advantage of complete independence of the mind-body tradition enjoyed by the field behaviorist. He is able to obviate completely the construction that psychological happenings require some biological or neural basis.[2] The point here is that Watsonian behaviorists, in common with the traditional mentalist, perpetuate the view that psychological data are diaphanous, unapproachable happenings requiring some more solid foundation. Here is a paradoxical situation. Those psychologists who propagate the notion that psychological events have a biological or neural basis assume that this notion reinforces the scientific character of psychology. Actually, the opposite happens. The stress on biological factors simply makes room for vague and even false interpretations. Consider the standard description of a sensory reaction which I quote from the *Handbook of Experimental Psychology*.

The external ear delivers sound waves through the external auditory canal to the middle ear, and thence they pass to the inner ear. There, in the cochlea, the sensory cells of the organ of Corti are stimulated and initiate nerve impulses in the fibres of the auditory nerve. The impulses pass through a series of nuclei and fiber tracts in the medulla and midbrain to the auditory area of the cerebral cortex; and there *somehow*, they generate the sensations that we know subjectively as "sounds" (our italics).[3]

Although the Watsonian behaviorist claims to be free from the constructs of the introspectionist he really is committed, in part at least, to the same doctrine. His refusal to accept the rest of the introspectionist's system lays the Watsonian behaviorist open to the charge of not doing justice to the total cognitive situation.

Let us note that there are two problems here. One is to describe what occurs when an organism discriminates a color, a taste, an odor or some other sensory quality. The other is to describe what the organic structures of the organism do when a discrimination is made. It is obvious that a sensory or a discrimination event cannot be reduced to the functioning of biological processes. Neural conduction or cortical excitation cannot be identified with sensory qualities and clearly there is no color in light rays, as Newton knew in his time.

Psychologists face a striking dilemma in the study of sensory processes. On the one hand, it is impossible to accept the mentalistic interpretation

[2] Biological Basis is to be distinguished from Biological Participation.
[3] Stevens 1951, p. 1116.

that a sensation arises when energy impinges on a sense organ and sets up a conduction pattern in the brain. And on the other hand, to accept only the stimulation and conduction factors is to leave sensory qualities out of the picture.

The removal of this dilemma requires that account be taken of the complex physical and chemical traits of stimulus objects. For example, in the analysis of the discrimination of the red of blood or the green and other colors of plants it is inadvisable to neglect the chemistry of chlorophyll, of the anthocyanins, and of hemoglobin.

Basic to the errors of both the Watsonian behaviorist and the introspectionist is the indiscriminate borrowing of abstract constructs from other disciplines even when they have clearly a negative or harmful effect upon psychological descriptions. For example, both types of psychologists, when describing visual events, take over the constructs of wave lengths and frequencies in order to transform them into stimulus data despite the fact that organisms respond to colored or bright objects and not to the physicist's abstractions.

Nothing that I have said goes counter to the undeniable fact that when an organism responds there are many biological occurrences in the situation. But this is merely to note that psychological events are also biological and physiochemical events. What must be emphasized is that the biological features of the situation, when they are not aspects of stimulating objects, are only participating factors in the response phase of the stimulus and response event.

On the response side, all psychological events are performances of biological organisms. Obviously, then, psychological actions include organic activities as components. Every tissue, organ, or system contributes to the total response. It is an error, however, to think that the neural, muscular, or glandular functions are the basis of some other kind of process. Rather they are part of the pattern of action which is coordinate with the action of the stimulus object. It is in this sense that we must distinguish between biological concomitants or bases of action and the intimate participants of action. The concomitant view is born of the traditional mind-body diremption while the participation view comports with actual observation.

Recently, the expression has become popular that biological actions are the bases of behavior. This expression suggests the same sort of dualism we have just been considering. Behavior is separated from biological action and made to parallel it. Whatever is objectionable in this sort of construction is obviated by the participation description.

Another great difference between Watsonian and field behaviorism is that the latter is far removed from the organocentrism which localizes a psychological event in or about an organism. It is precisely the organocentric way of thinking that has led to the invention of psychic powers or internal forces to account for the activities of organisms. Thus constructs like instincts, drives, intelligence, and personality have come to be used for such powers and forces instead of as class names for the actions that are really stimulated and controlled by the contingencies of personal, domestic, and social life. For that reason an authentic behaviorism concerns itself with comprehensive fields that include in addition to the organism the stimulus objects and the many physiochemical, biological, and social setting factors.

A fourth great difference between the two types of behaviorism concerns the nature of stimulus and response. For Watsonian behaviorism the stimulus is anything that elicits a response. The stimulus may be some form of energy or an object. Corresponding to the simple stimulation is the response reduced to a movement or a secretion. The interbehavioral psychologist, on the other hand, differentiates between a stimulus object and a stimulus function. The latter is developed in correspondence with a response function during a prior contact of the organism and an object. The basic datum of psychology is, then, the occurrence of stimulus and response functions in complex fields organized in earlier contacts between organisms and objects or conditions. In this way account may be taken of all sorts of complex behavior; the psychologist is not restricted to elementary reflexes nor is he constrained to build his interpretations with reflexes as models.[4]

As a fifth and final differentiation between interbehavioral and behavioral psychology we must point out the completely different protopropositions or philosophical assumptions that underlie them. Despite all its resolute efforts to avoid the mental, Watsonian behaviorism still stands under the banner of the dualistic tradition. In contrast, interbehavioral psychology claims to be entirely free of the idealistic or other metaphysical philosophical traditions, and thus avoids altogether the problems of creative processes, which produce objects of knowledge, or even the need to sidestep such problems by reducing the qualities of objects to organic processes. Basically, this means that interbehavioral psychology does not stand in the shadow of any traditional form of philosophy. If some philosophical foundation is regarded as necessary, it is of a new type and absolutely different from the philosophy which has flourished since the Judeo-Christian way of thinking became established.

In completing our comparison of Watsonian and authentic behaviorism we may draw two conclusions: first, that scientific psychology is a particular type of behaviorism and, second, that all types of behaviorism have been successively evolved and illustrate the corrigibility of science. I will conclude my discussion by considering several of the most outstanding characteristics of authentic behaviorism.

[4] For a more elaborate statement of stimulus and response functions see Kantor 1933b and 1942.

Outstanding Characteristics of Authentic Behaviorism

We have already dwelt sufficiently upon the fact that authentic behaviorism demands the derivation of all data from confrontations with observed events. For any discipline to be a science there is a further demand: namely, that the data be organized and interpreted by means of a suitable set of postulates.

What guarantees the scientific character of field behaviorism is the precise conformity of its postulations with its operations. We have seen that experimental operations alone do not suffice to make psychology scientific, the classic example being Fechnerian experimental psychology. Though Fechner's operations were excellent, especially his manipulation of data, they had nothing at all to do with his mystic assumptions. Consequently, while Fechnerian experiments contributed greatly to the eventual evolution of scientific psychology, his work on the whole belongs only to the protobehavioristic period of psychological history. For the most effective progress of science it is imperative that the assumptions be drawn from operations and the criticism of operations, and also they must later be applied and tested by additional experiments, that is by confrontations with events. In other words, postulates must be congruent and convergent with operations.

Two important advantages ensue from the congruence and convergence of postulates and operations. The first is the inhibition of all substitution of the data or methods of other sciences for those of psychology. Probably because of the persistence of spiritistic postulation, under the name of psychology many workers occupy themselves with events that belong to the older naturalistic disciplines. They may concern themselves with neurological, statistical, and general biological tasks, or even problems of physics. It is hardly an advantage for psychology to substitute the data of physiology, pharmacology, or physics for psychological events. When such substitution is made we can, at best, hope only for some remote advantage to psychology.

All scientific events are interrelated; accordingly there is great merit in interdisciplinary study. But to take account of what is going on in the neighboring sciences and to cooperate with their workers is no warrant for neglecting to respect the importance and integrity of psychology as a science.

The most aggravated form of substitution is illustrated by psychologists who go even farther afield than neighboring sciences and confine themselves to practical work of some kind, substituting some professional activity for basic scientific study. The plea that this is a way of avoiding unsuitable postulation really reflects a complete escape from science. Our objection here is not to a field instead of a laboratory source of data, but to the inevitable danger of either neglecting scientific problems or, even worse, employing psychic interpretations in handling the data. The latter eventuality is daily observed when psychologists apply constructs borrowed from classical Greek mythology to human nature and its deviations.

The second advantage of converging postulates and operations is that psychological studies can be carried out on even the most elaborate types of behavior, such as imagining, feeling, and thinking, without transmuting them into organic processes or simpler psychological acts, or denying their existence altogether. As long as we cleave to the fundamental principle that psychology is the study of the interactions between response functions and stimulus functions there is no type of behavior that eludes observation. In dealing with the most refined and difficult behavior we need only exclude the influence of venerable traditions. Imagery, for example, can be readily described in terms of incipient and vestigial action based upon prior contacts with particular objects and surrounding circumstances.[5]

With even greater assurance we may assert the capacity of interactional theory to describe and interpret the more overt ranges of behavior. We all recall the criticisms directed by the psychopathologists against academic psychology. They complained that psychologists have been so intent upon the judgment of lifted weights or differences in brightness discrimination as to have no interest in man's important complex behavior. This criticism grew out of the claims of the extreme introspectionist that only rigidly introspective studies were truly scientific. The authentic behaviorist, however, is in principle enjoined from discriminating against any form of action, whether human or non-human.

One of the most valuable achievements of authentic behaviorism still remains to be mentioned. It encourages the distinction between constructs and events and between different constructs. When we respect this analytic differentiation we cannot but be struck by the building up of fantastic constructs such as ego, id, or death instinct as descriptions of deviant behavior. Our basic point is that any description or interpretation in psychology must begin and end with definite interactions of persons in favorable or unfavorable conditions. To draw constructs from mythology or metaphysical historical traditions is to take psychology out of the range of science.

Conclusion

In concluding this sketch of the nature and development of behaviorism, I want to refer once more to the tortuous career of psychology as a science. As we know, psychology early attained a scientific status soon to be lost. Indeed it is interesting to contemplate the high estate that Greek psychology would have reached had it not been cut off in its infancy. What followed was a different cultural world which abolished be-

[5] See Kantor 1924, Ch. 10 and 1933, Ch. 11.

haviorism in psychology as well as in the other disciplines and reduced them all to supermundane traditions. This transcendental intellectual orientation lasted for some seventeen centuries and, though gradually modified, left numerous institutional survivals. Slowly, however, with the changing conditions of social and economic life, science was allowed a place beside theology and eventually reached a lofty peak. In the case of psychology the steps by which this was accomplished were (a) a gradual departure from theological speculation, (b) the postulation that the mental aspects of man were somehow natural, (c) the growing belief that the mind was dependent upon the body, (d) the development of manipulations and experiments, and finally, (e) the insistence that observable interbehavioral events were the actual data. Today there exists again an authentic behaviorism which has made considerable progress in penetrating into the psychological domain. Still, a survey of the current psychological field reveals the perseverance of many traditional doctrines so that authentic behaviorism has by no means achieved a dominant position.

REFERENCES

AUGUSTINE, 1938. *Confessions.* London: Everyman Library.

KANTOR, J. R., 1924. *Principles of psychology.* Vol I. New York: Knopf.

————. 1933a. *A survey of the science of psychology.* Bloomington, Ind.: Principia Press.

————. 1933b. In defense of stimulus-response psychology. *Psychol. Rev.,* **40,** 324–366.

————. 1942. Preface to interbehavioral psychology. *Psychol. Rec.,* **5,** 173–193.

STEVENS, S. S. (Ed.) 1951. *Handbook of experimental psychology.* New York: Wiley.

38

TENETS OF NEOBEHAVIORISM

HOWARD H. KENDLER *and* JANET T. SPENCE

Explanation in Psychology

CONTEMPORARY psychology is confronted with an explanatory crisis. Conflicting interpretations of explanation accepted by different segments

FROM H. H. Kendler and J. T. Spence, Eds., *Essays in Neobehaviorism: A Memorial Volume to Kenneth W. Spence,* © 1971, pp. 21–40. Reprinted by permission of Prentice-Hall, Inc., Englewood Cliffs, New Jersey.

of the psychological community are at the roots of many of the significant controversies that rage within the discipline of psychology, and different conceptions of the nature of explanation appear to mold psychological knowledge into strikingly different forms.

The neobehavioristic tradition on the nature of scientific explanation clearly is at odds both with that segment of the behavioristic community (Skinner, 1950) that assumes a radical positivist position, denying any need for theories, and with varieties of phenomenology (e.g., Allport, 1955; Smedslund, 1969) which in one way or another seek the explanation of human conduct in terms of the phenomenology of the experiencing individual. After describing briefly the explanatory position of the neobehaviorists and contrasting it with competing conceptions, we will direct our main effort to clarification of the fundamental causes of the existing differences in explanatory goals and their implications for the future.

The neobehavioristic decision concerning the nature of explanation is, in principle, both clear and simple. Explanation is equated with theoretical deduction: an event is explained by deducing it from one or more general propositions. The deductive process is analogous to mathematical proof although its precision can vary from mathematical verification to the logical use of ordinary language. The constructs used in the theoretical propositions must in some manner be representative of the concepts involved in the events to be explained. In other words the theoretical constructs must be coordinated with the empirical events.

Accepting the deductive model of explanation does not imply any preference for a particular strategy, such as an axiomatic system, inductive generalizations, formulating intervening variables, reductionistic hypotheses, etc. The deductive model sets the goal for explanation but not the means by which it is to be attained.

THE ROLE OF THEORY IN SCIENCE

In opposition to the deductive model of explanation is the radical positivistic position, at times enunciated by Skinner (1950), that theories are unnecessary. The scientist's task is to manipulate experimentally events that are directly observable in order to discover the facts as they are, and nothing more. One historical factor encouraging this atheoretical position was the desire of the early behaviorists to rid psychology of vague subjective concepts. A suspicion developed that the ambiguity of mentalism would reenter psychology in the form of theoretical constructs.

Skinner's atheoretical position has generated much confusion simply because it is itself unclear. It is one thing to state that at a particular time in the history of psychology the systematic collection of data without any theoretical preconceptions, but with a desire to control phenomena, may be more productive than self-conscious efforts to erect theoretical structures that cannot be supported by available empirical evidence. It is quite another thing to state that theories are unnecessary and should be ignored as a scientific goal. Skinner seems to maintain both of these positions, frequently arguing in favor of the latter, but defending it in terms of the former (see Scriven, 1956).

In truth, the denial of the significance of the theoretical goal in psychology has been more of a debator's point than a controversy that reflects in actual practice two forms of scientific effort. Skinner himself has theorized extensively, in his efforts both to systematize the variables that determine behavior and to generalize from the operant-conditioning situation to all aspects of life. But his theorizing has been covert and thus he has felt no need to defend his speculations. In addition, many of his students have discovered that scientists cannot live by facts alone and have self-consciously entered the theoretical arena (e.g., Terrace, 1968). Thus we are forced to conclude that a fundamental disagreement about one of the most central issues in science, the role of theory, does not prove to exert as great an impact as would be expected from the extent of the divergence of the competing views.

DEDUCTIVE EXPLANATION VS. INTUITIVE UNDERSTANDING

The issue of understanding behavior within a phenomenologically oriented psychology raises a difference that is fundamental not only in conception but also in practice. Whereas behavioristic psychology views behavior, whether of animals or men, from the "outside," just as a natural scientist observes the phenomena which he investigates, the phenomenological psychologist desires to understand behavior from the "inside" in terms of what the action means to the person who is behaving. Whereas a neobehaviorist explains behavior by deducing consequences through propositions formulated from previously observed regularities, the phenomenological psychologist explains behavior by "crawling into a person's mind" and showing how his resulting behavior was inevitable.

Implicit in this "outside-inside" difference are several independent problems that should be identified before this discussion continues. The first is the existence of phenomenal experience in man. Reference to this problem has been made previously and it was concluded that the observations of *both* private and public events involve personal conscious experience. Thus if we limit our interest to humans, who are capable of reporting subjective events, then we must conclude that the problem of accepting conscious experience as a valid event is not a source of dispute between the neobehaviorist and the phenomenologist. Two related questions are at issue. The first is whether phenomenal experience should be investigated. Assuming a positive response, the second is, how should it be done?

The decision to investigate phenomenal experience will depend upon the place one assigns to it in psychology. If phenomenal experience is considered, by definition, to be the major object of investigation, as the structuralist decided, then the only choice is to investigate it. But this justification does not entail a specific method of procedure. One possibility is to investigate phenomenological experience within a conception of science that demands intersubjective agreement and deductive explanation, the same framework that guides the work of neobehaviorists. Whether phenomenological research can meet such demands is an open question. Some psychologists either forget or ignore the point that the methods of structuralism are not the only ones that can be applied to the investigation of phenomenal experience. It can be argued that the failure of structuralism should not be interpreted as a general indictment of the pursuit of phenomenological experience, but instead as a condemnation of a particular method.

Another possibility is that phenomenological research can adopt a different epistemological framework. To pursue this alternative the distinction between *deductive explanation* and *intuitive understanding* should be made. The clearest example of deductive explanation is a successful mathematical model capable of generating deductions in agreement with empirical data. Yet models that provide only a mathematical description in the absence of any conceptual interpretation fail to generate in some psychologists an intuitive understanding of the causal formations of a set of facts. Consider conditioning. One can represent the conditioning process exclusively in terms of mathematical changes as a function of practice or one can inject, as Estes (1959) did, a conceptual analysis (stimulus sampling) of the conditioning process. From the explanatory point of view these two conceptions, assuming the mathematical properties are the same, are not fundamentally different. However, from the viewpoint of intuitive understanding the conceptions differ in the phenomenal experience they evoke, at least for some persons.

Intuitive understanding, however, does not depend upon deductive explanation. One can obtain a sense of deep understanding of behavior from the writings of a perceptive novelist, such as Dostoevsky or Camus. One can speculate that this intuitive understanding stems from the ability of the literary work to generate empathic reactions which create in the reader an intuitive understanding of the character's, and perhaps even the reader's own, behavior. These literary descriptions possess no deductive consequences as does a logically constructed theory and therefore do not qualify as deductive explanations, even though they do generate intuitive understanding. Our aim, it should be noted, has not been to characterize all aspects of intuitive understanding, a task more appropriate for phenomenologists than for neobehaviorists, but instead to emphasize the distinction between two forms of understanding, the deductive and the intuitive.

This analysis suggests that two kinds of data, objective responses and personal phenomenal experience, and two types of interpretations, deductive explanation and intuitive understanding, are available to psychologists. Neobehaviorism has clearly opted for objective responses as the dependent variable in psychology and for deductive explanation as the method of interpretation. In opposition are varieties of phenomenological psychology which recently have become popular as a consequence of the interior immigration within all segments of society from the objective to the subjective world. These phenomenological orientations assign a central role to phenomenal experience in psychology and accept as an explanation some criterion of shared experience between an observer and the person whose behavior he seeks to understand. The objection of neobehaviorism to phenomenological psychology is not in the recognition of phenomenal experiences as an observable event, or even in acknowledging their special importance, but instead in the failure of the conceptualization and explanation of phenomenal experience to meet the requirements of their epistemological principles.

The adoption by the neobehaviorists, as well as most other experimental psychologists, of a deductive model of explanation frequently has been attributed to their frank desire to emulate physics. Assigning motivations to actions, particularly those involved in intellectual pursuits, is a tricky business and perhaps should be avoided, or at least expressed in less confident terms. Brodbeck (1962) argues that accepting the deductive model does not mean that physics is being imitated but instead that physics is being admired. The most compelling point about the deductive model is its conclusiveness. Proof is in the explanatory statements available to all, rather than in the mind of the person asserting them. In any case it may be best to consider the intrinsic worth of the deductive model instead of trying to discover the psychological reasons for its adoption. Nobody should be surprised, however, that a systematic position that values intersubjective agreement should embrace the deductive model of explanation.

The Strategy of Neobehaviorism

Epistemological decisions must be distinguished from the strategy with which any scientific discipline implements them in an attempt to develop an empirical body of knowledge. The decisions themselves, such as adopting the deductive model of explanation, do not imply any strategy by which the intent of the decision can be accomplished. The decision establishes the objectives; the strategy describes the intellectual methods used to achieve them. But since any particular strategy is not demanded by any given decision, that is, others are possible, the strategy itself is not as central to a particular orientation, such as neobehaviorism, as is an epistemological decision. Nevertheless, the strategies are important in characterizing a given systematic position because they differentiate it from other approaches that share the same epistemological commitments. Several schools of psychology considered the mind to be the subject matter of psychology but it was the strategy of observing the mind by introspection and analyzing it into its basic elements that distinguished structuralism from other mentalistic approaches. Similarly Tolman (1932) shared with neobehaviorism the epistemological decision to regard behavior as the object of study but differed in terms of the strategy he advocated in developing a theory of behavior.

STRATEGY OF THEORETICAL DEVELOPMENT

Neobehaviorism, in its early stages of development, chose to pursue the task of theoretical development by using classical conditioning phenomena as a source for primary theoretical assumptions. This approach was seen to possess two advantages. Principles of conditioning, considered the simplest form of learning, presumably would also enter in more complex forms of learning. Classical conditioning also was a highly controlled and flexible experimental technique that could generate additional information that would be needed to refine and expand the theoretical structure.

However, if we look upon the choice of an experimental paradigm to reflect theoretical principles in a somewhat more detached manner, other alternatives to classical conditioning in the field of learning were available. Tolman preferred T-maze learning because he believed that choice behavior was fundamental to all behavior, while Skinner chose free-operant conditioning because he felt that the probability of a response was the basic measure of behavior and that the schedule of reinforcement was the most important psychological variable. How are these discrepancies in choice of a fundamental experimental situation to be explained? Do they result from information which, if properly understood, would lead to the unanimous selection of one particular situation? Or is the choice determined by some pretheoretical model of behavior which expresses an intuitive a priori judgment about the nature of the process which is being investigated?

Neobehaviorists, particularly Hull and Spence, have argued that the classical conditioning situation is simpler than other laboratory paradigms, or at least can and typically has been arranged to be. In single and multiple T-mazes, puzzle boxes, and other trial-and-error situations popular during the initial development of neobehaviorism, performance was said to reflect the simultaneous *acquisition* of one response or response chain and *extinction* of a number of competing responses. In contrast, the relative simplicity that could be built into the classical conditioning arrangement—that is, the limited number of stimulus variables assumed to determine performance and the possibility of strict control in such matters as stimulus reception, made it the paradigm of choice for discovering many basic phenomena. Thus, not only could the acquisition and extinction of a single S-R association be studied in isolation, but other processes such as motivational and inhibitory ones could be as well. Skinner's lever-pressing paradigm—whether free-operant or discrete-trial—was characterized by Spence as "limiting cases of selective learning [1956, p. 39]," a situation in which competing response tendencies were minimized and the organism under greater external control and thus more closely approximating the classical conditioning situation.

Too little work had been done with the operant technique, in any event, to be of much assistance to the early neobehaviorists. Thus when Hull was developing his systematic behavior theory, he leaned heavily on Pavlovian concepts as well as classical conditioning phenomena in attempting to describe the basic laws of learning. Hull himself did very little research in classical conditioning. Spence, whose major early work was with discrimination learning, used phenomena discovered in the context of classical conditioning as a source of his theoretical hypotheses but did not engage in classical conditioning research until the late 1940s, his first empirical investigation being published in 1950 (Spence & Norris, 1950). His purpose in turning to classical conditioning is described in the following statements, which were intended as a broader justification of the predilection of objective psychologists to confine their research to simple laboratory situations:

The primary criterion that has guided us in any priorities that we have given to various areas of psychological study has been our estimate of the likelihood of successful accomplishment of our aim of discovering scientific laws about the phenomena. Being guided by such purely scientific objectives, and not having any special interests, humanitarian, religious, social betterment or otherwise, no particular area of human or animal behavior is seen as more important than another. We have chosen to investigate simpler phenomena first because we are of the belief that progress in the formulation of psychological laws and theories will be more rapid in this area than in the case of more complex behavior. We also believe that many of the variables and laws isolated in the study of simpler forms of behavior will be operative in more complex instances, interacting presumably with the additional factors introduced into these more complex situations. If such is the case it would appear to be more efficient in the long run to investigate the simpler phenomena first [Spence, 1957, p. 103].

It is critical to note Spence's assumption that there are basic trans-situational laws. The experimental operations defining classical conditioning are obviously not identical to those defining instrumental conditioning, yet, in theoretical terms, the growth of the learning construct, habit (H), for example, was assumed to have the same functional relationship to the number of reinforced trials (N), in both instances. His remarks further assume that experimental paradigms in which learning is being investigated can be roughly arranged on a simplicity-complexity continuum, with classical conditioning being at one extreme.

Although these arguments are reasonable they are not compelling. Justifying any given experimental situation as being more fundamental or simple than any other involves circular reasoning. The pretheoretical model demands a particular basic experimental design which in turn is justified by the same pretheoretical model. But it must be remembered that the pretheoretical model is justified not by a validated theory but only by an unproven judgment. When viewed in this light other pretheoretical models are possible, and if persuasively rationalized, equally defensible.

The analysis of the rational underpinnings of a choice of a primary source of theoretical principles is not offered as a criticism of the decision to afford classical conditioning a central role in the development of a theory of learning. No other method exists for selecting a basic experimental paradigm. Prejudgments must be made without guarantees of their eventual value. A theorist must gamble. But it must not be forgotten that the final test of a basic experimental paradigm is not the rationalization offered in its support; it is its ultimate fruitfulness.

A problem for contemporary neobehaviorists who are interested in extending their formulations to complex behavior is to judge the potential of classical and other forms of conditioning, single-trial instrumental and operant, to continue as primary sources of theoretical assumptions as well as of productive experimental procedures.

Although Spence never wavered in his belief that classical conditioning was both a fertile source of theoretical hypotheses and an invaluable experimental technique, he was always alert to the problems of boundary conditions of his theoretical formulations, particularly when verbal processes were involved. Early in his career, when discussing his discrimination-learning theory (1936), he hinted at the limitations of conditioning postulates, "It is possible only with the advent of verbal processes that the simple mechanism of learning discrimination problems we have proposed, is transcended [Spence, 1937, p. 99]." Accepting this suggestion, his student Margaret Kuenne investigated transposition in young children, and concluded that

there are at least two developmental stages so far as the relation of verbal responses to overt choice behavior is concerned. In the first, the child is able to make differential verbal responses to appropriate aspects of the situation, but this verbalization does not control or influence his overt choice behavior. Later, such verbalizations gain control and dominate choice behavior [Kuenne, 1946, p. 488].

The acknowledgment of a theoretical distinction between single-unit behavior, which involves a response directly controlled by a stimulus (as was postulated in Spence's [1936] original discrimination theory), and mediated behavior, in which implicit symbolic responses exert control over behavior, raises the issue of whether a strategy that uses conditioning principles and heavily emphasizes conditioning as a research tool is appropriate for the analysis of verbal behavior. This issue is to some extent central to a current debate raging over the relationship between learning theory and language behavior. At one extreme is the attempt to analyze verbal behavior in terms of principles of operant conditioning (Skinner, 1957). At the other extreme is an unqualified denial that this is possible (Chomsky, 1959), or that any associative-learning theory can properly interpret the more significant aspects of verbal behavior such as language acquisition (Bever, Fodor, & Garrett, 1968). In regard to neobehaviorism, these latter arguments lose sight (a) of the skimpiness of the empirical information concerning language acquisition, (b) of the fact that most associative-learning theories, most notably neobehavioristic theory, are neither closed systems nor exclude nonassociative theoretical mechanisms including genetic ones, and (c) of the possibility that maturational factors can be considered to complement rather than conflict with learning processes.

A more reasonable position, in our view, is to consider the relevance of conditioning principles and procedures to verbal behavior as an open issue to be resolved by future achievements instead of current prejudgments. However, this strategy should not conceal the impact of certain neobehavioristic preconceptions on empirical and theoretical efforts, and thus prevent their possible reexamination. The fact that classical and other forms of conditioning have provided interesting data in the field of verbal behavior (e.g., Cerewicki, Grant, & Porter, 1968; Razran, 1961) should not encourage one to ignore the question of whether other experimental procedures might better reveal the basic phenomena of verbal behavior. And in regard to conditioning principles, a similar consideration of alternatives should be in order. When interpreting behavior, neobehaviorists tend to invoke theoretical principles that represent the influence of motivation, past training, and the present situation, to the exclusion of other possible processes, such as the behavioral capabilities of the organism. Nothing inherent in the neobehavioristic model prevents incorporation of principles based on differences in behavioral capacities whether they result from phylogenetic, ontogenetic, or individual sources. Spence was addressing himself to this kind of difference in capacity when he suggested limits on the generality of his discrimination-learning theory. He also investigated such differences when investigating the influence of emotional responsiveness on classical conditioning (Spence, 1958). And within the neobehavioristic tradition, a coordinated single-unit and mediational formulation has been proposed (Kendler & Kendler, 1968, 1970) which postulates that the ontogeny of discrimination learning is characterized by an initial stage in which the behavioral capability is limited to instrumental responses, but that with development, the child acquires the capacity to generate internal modes of representation. This mediated representational stage presumably has its own course of development with successively more abstract symbolic representations becoming available to the child as he matures.

The implication of our remarks is that conditioning may have been and perhaps will continue to be a fruitful source of empirical data and theoretical postulates, but as neobehaviorism enlarges its empirical domain, other standard experimental paradigms and theoretical processes should be considered. No recipe can be offered for successfully implementing this advice, except that actively considering new empirical and theoretical alternatives is the first step.

THE ROLE OF MATHEMATICS IN PSYCHOLOGICAL THEORY

At its inception neobehaviorism explicitly and enthusiastically adopted mathematical representation of theory as a goal for psychology as it has been for physics. This decision was a natural consequence of adopting a deductive model of scientific explanation. Mathematical theorizing was not to be postponed to some future date when some signs would indicate that psychology had achieved an appropriate level of maturity. The attitude was to proceed with mathematical representation and then judge its value. The early attempts at mathematical theorizing about the goal-gradient hypothesis (Hull, 1932) and discrimination learning (Spence, 1936) succeeded in explaining certain facts and in stimulating new research and theorizing. But the mathematics used was rather simple as compared to the streamlined probabilistic models that began to appear later (Bush & Mosteller, 1951; Estes, 1950).

Perhaps the most ambitious mathematical theorizing about a broad range of phenomena in the history of neobehaviorism was Hull's *Principles of Behavior* (1943). As a mathematical formulation it was largely unsuccessful, although it did encourage the development of later mathematical theories. In certain respects, aside from its relatively primitive mathematical base, it was different from contemporary models. Hull aspired to formulate a set of theoretical postulates that would be relevant to all forms of behavior. Although this expressed a self-conscious romantic ideal it nevertheless shaped the subsequent development of neobehaviorism. It led, among other things, to the tactic of selecting intervening variables which presumably possessed broad theoretical implications.

The aspiration to formulate a general behavior theory was shared by some of the early mathematical modelers; Estes (1950), for example, conceptualized the learning process in terms of stimulus sampling, an interpretation that also possessed general implications for a wide range of learning and motivational phenomena. But interest in mathematical models with broad implications seemed to dissipate in proportion to the increased concern with the fine-grain analysis of various properties of the learning process. Over the years mathematical models have moved toward more circumscribed representations of empirical events. Within a historical context, the more modest aspiration of the mathematical modelers in regard to a general behavior theory can be viewed as an appropriate reaction to the lack of success of such general theorists as Hull, Lewin, Tolman, and Koffka. Even within the neobehavioristic tradition one can observe a definite backtracking from the goal of general behavior theory to the development of more specific formulations. Whereas Hull (1943) regarded his *Principles of Behavior* "as a general introduction to the theory of all the behavioral (social) sciences [p. v]," Spence (1956) more cautiously described his *Behavior Theory and Conditioning*, which actually covers a wider range of empirical phenomena, as having "as its primary purpose the integration (derivation) of [data from a number of simple conditioning situations and] . . . to show how the theory . . . may be extended to more complex types of behavior phenomena such as selective and paired-associate learning [p vi]." And as the following essays suggest, most of the current theoretical attempts within the neobehavioristic tradition have been concerned with an even more restricted range of phenomena.

Perhaps general theories that cover an entire scientific discipline or even a large area within it are unrealizable dreams, especially in psychology. But the neobehavioristic tradition of pointing one's formulations in the direction of general theory will no doubt persist. It will be expressed by theoretical constructs with conceptual properties that extend beyond the empirical confines of a specific experimental paradigm. The success of such efforts will depend on the standards set for the theoretical deductions both in regard to their level of precision and the range of data involved. Precision and generality can be countervailing forces in the development of psychological theories and any orientation that simultaneously seeks to achieve both, as did neobehaviorism, is perhaps bound to suffer failures in each.

STIMULUS-RESPONSE LANGUAGE

Of all the strategies that the neobehaviorists have adopted, the choice of stimulus-response associationism as a theoretical framework has generated the greatest opposition and the most controversy. To some extent the source of the dispute lies in the fact that the concept of S-R associationism has several facets. Mistaken interpretations added to these multiple meanings have generated needless disputes and confusion. To make a proper assessment of S-R associationism, it is imperative to treat the various components separately.

One of us (Kendler, 1965) has suggested that the S-R concept can be divided into four components: (a) a technical language that analyzes psychological events into three major categories: stimuli, responses, and the associations between them, (b) a methodological orientation that can be succinctly characterized as physicalistic, operational, and experimental (Estes, 1959), (c) a pretheoretical model that is used as an informal conception of behavior and operates as an analogy (e.g., concept formation is conceived as analogous to discrimination learning), and (d) a group of theories with different, and frequently conflicting, theoretical assumptions.

Of these four components only the first and third qualify as strategic decisions. Since the third has already been discussed when we evaluated classical conditioning as a paradigm for other forms of behavior, we will now examine the first category—the implication of using S-R language.

Stimulus-response language, as we have said, is used to represent psychological phenomena in terms of three important sets of variables: stimuli, responses, and the association—the hyphen—between them. This language can be applied to both empirical events and theoretical constructs. On the empirical level, an auditory conditioned stimulus in classical conditioning could be defined by the frequency of the sound waves and the response by the frequency of the conditioned eyeblink. The association between them, on the purely empirical level, is represented by the functional relationship between the two. But these three constructs can be conceptualized as possessing abstract properties above and beyond their specific empirical referents. A sound wave belongs to a class of physically or socially defined events (e.g., a light wave of 660 nanometers, an American flag) that possess a tendency to evoke a response. Similarly, no eyeblink response belongs to a set of events that characterize physical or social attributes of an organism's behavior (e.g., leg flexion, a hostile remark) which are functionally related to stimulus events. Stimuli and responses can also be inferred; a child of a certain mental age who is discriminating between sets of pictures of animals and fruits can be assumed to be making implicit conceptual responses appropriate to each picture and these inferred responses can be assumed to produce cues that control his discriminative behavior. The justification of such inferences obviously depends on their value for interpreting data.

Stimulus-response language, either when used to refer to empirical events or to characterize theoretical processes, is not demanded by the nature of psychology. Its justification is purely pragmatic, and the verdict of neobehaviorism is that S-R language can play a useful role both in collecting data and in constructing a theory. The exact influence of S-R language on neobehaviorism is difficult to assess because no historical comparison is available between neobehaviorism and a similar orientation with a different language system. In isolating the influence of S-R language, it therefore becomes necessary to identify those special characteristics of neobehaviorism that seem to emanate from its adopted language.

Probably the greatest impact of S-R language on neobehaviorism and other systematic positions that use this language is that it forces psychologists to think in terms of manipulative environmental variables and measures of objective behavior. To use the language properly one must specify characteristics of both the environment and behavior. Identifying these two sets of variables stimulates research directed at relating them and simultaneously forces the theorist to specify the dependent variables he seeks to predict. In sum, S-R language clarifies the experimental and theoretical task of the psychologist by focusing attention on the empirical relationships to be investigated and explained.

Neobehaviorists adopted stimulus-response language because it represented important traditions from which their orientation emerged: British associationism, classical conditioning methodology, and a methodological commitment to objectivity. Because of this background, the use of S-R language encouraged learning research while it simultaneously slighted perception and many nonassociative processes. The significant question is whether some intrinsic characteristic of S-R language makes it difficult or impossible to incorporate other than learning processes within its representational system. We think not; neobehaviorism from its inception has shown a concern for motivational processes and more recently has attempted to deal with problems of perception and representational responses (as several essays in this volume illustrate). Constructs other than stimulus, response, and association can and have been incorporated into an S-R theoretical representation.

Stimulus-response language has no doubt encouraged neobehaviorists to investigate how behavior changes (e.g., lever pressing, an approach response to black) as a function of practice in a relatively unchanging environment. This interest reflects the concern with the theoretical construct of habit which conceptually characterizes the change in the tendency of a particular stimulus to evoke a particular response. The concept of habit works well in explaining facts from situations in which the response measure remains unchanged throughout the experiment. But in transfer of training designs where the organism is required to exhibit new responses, neobehaviorists, as well as other S-R psychologists, are confronted with the task of postulating theoretical mechanisms that will permit one particular response to be transformed into another. It is an open question whether this can be accomplished most effectively by (a) formulating principles that govern relationships among different response systems via some mechanism of response generalization or by (b) postulating response systems that are organized into some hierarchical system in which the acquisition of a superordinate response will enable an organism to respond appropriately to a range of situations. S-R language itself does not imply any universal principle about the specificity of the learning process. Instead it encourages theoretical response-estimates, thus avoiding the embarrassment, as Guthrie (1952) once remarked in discussing Tolman's cognitive theory, of leaving the organism "buried in thought [p. 143]."

All theories that accept behavior as the dependent variable in psychology must be response theories in the sense of yielding theoretical estimates of behavior; and the nature of the S-R language, as noted, helps to ensure that this demand will be met. Nevertheless it must be recognized that it is most difficult to meet this demand, and probably elaborate modifications of the theoretical structure will be required when problems of transfer of training, particularly in human intellectual tasks, are analyzed.

PHYSIOLOGY AND PSYCHOLOGY

Discussions about the relationship between behavior and physiology frequently have been marked by extreme positions, such as assumptions that behavior *must* be explained in terms of physiological events, or that it *cannot* be so explained. For the most part, neobehaviorists have been free from such prejudices, although they have tended to take an aphysiological position. Spence in particular shared Tolman's early view that "psychological facts and laws have . . . to be gathered in their own right. A psychology cannot be explained by physiology until one has a psychology to explain [1936, p. 92]." This strategy served both as a justification and an impetus for purely behavioral research. But the strategy that has been followed through the years neither prejudges nor prescribes the nature of the relationship between the two disciplines, but instead permits the state of knowledge to dictate whether the development of a theory of behavior can be assisted by physiological procedures and information. Within such a framework the empirical problem determines the relevance of physiology to psychology. Rarely do sensory psychologists ignore physiology, while only a small minority of social psychologists consider physiological processes.

The relevance of the neurophysiology of the time to the major concern of most behaviorists, the psychology of learning, has always been difficult to gauge. Hence the wisdom of interpreting learning within a physiological framework has been a source of disagreement, even among neobehaviorists. Hull felt compelled to offer some highly problematical physiological analogue to his theoretical constructs while Spence expressed a fear that such speculations would produce confusion and avoided any physiological interpretations of his theories. However, in 1956 he wrote,

With the advent of the functional and behavioristic viewpoints interest in physiological research declined markedly until it now represents a relatively small proportion of the current research activity of psychologists. Presumably, as psychology attains a fairly well-developed body of environmento-behavioral laws, more and more attention will once again be directed to these physiological variables [Spence, 1956, p. 17].

Soon after he wrote this Spence's prediction was borne out by a rapid increase in physiologically oriented research among psychologists, although the increase resulted more from the impact of the development of new electrical brain stimulation techniques than from the advances in behavior theory. The greater knowledge of behavioral laws served as a framework to judge the influence of specific physiological variables. Within the neobehavioristic tradition, the efforts of Neal Miller exemplify how physiological techniques can be combined with behavioral research to illuminate psychological theory.

The fundamental epistemological relationship between behavior and physiology has for the most part been ignored. This is understandable because at present our knowledge of both is so incomplete that questions about their ultimate relationship seem almost irrelevant. But perhaps something can be gained from considering the meaning of reductionism, so that strategies which demand or reject it as an achievable goal can be evaluated.

To assume that behavior can be reduced to neurophysiology depends not only upon formalizing a behavior theory, as Tolman (1963) suggested, but also a neurophysiological theory. If the primary assumptions of the behavior theory can be deduced from the neurophysiological theory, then it can properly be stated that behavior has been reduced to neurophysiology. Expressed in this fashion reductionism is a much more demanding task than is usually realized when one casually assumes that behavior can be reduced to neurophysiology.

Problems of reductionism have contemporary significance for only those areas of sensory physiology in which certain perceptual phenomena can be predicted from our knowledge of patterns of neural impulses (e.g., Ratliff, 1965). For the rest of psychology the closest approach to reductive success has been in the *interpretation* of behavior in terms of neurophysiological processes. Examples are the interpretation of reinforcement in terms of electrical changes in the brain (Olds & Olds, 1965) or the interpretation of motivation in terms of hypothalamic functioning (Stellar, 1954).

Although these interpretations are in the direction of reducing behavior to physiology, two points must be recognized. First, such interpretations are far removed from formal reduction, and second, the reduction of behavior to neurophysiology is not inevitable. Kaplan's (1964) reaction to the question of whether laws of behavior are reducible to laws of neurophysiology (or chemistry or physics) summarizes rather well a position that would be consistent with the pragmatic orientation of neobehaviorism:

An affirmative answer . . . as a matter of doctrine, seems to be . . . both unwarranted and useless. . . . As a methodological presupposition . . . it provides a valuable perspective in which the behavioral scientist can see continuing possibilities for turning to his own use the findings of other sciences. But the significance of such possibilities appears only as they are actualized; otherwise their affirmation expresses only a hope. It may well be that the psychologist can derive the whole of his discipline from neurology, biochemistry and the rest: it is not destructive skepticism but productive pragmatism to say, "I'd like to see him do it!" [Pp. 124–125]

PHENOMENOLOGY AND BEHAVIOR

Reference has already been made to the distinction between *metaphysical behaviorism* and *methodological behaviorism* (Bergmann, 1956), the former denying the existence of mental states, the latter asserting that behavior rather than mental states is the primary datum of psychology. Watson ultimately adopted the extreme position of metaphysical behaviorism in his polemics against structuralism but neobehaviorism, as has been noted, had to reject such a position if only to be consistent with its assumption about the fundamental role of experiential data in scientific knowledge and the importance of achieving intersubjective agreement in scientific communication. The doctrine of *methodological behaviorism,* adopted by neobehaviorism, demands that the dependent and independent variables, as well as the theoretical constructs, be defined in terms of intersubjectively agreed-upon events.

What, if any, role can phenomenal experiences play in neobehaviorism? A person's behavior cannot be explained by his state of mind, certainly, because his private experience is unavailable to the inspection of other observers. But a person's report of his inner state, expressed as a verbal description or as a pattern of responses to a series of questions in a personality inventory, is a public event. Observers can agree on what the person said or what his inventory responses were; in principle, these self-reports are no different than any other type of behavior, and may therefore enter into an explanatory system. This epistemological position is succinctly expressed in Max Meyer's (1921) informative title of his book, *The Psychology of the Other One.* Thus personal phenomenal experience is excluded from any formal explanation of behavior, but reports of such events are not if they are used within a theoretical network that meets both the demands of intersubjective agreement of meaning and the demands of the deductive model of explanation. The methodological disagreement between the phenomenologist and the neobehaviorist, then, is that while the former tends to regard self-report as having a high degree of correspondence with private experience and thus acts as though these experiences were raw data, the neobehaviorist makes no further assumptions and gives verbal reports no special status.

Whether or not phenomenological data (i.e., self-reports) should be incorporated into a neobehavioristic system is another issue. Three possible strategies suggest themselves. (a) The first is to ignore such data, the argument being they cannot help, and possibly can harm by sowing confusion and directing attention from significant variables. Using arguments of this sort, behaviorists such as Skinner, to give only a contemporary example, have spurned the introduction of phenomenological experience into their system. Neobehaviorists have been less militant although they have never used introspective data extensively, in part because of their historical identification with the early behavioristic struggle to reject mind as the subject matter of psychology, but also because of their preoccupation with relatively simple experimental situations. Much of their research has involved animal Ss, and more recently young children, thus precluding the use of phenomenal data. In instances where adult human Ss were used, the theoretical model implicitly suggested that phenomenal data would not be particularly useful, a position that has been challenged with increasing frequency in recent years. (b) The second possibility is to use phenomenal reports as a source of theoretical hypotheses. For example, in the study of memory, where encoding processes are beginning to assume a central theoretical role, introspective reports can serve as a rich source for stimulating, interesting conjectures. (c) The third alternative is to develop a theoretical structure to represent conscious experience. The rationale for such an effort, a model of the mind, is that in many situations the most useful information for predicting behavior would be introspective evidence. If this is so, a theoretical representation of inner states could prove to be a fruitful model in interpreting behavior.

It may very well prove that a uniform strategy for relating phenomenology to behavior will not be the most effective method because each strategy might have special advantages for particular forms of behavior. The key methodological issue in treating phenomenal experience within neobehaviorism is to recognize that the S's phenomenal data, unlike those of the experimenter, are inferred, and not directly observed. Since phenomenal experience is inferred, and not directly observed, its epistemological status is that of a theoretical construct instead of a raw datum.

The key pragmatic issue, and one that can be easily overlooked, is that the S's observation of his own phenomenal experience is not a simple task devoid of all subtleties and complexities. The history of structuralism and other mind-oriented psychologies testifies to this point. Perceptions of external events are influenced not only by what the S observes, but by how he observes it. The same principle no doubt operates with self-observation (see Natsoulas, 1970). The potential contributions of phenomenal experience to behavior theory will no doubt vary with the methods used by Ss to observe and report phenomenological events.

Concluding Remarks

Almost a hundred years have passed since the establishment of the first psychological laboratories; psychology is beginning to have a history as well as a past. Although the goal of this essay has been to describe the epistemological bases and strategic decisions of neobehaviorism, an appreciation of even these purely methodological commitments requires that neobehaviorism be placed in historical context.

By the turn of the century functionalists such as Dewey and Angell had broadened the limited view of the structuralists that psychology had consciousness as its subject matter, to include as well the study of behavior. But it was not until the 1910s that Watson carried the functionalist movement to its logical extreme by proposing that psychology be solely the science of behavior. Spirited intellectual battles over what kind of science psychology was to be ensued, and it was not until the early 1930s that it could safely be said that experimental psychology in this country had cast its methodological lot with behaviorism.

The struggle over, the period of the 1930s and early 1940s was highly creative, as behaviorism sought to find a solid methodological base, as well as to get on with the business of developing a science of psychology. The intervening variable approach to theorizing was introduced by Tolman (1936), while Hull became intrigued with the method of formal postulates which he used most formidably in his *Mathematico-Deductive Theory of Rote Learning* (1940). Stimulated by the contributions of logical empiricists such as Carnap (1934), the epistemology of behaviorism was developed, most notably by Spence, often in collaboration with the philosopher Gustav Bergmann.

During this same period, there appeared three remarkable books, all behavioristic in orientation, whose influence dominated experimental psychology for the next several decades: Tolman's *Purposive Behavior in Animals and Men* (1932), Skinner's *The Behavior of Organisms* (1938), and Hull's *Principles of Behavior* (1943). Tolman's intellectual ancestry was closer to European phenomenology, with its emphasis on perception and organization, than to British associationism, but he shared with Hull and Skinner the methodological tradition of behaviorism and a commitment to a deductive theoretical model. Of the three attempts to develop a general behavior theory (Skinner's rejection of theory for the ultrapositivistic approach came later), Hull's was the most ambitious in its detail and theoretical formality and proved to be the most immediately and directly influential.

The early neobehaviorists were infected by a heady optimism. Having found the proper direction in which to go and the methodological vehicles to take them, they believed not only that a general behavior theory was possible to construct but that its development would be relatively rapid. Scientific progress would be further facilitated, they believed, if instead of complex learning and cognitive processes, "simple" phenomena such as classical and instrumental conditioning were studied first. The lack of success of their predecessors and contemporaries in advancing scientific understanding of "complex" phenomena gave impetus to the tactic of using conditioning as a source of deductive principles.

The easy optimism of the early years has not been justified, even "simple" situations proving to be unexpectantly recalcitrant to both empirical and theoretical analysis. Neobehaviorists have largely abandoned their attempts to erect a theoretical structure with broad implications, and along with others with whom they share the behavioristic tradition, including most of the builders of mathematical models, attack limited problem areas about which they develop "miniature systems."

Emboldened perhaps by the successes of neobehaviorism as well as by its failures, and often guided by theoretical models of quite different origins, many contemporary psychologists have redirected their interests to cognitive-perceptual problems which neobehaviorism historically has tended to slight, either because of its preoccupation with learning or of its tactical decision to concentrate on the investigation of relatively simple phenomena. At least the more enthusiastic proponents of these new theoretical developments claim for them the same broad, all-encompassing implications that were the original goal of neobehaviorism. Whether these or any general theoretical efforts will succeed, or whether problem areas rather than general theories will prove to be the cohesive force of the future cannot yet be foretold.

With the death of Clark L. Hull and Kenneth W. Spence, the two most eminent of the neobehavioristic theorists and the driving forces in erecting a theoretical structure with broad implications, perhaps the neobehavioristic tradition will merge with other less ambitious behavioristic orientations. Hull aspired to be a Newton, while Spence would have been pleased to be a Galileo. In fact their influence may prove to be more like that of Darwin: providing a conception that structured a field and led to subsequent discoveries and theoretical developments. This comment does not suggest that a neobehavioristic theoretical model has achieved a level of integrating facts resembling that of Darwin's theory of evolution—no psychological theory has. But it does imply that both conceptions share a common quality of relative imprecision by the standards of physical sciences but nevertheless offer integrative power and heuristic value.

Only the future can tell whether the boundaries between neobehaviorism and other objectively oriented psychologies will continue to become fainter and finally disappear or whether neobehaviorism will, among future generations of psychologists, retain and sustain some of its original character.

REFERENCES

ALLPORT, G. *Becoming: Basic considerations for a psychology of personality.* New Haven: Yale University Press, 1955.

BEVER, T. G., FODOR, J. A., & GARRETT, M. A formal limit of associationism. In T. R. Dixon & D. L. Horton (Eds.), *Verbal behavior and general behavior theory.* Englewood Cliffs, N.J.: Prentice-Hall, 1968. Pp. 582–585.

BRODBECK, M. Explanation, prediction, and "imperfect" knowledge. In H. Feigl & G. Maxwell (Eds.), *Minnesota studies in the philosophy of science.* Vol. III. Minneapolis: University of Minnesota Press, 1962. Pp. 231–272.

BUSH, R. R., & MOSTELLER, F. A. A mathematical model for simple learning. *Psychological Review,* 1951, **58**, 313–323.

CARNAP, R. *The unity of science.* London: Kegan Paul, Trench, Trubner, 1934.

———. Testability and meaning. *Philosophy of Science,* 1936, 1937, **4**, 1–40.

CEREWICKI, L. E., GRANT, D. A., & PORTER, E. C. The effect of number and relatedness of verbal discriminanda upon differential eyelid conditioning. *Journal of Verbal Learning and Verbal Behavior,* 1968, **7**, 847–853.

CHOMSKY, N. A review of B. F. Skinner's "Verbal Behavior." *Language,* 1959, **35**, 26–58.

ESTES, W. K. Toward a statistical theory of learning. *Psychological Review,* 1950, **57**, 94–107.

———. The statistical approach to learning theory. In S. Koch (Ed.), *Psychology: A study of a science.* Vol. 2. New York: McGraw-Hill, 1959. Pp. 380–491.

GUTHRIE, E. R. *The psychology of learning.* (Rev. ed.) New York: Harper & Row, 1952.

HULL, C. L. The goal gradient hypothesis and maze learning. *Psychological Review,* 1932, **39**, 25–43.

———. *Principles of behavior.* New York: Appleton-Century, 1943.

———, HOVLAND, C. I., ROSS, R. T., HALL, M., PERKINS, D. T., & FITCH, F. B. *Mathematico-deductive theory of rote learning.* New Haven: Yale University Press, 1940.

KAPLAN, A. *The conduct of inquiry.* San Francisco: Chandler, 1964.

KENDLER, H. H. Motivation and behavior. In D. Levine (Ed.), *Nebraska symposium on motivation,* 1965. Lincoln: University of Nebraska Press, 1965. Pp. 1–23.

KENDLER, H. H., & KENDLER, T. S. Mediation and conceptual behavior. In K. W. Spence & J. T. Spence (Eds.), *Psychology of learning and motivation.* Vol. 2. New York: Academic Press, 1968. Pp. 197–243.

KENDLER, H. H., & KENDLER, T. S. Developmental processes in discrimination learning. *Human Development,* 1970, **13**, 65–89.

KUENNE, M. R. Experimental investigation of the relation of language to transposition behavior in young children. *Journal of Experimental Psychology,* 1946, **36**, 471–490.

MEYER, M. F. *Psychology of the other one.* Columbia, Missouri: Missouri Book, 1921.

NATSOULAS, T. Concerning introspective "knowledge." *Psychological Bulletin,* 1970, **73**, 89–111.

OLDS, J., & OLDS, M. Drives, rewards, and the brain. In *New directions in psychology.* New York: Holt, Rinehart and Winston, 1965. Pp. 329–410.

RATLIFF, F. *Mach bands.* San Francisco: Holden-Day, 1965.

RAZRAN, G. The observable unconscious and the inferable conscious in current Soviet psychophysiology: Interoceptive conditioning, semantic conditioning, and the orienting reflex. *Psychological Review,* 1961, **68**, 81–147.

SCRIVEN, M. A study of radical behaviorism. In H. Feigl & M. Scriven (Eds.),

Minnesota studies in the philosophy of science. Vol. 1. Minneapolis: University of Minnesota Press, 1956. Pp. 88–130.

SKINNER, B. F. *The behavior of organisms.* New York: Appleton-Century, 1938.

———. Are theories of learning necessary? *Psychological Review,* 1950, **57,** 193–216.

———. *Verbal behavior.* New York: Appleton-Crofts, 1957.

SMEDSLUND, J. Meanings, implications and universals: Towards a psychology of man. *Scandinavian Journal of Psychology,* 1969, **10,** 1–15.

SPENCE, K. W. The nature of discrimination learning in animals. *Psychological Review,* 1936, **43,** 427–449.

———. Analysis of the formation of visual discrimination habits in chimpanzee. *Journal of Comparative Psychology,* 1937, **23,** 72–100.

———. *Behavior theory and conditioning.* New Haven: Yale University Press, 1956.

———. The empirical basis and theoretical structure of psychology. *Philosophy of Science,* 1957, **24,** 97–108.

———. A theory of emotionally based drive (D) and its relation to performance in simple learning situations. *American Psychologist,* 1958, **13,** 131–141.

SPENCE, K. W., & NORRIS, E. Eyelid conditioning as a function of the intertrial interval. *Journal of Experimental Psychology,* 1950, **40,** 716–720.

STELLAR, E. The physiology of motivation. *Psychological Review,* 1954, **61,** 5–22.

TERRACE, H. S. Discrimination learning, the peak shift, and behavioral contrast. *Journal of Experimental Analysis of Behavior,* 1968, **11,** 727–741.

TOLMAN, E. C. *Purposive behavior in animals and men.* New York: Appleton-Century, 1932.

———. Operational behaviorism and current trends in psychology. In H. W. Hill (Ed.), *Proceedings, 25th American celebration of the inauguration of graduate studies, The University of Southern California.* Los Angeles: The University of Southern California Press, 1936. Pp. 89–103.

39

A SCIENCE OF BEHAVIOR

B. F. SKINNER

A CRITIC contends that a recent book of mine (Skinner, 1971) does not contain anything new, that much the same was said more than four cen-

FROM B. F. Skinner, The steep and thorny way to a science of behavior, in Rom Harré (Ed.), *Problems of Scientific Revolution,* © Oxford University Press, 1975. Reprinted by permission of the Oxford University Press, Oxford.

turies ago in theological terms by John Calvin. You will not be surprised, then, to find me commending to you the steep and thorny way to that heaven promised by a science of behavior. But I am not one of those ungracious pastors, of whom Ophelia complained, who "recking not their own rede themselves tread the primrose path of dalliance." No, I shall rail at dalliance, and in a manner worthy, I hope, of my distinguished predecessor. If I do not thunder or fulminate, it is only because we moderns can more easily portray a truly frightening hell. I shall merely allude to the carcinogenic fallout of a nuclear holocaust. And no Calvin ever had better reason to fear his hell, for I am proceeding on the assumption that nothing less than a vast improvement in our understanding of human behavior will prevent the destruction of our way of life or of mankind.

Why has it been so difficult to be scientific about human behavior? Why have methods that have been so prodigiously successful almost everywhere else failed so ignominiously in this one field? Is it because human behavior presents unusual obstacles to a science? No doubt it does, but I think we are beginning to see how these obstacles may be overcome. The problem, I submit, is digression. We have been drawn off the straight and narrow path, and the word *diversion* serves me well by suggesting not only digression but dalliance. In this article I analyze some of the diversions peculiar to the field of human behavior which seem to have delayed our advance toward the better understanding we desperately need.

A Science of Behavior

I must begin by saying what I take a science of behavior to be. It is, I assume, part of biology. The organism that behaves is the organism that breathes, digests, conceives, gestates, and so on. As such, the behaving organism will eventually be described and explained by the anatomist and physiologist. As far as behavior is concerned, they will give us an account of the genetic endowment of the species and tell how that endowment changes during the lifetime of the individual and why, as a result, the individual then responds in a given way on a given occasion. Despite remarkable progress, we are still a long way from a satisfactory account in such terms. We know something about the chemical and electrical effects of the nervous system and the location of many of its functions, but the events that actually underlie a single instance of behavior—as a pigeon picks up a stick to build a nest, or a child a block to complete a tower, or a scientist a pen to write a paper—are still far out of reach.

Fortunately, we need not wait for further progress of that sort. We can analyze a given instance of behavior in its relation to the current setting and to antecedent events in the history of the species and of the individual. Thus, we do not need an explicit account of the anatomy and physiology of genetic endowment in order to describe the behavior, or the behavioral processes, characteristic of a species, or to speculate about the contingencies of survival under which they might have evolved, as the ethologists have convincingly demonstrated. Nor do we need to consider anatomy and physiology in order to see how the behavior of the individual is changed by his exposure to contingencies of reinforcement during his lifetime and how as a result he behaves in a given way on a given occasion. I must confess to a predilection here for my own specialty, the experimental analysis of behavior, which is a quite explicit investigation of the effects upon individual organisms of extremely complex and subtle contingencies of reinforcement.

There will be certain temporal gaps in such an analysis. The behavior and the conditions of which it is a function do not occur in close temporal or spatial proximity, and we must wait for physiology to make the connection. When it does so, it will not invalidate the behavioral account (indeed, its assignment could be said to be specified by that account), nor will it make its terms and principles any the less useful. A science of behavior will be needed for both theoretical and practical purposes even when the behaving organism is fully understood at another level, just as much of chemistry remains useful even though a detailed account of a single instance may be given at the level of molecular or atomic forces. Such, then, is the science of behavior from which I suggest we have been diverted—by several kinds of dalliance to which I now turn.

Feelings and Their Relation to Behavior

Very little biology is handicapped by the fact that the biologist is himself a specimen of the thing he is studying, but that part of the science with which we are here concerned has not been so fortunate. We seem to have a kind of inside information about our behavior. It may be true that the environment shapes and controls our behavior as it shapes and controls the behavior of other species—but *we* have feelings about it. And what a diversion they have proved to be. Our loves, our fears, our feelings about war, crime, poverty, and God—these are all basic, if not ultimate, concerns. And we are as much concerned about the feelings of others. Many of the great themes of mythology have been about feelings —of the victim on his way to sacrifice or of the warrior going forth to battle. We read what poets tell us about their feelings, and we share the feelings of characters in plays and novels. We follow regimens and take drugs to alter our feelings. We become sophisticated about them in, say, the manner of La Rochefoucauld, noting that jealousy thrives on doubt, or that the clemency of a ruler is a mixture of vanity, laziness, and fear. And along with some psychiatrists we may even try to establish an independent science of feelings in the intrapsychic life of the mind or personality.

And do feelings not have some bearing on our formulation of a science of behavior? Do we not strike because we are angry and play music because we feel like listening? And if so, are our feelings not to be added to those antecedent events of which behavior is a function? This is not the place to answer such questions in detail, but I must at least suggest the kind of answer that may be given. William James questioned the causal order: Perhaps we do not strike because we are angry but feel angry because we strike. That does not bring us back to the environment, however, although James and others were on the right track. What we feel are conditions of our bodies, most of them closely associated with behavior and with the circumstances in which we behave. We both strike *and* feel angry for a common reason, and that reason lies in the environment. In short, the bodily conditions we feel are *collateral products* of our genetic and environmental histories. They have no explanatory force; they are simply additional facts to be taken into account.

Feelings enjoy an enormous advantage over genetic and environmental histories. They are warm, salient, and demanding, where facts about the environment are easily overlooked. Moreover, they are *immediately* related to behavior, being collateral products of the same causes, and have therefore commanded more attention than the causes themselves, which are often rather remote. In doing so, they have proved to be one of the most fascinating attractions along the path of dalliance.

Environment and Its Relation to Behavior

A much more important diversion has, for more than 2,000 years, made any move toward a science of behavior particularly difficult. The environment acts upon an organism at the surface of its body, but when the body is our own, we seem to observe its progress beyond that point; for example, we seem to see the real world become experience, a physical presentation become a sensation or a percept. Indeed, this second stage may be all we see. Reality may be merely an inference and, according to some authorities, a bad one. What is important may not be the physical world on the far side of the skin but what that world means to us on this side.

Not only do we seem to see the environment on its way in, we seem to see behavior on its way out. We observe certain early stages—wishes, intentions, ideas, and acts of will—before they have, as we say, found expression in behavior. And as for our environmental history, that can also be viewed and reviewed inside the skin, for we have tucked it all away in the storehouse of our memory. Again this is not the place to present an alternative account, but several points need to be made. The behavioristic objection is not primarily to the metaphysical nature of mind stuff. I welcome the view, clearly gaining in favor among psychologists and physiologists and by no means a stranger to philosophy, that what we introspectively observe, as well as feel, are states of our bodies. But I am not willing to give introspection much of a toehold even so, for there are two important reasons why we do not discriminate precisely among our feelings and states of mind and hence why there are many different philosophies and psychologies.

In the first place, the world within the skin is private. Only the person whose skin it is can make certain kinds of contact with it. We might expect that the resulting intimacy should make for greater clarity, but there is a difficulty. The privacy interferes with the very process of coming to know. The verbal community which teaches us to make distinctions among things in the world around us lacks the information it needs to teach us to distinguish events in our private world. For example, it cannot teach us the difference between diffidence and embarrassment as readily or as accurately as that between red and blue or sweet and sour.

Second, the self-observation that leads to introspective knowledge is limited by anatomy. It arose very late in the evolution of the species because it is only when a person begins to be asked about his behavior and about why he behaves as he does that he becomes conscious of himself in this sense. Self-knowledge depends on language and in fact on language of a rather advanced kind, but when questions of this sort first began to be asked, the only nervous systems available in answering them were those that had evolved for entirely different reasons. They had proved useful in the internal economy of the organism, in the coordination of movement, and in operating upon the environment, but there was no reason why they should be suitable in supplying information about those very extensive systems that mediate behavior. To put it crudely, introspection cannot be very relevant or comprehensive because the human organism does not have nerves going to the right places.

One other problem concerns the nature and location of the knower. The organism itself lies, so to speak, between the environment that acts upon it and the environment it acts upon, but what lies between those inner stages—between, for example, experience and will? From what vantage point do we watch stimuli on their way into the storehouse of memory or behavior on its way out to physical expression? The observing agent, the knower, seems to contract to something very small in the middle of things.

In the formulation of a science with which I began, it is the *organism as a whole* that behaves. It acts in and upon a physical world, and it can be induced by a verbal environment to respond to some of its own activities. The events observed as the life of the mind, like feelings, are *collateral products*, which have been made the basis of many elaborate metaphors. The philosopher at his desk asking himself what he really knows, about himself or the world, will quite naturally begin with his experiences, his acts of will, and his memory, but the effort to understand

the mind from that vantage point, beginning with Plato's supposed discovery, has been one of the great diversions which have delayed an
analysis of the role of the environment.

Observation of a Behaving Organism

It did not, of course, take inside information to induce people to direct
their attention to what is going on inside the behaving organism. We almost instinctively look inside a system to see how it works. We do this
with clocks, as with living systems. It is standard practice in much of
biology. Some early efforts to understand and explain behavior in this
way have been described by Onians (1951) in his classic *Origins of
European Thought*. It must have been the slaughterhouse and the battle-
field that gave man his first knowledge of anatomy and physiology. The
various functions assigned to parts of the organism were not usually those
that had been observed introspectively. If Onians is right, the *phrénes*
were the lungs, intimately associated with breathing and hence, so the
Greeks said, with thought and, of course, with life and death. The
phrénes were the seat of *thumós,* a vital principle whose nature is not
now clearly understood, and possibly of ideas, in the active sense of
Homeric Greek. (By the time an idea had become an object of quiet
contemplation, interest seems to have been lost in its location.) Later,
the various fluids of the body, the humors, were associated with disposi-
tions, and the eye and the ear with sense data. I like to imagine the
consternation of that pioneer who first analyzed the optics of the eyeball
and realized that the image on the retina was upside down!

Observation of a behaving system from without began in earnest with
the discovery of reflexes, but the reflex arc was not only not the seat of
mental action, it was taken to be a usurper, the spinal reflexes replacing
the *Rückenmarkseele* or soul of the spinal cord, for example. The reflex
arc was essentially an anatomical concept, and the physiology remained
largely imaginary for a long time. Many years ago I suggested that the
letters CNS could be said to stand, not for the central nervous system,
but for the conceptual nervous system. I had in mind the great physiologists Sir Charles Sherrington and Ivan Petrovich Pavlov. In his epoch-
making *Integrative Action of the Nervous System*, Sherrington (1906)
had analyzed the role of the synapse, listing perhaps a dozen characteristic properties. I pointed out that he had never seen a synapse in action
and that all the properties assigned to it were inferred from the behavior
of his preparations. Pavlov had offered his researches as evidence of the
activities of the cerebral cortex though he had never observed the cortex
in action but had merely inferred its processes from the behavior of his
experimental animals. But Sherrington, Pavlov, and many others were
moving in the direction of an instrumental approach, and the physiologist
is now, of course, studying the nervous system directly.

The conceptual nervous system has been taken over by other disciplines—by information theory, cybernetics, systems analyses, mathematical models, and cognitive psychology. The hypothetical structures they describe do not depend on confirmation by direct observation of the nervous system, for that lies too far in the future to be of interest. They are to be justified by their internal consistency and the successful prediction of selected facts, presumably not the facts from which the constructions were inferred.

These disciplines are concerned with how the brain or the mind must work if the human organism is to behave as it does. They offer a sort of thermodynamics of behavior without reference to molecular action. The computer with its apparent simulation of Man Thinking supplies the dominant analogy. It is not a question of the physiology of the computer —how it is wired or what type of storage it uses—but of its behavioral characteristics. A computer takes in information as an organism receives stimuli and processes it according to an inbuilt program as an organism is said to do according to its genetic endowment. It encodes the information, converting it to a form it can handle, as the organism converts visual, auditory, and other stimuli into nerve impluses. Like its human analogue it stores the encoded information in a memory, tagged to facilitate retrieval. It uses what it has stored to process information as received, as a person is said to use prior experience to interpret incoming stimuli, and later to perform various operations—in short, to compute. Finally, it makes decisions and behaves: It prints out.

There is nothing new about any of this. The same things were done thousands of years ago with clay tiles. The overseer or tax collector kept a record of bags of grain, the number, quality, and kind being marked appropriately. The tiles were stored in lots as marked, additional tiles were grouped appropriately, the records were eventually retrieved and computations made, and a summary account was issued. The machine is much swifter, and it is so constructed that human participation is needed only before and after the operation. The speed is a clear advantage, but the apparent autonomy has caused trouble. It has seemed to mean that the mode of operation of a computer resembles that of a person. People do make physical records which they store and retrieve and use in solving problems, but it does not follow that they do anything of the sort in the mind. If there were some exclusively subjective achievement, the argument for the so-called higher mental processes would be stronger, but as far as I know, none has been demonstrated. True, we say that the mathematician sometimes intuitively solves a problem and only later, if at all, reduces it to the steps of a proof, and in doing so he seems to differ greatly from those who proceed step by step, but the differences could well be in the evidence of what has happened, and it would not be very satisfactory to define thought simply as unexplained behavior.

Again, it would be foolish of me to try to develop an alternative account in the space available. What I have said about the introspectively observed mind applies as well to the mind that is constructed from observations of the behavior of others. The *accessibility* of stored memories, for example, can be interpreted as the *probability* of acquired behaviors, with no loss in the adequacy of the treatment of the facts, and with a very considerable gain in the assimilation of this difficult field with other parts of human behavior.

An Inner Life

I have said that much of biology looks inside a living system for an explanation of how it works. But that is not true of all of biology. Sir Charles Bell could write a book on the hand as evidence of design. The hand was evidence; the design lay elsewhere. Darwin found the design, too, but in a different place. He could catalog the creatures he discovered on the voyage of the *Beagle* in terms of their form or structure, and he could classify barnacles for years in the same way, but he looked beyond structures for the principle of natural selection. It was *the relation of the organism to the environment* that mattered in evolution. And it is the relation to environment that is of primary concern in the analysis of behavior. Hence, it is not enough to confine oneself to organization or structure, even of the most penetrating kind. That is the mistake of most of phenomenology, existentialism, and the structuralism of anthropology and linguistics. When the important thing is a relation to the environment, as in the phylogeny and ontogeny of behavior, the fascination with an inner system becomes a simple digression.

We have not advanced more rapidly to the methods and instruments needed in the study of behavior precisely because of the diverting preoccupation with a supposed or real inner life. It is true that the introspective psychologist and the model builder have investigated environments, but they have done so only to throw some light on the internal events in which they are interested. They are no doubt well-intentioned helpmates, but they have often simply misled those who undertake the study of the organism as a behaving system in its own right. Even when helpful, an observed or hypothetical inner determiner is no explanation of behavior until it has itself been explained, and the fascination with an inner life has allayed curiosity about the further steps to be taken.

I can hear my critics: "Do you really mean to say that all those who have inquired into the human mind, from Plato and Aristotle through the Romans and scholastics, to Bacon and Hobbes, to Locke and the other British empiricists, to John Stuart Mill, and to all those who began to call themselves psychologists—that they have all been wasting their time?" Well, not all of their time, fortunately. Forget their purely psychological speculations, and they were still remarkable people. They would have been even more remarkable, in my opinion, if they could have forgotten

that speculation themselves. They were careful observers of human behavior, but the intuitive wisdom they acquired from their contact with
real people was flawed by their theories.

It is easier to make the point in the field of medicine. Until the present
century very little was known about bodily processes in health and
disease from which useful therapeutic practices could be derived. Yet
it should have been worthwhile to call in a physician. Physicians saw
many ill people and should have acquired a kind of wisdom, unanalyzed
perhaps but still of value in prescribing simple treatments. The history of
medicine, however, is largely the history of barbaric practices—blood-
letting, cuppings, poultices, purgations, violent emetics—which much
of the time must have been harmful. My point is that these measures
were not suggested by the intuitive wisdom acquired from familiarity
with illness; they were suggested by *theories*, theories about what was
going on inside an ill person. Theories of the mind have had a similar
effect, less dramatic, perhaps, but quite possibly far more damaging.
The men I have mentioned made important contributions in government,
religion, ethics, economics, and many other fields. They could do so with
an intuitive wisdom acquired from experience. But philosophy and psychology have had their bleedings, cuppings, and purgations too, and they
have obscured simple wisdom. They have diverted wise people from a
path that would have led more directly to an eventual science of behavior. Plato would have made far more progress toward the good life
if he could have forgotten those shadows on the wall of his cave.

The Individual as a Creator

Still another kind of concern for the self distracts us from the program
I have outlined. It has to do with the individual, not as an object of self-
knowledge, but as an agent, an initiator, a creator. I have developed this
theme in *Beyond Freedom and Dignity*. We are more likely to give a
person credit for what he does if it is not obvious that it can be attributed
to his physical or social environment, and we are likely to feel that truly
great achievements must be inexplicable. The more derivative a work
of art, the less creative; the more conspicuous the personal gain, the
less heroic an act of sacrifice. To obey a well-enforced law is not to show
civic virtue. We see a concern for the aggrandizement of the individual,
for the maximizing of credit due him, in the self-actualization of so-called
humanistic psychology, in some versions of existentialism, in Eastern
mysticism and certain forms of Christian mysticism in which a person is
taught to reject the world in order to free himself for union with a divine
principle or with God, as well as in the simple structuralism that looks
to the organization of behavior rather than to the antecedent events
responsible for that organization. The difficulty is that if the credit due a
person is infringed by evidences of the conditions of which his behavior is

a function, then a scientific analysis appears to be an attack on human worth or dignity. Its task is to explain the hitherto inexplicable and hence to reduce any supposed inner contribution which has served in lieu of explanation. Freud moved in this direction in explaining creative art, and it is no longer just the cynic who traces heroism and martyrdom to powerful indoctrination. The culminating achievement of the human species has been said to be the evolution of man as a moral animal, but a simpler view is that it has been the evolution of cultures in which people behave morally although they have undergone no inner change of character.

Even more traumatic has been the supposed attack on freedom. Historically, the struggle for freedom has been an escape from physical restraint and from behavioral restraints exerted through punishment and exploitative measures of other kinds. The individual has been freed from features of his environment arranged by governmental and religious agencies and by those who possess great wealth. The success of that struggle, though it is not yet complete, is one of man's great achievements, and no sensible preson would challenge it. Unfortunately, one of its by-products has been the slogan that "all control of human behavior is wrong and must be resisted." Nothing in the circumstances under which man has struggled for freedom justifies this extension of the attack on controlling measures, and we should have to abandon all of the advantages of a well-developed culture if we were to relinquish all practices involving the control of human behavior. Yet new techniques in education, psychotherapy, incentive systems, penology, and the design of daily life are currently subject to attack because they are said to threaten personal freedom, and I can testify that the attack can be fairly violent.

The extent to which a person is free or responsible for his achievements is not an issue to be decided by rigorous proof, but I submit that what we call the behavior of the human organism is no more free than its digestion, gestation, immunization, or any other physiological process. Because it involves the environment in many subtle ways it is much more complex, and its lawfulness is, therefore, much harder to demonstrate. But a scientific analysis moves in that direction, and we can already throw some light on traditional topics, such as free will or creativity, which is more helpful than traditional accounts, and I believe that further progress is imminent.

The issue is, of course, determinism. Slightly more than 100 years ago, in a famous paper, Claude Bernard raised with respect to physiology the issue which now stands before us in the behavioral sciences. The almost insurmountable obstacle to the application of scientific method in biology was, he said, the belief in "vital spontaneity." His contemporary, Louis Pasteur, was responsible for a dramatic test of the theory of spontaneous generation, and I suggest that the spontaneous generation of behavior in the guise of ideas and acts of will is now at the stage of the spontaneous generation of life in the form of maggots and miscroorganisms 100 years ago.

The practical problem in continuing the struggle for freedom and dignity is not to destroy controlling forces but to change them, to create a world in which people will achieve far more than they have ever achieved before in art, music, literature, science, technology, and above all the enjoyment of life. It could be a world in which people feel freer than they have ever felt before, because they will not be under aversive control. In building such a world, we shall need all the help a science of behavior can give us. To misread the theme of the struggle for freedom and dignity and to relinquish all efforts to control would be a tragic mistake.

But it is a mistake that may very well be made. Our concern for the individual as a creative agent is not dalliance; it is clearly an obstacle rather than a diversion, for ancient fears are not easily allayed. A shift in emphasis from the individual to the environment, particularly to the social environment, is reminiscent of various forms of totalitarian statism. It is easy to turn from what may seem like an inevitable movement in that direction and to take one's chances with libertarianism. But much remains to be analyzed in that position. For example, we may distinguish between liberty and license by holding to the right to do as we please provided we do not infringe upon similar rights of others, but in doing so we conceal or disguise the public sanctions represented by private rights. Rights and duties, like a moral or ethical sense, are examples of hypothetical internalized environmental sanctions.

In the long run, the aggrandizement of the individual jeopardizes the future of the species and the culture. In effect, it infringes the so-called rights of billions of people still to be born, in whose interests only the weakest of sanctions are now maintained. We are beginning to realize the magnitude of the problem of bringing human behavior under the control of a projected future, and we are already suffering from the fact that we have come very late to recognize that mankind will have a future only if it designs a *viable* way of life. I wish I could share the optimism of both Darwin and Herbert Spencer that the course of evolution is necessarily toward perfection. It appears, on the contrary, that that course must be corrected from time to time. But if the intelligent behavior that corrects it is also a product of evolution, then perhaps they were right after all. But it could be a near thing.

Diversions and Obstacles

Perhaps it is now clear what I mean by diversions and obstacles. The science I am discussing is the investigation of the relation between behavior and the environment—on the one hand, the environment in which the species evolved and which is responsible for the facts investigated by the ethologists and, on the other hand, the environment in which the individual lives and in response to which at any moment he behaves. We have been diverted from, and blocked in, our inquiries into the relations between behavior and those environments by an absorbing interest in the organism itself. We have been misled by the almost instinctive tendency to look inside any system to see how it works, a tendency doubly powerful in the case of behavior because of the apparent inside information supplied by feelings and introspectively observed states. Our only recourse is to leave that subject to the physiologist, who has, or will have, the only appropriate instruments and methods. We have also been encouraged to move in a centripetal direction because the discovery of controlling forces in the environment has seemed to reduce the credit due us for our achievements and to suggest that the struggle for freedom has not been as fully successful as we had imagined. We are not yet ready to accept the fact that the task is to change, not people, but rather the world in which they live.

A Different Approach

We shall be less reluctant to abandon these diversions and to attack these obstacles, as we come to understand the possibility of a different approach. The role of the environment in human affairs has not, of course, gone unnoticed. Historians and biographers have acknowledged influences on human conduct, and literature has made the same point again and again. The Enlightenment advanced the cause of the individual by improving the world in which he lived—the Encyclopedia of Diderot and D'Alembert was designed to further changes of that sort, and by the nineteenth century the controlling force of the environment was clearly recognized. Bentham and Marx have been called behaviorists, although for them the environment determined behavior only after first determining consciousness, and this was an unfortunate qualification because the assumption of a mediating state clouded the relation between the terminal events.

The role of the environment has become clearer in the present century. Its selective action in evolution has been examined by the ethologists, and a similar selective action during the life of the individual is the subject of the experimental analysis of behavior. In the current laboratory, very complex environments are constructed and their effects on behavior studied. I believe this work offers consoling reassurance to those who are reluctant to abandon traditional formulations. Unfortunately, it is not well known outside the field. Its practical uses are, however, beginning to attract attention. Techniques derived from the analysis have proved useful in other parts of biology—for example, physiology and psychopharmacology—and have already led to the improved design of cultural practices, in programmed instructional materials, contingency management in the classroom, behavioral modification in psychotherapy and penology, and many other fields.

Much remains to be done, and it will be done more rapidly when the role of the environment takes its proper place in competition with the apparent evidences of an inner life. As Diderot put it, nearly 200 years ago, "Unfortunately it is easier and shorter to consult oneself than it is to consult nature. Thus the reason is inclined to dwell within itself." But the problems we face are not to be found in men and women but in the world in which they live, especially in those social environments we call cultures. It is an important and promising shift in emphasis because, unlike the remote fastness of the so-called human spirit, the environment is within reach and we are learning how to change it.

And so I return to the role that has been assigned to me as a kind of twentieth-century Calvin, calling on you to forsake the primrose path of total individualism, of self-actualization, self-adoration, and self-love, and to turn instead to the construction of that heaven on earth which is, I believe, within reach of the methods of science. I wish to testify that, once you are used to it, the way is not so steep or thorny after all.

REFERENCES

ONIANS, R. D. *The origins of European thought.* Cambridge, England: University Press, 1951.

SHERRINGTON, C. S. *Integrative action of the nervous system.* New Haven, Conn.: Yale University Press, 1906.

SKINNER, B. F. *Beyond freedom and dignity.* New York: Knopf, 1971.

40

THE CASE FOR BEHAVIORISM *

WILLARD DAY

IN THE program for this series the topic announced for my remarks is "The Trouble with Freedom." However, since this is the opening talk in the series it seems to me more appropriate that I deal with behaviorism somewhat more broadly than would be the case if I were to restrict myself to certain problems that arise from ways in which we commonly

---

* Written for this volume.

use the concept of freedom. What really needs to be done, in view of the tension between popular public animosity toward behaviorism and the increasing evidence of the effectiveness of behaviorist technology in the treatment of certain types of behavior problems, is for the heart of the basic case that behaviorism has to be made clear. That is what I am going to try to do here. What follows is the case for behaviorism as I see it. What I am going to do is to state as succinctly, as starkly, and as directly as I can the essence of what I think behaviorism has going for it, and why. I will have occasion, in passing, to say something about certain difficulties we get ourselves into when we think about freedom in a particular way.

What I have to say is organized in the following way. First I am going to make a statement of what I take to be the very heart of the behaviorist outlook in psychology. It is the case for this particular outlook that I will be arguing here. I will equate the behaviorism I am talking about with three specific propositions, which I will state at the outset. The body of my remarks will consist of a discussion of certain implications of each of these propositions considered in order, particularly as they bear on the issues brought to a head by B. F. Skinner in the publication of his book *Beyond Freedom and Dignity* two years ago.

The three propositions in terms of which I define the behaviorist outlook are these. First, behaviorism is at heart a concern with the *contingencies* involved in behavioral control. Second, behaviorism has a negative aspect to it: it is opposed to something called *mentalism*, although in *Beyond Freedom and Dignity* this same negative element appears as Skinner's opposition to what he calls "autonomous man." Third, behaviorism involves at heart a particular conviction with respect to social planning, namely, that if we are to survive as a species we should begin at once to restructure our social environment, in a piecemeal fashion, so that it acts to produce people who have the behavioral equipment necessary for us all to survive. These three things—a focal interest in the contingencies involved in behavioral control, an opposition to a particular way of thinking about human affairs called mentalism, and an active interest in a particular kind of social planning—constitute to my mind the heart of the behaviorist outlook, a case for which I shall attempt to develop as I proceed.

I take up first the behaviorist's focal concern with the analysis of contingencies involved in behavioral control. But what is a contingency anyway, and what do we mean by behavioral control? Basically, a contingency is any connection we have reason to believe exists between behavior and the factors operating on a person to which we believe his behavior is related. Thus contingencies are essentially *relationships* which are taken to obtain between behavior and whatever factors we have reason to believe have acted to give it its particular form. When a behaviorist looks at a particular instance of behavior for purposes of accounting for its occurrence, or of understanding it, or of trying to figure out what might be done to change it, he thinks in a particular way: he tries to make an assessment of what it was about the situation the person has had to live in that would lead him to behave in the particular way he now does, and of what he might do to change the circumstances under which he lives so that more appropriate behavior might be strengthened. Assessments of this kind are what the behaviorist means when he speaks of an analysis of contingencies. When he goes on to speak of behavioral *control,* or of the "variables" involved in behavioral control, what he is talking about is the pattern of contingencies he believes must underlie the fact that behavior in a particular case has assumed the particular form that it has. Thus for behaviorists the word *control* means precisely, yet simply, patterns of operating contingencies. To say "patterns of controlling contingencies" means precisely the same thing as, and no more than, "patterns of operating contingencies." When a behaviorist speaks of *variables,* as in the expression "controlling variables," he means by the word *variable* just what we mean when we speak of *factor.* Thus when he refers to "variables that have acted to shape a particular pattern of behavior" he has in mind precisely what would more commonly be spoken of as factors or circumstances which are in some sense responsible for the fact that particular people are likely to engage in one particular, rather than another, type of behavior.

I have gone into this discussion of what behaviorists mean by such expressions as *behavioral contingencies* and *controlling variables* for the purpose of showing that insofar as the behaviorist is centrally involved in his work with the analysis of contingencies controlling behavior, as he in fact is, he is zeroing in on what must be a vital part of anything that can seriously be considered significant psychological knowledge of any kind on the part of anybody. In some sense, psychological knowledge, if it is knowledge, can be construed in a way so that it bears upon the general problem of "the determinants of behavior," or of "the factors involved in accounting for behavior," or some such expression. This means, for instance, that if a competent psychoanalyst can be regarded as knowing anything at all about the psychological situation of his patient, about the factors at least to some extent likely to have been involved in the source of the patient's problems, and about possible courses of action available to the analyst that may be helpful to the patient, then at some point the psychoanalyst is to some extent in contact with what the behaviorist would regard as significant controlling contingencies. The potential power of the behaviorist outlook lies in the explicitness and directness with which he focuses his attention centrally upon the search for, the precise specification of, and the careful evaluation of whatever contingencies are involved. Once again, the behaviorist's focal interest in the analysis of behavioral controlling contingencies leads him to attend seriously to any nontrivial claim to psychological knowledge. However, the professional utility of his outlook lies precisely in the concentration of his interest specifically upon the search for whatever contingencies can be found to underlie the knowledge claim.

What I have been saying about the inescapable linkage between genuine psychological knowledge of any kind and the behaviorist's pressing concern with the assessment of contingencies undoubtedly raises questions in the minds of some of you concerning just how it is that the inevitable contingencies are identified, specified, and evaluated. It is true indeed that behaviorists without exception would want to accord to contingencies identified as such the professional confidence generally associated with respectable science. I must also say that, at least in my opinion, the image behaviorists often like to give of themselves as being "purer" or more "hard-headed" than other psychologists in their commitment to "science" is as a rule more incredible than credible. It is true that some behaviorist thinkers, and Murray Sidman is a conspicuous case in point, have made contributions of great significance to our understanding of profitable strategies for the conduct of laboratory research. Yet the crux of the matter in the identification and evaluation of contingencies is the degree to which claims to the effect that under certain circumstances contingencies of a particular kind are operating merit public confidence and trust. Indeed it is part of the particularly valuable emphasis of behaviorism that the evidence upon which contingency claims are based be carefully and scrupulously displayed. However, it is entirely mythical to believe that it is only in the laboratory where refined experimental control is often possible that contingency claims can be legitimately evaluated by some kind of test, or that one or another innovation in baseline methodology must serve as the criterion for public confidence in contingency claims in the applied areas.

It is simply fact that the most important contingencies operating in the control of human behavior are impossible to bring into the laboratory for investigation, no matter how much the research ingenuity of the experimenter. This fact, moreover, does not leave us without other recourse than to resort to established procedures for carrying out research in the field. Once again, it is one of the great strengths of behaviorism as an intellectual outlook that it can lead us with integrity out of our habitual methodological preconceptions. The thrust of behaviorism is to encourage public trust and confidence in claims about human functioning that bear the closest possible relation to direct observation. For me to speak of verbal claims bearing a certain type of *relation* to direct observation is, as you will have recognized, for me to speak of a particular type of controlling contingency. In other words, we are urged by the behaviorist to place most public confidence and trust in contingency claims that, as aspects of behavior, are themselves controlled—that is, are themselves parts of contingencies—in ways where direct observation is conspicuously important. Such contingency claims, in which we are encouraged to have confidence and trust and which are heavily controlled by practices of direct observation, contrast, for example, with the overwhelming preponderance of conclusions commonly proferred as psychological knowledge, where the control exercised by direct observation is quite remote.

For me to speak as I have just been doing of the control of verbal behavior is of course absolutely central to the behaviorist outlook. With the possible exception of certain intentionalistic approaches to the analysis of rhetoric, to my knowledge the interests of behaviorism in a functional analysis of verbal productions is unique in contemporary psychology. However, now that I have brought up behaviorist interest in the functional analysis of verbal behavior, and in view of the fact that I am shortly to turn to behaviorist objections to what is regarded as mentalism in psychology, let me simply say at this point what mentalism is *not*. By *mentalism* the behaviorist does not mean the use of particular kinds of words, to which he objects. For example, to use the word *mind*, as I already have several times in these remarks, is not thereby to be mentalistic. The behaviorist has no objection to the use of any words, so long as they are used meaningfully, and most verbal behavior is emitted meaningfully, whether by the most esoteric professional psychologist or by the man in the street. It is indeed one of the valuable contributions that behaviorism can make to professional understanding by clarifying what it is that professional people say, through an analysis of the contingencies involved in its production.

Let me close this discussion of the behaviorist's focal interest in the analysis of contingencies by taking note of a particular irony. In view of the prejudice commonly expressed on the part of behaviorists against, let us say, "humanistic" practices of psychotherapy, it strikes me as ironic indeed that it is the professional behavior of clinical psychologists that functions so heavily under the control of little more than what can be directly observed from the behavior of their clients. To be sure, it is a rare clinical psychologist who hears the behaviorist's advice that records of therapeutic encounter be systematically scrutinized for the evidences of important contingencies they contain. Yet the behaviorist should envy the clinician for his opportunities to have contact with the contingencies most important in determining the outcome of people's lives. The point becomes particularly pressing in connection with the behaviorist's interests in social planning, because it is precisely the contingencies currently most accessible to the clinical psychologist that will have to be taken predominantly into consideration in making recommendations for societal change.

I turn now to a consideration of behaviorism's objections to an exceedingly widespread practice in the interpretation of human affairs that is variously identified as an objection to "mentalism" or as an objectionable reliance upon conceptualizing human beings as inherently "autonomous" agents. The first thing to realize about this objection is that it is not primarily a "theoretical" or systematic issue directed largely at psychologists. Psychologists get involved in mentalistic practices of making sense out of their own behavior or that of others for the most part only to the extent to which they revert to nonprofessional patterns of thinking picked up from the lay culture at large. To the extent that a psychologist actually possesses genuine psychological knowledge, and makes use of it in his daily interactions with people, he is not likely to manifest the inefficient and misguided practices to which the behaviorist objects as mentalistic. To be sure, mentalism remains rampant among psychologists of the primarily academic type, presumably either because in spite of what they preach they do not actually have much genuine psychological knowledge or because their area of professional competence is so narrow that it does not significantly engage the circumstances of human interaction that they characteristically face in daily life.

At heart, behaviorists mean by mentalism a conception of the nature of man that is tacitly assumed or taken for granted to be true and that is deeply ingrained in our culture as a part of Western civilization. (Actually, it is genuinely mentalistic of me to speak as I just have of a "conception" of man's nature that is "assumed" to be "true." It is mentalistic of me because as a psychologist I know better than to think that people treat each other as they do largely because of assumptions they regard as true. I speak loosely here because neither you nor I have the time or knowledge to analyze mentalistic behavior in technical detail.) However, perhaps I can get to the nub of the matter by asking you to consider how very much a part of us it is to rely on other people being at least roughly rational in their relation to us. From the Greeks we have it that the most important thing about a human being is his capacity for rationality: man is a rational animal. Yet the concept of rationality can not go very far by itself in enabling us to make sense out of behavior. The mentalistic outlook involves a complete system of primitive psychology. Our rationality consists of our making use of *ideas* in a fashion that is *logically satisfactory;* our words have meaning because they are external symbols of our ideas, and all it takes for communication to be successful is to speak distinctly with words the other person is familiar with; behavior is rational if it follows a *decision* reached as a result of clear thinking; action following a decision manifests the human capacity for *choice*: it is up to the individual as an *autonomous agent* to act on his decision or not; he makes his choices and acts on his decisions according to his *will;* his will is *free*, since, as I have said, it is up to the individual to act on his own decison or not; however, man's freedom carries with it the *responsibility* each person must bear for the consequences of his acts, and hence we are appropriately liable to the *judgment* of others and subject to their *condemnation* and *blame* (or approval, as the case may be). And so the primitive psychological account goes on. I think you can see that once the commitment is made to a primary emphasis upon man's capacities for rationality, it is not difficult to generate the whole package of the mentalistic outlook that is the focus of Skinner's attack in his book *Beyond Freedom and Dignity*.

However, the difficulty most people have with behaviorism is that they do not see what is so *wrong* with the mentalistic outlook that I have described. The great wrong is precisely this: the mentalistic picture does not conform to psychological reality. Man in his functioning is not primarily a rational creature. It is true that from time to time, and under certain circumstances, particular people can and do act in ways that we regard as rational. However, their capacities to do so must be carefully constructed in them by their experience. The human potential for rational behavior that most of us are endowed with by our genetic and physiological make-up will assume in each of us that particular form that is determined by the opportunities for the relevant shaping that actually exist in the environment in which we function.

Or consider our capacities for communicating with each other verbally. The reality of whether or not we really understand each other when we speak together is not at all simply a matter of our being able to understand the meaning of individual words correctly ordered in a sentence in some way that we think expresses our idea accurately. Whether or not communication will take place depends critically upon exactly what the background of each person has been in the shaping of the relevant verbal repertoires. It is not enough, for example, to think that just because college students are relatively fluent in the language they can thereby really learn from listening to a lecture or from reading a book. There are many different ways to read a book, or to listen to a lecture, only some of which participate in the contingencies necessary for learning to take place.

Or take the problem faced by the therapist in trying to help his patient. It is hardly ever the thing to do to give advice, hoping that the patient will then simply understand how to solve his problem. Nor is it the thing to do to exhort the patient to try harder, to exercise his will power. Nor is it effective simply to explain to him in great detail the psychological determinants of his problem, hoping that his new insight will lead to more adaptive decisions on his part. It is of course obvious that it is a rare therapist indeed who makes use of the primitive psychology of mentalism in this way to do his work. Presumably if the therapist is an effective one it is because to some extent he has knowledge of psychological reality and in one way or another makes use of particular contingencies that he has learned from his experience are to the point.

However, once again, it is not primarily to the professional psychologist that the concern with mentalism is directed. The behaviorist's concern here is with the general public, with society at large. It is parents, teachers, civil servants, our friends and neighbors who vote, our lawmakers, and political leaders, who give advice, exhort the will, levy blame and condemnation, think their thoughts are rational, and expect people to take their speeches seriously. The enormous potential of behaviorism lies in its aspirations to change society in the way it thinks about, interprets, and deals with human beings. In this it wants society to assess human conduct in a fashion that maps accurately onto the realities of the human condition. It wants society at large to be knowledgeable about the kinds of contingencies that are actually at work in the control of behavior and to take action in human affairs that is enlightened and informed by such knowledge.

I believe, before turning to the behaviorist's serious interest in social planning, that I am now in a position to make a point with respect to the concept of freedom. As with most words linked to abstract concepts the term *freedom* has many uses. By no means all, or even most, of these uses function in verbal contexts that are objectionable to the behaviorist. However, in one sense it is clearly objectionable to regard people as "free," namely, in that sense in which it functions as part of the primitive psychology of mentalism, in which the notion of freedom directly confronts serious professional interest in the psychological determinants of behavior.

I turn now to discussion of the third fundamental element in the behaviorist outlook, namely, the intense and serious interest in long-range social planning. Behaviorists are of course not the first to be interested in social planning in the history of Western civilization, and in view of the current widespread advocacy of social planning for the protection of our natural resources and the ecological necessities of our environment if we are to survive, let me say that undoubtedly only a very small proportion of these advocates of social planning are behaviorists. There are many in this country who read Skinner's assault on the concepts of freedom and personal pride for what they take to be its political implications, and who see in it little more than an invitation to Communism. On the other hand, I have known sophisticated European Marxists who regard behaviorist talk of widespread social control unaccompanied by any discussion of the rights of individuals to be a spur to latent tendencies toward Fascism. In any case, ignoring political overtones altogether, many, many people today regard any application of behaviorist technology as an unwanted increment to an already over-technologized society, and they cry for increased public education in the humanities or in other "humanistic" disciplines that call for renewed respect for human individuality.

In the remainder of my remarks I will try to show that, far from leading inevitably to man's dehumanization, making increasingly vigorous attempts to gain new knowledge of the contingencies actually functioning in behavioral control, and incorporating whatever knowledge of relevant contingencies we have in self-conscious attempts to restructure our social environment, is perhaps the only option now remaining open to us for protecting and preserving those aspects of our humanity that are precisely the most valuable to us.

Let me be quite blunt about the matter. To be sure, the point of behaviorist social planning is to remake people where necessary and possible, and to arrange social institutions so that they function to build people to begin with so that their socially and personally desirable qualities are maximized. However, the aim is not to change human nature itself. Our nature as humans is given to us by our genetic environment; yet *what we turn out to be* as humans is determined by the interaction of that endowment with the environmental circumstances under which we live. When people worry about *human nature,* they do not mean just the way individual people turn out to be. Yet it is with the way people turn out to be that behavior shaping is concerned. It is one thing to be pleased or displeased with the native equipment and capacities we have as humans that are given in our genetic endowment. Yet it is something quite different (and this is the province of behaviorism) to like or dislike the extent to which a person appears to have realized much of his native potential as a human, which one judges by looking at the way he acts or at the way he appears to be able to act in view of the particular circumstances his life has happened to involve.

I do not deny that with our burgeoning new knowledge of genetic mechanisms there are now those who actively speculate about the possibilities of direct genetic manipulation of human nature itself. Nor do I deny that such speculation raises ethical problems similar to those raised by far-reaching speculation in connection with behaviorist social planning. However, my point is much more specific. When a behaviorist speaks of changing the social environment so that it changes behavior in a particular way, he is not talking about the kinds of things people fear when they think of what might be involved in changing our very natures as human beings.

These issues arise because of the explicit interest on the part of the behaviorist in influencing the way our behavioral repertoires are shaped by our experience. The behaviorist is interested in influencing us in what happens to us by way of learning. Yet it is simply not the case that the acquisition of specific behavioral repertoires through shaping in and of itself makes us more like robots. People do not turn out to be essentially the same who possess roughly analogous capacities to read, to play football, to invest themselves deeply in interpersonal relations, and so forth. Explicit behavior shaping does not make people more "mechanical" than they already are, nor is it good philosophy to believe that if one acknowledges the reality of psychological determinants of behavior he is thereby somehow committed to a belief that people are no more than machinelike things to begin with. People are people, and the "humanity" that any human being has ever had is presumably the product of his genetic endowment and the opportunities for behavioral shaping provided by his environment. Behavior shaping does not fix people in chains of conditioned reflexes. It *enables* people to perform in new ways; it gives them new behavioral repertoires with which they can respond to environmental circumstances as they occur.

The issue of "mechanical" man versus "fully human" man is very much alive in people's thoughts today. Yet the current vitality of this issue has not arisen because of *behaviorism*, the practical application of which in the amelioration of human problems is still much in its infancy. The issue has arisen precisely because of the consequences of the deplorable circumstances that define the social environment as it exists *right now*. The expression "mechanical man" is used metaphorically by psychotherapists and social commentators to apply to the general condition of people in our society right now. It is true that it has not been the behaviorists who have called attention to the machinelike apathy of most of us at the present time. But I, for one, look first to the behaviorist for help in rearranging the circumstances of people's lives so that the more viable aspects in their "humanity" can be restored.

However, I am after another point. It is important to attend to the fact that it is not all that difficult for people to understand what social critics are objecting to when they complain of the dehumanized, mechanical apathy on the part of large segments of our present society, and are able to conceive of a more vital, successfully human personhood on the part of these people that it would be better for them to have. This gives evidence that the problem of what values *should* be shaped in a planned society is not simply some inherently unsolvable problem in ethical philosophy. As the logic in Skinner's *Beyond Freedom and Dignity* attempts to make clear, it is simply a matter of *fact* that people have values. To be sure the nature of the values of particular people is determined to a certain extent by the environmental circumstances under which they have lived. Yet the problem of the origin of people's values can be separated out from the issue of which particular values should act to guide efforts at social planning. It is simply a matter of fact that the particular behavioral repertoires selected for special strengthening by behavior modifiers at the present time reflect values that are relatively broadly held among the general population at large. Similarly, whatever planning is foreseeable in the relatively immediate future is likely to involve a strengthening of repertoires relevant to values widely agreed upon as desirable among most members of our society, such as the capacity to read and to express oneself with facility, the capacity to learn the skills required in available and preferred employment, the capacity to relate in a nondestructive fashion to members of one's family, and so forth. So long as the distribution of power remains roughly in our society as it is at the present time, it seems to me quite clear that the values reflected in the behavioral repertoires selected for special strengthening in piecemeal planning will continue to be values widely regarded as desirable in the population at large.

However, in the long run behaviorism can promise to offer much more than that. There is no reason why behaviorists, and particularly those especially interested in social planning, should not turn their attention specifically to the contingencies involved in enabling people to live those lives that are regarded now as most richly fulfilling in the sense of most adequately realizing the potential inherent in our natures as human beings. Exactly what this would mean is not widely understood with much verbal sophistication on the part of the general public at large. Yet perceptive and broadly experienced psychotherapists are quite able now to talk with much credibility about the major psychological dimensions that are involved in living a richly fulfilled life. Involved here are such matters as the capacity to form and maintain deeply intimate personal relationships; the capacity to discriminate and verbalize the feelings that one actually has; the capacity to accept the consequences of one's own behavior; the capacity to deal in a socially acceptable way with one's impulses to aggression; the capacity to make decisions on the basis of a realistic assessment of one's situation; the capacity to stand up to such crises of life as aging, debilitating illness, or death; the capacity to invest oneself creatively in new opportunities for learning; the capacity to be concerned in a caring way for others in one's own community; and so forth. There is no reason why initiative should not be undertaken by behaviorists right now, at the present time, toward serious social planning directed toward strengthening the repertoires requisite for such deeply fulfilling human values as these.

I recognize that the objection is not without force that behaviorists have so far been slow in involving themselves much in humanistic concerns of this kind, even though they would have to be in the forefront of consideration in any serious social planning of a global or far-reaching nature. I suppose that the fact that there are barely enough behaviorists around now to fill the needs of existing institutions of social rehabilitation is but a poor excuse. Even so, the direction in which the behaviorism of the future is likely to expand seems clear enough to me. The time is ripe now for behaviorists to turn their attention increasingly to an assessment of the contingencies involved in the rich fulfillment of people's lives as fully developed human beings. There are many problems to be overcome in doing this. Behaviorists still remain uncomfortable in assessing contingencies based on personal observation alone or where contingencies have to be extracted from the verbal records of such interactions as therapeutic sessions. Even more difficult is the challenge of extracting potential contingencies from semitheoretical efforts at interpretation offered by experienced clinicians. However, the task is not impossible, and indeed it is absolutely necessary if behaviorist interests in productive social planning are seriously to be pursued. As a place to start, let me recommend to my fellow behaviorists that they read carefully the two latest books by Rollo May: *Love and Will* and *Power and Innocence*. These books, enlightened as they are by intimate knowledge of heavily Freudian psychoanalysis, Jungian analysis, existentialism, religion, humanistic psychology, and phenomenological psychology, should provide an introduction that is indeed heavy enough to match the complexity of the task involved in assessing the behavioral contingencies that face analysis.

On this note let me rest my case. However, as a parting comment I would like to acknowledge the mentalism I have engaged in in resting my argument so strongly on the notion of "psychological knowledge." I would just like you all to know that I am very fully aware that what I have spoken of as "psychological knowledge" is more accurately spoken of as a special class of professional behaviors that are themselves under relatively identifiable varieties of environmental control.

41

BEHAVIOR MODIFICATION

PERRY LONDON

WHEN little "behavior modifiers" sit at their professional daddys' knees and ask, "Where did I come from?" they are usually told a story about the "principles of learning" that spawned them, the evil clinicians who left them to perish on a hillside, and the kindly shepherd doctors who found them, raised them as their own, and eventually restored them to their rightful position as the benefactors of behavior. When they grow up, confer their own benefits, and spawn their own little behavior modifiers, they become disabused of the myth. But not entirely—there remains, at the very least, a tradition of deferring to the principles of learning as the ultimate source of all good modifications and a parallel ritual of knocking psychoanalysts, Rogerians, existentialists, and general

FROM P. London, The end of ideology in behavior modification, *American Psychologist*, 1972, 27, (10), 913–920. Copyright 1972 by the American Psychological Association. Reprinted by permission.

psychiatrists who have not yet mastered or endorsed the jargon of respondents, operants, and reinforcements.

Like most myths, this tale has been based on some true events and has proved useful for the promotion of behavioristic patriotism and for extending the frontiers of experimentation and the clinical and technical growth of the field. And it makes a good story. But enough is enough. The borders are secure now, the settlers are thriving, the dark untrammeled forests are trammeled and cut down, the stumps blown, the fields plowed. It is time now to build this domain, not defend it.

Building it requires three things: first, abandoning strife with other modalities and developing peaceful commerce to see what they have to offer and exchange; second, examining the constructs that underlie modifying operations and that give clues for the design of new ones; and finally, devoting ourselves to "criterion validity," that is, to building treatment methods that work. The entire field has been moving in these directions during the past few years, but only partly I think, as a result of the intelligent pressures of people making these recommendations. The shift results also from technological changes in related disciplines and from attitude changes in the entire society that supports them. New equipment brings new possibilities for use and a new social readiness to use it, and the speed with which it gets advertised and talked about pushes advances in practice that no theory is likely to keep up with. This article argues that it is probably just as well.

For public purposes, behavior modifiers of the 1960s usually described their activities as logically inevitable corollaries of theorems or principles of learning and of ongoing discoveries about how they applied to disordered human behavior. Actually, there were only about three principles that they ever referred to, all of which can be reduced to one or one and a half principles—namely, that learning depends on the connections in time, space, and attention between what you do and what happens to you subsequently (Franks, 1969; Lazarus, 1971). In addition, the special application to human behavior was predicated less on ongoing scientific discoveries about learning or about people than on the idea that human neuroses are probably about the same as animal neuroses (Wolpe, 1958). The critical principles of learning involved had all been spelled out rather elaborately between 1898 and 1938, and the business about animal neuroses was posited by Pavlov in the same period. During that period, in fact, Pavlov, Watson, Jones, Mowrer, and Guthrie pretty much spelled out all of the major behavior therapy methods that became popular for treating people since 1958, with the possible exception of desensitization and operant behavior shaping (London, 1964). And they are exceptions only because the former is not derived from the usual learning principles and cannot be, and because the latter is something everybody knew about anyhow but never applied ingeniously until Skinner laboriously spelled out its monumental implications.

Evolution of Behavior Modification

The early growth of behavior modification as a professional specialty was largely polemical and political, not theoretical, and most of its scientific hoopla evolved to serve the polemical needs of the people who made it up—not all of it, however, and not only polemical needs.

The study of learning for behavior therapists, in fact, was always more for the purpose of metaphor, paradigm, and analogy than for strict guidance about how to operate or about what it all means. Whatever value theory may have for dictating laboratory procedures, therapeutic operations have been essentially seat-of-the-pants affairs, and still are, because they address immediate practical problems that require solutions in fact, not in principle. The disregarding of principles to see what really works, in this connection, reflects the intelligence and scientific good sense of therapists. The search for principles to explain what works, on the other hand, reflects their integrity and their anxiety—integrity because only fools would accept their own results without question, anxiety because therapists seek principles as much to increase their confidence as to reduce their ignorance. People also look for principles to help fight intellectual battles. Conventional therapies could be assaulted for their ineffectiveness, but the basis for offering new ones had to be more than a simplistic appeal to "what works." Of all popular therapies, psychoanalysis in particular was based on a pretentious, respectable, and smart *theory*. It could not be challenged with less than a theory.

Learning theory was an obvious choice: first, because there is a history of suggested therapeutic applications of learning principles, from Thorndike and Pavlov through Mowrer and Guthrie; and second, because the heart of any *psycho*therapy is changing people's behavior without changing their body structure or gross functions—which means, in plain language, teaching them and getting them to learn.

Even so, the evolution of behavior modification did not go so neatly. It could not make much use of learning theory, except for the broadest principles of learning, because most of the principles either do not yet have any really systematic application to disorders, or because they are much more in dispute than naive students realize.

The polemics actually used attacked evident flaws in psychoanalytic and other psychiatric formulations, sometimes also getting a little professional jealousy of psychologists for doctors into the act. Their main points were (a) an attack on "the medical model"; (b) the insistence that the origins of disorder were in *learning* instead of biochemical or genetic events; (c) the proposition that effective therapeutics should treat symptoms instead of their causes, that is, that disorders are identical with their symptoms; and finally, (d) the demand that even the name of the game should be changed from psychotherapy to behavior therapy, so no one thinks we are mentalistic or unscientific, as other therapies obviously are (sic).

This description is not exaggerated at all. Eysenck's (1959) tabulation of "the more important differences between Freudian Psychotherapy and Behavior Therapy," for instance, says that Freudian therapy is "based on inconsistent theory never properly formulated in postulate form," while behavior therapy is "based on consistent, properly formulated theory leading to testable deductions." Similarly, Freudian practice is "derived from clinical observations made without necessary control, observation or experiment," while behavior therapy is "derived from experimental studies specifically designed to test basic theory and deductions made therefrom [p. 67]." Franks (1969) is kinder than Eysenck, but even he says, a decade later, "for most behavior therapists, the preferred sequence of events is from experimental observation to clinical practice. This may be contrasted with the approach of traditional psychotherapists, in which the sequence is often reversed [p. 3]."

These arguments are not entirely pointless, but they are not entirely apropos of anything either, except who is smart and who will get the last word. What makes them largely irrelevant is that explanatory concepts are only necessary to explain what is going on—and until you know that, you do not need a theory, at least not much of one. Such theory, at this point in this enterprise, has to be stretched to fit facts rather than tailored to them. And it is damaging in the long run because people may start believing it and making up nonsense to plead silly cases that confuse everybody and enlighten no one. Enormous time and space have been wasted in pious debates on irrelevant aspects of most of the popular polemic issues of psychotherapy.

Discussions of "the medical model," for instance, often contrast "learning theory" approaches to "psychodynamic" approaches. There is a real question about the relative utility of *organic* versus *dynamic* perspectives on some behavior disorders, but all learning theory formulations are, in fact, dynamic ones. Also, there are many medical models, and the general attack on "the" medical model is only applicable to the *infectious disease* model, and only usable against psychoanalysis by lamely borrowing against Freud's (1961) unfortunate statement about putting demonology inside peoples' heads. Medical *epidemiological* models should have some appeal to Skinnerians, in fact, with their emphasis on environmental determinants of disorder, just as psychological models of habit formation are good for understanding the course of some developmental or degenerative medical conditions like heart disease.

The controversy about (learned versus structural) origins of disorder is mostly pointless because it is mostly irrelevant to treatment. The behaviorist attack commonly assumes that a genetic or biochemical view of etiology is bad because if disorder is learned, then treatment must be a learning process. This is nonsense. Etiology and treatment have no logical connection in either direction. Anxiety, for example, may be the result of prior experience, but can be alleviated chemically; or it may be aroused by essentially chemical circumstances (like fatigue plus mild arousal to danger), but can be soothed physically or verbally (Davison, 1968).

The only treatment question of relevance is that of the functional relationship between the problem and its solution. The process is what matters and nothing else.

The biggest polemic, of course, about treating symptoms versus causes has occurred largely because of the uncertain danger of symptom return or symptom substitution. Everywhere, much confusion has occurred, mostly because of confusion about the "medical model"—in this instance, about the exact meaning of symptom. If symptom means trouble, surely it should be treated. If not, maybe not. The polemic has been around the question of symptoms as "the main trouble"; this is because of the widespread belief, largely from psychoanalysis, in symptom return or substitution. (Buchwald and Young [1969] point out, incidentally, that some analysts, such as Fenichel and, later, Alexander, thought that symptoms should be treated directly.)

The real issue, in any case, is the consequence of the treatment for the person's condition—or his life. Sometimes too, the issue is prophylactic or preventive rather than ameliorative. This becomes clear by comparing the infectious disease and chronic ailment models in medicine. Behavior disorders are more like chronic ailments, where medical treatment generally aims at the symptoms only. The control of diabetes, on the other hand, is not treatment of symptoms, but their prevention. Is the shaping of behavior likewise? For changing the table manners of psychotics' ward behavior, maybe not; for molding children's manners, maybe so. The same question may be addressed to assertive training or to aversion training. Is teaching someone to talk back to his mother-in-law "reducing his anxiety" or preventing it from happening? Is teaching a homosexual man to attend to women when aroused and to feel repugnance for sex with men relieving his symptom or preventing a disorder (which does not exist legally until he "goes for" the man), teaching a habit pattern or unteaching one, changing a life style, altering a phenomenological field, shifting ego boundaries, redirecting id impulses or superego functions, or cathexis? And if he "feels" different or thinks about it differently, is it still behavior therapy?

These are silly questions. The change in the homosexual is all those things, depending on how you want to talk about them. Understanding the process is what matters, not belaboring the different styles of talking about it. The only important question about systematic treatment is that of the simultaneous relevance of the treatment technique to the person's manifest trouble and to the rest of his life.

Sometimes it accounts for both at once—as when he is suicidal. Sometimes it accounts for the rest of his life but not for the symptom—which is the behavior modifier's claim against insight types' preoccupation with motivation. Sometimes it accounts for only the manifest trouble—which is the insight therapists' accusation against behavior modifiers, based on the specious presumption that everything in a person's life is integral to it.

All of these polemics were not so much meaningless as overdone. The assault on psychoanalysts and existentialists was too extreme; the scientific claims on learning were too grandiose (Buchwald & Young, 1969; Franks, 1969). Changing from psychotherapy to behavior therapy may have been useful for people brought up on mind-body dualism, but for those of us who always thought the mind hung around the brain and that behavior meant "what happened," the distinction was graceless and gratuitous.

When you eliminate the polemics and politics and gratuities, however, what remains of theory to define the field and to tell you what it is about? Not a whole lot. The definition of the field either becomes very inclusive (Lazarus, 1971; Marks, 1971; Marston, 1970; Paul, 1969; Skinner, 1971) or very narrow (Eysenck, 1960; Skinner, 1963; Wolpe, 1968). This probably makes no serious difference to anything. As Kuhn (1962) said, "Can a definition tell a man whether he is a scientist or not [p. 160]?"

But what about theory? If behavior modification lacks theory, then is it not reduced to a technology rather than a science? Yes it is, and I believe that is what it should be, just as medicine is technology rather than science.

There is some dispute in the field about this point. The sides are well represented by Lazarus, who agrees with my view, and Franks, who does not. Lazarus (1971) said, in his latest book:

The emphasis of the volume is upon techniques rather than upon theories. . . . Methods of therapy are often effective for reasons which are at variance with the views of their inventors or discoverers. Technical eclecticism (Lazarus, 1967) does not imply a random melange of techniques taken haphazardly out of the air. It is an approach which urges therapists to experiment with empirically useful methods instead of using their theories as a priori predictors of what will and will not succeed in therapy (Eysenck, 1957, p. 271). The rationale behind the methods described in this book is predicated upon London's (1964) observation that: "However interesting, plausible, and appealing a theory may be, it is techniques, not theories, that are actually used on people. Study of the effect of psychotherapy, therefore, is always the study of the effectiveness of techniques" [p. 33].

Franks (1969) argued, to the contrary:

It would seem to be highly desirable for the therapist to aspire to be a scientist even if this goal were difficult to realize. To function as a scientist, it is necessary to espouse some theoretical framework. For reasons too obvious to detail here, this is true of the behavioral therapist. . . . How the behavior therapist practices (including his choice of technique, his approach to the problems of general strategy, and his specific relationships with his patient) thus depending both upon his explicit theoretical orientation and upon his implicit philosophical and cultural milieu [p. 21].

The argument that behavior modification should view itself as technology rather than as science is not meant to denigrate the importance of theory, either scientifically or heuristically. Scientifically, theory is valuable because it directs the systematic search for new information by interpreting and integrating what is already known. Heuristically, theory is valuable because it lays our biases out in the open and, by explicating them, makes it easier for us to disavow them when they are found to be inadequate.

The question with respect to behavior modification is twofold: First, is current theory very good (scientifically) in this case? Second, is any theory very useful for the current development of this field at this time? I think the answer to both questions is no.

In reality, behavior therapists never did have so much a theory as an "ideology"; in my own paraphrase of Bell (1960) and Tomkins (1964), "Ideology does not mean just ideas, but ideas to be acted on . . . [London, 1969]." What behavior therapists called theory actually served as bases for commitment or a rallying point for talking about disorder and treatment in a certain way and, more important, about acting on it within particular sets of limited operations, that is, technical limits. In this case, the commitment is to the *functional analysis of problems*. And it is for this reason that the domain incorporated within the legitimate purview of the field becomes broader and broader and the polemics milder and milder—as it is recognized that even Rogerians and humanists and psychoanalysts may analyze some things functionally and act on them accordingly.

What results from the increasing functional analysis of problems is an increasing number of plausible methods for coping with them—until the proliferation of methods is tested and found to work, no theory is really very necessary to explain *why* they work. For practitioners, none may be needed even then, if they work well. In any case, theory will largely grow from practice (Lazarus & Davison, 1971) and practice from instrumentation, in the broadest sense; this will happen to behavior modification just like it did to psychoanalysis, but with two generations' more experience, the results, hopefully, will be more scientific.

The status of theory comes largely from the belief that technique develops out of theory, that is, that science underlies engineering. But this is only partly true even among very "hard" sciences, less so among "soft" sciences, like the social and behavioral sciences, and not at all true for many endeavors where the existence of the technological capacity and the practical need is what produces the technical application and, indeed, what "nourishes" much of the theoretical development itself (Oppenheimer, 1956).

This does not mean that the alternative to rude theory is rude empiricism; rather, it suggests a close-to-the-situation functional analysis instead of a premature and precocious search for general principles from which to get overextended, or for a professional ideology to which to be committed. Such a development seems to be proceeding now, with practitioners using the techniques of behavior modification but declining the identity (Paul, 1969b), and scholars recommending heterodoxies like "technical eclecticism" without shame (Lazarus, 1971). The rest of this article spells out what this development means, so we will see clearly what we are doing, with the view to doing it better.

By deducing the intellectual condition of behavior modification from the technology it uses, there seem to be two kinds of conceptual schemes which characterize it. Borrowing from Price's (1971) book, *Abnormal Psychology: Perspectives on Conflict*, in turn derived from Kuhn's (1962) *Structure of Scientific Revolutions*, these are first, *metaphors* or analogies, and second, *paradigms* or models.

In the conventional classification of how much we seem to know what we are talking about in science, these concepts fit the lower end of the scale of certainty whose upper rungs are called "theories" and "laws." A scientific law, in other words, is an idea that seems absolutely to comprehend all of the facts it talks about; a theory is one that hopes to do so, but is not so compellingly known to do so. The activities involved in behavior modification are a good distance below both those points on the same continuum. A few are paradigms or models, that is, ideas that seem to explain a group of facts pretty precisely; most are metaphors or analogies, that is, ideas that look like they might fit a group of facts, where there is no clear evidence that they really do.

In general, the treatment methods derived from speculations about conditioning studies of animals are metaphorical or analogous, especially desensitization and implosion, or flooding. In general, the treatment methods that fall under the heading of education or training or, in jargon, of instrumental learning are paradigmatic or exemplary, including modeling, shaping, and possibly aversion techniques.

The difference between the metaphoric and the paradigmatic treatments is not in how well they work, but only in how well their workings are understood. This, in turn, reduces to how much of the mechanics involved can be predicted or explained with what degree of precision, which reduces still further to how many of the details are visible or can be inferred with different degrees of correlation. For practical purposes, the difference is simply one of the extent to which you can see what is going on enough to figure out how variations in your approach will affect it. The more you can peer intellectually into the "black box" in other words, and the prediction proves correct, the more you are dealing with a paradigm rather than a metaphor. A paradigm, in other words, is an attempt to construct a direct model or example of how something works. A metaphor is a more oblique comparison, in which the flaws in the analogy are obvious, but the similarities are still big enough to allow us to ask whether the comparison might "work."[1]

Desensitization is only a metaphor or analogy to conditioning: first, because it involves a specific cognitive process (the use of language) that classical conditioning does not; second, because it involves a mechanism of sequential imagination that can only be guessed at from conditioning studies; and third, because it is subject to a variety of successful variations that could not be predicted from the situations from which the metaphor was derived in the first place. Finally, desensitization does the same thing that implosion or flooding does, though it appears to be an opposite method.

Implosion is a better analogy than desensitization because Stampfl's original experiment (London, 1964) seems to parallel both Mowrer's (1950) theoretical statement, Solomon, Kamin, and Wynne's (1953), and Black's (1958) animal experiments more closely than Wolpe fits Masserman's cats or Pavlov's dogs. Also, implosion technique does predict all of its own variants—including Watson, Gaind, and Marks' (1971) finding that practice helps to extinguish phobic reactions and that using real objects instead of imagination as fearful stimuli also is helpful— but it is metaphorical nonetheless because it is between people, and because it is administered in social situations where the pressure *not* to escape is obviously coming from the thoughts that the patient has about the situation, not from physical restraints on his action.

Shaping is more exemplary or paradigmatic than conditioning treatments because it presumes less, in the first place, on the black box— modeling, likewise. Stated differently, both shaping and modeling methods can aim for precision in establishing the conditions that will work the desired effects without having to worry much about what is going on in the person that makes them work. *Aversion* treatment is more paradigmatic than metaphoric because its critical stimulus is not cognitive; that is, it hurts the patient physically. Giving a person an electric shock is much more like shocking a dog than telling scary stories to a person is like blowing air up a rat's behind; ergo, it is more paradigmatic than metaphoric.

Neither metaphors nor paradigms are scientific theories by some distance, but both of them are useful intellectual tools. *Metaphor* and *analogy* are good heuristically—they help to turn images into thoughts and inchoate hunches into articulate propositions. *Paradigms* are more

[1] Oppenheimer (1956) distinguished analogy from metaphor because the "structural similarity" of analogous events implies more precision in their comparison than is ordinarily true of metaphoric comparisons. I am putting them together here, however, to distinguish them both from paradigm.

literally useful—they model to scale what you need to do, or give a mathematical formula into which you can put specific quanta.

Notice, however, that none of this has anything to do with whether anything works for any practical problem. Desensitization may be a poor deduction from conditioning, but it is a fine treatment for phobias. Behavior shaping may be an excellent paradigm for getting autistic children to hug people, but it does not teach them syntactical speech.

Whatever scientific concern people have about the intellectual status of the field, at this point in the development of this enterprise, none of this material is yet very important to practitioners, and it is barely important to clinical research. What *is* important, at this juncture, is the development of systematic practice and of a technology to sustain it. My thesis is that, in the long run, scientific understanding will derive from them.

The practitioner tries to figure out what will work, for the most part, and then, if he is scientifically inclined, looks for a way to rationalize it if it does. The technologist devises machinery to support him. This is not a bad idea, even if it doesn't add up to test-tube-pure, white-coat science. Systematic desensitization is a good example of this process because, by "working" in the first place, it has given rise to technological refinements of itself that also work and that still leave the reasons unexplained. In the long run, this must force better and better logical and experimental confrontations with the reasons for the phenomenon —which success alone would not have done.

New equipment, new drugs, new gimmickry and gadgetry should now be the basis for systematically developing new methods of behavior modification and for streamlining the established techniques with controlled experimental testing. Instead of looking for new principles, or justifying worn-out ones, we should look for new applications: What could we do to treat such-and-such if we had such-and-such machinery? What would be required to build it? To test it? And then, finally, to determine what it means?

The critical point is that *good technology always undermines bad theory.* "Bad" is not meant to be pejorative here; it means metaphoric. Precise technology reveals the empirical error in metaphoric reasoning and in the operations that result from it. So Lang's (1969a, 1969b) on-line computer removes the therapist from the desensitization process; Quirk's (1970) machine removes the imagining and the relevance of the phobic subject matter; and Wolpin's (Jacobs & Wolpin, 1971; Wolpin, 1969; Wolpin & Raines, 1966) removes the need for hypnosis, for the fear hierarchy, and, indeed, for relaxation. Since the method still works, the need for explanation becomes more and more apparent (Davison, 1969), as does the inadequacy of the very plausible metaphor that launched Wolpe (1958) on the whole business.

Technology promises, in fact, more and more to turn metaphor to paradigm, if not paradigm to theory, by going directly into the black box and doing funny things to it and, increasingly, by bringing the black box out into the open where we can see more and more what has been happening in it. For the former, I refer to drug research and to the work in progress on electrical stimulation of the brain (Cohen, 1969; Delgado, 1969; London, 1969). These activities undercut specious distinctions between learned and unlearned patterns, either by manipulating the patterns out of hand or by potentiating learning so effectively that the issue of its importance disappears.

Bringing the black box out into the open is one of the main results likely to accrue from *biofeedback* research, and it is probably the best illustration one can find of technology feeding science with one hand as it enhances practice with the other. All of the biofeedback methods work on a single principle, whether they teach people to ring buzzers from a switch in their heads or to alter their blood pressure or heartbeat or skin resistance by monitoring lights and guages. The principle is finding a means of accurately externally recording some internal process, then of projecting that record into the person's consciousness so that he can literally see or hear what his blood vessels or brain waves or heart muscles are doing. Then let him learn to manipulate his conscious sensory experience in whatever way people learn to do anything consciously—something about which we really know next to nothing.

The clinical value of biofeedback methods remains to be seen and will certainly not be what alpha-machine hucksters seem to wish— instant cool for overheated psyches. Its clinical utility is not yet the point, only its technological sophistication and the scientific potential that comes from that.

To turn the point around, I am saying that theory has worn itself out in behavior modification and that technology, essentially of treatment, should now be a primary focus, perhaps, in the long range, even for serving scientific purposes. What began with the Mowrers' quilted pad in 1938 is extending now into therapeutic on-line computers, electric pottie chairs, electronic skin braille, and an almost self-generating brace of valuable hardware for therapeutic purposes. A summary of much of it will appear soon in a book by Robert and Ralph Schwitzgebel (in press) entitled *Psychotechnology.*

But the proper development that I am suggesting is not limited to hardware and is not self-generating, but reaches to the systematic exploration of all kinds of therapeutic things without inhibition or concern as to whether they fit ostensible *principles* of learning, or reinforcement, or whatever, but with a singular focus on whether they fit the *facts* of human experience. No one has been more forthright or resourceful in this connection than Lazarus (1971), whose latest work, *Behavior Therapy and Beyond,* goes into such things as imagery exercises for depression; thought control, straight out, for whatever it works for;

hypnosis for all kinds of things; exaggerated role taking à la the late George Kelly; differential relaxation; covert sensitization for aversive imaging; and Masters and Johnson's penis squeezing for premature ejaculation. It would take a genius or a madman to shelter this whole array of techniques under the intellectual umbrella of conditioning, or learning, or any other single psychological theory. It would take a fool to want to. The first issue, scientifically as well as clinically, is the factual one—Do they work? On whom? When? The how and why come later.

With the era of polemics virtually ended, and Skinner (1971) citing Freud over and over again in his latest work, and the American Psychoanalytic Association at a recent convention casually incorporating behavior modification into its discourses on psychotherapy, the political utility of learning theory, so called for the definition of the field, is ended. It was never really theory anyhow, as we used it, but ideology for professional purposes and mostly metaphor for clinical ones. It is time now, I think, for the remedial branch of this business to stop worrying about its scientific pretensions, in the theoretical sense, as long as it keeps its functional nose clean, and to devise a kind of engineering subsidiary, or more precisely, a systems analysis approach to its own operations. We have gotten about as much mileage as we are going to out of old principles, even correct ones, but we have barely begun to work the new technology.

REFERENCES

Bell, D. *End of ideology: Exhaustion of political ideas in the fifties*. Glencoe, Ill.: Free Press, 1960.

Black, A. H. The extinction of avoidance responses under curare. *Journal of Comparative and Physiological Psychology*, 1958, **51**, 519–524.

Buchwald, A. M., & Young, R. D. Some comments on the foundations of behavior therapy. In C. M. Franks (Ed.), *Behavior therapy: Appraisal and status*. New York: McGraw-Hill, 1969.

Cohen, S. I. Neurobiological considerations for behavior therapy. In C. M. Franks (Ed.), *Behavior therapy: Appraisal and status*. New York: McGraw-Hill, 1969.

Davison, G. C. Systematic desensitization as a counter-conditioning process. *Journal of Abnormal Psychology*, 1968, **73**, 91–99.

———. A procedural critique of "desensitization and the experimental reduction of threat." *Journal of Abnormal Psychology*, 1969, **74**, 86–87.

Delgado, J. M. R. *Physical control of the mind*. New York: Harper & Row, 1969.

Eysenck, H. J. Learning theory and behavior therapy. *Journal of Mental Science*, 1959, **105**, 61–75.

——— (Ed.) *Behavior therapy and neuroses*. London: Pergamon Press, 1960.

Franks, C. M. *Behavior therapy: Appraisal and status*. New York: McGraw-Hill, 1969.

FREUD, S. *The standard edition of the complete psychological works of Sigmund Freud.* London: Hogarth Press, 1961.

JACOBS, A., & WOLPIN, M. A second look at systematic desensitization. In, *Psychology of private events.* New York: Academic Press, 1971.

KUHN, T. S. *The structure of scientific revolutions.* Chicago: University of Chicago Press, 1962.

LANG, P. J. The mechanics of desensitization and the laboratory study of human fear. In C. M. Franks (Ed.), *Behavior therapy.* New York: McGraw-Hill, 1969. (a)

LANG, P. J. The on-line computer in behavior therapy research. *American Psychologist,* 1969, 24, 236–239. (b)

LAZARUS, A. A. *Behavior therapy and beyond.* New York: McGraw-Hill, 1971.

LAZARUS, A. A., & DAVISON, G. C. Clinical innovation in research and practice. In A. E. Bergin & S. L. Garfield (Eds.), *Handbook of psychotherapy and behavior change.* New York: Wiley, 1971.

LONDON, P. *The modes and morals of psychotherapy.* New York: Holt, Rinehart & Winston, 1964.

———. *Behavior control.* New York: Harper & Row, 1969.

MARKS, I. M. The future of the psychotherapies. *British Journal of Psychiatry,* 1971, 118, 69–73.

MARSTON, A. Parables for behavior therapists. Address given to Southern California Behavior Modification Conference, Los Angeles, October 1970.

MOWRER, O. H. *Learning theory and personality dynamics.* New York: Ronald Press, 1950.

OPPENHEIMER, R. Analogy in science. *American Psychologist,* 1956, 11, 127–135.

PAUL, G. L. Behavior modification research: Design and tactics. In C. M. Franks (Ed.), *Behavior therapy: Appraisal and status.* New York: McGraw-Hill, 1969. (a)

———. Outcome of systematic desensitization: II. Controlled investigations of individual treatment, technique variations and current status. In C. M. Franks (Ed.), *Behavior therapy.* New York: McGraw-Hill, 1969. (b)

PRICE, R. *Abnormal psychology: Positions in perspective.* New York: Holt, Rinehart & Winston, in press.

QUIRK, D. A. *Stimulus conditioned automatic response suppression: A behavioral therapy.* Toronto: University of Toronto, Clarke Institute of Psychiatry, 1970.

SCHWITZGEBEL, R. L., & SCHWITZGEBEL, R. K. *Psychotechnology.* New York: Holt, Rinehart & Winston, in press.

SKINNER, B. F. Behaviorism at fifty. *Science,* 1963, 140, 951–958.

———. *Beyond freedom and dignity.* New York: Knopf, 1971.

SOLOMON, R. L., KAMIN, L. J., & WYNNE, L. C. Traumatic avoidance learning: The outcomes of several extinction procedures with dogs. *Journal of Abnormal and Social Psychology,* 1953, 48, 291–302.

TOMKINS, S. The psychology of knowledge. Invited address to Division 8 presented at the meeting of the American Psychological Association, Los Angeles, September 7, 1964.

WATSON, J. P., GAIND, R., & MARKS, I. M. Prolonged exposure: A rapid treatment for phobias. *British Medical Journal,* 1971, 1, 13–15.

Wolpe, J. *Psychotherapy by reciprocal inhibition*. Stanford: Stanford University Press, 1958.

Wolpin, M. Guided imagining to reduce avoidance behavior. *Psychotherapy: Theory, Research and Practice*, 1969, 6, 122–124.

Wolpin, M., & Raines, J. Visual imagery, expected roles and extinction as possible factors in reducing fear and avoidance behavior. *Behavior Research and Therapy*, 1966, 4, 25–37.

42

A FEEDBACK MODEL

William T. Powers[*]

The basis of scientific psychology is a cause-effect model in which stimuli act on organisms to produce responses. It hardly seems possible that such a simple and venerable model could be in error, but I believe it is. Feedback theory shows in what way the model fails, and what must be done to correct our concepts of organized behavior.

Responses are dependent on present and past stimuli in a way determined by the current organization of the nervous system; that much is too well documented to deny. But it is equally true that stimuli depend on responses according to the current organization of the environment and the body in which the nervous system resides. That fact has been left out of behavioristic analyses of human and animal behavior, largely because most psychologists (especially the most influential early psychologists) have lacked the tool of feedback theory.

Norbert Wiener and later cyberneticists notwithstanding, the full import of feedback in behavioral organization has yet to be realized. The influence of behaviorism, now some 60 years old, is pervasive and subtle. Shaking ourselves free of that viewpoint requires more than learning the terms associated with feedback theory; it requires seeing and deeply appreciating the vast difference between an open-loop system and a closed-loop system.

Traditional psychology employs the open-loop concept of cause and effect in behavior; the effect (behavior) depends on the cause (stimuli) but not vice versa. The closed-loop concept treats behavior as one of

[*] The author is a research associate at the Western Behavioral Sciences Institute, La Jolla, California.

from W. T. Powers, Feedback: Beyond behaviorism, *Science*, 1973, 179, 351–356.

the causes of that same behavior, so that cause and effect can be traced all the way around a closed loop (1). When any phenomenon in this closed loop (such as the force generated by a muscle) persists in time, effectively averaging the antecedent causes over some period, the character of the system-environment relationship changes completely—cause and effect lose their distinctness and one must treat the closed loop as a whole rather than sequentially. That is where feedback theory enters the picture. Feedback theory provides the method for obtaining a correct intuitive grasp of this closed-loop situation in the many situations where the old open-loop analysis leads intuition astray.

In this article I intend to show as clearly as I can how a new theoretical approach to behavior can be developed simply by paying attention to feedback effects. There is nothing subtle about these effects; they are hidden only if they are taken for granted. All behavior involves strong feedback effects, whether one is considering spinal reflexes or self-actualization. Feedback is such an all-pervasive and fundamental aspect of behavior that it is as invisible as the air we breathe. Quite literally it is behavior—we know nothing of our own behavior but the feedback effects of our own outputs. To behave is to control perception.

I will not try here to develop all these concepts fully; that is being done elsewhere (2). I will provide only some essential groundwork by discussing the development of a hierarchical control-system model of behavioral organization beginning with the same sort of elementary observations that led to behaviorism. I hope it will thus become evident that a fully developed feedback model can do what no behavioristic model has been able to do: it can restore purposes and goals to our concept of human behavior, in a way that does not violate direct experience or scientific methods. The human brain is not simply a switchboard by means of which one environmental event is connected to another environmental event. These ideas are not new, but perhaps my synthesis is.

Act Versus Result

Behaviorists speak of organisms "emitting" behavior under stimulus control, this control being established by use of reinforcing stimuli. The effectiveness of reinforcers cannot be denied, but behavior itself has not been thoroughly analyzed by behaviorists. Behaviorists have not distinguished between means and ends—acts and results (3)—because they have not used the model that is appropriate to behavior.

When a pigeon is trained to walk in a figure-eight pattern, there are at least two levels at which the behavior must be viewed. The first, which is the one to which the behaviorist attends, is that of the pattern which results from the pigeon's walking movements. The other consists of those movements themselves (4).

The figure eight is created by the walking movements: the act of walking produces the result of a figure-eight pattern in the observer's perceptions. The observer sees a consistent behavior that remains the same from trial to trial. He generally fails to notice, however, that this constant result is brought about by a constantly changing set of walking movements. Clearly, the figure-eight pattern is not simply "emitted."

As the pigeon traces out the figure eight over and over, its feet are placed differently on each repeat of the same point in the pattern. If the cage is tipped, the movements become still more changed, yet the pattern which results remains the same. Variable acts produce a constant result. In this case the variations may not be striking, but they exist.

As behaviors become more complex the decoupling of act and result becomes even more marked. A rat trained to press a lever when a stimulus light appears will accomplish that result with a good reliability, yet each onset of the stimulus light produces a different act. If the rat is left of the lever it moves right; if right it moves left. If the paw is beside the lever the paw is lifted; if the paw is on the lever it is pressed down. These different, even opposite, acts follow the same stimulus event.

The more closely the rat's acts are examined, the more variability is seen. Yet in every case the variations in the acts have a common effect: they lead toward the final result that repeats every time. In fact, if precisely those variations did not occur, the final result would not be the same every time. Somehow the different effects apparently caused by the stimulus light are exactly those required to compensate for differences in initial conditions on each trial. This situation was clearly recognized by the noted philosopher of behaviorism, Egon Brunswik (5).

The accepted explanation for this phenomenon of compensation is that the changed initial conditions provide "cues," changes in the general background stimuli, which somehow modify the effect of the main stimulus in the right way. There are three main problems created by this explanation. First, these hypothetical "cues" must act with quantitative accuracy on the nervous system employing muscles which, because they are subject to fatigue, give anything but a quantitative response to nerve impulses. Second, these "cues" are hypothetical. They are never experimentally elucidated in toto, and there are many cases in which one cannot see how any cue but the behavioral result itself could be sensed. Third, the compensation explanation cannot deal with successful accomplishment of the behavioral result in a novel situation, where presumably there has been no opportunity for new "cues" to attain control of responses.

The central fact that needs explanation is the mysterious fashion in which actions vary in just the way needed to keep the behavioral result constant. The "cue" hypothesis comes after the fact and overlooks too many practical difficulties to be accepted with any comfort. Yet what is the alternative? It is to conclude that acts vary in order to create a constant behavioral result. That implies purpose: the purpose of acts is to produce the result that is in fact observed. This is the alternative which I recommend accepting.

Feedback Control

Behaviorists have rejected purposes or goals in behavior because it has seemed that goals are neither observable nor essential. I will show that they are both. There can be no rational explanation of behavior that overlooks the overriding influence of an organism's present structure of goals (whatever its origins), and there can be no nontrivial description of responses to stimuli that leaves out purposes. When purposes are properly understood in terms of feedback phenomena, acts and results are seen to be lawfully related in a simple and direct way. We will see this relationship using a simple canonical model of a feedback control system.

Engineers use negative feedback control systems to hold some physical quantity in a predetermined state, in an environment containing sources of disturbance that tend to change the quantity when it is uncontrolled. Every control system of this kind must have certain major features. It must sense the controlled quantity in each dimension in which the quantity is to be controlled (*Sensor function* in Fig. 1); this implies the presence of an inner representation of the quantity in the form of a signal or set of signals. It must contain or be given something equivalent to a reference signal (or multiple reference signals) which specifies the "desired" state of the controlled quantity. The sensor signal and the reference signal must be compared, and the resulting error signal must actuate the system's output effectors or outputs. And finally, the system's outputs must be able to affect the controlled quantity in each dimension that is to be controlled. There are other arrangements equivalent to this, but this one makes the action the clearest.

This physical arrangement of components is further constrained by the requirement that the system always oppose disturbances tending to create a nonzero error signal; this is tantamount to saying that the system must be organized for negative (not positive) feedback, and that it must be dynamically stable—it must not itself create errors that keep it "hunting" about the final steady-state condition. There is no point in concern with unstable systems, because the (normal) behavior we wish to explain does not show the symptoms of dynamic instability—and we do not have to design the system.

This system is modeled after Wiener's original concept (6). In the system I describe, however, there are certain changes in geometry, particularly the placement of the system boundary and the identification of the sensor (not reference) signal as the immediate consequence of a stimulus input. This is a continuous-variable (analogue) model, without provision for learning.

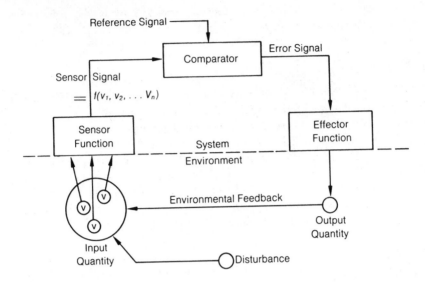

FIGURE 1. *Basic control-system unit of behavioral organization. The Sensor function creates an ongoing relationship between some set of environmental physical variables (v's) and a Sensor signal inside the system, an internal analog of some external state of affairs. The sensor signal is compared with (subtracted from, in the simplest case) a Reference signal of unspecified origin (see text). The discrepancy in the form of an Error signal activates the Effector function (for example, a muscle, limb, or subsystem) which in turn produces observable effects in the environment, the Output quantity. This quantity is a "response" measure. The environment provides a feedback link from the output quantity to the Input quantity, the set of "v's" monitored by the sensor function. The input quantity is also subject, in general, to effects independent of the system's outputs; these are shown as a Disturbance, also linked to the input quantity by environmental properties. The disturbance corresponds to "stimulus." The system, above the dashed line, is organized normally so as to maintain the sensor signal at all times nearly equal to the reference signal, even a changing reference signal. In doing so it produces whatever output is required to prevent disturbances from affecting the sensor signal materially. Thus the output quantity becomes primarily a function of the disturbance, while the sensor signal and input quantity become primarily a function of the reference signal originated inside the system. For all systems organized in this way, the "response" to a "stimulus" can be predicted if the stabilized state of the input quantity is known; the stimulus-response law is then a function of environmental properties and scarcely at all of system properties.*

A system that meets these requirements behaves in a basically simple way, despite the complexities of design that may be required in order to achieve stable operation. It produces whatever output is required in order to cancel the effects of disturbances on the signal generated by the sensor. If the properties of the sensor remain constant, as we may usually assume, the result is to protect the controlled quantity against the effects of unpredictable disturbances of almost any origin.

Goal-Directed Behavior

The reference signal constitutes an explanation of how a goal can be determined by physical means. The reference signal is a model inside the behaving system against which the sensor signal is compared; behavior is always such as to keep the sensor signal close to the setting of this reference signal.

With this model we gain a new insight into so-called "goal-seeking" behavior. The usual concept of a goal [for example, William Ashby's treatment (7)] is something toward which behavior tends over some protracted period of time. We can see that idea now as describing the behavior of a sluggish control system, or a control system immediately after an overwhelming disturbance. Many complex control systems are sluggish, but only because any faster action would lead to dynamic instability. The appearance of "working toward" a goal may result from nothing more than our viewing the system on an inappropriately fast time scale.

It is useful to separate *what* a control system does from *how* it does what it does. Given two control systems controlling the same quantity with respect to the same reference signal, one system might be able to resist disturbances lasting only 0.1 second while the other could not oppose a disturbance lasting less than 1 second. After a disturbance, one system might restore its error signal nearly to zero in one swift move, while the other makes that correction slowly and after several over- and undershoots of the final steady-state condition. These are dynamic differences, and have to do with the details of system design. Both systems, however, do the same thing when viewed on a slow enough time scale: they control a given quantity, opposing disturbances tending to affect that quantity. On a time scale where we can see one system "working toward" the goal state, we might see the other as never allowing significant error to occur—as reacting simultaneously with the disturbance to cancel its effects.

The proper time scale for observing what a control system does is that on which the response to an impulse-disturbance is apparently zero. That automatically restricts our observations of disturbances in the same way: all disturbances appear to be slow. On such a slow time scale, it is apparent that a control system keeps its sensor signal nearly matching its reference signal by producing outputs equal and opposite to disturbances, in terms of effects on the controlled quantity.

The normal behavior of a good control system, viewed on the appropriate time scale, is therefore not goal-seeking behavior but goal-maintaining behavior. The sensor signal is maintained in a particular goal state as long as the system is operating within its normal range, in the environment to which its organization is matched. If the properties of the sensor do not change, this control action results in the external controlled quantity being maintained in a state we may term its reference level.

Much of what we interpret as a long process of goal-seeking (and perhaps all) can be shown to result from higher-order goal maintenance that involves a program of shifting lower-order reference levels, but that anticipates what has yet to be developed here.

Controlled Quantities

The key concept in this model, as far as observable behavior is concerned, is that of the controlled quantity. If it were possible to identify a controlled quantity and its apparent reference level, the model just given would provide an adequate physical explanation for existence of this quantity and its goal state, just as the telephone-switchboard model of the brain has heretofore been taken as an adequate physical explanation for stimulus-response phenomena. To be sure, the source of the reference signal that sets the system's goal remains unspecified, but that is of no consequence in a part-model of a specific behavior pattern. We are concerned here with immediate causation, not ultimate causes.

If a quantity is under feedback control by some control system, that fact can be discovered by a simple (in principle) procedure, based on the fact that the system will oppose disturbances of the controlled quantity.

Suppose we can observe the immediate environment of a control system in terms of detailed physical variables $(v_1, v_2, \ldots v_n)$. We postulate a controlled quantity $q_c = f(v_1, v_2, \ldots v_n)$, where f is a function of the variables. According to the definition and known physical principles, we can then devise a small disturbance d affecting some v's such that (in the absence of behavioral effects) $\triangle q_c = g(d)$, where g is the function describing the environmental connection between the disturbance and the controlled quantity. Applying the disturbance we predict a change in q_c, and compare it with the observed change, $\triangle^* q_c$. If we have hit upon a definition of q_c that is accurate, and if a reasonably good control system is acting, we will find $\triangle^* q_c / \triangle q_c \ll 1$.

By progressively changing the definition of q_c [that is, the form of f in $f(v_1, v_2, \ldots v_n)$], we can find a minimum in the ratio $\triangle^* q_c / \triangle q_c$; that is, we can find a definition of the controlled quantity such that the observed effect of a disturbance is far less than the effect predicted according to physical principles, omitting the behavior of the system.

The reason for the "failure" of the prediction is of course the fact that the control system actively opposes effects of d on q_c. Let h be the function describing the environmental connection between the output o of the system and the controlled quantity. If the output o affects q_c additively according to the relationship $\triangle q_c = h(o)$, then the total effect on q_c is the sum of the effects of the disturbance and the system's active output: $\triangle q_c \cong g(d) + h(o)$. When control is good, this sum will be nearly zero.

Defining the zero points of the controlled quantity and the system's output as their undisturbed values, we can see that the controlled quantity will remain nearly at its zero point ($\triangle q_c \approx 0$), while the disturbance and the system's output will be related by the approximation, $g(d) \approx - h(o)$.

Here is a very simple example. Suppose we observe a soldier at attention, and guess that one controlled quantity involved in his behavior is the vertical orientation of one of his arms, seemingly being held in a straight-down position (the zero point). If this quantity were not under active control, we could predict that a sideways force of 1 kilogram would raise the arm to about a 30-degree angle from the vertical. Applying the force, we observe that in fact the arm moves only 1 degree, or 1/30 of the predicted amount. The effective force-output of the soldier is thus just a trifle under 1 kilogram in a direction opposite to our 1-kilogram disturbance, the trifle being the restoring force due to the slightly deflected mass of the arm, and gravity. This is a reasonable verification of the initial guess, and we may claim to have found a control system in the soldier by identifying its controlled quantity.

The reference level of a controlled quantity can better be defined as its value when the system's output is totally unopposed (even by friction or gravity). Because that state normally implies no error-correcting output, the reference level of the controlled quantity can also be defined as that level (state, for multidimensional quantities) which results in zero error-correcting output.

A controlled quantity need not have a reference level of zero. The soldier, for example, might be persuaded to raise his arm to the horizontal position, so that in the same coordinate system used before, the apparent reference position is now 90 degrees. The weight of the arm now constitutes a natural disturbance, and we would guess that the system's output is now equivalent to an upward force equal to the weight of the arm. If that force were 10 kilograms, we would also predict that an upward force disturbance of 10 kilograms would cause the arm muscles to relax completely, or at least that the net force-output would drop to zero (arm muscles can oppose one another). Our pushing upward with a force of 11 kilograms should result in an output of ½ kilogram downward.

Hierarchies of Controlled Quantities

Suppose that the soldier is now ordered to point at a passing helicopter. He will raise his arm and do so. We can verify that arm position is still a controlled quantity by applying force-disturbances, but now the picture is complicated. The test still works for relatively brief (but not too brief) disturbances, but over a period of some seconds we find that arm position does not remain constant. Instead, it moves slowly and uniformly upward and sideways, as the helicopter approaches.

This suggests that a second controlled quantity has entered the picture. If the helicopter stops and hovers, this new controlled quantity is invisible—the force-test cannot distinguish it, for the arm simply remains almost still as before. But if we radio the helicopter pilot to move his craft in various ways, we can test the hypothesis that the soldier is controlling the angular deviation of his pointing direction from his actual line of sight to the helicopter. If that were not a controlled quantity, the pilot's moving the helicopter would create a predictable deviation. In fact, movement of the helicopter results in no observable deviation at all (barring slight tremors). We are reasonably assured that the pointing direction relative to the direction of the helicopter (and nothing else) is a two-dimensional controlled quantity, with a reference level of zero deviation.

Now we have a slight dilemma. We established, and could reestablish at any time, arm position as a controlled quantity. (The position-control system will react to disturbances within the lag time of the pointing-control system.) Yet control of the new controlled quantity requires a change in arm position, which would constitute a disturbance of the first system. Why does the first control system not resist this change?

The answer is obvious. The second control system opposes disturbances not by direct activation of force outputs, but by altering the reference level, by means of changing the reference signal for the arm-position control system.

Now two controlled quantities (and implied control systems) exist in a relationship that is clearly hierarchical. One controlled quantity is controlled by means of changing the reference level with respect to which a second quantity is controlled.

This immediately suggests a partial answer to the question raised by Fig. 1: Where does the reference signal come from? It is clearly the output of a higher-order control system, a system that senses a different kind of quantity and controls it with respect to an appropriate reference signal by using the whole lower-order system as its means of error prevention (the appropriate time scale for the higher-order system will be slower than that for the lower).

We now have a plausible physical model for a two-level structure of goals. The goal of pointing is achieved by setting—and altering—a goal for arm position. In fact the higher-order system must adjust reference levels for two lower-order control systems, one governing horizontal arm position and one governing vertical arm position: both can be shown to be under feedback control. Of course we do not know yet the actual nature of the lower-order systems—any two noncollinear directions of control would give the same observed results. But we have achieved a first approximation.

The source of the lower-level reference signals has been identified but the question of the ultimate source of reference signals has simply been pushed up a level. The range of explanation for immediate causes, however, has been considerably extended.

This hierarchical analysis of behavior can now be continued indefinitely, the only restriction on the number of levels being that imposed by experimental findings. The model of the brain's organization (for that is what it is) can be extended accordingly. Each time a new level of control is found, the range of explanations of immediate causes of behavior is extended to cover more kinds of behavior and to span longer periods of time. Each such extension redefines the question of ultimate causes, for each new level of reference signals represents goals of greater generality.

Our going up a level in this analysis is equivalent to our asking what purpose is served by achievement of a given set of lower-order goals: *why* is the man doing that? Why does the soldier raise his arm? In order to point at the helicopter. Why does he point at the helicopter? Perhaps—we would have to verify this guess by test—perhaps to comply with an order. And why comply with an order . . .?

Going down a level is equivalent to asking *how*. How must the man behave in order to point? He must control his arm position. How must he behave in order to control arm position? He must control net muscle-generated forces. And the chain extends further down, to the control systems in the spine which control the effort in whole muscles, as sensed kinesthetically. Each level must be verified by finding a way of disturbing the controlled quantity without affecting lower-order quantities.

Oddly enough, behaviorists may have already found the answer to the ultimate *why* at the top level of this model. Why are the highest-order behavioral goals set where they are set? In order to control certain biologically important variables, which Ashby called critical variables and which I term intrinsic quantities. These are the quantities affected by deprivation and subsequent reinforcements that erase, or at least diminish, the errors caused by deprivation. This makes the highest order of reference levels into those extremely generalized ones that are inherited as the basic conditions for survival. But that takes us to the verge of learning theory, which is beyond the intent of this article. Briefly, I view the process of reorganization itself as the error-driven "output" of a basic inherited control system which is ultimately responsible for the particular structure of an adult's behavioral control system (8). For a human being, the "intrinsic reference levels" probably specify far more than mere food or water intake. We cannot arbitrarily rule out any goal at this level—not even goals such as "self-actualization."

Implications for Behaviorism

The most important implication of this analysis for the traditional view of cause and effect in behavior lies in the fact that control systems control what they *sense*, not really what they *do*. In the total absence of disturbances, a control system hardly needs to do anything in order to keep a controlled quantity at a reference level, even a changing reference level. By far the largest portion of output effort is reserved for opposing disturbances.

This is expressed in the approximate relationship, $g(d) \cong -h(o)$. Because of the way negative feedback control systems are organized, the system's output is caused to vary in almost exact opposition to the effects of disturbances—the chief determinant of output is thus the disturbance. If we read "stimulus" for disturbance and "response" for some measure of output, stimulus-response phenomena fall into place within the feedback model.

Stimuli do cause responses. If one knew the controlled quantity associated with a given stimulus-response pair, one would see more regularity in the relationship, not less. In fact one would see an exact quantitative relationship, for the effects of the response on the controlled quantity must come close to canceling the effects of the stimulus on that same quantity, and both these effects are mediated through the environment, where the detailed physical relationships can be seen. That implies, of course, that given knowledge of the controlled quantity one can deduce the form of stimulus-response relationships from physical, not behavioral laws (9).

Knowledge of the controlled quantity makes the stimulus-response relationship even clearer by pointing out the right response measure and the right measure of the disturbance, or stimulus. An organism's muscle efforts produce many consequent effects, no one of which can be chosen on the basis of behavioristic principles as being a "better" measure than any other. A stimulus event impinges on an organism and its surroundings in many ways and via many paths, again undistinguishable under the philosophy of behaviorism. Knowledge of the controlled quantity eliminates irrelevant measures of stimulus and response.

Let us consider a rat in a Skinner box. The rat responds to a light by pressing a lever for food. Whatever the immediate controlled quantity may be, it is clearly not affected by the current that flows to the apparatus when the lever is depressed: opening the circuit will not in any way alter the rat's next press of the lever. But holding the rat back with a drag-harness as it moves toward the lever would create immediate forward-pushing efforts, so we would know that the rat's "motion" is close to a controlled quantity. We would of course try to do better than that.

Even though the current to the experimental apparatus does affect the appearance of food, which is quite likely to be a controlled quantity (q_c), the current is still not a controlled quantity, for we could leave the circuit open and actuate the food dispenser in a different way, and the rat would still do nothing in opposition, nothing to restore the current. There is no need to assume what is controlled except as a starting hypothesis, and this method can disprove wrong hypotheses.

The irrelevance of some stimulus measures is common knowledge; rats, for instance, have been found to respond quite well to a burned-out stimulus light, provided that the actuating relay still clicked loudly enough.

Systematic experimental definition of controlled quantities will eliminate irrelevant side effects of stimuli and responses from consideration. But it will also negate the significance of most stimulus-response laws, for once a controlled quantity has been identified reasonably well, a whole family of stimulus-response laws becomes trivially predictable. Once it is known why a given response follows a given stimulus, further examples become redundant. Knowing why means knowing what is being controlled, and knowing the reference level.

When a controlled quantity is found, variability of behavior is drastically lowered, simply because one no longer considers irrelevant details. The remaining variability is lowered even further as one explores the hierarchy of controlled quantities. If all we observed about the soldier in the example were his force outputs, we would have to fall back on statistics to predict them. If we then understood that the soldier was using these outputs to control arm position we could find many cases in which there would be scarcely any variability; applying the correct stimuli (forces) would result in quantitatively predictable force outputs. There would still be many unpredicted changes, but a good fraction of those would become precisely predictable if we understood that the soldier was using his arm position in order to point at a specific moving object. Of course as we push toward higher and higher orders of control organization we will find more complex systems employing many lower-order systems at once so that prediction depends on our determining which of several apparently equivalent subsystems will be employed. In principle, however, we can become as thoroughly acquainted with one individual's structure of controlled quantities as we please, if cooperation continues to satisfy his higher-order goals.

Control systems, or organisms, control what they sense. The application of a disturbing stimulus does not affect for long what matters to the organism at the same level as the disturbance, because the organism will alter its lower-order goals in such a way as to cancel the effects of the disturbance. If a position disturbance is applied, the organism will alter its force goals and prevent disturbance of position. If a relative position disturbance (movement of the helicopter) is applied, the organism will alter its absolute position goals and prevent disturbance of relative position.

In this way the system continues to oppose disturbances, making adjustments at every level in the hierarchy of control. The organism will not let *you* (the experimenter) alter what it senses (if it can prevent it), but it will without hesitation alter the very same quantity itself in order to prevent the experimenter's disturbing a higher-order controlled quantity. Hence the well-known perversity of experimental subjects!

It is this hierarchical character of control systems that makes it seem that organisms value self-determinism. And that is not only appearance: organisms are self-determined in terms of inner control of what they sense, at every level of organization except the highest level.

Only overwhelming force or insuperable obstacles can cause an organism to give up control of what it senses, and that is true at every level. In order to achieve ultimate control over behavior, one must obtain the power to deprive the organism of something its genes tell it it must have, and make restoration contingent on the organism's setting particular goals in the hierarchy of learned systems, or even on acquiring new control systems. But one attempts that at risk. Human beings are more prone to learn how to circumvent arbitrary deprivation than they are to knuckle under and do what someone else demands in order to correct intrinsic error. In the sequence deprive, reward, deprive, reward . . ., one person may see the reward as terminating deprivation, but that is only a matter of perceptual grouping. Another person may learn that reward leads to deprivation, and take appropriate action against the cause of deprivation. Pigeons in Skinner boxes, of course, do not have that option.

Summary

Consistent behavior patterns are created by variable acts, and generally repeat only because detailed acts change. The accepted explanation of this paradox, that "cues" cause the changes, is irrelevant; it is unsupported by evidence, and incapable of dealing with novel situations.

The apparent purposefulness of variations of behavioral acts can be accepted as fact in the framework of a control-system model of behavior. A control system, properly organized for its environment, will produce whatever output is required in order to achieve a constant sensed result, even in the presence of unpredictable disturbances. A control-system model of the brain provides a physical explanation for the existence of goals or purposes, and shows that behavior is the control of input, not output.

A systematic investigation of controlled quantities can reveal an organism's structure of control systems. The structure is hierarchical, in that some quantities are controlled as the means for controlling higher-order quantities. The output of a higher-order system is not a muscle force, but a reference level (variable) for a lower-order controlled quantity. The highest-order reference levels are inherited and are associated with the meta-behavior termed reorganization.

When controlled quantities are discovered, the related stimulus-response laws become trivially predictable. Variability of behavior all but disappears once controlled quantities are known. Behavior itself is seen in terms of this model to be self-determined in a specific and highly significant sense that calls into serious doubt the ultimate feasibility of operant conditioning of human beings by other human beings.

REFERENCES AND NOTES

1. L. VON BERTALANFFY, in *Toward Unification in Psychology*, J. R. Royce, Ed. (Univ. of Toronto Press, Toronto, 1970), p. 40.
2. W. T. POWERS, *Behavior: The Control of Perception* (Aldine, Chicago, in press).
3. This distinction is akin to the older distinction between movement and action, the more recent distinctions between molecular and molar, or proximal and distal aspects of behavior. What I term an *act* is a behavior that is arbitrarily left unanalyzed, while a *result* is defined as an understandable physical consequence of an act. Act and result are relative terms, whereas those they replace are absolute. In some circumstances it may be appropriate to consider a movement as a result, in which case the *acts* would be the tensing of muscles. What is proximal or molecular at one level of analysis may be distal or molar at another level. "Distal achievement," in this feedback theory, becomes *perceptual* achievement, and is multiordinate.
4. W. W. ROZEBOOM, in *Toward Unification in Psychology*, J. R. Royce, Ed. (Univ. of Toronto Press, Toronto, 1970), p. 141.
5. E. BRUNSWIK, *The Conceptual Framework of Psychology* (Univ. of Chicago Press, Chicago, 1952).
6. N. WIENER, *Cybernetics: Control and Communication in the Animal and the Machine* (Wiley, New York, 1948).
7. W. R. ASHBY, *Design for a Brain* (Wiley, New York, 1952).
8. W. POWERS, R. K. CLARK, R. L. MACFARLAND, "A General Feedback Theory of Human Behavior," in *General Systems—Yearbook of the Society for General Systems Research 1960*, L. von Bertalanffy, Ed. (Society for General Systems Research, Ann Arbor, Mich., 1960), pp. 63–83.
9. W. T. Powers, *Behav. Sci.*, **16**, 588 (1971).
10. This article is adapted from a series of lectures given at a faculty seminar on "Foundations of Science," held at Northwestern University, 1971.

TOWARD UNIFICATION

THIS *final section of the book attacks the tough, persistent issue of how best to unite the divided discipline of psychology. Focusing the subject matter of our discipline on three different levels of data has created this troublesome and enduring issue. Psychology has been and remains segmented in both subject matter and method. Probably the easiest and most frequently attempted resolution of this problem is exclusion. For example, Titchener rejected all data other than those pertaining to experience, and some contemporary neobehaviorists give similar priority to overt response. Another solution, somewhat broader and almost as popular, has been subsumption (usually called reduction when the movement is toward physiology). A behaviorist might subsume all the data about experience or physiology by defending the view that such data are always given in terms of verbal reports or instrument readings. Conversely, those fixed on the experiential level have defended the priority of their data by arguing that all reactions, whether by an organism or a machine, must be represented sooner or later in the experience of the observer. Those of physiological bent are not outdone. They have maintained, and still maintain, that unless one believes in spirits or empty organisms, every thought and action must be centered in some biological process. Still another solution has been inclusion. In the opening paper of this division, for example, Goodson and Morgan defended the view that the task of psychology is to determine how the organism works and that including data from all three levels is necessary if this goal is to be achieved.*

Efforts to cope with the troublesome issue of psychology's tripartite subject matter are varied and ingenious, as the following selections show. In the first selection, by Salzinger, the contributions of cognitive psychology and phenomenology are evaluated and avenues are suggested for rapprochement with behaviorism. In the next paper, Day suggests that the separation that exists between radical behaviorism (Skinnerian psychology) and phenomenology may be largely due to misconceptions and that a rapprochement is not only desirable but possible, because complementary avenues of research and discourse are implicit in both positions. In the final selection, Kendler analyzes the problems of reduction as they pertain to the three levels of psychological data and presents some thoughtful suggestions concerning the essential unity of psychology.

43

COGNITION AS A UNIFYING CONCEPT[1]

Kurt Salzinger[2]

Is it true what they say about us behaviorists? Do we really believe that looking inside the organism is like opening Pandora's box? According to the myth, Pandora received a gift from Zeus. The gift was a box containing all the ills of humankind. When Pandora opened it, she released all the ills and in doing so supplied us with an early explanation of human behavior. I think it would be well to point out right at the start that even if John B. Watson suffered from a Pandora's-box complex, contemporary behaviorists have long ago peered inside with no ill effects at all. Even Watson himself was very much interested in proprioception, a form of stimulation that is certainly inside the organism. Behavioral research has not only theorized about stimuli inside the organism (e.g., Schoenfeld and Cumming, 1963; Skinner, 1945, 1953, 1957) but has produced a good deal of exciting experimental work (Jacobs and Sachs, 1971; Kendler, 1971; McGuigan, 1966; N. E. Miller, 1969; Razran, 1971).

I have two objectives in writing this paper. The first is to acquaint those of us of a behavioristic persuasion with some of the theories, concepts, and data of cognitive psychology; the second is to show how radical behaviorism's concepts can address themselves to the problems that our cognitive psychologist colleagues have (temporarily) sequestered unto themselves.

The Cognitive Point of View

Cognitive psychologists believe that a behavioristic approach to psychology is grossly inadequate and too confining. Even Neisser (1967), who largely ignored the behavioristic literature, made some negative remarks about the approach. A mere generation ago, he tells us, "a book

[1] A review of Ulric Neisser's *Cognitive Psychology* (New York: Appleton-Century-Crofts, 1967).

[2] The author wishes to thank Suzanne Salzinger and Richard S. Feldman for their comments on this manuscript. He is also grateful to Joseph Zubin, who has provided the environment in which the writing of such papers is fostered. The writing of this paper was supported in part by NIMH Grant HD 04516 and a General Research Support Grant from the New York State Psychiatric Institute.

FROM K. Salzinger, Inside the black box, with apologies to Pandora. A review of Ulric Neisser's *Cognitive psychology*. *Journal of the Experimental Analysis of Behavior*, 1973, 19, 369–378. Copyright 1973 by the Society for the Experimental Analysis of Behavior, Inc.

like this one would have needed at least a chapter of self-defense against the behaviorist position" (p. 5); now, apparently, it suffices to point out that radical behaviorists eschew categories, images, and ideas. Segal and Lachman (1972), in agreement with Neisser, spoke of the "demise" of behaviorism, its weakening, or its metamorphosis into neo- or non-behaviorism. In an introduction to a symposium on cognition and affect, Antrobus (1970) claimed that radical behaviorists have given up the study of cognition. He went on to say that while some psychologists were content with the achievements of radical behaviorism (and he admits these achievements), there are "others whose curiosity can be contained neither by epistemological constraints nor by the achievements of radical behaviorism . . . they wish to know what internal events produce 'spontaneous' behavior in the absence of any particular external stimulus. What are the internal processes that make it possible for an individual to perceive, speak, think, recall, and dream?" (Antrobus, 1970, p. 2).

Cognitive psychologists talk about two kinds of "internal" events when they reach into Pandora's box. The first is an internal *stimulus*. No behaviorist, contrary to what some cognitivists think, objects to the search for a real stimulus, no matter where it is. The second type of internal event, however, is quite different. It constitutes an answer to such questions as: What happens to the stimulus after it comes to the subject? How is it changed? How is it stored? Both the external initiating stimuli and the external responses are events that cognitivists tolerate because they are the ones that they measure; nevertheless, they would just as soon do without them. It is the second kind of internal event to which behaviorists object. Neisser (1967) called our attention to this kind of internal event in his definition of cognition: it "refers to all the processes by which the sensory input is transformed, reduced, elaborated, stored, recovered, and used. It is concerned with those processes even when they operate in the absence of relevant stimulation, as in images and hallucinations. Such terms as *sensation, perception, imagery, retention, recall, problem-solving,* and *thinking,* among many others, refer to hypothetical stages or aspects of cognition" (p. 4, author's italics). The confrontation between cognitive psychology and behaviorism is clear, for the italicized words are the ones that Skinner has for years avoided as hypothetical constructs. The question to which we will address ourselves is whether behaviorism can, by shunning these terms, still study the substantive area that is of interest to cognitivists. Even though the cognitivist professes an interest in structure and the behaviorist in functional relationships, both approaches try to account for all of behavior.

One final point by way of introduction. Why are we talking about the myths of yesteryear? Did we not show the bankruptcy of the Gestalt approach to psychology many years ago? Is there really anyone who would like to revive the confusion of introspectionism? The answer is that the cognitivist approach is no more the same as the Gestalt approach or introspectionism than the radical behaviorist approach is the same as Watson's. In both cases we are discussing only the predecessors of current thinking. In the same way that Neisser feels uncomfortable with the Gestalt concepts of the template and the memory trace, which suggest a copying process of the stimulus, behaviorists reject Watson's idea of the verbal report because it invests speech with a superior status, derived from the special entree it has to information that is somehow barred to nonverbal behavior. The present paper will not only point out those current aspects of cognition and behaviorism that are in direct conflict with one another, but it will also list some of the views that are no longer held.

Neisser speaks of construction as the central concept of his cognitive approach. "Perception is not a passive taking-in of stimuli, but an active process of synthesizing or constructing a visual figure" (Neisser, 1967, p. 16). He compares perception to the activity of the paleontologist who "extracts a few fragments of what might be bones from a mass of irrelevant rubble and 'reconstructs' the dinosaur" (p. 94). Essentially, Neisser proposes a theory of stimulus input → (analysis-by-synthesis) → response output, and although he admits that it is "little more than a metaphor," he justifies this approach by insisting that "a man who sees things that are not present must be constructing them for himself" (p. 95). In explanation, interestingly enough, Neisser rejects as quite naive the notion that a precise replica of the stimulus is stored inside the subject, but insists, nevertheless, that the information of the stimulus is stored and then constructed or reconstructed to give rise to perception, hallucinations, or remembering. The problem, however, stems not from the way the stimulus is followed inside the organism (although the proof or disproof of its travels is not immediately obvious) but rather from an incomplete analysis of the term "see." Skinner (e.g., 1945, 1953) has often stated that such responses must be analyzed in terms of the stimuli (and there are many) that determine them. To take the term "see" as an example, an observer will require a relatively long time to recognize an individual who is transposed into a new context consisting of different clothing or of an environment in which he had not previously been encountered. This is a case in which some of the usual supporting stimuli, or parts of the original compound stimulus, are absent, resulting in a reduction of the response strength of "seeing." On the other hand, an observer will also "see" a person he has been waiting for, at some appointed time and place, who has not actually arrived. This is a case where a few strong stimuli (the fact of the appointment, experience with the person in the past coming on time, etc.) in conjunction with other parts of the compound (general appearance of the individual) produces a response we would not ordinarily call "seeing."

Neisser discusses this term with respect to Goldiamond and Hawkins's (1958) experiment. They produced "seeing" by presenting a number of strong discriminative associated but not principal stimuli. Before the experiment, subjects were given a number of nonsense syllables to read and it was explained that they would be presented again later for very brief exposure times; during the experiment only smudges were presented at high speed, to which subjects responded as if they were nonsense syllables. Goldiamond and Hawkins concluded that the typical perception experiments contained response biases reflecting the observer's tendency of *saying* rather than *seeing*, since in their own "non-stimulus" procedure "seeing" responses occurred quite regularly. I agree with Neisser in so far as he objects to separating saying from seeing. I prefer to consider saying as controlled by a continuum of stimuli. Although the retinal image is an important stimulus in determining what we "see," we often "see" in its absence. On the other hand, I disagree with Neisser's calling all "seeing" responses perception; "seeing" is simply a response under the control of *various* stimuli. If given a choice, I would prefer the term "saying" under varying conditions of stimulus control to "seeing" with varying degrees of justification.

Neisser explains visual imagery as follows: "My own usage will be as follows: 'visual image' is a partly undefined term for something *seen* somewhat in the way real objects are seen, when little or nothing in the immediate or very recent sensory input appears to justify it" (Neisser, 1967, p. 146). You have an image when you count the number of windows in your apartment or house without looking at it, or, for that matter, when you remember on what part of a page a certain bit of information can be located. Neisser cites the work of Antrobus, Antrobus, and Singer (1964) to show the importance of various motor components of "seeing" to explain images. In that experiment, more eye movements accompanied a subject's imagining an active (e.g., tennis) than a passive (e.g., an illuminated face in a darkened room) scene. With respect to dream imagery, Roffwarg, Dement, Muzio, and Fisher (1962) were able to match the dream content to the rapid eye movements measured while the dream took place. Thus, we have a relationship between the subject's motor activity component (response-produced stimuli) of seeing and what he "sees." Neisser summarizes (p. 153): "Visual synthesis of an image without eye motion may be possible, but the better the image the more likely it is to involve some sort of scanning." Then, having said that, he goes on to explain that the image is not merely motoric; it is also visual.

Neisser also rejects the notion that the brain stores a permanent record (a replica) of what the brain owner perceives; unlike Penfield, he views the electrical stimulation of the cortex as a way of producing what he calls perceptual synthesis. For Neisser, there are operations of synthesis that make use of the *information*, which is what is stored in the brain— always construction or synthesis.

In one very important sense the behaviorist agrees with this view: a stimulus does not become incorporated into the organism. It controls the organism's behavior. The organism neither copies nor categorizes the stimulus; it merely responds. Stimuli vary from time to time and because of the various effects of repeated stimulation (habituation, learning, extinction, etc.), even when the same stimulus occurs, early stimulation differs from stimulation that follows it. This implies that the same response may be evoked in different strengths or that altogether different responses may be evoked by stimuli that the organism experienced a different number of times.

The idea of construction is also forcefully brought to our attention in the context of verbal behavior. Psycholinguists, a large group of whom form a significant subset of cognitivists, invoke some sort of construction process to explain how one individual understands the speech of another. The most important adherents to an analysis-by-synthesis theory in speech are members of the Haskins laboratory. This group of investigators (e.g., Liberman, Harris, Hoffman, and Griffith, 1957) found that, unlike the judgments of other physical stimuli, which vary gradually over the entire sensed continuum, the judgments of phonemes change abruptly from one to another in a categorical manner. The Haskins group concluded that since the acoustic cues are inadequate to explain how an individual perceives speech, and since its perception is categorical (that is, various stimuli either are or are not members of a particular category), the perception of speech must take place with reference to articulation. In other words, when a subject hears a sound, he discriminates it from another one by matching it to the way he would produce such a sound. Since there are many obvious situations where a hearer could not do this fast enough, the Haskins group modified their theory to say that the matching takes place with respect to neuromotor commands rather than with reference to actual movements. They further bolster this theory by pointing to the greater efficiency (and parsimony) of having one mechanism to explain both the production and the perception of speech.

A number of investigators have criticized this theory. Lane (1965, 1967) suggested that the categorical perception phenomenon is not necessarily restricted to speech but relates to the type of conditioning paradigm involved in the learning of speech. When two stimuli are selected from a physical continuum and are made discriminative stimuli for two different responses, the same kind of abrupt change occurs from one stimulus to another, as is found in speech sounds. Studdert-Kennedy, Liberman, Harris, and Cooper (1970), however, were unable to produce categorical perception by a conditioning paradigm. In contrast, Kopp and Udin (1969) were successful in replicating Lane's procedure for the labelling of pure tones varying in frequency, while Pisoni (1971) concluded that the effectiveness of such training appears to vary from subject to subject.

Another interesting criticism of the motor theory of perception is contained in a paper by MacNeilage (1970). He rejected the theory because it would take at least 17,000 different motor commands to emit the phonemes, since their utterance differs not only with respect to identity but also as a function of which phoneme precedes and which follows it; and that omits such further common variations in speaking as stress, speaking rate, and segmenting. Instead of motor commands to explain speech production, he suggests an "internal specification of certain spatial targets." The metaphor is tennis: an individual's response depends on where he tries to direct the ball. Of interest to behaviorists is the fact that this kind of response specification is the way in which responses are commonly grouped, that is, in terms of their common effect on the environment (Salzinger, 1967). It suggests that perception of speech precedes its production; otherwise the effects would not control the responses. In any case, it contradicts Neisser's analysis-by-synthesis idea for speech.

But Neisser bases his construction interpretation of speech perception on other evidence as well. That evidence is based on Chomsky's (1957) transformation grammar, which made its first bow in linguistics and subsequently took over the fledgling field of psycholinguistics. Neisser begins his discussion of psycholinguistics by speaking of the "irrepressible novelty" of verbal behavior. Like Chomsky, he maintains that the uniqueness of sentences is characteristic of verbal behavior.

To explain the regularity of speech, he relies on structural rules for the formation of sentences. Such structural rules relate to the problem of ambiguity as well. In order to interpret an ambiguous sentence such as, "They are eating apples," the generative grammarian psycholinguist insists that you must know its structure. In one structure the word "eating" is an adjective; in another, it is a verb. Diagrammatic analysis makes clear that these two structures are possible. It is known as phrase structure analysis and it describes the surface structure of utterances. However, there are sentences that cannot be understood without delving into the "deeper structure." Thus, they also posit a common deep structure, such as the one underlying all of these sentences: "He appreciated Chomsky's theory." "Chomsky's theory was appreciated by him." "He did not appreciate Chomsky's theory." "Did he appreciate Chomsky's theory?" "Didn't he appreciate Chomsky's theory?" "Wasn't Chomsky's theory appreciated by him?"

Miller (1962) summarized data in support of the notion that a listener recorded the basic kernel (best approximated by the simple declarative sentence of these various sentences) with a footnote as to how to transform it into the particular sentence that he heard. Those sentences that took a larger number of transformations, such as the passive negative question, resulted in the greatest distortion in memory because they ostensibly required the largest number of footnotes. Some psycholinguists have even suggested that such structures are built into the brain of the speaker/hearer so that the simpler structures always result in easier comprehension and better recall than the more complex structures. Following Chomsky, they have maintained that the grammatical structure has nothing to do with the meaning of sentences; the two aspects of verbal behavior were said to be independent of one another.

The behaviorist takes a different approach to the problem of ambiguity. To begin with, ambiguity in normal conversation is probably quite rare. Note, we are not saying that misunderstanding is rare; it is relatively frequent. But under normal circumstances the stimuli surrounding the emission of speech generally ensure that any sentence will lead to a particular response on the part of a hearer; the response itself is made without uncertainty, even though the hearer's interpretation may well be wrong. Exceptions occur when ambiguity is purposefully employed to befuddle or amuse the audience, which is probably why ambiguity is maintained in the language rather than becoming extinguished. It sometimes pays to be ambiguous; thus, one can insult an individual without incurring the consequences of his wrath, since such sentences are weak discriminative stimuli for responses that are aversive to the speaker.

The two explanations for ambiguity bring up the controversy over Chomsky's contention that knowledge of grammatical structure is sufficient, without meaning, for understanding sentences. To test Chomsky's idea of the independence of grammar and meaning, Salzinger and Eckerman (1967) constructed the simplest kind of sentences (simple, active declarative sentences) and much more complicated ones (passive negative questions) out of nonsense syllables and function words and tested for differences in recall. An example of the simple declarative sentence in the active mood was: "And the piqy kews were beboving the nazer zumaps dygly." An example of the same sentence in the passive negative question form was: "Weren't the nazer zumaps dygly beboved by the piqy kews?" Each of the forms was also represented in a random order; various groups of comparable subjects were given the opportunity to learn two different sentences in the same form.

The results showed a number of significant differences. The function words (e.g., by, the) were more easily recalled than were the nonsense words; sentences were more easily recalled than random arrays of items; and the second sentence that a subject learned was more easily recalled than the first. In contrast, differences due to grammatical structure, that is, differences between the simple declarative sentence and the more complicated one, failed to emerge. Furthermore, the small, statistically nonsignificant difference due to sentence types, that existed for the first sentence, vanished entirely for the second sentence of the same type. Finally, the small difference that existed for the first sentence expressed itself only in the *randomly* ordered strings, rather than in the "correctly" ordered sentences.

The results are rather clear. Subjects recalled better those kinds of strings of verbal items to which they had more frequently been exposed.

Thus, although there was a tendency for the simple declarative sentence in the active mood to be more easily recalled than the passive negative question (a difference probably reflecting relative frequency of exposure and/or emission), this difference quickly disappeared after a few trials of learning (in which frequency of exposure of the initially infrequent sentence type was increased). Surely this cannot reflect an *innate* structure that forces a subject to recall material in terms of a kernel sentence plus some notation on the number of transformations needed to produce the sentence form required. The more parsimonious interpretation, that differences among sentences varying in "structure" merely reflect a difference in frequency of exposure, is much more cogent. The question as to why some sentence structures do in the first place occur less frequently than others can also be answered in terms of known psychological principles from behavior theory, without having to turn back to innate ideas.

Cognitivists believe that language is "structured." Neisser presents it as an obvious case of analysis-by-synthesis. How else, he asks, can we understand so-called embedded structures? "The man who came to dinner is a friend of mine." Here the words "is a friend of mine" must not be uttered until the intervening verbal behavior "who came to dinner" has been emitted. The generative grammarians tell us that in language one can increase the amount of embedded material indefinitely (if only it weren't for man's limited memory). This kind of approach neglects the importance of the consequences of behavior. If what we said made us forget how we began to say it, the consequence would be an absence of positive reinforcement (such as getting what we were asking for, or, for that matter, merely retaining the hearer's attention) and extinction of such behavior.

Neisser also treats the complex problems of memory and thought. He begins by rejecting what he calls the Reappearance Hypothesis. It states that a memory can be locked up inside the organism and produced at a later time as needed. As a substitute for it he suggests the Utilization Hypothesis, according to which remembering takes place "after an elaborate process of *re*construction" (Neisser, 1967, p. 285, author's italics). The person who recalls does so by using the "traces of *prior processes of construction*" (p. 285). This, it should be noted again, is an active process that Neisser places inside the organism.

The criticism is obvious. Where is the locus of control for such an internal process? In fact, the question of control is not answered by such models, merely postponed—or, if the theoretician is clever enough, quite obscured. Let me say immediately that Neisser is aware of the problems involved. He admits that a *homunculus* is "unpalatable," but then he adds that it cannot be avoided. "If we do *not* postulate some agent who selects and uses the stored information, we must think of every thought and every response as just the momentary resultant of an interacting system, governed essentially by laissez-faire economics" (p. 293).

Neisser then posits two stages of remembering: one he calls "primary process," a sort of crude process, and one he calls "secondary process," which includes an active agent within the organism that manipulates the information toward some end. This active agent is analogous to the executive routines of the computer. The executive decides which subroutines to use, but it is not itself used by any other higher executive. Apparently what Neisser means by this secondary process is the way the built-in capacities of the organism respond to the environment. Finally, at the end of his book, Neisser expresses regret that cognitive psychology is after all incomplete. It cannot take into account motivation. "However, the course of thinking or of 'inner-directed' activity is determined at every moment by what the subject is trying to do. Although we cannot always see only what we want to see, we can generally think what we like" (Neisser, 1967, p. 305). Free will is simply taken for granted.

The Behaviorist Answer

So much for the first objective of my paper. I have tried to present some of the leading ideas in cognitive psychology, at least as viewed by a leader in that field. Along the way I could not entirely refrain from commenting or even arguing against some of the concepts. Now I will try to deal with the cognitive *versus* behavioristic approaches in a more general way.

First, it is important to understand what behaviorism is willing to include and what it insists on excluding in its approach. Cognitivists have made much of feeling confined by behavioristic principles. Lest some of us take these criticisms as merely the statements of those who do not understand behaviorism, let us hear them again from an unimpeachable source. In an article on "The experimental analysis of behavior (TEAB)," Kantor (1970), a foremost behaviorist himself, urges us "to include the free investigation of human organisms." Although the implication that no human work had been done is not entirely just, it is true that most behaviorists have failed to work with human subjects, thus avoiding the kinds of problems regularly met by cognitivists, who in turn have confined their work to human beings. Kantor states (p. 103) that "TEAB methods and postulates" must be applied to the "investigation of all types of adjustments including perceiving, remembering, thinking, and feeling behavior among other classes as performed by organisms of all genera and species."

Let us not, however, conclude that the study of human behavior has been entirely avoided. Skinner (1953, 1957, 1968, to take but a few of the most outstanding examples) has for a long time had quite a bit to say about human behavior. What we need now is more experimental work. I say this without in the least trying to slight the very interesting work that many behaviorists have in fact done in the areas of abnormal psychology, in programmed instruction, in perception, in verbal behavior, etc., and I say this despite the fact that almost all of my work has been with human beings.

Among the concepts that cognitivists accuse behaviorists of excluding, perhaps the most important is the image. Aside from Skinner's own interest in private events, there exists a compilation of studies in this area by McGuigan (1966) and a recently edited volume by Jacobs and Sachs (1971), which focussed on a variety of private events that are susceptible to experimental analysis. Experiments in this area have shown that one can condition images, hallucinations, or whatever name one gives them (e.g., Ellson, 1941; Leuba, 1940; Leuba and Dunlap, 1951; Hefferline and Perera, 1963). In the last-cited study, the subject reported the existence of two tones when one was produced by conditioning and the other was presented a fraction of a second later. Furthermore, Staats (1967; 1968) made use of the conditioning of images as a central aspect of his theory of the acquisition of meaning. Even Paivio (1971), who rejects the conditioning model as a complete explanation for the image, admits that no explanation would be complete without it.

Behaviorists are quite comfortable with the concept of image—as long as it is viewed as a stimulus to be measured and manipulated rather than as a *post hoc* attempt to explain a result, without even the potential of measurement. This is not to say that the problems of measurement of images (or, for that matter of other private events) have by any means been completely solved. Behavior is multiply determined and the subject's verbal response, "I see an image" may simply be determined by reinforcement contingencies unrelated to an image as a discriminative stimulus (S^D); the critical S^D may be the instructions of the experimenter, especially if the reinforcer is large enough in magnitude. Paivio's (1971) experimental work is certainly intriguing but his operational definition of imagery in terms of a rating scale is not entirely satisfying. Nevertheless, the large amount of supporting data amassed by Paivio and his students for the role of imagery in learning and comprehension cannot be ignored any more than the reality of private events.

One final point about images. It is a logical extension of the concept of stimulus control, to move from public events in the external environment to private events that are response-produced. The highly sophisticated methods of operant and respondent conditioning should certainly be useful in shedding some light on the acquisition of images, their evocation, their maintenance, and their loss. Research on animals would do a great deal to aid us in understanding the image, since no amount of verbal fudging (whether intentional or not) that sometimes creeps into experiments with human beings through instructions or biased analysis of subjects' verbal responses can enter an animal experiment.

Cognitivists pose as an additional problem for the behaviorist the phenomenon of spontaneous behavior—the behavior that is not, Neisser tells us, controlled by "relevant" stimulation. The solution is that behaviorists no more believe in responses without stimuli than they believe in free will. Behaviorists assume that responses are controlled by stimuli. The control may not always be obvious; it may not always be strong; in terms of today's technology, it may even be impossible to specify the particular stimulation that is controlling a particular response. But stimuli do control responses. It must be added that behaviorists are not interested in predicting the precise member of a class of stimuli that controls the precise member of a class of responses; their interest is in predicting what stimulus classes control what response classes. Contrary to Neisser's contention, there is no such thing as an irrelevant stimulus controlling a response. If a stimulus controls a response, then it is by definition relevant. To describe an hallucination as controlled by irrelevant stimuli is to make the value judgment that it is better to be influenced by one's retinal image than by a conditioned stimulus in seeing. This approach leads away from the experimental analysis of the phenomenon. We must never discard stimuli that we think ought not to control responses; we must find out how they, like the supposedly more appropriate stimuli, come to control the responses, how they maintain control, and how their control can be reduced.

Cognitivists believe that behaviorists confine their interest to atomistic responses and stimuli. Contrary to this belief, behaviorists define stimulus and response as classes (Skinner, 1935). It is this concept of response *class* that makes some of the criticisms of the behavioral approach quite beside the point. G. A. Miller (1962) has set up the straw man that there are too many combinations of words for a child to learn to emit all the sentences he will eventually say, without benefit of generative rules of grammar. But behaviorists (Skinner, 1957) never did discuss single responses only. Language is acquired in the form of response classes and their interrelationships. In 1967, I devoted a paper to a discussion of verbal response classes. In 1968, Chomsky (1968, p. 87) responded: "Unfortunately, this is empty verbiage until the condition that defines membership in this class is established." My article did go about the job of defining some of the many conditions that define membership. Single words as well as combinations are members of a vast variety of different response classes. The word "table," for example, is a member of response classes defined by the following controlling operations: physical discriminative stimuli—What is this (point to a table)?; verbal discriminative stimuli—Complete this sentence: He put the chairs around the ——————; List as many words as you can beginning with the letter ta_____; On what do you place a plate of food?; List some examples of furniture; Read some material containing the word "table" in it; Describe the furniture you have in your dining room; etc. Obviously a verbal response can be a member of many different classes; and so, incidentally, can nonverbal responses. Neither verbal nor nonverbal responses require structural analysis. The hand movement you employ to squash a mosquito may well be the same topographically as the one used to call a dog, applaud a famous singer, or express joy, etc.

As to the problem of units of verbal behavior, behaviorists know that verbal response units are indeed quite variable from time to time and from occasion to occasion (see Salzinger, 1973). Like the definition of response class, the definition of response unit is functional. Under certain circumstances the response, "Fire!" may have the same function as (i.e., be considered a single integral unit as much as) "Hey, I think there's a fire there!" On the other hand, it is equally clear that the word "fire" in the sentence above is not a single integral unit. We do not need a generative grammar to provide us with definitions of response classes even when we talk of sentences, as Chomsky(1968) implies. Some of the differences attributed to "structure" are better explained in terms of differences in image (Paivio, 1971). We must add to this the important fact that people emit verbal behavior in nonsentences, thus making the entire generative grammar effort incomplete, at best, for the analysis of speech. For additional criticisms of the generative grammatical approach the reader is directed to Goodman (1967), Quine (1970), Salzinger (1967; 1970), Staats (1971) and Verhave (1972). Critics of generative grammar have recently been joined by linguists, particularly with respect to the problem of semantics (see, for example, Steinberg and Jakobovits, 1971).

The final question is: Is the trip inside the organism really necessary? Note that the trips inside are not charted by physiology or biochemistry. Neisser is no more interested in those topics than are most behaviorists. As an experimentalist, he collects data in such a way that one can replicate his experiments and interpret his results because his data are reliable and available. Trips inside may be viewed as small excursions not critical with respect to evaluation of the data, i.e., not critical, to complete the metaphor, to determine where the trip ends.

There is another way to ask the question about the necessity of delving inside the organism: What function do the "inside" concepts have? They are obviously useful to at least some people in organizing the next experiment or the next theoretical question. In that way, such concepts may stimulate experimenters to think in novel ways. Novelty in science should always be fostered.

There is, however, one way in which some of the cognitive concepts are deleterious: in supplying answers by naming problems rather than by investigating them. In so doing they fail to promote further needed research. As an example of this, consider the fact that the concept of competence, which is so dear to generative grammarians and has done so much to keep alive their theory of grammar, has actually proposed that the speaking behavior of the individual is not to be trusted for information as to how well the individual speaks!

In reply to my criticism (Salzinger, 1967) that the notion "grammatical is equivocal as a scientific concept because there is no agreement among subjects in classifying sentences in this manner," Chomsky (1968) rejected the empirical evidence rather than the concept. "Obviously, the failure indicates nothing more than that the tests were ineffective" (Chomsky, 1968, p. 88). However, a concept should be capable of empirical refutation if it is to be retained in a science. The concept of competence presents a similar problem. It also denigrates the value of data without providing anything better than the investigator's opinion in opposition.

We must, instead, deal with the important observation that organisms emit different behaviors under different circumstances. Thus, when we say that an individual emits ungrammatical sentences but "recognizes" that they are ungrammatical, thereby revealing his competence in the language, we are merely singling out one class of responses to one set of discriminative stimuli and asserting that it has priority over another for exhibiting his "underlying" ability. The arbitrary character of this procedure emerges clearly when we consider an individual who emits grammatical sentences but fails to "recognize" them, for he would be considered less competent than the individual mentioned above.

Finally, a word about the concept of construction, since it is central to Neisser's book. Despite Neisser's protestations to the contrary, he requires the concept only because he accepts a theory very much akin to the Reappearance Hypothesis. If he gave up the notion that any part of the stimulus has to be incorporated into the organism, he would not have to talk about constructing a stimulus that is not there, not to speak of reconstructing such stimuli for purposes of recall. Memory, or more concretely, recall, must be evoked by stimuli, some of which are external and some internal. Stimuli evoke responses that vary in strength. The way in which an organism is modified after learning is in its responding to a stimulus it did not formerly react to.

The difference between perception and memory does not reside in the concepts of construction and reconstruction. Rather it more typically inheres in the strength with which the evoking stimuli control the responses that interest the experimenter. For in perception, a subject responds to a stimulus manipulated by the experimenter at the time he is required to respond, whereas in memory, a subject is required to respond to a related (part of the) stimulus some time after the earlier perceived stimulus has been presented.

I don't quite know how one proves that it is less elegant to describe subjects as "constructing" stimuli to which they respond than to think of them as varying in sensitivity in responding to various stimuli with various responses. I do believe that my speculation is more parsimonious in that it requires only a change in how responses are evoked rather than a change that consists essentially of having organisms incorporate ever larger and larger and more intricately organized chunks of the external environment as they grow older. On the other hand, I am not certain that Neisser's experiments would be any different if he had used my model instead of his. Are theories of cognition necessary?

REFERENCES

ANTROBUS, J. S. (Ed.) *Cognition and affect.* Boston: Little, Brown, 1970.

ANTROBUS, J. S., ANTROBUS, J. S., and SINGER, J. L. Eye movements accompanying daydreaming, visual imagery, and thought suppression. *Journal of Abnormal and Social Psychology,* 1964, **69**, 244–252.

CHOMSKY, N. *Syntactic structures.* The Hague, Mouton, 1957.

———. *Language and mind.* New York: Harcourt, Brace & World, Inc., 1968.

ELLSON, D. G. Hallucinations produced by sensory conditioning. *Journal of Experimental Psychology,* 1941, **28**, 1–20.

GOLDIAMOND, I. and HAWKINS, W. F. Vexierversuch: the log relationship between word-frequency and recognition obtained in the absence of stimulus words. *Journal of Experimental Psychology,* 1958, **56**, 457–463.

GOODMAN, N. The epistemological argument. *Synthese,* 1967, **17**, 23–28.

HEFFERLINE, R. F. and PERERA, T. B. Proprioceptive discrimination of a covert operant without its observation by the subject. *Science,* 1963, **139**, 834–835.

JACOBS, A. and SACHS, L. B. *The psychology of private events.* New York: Academic Press, 1971.

KANTOR, J. R. An analysis of the experimental analysis of behavior (TEAB). *Journal of the Experimental Analysis of Behavior,* 1970, **13**, 101–108.

KENDLER, H. H. Environmental and cognitive control of behavior. *American Psychologist,* 1971, **26**, 962–973.

KOPP, J. and UDIN, H. Identification and discrimination functions for pure tone auditory frequencies. *Psychonomic Science,* 1969, **16**, 95–96.

LANE, H. L. The motor theory of speech perception: A critical review. *Psychological Review,* 1965, **72**, 275–309.

———. A behavioral basis for the polarity principle in linguistics. In K. Salzinger and S. Salzinger (Eds.) *Research in verbal behavior and some neurophysiological implications.* New York: Academic Press, 1967. Pp. 79–96.

LEUBA, C. Images as conditioned sensations. *Journal of Experimental Psychology,* 1940, **26**, 345–351.

LEUBA, C. and DUNLAP, R. Conditioning imagery. *Journal of Experimental Psychology,* 1951, **41**, 352–355.

LIBERMAN, A. M., HARRIS, K. S., HOFFMAN, H. S., and GRIFFITH, B. C. The discrimination of speech sounds within and across phoneme boundaries. *Journal of Experimental Psychology,* 1957, **54**, 358–368.

MacNeilage, P. F. Motor control of serial ordering of speech. *Psychological Review*, 1970, **77**, 182–196.

McGuigan, F. J. *Thinking: studies of covert language processes.* New York: Appleton-Century-Crofts, 1966.

Miller, G. A. Some psychological studies of grammar. *American Psychologist*, 1962, **17**, 748–762.

Miller, N. E. Learning of visceral and glandular responses. *Science*, 1969, **163**, 434–445.

Neisser, U. *Cognitive psychology.* New York: Appleton-Century-Crofts, 1967.

Paivio, A. *Imagery and verbal processes.* New York: Holt, Rinehart & Winston, 1971.

Pisoni, D. B. *On the nature of categorical perception of speech sounds.* Unpublished doctoral dissertation, University of Michigan, 1971.

Quine, W. V. Methodological reflections on current linguistic theory. *Synthese*, 1970, **21**, 386–398.

Razran, G. *Mind in evolution.* New York: Houghton Mifflin Co., 1971.

Roffwarg, H. P., Dement, W. C., Muzio, J. N., and Fisher, C. Dream imagery: relationship to rapid eye movements of sleep. *Archives of General Psychiatry*, 1962, **7**, 235–258.

Salzinger, K. The problem of response class in verbal behavior. In K. Salzinger and S. Salzinger (Eds.) *Research in verbal behavior and some neurophysiological implications.* New York: Academic Press, 1967. Pp. 35–54.

———. Pleasing linguists: a parable. *Journal of Verbal Learning and Verbal Behavior*, 1970, **9**, 725–727.

———. Some problems of response measurement in verbal behavior: The response unit and intraresponse relations. In K. Salzinger and R. S. Feldman (Eds.) *Studies in verbal behavior: An empirical approach.* New York: Pergamon, 1973. Pp. 5–15.

Salzinger, K. and Eckerman, C. Grammar and the recall of chains of verbal responses. *Journal of Verbal Learning and Verbal Behavior*, 1967, **6**, 232–239.

Schoenfeld, W. N. and Cumming, W. W. Behavior and perception. In S. Koch (Ed.) *Psychology: A study of a science.* New York: McGraw-Hill, 1963, Vol. 5. Pp. 213–252.

Segal, E. M. and Lachman, R. Complex behavior or higher mental process: Is there a paradigm shift? *American Psychologist*, 1972, **27**, 46–55.

Skinner, B. F. The generic nature of the concepts of stimulus and response. *Journal of General Psychology*, 1935, **12**, 40–65.

———. The operational analysis of psychological terms. *Psychological Review*, 1945, **52**, 270–277.

———. *Science and human behavior.* New York: Macmillan, 1953.

———. *Verbal behavior.* New York: Appleton-Century-Crofts, 1957.

———. *The technology of teaching.* New York: Appleton-Century-Crofts, 1968.

Staats, A. W. Emotions and images in language: A learning analysis of their acquisition and function. In K. Salzinger and S. Salzinger (Eds.) *Research in verbal behavior and some neurophysiological implications.* New York: Academic Press, 1967. Pp. 123–145.

————. *Learning, language, and cognition.* New York: Holt, Rinehart & Winston, 1968.

————. Linguistic-mentalistic theory versus an explanatory S-R learning theory of language development. In D. I. Slobin (Ed.) *The ontogenesis of grammar.* New York: Academic Press, 1971. Pp. 103–150.

STEINBERG, D. D. and JAKOBOVITS, L. A. (Eds.) *Semantics.* Cambridge: Univ. Press, 1971.

STUDDERT-KENNEDY, M., LIBERMAN, A. M., HARRIS, K. S., and COOPER, F. S. The motor theory of speech perception: a reply to Lane's critical review. *Psychological Review,* 1970, 77, 234–249.

VERHAVE, T. The language and mind of a polemicist: some reflections on *Language and mind. Journal of Psycholinguistic Research,* 1972, 1, 183–195.

44

RECONCILIATION OF BEHAVIORISM AND PHENOMENOLOGY

WILLARD F. DAY

MUCH of the material which follows is under partial audience-control of the symposium on behaviorism and phenomenology held in the spring of 1963 at Rice University. The papers presented at this symposium, together with the discussion among the speakers and members of the audience, have been published in a recent book edited by Wann (1964) and entitled *Behaviorism and Phenomenology: Contrasting Bases for Modern Psychology.* Of the six speakers at the symposium two, Sigmund Koch and B. F. Skinner, are acknowledged authorities on the practice of behaviorism; two, R. B. MacLeod and Carl R. Rogers, are widely held to be advocates of phenomenology in psychology; and two, Norman Malcolm and Michael Scriven, are prominent professional philosophers, both known for their interest in the philosophical implications of contemporary psychological thought. The significance of the Rice symposium should not be underestimated by psychologists. The papers presented are instances of professional comment of unusually high quality, and they cast an especially instructive light on the current state of affairs of psychology as a science.

FROM W. F. Day, Radical behaviorism in reconciliation with phenomenology, *Journal of the Experimental Analysis of Behavior,* 1969, 12 (2), 315–328. Copyright 1969 by the Society for the Experimental Analysis of Behavior, Inc.

In overview, two significant conclusions appear to have emerged from the Rice symposium. The first of these is that behaviorism, in the sense in which the term is widely used among psychologists, is essentially an unproductive and unrealistic framework within which to pursue psychological research. This is to put the matter as mildly as possible, for the point was pursued with much force and clarity by Koch in his paper, and it was strongly seconded by Scriven, as part of his broader appraisal of the long-range potentialities of professional psychology. In a particularly choice statement, Koch expressed what appears to be to some extent his reaction to the symposium as a whole: "I would be happy to say that what we have been hearing could be characterized as the death rattle of behaviorism, but this would be a rather more dignified statement than I should like to sponsor, because death is, at least, a dignified process" (p. 162).[1] The following is representative of what Scriven had to say on the same topic.

So I would conclude by saying that Professor Koch's criticisms of behaviorism effectively destroy a specter which was, indeed, haunting and which has continued to haunt the subject. I think of behaviorism, as I know he does, as something which will leave its mark on a generation of graduate students now arising and will thus be with us for thirty or fifty years. I spend my life going around campuses and finding in each new psychology department a new burst of colossal enthusiasm; the leading lights of the graduate student body turn out to be enthusiastic, tough-minded positivists circa 1920. And they are now in their twenty-second year of age and, unfortunately, are likely to live a very long time. Some of them will presumably retain this approach to the subject. This is one reason why I believe that philosophy has an enormous influence on psychology though it has often been very bad. But that is, of course, because it was the wrong philosophy! (pp. 181–182)

Were anyone to search the symposium for disagreement with the conclusion that if conventional behaviorism is not now dead we should certainly all be better off if it were, he would have to content himself, rather remarkably, with certain statements of Carl Rogers. At one point in the discussion Rogers remarks that it had not been his purpose to point out "any theoretical flaw in behaviorism. There is a lot about behaviorism that I accept. I was simply trying to go beyond it" (p. 157). To be sure, Rogers calls attention to what he considers certain weaknesses of behaviorism. "Valuable as have been the contributions of behaviorism, I believe that time will indicate the unfortunate effects of the bounds it has tended to impose. To limit oneself to consideration of externally observable behavior, to rule out consideration of the whole universe of inner meanings, of purposes, of the inner flow of experiencing, seems to me to be closing our eyes to great areas which confront us when we look at the human world" (p. 119). However, the spirit of his paper

[1] Where no date is given, references apply to page numbers in Wann (1964).

is essentially conciliatory. "There are without doubt some individuals in this current of thought who maintain the hope that this new point of view will supplant the behaviorist trend, but to me this is both highly undesirable and highly unlikely. Rather it will mean, I believe, that psychology will preserve the advances and contributions that have come from the behaviorist development but will go beyond this" (p. 118). Rogers proceeds to argue for the measurement of new phenomenological variables, employing "thoroughly objective measures, whose results are publicly replicable" (p. 120), "using methods which are strictly operational" (p. 121), etc. Such procedures would presumably yield knowledge stemming from only one of the "three ways of knowing" that he differentiates in his paper.

The reader need not look to the paper by B. F. Skinner for a defense of conventional behaviorism. Skinner's radical behaviorism stands sharply in contrast to the more popular varieties of behaviorism criticized so effectively by Koch and defended in part by Rogers. The theme of Skinner's antagonism to conventional behaviorism runs through much of his later work. His objections to the inroads upon behaviorism of logical positivism and of what he calls "the operationism of Boring and Stevens" can be seen explicitly in as early a work as his revolutionary paper on operationism (1945). It is clear that Koch did not intend to exempt Skinner from the force of the attack developed in his paper. Yet it is equally clear that Skinner did not feel that the major points of Koch's argument applied to him. In the discussion following Koch's paper Skinner insisted that he does not "subscribe to any of the strategems of science" Koch described (p. 42). A member of the audience remarked that what Professor Koch presented did not seem "truly representative of what Skinner has to say" (p. 42). Even Scriven, in his formal critique of Koch's paper, emphasized the need for keeping clearly in mind the differences between conventional behaviorism and Skinner's views: "We notice that it is characteristic of Skinner's behaviorism that he does not saddle himself with this apparatus of the logic of science, which Koch so rightly criticizes. I would, therefore, put in a plea here for making a very careful distinction between the standard forms of behaviorism and Skinner's, which really meets only two of Koch's five criteria for behaviorism, and these, in a rather special way" (p. 181). However, Koch was not unaware of the fact that certain differences exist between conventional behaviorism and Skinner's point of view. He seemed, rather, to feel that the Skinnerian position is in some fundamental way internally inconsistent. He referred to the position as "strange and equivocal," "systematically ambiguous," and "Pickwickian" (p. 43). Other more specific objections are mentioned. Although Koch persisted throughout the symposium in his view that Skinner's radical behaviorism is little more than a rather unusual variety of neo-neobehaviorism, in one of the discussions he made the following comment concerning the need to clarify the differences between conventional and radical behaviorism: "[Skinner's formulation in the paper presented was so] extraordinarily libertarian . . . that one begins to wonder what the actual defining characteristics of the behaviorist thesis or the behaviorist method might be in his particular case" (p. 98).

The second general conclusion to emerge from the Rice symposium was that in spite of the patent difficulties of a conservative and conventional behaviorism, there are marked indications of an increasing *rapprochement* between the interests of behaviorism and phenomenology. This conclusion was apparently not expected by those who organized the symposium. Wann appeared surprised to have to conclude that the major trend in the symposium was a "blunting rather than a sharpening of the contrasts between behaviorism and phenomenology," and that "Professors MacLeod, Malcolm, Rogers, and Scriven, in one way or another, suggest the possibility of coexistence" (p. vii). Even Koch was aware of this trend, although he found it deplorable (p. 162). There was little uniformity of opinion concerning the nature of the implied compatibility. MacLeod suggested, with some diffidence, that the phenomenological approach in psychology might lead in part into some kind of "sophisticated behaviorism" (p. 55), and Scriven spoke specifically of the reconciliation of what he called *defensible* forms of phenomenology and behaviorism (p. 180). Malcolm was led to the conclusion "that Skinner had stated here an absolutely decisive objection to introspectionism," and he devoted considerable attention to giving "an account of the hard core of logical truth contained in behaviorism" (p. 149). Malcolm qualified his endorsement by stating that the Achilles' heel of behaviorism lay in its treatment of psychological sentences in the first-person-present tense. Skinner, for his part, thanked Malcolm for his support and suggested that perhaps agreement could be reached, even with respect to first-person statements (p. 155).

However, Wann is not so sure that Skinner's views as presented in the symposium are compatible with the interests of phenomenology. In his introduction, Wann leaves it for the reader to decide whether Skinner joins the majority of the symposium in seeing the possibilities of a reconciliation (p. viii). On the inside flap of the book's jacket it is stated that "only Koch and Skinner dissent from the view that coexistence is possible." Certainly this hesitancy to regard Skinner's position as in any way compatible with phenomenology is characteristic of the attitude maintained by a majority of contemporary psychologists. The purpose of this paper is to show that Skinner's radical behaviorism is indeed capable of encompassing a productive phenomenology. In the material that follows there is first a description of what I shall call the basic dimensions of radical behaviorism. This is partly in response to Koch's request for a statement of the "defining characteristics" of Skinner's position. Next, I shall attempt to illustrate the way in which radical behaviorism might profitably proceed to interact with problems that are often considered phenomenological in nature. Finally, I shall close with a brief discussion of some of the major problems that are faced in bringing about an effective reconciliation of radical behaviorism and phenomenology.

The Basic Dimensions of Radical Behaviorism

In this section I shall try to describe what I consider to be the basic dimensions of Skinner's radical behaviorism. I feel that almost all of what I have to say is rigidly under the control of a careful study of Skinner's work in breadth and depth. Nevertheless, I am prepared to accept responsibility if some defense should be necessary of the presentation that I make. I have chosen this course of action largely for reasons of simplicity and convenience. Skinner's work is difficult to understand, and a detailed textual explication of the relevant material scattered throughout his writing would involve a tiresome analysis of specific contexts.

As an example of the problem faced in detailed explication, consider the following two statements by Skinner which bear directly upon the difference between radical and conventional behaviorism. First, in the early symposium on operationism Skinner discusses the difficulties which arise in making a distinction between things that are public and those that are private. He criticizes "the arid philosophy of 'truth by agreement,'" a perspective often adopted by conventional behaviorists who claim that scientific knowledge must somehow be essentially public in nature. Skinner proceeds to state that "the distinction between public and private is by no means the same as that between physical and mental. That is why methodological [or conventional] behaviorism (which adopts the first) is very different from radical behaviorism (which lops off the latter term in the second)" (1945, p. 294). Secondly, in response to a question raised by Scriven in the Rice symposium concerning how he can justify calling himself a radical behaviorist, Skinner replies that, "I am a radical behaviorist simply in the sense that I find no place in the formulation for anything which is mental" (p. 106). These comments by Skinner are likely to appear somewhat cryptic to someone who has not studied Skinner's published work intensively. It is clear that Skinner is objecting here not to things that are private but to things that are mental. It is true that the distinction between radical and conventional behaviorism hinges in a number of ways on the issue of mentalism. It is also true that one of Skinner's most persistent objections to conventional behaviorism is directed at a fundamental mentalism which he sees as all too thinly disguised. Yet actually, the issues involved in what Skinner means by "mentalism" are quite complex. The careful clarification of what Skinner is getting at in such statements as these requires a more detailed analysis than can be given here.

A FOCAL INTEREST IN THE CONTROL OF BEHAVIOR

Perhaps the most conspicuous characteristic of radical behaviorism is its focal interest in the control of behavior. Radical behaviorists view themselves as essentially engaged in a search for what they call controlling variables, even though the term *variable* is often used in a sense only distantly related to its etymology. Events are considered controlling variables when they are seen, or perceived, to be related to behavior in some way. However, many times the identification of controlling variables does not follow from anything so simple as an observation of the temporal contiguity of phenomenal events. The identification is often likely to be emitted more after the fashion of what might be called a guess, a hunch, or an insight. Verbal behavior describing a relation between behavior and controlling variables is called the statement of a functional relationship, and a more or less systematic attempt to describe functional relationships is called a functional analysis of behavior. In the statement of a functional relationship, the controlling variable is called a stimulus, and that aspect of behavior seen in relationship to the controlling variable is called a response.

In using such words as *seen, perceived, observation, guess, hunch,* and *insight,* as in the preceding paragraph, the radical behaviorist does not feel that he is specifying with very much precision what many psychologists would call either behavioral or mental processes. He is simply talking as best he can—actually, in this case he is not talking as carefully as he might—and he is responding to discriminable events which have not been very consistently differentiated by whatever factors govern the way in which we learn to talk as we do. He calls a stimulus a stimulus for reasons that are presumably similar to those which make people speak of cows as cows, and he can be led to attempt to define a stimulus under circumstances (and with characteristic difficulties) that are much the same as what one might expect to find in being called upon to define a cow. Yet why struggle to define a cow when any child sufficiently exposed to the ordinary verbal community can identify one on sight? Similarly, the capacity to identify a stimulus as such presumably depends largely upon the reinforcing practices of some scientific verbal community.

The practice of looking for functional relationships is obviously similar in certain respects to the effort to find relations between cause and effect. Yet in attempting to discover functional relationships the radical behaviorist does not accept any *a priori* logical assumption of a universe that is orderly in a mechanical sense upon which he feels he must base his scientific work. To be sure, he can easily be led, by appropriate verbal manipulation, to state that he "[assumes] that nature is orderly rather than capricious" (Skinner, 1950, p. 193). However in doing so, nothing of the least systematic significance is asserted. A rancher can undoubtedly be led to state that he assumes cattle are on a particular range where he expects to find them, yet it is absurd to look to a cowboy for profound philosophy.

The interest of the radical behaviorist in the concept of control reflects his conviction that if knowledge is to be trusted it is often likely to lead ultimately to effective action. He is most confident in his statement of a functional relationship if it plays some part in guiding him eventually to the successful manipulation, i.e., control, of specific behavior. Furthermore, a focal interest in the control of behavior does not prejudice the case for the importance in human functioning of genetic or constitutional factors, nor does it lead to any such grandiose hypothesis as that all behavior is controlled by reinforcement.

THE FOCAL AWARENESS THAT ANY SCIENTIST IS HIMSELF A BEHAVING ORGANISM

A second basic dimension of radical behaviorism is its insistence that scientists are themselves no more than behaving organisms. Science is at heart either the behavior of scientists or the artifacts of such activity, and scientific behavior is in turn presumably controlled by much the same kind of variables as those which govern any other aspect of complex human behavior.

However, as commonplace as this notion may appear to most psychologists, it leads in the mind of radical behaviorists to conclusions that are likely to seem strange to many persons. The radical behaviorist faces the fact that the ultimate achievement of his scientific activities is for the most part either further verbal behavior on his own part or a new set of acquired behaviors which hopefully enable him to control nature more effectively. Yet in viewing his own verbal and intellectual behavior as significantly controlled in a number of ways, he is led in a sense not to trust it at face value. He is aware, for example, that much of what he says in offering systematic psychology is likely to reflect psychological distinctions that are modeled after linguistic practices uncritically acquired simply in learning to speak the lay vocabulary. He is particularly conscious of the fact that much psychological talk reflects stereotyped conceptions both of the nature of the knowing process and of the relation between our knowledge of things and the structure of whatever it is that is taken to be the object of psychological investigation. For example, he is suspicious of primitive animism, which embodies nature with man-like powers, strengths, and forces, as well as of a facile determinism, which views the aim of research as isolating the fundamental elements of nature which are thought of as existing in some kind of mechanical interrelationship.

His resistance to such hidden epistemology leads at times to an obstinate refusal to think in terms of a particular common-sense theory of what it is to have knowledge about one or another subject matter.

This is the notion that whenever we have significant knowledge, this knowledge consists of an at least partial identification of the inherent nature of what it is that is known about. The notion is, in other words, that in knowing about something the expression of our knowledge consists in a comment on the *nature* of the object of knowledge or of a statement of what the object of knowledge *is*. It is as if in verbalizing our knowledge of things we have always to express an identification of one or another aspect of the permanent structure of nature. Yet the radical behaviorist is aware that we may attribute thing-ness to events largely because we are accustomed to speak of the world about us as composed of objects which are felt to possess an inherent constancy or stability. He is reluctant to take for granted that all useful knowledge must be conceptualized in terms of verbal patterns of thought derived simply from our experience with material objects. Consequently, he is led to a position which is peculiarly anti-ontological.

In particular, he objects to speaking of the events associated in a functional relationship as if they were things and objects having a more or less permanent identity as real elements of nature. He does not believe that the functional relations he describes constitute an identification of anything which might be called "true laws of nature," in the sense that the systematic collection of such functional relations can ultimately be expected to fit together into a completed picture of an account of human interaction with the environment. Rather, he is content for the most part simply to describe whatever natural consistency he can actually see, and to hope that the report he makes of his observations will in turn generate ultimately more productive behavior in the control of human affairs. He adopts this course of action out of an interest in increased efficiency and a conviction that only the analysis of behavior will lead some day to a more trustworthy set of guidelines for the acquisition of knowledge.

Consider several illustrations of this point of view. The statement made above that science is the behavior of scientists is not viewed by the radical behaviorist as a reductionist treatment of what might be viewed as an ontological assertion. It is regarded instead as a highly abstract description of what we are probably looking at when we identify events as constituting science. In the Rice symposium Skinner bluntly states that he is not interested in the nature of reinforcement. He comments: "I do not know why [food is reinforcing to a hungry animal] and I do not care" (p. 104). Skinner is also well known for his repudiation of reference theories of meaning (e.g., 1957, p. 7f., p. 114f.). Such theories generally assume that words are objects which are somehow attached to other objects or entities which are called meanings. In what Skinner calls mentalism, inner psychological processes are given homuncular power to cause other more behavioral events to come about. It is not so widely recognized that it is possible to "mentalize" environmental events, as where reinforcers are endowed, often in the thinking of avowed Skinnerians, with some sort of demoniacal power to forge the chains of a reified conception of conditioning.

The reader is likely to resist strenuously such an anti-ontological outlook. Consider the following remarks by Koch: "More generally, I think there is something frightening about the way neo-neobehaviorism is treating the newly reclaimed subject-matter. . . . Scientific knowledge is, of course, 'selective'—but when ontology is distorted, denied, or evaded past a certain point, one is no longer in the context of serious scholarship" (p. 32). Similarly, MacLeod has the following to say: "To build a science of psychology one must begin with the phenomenal world, but then one must transcend it. . . . Every scientist is a metaphysician, whether or not he likes to admit it, at least to the extent that he asserts the existence of something which he does not fully understand but which he is determined to investigate" (p. 54).

Still, the force of radical behaviorism presses for the formulation of a radically new epistemology. The most conspicuous characteristic of this new epistemology will be that it will have been obtained by the psychological analysis of the behavior, both public and private, of scientists, scholars, and whatever other persons can reasonably be said to know things. It will involve, more specifically, the analysis of the variables controlling the verbal behavior of whosoever uses the word *knowledge* and related terms in an interesting and significant way. Skinner has called at great length and over a period of many years for the formulation of such an epistemology (e.g., 1945, p. 277; 1957, Ch. 18; 1961, p. 392; 1964, p. 104), but as yet no serious attempt at the requisite behavioral analysis has been undertaken.

Even so, in the last analysis the radical behaviorist is committed to an exceedingly liberal position with respect to the verbal behavior of his professional colleagues. Admittedly, the reliance upon a speculative epistemology is deplorable, especially when unrecognized or unintended, but objection is ultimately to be raised only on pragmatic grounds. Anyone is basically free to speak as he does. A man says what he can say; he says what he *does* say, and all this is in principle acceptable to the radical behaviorist, since whatever is said is as such a manifestation of complex human functioning and is consequently the legitimate object of behavioral investigation. In responding to professional language, the radical behaviorist has his own new course to follow: he must attempt to discover the variables controlling what has been said. Even the most mentalistic language is understandable and valuable in this sense. The meaningfulness of psychological and mental terms provides no insuperable problem, provided the verbal practices of both speaker and hearer have been shaped by overlapping verbal communities. The meaning of such terms can be clarified by an attempt to assess the observable (not necessarily publicly observable) events that act as discriminative stimuli in control of emission of the term. This kind of analysis is what Skinner has in mind when he speaks of "operational definition" (1945, p. 271).

THE FOCAL INTEREST IN VERBAL BEHAVIOR CONTROLLED BY DIRECTLY OBSERVED EVENTS

The radical behaviorist is further characterized by the heavy value he places on the consequences of direct observation. In his view, the more he can bring his own verbal behavior under the control of what he has actually observed, the more productive and useful it is likely to be. The control exercised by the observed event may be relatively direct, as in simple description, or rather more complex, as in the identification of controlling variables or in the behavior of deciding which of a variety of potential variables next to manipulate. In the early stages of research, or when an overabundance of theoretical speculation has become involved, there is generally a preference for simple description. The power of simple description as a method for generating knowledge appears to have been grossly underestimated. Of course, nothing in the Skinner system requires that the observer restrict his talk simply to the emission of descriptive statements. Once the observation of behavior has taken place, the observer should be encouraged to talk interpretatively about what he has seen, not necessarily restricting himself to the identification of controlling variables. To be sure, the radical behaviorist recognizes that the particular interpretation that he makes will be a function of his own special history, and clearly interpretation guided by extensive observation of relevant behavior is to be preferred to speculation by the novice. It is, of course, only under very special circumstances that the interpretations that an observer makes of what he has seen should be identified as a contribution to psychological "theory."

This outlook is viewed as markedly in contrast with most popular approaches to psychological research. The standard machinery of experimental method in psychology is seen as yielding results that are much too distantly related to anything directly observable. To be sure, in most psychological studies subjects are required at some point or other to do at least something which is capable of being seen. But how often does the psychologist actually watch his subjects in action, hoping simply that what he sees will lead him to talk more informatively about what he is investigating? All too frequently, the principal investigator of a research project merely surveys an orderly collection of numbers, usually purported to be composite "measures" of something or other. These numbers have in turn been written down by some more fortunate graduate student who presumably had at least the opportunity to observe the relevant behavior as it actually took place. Even in circumstances where the behavior of immediate interest is preserved intact, as in the verbal protocols used in content analysis, how frequently is the experimenter himself in a position to observe the specific stimulating conditions under which the behavior has been emitted? Without the most skillful practices of observation on the part of the experimenter himself, why should one expect a relation between stimulus and response ever to be perceived? It is not that conventional experimental method is incapable of generating the observed functional relationships so much of interest to the radical behaviorist, especially when the method has been purged of statistical over-refinement. The point is only that most psychologists rarely take active advantage of the opportunity to inspect both behavior and its controlling stimulation as closely as they might. Cumulative records are valued by Skinner precisely because he feels they make certain interesting changes in behavior conspicuously *visible*.

However, the interest of the radical behaviorist in the effects of observation is neither complex nor profound. He merely hopes that what he sees will come to exert an increasing influence on what he says. In this he is not unlike the unpedantic clinical psychologist who simply behaves in the therapeutic situation in a way that he regards as the natural outcome of his past experience in treating patients. Usage here of the term *observation* does not imply any special mental or behavioral process. The verbal community teaches us all to distinguish observation from reflection, speculation, wool-gathering, thinking, and other psychological activities, although the extent to which the differential reinforcement involved is consistent has not as yet been described. Neither does the focal interest in observation commit the radical behaviorist to the notion that observation must somehow be essentially public. In fact, most of the time it is easiest to view observation as something private, in the sense that no more than one individual participates in the behavioral event we identify as a single act of observation. Similarly, there is no restriction of interest to events which are considered to be observable "in principle" by someone else. The radical behaviorist feels as free to observe or otherwise respond to his own reactions to a Beethoven sonata as he is to observe those of someone else.

THE FOCAL AWARENESS OF THE IMPORTANCE OF ENVIRONMENTAL VARIABLES

The radical behaviorist is interested in the environment for a variety of reasons. First of all, it is simply obvious that a great deal of behavior is to some extent under environmental control. However, it is not so obvious that the grain of the environmental control of behavior is much finer than is commonly appreciated; the slightest difference in stimulating conditions (which the experimenter is often not prepared to appreciate) may lead to very gross differences in behavior. For example, in an experimenter's attempt to get a human subject to press a button over and over again in a standard rate of response study, the instruction, "Following your first press, if you wish to continue to press the button, you may do so," is observed to lead some subjects simply to keep the button depressed for as long as 15 minutes, with no environmental change taking place. Similarly, in teaching machine programming, it generally requires very subtle environmental engineering to make it highly likely that the experimental student will emit the desired response.

An interest in the environment also follows from the inherently practical orientation of the radical behaviorist. In so far as he is interested in manipulation and control, he becomes committed to a basic concern with the environment. Whatever is done by way of any manipulation inevitably consists of some change in the environment of the person whose behavior is to be affected, and one has little reason to expect a manipulation to be successful unless it reflects some functional relation between behavior and the relevant environmental change. To precisely the same extent as one is interested in manipulation he becomes concerned with ways in which the environment is related to behavior. However, the radical behaviorist is interested in manipulation not only for its immediate effect upon the behavior he is attempting to control, but also because he wants the manipulation to have some effect upon his own behavior as a scientist. The extent to which he is able to manipulate behavior successfully is perhaps the most important variable that acts to shape his own research activities. He is likely to feel that the most effective means of acquiring knowledge about some aspect of behavior is to attempt to learn how to shape up that very behavior in which he is interested. In speaking of the need for an empirical epistemology, Skinner states that "it is possible that we shall fully understand the nature of knowledge only after having solved the practical problems of imparting it" (1961, p. 392).

The radical behaviorist is interested in the environment for a still more basic reason. He holds the view that *all* verbal behavior, no matter how private its subject matter may appear to be, is to some significant extent controlled by the environment. Although he recognizes that the range of phenomena related to human verbal functioning varies from the most intimately personal to the most spectacularly social, he sees that all meaningful language is shaped into effective form by the action of an environmental verbal community. It is this contact of language with the environment that enables us to respond effectively to it. We know, in other words, what language means because some common environmental contingency controls both our own behavior and that of the speaker whose talk is of interest to us. To be sure, it is only rarely possible for us to perceive directly the relevant environmental variables as they operate to shape the verbal behavior with which we are concerned. Yet the problem here is no different in kind from that faced in attempting to infer the contingencies controlling any aspect of a person's previous history. The verbal community has taught us a variety of practices by which we guess at relevant factors, some more useful than others.

The case is not prejudiced for an interest in what someone has to say about what he considers his own private experience. Verbal behavior constitutes by far the most convenient avenue of access to anything that might be considered a significant aspect of human knowledge, including one's own knowledge of himself. If we want to find out more about what a man is experiencing in a certain situation, one of the simplest things to do is to try to get him to talk. Of course, whether or not we happen to trust the speaker depends upon the nature of the environmental control exercised by him over our own behavior. Yet the radical behaviorist is not basically concerned with whether or not a speaker is telling the truth. What he wants to know is what makes him say the things that he does. This leads him inevitably to a concern, at least in part, with the environmental events that have acted to teach him to talk. It leads also to an interest in possible events in the present and recent environment of the speaker that bear some similarity to the stimulation available to the verbal community in providing initial differential reinforcement. In searching for such influences he will be himself for the most part responding in some way to the environment. It is the belief of the radical behaviorist that by tracing the environmental chain of command over verbal behavior as far as possible, he can extend the range of his effective action as a scientist most profitably. Suppose, for example, that a student begins to suspect that he senses some order of a particular kind in human functioning. What must he do? He must not fail to proceed directly to an explicit verbal description of *what he has seen* that appears to make him think he has found something. This first step involves, of course, an analysis of the environmental control of his own behavior.

There is yet a fourth way in which the radical behaviorist is interested in the environment. He tends to regard explanations as simply incomplete if they do not involve tracing the observable antecedents of behavior back as far as possible into the environment. Many current psychological explanations are thus seen as incomplete, since they often do little more than specify some inner process as the cause of a particular aspect of behavior. Issues of ontology are again involved here, since explanatory inner processes are generally regarded as having a kind of power metaphorically related to primitive animism. However, if the ontological pattern of language is insisted upon, it is only reasonable to ask what makes the inner process work as it does. Since an answer to this question is usually not provided, the radical behaviorist regards such explanations as incomplete.

The case is different if the explanation involves no more than the description of a relation between behavior and some observed private event. Such a relation constitutes a legitimate functional relationship in precisely the same way as does the statement of a relation between behavior and the environment. Here the radical behaviorist asks only that the situation be more closely examined to see if the private event in turn cannot be seen to bear some relation to the environment. If it can, then the functional relation as stated is clearly incomplete as an explanation of the behavior. In those cases where the private event is conspicuously related to the environment, then reference to the private event is likely to be considered irrelevant or unnecessary for purposes of manipulation and control. In those absurd situations where private events are said to control behavior even though they are not themselves directly observable even to a single observer, as in much of Freud and in certain uses of the term *self*, then the explanation is of interest only as a sample of very complexly constructed verbal behavior.

However, the preference for environmental explanation does not mean that it is the only meaningful form of explanation. The radical behaviorist makes no prior epistemological assumption that an explanation is complete only when environmental controlling variables have been identified. Many patterns of verbal behavior pass as successful explanation to many people, and indeed common practices of explanation provide an interesting area for empirical investigation. The complex verbal material that composes psychological theory is not to be abhorred on principle. The radical behaviorist simply calls attention, again, to the fact that psychological theory is after all directly observed as verbal behavior on the part of the theorist, and it seems good advice to suggest that the theorist at least attempt to understand the factors that operate to make him generate his theory in the way that he does. Even a fairly casual inspection of most of the verbal material that is considered by many to be psychological theory can be seen to manifest conspicuous control by ordinary language habits, extensive chains of familiar interverbals, and one or another preconception about the inherent nature of scientific explanation.

Radical Behaviorism and Phenomenological Research

It is probably already clear there is no inherent incompatibility between a robust interest in phenomenology and the basic dimensions of radical behaviorism. Koch himself has stated the terms that must be met before a harmonious coexistence between behaviorism and phenomenology is possible. He argues that psychology has to be a "conceptually heterogeneous" science. He would "no longer have any objection to neo-neo-behaviorists" if "even the most libertarian" among them would "permit" such conceptual heterogeneity (p. 186). Clearly these terms are met by radical behaviorism. Any kind of professional language, no matter how esoteric, is of interest to the radical behaviorist as a sample of verbal behavior. What he wants to know is what sort of factors have been involved in leading the speaker to say what he does. Still, it seems natural to protest that when professional psychological talk is viewed simply as a sample of verbal behavior, what the psychologist is really trying to say has not been taken very seriously. Yet such a reaction reflects a misunderstanding of how earnestly the radical behaviorist is prepared to try to understand whatever factors control the emission of any interesting psychological talk. To know thoroughly what has caused a man to say something is to understand the significance of what he has said in its very deepest sense.

It is true that Skinner has not rushed to embrace with star-eyed enthusiasm the sentimental, emotional, common-sensical, or obscure out-pourings that often pass as pleas for phenomenology in psychology. Why should he? Skinner has his own row to hoe in attempting to advance an explicit interest in the analysis of behavioral control, which is what many psychologists are basically interested in anyway. He does this in the face of a frankly embarrassing professional shallowness in the interpretation of his work. The popular "Skinnerian" myth that any concern with private experience must be "mentalistic" and is hence unbecoming to the radical behaviorist simply flies in the face of some of Skinner's best thought. Consider the following quotation from Skinner's contribution to the Symposium on Operationism.

"Science does not consider private data," says Boring. (Just where this leaves my contribution to the present symposium, I do not like to reflect.) But I contend that my toothache is just as physical as my typewriter, though not public, and I see no reason why an objective and operational science cannot consider the processes through which a vocabulary descriptive of a toothache is acquired and maintained. The irony of it is that, while Boring must confine himself to an account of my external behavior, I am still interested in what might be called Boring-from-within. (1945, p. 294)

In the Rice symposium only Scriven seems really to appreciate what Skinner is basically up to, and Scriven is a philosopher. Both Rogers (p. 140) and Koch (p. 186) consider Skinner's verbal behavior as in some way inherently intolerant. But a specialization of interest does not imply intolerance, nor is intolerance implied by a decreasing interest in verbal behavior as its control by observable events becomes more hopelessly obscure.

The radical behaviorist understandably reacts slowly to phenomenological talk that is to some extent too distantly removed from the direct observations that have made the speaker excited to begin with. Even MacLeod, a phenomenologist to whom the radical behaviorist can look squarely with respect, remarks, "To be quite frank, I must confess that I find Heidegger as deadly as Hegel and that many existentialist plays leave me simply uncomfortable" (p. 51). It is easiest, for example, simply to try to swim along with Rogers through the first page of his paper for the Rice symposium, where the composition is heavily controlled by a torpid oceanic metaphor. "Like the flotsam and jetsam which float on each ocean current, certain words and phrases identify, even though they do not define, these separate flowing trends" (p. 109). Or, "Toward what shores, what islands, what vastnesses of the deep is its compelling current carrying us" (p. 100)? With respect to the second of these quotations, it could in fact be helpful, in trying to get an idea of what Rogers must have seen in his relevant therapeutic experience, to know to what extent and in what way the composition of this particular statement of his was under partial control of "The Tyger" by Blake.

However, it is more the purpose of this paper to clarify the possibilities of active reconciliation, rather than mere peaceful coexistence. There are numerous ways in which a flourishing phenomenology and radical behaviorism need each other. Consider first the case of radical behaviorism, whose current situation presses for the more explicit study of phenomenological functional relationships. Skinner's analyses of obviously phenomenological subject matter, as his chapter on "Private Events in a Natural Science" in *Science and Human Behavior* (1953, Ch. 17), or the paper on operationism (1945), or his contribution to the Rice symposium (1964), are clearly under the control of considerable self-observation on the part of Skinner himself. It is not that what Skinner has to say in this material needs "experimental test." What is needed is extensive descriptive analysis of verbal behavior controlled by observable events that are likely to be identified by the speaker as his own conscious experience, his inner subjective feelings, or his private hopes, fears, and aspirations. Without such a behavioral analysis, coverage of the obviously interesting aspects of human functioning will remain incomplete. Perhaps one need not expect to find in the analysis of phenomenological verbal behavior important causes of the social and personal-adjustmental behavior so much of current interest. However, the careful description of such functional relations can be expected to have an ameliorative influence upon the extent to which inner mental processes are called upon in the explanation of behavior. A sound phenomenology is the best defense against a facile mentalism.

Similarly, radical behaviorism needs to attend to other, more complex aspects of behavior which are coming to be identified as phenomenological in a looser usage of the terms. There is great current interest in questions pertaining to the value, meaningfulness, and significance of a person's experience, and this interest is increasing. Except for want of time, there is no reason for the radical behaviorist to neglect to analyze the complex behavioral situations that are taken to be the signs of these broader phenomenological concerns. In making sense out of this behavior, he has no other recourse than to put himself in a position to make the same kind of observation—often clinical, literary, social, religious, or aesthetic in nature—that gives rise to such phenomenological talk. Extensive observation of the extraordinarily wide range of human functioning, from the contemplative behavior of the mystic through the puzzling behavior of the leather-jacketed cyclist, is urgently needed. How can we expect a viable psychology, when we find that so many psychologists are themselves simply rather narrowly experienced people? At the present time, radical behaviorism rapidly advances to the study of higher intellectual functioning in education, the rehabilitation of juvenile delinquents and criminals, the appreciation of music and art, and the behavior of psychotics and people who seek psychotherapy. In all this, the simple observation and description of the relevant behavior, conspicuously including what the persons involved have to say themselves, becomes of increasing importance. The current work of Murray Sidman (see, e.g., Sidman and Stoddard, 1966) on the rehabilitation of mentally defective children is exemplary of the way in which a radical behaviorist can profitably take advantage many times of analyses which might easily be called phenomenological in nature.

As for the phenomenologist, he is for the most part still grossly unaware of the first lessons to be learned from the experimental analysis of behavior. The ways in which radical behaviorism impinges upon the domain of phenomenology have been delineated to a great extent by Skinner in the works referred to above. This paper has also attempted to clarify the radical behaviorist point of view so that its relevance to phenomenological interests can be appreciated. However, it should perhaps be stressed again, by way of summary, that insofar as the phenomenologist is in any way in contact with human functioning, he is looking at, and responding to, *behavior*, even though it may not be public in nature. Much of both his own behavior and that in which he is interested is under complex control, a control that is likely to be to a considerable extent environmental in nature. The phenomenologist needs greatly to recognize that a little less metaphor and theory, and a lot more simple description of the things that he has actually observed, would be of much help to others in understanding the problems he faces. For example, it is relatively exciting to learn that Rogers suspects some relationship between a patient's "willingness to discover new feelings and new aspects of himself" and "personality change." Yet it is not so interesting to watch him then go out and get a small gun from the arsenal of statistics and victoriously reject the notion of precisely zero correlation between some measure of self-exploration and another measure of personality change (p. 124). Here the perceived functional relation is directly of interest in itself. It is enough that it control verbal behavior. There is no need to use statistics to bolster one's self-confidence or to justify one's right to talk about behavior. The practical value of statistics lies elsewhere than in providing a simple criterion for deciding whether or not one knows anything about behavior.

The phenomenologist should be especially wary of the ways in which his previous experience acts to influence however he happens to talk, particularly in constructing theories, planning research, and reaching explanatory conclusions. He should, at least to some extent, attempt to assess the variables in his own history which affect his professional performance in any of its significant facets. When he places heavy emphasis on a word taken from the lay vocabulary, he must not fail to examine carefully the observable events which control his usage of the term and guarantee its successful effect upon the behavior of others. He should satisfy himself, in making use of a psychological test, that he really wants to regard the elicitation of specific samples of behavior as the "measurement" of some inner "thing," supposedly in part an element of the psychic apparatus. If he happens to prefer practices of explanation in which powers or forces are attributed to entities of any kind, he should try to form some notion of how he has come to acquire this particular preference. In the study of complex mental processes he must be sure he had observable evidence to help him decide what is chicken and what is egg, the prior environment or some inner mental entity presumed to influence behavior. When a mental process is purported to exist, he must know clearly in his own mind precisely to what extent the process is observable, *directly* observable, at least to someone.

Finally, the phenomenologist should recognize that he engages blindly in efforts at manipulation unless he is clearly aware of the pertinent relations between the environment (including his own behavior) and the behavioral change he is interested in making. He should keep in mind that an environmentalistic frontal attack on any problem of control may be considerably more profitable than recourse to verbal interpretations involving mental states. The best way to change a mental condition may be to try to change other, more conspicuous aspects of behavior first; the desired changes in covert behavior may occur as a result. For example, it is one thing to get a subject to respond on a paper-and-pencil test and quite something else again to know what the same Caucasian subject will feel when he first learns that his children will soon have to attend a predominantly non-white school. A particular manipulation may well succeed for rather trivial reasons in changing performance on a paper-and-pencil test; yet clearly much more complex problems of control are involved in shaping vigorous support for integration in the public school system. It is entirely possible that the best way to get a person to feel comfortable inside himself about issues of civil liberties is to attempt *first* to control his overt behavior in relevant social situations. One would possibly then find that the observable covert or overt behaviors taken as evidence of his attitudes on the subject have also changed.

Practical Problems in Reconciliation

In closing, let me mention four problems that seem to me to stand particularly in the way of a healthy interaction between radical behaviorism and phenomenology. The first of these is the superficiality with which the profession at large is familiar with Skinner's work. A couple of survey courses in learning theory, possibly a reading of *The Behavior of Organisms*, a glance at *Science and Human Behavior* or *Wal-*

den Two, the isolated study of such papers as "Are Theories of Learning Necessary?", or primary reliance on such digests as Hilgard and Bower's *Theories of Learning* (1966) will not do. If radical behaviorism is to be understood, Skinner's work must be studied by professionals with precisely the same diligence as that we take for granted from our better graduate students. In particular, the paper on operationism (1945), *Verbal Behavior* (1957), the later papers on programmed instruction (*e.g.*, 1961), and the paper for the Rice symposium (1964) must be mastered. By way of help, Verplanck's critique of Skinner's views in *Modern Learning Theory* (1954) can be taken as authoritative, in spite of the fact that it is now very much out of date.

The lack of careful study of Skinner's work has led to professional absurdities too numerous to review in detail. Strange blends of Skinner and conventional behaviorism abound. I would rather not identify the even relatively prominent Skinnerians who fail to concede that private events have any place in a natural science. Others view *Science and Human Behavior* as somehow beneath their empirical dignity; the word is passed around that the sticky parts of the book are to be excused because it is, after all, no more than a sophomore level text—this in spite of the fact that in a work as crucial as *Verbal Behavior*, Skinner refers the reader back again to *Science and Human Behavior* for his most thorough analysis of the issue of private experience (1957, p. 130). Mentalism among Skinnerians is rampant, and they are quickly trapped by the operationism of Boring and Stevens. Unfortunately, only very few people have an accurate idea of what Skinner means by operational definition. I have taken the liberty of speaking here directly to some of those who preach most loudly a supposedly Skinnerian line. One hardly knows where to begin to analyze the grossly uninformed verbal material that is generated concerning Skinner's work by the typical psychologist.

A second problem is the failure to distinguish sharply enough between radical and conventional behaviorism, a point much emphasized in this paper. Operationism and the logical positivism of the 1930's operate to influence both points of view but in markedly different ways. Skinner came quickly to detest logical positivism. In the Rice symposium, one would have expected Koch to focus his intelligence on radical rather than on conventional behaviorism, since it was Skinner who was obviously intended to champion the most vigorous practice of behaviorism at the time. It is much to be hoped that Koch will not long delay in accepting the challenge of a critique of radical behaviorism. The radical behaviorist cannot look profitably for relevant criticism to the painstaking review of *Verbal Behavior* made by Chomsky (1959). Chomsky writes under the misconception that Skinner's work is more or less another form of conventional behaviorism dominated by logical positivism in the usual way. The same misconception leads Malcolm in the Rice symposium (p. 144f.) to try to clarify the philosophical implications of

Skinner's views by extensive quotations from Carnap and Hempel. We can similarly excuse Malcolm's unfortunate remark that, "In his brilliant review . . . of Skinner's *Verbal Behavior*, Noam Chomsky shows conclusively . . . that Skinner fails to make a case for his belief that 'functional analysis' is able to deal with verbal behavior" (p. 154). The philosophical character of Skinner's work is considerably closer to what is often now called "analytic philosophy" or "ordinary language analysis" than to the narrow forms of logical positivism that have influenced psychological thinking to so great an extent. Koch (p. 23) suspects that behaviorism might try to look to analytic philosophy for its defense, and Scriven (p. 179) associates Skinner's analysis of the language of private experience with the central problem of the *Philosophical Investigations* of Ludwig Wittgenstein (1953). Wittgenstein's later work forms the basis of much of the force of analytic philosophy, and a number of similarities between his views and Skinner's are pointed out in a paper now in press (Day, 1969). The student of radical behaviorism is well advised to read the *Philosophical Investigations* as an antidote to the inroads of logical positivism upon psychology. It would also make the reading of Skinner's work somewhat easier.

A third and related problem faced in the effective reconciliation of radical behaviorism and phenomenology is the lack of training among psychologists in contemporary philosophy. The traces of an Oedipal resentment of philosophy by psychology still persist, much to the detriment of effective self-criticism among psychologists. Unfortunate preconceptions about the nature of science are currently under considerable philosophical attack, and this theme runs throughout much of Koch's paper for the Rice symposium. There is presently a new and vigorous excitement about phenomenology in professional philosophy. The relevance of these philosophical interests to practical problems in psychology is coming increasingly to be appreciated. Witness the birth of the new division of philosophical psychology in the American Psychological Association. Scriven's lengthy paper for the Rice symposium is essentially philosophical in nature, yet it will afford an eye-opening experience for any psychologist who takes the time to give it careful study. In two pages Scriven takes the trouble to list no less than 13 "other philosophical topics that have been deeply involved . . . in the course of the symposium" (p. 178f.). Yet how many psychologists have learned simply to turn a philosopher off when he starts to say something they do not like to hear? In the discussion following his paper, Scriven bluntly comments that "pure research in social psychology is among the most unproductive fields of human endeavor today" (p. 190). In another context he notes that "steaming somebody up to think that the only way to do psychology is via phenomenology and that all behaviorists are wicked may well turn out to be a good way of getting him to do something worthwhile, but it is certainly an unfortunate comment on psychology if psychologists need to do this. Do we *have* to feed ourselves fibs as fuels for our forward movement" (p. 177)? How many of us psychologists are sufficiently prepared to understand Scriven when he talks?

Finally, a fourth problem lies in certain practical difficulties faced in attempting to carry out explicitly descriptive research. These difficulties stem from the complex set of professional practices that define what is, and what is not, acceptable as psychological research. A simple interest in behavior no longer suffices to lead a man to try to make the relevant observations. He must first justify, often with hypocrisy, and inevitably with great caution, whatever interest in behavior he may have. The justification of research must walk the razor's edge of sufficient but not too much similarity to the research activities of other scientists. What is the hypothesis tested? What possible outcomes are anticipated? Except in those areas where we already have considerable knowledge and consequently need research the least, how can a man be expected to know what he may find in his research? Conspicuously exploratory research is frowned upon; it is tolerated only when the researcher's competence is buttressed by a formidable list of publications, often in some picked-over area. To remonstrate that the very canons of the respected establishment are under attack is to no avail. Who would suspect that simply by looking carefully at whatever one is interested in, no matter how complex the behavior may be, and by trying to push it around a bit, one can come to know a great deal more about the subject?

The profession greatly needs a lot more writing that consists of little more than careful description of what is actually observed by psychologists. One is understandably anxious in research to go beyond the stage of mere description to the statement of significant conclusions concerning behavioral control. It is understandable also that conclusions, rather than descriptions, find themselves the prized commodity in the market of publication. However, conclusions are specimens of verbal behavior that involve a very complex kind of control. Equally profitable in the control of productive professional behavior are the direct observations that presumably govern the published conclusions. The need for simple descriptions of observed behavior is especially great in precisely those areas of psychology where clear-cut conclusions are difficult to draw. Although someone is able to make only the most tentative conclusions—here, of course, he is conditioned to hesitate even to speak, much less to publish—the professional community still needs the benefit of his experience. Similarly, the man who looks but fails to find at all must nonetheless be encouraged to report what he has seen. Without publication, the possibility that his observations may have some more fortunate effect on the behavior of someone else is lost. Unless the beginning psychologist can rely on having access to the direct observations of others, he must face the bleak prospect of a career in research that even he himself may view as trivial, or he must undertake the uphill fight of analyzing behavior essentially by himself, alone.

In short, the hearty interaction of radical behaviorism and phenomenology is hindered only by one or another form of narrowness of outlook. With a deeper and wider scholarship on the part of the interested psychologist, with a considerably enlarged familiarity on his part with the rich spectrum of human activities, and with a greater freedom to make the observations upon which a broader understanding of behavior must depend, then the inherent liberalism of radical behaviorism can find successful reconciliation with the libertarian aspirations of phenomenology.

REFERENCES

CHOMSKY, N. Review of Skinner's *Verbal Behavior*. *Language*, 1959, **35**, 26–58.

DAY, W. F. On certain similarities between the *Philosophical Investigations* of Ludwig Wittgenstein and the operationism of B. F. Skinner. *Journal of the Experimental Analysis of Behavior*, 1969 (in press).

HILGARD, E. R. and BOWER, G. H. *Theories of learning.* (3rd ed.) New York: Appleton-Century-Crofts, 1956.

SIDMAN, M. and STODDARD, L. T. Programming perception and learning for retarded children. *International Review of Research in Mental Retardation*, 1966, **2**, 151–208.

SKINNER, B. F. The operational analysis of psychological terms. *Psychological Review*, 1945, **52**, 270–277, 291–294.

———. Are theories of learning necessary? *Psychological Review*, 1950, **57**, 193–216.

———. *Science and human behavior.* New York: Macmillan, 1953.

———. *Verbal behavior.* New York: Appleton-Century-Crofts, 1957.

———. Why we need teaching machines. *Harvard Educational Review*, 1961, **31**, 377–398.

———. Behaviorism at fifty. *Science*, 1963, **140**, 951–958, and in T. W. Wann (Ed.), *Behaviorism and phenomenology.* Chicago: University of Chicago Press, 1964. Pp. 79–97.

VERPLANCK, W. S. In W. K. Estes, S. Koch, K. MacCorquodale, P. E. Meehl, C. G. Mueller, Jr., W. N. Schoenfeld, and W. S. Verplanck, *Modern learning theory.* New York: Appleton-Century-Crofts, 1954. Pp. 267–316.

WANN, T. W. (Ed.) *Behaviorism and phenomenology.* Chicago: University of Chicago Press, 1964.

WITTGENSTEIN, L. *Philosophical investigations.* New York: Macmillan, 1953.

45

THE UNITY OF PSYCHOLOGY[*]

Howard H. Kendler

By belonging to the Division of General Psychology one accepts a challenge typically avoided or ignored by members of other divisions. That challenge has to do with the presumed integrity of the science of psychology. Does the discipline of psychology possess a unity despite the apparent diversity of its methods, facts and theories? Or more concisely, is the unity of psychology a reality or an illusion?

This question has been entertained in various forms even before psychology achieved an independent status. Not unexpectedly, because the issue does not lend itself to any purely logical or empirical resolution, no proposed answer has gained universal acceptance. Nevertheless, in this era, when psychology is becoming more fractionated and communication among psychologists more confusing, a need exists to examine once again the question of the unity of psychology, not in order to justify romantic notions or emotional prejudices, but instead to reveal the structure of contemporary psychology. By *structure of psychology* I refer to the manner in which the various parts of psychology, represented by different methodologies and problem areas, are interrelated and organized. If the structure of psychology can be revealed, its apparent unity, or lack of it, can be discerned.

The structure of psychology is basically an epistemological issue, an issue that concerns the ordering of psychological knowledge and the methods on which it is based. As already suggested, the question under consideration does not submit to any predetermined set of logical or empirical operations. The reason is simple. In any epistemological analysis one must make arbitrary assumptions to guide his rational analysis. We cannot demand acceptance of these assumptions in the same sense that we can ask for agreement when displaying a logical proof or an experimental fact.

Although arbitrary, epistemological assumptions cannot be adopted

[*] This paper was given as the presidential address of the Division of General Psychology at the 1968 meeting of the American Psychological Association in San Francisco. The problems discussed in the paper are to some extent an outgrowth of the author's research in the area of cognitive behavior which is supported by grants by the National Science Foundation (GB-6660) and The Office of Naval Research (Nonr-4222-04).

---

from H. H. Kendler, The unity of psychology. *Canadian Psychologist*, 1970, **11** (1), 30–47. Reprinted by permission of the author, the *Canadian Psychologist*, and the Canadian Psychological Association.

capriciously or idiosyncratically if one seeks social acceptance of his views—which I do. My intention is not to deny the status of a psychologist to any member of APA. Excommunication, even if The Council of Representatives approved its practice, would not resolve the intellectual controversy that exists in psychology today and certainly would do nothing to clarify the issues.

As an alternative to dogmatism, I wish to offer a detached analysis of the structure of psychology that will identify the common themes and discordant notes in contemporary psychology. This analysis will be guided by a set of five predilections. First, psychology will be described as it is and not in any idealized version. Second, the methodological analysis offered will be that of a practicing psychologist rather than an aspiring philosopher of science. Third, since knowledge is an end-product of human behavior, I will not refrain from speculating on psychological processes involved in the search for scientific truth. Fourth, the goal of my methodological analysis will be illumination and not prescription. Fifth and last, my aim will be to achieve collective understanding.

Let me now clarify and justify these orienting attitudes:

1. I see no virtue in arguing about any Platonic notion of the true psychologist. A simple operational approach may have some merit. Psychology is what the psychologist does. If we discover that psychologists do basically different things then we can conclude that there are basically different kinds of psychologists.

2. Like most psychologists I do not qualify as a philosopher of science neither in skill nor training but my actions as a psychologist frequently demand that I behave as one. Being a professional psychologist and an amateur philosopher, nevertheless, has advantages. Viewing psychology from within allows you to detect certain problems that are not apparent from without. In addition, one can avoid entanglements in subtle philosophical issues that have no bearing on psychology.

3. The nice neat analysis of scientific knowledge into distinct epistemological categories to which the early logical empiricist aspired, failed to materialize. The main reason was that the consequences of behavior of the scientist could not be easily extirpated from logical, empirical, and theoretical constructs. If knowledge is shaped by the scientist's behavior will not deeper insights into the structure of knowledge be achieved by considering the psychology of the scientist?

4. Methodological analyses of psychology in the past have frequently resulted in prescriptions which unhesitatingly offer eternal truths as how research is to be done, how behavior should be measured, what psychological processes are fundamental, what questions are relevant, what answers are trivial, and what constitutes true explana-

tion. Fortunately or unfortunately no firm guidelines presently exist as to the precise procedures a scientist should follow in pursuing truth and wisdom. Nevertheless, an epistemological analysis can serve a useful function if it illuminates issues and clarifies problems so that the scientist is alerted to alternatives he may have misunderstood or ignored.

5. In search for collective understanding, I will be forced to ignore the individual scientist who denies that intersubjective agreement has some merit in the scientific enterprise. I would be the last person to disrupt the solipsistic serenity of any scientist since I recognized that his insulated existence is impervious to penetration. Consequently I exclude from my audience any methodological solipsist, not in order to criticize his position but instead in recognition of the obstacles to communication.

Now that the guidelines of my analysis of the structure of psychology have been described, I can proceed with the task itself.

The Subject Matters of Psychology

My initial point will be boldly stated. Psychology has three "subject matters." They are *behavior, neurophysiological events,* and *phenomenal experience.* Discriminating among them implies nothing about the nature of their interrelationship or their potential for being integrated within a unified science of psychology. The identification of these three "subject matters" reflects only a surface description of the activities of different groups of contemporary psychologists.

My representation of the current psychological landscape would be questioned by some who believe a simpler description is more accurate. Such a characterization could either be achieved by denying legitimate status to any one of these "subject-matters" or by insisting that one or two could be reduced to another. Either simplification is unwarranted. They both represent prejudgments, gratuitous assumptions that encourage those endless methodological disputes that plague psychology. My own position is that all three "subject matters" represent legitimate areas of investigation. Their ultimate interrelationships cannot be legislated but instead depend upon future empirical and theoretical developments. Although speculating about those future developments is interesting, proposing *the* blueprint about their future organization is inappropriate.

Before discussing problems of interrelationships, let us be sure agreement prevails about the meaning of the proposed three "subject matters." Although the meaning of each has encouraged debate, an adequate understanding can be achieved if first, we refrain from exchanging our robes as empiricists for those of the philosopher and second, if we recognize that all concepts are to some extent open-ended since their meaning is modified by the network of constructs in which they are embedded.

Behavior can be defined either directly or indirectly: either in terms of the observable changes in the activity (muscular or glandular) of an organism or in the consequences of these changes on the environment. The traditional examples of direct measurements are the salivary response and muscular contraction that serves as the dependent variable in classical conditioning. Lever depression and disk displacement in instrumental conditioning are examples of indirect measures of behavior. Muscular contraction during human speech is a direct measure while speech records on tape is an indirect measure.

Internal physiological events associated with neural functioning are being investigated more frequently in psychophysiological research. Recordings of impulses from single nerve fibers, electrical changes in the brain, chemical changes at the synapse are examples of dependent variables that have had revolutionary impact on physiological psychology. It can be argued that strictly speaking these dependent variables belong to physiology alone; their relevance to psychology is in the light that they can throw on laws of behavior. Although understandable such an attitude is unnecessarily restrictive; first because it denies neural action a status in psychology equivalent to glandular and muscular changes and second, because it limits the purpose of studying neural functioning to the understanding of overt behavior and not, for example, conscious experience. It should be mentioned that the impact of these potential sources of disagreement has been minimal and in general the methodological relationships between behavioral and physiological psychologists have been cordial and free of strident debates, due mainly to their commitments to the "objective" orientation in psychology.

The role of phenomenal experience, our third "subject matter," generates much controversy. This is not surprising considering that the Behavioristic revolution against the mind-oriented position of Structuralism was successful but not complete. Although behavioristic methodology won the day by gaining the allegiance of the most influential leaders in American psychology and by dominating graduate education, pockets of resistance always remained, arguing in one form or another that phenomenal experience was a legitimate subject matter in the science of psychology. The issues involved in this debate have become unnecessarily confused partly because of the simplistic solutions initially offered. For the time being, however, I just wish to insist that phenomenal experience represents a legitimate area of investigation for the simple reason that phenomenal experience exists. To deny the existence of human consciousness is equivalent to denying the existence of an external environment. An image of a lake in Vermont, which I can generate at will, is as real to me as is my audience. If anyone is disturbed by this comparison they should know that the imagined lake is serene and sparkling.

My position, affirming the existence of human phenomenal experience, should not be confused with the strategy of advocating its investigation. I am simply stating that a person's phenomenal experience is an observable event, at present to him alone, and is neither equivalent to behavior nor to neurophysiological events as I have already defined them. Behavioral and physiological interpretations of phenomenal experience are possible but such interpretations are not equivalent to raw phenomenal experience.

Even if investigations of phenomenal experience are considered strategically ill-advised at the present time, their results cannot automatically be rejected. It is quite proper, and somewhat romantic, for a psychologist to assume a position not unlike that of a mountain climber. Because it is there, a mountain demands to be climbed. Because it exists, phenomenal experience invites analysis. In anticipation of future discussion it may be noted that the conquest of Mount Everest had to await technological developments to make the ascent possible.

Reductionism and Explanation

If we do have three distinctive subject matters in psychology what possible relationships might exist among them? Although I have maintained that this question has both empirical and theoretical components, it nevertheless can be scrutinized by considering the possible interrelationships that will prevail. By doing so the relevance and significance of present-day controversies can be properly understood and evaluated. In my analysis reference to two related concepts will be frequently made; *explanation* and *reductionism*. Our purposes will be best served to describe each briefly with our initial attention focused on the latter.

On the most general level *reductionism* can be described as substituting ". . . for one set of assertions another set whose members are more basic than those of the original" (Turner, 1965). Although the assumption that behavior can be reduced to neurophysiology has not been universally accepted (e.g., Jessor, 1958) it seems to be a self-evident truth to many, if not all psychologists. More concern has been shown for the implications of this assumption for research and theory than for the complex problems associated with its verification. The assumption that behavior can be reduced to neurophysiology has suggested to some psychologists that behavior theory must be developed first in order to guide the direction of psychophysiological research. In contrast, the same reductionistic assumption has suggested to others that any analysis of behavior must be made in terms of underlying neurophysiological processes. Both of these conflicting prescriptions appear eminently reasonable but their relative merits will have to await future developments. Although such prescriptions may alert some to strategies previously ignored, their major contribution probably is the justification they afford to the actions of those who propose and accept them. Strong convictions are excellent motivational devices to overcome the tedium of laboratory work.

The validation of the thesis that behavior can be reduced to neurophysiology depends upon formalizing both a behavior theory and a neurophysiological theory. If the primary assumptions of the behavior theory can be deduced from the neurophysiological theory then we can properly state that reductionism has been achieved. Expressed in this fashion reductionism is a far more demanding task than is usually realized when the assumption that behavior can be reduced to neurophysiology is casually accepted. Problems of reductionism have contemporary significance for only some areas of sensory physiology where certain perceptual phenomena can be predicted from our knowledge of patterns of neural impulses (e.g., Ratliff, 1965). For the rest of psychology the closest approach to reductive success has been the *interpretation* of behavior in terms of neurophysiological processes, e.g., reinforcement has been interpreted in terms of electrical changes in the brain (Olds & Olds, 1965), motivation has been interpreted in terms of hypothalamic function (Stellar, 1954).

Although conceivably these interpretations are the first steps in reducing behavioral phenomena to underlying neurophysiological events, two points must be recognized. First, such interpretations are far removed from formal reduction, and second that the reduction of behavior to neurophysiology is not inevitable. The first point is obvious if the complex problems of deducing an axiomatic behavior theory from an axiomatic neurophysiological theory are realized. The second point—the reduction of behavior to neurophysiology is not inevitable—is usually ignored because of the compelling nature of the assumption that neurophysiological changes must underlie behavioral events. Nevertheless two possible obstacles could prevent achieving reductive success. The first is that an empirically sound and theoretically formal behavior theory may not prove to be isomorphic with an empirically sound and theoretically formal neurophysiological theory. A behavior theory may be able to predict many behavioral events, which of course is what we demand of a theory, but yet not prove to be congruent with a neurophysiological theory. If we accept the idea that any theory has a limited range of empirical validity, then we cannot fault either a successful behavioral or neurophysiological theory for their failures to implement a successful reduction. The second obstacle to reductive success is that intrinsic properties of certain behavioral events prevent their being subsumed under neurophysiological processes. Several reasons, ranging from a failure to find a neurophysiological correlate of a specific response to some emergent behavioral process (an alternative best considered as a last resort) may underly reductive failures. For the present, Kaplan's (1964) reaction to the question of whether laws of behavior are reducible to laws of neurophysiology (or chemistry or physics) is both sensible and proper:

> An affirmative answer . . . as a matter of doctrine, seems to be . . . both unwarranted and useless. . . . As a methodological presupposition . . . it provides a valuable perspective in which the behavioral scientist can see continuing possibilities for turning to his own use the findings of other sciences. But the significance of such possibilities appears only as they are actualized; otherwise their affirmation expresses only a hope. . . . It may well be that the psychologist can derive the whole of his discipline from neurology, biochemistry and the rest: it is not destructive skepticism but productive pragmatism to say, "I'd like to see him do it!" [pages 124–125].

The relationship between psychology and neurophysiology has been examined within the context of *reductionism* and the conclusion was drawn that the assumption that behavior is reducible to neurophysiology, or to more "basic" discipline such as chemistry or physics, is gratuitous. Implicit in this discussion of reductionism was the acceptance of a specific meaning of scientific explanation, namely that an event, or law, or set of laws, or a theory, can be explained if it can be logically deduced from a prior set of assumptions or a higher level theory. This deductive model of explanation has gained wide acceptance among theoretically oriented behavioral and physiological psychologists. Consequently the nature of explanation has never appeared to be a significant source of disagreement between the communities of behavioral or neurophysiological psychologists. It is my contention however, that a fundamental source of misunderstanding and friction between psychologists with a phenomenal bent and those who operate within a behavioral and neurophysiological framework stems from radically different conceptions of explanation. So in order to prepare for our discussion of phenomenal experience it becomes necessary to analyze the possible meanings of explanation.

Explanations can be examined within two different frameworks, epistemological and psychological. Explanation as a deductive process represents an epistemological analysis. Within this framework the issue has been raised whether deduction is a necessary or sufficient requirement for explanation. According to some, not only must an event be deduced to be explained but must also be interpreted within some comprehensive schema.

This distinction can perhaps be illuminated by reference to mathematical models in psychology. Some model builders deal with quantitative descriptions of data alone while puritanically avoiding any psychological interpretation. Others, in contrast, feel compelled to inject a conceptual analysis of behavior (e.g., stimulus sampling theory of Estes, 1959) into their mathematical model. Are these two interpretations of explanation, the deductive vs. contextual model, qualitatively different? From the epistemological point of view, I think not. Both demand a deductive requirement for explanation. They differ in that the contextual model demands a deductive capacity of much wider range.

My interest is not in examining the epistemological difference between these two models too closely or critically. Instead I wish to emphasize the significant psychological difference between a deductive and contextual interpretation of explanation. A purely quantitative deduction in the absence of any conceptual interpretation provides no "a-ha" experience, no psychological understanding. I realize that I cannot offer any definitive experimental data to back up my view but my own phenomenal experience and the reports of some other psychologists who introspect on occasion do suggest that scientific explanation is not equivalent to psychological understanding. It may very well be that theoretical advances are triggered by psychological understanding which in turn are reconstructed as logical explanations. My concern however is not with analyzing the possible relationships between scientific explanation and psychological understanding but instead to emphasize the point that intrinsically they are different; the former depending on socially-based requirements of meaning and logic, the latter on an individual's phenomenal experience.

The distinction between scientific explanation and psychological understanding is perhaps best illustrated by the fact that a deductive component is not required for psychological understanding. As an illustration I refer to the deep understanding one can achieve from the writings of a perspective novelist, such as Dostoyevsky. I recall that when I was an undergraduate major in psychology, I attended a symposium in which all the members of the psychology department participated in a discussion of *human nature*. Practically without exception every participant illustrated his viewpoint by quoting a passage from some famous literary work. While listening to these quotations it occurred to me that if I really wanted to study psychology I should major in English. But at that time members of the English Department were offering Freudian interpretations of literature. I decided to continue to major in psychology more as a matter of convenience than as a result of keen epistemological insights. But in any case, it seemed obvious then, and does today, that one can achieve a deep understanding of behavior from literary masterpieces. I would speculate that this psychological understanding stems from the ability of a literary work to generate phenomenal experiences similar to those evoked by "real-life" situations. These literary descriptions however possess no deductive consequences as does a logically constructed theory and therefore do not qualify as scientific explanations even though they evoke psychological understanding.

Phenomenal Experience

Now that I have broken down the concept of explanation into two components, scientific explanation and psychological understanding, and noted the distinction between them, I am prepared to discuss phenomenal experience. Initially phenomenal experience as observational data will be analyzed followed by an examination of its relationships to behavior and to neurophysiological events.

I have already acknowledged the reality of phenomenal experience. Its raw observational character is no different from the raw observational character resulting from perceiving an event in the external environment. Consequently I must reject the common distinction between subjective and objective which implies a qualitative difference between the observational base of internally-induced phenomenal experience and the perception of external events.

The scientific enterprise involves not only observations but also their communication. At the level of communication we can detect differences between observations of conscious experience and observations of the external environment; the main difference being that intersubjective agreement is more easily achieved with the observations of external events. Why is this so? Let us examine this question.

Our observations of external events, such as a rat learning to choose correctly in a T-maze, or a college student learning to respond appropriately in a concept-identification problem, are anchored to socially approved criteria. If intersubjective agreement is not attained in the observation of such events then the source of the disagreement is easily located and methods instituted to improve agreement. The dimensions of the maze and the presentation rate of the items in the concept-indentification task can be observed within a framework of physical measurement; a frame of reference that has been successful in producing intersubjective agreement. Disagreements about the behavior of the subjects can also be easily resolved. Did the rat turn left or right? Although psychologists innocent of animal experimentation may be surprised to discover that such a simple response measure could generate uncertainty, the fact is that rats are known to dart into one alley and then suddenly reverse themselves and enter the other one. Was it a left or right response? Agreement is easily reached when lines of penetration or electric eyes are used to define the turning response. Similarly in concept-identification experiments disagreements concerning the subjects' responses are minimized by defining his behavior in terms of some environmental event such as pressing a key.

Although intersubjective agreement has been improved by employing physical measurement, two limitations of physical measurement should be mentioned. The first is that it does not guarantee intersubjective agreement. The hope, once encouraged by the logical empiricists, that vagueness and disagreements about the observational base of science could be banished by the use of a physicalistic language—the doctrine of immaculate perception—has not been realized. Numerous personal factors, perhaps most importantly, theoretical preconceptions, can influence our observations as scientists. Experiments in perception have frequently indicated that a set can determine what is observed, e.g., Bruner and Postman (1949) demonstrated that an incongruous red four-of-spades was misperceived in line with previous experience; either as a red four-of-hearts or a black four-of-spades. Psychologists therefore should not be surprised that theoretical sets can influence the observations of the scientist. But the influence is not as great as some philosophers of science would have us believe. Because observations are sometimes influenced by personal factors we should not conclude that they always must be. We should distinguish between what is observed and how that observation is interpreted. Differences in raw observations have not been at the root of the controversies involving heredity and environment or one-trial learning but rather the interpretation of the observations. I find it difficult to believe that contradictory perceptions of the same behavioral and neurophysiological data cannot be eliminated, regardless of what theoretical orientations are adopted, if concerted effort is made to do so (which usually is not made because of greater interest in retaining theoretical differences than eliminating them).

Observational disagreements in behavioral and neurophysiological psychology do not stem primarily from different perceptions of the same events. Instead they result from the fact that in the same experimental situation entirely different theoretical orientations, will attend to different events, e.g., in an instrumental conditioning situation a Guthrien will attend to the pattern of movements a subject makes when pressing the bar whereas a Skinnerian will attend to the rate of lever depressions.

Physically-based measurement not only does not guarantee observational agreement, but also tends to encourage researchers to avoid phenomena to which physical measurement cannot be easily applied. In concept identification tasks the subject's sense of commitment to do the very best he can or his sense of despair when he cannot decipher the task are typically ignored. It can be argued that these are not significant variables in studying cognitive processes and therefore can be disregarded. That may be so, but it also can be argued, with equal cogency, that these phenomenal states may be significant facts in their own right as well as be causally related to behavioral and neurophysiological events.

The two limitations of physically based observations were not mentioned in order to criticize this useful mode of definition and measurement but instead to encourage a sympathetic attitude to the analysis of phenomenal experience. If we have not devised methods by which complete intersubjective agreement is guaranteed by physically-based observations perhaps we should become more tolerant of ambiguities in describing phenomenal experience. If the use of physically-based observations encourages researchers to disregard certain phenomena, we can become tolerant of those who ignore other phenomena when they focus their attention on conscious experience.

How can the phenomenal experience of a single individual be anchored by events that will permit some degree of intersubjective agreement? The answer to this question depends upon the criterion of explanation used (scientific explanation or psychological understanding) and the relationships sought between phenomenal experience and behavioral and neurophysiological events.

The most common mooring for phenomenal experience is the verbal report of the person who is examining his own conscious experience. One can assume, as did the Structuralists, that verbal reports can be used to reflect phenomenal experience. But as they were forced to discover, these verbal reports were influenced by the training of the observer and consequently did not simply mirror phenomenal experience. The inability of the Structuralists to unravel the influence of the observer's training from his description of personal phenomenal experience led to the abandonment of their methodological system. Were the Structuralists foredoomed to failure because of the intrinsic limitations of self-observation or because of some defect of their particular method? I do not know. I often wonder what would happen to a systematic analysis of conscious experience if it were conducted with the Structuralists' dedication to experimentation but in the absence of their theoretical preconceptions. Although it is difficult to imagine that conscious experience described in terms of verbal reports could factor out the effects of verbal processes, it is equally hard to believe that the descriptions of phenomenal experience performed by the Structuralists, in spite of their defective methodology, had some relevance to sensory discriminations and sensory physiology.

If phenomenal experience is interpreted by verbal reports how can the validity of the interpretation be evaluated? One possible way is to transform the description into some logical network of constructs that would generate deductions about the characteristics of phenomenal experience under various conditions. The validity of the interpretation would be tested in the same manner as in any other theoretical formulation, viz., determining whether the deductions are consistent with observations.

An alternative method of judging the validity of a phenomenal description is to determine whether it generates psychological understanding. Empathy, not valid deduction, is sought. This effort at generating psychological understanding can produce some degree of intersubjective agreement about phenomenal experience. A description by one person of his existential commitment or existential dilemma can produce a feeling of shared experience by some members of his audience. Such phenomenally "accurate" descriptions can aid in predicting behavior if it is discovered that they are correlated with overt behavior. If the phenomenologically-oriented investigator is interested in arriving at a psychologically-true description so that future behavior can be predicted, then his efforts can be transformed into a deductive explanatory system. The question that must be posed in evaluating descriptions of phenomenal experience is whether they have as their ultimate aim the ability to generate psychological understanding (shared experience) or as the fundamental data of a theory that seeks to deduce events of phenomenal experience or behavior.

No way exists to resolve the difference between these two explanatory frames of reference. One or the other must serve as the ultimate criterion to judge the validity of a psychological theory. The current scene in psychology would be better understood if investigators and theorists make clear the type of explanation they seek so that their ideas will not be misjudged or misunderstood. With equal justification we can encourage critics to recognize the distinction between these two models of explanation so that their comments will be relevant to the notions they seek to evaluate. If a phenomenologically-oriented theorist seeks deductive explanations then his efforts fit into the mainstream of behavioral and physiological psychology. His epistemological aims are the same but his subject matter is different. If, however, the description of phenomenal experience is an end in itself, to be judged by criteria of "shared experiences," then it must be recognized that these efforts represent a discipline that is dissimilar to the one that searches for scientific explanation.

Instead of describing phenomenal experience one can attempt to abstract from it those characteristics that are significant in understanding behavioral and neurophysiological events. These abstractions can form the basis of a model of the mind. Constructing such a model presupposes that phenomenal experience serves as an important causal link in the occurrence of other psychological events. Such an assumption is certainly not demanded. Numerous psychological theories with predictive capacities deny or ignore the significance of processes associated with phenomenal experience. However, the fact that such processes can sometimes be ignored does not mean that they should be neglected. In many situations a better prediction of a person's behavior will come from knowledge of his phenomenal experience than from information of his past behavior or present neurophysiological condition. From the viewpoint of strategy, a consideration of phenomenal experience can certainly be defended.

A survey of contemporary psychology suggests that models of phenomenal experience are becoming more popular especially in the cognitive and personality areas. Such concepts as *strategies, rules, existential dilemmas* testify to this point. Two major problems exist for theorists who construct such models. The first is the discovery of a fruitful source of conceptual properties that can be assigned to the constructs of the model. The second is the theoretical problem of postulating processes that will transform the model into observable events.

In characterizing the properties of the model of phenomenal experience one would expect that a rich source of hypotheses would come from introspection. It is interesting to note that Tolman (1936), at the time he was immersed in constructing his cognitive theory of behavior, wrote as follows:

> Is not introspection after all, at least in the case of men, a significant method by which one can get at and define these intervening variables in a direct and really reliable fashion? I doubt it. I believe that introspection is a form of social response—a type of final behavior . . . which has very complicated conditions . . . it seems to me obvious and already well demonstrated that in most cases introspective behavior is far less successful in such a direct mirroring than are most gross forms of behavior; for these latter are not, as is introspection, subject to distortion by being directed toward an audience. The very essence of introspection lies in the fact that it is a response to audiences—external and internal. And, such being the case, it seems less likely to mirror most types of intervening variable so directly and correctly as do more gross nonsocial forms of behavior.

A somewhat different strategy of characterizing the conceptual properties of the mind is suggested by Stoyva and Kamiya (1968) who argue that consciousness may be best studied by considering it a hypothetical construct related simultaneously to verbal reports and neurophysiological measures. Presumably, the argument goes, a more valid characterization of the mind emerges when neurophysiological measures are combined with verbal reports.

I have already indicated my personal wariness of any methodological prescriptions; whether in favor or against a particular strategy. Tolman was reasonable in expressing reservations about introspection as a source of theoretical ideas for a model of the mind. Any such model need not be exclusively or even partly based on self-observation. Stoyva and Kamiya are reasonable in pointing out the strategic advantages of combining verbal reports with correlated physiological measures. Both are wrong however in implying the validity of their particular strategy. A more pragmatic and less controversial approach is to judge one's strategy not by its reasonableness but instead by its fruitfulness.

Although theoretical constructs that reflect properties of phenomenal experience have intuitive appeal (perhaps because they generate "psychological understanding") they do present a special problem that is best characterized by Guthrie's criticism (1952) that Tolman left his rats "buried in thought." The problem is how to transform these hypothetical states of mind into observable events. This problem has plagued phenomenally oriented theories and no simple theoretical solution has yet been proposed. The requirements of scientific explanation demands that this problem be solved. Theorists who construct models of the mind would be well-advised to pay as much attention to the relationships between their theoretical constructs and dependent variables as they do the conceptual properties of their theoretical constructs.

I hesitate to make my last point about phenomenal experience because the proposal is so removed from current reality. But one possible method of constructing a model of the mind is to base it upon the observations of phenomenal experience from the outside. Perhaps someday it will be possible for a person's phenomenal experience to be perceived by a group of outside observers. An interesting parlor game for psychologists is to formulate experimental designs, unhampered by current technological limitations, that will allow you to observe another person's phenomenal experience. I believe it is possible to design such an experiment that will answer such age-old question of whether two people have the same sensation or perceive the same image. My interest, however, is in scientific methodology and not science fiction, and therefore will refrain from discussions of such designs. The methodological point that I am making is simply that the observation of another person's phenomenal experience is presently impossible, not because of logical considerations but instead because of technical limitations.

Conclusion

Before closing, I would like to return to the question that provoked this paper. Is the unity of psychology a reality or an illusion? It is neither. A unified psychology does not exist today and there is no guarantee that it will ever be achieved. But the unity of psychology is not beyond the realm of possibility and consequently it cannot be considered to be completely unreal. Whether a unity is achieved or not will depend on the psychological community accepting a criterion of explanation that will permit a framework by which the relative merits of competing interpretations can be judged, not necessarily to provide a single unequivocal overall evaluation but instead to identify the assets and liabilities of each. It may seem naive to think that a common explanatory frame of reference can be agreed upon by such an already fragmented community but a look at the annals of more mature sciences testifies to the ability of historical processes to settle what initially appeared to be unresolvable controversies.

The most likely candidate for a mutually acceptable explanatory frame of reference is one that requires a deductive component. The significant question for the future will be whether such a requirement is meaningful and acceptable to those whose interests are in the analysis of phenomenal experience. If not an inevitable split must occur in the intellectual discipline we now refer to as psychology. If however a deductive model of explanation prevails then the unity of psychology will depend on the ingenuity of future psychologists to create theories that in some manner will integrate behavior, phenomenal experience, and neurophysiological events. But whatever the future holds, I do hope my comments have clarified the present structure of psychology and in so doing perhaps will discourage, or at least minimize, those endless, fruitless debates on the undebatable issues of the *true* nature and *proper* methods of the science of psychology.

REFERENCES

BRUNER, J. S., and POSTMAN, L. On the perception of incongruity: A paradigm. *J. Pers.*, 1949, 18, 206–223.

ESTES, W. K. The statistical approach to learning theory. In S. Koch (Ed.) *Psychology: A study of a science.* Vol. 2. New York: McGraw-Hill, 1959, pp. 380–491.

GUTHRIE, E. R. *The psychology of learning* (Rev. ed.). New York: Harper, 1952.

JESSOR, B. The problem of reductionism in psychology. *Psychol. Rev.*, 1958, 65, 170–178.

KAPLAN, A. *The conduct of inquiry.* San Francisco: Chandler, 1964.

OLDS, J., and OLDS, M. Drives, rewards, and the brain. In *New directions in psychology.* New York: Holt, Rinehart and Winston, 1965, pp. 329–410.

RATLIFF, F. *Mach bands.* San Francisco: Holden-Day, 1965.

STELLAR, E. The physiology of motivation. *Psychol. Rev.*, 1954, 61, 5–22.

STOYVA, J., and KAMIYA, J. Electrophysiological studies of dreaming as a prototype of a new strategy in the study of consciousness. *Psychol. Rev.*, 1968, 75, 192–205.

TOLMAN, E. C. Operational behaviorism and current trends in psychology. *Proc. 25th Amer. Celebration Inaug. Grad. Stud.*, Los Angeles: The University of Southern California, 1936, pp. 89–103.

TURNER, M. B. *Philosophy and the science of behavior.* New York: Appleton-Century-Crofts, 1967.

SUBJECT INDEX

A

Abduction, 300, 305–308
Abnormal psychology, 7, 396, 486, 581
Abstraction, 213
Acceptance, 138
Act psychology, 395, 399
Adaptation-level theory, 135, 145, 148
Adequate stimulation, 385
A-factors (A variables), 109
Affection, 141
"Aha" reaction, 142, 616
Altruism, 365
Ambiguity, 103, 577
Anarchy, 165, 177–201
Antibehaviorism, 488, 489–492
Anxiety, 138, 549
Applied science, 51–52, 251
Apprentice system, 264–265, 267–268, 278
Archaic behaviorism, 488–489
Association, 376, 394, 477
Associationism, 125, 235, 512–515
Attention, 126, 135, 139–151, 458, 460
Attitude, 109, 125
Authentic behaviorism, 488, 496–501
Autonomic variables, 150
Auxiliary condition, 257–258, 278
Aversion treatment, 553

B

Basic (pure) science, 47, 48, 51, 52
Behavior, 152–164, 522–534
Behavioral therapy, 149
Behaviorism, 11, 19, 99, 100, 103, 107, 108, 114, 119, 126, 204, 217, 221, 222, 389, 390, 396, 397, 398, 453, 487–502, 534–545, 567–569, 587–608, 612
Behavioristics, 4

Behavior modification, 545–558
Bergmann coefficient, 303
Biofeedback, 273, 555
Biographic history (of science), 100
Blood–brain barrier, 480
Boyle-Charles law, 225
Brain, 450, 451, 458–468, 468–485
Brain reinforcing areas, 144
Brain processes, 413
Bridge laws, 164, 174, 175, 225, 226, 230

C

Cardiac deceleration, 142, 143
Causality, 108, 109, 380, 468
Classical conditioning, 507, 612
Classification, 161, 162
Cognition, 152, 155, 157, 409
Cognitive dissonance theory, 236, 238, 278–279
Cognitive processes, 103, 127
Cognitive psychology, 119, 120–130, 153, 435, 436, 528, 571, 572–587
Cognitive states, 126, 135, 412
Color perception, 321–324
Communicability (of theory), 294–295
Complementarity, 346–358
Computer technology, 103, 126, 127, 131, 436, 439, 447, 528
Concept, 279, 302
Concept formation, 125, 126, 160, 213, 513
Conditioning, 125, 138, 147, 258, 408, 553, 554
Conjoint structures, 312–320
Consciousness, 125, 206, 210, 213, 214, 222, 223, 235, 393, 397, 412, 413, 426, 428, 431, 435–451, 451–457, 474, 475, 476, 491, 493, 495, 496, 612, 621
Consistency (of theory), 292–293, 306
Constructs, 238, 240–241, 279

NAME INDEX

A

Abelson, R. P., 238, 381
Achinstein, P., 175
Albert, Saint, 491
Alexander, F., 195, 549
Allais, M., 328
Allen, F. S., 69, 84
Allport, F., 286, 288, 297, 298
Allport, G. W., 34, 255, 281, 520
Ames, A., 340
Ampère, André-Marie, 76, 85
Amsel, A., 236, 281
Anderson, N. R., 329
Andrade, E. N. da, 121, 131
Angell, J. R., 519
Antrobus, J. S., 573, 575, 586
Aquinas, Thomas, 195, 491
Arbib, M. A., 444, 449
Aristophanes, 187
Aristotle, 61, 63, 166, 235, 488, 489, 529
Armstrong, D. M., 438, 446, 449
Aronfreed, J., 146, 151
Aronson, E., 281, 284
Arrow, K. J., 328
Asch, S. E., 421, 425
Ashby, W. R., 561, 570
Astin, A., 378
Atkinson, R. C., 126, 131, 274, 281
Attneave, F., 437, 449
Augustine, Saint, 193, 490, 491, 502
Avagadro, Amedeo, 62
Ayer, A. J., 23, 24, 29, 208
Azrin, N. H., 129, 132

B

Back, Kurt, 89, 97
Bacon, Roger, 491, 529
Bain, A., 394
Bainbridge, P., 274, 282
Bakan, D., 255, 281, 430, 434

Bakunin, M. A., 179
Baldwin, A. L., 136, 137, 151, 286, 288, 298
Barker, S. F., 175
Barron, F., 41, 84, 85
Bartlett, F. C., 106, 107, 111, 117
Barzun, J., 210
Bass, L. W., 269, 283, 468
Bateson, P. P. G., 145, 151
Bayley, N., 136, 152
Beals, R., 329
Beasley, N. A., 109, 117
Becker, W. C., 136, 151
Beckner, M., 438, 449
Beer, G. de, 85
Bell, Charles, 529
Bell, Daniel, 68, 83, 551, 556
Bell, E. T., 9, 19, 29
Bem, D. J., 274, 281
Bem, S. L., 274, 281
Benjamin, A. C., 3, 29, 241, 281
Benn, G., 181
Bentham, J., 210
Bentley, A. F., 6, 12, 15, 16, 29
Bergin, A. E., 557
Bergmann, G., 61, 284, 286, 299, 301, 303, 308, 517, 519
Bergson, Henri, 95
Berkeley, G., 380, 383, 384, 392, 492
Bernard, Claude, 531
Berne, E., 378
Bernstein, N. A., 440, 443, 444, 449
Bertalanffy, L. von, 570
Bessel, W. F., 382, 383, 392
Bever, T. G., 130, 132, 510, 520
Bills, A. G., 7, 11, 12, 29
Binder, A., 378
Binet, A., 396
Bitterman, M. E., 274, 282
Bittle, W. E., 164
Black, A. H., 553, 556

631

C

K

Kagan, J., author, selection 11: pp. 134–152; 103, 134, 136, 138, 141, 151, 152

Kalhorn, J., 136, 151

Kamin, L. J., 553, 557

Kamiya, J., 621, 623

Kangro, H., 84

Kant, I., 15, 27, 65, 159, 210, 222

Kantor, J. R., author, selection 37: pp. 487–502; 7, 11, 30, 486, 487, 501, 502, 580, 585

Kaplan, A., 516, 521, 615, 623

Karlin, S., 328

Katz, B., 7

Kaufmann, F., 35, 39

Kearney, H. F., 80, 86

Keats, J., 222

Keele, S. W., 445, 450

Kelley, H. H., 125, 132

Kelly, G., 556

Kemeny, J. G., 133

Kendler, H. H., author, selection 38: pp. 502–522; author, selection 45: pp. 609–623; 128, 130, 133, 486, 502, 510, 512, 521, 571, 572, 585, 609

Kendler, T. S., 510, 521

Kepler, J., 80, 83, 189, 331

Kessen, W., 285

Kiang, C. S., 83

Kierkegaard, S., 184, 186, 197, 198

Kim, J., 225, 227

Kimble, D. P., 459, 467

King, A. L., 70, 84

Kittel, C., 67, 83

Klein, M., 70

Klemperer, V., 191

Klopfer, P. H., 145, 152

Knight, W. D., 83

Koch, S., 110, 117, 118, 128, 132, 133, 236, 245, 246, 253, 275, 282, 283, 284, 285, 299, 421, 425, 587–608

Koestler, A., 83

Koffka, K., 455, 457, 512

Kohler, W., 108, 420, 421, 455, 457

Kohne, D., 471

Kopp, J., 576, 585

Körner, S., 176

Korzybski, A., 27

Kottenhoff, H., 339, 344

Koyré, A., 71, 72, 80, 84, 86

Kraepelin, E., 396

Krantz, D. H., author, selection 22: pp. 309–329; 300, 309, 316, 328, 329

Krutch, J. W., 210

Kuenne, M., 509, 521

Kuhn, T. S., author, selection 3: pp. 41–52; 40, 41, 42, 52, 53–61, 69, 73, 82, 84, 85, 86, 119, 128, 133, 253, 271, 276, 282, 285, 288, 292, 299, 359, 394, 407, 550, 552, 557

Külpe, O., 395, 431

Kundera, M., 195

L

Lachman, R., author, selection 10: pp. 119–134; 103, 119, 130, 133, 573, 587

Laing, R. D., 88, 91, 93, 97, 199

Lakatos, I., 56, 85, 187, 194, 195

Landshut, S., 187

Lane, H. L., 576, 585

Lang, P. J., 554, 557

Laplace, P. S., 79, 86

Lashley, K. S., 24, 100, 108, 339, 420, 458, 496

Lasson, G., 192

Latané, B., 266, 282

Lavoisier, A. L., 72

Lawrence, D. H., 238, 282

Lazarus, A. A., 546, 550, 555, 557

Lee, H. N., 301, 302, 306, 307, 308

Legge, D., 450

Leibnitz, G. W., 19, 492

Le Grand, Y., 329

Lenin, V. I., 178, 186, 187, 194, 197, 198

Lennard-Jones, J. E., 78

Lenzen, V. F., 176

Leonard, G., 97

Leuba, C., 140, 152, 581, 585

Levin, H., 136, 152

Levine, D., 521

Levine, J., 141, 151

Lewin, K., 30, 33, 267, 421, 512

Lewis, C. I., 65, 167

Lewis, G. N., 346, 357

Lewis, M., 141, 151

Liberman, A. M., 576, 585, 586, 587

Lindsay, R. B., 12, 30, 84

Lindzey, G., 117, 284

Locke, J., 384, 392, 394, 492, 529

Loeb, J., 495

Loewith, K., 197

Logan, F. A., 236, 282